ONE WEEK LOAN

KEY TEXT
REFERENCE

HANDBOOK OF BEREAVEMENT RESEARCH AND PRACTICE

HANDBOOK OF BEREAVEMENT RESEARCH AND PRACTICE

Advances in Theory and Intervention

Edited by Margaret S. Stroebe, Robert O. Hansson, Henk Schut, and Wolfgang Stroebe

American Psychological Association • *Washington, DC*

Published by
American Psychological Association
750 First Street, NE
Washington, DC 20002
www.apa.org

To order
APA Order Department
P.O. Box 92984
Washington, DC 20090-2984
Tel: (800) 374-2721; Direct: (202) 336-5510
Fax: (202) 336-5502; TDD/TTY: (202) 336-6123
Online: www.apa.org/books/
E-mail: order@apa.org

In the U.K., Europe, Africa, and the Middle East, copies may be ordered from
American Psychological Association
3 Henrietta Street
Covent Garden, London
WC2E 8LU England

Typeset in Goudy by Circle Graphics, Inc., Columbia, MD

Printer: Data Reproductions, Auburn Hills, MI
Cover Designer: Naylor Design, Washington, DC
Technical/Production Editor: Harriet Kaplan

The opinions and statements published are the responsibility of the authors, and such opinions and statements do not necessarily represent the policies of the American Psychological Association.

Library of Congress Cataloging-in-Publication Data

Handbook of bereavement research and practice : advances in theory and intervention / edited by Margaret S. Stroebe . . . [et al.]. — 1st ed.
    p. cm.
  Includes bibliographical references and index.
  ISBN-13: 978-1-4338-0351-2
  ISBN-10: 1-4338-0351-8
  1. Bereavement—Psychological aspects. 2. Grief. I. Stroebe, Margaret S.
  BF575.G7H353 2008
  155.9'37—dc22
                            2007047614

British Library Cataloguing-in-Publication Data
A CIP record is available from the British Library.

Printed in the United States of America
First Edition

For Aubrey (Robert O. Hansson)

For Scottie (Henk Schut)

For Katherine and Bernard (Margaret S. Stroebe and Wolfgang Stroebe)

CONTENTS

CONTRIBUTORS

John Archer, University of Central Lancashire, Lancashire, England

Tim S. Ayers, Arizona State University, Tempe

Kathrin Boerner, Lighthouse International, New York, NY

George A. Bonanno, Teachers College, Columbia University, New York, NY

Deborah Carr, Rutgers University, New Brunswick, NJ

Wai Chow, Arizona State University, Tempe

Stefany Coxe, Arizona State University, Tempe

Christopher G. Davis, Carleton University, Ottawa, Ontario, Canada

Kenneth J. Doka, The College of New Rochelle, New Rochelle, NY

Nigel P. Field, Pacific Graduate School of Psychology, Palo Alto, CA

Helen Fisher, Rutgers University, New Brunswick, NJ

Robert O. Hansson, Professor Emeritus, University of Tulsa, Tulsa, OK

Judith C. Hays, Duke University School of Nursing, Durham, NC

Bert Hayslip Jr., University of North Texas, Denton

Randy S. Hebert, University of Pittsburgh, Pittsburgh, PA

Cristina C. Hendrix, Duke University School of Nursing, Durham, NC

Nancy S. Hogan, Loyola University Chicago, Chicago, IL

Robert Kastenbaum, Arizona State University, Tempe

David W. Kissane, Memorial Sloan-Kettering Cancer Center, New York, NY, and Weill Medical College of Cornell University, New York, NY

Anna Laurie, University of Memphis, Memphis, TN

Wendy G. Lichtenthal, Memorial Sloan-Kettering Cancer Center, New York, NY

Linda J. Luecken, Arizona State University, Tempe, and the University of Arizona College of Medicine, Phoenix

Paul K. Maciejewski, Yale University School of Medicine, New Haven, CT

Ruth Malkinson, Tel Aviv University, Tel Aviv, Israel

Mario Mikulincer, Bar-Ilan University, Ramat Gan, Israel

Shirley A. Murphy, Professor Emeritus, University of Washington, Seattle

Janice Winchester Nadeau, Minnesota Human Development Consultants, Minneapolis

Robert A. Neimeyer, University of Memphis, Memphis, TN

Colin Murray Parkes, St. Christopher's Hospice, Sydenham, Kent, England, and St. Joseph's Hospice, Hackney, London, England

Holly G. Prigerson, Dana-Farber Cancer Institute, Boston, MA

Paul C. Rosenblatt, University of Minnesota, St. Paul

Simon Shimshon Rubin, University of Haifa, Haifa, Israel

Irwin N. Sandler, Arizona State University, Tempe

Richard Schulz, University of Pittsburgh, Pittsburgh, PA

Henk Schut, Utrecht University, Utrecht, the Netherlands

Phillip R. Shaver, University of California, Davis

Margaret S. Stroebe, Utrecht University, Utrecht, the Netherlands

Wolfgang Stroebe, Utrecht University, Utrecht, the Netherlands

Jenn-Yun Tein, Arizona State University, Tempe

Karolijne van der Houwen, Utrecht University, Utrecht, the Netherlands

Lauren C. Vanderwerker, Harvard Medical School, Boston, MA

Tony Walter, University of Bath, Bath, England

Robert S. Weiss, Professor Emeritus, University of Massachusetts, Boston

Diana L. White, Oregon Health and Scientific University, Portland

Eliezer Witztum, Ben-Gurion University, Beer-Sheva, Israel

Sharlene A. Wolchik, Arizona State University, Tempe

Camille B. Wortman, Stony Brook University, Stony Brook, NY

PREFACE

With the publication of this volume we have completed a trilogy of handbooks on bereavement. Our continued aim has been to provide a synthesis of scientific knowledge about the phenomena and manifestations of bereavement from a standpoint that emphasizes theoretical approaches and scientific method. It is important to note that the current volume is not a revised edition; it is an entirely different book. Each of the volumes grew from the previous one: New questions emerged, new topics were suggested, and new insights were provided, which led us to redefine the focus of each of the succeeding volumes. Thus, the structure and content of the current volume have again changed radically to reflect contemporary research developments, with the majority of chapters being contributed by new teams of authors. In particular, we felt it was timely to focus more explicitly on relating bereavement research to contemporary societal and practice issues. It will become apparent in the following pages that there are remarkable developments concerning these topics in the field of bereavement research as well as ongoing controversies and healthy debates about them. With this *Handbook*, then, we complement and extend those that have gone before in both scope and content, hoping to promote the cause of thorough review of the bereavement research field in the 21st century.

Our work on the current volume began soon after the completion of the previous one, thus spanning a period of more than 5 years. During this time, there was scarcely a day when one of the editors was not busy with handbook business. As with our previous handbooks, working on this volume has never been an ordeal; it has frequently been a delight, and it has always been a learning experience—both personally and professionally. Production of the chapters individually and creation of the volume as a whole have been marked by many differences of opinion among us but no coming to blows. We have been incredibly supported in the editorial process by our authors, who have frequently encouraged us and who have undergone an unusually arduous reviewing process. We are grateful to all of them, not only for their commitment but also for their excellent chapters. Thus, first and foremost we thank our authors for contributing to this volume, and we acknowledge that it has been a great pleasure to work with them.

The American Psychological Association is an exceptional publisher in many respects, and we are delighted to have been able to bring this project to a happy conclusion with them. In particular, we thank Lansing Hays, the acquisitions editor who commissioned the volume and accompanied us through the earlier stages of production and, more recently, development editor Ron Teeter, whose editorial feedback went way beyond the organizational and structural aspects to insightful review of the chapters. In the final stages of production, we have been most grateful to production editor Harriet Kaplan, in particular for her skills in polishing the manuscript. Working with such excellent editors has helped us enormously to produce this volume.

Finally, we would like to give special mention to the lovely cover artwork, which depicts a painting by the Dutch artist Emmy van den Blink (1946–2007), entitled *Waiting for Better Times*. We pay tribute to her life and work.

I

INTRODUCTION

1

BEREAVEMENT RESEARCH: CONTEMPORARY PERSPECTIVES

MARGARET S. STROEBE, ROBERT O. HANSSON, HENK SCHUT, AND WOLFGANG STROEBE

Understanding of the bereavement experience has broadened and deepened in recent decades. Earlier assumptions have been put to empirical test; new and creative research designs have been introduced; innovative statistical techniques have been applied; and there have been novel attempts at theoretical integration, lively disputes about controversial issues, and significant developments in intervention programming. We have come to understand as well the influence of dramatic societal change and the ways in which events of national and international scope have altered the circumstances of bereavement to which people must adapt, affecting how they grieve personally and mourn publicly. Bereavement research continues to reflect the involvement of many clinical and academic disciplines and investigators from many countries and cultures.

These developments, then, suggest the timeliness of the present volume. With the turn of the century not long behind us, it is appropriate to take stock, to sort through and attempt an integration of the new knowledge base, and to come to some consensus regarding priorities and directions for future research efforts.

Our objective for this volume was to continue to provide an up-to-date, state-of-the-art account of bereavement research, as we have attempted to provide in our previous *Handbooks* on the topic of bereavement (M. Stroebe, Hansson, Stroebe, & Schut, 2001; M. Stroebe, Stroebe, & Hansson, 1993). However, in the current volume we have tried to relate bereavement research more explicitly to contemporary societal and practice issues than was done in earlier volumes. In this context, it is important to emphasize that this volume is not a sourcebook for practitioners seeking practical tips. It is instead intended to provide—insofar as this is possible in a single volume—a comprehensive overview of research in relationship to practice, identifying developments in the field, discussing contemporary controversial issues, encouraging debate about them, and proposing research and implementation agendas for the future.

All the chapters in this volume are new, except for chapter 7 (which we discuss in more detail later in this chapter). Chapter 7 is an update and considerable expansion of a similar chapter in the previous *Handbooks*. The remaining chapters all address topics and perspectives that complement and build on the contents of previous *Handbooks*. Chapters were sought from many new authors on emerging, innovative topics and lines of research on bereavement.

In the following sections of this chapter, we have three goals. First, for the reader's convenience, we define and discuss fundamental concepts in the bereavement field, ones that are frequently used by the contributors to this volume. We then trace the major historical shifts that have taken place in scholarly thinking about bereavement to set the stage for the contemporary developments in research and practice. Finally, we introduce the reader to the structure and scope of the volume itself and outline the unique contributions of the individual chapters.

BEREAVEMENT RESEARCH: DEFINITIONS OF FUNDAMENTAL CONCEPTS

In the paragraphs that follow, we provide definitions of the basic concepts and manifestations associated with bereavement. These definitions are followed with reasonable consistency by the authors in this book and across the bereavement research field in general (cf. Archer, 1999; Averill, 1968; Parkes, 1996; M. Stroebe et al., 2001). Despite the concordance, it will become evident to the reader that none of these definitions are actually cut and dried and that thoughtful consideration and ongoing discussion about the basic concepts are still necessary.

Bereavement, Grief, and Mourning

Bereavement is the term used to denote the objective situation of having lost someone significant through death. This naturally leads to the question of how to define *someone significant*. The category is generally taken to include personal losses experienced across the life span: the deaths of parents, siblings, partners, friends, and—against the expectations of parents—one's own child. Bereavement is associated with intense distress for most people. This is one of the main reasons for the burgeoning body of research on the topic; a major concern is to understand and try to relieve the suffering of bereaved people.

Grief is the term applied to the primarily emotional (affective) reaction to the loss of a loved one through death. It is a normal, natural reaction to loss: As Archer (1999) expressed it, "Grief . . . is the cost we pay for being able to love in the way we do" (p. 5). Although grief is understood to be primarily a negative affective reaction, it also incorporates diverse psychological (cognitive, social–behavioral) and physical (physiological–somatic) manifestations. It is a complex syndrome, within which a variety of symptoms may be apparent. The symptom picture, however, is understood to vary considerably from one bereaved person to another, from one culture to another, and across the course of time even for a single grieving individual (and again—across the course of time—between cultures).

As an illustration of differences in grief symptoms, consider the following examples (cf. Rosenblatt & Wallace, 2005): One person's grief may be dominated by intense feelings of loneliness, another's by anger at being abandoned by the loved one. Bereaved people from one ethnic group may experience (or express) feelings of grief that vary in nature and intensity from those experienced or expressed by other ethnic groups. One person may show few signs of grief early on but intense reactions later, whereas another person may manifest the opposite duration-related effects.

Mourning, in our view, is a term that should be distinguished from grief.[1] We consider *mourning* to refer to the public display of grief, the social expressions or acts expressive of grief that are shaped by the (often religious) beliefs and practices of a given society or cultural group. For a fascinating review of culture contrasts in mourning customs and rituals, we refer the reader to a volume by Parkes, Laungani, and Young (1997), whose descriptions of rituals and beliefs surrounding death range from those that are permeated and guided by Buddhist religious doctrine among traditional Tibetans (Gielen, 1997) to those influenced by secular, rational, humanistic philosophy in the West (Walter, 1997).

Although we define them separately, mourning and grief have at times been difficult to distinguish (an issue that is raised again by Rosenblatt in chap. 10 of this volume). For example, it may be unclear whether an overt expression of distress is a reflection of an emotional, personal reaction or

---

[1]*Mourning* is sometimes taken to mean the emotional reaction to loss, which we have defined as *grief*. Such usage is followed particularly by researchers and practitioners adhering to the psychoanalytic tradition, who sometimes use the terms *grief* and *mourning* interchangeably.

whether the bereaved individual is following a societal norm to express emotion (e.g., in the case of spontaneous vs. ritual crying). Grief may influence mourning, and mourning may equally influence feelings of grief. Such possibilities are illustrated in a recent account by Rubin and Yasien-Esmael (2004) of Muslim traditions in Israel, which are also likely to contrast with the experience of grief and mourning among those from other cultural and religious backgrounds:

> The extent to which the bereaved may remember and long for the deceased in Islamic tradition at the level of private psychological experience is not clearly set forth. It would seem that the bereaved is allowed to experience the complex of memories and emotions vis-à-vis the deceased from a generally positive psychological valence, and with a sense that the beloved is with God. . . . Mourning practices and their place in the psychological, communal, and religious life of Muslims within Israel today leave room for ongoing personal attachments to the deceased. The religious and behavioral focus is on acceptance of fate, the reality of the loss, and the primacy of following religious practices in the relationship to God, even at one's moments of great pain and upheaval. (pp. 158–159)

According to this account, then, rituals among members of this Muslim community positively affect feelings of grief over the deceased person.

Normal and Complicated Grief

Researchers are generally hesitant to define *normal* grief versus *complicated* grief,[2] given that grief is a complex emotional syndrome, encompassing myriad reactions, durational changes, and cultural differences. In accordance with our definition of grief, *normal* grief could be defined as an emotional reaction to bereavement, falling within expected norms, given the circumstances and implications of the death, with respect to time course and/or intensity of symptoms. This definition, however, raises further questions; for example, what are the expected norms? On what basis should loss experiences be classified with respect to circumstances and implications for the bereaved? What are people's expectations with respect to duration of symptoms, and how can a cutoff point for intensity be established?

Additional difficulties arise in trying to characterize complicated grief. Complicated grief is not a single syndrome; it is subject to cultural variation; it is sometimes difficult to differentiate from related disorders (e.g., depression, anxiety disorders, posttraumatic stress disorder) and, despite major contemporary efforts, researchers have yet to reach agreement regarding a definitive

---

[2]Other terms also are frequently used, for example, *pathological, traumatic, unresolved, prolonged.*

set of diagnostic criteria (or even whether diagnostic criteria are necessary and useful; see Parkes, 2005).

In this context, we can begin with our previous definition of *complicated* grief (M. Stroebe et al., 2001), namely, a deviation from the (cultural) norm (i.e., that could be expected to pertain, according to the extremity of the particular bereavement event) in the time course or intensity of specific or general symptoms of grief. However, such a definition fails to take dysfunction into account.[3] Intensity implies dysfunction, but daily functioning in various spheres of life following bereavement should probably be made more explicit, especially because this dimension is clinically relevant. The *Diagnostic and Statistical Manual of Mental Disorders* (4th ed.; *DSM–IV*; American Psychiatric Association, 1994) criteria for clinical significance (for mental disorders) usually include the specification that the condition "causes clinically significant distress or impairment in social, occupational, or other important areas of functioning" (p. 7). Thus, the roles of function and performance should also be taken into account in defining complicated grief. A two-pronged extension of our definition of complicated grief thus seems warranted: a clinically significant deviation from the (cultural) norm (i.e., that could be expected to pertain, according to the extremity of the particular bereavement event) in either (a) the time course or intensity of specific or general symptoms of grief and/or (b) the level of impairment in social, occupational, or other important areas of functioning.

Types of Complicated Grief

Various subtypes of complicated grief have received extensive attention in the clinical and research literatures. For example, *chronic* grief, which is similar to *prolonged* grief (see chap. 8, this volume), is characterized by long-lasting presence of symptoms associated with intense grief. *Delayed, inhibited,* or *absent* grief occurs when an individual shows little or no sign of grieving early on in bereavement but, in the cases of delayed and inhibited grief, does so intensely at a later time (again, pathology is not always indicated by early absence of symptoms). Absent grief can be linked with delayed and inhibited grief because of conceptual overlap: Although symptoms are apparently absent, they too may be manifested at some later time, or difficulties may be apparent in terms of some other grief-related debility or disorder, suggesting that the absence was indeed problematic. Like delayed and inhibited grief, absent grief is characterized by the nonappearance of overt symptoms typical of grief, with the continuation of life seemingly unaffected by the bereavement. As we suggested earlier, absent grief may also be problematic if the person man-

---

[3]We are grateful to E. Zech (personal communication, July 2006) for drawing attention to this point.

ifests symptoms that are not typical of grief (i.e., that take the place of grief symptoms); however, we need to emphasize that the absence of grief symptoms without the presence of other symptoms gives rise to caution in interpreting lack of apparent grief in terms of problems. Chronic (or prolonged) grief has been generally well accepted as a pathological category, whereas delayed, inhibited, and absent grief remain the subject of much debate.

In presenting these categories it is important to note that only a minority of bereaved persons suffer from complicated forms of grief and will need the professional help of counselors or therapists. Most bereavements involve no pathological indications. The majority of bereaved persons will undergo a period of intense suffering and some dysfunction but will be able to deal with their bereavement without professional referral.

Grief Counseling and Grief Therapy

Many different types of supportive intervention are available for bereaved persons in Western societies, and these are gradually extending to other cultures, notably in the wake of recent natural disasters. It is difficult to categorize the various programs meaningfully, but Worden (1982; see also Worden, 1991, 2001) has provided a useful distinction between grief counseling and grief therapy. *Grief counseling* refers to the facilitation through counseling of the process (tasks) of normal, uncomplicated grieving to alleviate suffering and help bereaved individuals to adjust well, within a reasonable time. An example is the Widow-to-Widow mutual help program, developed in the United States by Silverman (e.g., Silverman, 1986). *Grief therapy* refers to specialized techniques of intervention that guide an abnormal or complicated grief reaction (e.g., chronic grief) toward a normal coping process. Of course, in practice it may be difficult to make the distinction between these two types of intervention.

BEREAVEMENT RESEARCH ACROSS THE 20TH CENTURY

In this section, we provide an overview of the issues and concerns that have occupied scientists across the 20th century to place contemporary bereavement theory and research in a broader perspective. We focus on a few of the major researchers who have shaped the scientific study of bereavement (more comprehensive accounts can be found in Archer, 1999; Parkes, 1972, 1986, 1996; W. Stroebe & Stroebe, 1987).

Early Developments

Nearly a century ago, Freud's (1917/1957) classic paper "Mourning and Melancholia" provided the first systematic analysis of bereavement. The paper discussed reactions to the death of a loved one from Freud's psychoanalytic viewpoint, and his theoretical ideas became highly influential in shaping subsequent understanding of healthy and unhealthy coping with bereavement. His emphasis on the necessity for individuals to do grief work in coming to terms with a loss was to be taken up and elaborated for many decades to come—indeed, right up to the present. In subsequent decades, for example, both Deutsch (1937) and Klein (e.g., 1940) began to address, also within the psychoanalytic tradition, issues of complicated grief, with the former analyzing the phenomenon of absent grief and the latter the relationship of grieving to manic–depressive (i.e., bipolar) states. As already indicated, the demarcation of complicated grief is a topic that continues to occupy bereavement researchers today.

The early theoretical contributions to bereavement research reflected a psychoanalytic tradition. However, with the publication of Lindemann's (1944) article, titled "Symptomatology and Management of Acute Grief," researchers began to conduct empirical studies of grief and its consequences. The range of symptoms that Lindemann found to be associated with grief are still today reflected in assessments of bereaved persons. Even earlier, epidemiological studies in the 19th century, notably those by Durkheim (1951/1987) and Farr (1858/1975), had begun to explore the consequences of bereavement for mortality. This work was advanced in the middle of the 20th century by Kraus and Lilienfeld (1959), who showed that the mortality risk of the widowed was consistently higher than for married counterparts of the same age and sex. Bereavement-related mortality rates continue to hold the attention of contemporary researchers.

Mid 20th Century Onward

During the 1950s, researchers began a more systematic documentation of the manifestations and duration of grief. The work of Clayton and colleagues (e.g., Clayton, 1979) and Maddison and colleagues (e.g., Maddison & Viola, 1968; Maddison & Walker, 1967) made prominent contributions to this, and an important conceptual article by Averill (1968) brought focus to bereavement as a field of research by delineating central issues and concepts. Researchers began to map the mental and physical vulnerabilities of grieving persons with an eye to providing the right type of care to those who most needed it. Parkes's (1972) *Bereavement: Studies of Grief in Adult Life* consolidated much of the research that had been conducted up to that point. This classic book has continued to shape the field, with new editions appearing at regular intervals (Parkes, 1986, 1996).

During these years, with few exceptions, the focus centered on the grieving individual, the perspective being intrapersonal rather than interpersonal. Vachon's pioneering work (e.g., Vachon et al., 1982), however, extended the investigation to interpersonal issues to include social risk factors, the effectiveness of intervention programs for the bereaved, and the impact of bereavement on social networks (and vice versa). A feature of this historical period was that empirical research (despite the psychoanalytic tradition) was still largely issue rather than theory driven. For example, a major practical issue driving much research from the mid 20th century onward concerned the identification of high-risk categories of bereaved persons; given the vast individual differences in patterns of adjustment to the loss of a loved one, could researchers establish which subgroups of bereaved persons were most vulnerable, and to what specific health consequences?

These developments, and advances in the broader fields of stress and trauma, then led to further explorations of the nature of complicated grief. Investigations by Parkes (1965) and Parkes and Weiss (1983) resulted in a highly influential classification of the complications of grief based on a risk factor perspective. Jacobs (1993) subsequently made the link between complicated grief and the *DSM* system (cf. *DSM–IV*; American Psychiatric Association, 1994), suggesting a classification of so-called "pathologic grief" for potential inclusion in future editions of the *DSM*. In this period, also, Bowlby (1980) examined chronic and absent forms of grieving from his attachment theory perspective (see also Raphael, 1983).

Also by the later decades of the 20th century, stage models for adaptation to grief (e.g., Bowlby, 1980) and task models (e.g., Worden, 1982) had begun to shape researchers' understanding of the course of grieving. These were welcomed as guidelines by those counseling the bereaved. Unfortunately, there have been misinterpretations, particularly about Bowlby's (1980) stage model. Bowlby did not conceive of the postulated stages of grief as prescriptive with respect to where a given bereaved person should be at any particular duration of bereavement (although it is probably true to say that other stage theorists actually did so). There is much overlap in symptoms across proposed stages. Not all bereaved people show indications of going through phases or tasks, or in the sequence suggested, and there is typically no clear end point; bereaved people—at least in Western culture—do not simply recover or "get over" their loss and return to normal; there is no resolution or completion per se; instead, they adapt, adjust, and are to some degree changed forever (Weiss, 1993).

In recent decades, research has become increasingly theory guided; cognitive stress theory and attachment theory in particular have influenced research psychologists in the field, and attention has increasingly focused on the complexities of bereavement experience. Gradually, too, research designs, methods, and statistical techniques have become more sophisticated. Prospective, multivariate designs are now being used to address more finely grained processes underlying the manifestations of grief. Laboratory studies are beginning to become more frequent as well.

The Turn of the Century

Our *Handbook of Bereavement Research* (M. Stroebe et al., 2001) represented the state of affairs at the turn of the century, providing comprehensive reviews of theoretical and empirical advances in the field. That volume was organized around the three themes of "consequences," "coping," and "care." These three themes merit further investigation, and each one is well represented across the chapters of this new *Handbook*.

Consider the first theme, "consequences": By now it is well-known that the costs of bereavement in terms of mental and physical health can be extreme, and biological links have become much better established. Much still needs to be learned, however, about cultural differences in reactions (in terms of the relative frequency, intensity, duration, and even the nature and meaning of symptomatology). Researchers and practitioners also need to better understand resilience and to identify the personal and circumstantial factors that enable some persons to cope with a loss much better than others. There is a need as well to broaden the focus beyond health consequences (e.g., to social implications and to different types of dysfunction and debility).

Coping refers to processes, strategies, or styles of managing (reducing, mastering, tolerating) the situation in which bereavement places the individual. Grief work would be an example of coping. We noted elsewhere (M. Stroebe et al., 2001) that there is a thin line between the concepts of coping and symptomatology, but it remains important for theoretical and practical reasons to try to tease them apart (e.g., to retain clarity in the design of research by distinguishing process from outcome variables). Furthermore, although much interest in coping stems from a concern to identify more versus less successful strategies, the way one copes does not fully determine the outcome. Other factors, such as personality variables or circumstances of the death, may explain more variance in outcome than coping, and empirical studies involving multiple variables, instead of single-factor investigations, are needed (M. Stroebe, Folkman, Hansson, & Schut, 2006). Researchers also still need to identify the coping strategies that are effective (and for whom) and to better understand precisely what has to be coped with.

The third theme, "care," focused on

> ways that bereavement research can inform health care professionals and members of informal networks surrounding bereaved persons . . . includ[ing] knowledge about the nature of complications in the grieving process, the types of psychological and pharmacological interventions that are now available, and assessment of the effectiveness of such programs. (M. Stroebe et al., 2001, p. 10)

Bereavement researchers, ourselves included, are typically anxious to emphasize that grief is a normal reaction to the death of a loved one and that most people manage to come to terms with their loss over the course of time. Although associated for most people with a period of distress, it does not usually require the help of professional counselors or therapists (although if bereaved persons feel the need for intervention, it is important that assessment procedures be available to establish whether they could be helped). For a minority, though, mental or physical consequences can be extreme and sometimes persistent. Progress has been made over recent decades in designing and implementing a range of care services for bereaved persons. As the chapters of this volume show, researchers are continuing to grapple with the difficult task of establishing the efficacy of such programs, using controls in their designs that were lacking in many earlier studies.

Where does this leave us now? In the final chapter of the 2001 *Handbook*, we pinpointed core themes emerging from the preceding chapters, to suggest directions for future research (M. Stroebe et al., 2001). We also highlighted the major controversies in the field. In many ways, this current *Handbook* carries on where the last one left off, picking up new directions and neglected themes and furthering discussion of controversial issues.

SCOPE AND CONTENT OF THIS VOLUME

Before we describe the themes around which the chapters in this current volume are organized, it is important to say a few words about our particular theoretical orientation. Our view of bereavement research is based on several fundamental principles, some of which have probably already become evident. Perhaps the most fundamental is our belief that bereavement needs to be understood from a sound base of theoretically oriented and empirically derived knowledge and not purely on the basis of subjective descriptive accounts, not even those of skilled individuals. Although clinical reports are of considerable value in designing research and in understanding bereavement-related phenomena, we strive wherever possible to report methodologically stringent empirical research and to suggest ways that claims made in theoretical or clinical contexts can be put to rigorous test. Research should ultimately not only lead to deeper scientific understanding but also be practically useful; concern about the impact of loss on bereaved individuals and groups underlies the work of the contributors to this volume.

We advocate as well a broad scientific approach to bereavement. This volume includes the work of researchers from diverse disciplines, including medicine, public health, sociology, religion, gerontology, anthropology, social and clinical psychology, and so on. We view these different perspectives as integral to greater synthesis and deeper understanding of the bereavement experience. In this and previous *Handbooks* (e.g., M. Stroebe et al., 1993, 2001), we have also tried to include the work of scientists from different countries. So far, however, although fascinating studies are beginning to emerge from other countries, well-established programs producing sophisticated lines of research seem regretfully still pretty much limited to Western industrialized countries.

Finally, in this volume in particular, we have attempted to broaden and deepen our coverage of cultural and ethnic issues in bereavement. Cultural issues are a persisting concern, not least because of population trends in contemporary society. We need more comprehensive and differentiated knowledge about the ways that persons from very different cultures grieve and about the belief systems and mourning customs that shape and give meaning and expression to the grief experience. Yet cross-cultural investigation on an empirical level in the bereavement field is still in its infancy: It will take time for cross-cultural studies of bereavement to reach the level of maturity attained in other fields of investigation.

Turning now to the structure of this volume, the research perspectives covered here are organized around six themes. These make up the main parts of the book.

Contemporary Scientific Approaches and Issues

The chapters in Part II of this volume provide theoretical background and examine the major conceptual, methodological, and measurement issues in current-day bereavement research and provide a conceptual base for the remaining chapters in the book. At a general level, these chapters elucidate basic questions: What is grief? What theories best explain its manifestations? How have theoretical understandings changed over time, and as a function of societal systems? At a more specific level, the questions examine the following issues. How might further integration of theoretical perspectives prove useful? For example, can a theory of lost interpersonal relationships increase comprehension of who suffers most among bereaved persons? How can one actually measure grief and grieving, and how valid are researchers' attempts to do so across different ethnic and cultural groups?

In chapter 2, Robert S. Weiss probes the origins and nature of grief, tracing developments in the understanding of grief across the 20th century and exploring contemporary thinking on fundamental issues such as the course of grief and the nature and function of bonds with the deceased and mental representations of the deceased. Weiss illustrates, and places in perspective, the wealth of scholarship that has accumulated not only within the bereavement field but also in related fields, such as emotion, to provide scientific backing for contemporary formulations.

In chapter 3, John Archer provides a broad overview and critical commentary on theories that have been influential in past and current research, from evolutionary to social constructionist, and from analytic to holistic approaches. For example, he takes a critical look at research and theory on grief work, evaluating the utility of the concept and available evidence that bereaved persons actually need to confront and work through their grief to come to terms with it.

In chapter 4, the last of the three general theoretical chapters in this part, Robert Kastenbaum poses the following question: How might patterns of grieving and mourning change as we move deeper into the 21st century and beyond? He draws on his considerable experience in the fields of death, dying, and bereavement to assess ways that grief and grieving may influence individuals in the 21st century's evolving societies. Of particular importance is his consideration of grief not only within the individual but also within the context of societal death systems; he examines the interaction among individual experiences, cultural circumstances, and social forces. He examines as well how changing circumstances of dying can influence the ways in which people grieve. He then considers the phenomenon of grieving not only from one's personal bereavement perspective but also in terms of the loss of the world as it had been experienced and understood.

In chapter 5, Mario Mikulincer and Phillip R. Shaver turn from general theoretical issues to a specific, highly influential theory in recent bereavement research. Within the bereavement field, attachment theory's influence has increased phenomenally over the past 2 decades (this was a major topic in the last *Handbook* as well; M. Stroebe et al., 2001). There are good reasons to argue that this type of research is critical; attachment theory is a relationship theory that focuses on reactions to separation from a significant person. It follows that this perspective should offer insights into what happens when an attachment figure dies. Mikulincer and Shaver have used innovative methods to examine underlying processes relating to attachment patterns. In chapter 5, they outline the attachment theoretical perspective and review findings from their own and others' studies.

Also within the general theme of lost relationships is the question of whether an ongoing attachment to the deceased person should be continued during the grieving process or be relinquished. This remains a source of raging debate in the field. There has been a shift in recent decades, from an early–20th-century emphasis on the need to break bonds with a deceased person in order to adjust to loss and go on with life toward an emphasis on the need to sustain such bonds. Most recently, researchers have begun to approach this controversy in empirical as well as theoretical ways, examining the links between continuing and relinquishing bonds and adapting to grief. In chapter 6, Nigel P. Field reviews the continuing-bonds research and describes his own perspective. He presents his empirical research that has examined ways that people continue bonds and implications this might have for adjustment.

The topic of measurement also needs to be addressed. In the last *Handbook* (M. Stroebe et al., 2001), Robert A. Neimeyer and Nancy S. Hogan critically reviewed available quantitative and qualitative measures used in the study of grief. Since then, however, new instruments have emerged, and new, innovative techniques have been developed to examine the complex experience of grief. In chapter 7, with coauthor Anna Laurie, Neimeyer and Hogan update and extend their earlier review of quantitative and qualitative research approaches, addressing the following fundamental question: To what extent has the assessment of adaptation to bereavement moved toward greater psychometric rigor and sensitivity in recent years? Of particular importance in this chapter is that they appraise strategies and problems of measurement from a cross-cultural perspective: How can measures be adapted for use in various cultural and subcultural settings?

Contemporary Societal and Practical Concerns

The chapters in Part III explore contemporary practice and societal concerns associated with bereavement. The reader will note in this part considerable controversy surrounding a number of core questions; for example, how does one conceptualize those aspects of grief that require professional intervention? How does one ensure that bereavements among diverse components of a society are addressed with cultural competence? How does one ensure support for bereaved persons who may be isolated or whose grief may have become disenfranchised?

Perhaps the most important (and controversial) issue currently facing bereavement researchers and practitioners is whether complicated/prolonged grief should be included as a category of mental disorder in the next edition of the *DSM*. Given the significance of this issue, we devote two chapters in this book to consideration of the status of complicated grief as a category of mental disorder. In the first of these (chap. 8), Holly G. Prigerson, Lauren C. Vanderwerker, and Paul K. Maciejewski, strong proponents of introducing the new category, present a body of empirical research and argue the case that *prolonged grief disorder* (PGD; formerly known as *complicated grief*) constitutes a distinct mental disorder requiring inclusion in the *DSM* system. They elaborate on the features of PGD, identify specific risk factors for its occurrence, and describe possibilities for treatment. They also propose criteria for reliable and valid diagnosis of PGD and review trials they are conducting to assess the adequacy of the criteria for inclusion in the *DSM*.

There are good reasons to argue the case for inclusion of complicated grief/prolonged grief in the *DSM* system, not the least of which is to enable professional help to be given to those who most need it. However, there are also arguments against inclusion—for example, that it may unnecessarily medicalize grief or cause the natural family support network to withdraw if a grieving person is seen as needing and possibly receiving professional help. In chapter 9, then, Simon Shimshon Rubin, Ruth Malkinson, and Eliezer

Witztum discuss a number of challenges associated with *DSM* categorization of complicated grief. They draw on lessons learned from the classification of posttraumatic stress disorder in the planning for complicated grief, discuss the complications in conceptualization due to the interface of trauma and bereavement, and highlight difficulties associated with adopting a symptomatic phenomenological approach (e.g., assessment of the person's relationship with the deceased).

We have already argued the importance of expanding ethnic and cross-cultural research on bereavement, grief, and mourning. In chapter 10, Paul C. Rosenblatt addresses the need for cultural sensitivity, reviewing patterns of cultural influence and raising issues that all researchers need to be aware of. He advocates that for bereavement theory and research to advance, investigators must be sensitive to and informed by a cross-cultural perspective, including the belief that "culture creates, influences, shapes, limits, and defines grieving, sometimes profoundly" (p. 208). Attention to cultural perspectives in theory development in turn can enhance the provision of services and support to diverse grieving persons. Rosenblatt proposes an agenda for cross-cultural bereavement research in the future.

The concept of *disenfranchised grief* has had an enormous impact on the bereavement field, in large part because of the contributions of Kenneth J. Doka, author of chapter 11. The term denotes cases where grief has gone unrecognized, is marginalized, or has gone unsupported (e.g., in earlier times, loss of an out-of-wedlock partner; implications for mortality and ensuing bereavement because of positive DNA testing for Huntington's disease in contemporary society). From this viewpoint, then, a bereaved individual may be excluded from normative mourning and support processes, limiting his or her ability to acknowledge, experience, and adapt to loss. Doka describes the phenomenon of disenfranchised grief and its typologies, reviews research originating from different fields (e.g., psychological, sociological, and spiritual viewpoints), and considers complications for the grieving process and implications for counseling.

Another basic question is whether the concept of grief should be applied only to the loss of a loved one or close attachment figure. If so, what might be the meaning and significance of public demonstrations of grief that are seen with increasing frequency in the media, for example, for celebrities people have never met, or in response to traumatic events of national or international scope? In chapter 12, Tony Walter considers private and public mourning in the 20th century, introducing the concept of *new public mourning* (NPM)—the mourning for persons one did not know—and exploring its proliferation and transformation. He further examines the causes for this evolving phenomenon: Does the cause lie with the media, or does NPM have broader cultural, political, or psychological origins in changing society? Finally, he considers clinical and policy implications of NPM.

Patterns and Consequences of Grief: Phenomena and Manifestations

Since the publication of the last *Handbook* (M. Stroebe et al., 2001), important advances have been made with respect to understanding the experience and consequences of losing a loved one. This reflects scientific developments on many levels, from availability of prebereavement measurement in longitudinal studies and statistical advancements to the pinpointing of ways to establish neural correlates of emotion. These developments are extensively represented in Parts IV and V of this volume, which focus on patterns and consequences of grief. In Part IV, the chapter authors explore the course, manifestations, and diversity of grief reactions on both the psychological and physiological levels.

As in any other discipline, topics in bereavement go in and out of fashion, and the impact of the caregiving period before loss, including the possibility for anticipatory grief, has not been a popular research topic for some decades. Yet prebereavement experience is critically important. Richard Schulz, Kathrin Boerner, and Randy S. Hebert conducted a large-scale longitudinal investigation, which they describe in chapter 13, that followed the prebereavement caregiving of spouses and subsequent adaptation to bereavement. A main focus was on the impact of caregiving burden on subsequent adaptation. These authors also review existing research on the effects of bereavement when it is preceded by chronic illness, disability, and caregiving and describe their own research and the major findings, defining when and for whom a prebereavement period of preparation for death may be helpful versus harmful. They also suggest avenues for intervention and treatment.

In recent years, researchers have looked beyond stages or phases of grief through which bereaved persons were understood to proceed, postulating finely grained patterns of grieving. The availability of longitudinal data sets that include data collected before bereavement, to facilitate comparisons with patterns of adjustment after loss, has also enabled examination of trajectories of grieving and preloss predictors of different patterns. George A. Bonanno, Kathrin Boerner, and Camille B. Wortman, authors of chapter 14, have been at the forefront of this research. They have distinguished unique trajectories of bereavement outcome associated with different reactions to, and processing of, loss. In chapter 14, they provide a historical review and summarize their findings, enabling the reader to reassess such long-accepted notions as stages of grief, the role of denial, and the limits to resilience among the bereaved.

Whereas George A. Bonanno and his colleagues have greatly enhanced an understanding of resilience, Christopher G. Davis has made a major contribution with respect to the somewhat surprising phenomenon—given the devastating nature of loss—of personal growth during bereavement. In chapter 15, Davis describes his theoretical and empirical research on this topic. He views loss as a potential catalyst for change, as a challenge not only to the self but also to one's goal system. Growth involves significant changes in life direction and life goals, which come about through processes of renegotiation, leading to the establishment of new, intrinsically meaningful goals and priorities. He argues for the need to distinguish *growth* from *benefits*, which is a new, more sophisticated way of looking at posttraumatic growth.

The research programs we have just described have contributed to an understanding of the kinds of coping strategies or cognitive mechanisms that enhance resilience and promote growth after bereavement. A remaining puzzle, however, concerns the role of meaning-making systems in general and of religious coping in particular. Do religious beliefs help a bereaved person to explain, accept, and come to terms with loss? In chapter 16, Judith C. Hays and Cristina C. Hendrix examine the role of religious meaning-making and religious coping strategies in bereavement. They detail the types of investigations of religious coping that are now available, surveying studies across different faith traditions and reviewing the major findings in relationship to adjustment, and they examine implications for practitioners and intervention researchers.

In previous *Handbooks* (M. Stroebe et al., 1993, 2001), considerable attention was given to physiological concomitants of grief (e.g., immune system changes, physiological changes associated with intervention). However, there have also been remarkable developments in the examination of brain systems in recent years. Functional magnetic resonance imaging of the brain is a relatively new but widely used technique to investigate the neural circuits associated with emotion–motivation systems, such as romantic attraction. In view of the similarity between feelings of romantic rejection and the emotions experienced after bereavement, John Archer and Helen Fisher present in chapter 17 recent psychobiological research involving the neural mechanisms underlying the former state and examine its possible implications for the psychobiology of bereavement. It becomes clear that research at this level can help to illuminate the nature and functions of grief and grieving.

Patterns and Consequences of Grief: Relationship Perspectives

Despite a long tradition of research on risk factors for bereavement outcome, it is still difficult to predict who among the bereaved is likely to suffer most and to be most in need of help. Furthermore, research on some vulnerable subgroups has been neglected, and thus society is ill informed of their special risks and requirements. We need to learn more about particular reactions and needs that follow specific types of loss. Part V of this volume, then, is devoted to emerging research on diverse subgroups of bereaved people, grieving under different circumstances. We have already highlighted the importance of focusing on the lost relationship in outlining the chapters (5 and 6) that focus on attachment theory and continuing bonds. We pick up this theme in Part V, selecting four types of loss that represent contrasting relationships to deceased persons. The research described in these chapters suggests new insights regarding the dynamics of the grief and grieving of differing populations and how they may need special consideration both in research and practical support contexts.

The death of a child from any cause has been shown to have an extreme impact on parents, worse than any other type of bereavement. It has even been established that death of a child increases the mortality risk of mothers and fathers, particularly in the early weeks and months of bereavement (Li, Precht, Mortensen, & Olsen, 2003). Thus, researchers must continue to try to increase their understanding of parental bereavement. Of particular interest is the question of whether there might be even greater risk among parents of a child who has died from violent causes. With murder and suicide rates of young people increasing, answers to such key questions are urgently needed to enable appropriate interventions to be directed to parents who most require them. In chapter 18, Shirley A. Murphy describes her research program on parental bereavement specific to the violent subset of deaths (i.e., deaths due to accident, suicide, and homicide). To place these deaths in comparative perspective, she also summarizes the available research findings for parents whose children have died after an extended illness. She discusses difficult and sometimes controversial issues, for example, whether one violent cause of death of a child influences parents' outcomes more than another, or whether deaths due to suicide are particularly harrowing for parents.

There has been a long-standing debate in the scientific literature about the long-term effects on children of the death of a parent. Some investigators have found negative effects (into adulthood), whereas others have failed to confirm such connections. In chapter 19, Linda J. Luecken reviews evidence concerning both the short- and long-term impact of early loss of a parent on psychological and, of particular importance, on physiological outcomes (on which much new research is available). She examines alterations in the development of biochemical, hormonal, emotional, and behavioral responses to the environment and later life stressors. An important question here concerns why some children are resilient in the long term, whereas others appear much more vulnerable to the early loss event in their lives. Luecken examines social and environmental influences present both before and after the death, to establish moderators of the potential impact, including both risk and protective factors.

As life span expectancy has continued to increase over recent decades, issues surrounding the well-being and care of older adults are a cause for growing concern, especially as societies continue to struggle to provide adequately for their needs. A remarkable source of information about the bereavement experience among older persons has become available through the Changing Lives of Older Couples (CLOC) Study, a multiwave, large-scale prospective study of spousal bereavement. In chapter 20, Deborah Carr first reviews historical, social, and psychological factors that shape the experiences of bereaved older spouses. She then provides a comprehensive overview of the CLOC Study, highlighting findings specific to late-life bereavement and reflecting on the contexts in which bereavement takes place at this time of life (e.g., not only factors associated with increasing frailty but also those associated with more effective use of [inter]personal resources). Implications for theory, practice, and future research are discussed.

Bereaved grandparents are a terribly neglected group in the bereavement literature, despite the risk that they may grieve deeply, not only for their deceased grandchild but also for their own child, the parent who is also grieving. Such a loss can be especially distressing at a time of life when the grandparent him- or herself may be frail. In chapter 21, Bert Hayslip Jr. and Diana L. White consider the experience and consequences of grief among grandparents over the loss of a grandchild. Two conceptual frameworks guide their analyses of the experience of loss among grandparents: (a) the life course perspective on intergenerational relationships and family systems and (b) disenfranchised grief. They compare the bereavement experience with the impact of divorce on relationships with grandchildren and the losses associated with raising a grandchild. They identify common elements across these different types of loss and illustrate how each contributes to our understanding of grandparent bereavement.

Development and Efficacy of Intervention Programs

Continuing controversies, generated in part by chapters in our previous *Handbook* (M. Stroebe et al., 2001), focus on the provision of professional and informal help for bereaved persons. A number of questions remain at the center of the debates: Is intervention necessary and useful at all? If it is, who benefits most? Can the grief process itself be eased through intervention? Which subgroups need help? What kinds of intervention programs are currently available? What sort of help has been shown to be efficacious? How can help be provided to the bereaved at times of massive trauma and human losses? In part VI, the last substantive section of this volume, the chapter authors provide up-to-date reviews on important intervention issues. The chapters in this part also cover evaluations of different types of intervention for different subgroups of bereaved persons.

Bereavement following disasters, whether on a relatively small or a colossal scale, is known to be associated with complications in the grieving process. Many factors compound the risk of adjustment difficulties (bodies missing or mutilated; children lost; witnessing horrific events; survivor guilt; additional losses of home, livelihood, etc.). How, then, can psychological care for bereaved persons best be provided by professional and voluntary services following such disasters? In chapter 22, Colin Murray Parkes draws on his own considerable experience in organizing and providing care for bereaved people, from smaller scale, local disasters to international disasters. He carefully describes how the variability in the scope and magnitude of these disasters influences their impact and the nature of services necessary to cope with them. He also details other factors that influence the response, such as the duration of the event, cultural factors, and expectations of the bereaved individuals. He outlines the implications for bereavement practitioners and for community and national agencies of having to respond to a disaster.

A major advance in bereavement research has been the shift in focus from an intrapersonal perspective (on the grieving individual) to a broader, interpersonal perspective. After all, people do not grieve alone but among family and friends who may also be grieving, with mutual influence on the intensity and course of grief. This concern about including family and about group perspectives extends to therapy. Although in the past most interventions were designed to deal with a grieving person, there has been a more recent trend toward family-focused grief therapy. Given the importance of this broadened perspective, we include two chapters on family intervention. In chapter 23, David W. Kissane and Wendy G. Lichtenthal describe their family-focused grief therapy model and program. Family-focused grief therapy is a preventive intervention that begins during the terminal illness of a family member and continues beyond the person's death, intended to enhance family functioning and to encourage the sharing of grief among the family members. Kissane and Lichtenthal also describe controlled clinical trials that have assessed the therapy's efficacy. They place their own research within the perspective of other family-focused intervention programs, describing the principles underlying family approaches in general and the range of outcomes among different types of bereaved families.

In chapter 24, Janice Winchester Nadeau takes a very different type of family perspective. Nadeau focuses on interactive processes of family meaning construction, closely examining what goes on between and among family members during the time of bereavement. By what processes do families make sense of death? Nadeau addresses this basic question by drawing on her own research on family meaning-making and on her own considerable clinical experience. She integrates family theory, family therapy theory and methods, and relevant concepts from diverse scientific disciplines to provide ways to understand and appropriately intervene with families of the dying and bereaved. Again, in this chapter the need to link research with practice becomes evident: A family meaning-making model is presented that assumes that meanings attached to a death will affect bereavement outcomes in significant ways. Nadeau demonstrates how grief therapists might use the model and suggests guidelines for future research.

The research fields that have developed around bereavement and divorce have had little to do with each other, and there has been little cross-learning between these differing areas of expertise. Yet comparisons between these two life experiences are of interest on both theoretical and practical levels, not only to elucidate comparative consequences (as addressed in chap. 21) but also to provide insight into effective intervention on family and individual levels. Irwin Sandler and his colleagues have conducted extensive empirical research with families who have experienced either bereavement or divorce. In chapter 25, they describe the development and evaluation of their theoretically derived Family Bereavement Program. The program was designed to prevent mental health problems in children who had experienced the death of a parent. First, they examine risk and protective factors among children who have lost a parent, and then they discuss modifiable factors that were targeted in their Family Bereavement Program. They provide evidence for the efficacy of the intervention in assisting children and adolescents through their loss experiences and include assessments of mediators and moderators of the program's effects. They discuss ways in which the findings with bereaved children replicate and diverge from those of their research with children in divorced families.

In chapter 26, the final chapter of Part VI, Margaret S. Stroebe, Karolijne van der Houwen, and Henk Schut take a critical look at how contemporary technological advances offer new possibilities for bereavement support. What is the potential, and what are the drawbacks, of using the Internet and e-mail systems for the giving and seeking of support among bereaved persons? First the authors describe recent expansions of available support through the Internet (e.g., online memorial sites, chat rooms, support groups, mailing lists for specific types of bereavement). They review possibilities for research and intervention via the Internet. They raise the question of the efficacy of using such sites and consider the issue of whether assessment actually needs to be made (and how this could be done). They draw attention to the paucity of research in this area, to the need for caution in assuming benefits of Internet bereavement support, and to potential harm that may be caused. A major purpose of the chapter is to set a research agenda for the future.

In chapter 27, this volume's closing chapter, we provide an overview, as we did in the last *Handbook* (M. Stroebe et al., 2001). We summarize and comment on the themes and chapters, pick up on the debates and controversies and give our own views on these, suggest additional topics that might need further attention, and propose lines of research for the future.

CONCLUSIONS

Our goal for this volume, then, is to present the ideas and research that have broadened and deepened our understanding of the bereavement experience over the past decade. Important assumptions have now been put to empirical test, theoretical integration has progressed, and more sophisticated designs and methodologies and more advanced statistical techniques have been used and have provided new and more complex insights. In this context, important new controversies have arisen, causing much debate, and chapters in the volume address such issues from varying perspectives. New research has also shown how the bereavement experience itself has been changing in response to societal and cultural forces. Our hope is that this *Handbook* will provide a resource for bereavement researchers and practitioners alike, one that will be useful to them in their work with bereaved persons.

REFERENCES

American Psychiatric Association. (1994). *Diagnostic and statistical manual of mental disorders* (4th ed.). Washington, DC: Author.

Archer, J. (1999). *The nature of grief: The evolution and psychology of reactions to loss*. London: Routledge.

Averill, J. (1968). Grief: Its nature and significance. *Psychological Bulletin, 70*, 721–728.

Bowlby, J. (1980). *Attachment and loss: Vol. 3. Loss: Sadness and depression*. Harmondsworth, England: Penguin Books.

Clayton, P. (1979). The sequelae and nonsequelae of conjugal bereavement. *American Journal of General Psychiatry, 136*, 1530–1534.

Deutsch, H. (1937). Absence of grief. *Psycho-Analytic Quarterly, 6*, 12–22.

Durkheim, E. (1987). *Suicide: A study in sociology*. Glencoe, IL: Free Press. (Original work published 1951)

Farr, W. (1975). Influence of marriage on the mortality of the French people. In N. Humphreys (Ed.), *Vital statistics: A memorial volume of selections from reports and writings of William Farr* (pp. 438–441). New York: Methuen. (Original work published 1858)

Freud, S. (1957). Mourning and melancholia. In J. Strachey (Ed. & Trans.), *The standard edition of the complete psychological works of Sigmund Freud* (Vol. 14, pp. 152–170). London: Hogarth Press. (Original work published 1917)

Gielen, U. (1997). A death on the roof of the world: The perspective of Tibetan Buddhism. In C. M. Parkes, P. Laungani, & B. Young (Eds.), *Death and bereavement across cultures* (pp. 73–97). New York: Routledge.

Jacobs, S. (1993). *Pathologic grief: Maladaptation to loss*. Washington, DC: American Psychiatric Association.

Klein, M. (1940). Mourning and its relation to manic-depressive states. *International Journal of Psycho-Analysis, 21*, 125–153.

Kraus, A., & Lilienfeld, A. (1959). Some epidemiological aspects of the high mortality rate in the young widowed group. *Journal of Chronic Diseases, 10*, 207–217.

Li, J., Precht, D., Mortensen, P., & Olsen, J. (2003). Mortality in parents after death of a child in Denmark: A nationwide follow-up study. *The Lancet, 361*, 363–367.

Lindemann, E. (1944). Symptomatology and management of acute grief. *American Journal of Psychiatry, 101,* 141–148.

Maddison, D., & Viola, A. (1968). The health of widows in the year following bereavement. *Journal of Psychosomatic Research, 12,* 297–306.

Maddison, D., & Walker, W. (1967). Factors affecting the outcome of conjugal bereavement. *British Journal of Psychiatry, 113,* 1057–1067.

Neimeyer, R. A., & Hogan, N. S. (2001). Quantitative or qualitative? Measurement issues in the study of grief. In M. Stroebe, R. O. Hansson, W. Stroebe, & H. Schut (Eds.), *Handbook of bereavement research: Consequences, coping, and care* (pp. 89–118). Washington, DC: American Psychological Association

Parkes, C. M. (1965). Bereavement and mental illness. *British Journal of Medical Psychology, 38,* 1–26.

Parkes, C. M. (1972). *Bereavement: Studies of grief in adult life.* London: Routledge.

Parkes, C. M. (1986). *Bereavement: Studies of grief in adult life* (2nd ed.). London: Routledge.

Parkes, C. M. (1996). *Bereavement: Studies of grief in adult life* (3rd ed.). London: Routledge.

Parkes, C. M. (Ed.). (2005). Complicated grief: A symposium [Special issue]. *Omega: The Journal of Death and Dying, 52*(1).

Parkes, C. M., Laungani, P., & Young, B. (Eds.). (1997). *Death and bereavement across cultures.* New York: Routledge.

Parkes, C. M., & Weiss, R. (1983). *Recovery from bereavement.* New York: Basic Books.

Raphael, B. (1983). *The anatomy of bereavement.* New York: Basic Books.

Rosenblatt, P. C., & Wallace, B. R. (2005). *African American grief.* New York: Routledge.

Rubin, S., & Yasien-Esmael, H. (2004). Loss and bereavement among Israel's Muslims: Acceptance of God's will, grief, and relationship to the deceased. *Omega: The Journal of Death and Dying, 49,* 149–162.

Silverman, P. (1986). *Widow-to-widow.* New York: Springer Publishing Company.

Stroebe, M., Folkman, S., Hansson, R. O., & Schut, H. (2006). The prediction of bereavement outcome: Development of an integrative risk factor framework. *Social Science & Medicine, 63,* 2446–2451.

Stroebe, M., Hansson, R. O., Stroebe, W., & Schut, H. (Eds.). (2001). *Handbook of bereavement research: Consequences, coping, and care.* Washington, DC: American Psychological Association.

Stroebe, M., Stroebe, W., & Hansson, R. O. (1993). *Handbook of bereavement: Theory, research, and intervention.* New York: Cambridge University Press.

Stroebe, W., & Stroebe, M. (1987). *Bereavement and health: The psychological and physical consequences of partner loss.* New York: Cambridge University Press.

Vachon, M., Sheldon, A., Lancee, W., Lyall, W., Rogers, J., & Freeman, S. (1982). Correlates of enduring distress patterns following bereavement: Social network, life situation, and personality. *Psychological Medicine, 12,* 783–788.

Walter, T. (1997). Secularization. In C. M. Parkes, P. Laungani, & B. Young (Eds.), *Death and bereavement across cultures* (pp. 166–187). New York: Routledge.

Weiss, R. (1993). Loss and recovery. In M. Stroebe, W. Stroebe, & R. O. Hansson (Eds.), *Handbook of bereavement: Theory, research, and intervention* (pp. 271–284). New York: Cambridge University Press.

Worden, J. W. (1982). *Grief counseling and grief therapy*. New York: Springer Publishing Company.

Worden, J. W. (1991). *Grief counseling and grief therapy* (2nd ed.). New York: Springer Publishing Company.

Worden, J. W. (2001). *Grief counseling and grief therapy* (3rd ed.). New York: Springer Publishing Company.

II

CONTEMPORARY
SCIENTIFIC APPROACHES
AND ISSUES

2

THE NATURE AND CAUSES OF GRIEF

ROBERT S. WEISS

Darwin (1872/1998), in *The Expression of the Emotions in Man and Animals,* preceded a meticulous description of the facial muscles that convey grief by observing that there are distinct states of grief:

> After the mind has suffered from an acute paroxysm of grief, and the cause still continues, we fall into a state of low spirits; or we may be utterly cast down and dejected. . . . if we expect to suffer, we are anxious; if we have no hope of relief, we despair. (p. 176)

Darwin here introduced a stage theory of grieving. First there is "acute paroxysm," presumably a convulsive emotional expression in which self-control is overwhelmed. This is then followed, if "the cause still continues," by persisting low spirits or by either of two forms of more intense distress. In one of the latter, we are anxious; in the other, we despair.

Paul Ekman, commenting on Darwin's (1872/1998) observations, was concerned that by referring to all the states that followed loss as "grief," Darwin obscured the different emotions they expressed:

> Darwin uses the term grief . . . as a general term for two more specific emotions: distress and sadness. We have suggested that the term distress

be used for what Darwin describes as the violent and almost frantic movements of grief. We reserve the term sadness for the state which often follows distress, when . . . a person no longer wishes for action but becomes passively resigned to the feelings of grief. (Ekman, in Darwin, 1872/1998, p. 176)

The issue here is whether *grief* should be defined inclusively and refer to any state of distress produced by loss or more narrowly and refer only to emotional states that are identifiable as grief and nothing else.

It might seem little is lost by adopting the inclusive view that grief can be expressed in distinctly different ways. The inclusive view is certainly useful—indeed, it is required for stage theories of grief (Bowlby, 1980; Shuchter & Zisook, 1993), in which grief is viewed as moving from one manifestation to a quite different manifestation. This inclusive view also facilitates discussions of grief that does not abate with time (Prigerson & Jacobs, 2001), even when stage theories are disclaimed, because it recognizes that forms of grief may differ in intensity, duration, and perhaps in symptom picture (see chap. 8, this volume). In general, by bringing the consequences of relational loss under a single heading, an inclusive view of grief facilitates discussion of the trajectories of response to loss.

Definitions of grief in the bereavement literature uniformly adopt the inclusive view in which grief is a general term embracing many affective states. The following definition is both representative and authoritative: "This usual reaction to bereavement [i.e., intense distress] is termed grief, defined as a primarily emotional (affective) reaction to the loss of a loved one through death. It incorporates diverse psychological (cognitive, social–behavioral) and physical (physiological–somatic) manifestations" (M. S. Stroebe, Hansson, Stroebe, & Schut, 2001, p. 6).

Another definition of grief provides a listing of some of the distinctly different affective and cognitive states grief can include: "Grief includes depressed mood, yearning, loneliness, searching for the deceased, the sense of the deceased being present, and the sense of being in ongoing communication with that person" (Goodkin et al., 2001, p. 672).

In support of the idea that grief is a complex state in which a range of specific emotions may be expressed rather than being an emotion itself, Bonanno (2001) contrasted the characteristics of true emotions with the characteristics of grief. He noted three differences: (a) Whereas emotions happen quickly and are over quickly, grief can go on for months and years; (b) whereas an emotion tends to be responsive to an immediate situation, grief is expressive of a persisting awareness of a disruption in one's life; and (c) whereas emotions ordinarily are unconsidered responses to an event, grief typically involves, if anything, hyperawareness (p. 494; see also chap. 14, this volume.) *Grief*, Bonanno concluded, is best thought of as a term for any form of distress that is a response to loss.

This inclusive view of grief makes the concept of grief unique in the universe of concepts of affective states. Because grief, construed inclusively, can encompass many emotions, to know that a condition is grief it is necessary to know not its characteristics—sadness, restlessness, despair—but rather that it was produced by loss. I can think of no other conceptualization of an affective state that requires for its identification not how it displays itself but rather its cause. Boredom, disquiet, restlessness, pleasure—each of these can be identified by the characteristics it exhibits. None of them requires that one first know what led to the condition. However, emotions and affective states that are generated (to use Bonanno's [2001] word) by grief, such as agitation, sadness, and mental pain, can be said to be an expression of grief only if they result from loss. Furthermore, any negative feeling state can be said to be grief if it results from loss.

Does this mean that the term *grief*, as it is generally used is simply a way of referring to affective states stemming from loss? Is there no unique emotional state that can be characterized as grief, no matter when it occurs? What of Darwin's (1872/1998) "acute paroxysm of grief"? That state, it seems to me, can readily be recognized as grief even if there is no knowledge of the events that produced it. In addition, in my opinion it is distinct from the agitation, distress, sadness, and other emotional states that may follow it. To make evident the nature of this state, I describe my own experience.

My wife had just been operated on for ovarian cancer. I was in the postoperative waiting room. The surgeon came to tell me that the operation had gone well: He had achieved "optimal debulking," and there was no invasion of a vital organ. Yes, the cancer had metastasized; cancers of this sort usually have by the time they are found. He could guarantee us 2 or 3 years.

The surgeon was highly regarded, his surgical skills held almost in awe by colleagues. I could tell that he believed he had done well. I did not then know enough to realize how important optimal debulking is for prognosis, but I recognized that the surgeon was pleased to report that he had achieved it. However, even as I heard his statement that we would have 2 or 3 years for sure, I rejected it. I believed then (as I do now, several months later, when chemotherapy has brought the enzyme that tracks my wife's cancer well into normal range) that with treatment and luck my wife will have a normal life span.

The only emotion I was aware of was gratitude. Then, suddenly, I burst into tears. The tears were utterly unbidden. I was overwhelmed by them. I could not talk; neither could I stop sobbing. My mind was blank: I seemed to have no thoughts, no awareness of any feeling other than gratitude and, now, embarrassment for sobbing away.

It has been suggested to me that my tears might have been tears of gratitude. I do not think this is so. If, in the postoperative waiting room, the surgeon had told me that the tumor was benign and there would be no recurrence, I am pretty sure that my reaction would have been enormous relief and perhaps a dazed joy. What I think happened was that the surgeon's assurance of 2 or 3 years had in fact registered in my mind, though out of my awareness. My tears expressed grief at the loss I somewhere believed to be just down the road.

Note that it was not an actual loss but a sudden and unexpected *threat* of loss that triggered grief in this incident. When considering the cause of this instance of grief, the concept of loss must be construed broadly.

This instance of paroxysmal grief seems to me to escape Bonanno's (2001) objections to considering grief an emotion: It was sudden, a reaction to something happening right there, and it was utterly unconsidered. It may also meet two of what I consider the most relevant three of Ekman's (1999) criteria for a basic emotion: (a) that the state produce distinctive, universally recognized, signals and (b) that it appear automatically and unbidden.

The expression of paroxysmal grief seems to be universal in the sense of being a potential response to loss irrespective of culture. Cross-cultural ability to recognize an emotion is often taken as a proxy for cross-cultural similarity in the expression of the emotion. Grief seems to pass this test. Indeed, Darwin (1872/1998) seemed to believe that recognizable grief was displayed not only cross-culturally but also in other primate species (p. 134). Although there are many problems associated with the use of photographed emotion as a basis for deciding whether an emotion is universal (Russell, 1994), it is significant that Ekman, Sorenson, and Friesen (1969) found that the expression of sadness in photographs of the faces of western Europeans could be identified correctly by a majority of respondents native to New Guinea and Borneo who were relatively untouched by Western culture. We might expect the more florid expression of paroxysmal grief to be identified at least as easily.

That paroxysmal grief comes unbidden I will testify: Such was my experience in the incident I just described. However, paroxysmal grief may not be closely tied to a particular set of triggering conditions—the third of Ekman's (1999) criteria for emotions. Even though its apparent universality makes it likely that it is a hard-wired potential response, it is not an invariable response to relational loss. Relational loss that is physiologically significant, as demonstrated, for example, by increased heartbeat, can sometimes give rise to only minimal symptoms of grief (Bonanno, Keltner, Holen, & Horowitz, 1995). Furthermore, paroxysmal grief can result from traumatic experiences other than relational loss—for example, from victimization. Parkes (2005) argued that these considerations make it undesirable to define grief in a way that permits paroxysmal sobbing (or associated states, e.g., Bowlby's [1980] shock and numbing) to be seen as among its expressions. He would instead identify grief with separation distress following loss: "In my view [grief's] essential components are the experience of a loss and a reaction of intense pining or yearning for the object lost" (Parkes, 2005, p. 30). However, the objections to considering paroxysmal sobbing an emotional expression of grief might be overcome if one widened the list of potential antecedents of grief to include anticipated loss as well as widened the list of its expressions to include other manifestations of separation distress.

STAGE THEORIES OF GRIEF

It is a common belief that as time passes, grief ameliorates. That there is a succession of stages would seem likely, if not logically necessary. Darwin's (1872/1998) description of grief, noted earlier, constitutes a stage theory. Bowlby (1980), largely on the basis of studies of widows and widowers, offered a stage theory similar to Darwin's. The initial response of numbness and disbelief in Bowlby's theory is like Darwin's initial paroxysmal response in that ordinary functioning has been overwhelmed. Bowlby's subsequent stages of yearning and searching and of disorganization and despair correspond closely to Darwin's states of anxiety and despair (Bowlby, 1980, p. 85; see also Bowlby & Parkes, 1970, and Parkes, 1970).

Bowlby's stage theory dominated thinking about the course of grief for some 20 years from the time of its publication in the 1960s and 1970s (Bowlby, 1961; Bowlby & Parkes, 1970). More recently, it has come under criticism on two grounds: (a) that an invariable sequence of stages is not supported empirically and (b) that the assertion of stages implies more intercorrelation of the various expressions of grief than is found empirically.

Regarding the absence of a sequence among stages of grieving following loss, Wortman, Silver, and Kessler (1993) noted that the stage models severely understate the extent to which people differ in the emotional states they experience following loss. Although they applauded the descriptions of specific bereavement reactions provided by stage theorists, they found empirical support for the idea of a sequencing of stages neither in the bereavement literature nor in their own longitudinal study. In consequence, they endorsed the caution in the Institute of Medicine report (Osterweis, Solomon, & Green, 1984, p. 48) that use of the concept of stages could encourage inappropriate expectations of the course of grieving.

The more fundamental idea that grief takes the form of discrete affective states, quite apart from whether the states exhibit sequencing, also has itself been subject to scrutiny. There have been many efforts to use factor analysis to decide whether links can be established among component elements of grieving, such as agitation and pining. One review of this work reports little consistency from study to study in the way in which elements of grief are grouped. Furthermore, the elements of grief seem to abate at different rates: for example, distress shows a fairly rapid decline whereas preoccupation and restlessness decline more slowly (Archer, 1999, p. 99). These observations, taken together, suggest that there may be only limited clustering of grief's expressions.

However, the ideas that stages exist and that grief moves in some regular fashion from stage to stage are repeatedly used by investigators to capture something they find evident in their data. This is true not only for investigators who use Bowlby's (1980) stage theory but also for many who offer a stage theory different from Bowlby's. Shuchter and Zisook (1993), after cautioning that "Grief is not a linear process with concrete boundaries but, rather, a composite of overlapping, fluid phases that vary from person to person" (p. 23), offered a stage theory in which the bereavement experience moves from shock and disbelief, to somatic and emotional discomfort together with social withdrawal, and finally to restitution. Also, Malkinson and Bar-Tur (2005), in describing how parental grief for sons killed in war changes over a long stretch of time, found it useful to identify as stages "young grief," "mature grief," and "aging grief."

Despite the observation that individual cases show great variation in the sequencing and even the experience of particular affective states, the idea of a progression in grief states makes it easier to think about the changes in grieving that occur as time elapses. Given this, stage theories may best be seen as Weberian ideal types (Hempel, 1963). As ideal types, stage theories would be conceptual devices, useful insofar as they provide a framework for theory, observations, and expectations. What matters is that they help one think about what may be expected over the course of grief.

KINDS OF GRIEF

There has for some time been interest in grief that did not move from initial intensity to eventual resolution. In one account, three forms of such grief are identified: (a) *chronic grief*, in which there is no amelioration; (b) *delayed grief*, in which an initial absence of grief is followed after an interval of weeks or months by severe disturbance; and (c) *conflicted grief*, in which grief is complicated by intense guilt and anger (Parkes, 1991). The existence of chronic grief is well established. Research has shown that people can remain grief stricken for a very long time (Lehman, Wortman, & Williams, 1987). The existence of delayed grief and conflicted grief are less assured. Some clinicians say that they have seen instances in their practice, but survey studies of the bereaved seem not to find them (see Bonanno et al., 2002; Bonanno & Kaltman, 2001; W. Stroebe, Schut, & Stroebe, 2005).

Current work by two research teams, one directed by Mardi Horowitz, the other by Holly Prigerson, has raised interest in the identification of forms of grief that might be considered pathological because of their intensity, duration, accompanying behaviors, or dominant symptoms and complaints (Horowitz et al., 1997; Prigerson & Jacobs, 2001; see chap. 8, this volume). Prigerson (chap. 8, this volume) has proposed the term *prolonged grief disorder* for grief that does not abate with the passage of time.

A leading aim in work on prolonged grief disorder is to have it recognized as a diagnostic category in the *Diagnostic and Statistical Manual of Mental Disorders* (DSM; e.g., 4th ed.; American Psychiatric Association, 1994), thus supporting the idea that prolonged grief is a psychiatric disorder (Horowitz, 2005). Arguments for treating prolonged grief as a distinct psychiatric condition include that it is a syndrome that puts its sufferers at risk of severely undesirable outcomes; that its symptom picture overlaps only slightly with symptom pictures for other conditions, such as depression; and that it seems responsive to targeted treatments (Goodkin et al., 2005; see chap. 8, this volume; for an instance of targeted treatment, see Shear, Frank, Houck, & Reynolds, 2005). That people experiencing prolonged grief have a severely diminished quality of life seems unquestionable, as is the justification for helping them in any way possible.

Although prolonged grief disorder seems to be a distinguishable clinical entity, its difference from ordinary grief may be a matter of degree rather than kind. Many of the symptoms proposed for identification of prolonged grief disorder—for example, persistent yearning for the deceased person— are also found in ordinary grief and are different in prolonged grief disorder mainly in how long they continue. Like pathological anxiety and many other psychiatric diagnoses, pathological grief seems a way of characterizing one end of a continuum. It may be that although recognition of prolonged grief as a condition justifying clinical intervention is entirely desirable, its conceptualization as a distinct syndrome can be debated. (For arguments regarding the usefulness of the concept of prolonged grief, measures for its assessment, and justifications for its inclusion in the *DSM*, see the issue of *Omega: The Journal of Death and Dying* that was devoted to *complicated grief*, an earlier way of referring to prolonged grief [Parkes, 2005–2006]; see also chap. 9, this volume.)

WHAT GIVES RISE TO GRIEF?

The conditions that give rise to overwhelming, paroxysmal grief undoubtedly include the nature of the loss and the character of the person afflicted. Setting may also play a role: People may be able to inhibit their grief reaction if, for example, they are responsible for others. However, little systematic research has examined the conditions leading to its expression; neither do we have much understanding, in relation to any emotional state, of the underlying physiological linkages that might lead from awareness to emotion.

In contrast, there is a good deal of empirically based theoretical work providing explanation for the later expressions of grief, those that stretch over the months and years after loss. There seem to be three main approaches here, each linked to empirical findings of various kinds. The first focuses on bonds, the second focuses on meanings, and the third considers the dysregulation consequent to loss of a figure with whom life is shared.

Bonds and Their Mental Representations

The idea that it is a bond to a now-dead figure that is responsible for grief has long played a central role in the understanding of grief's nature. However, there are only three relational bonds whose loss is likely to give rise to persisting grief: (a) children's bonds to their caretakers; (b) the bonds of spouses or, more generally, of those who have established marriage-like emotional partnerships; and (c) the bonds of caretakers to children. To explain why it is these bonds whose loss reliably gives rise to grief, it is necessary to call on the attachment theory of John Bowlby (1969, 1973, 1980).

Bowlby's theory of grief can be seen as having three parts. First, it treats grief as a response to the loss of someone whose accessibility had fostered a sense of security: that is, an attachment figure. This idea helps explain, for one thing, that grief can be expressed both as restless preoccupation with the lost figure, because the griever is possessed by the need to regain that figure's presence, and as despair, as the griever accepts that the figure is permanently lost. Second, together with Mary Ainsworth, Bowlby developed a quite powerful theory of relational styles that provides explanations for what might otherwise be seen as chance-driven individual differences in response to loss (Fraley & Shaver, 1999, pp. 739–742). Third, Bowlby developed a theory of the way grief changes and abates with time. There has been a questioning of his belief that in most cases a return to earlier levels of functioning requires acknowledgement and acceptance of loss. Research suggests that although this is true for many people, it is not true for people who may be more guarded against awareness of their feelings (Bonanno et al., 1995; Fraley & Shaver, 1999). Such people may be able to manage grief by minimizing and denying it at least as well as others manage grief by full recognition of their feelings of loss.

Bowlby was primarily concerned with the bond linking children to parents, although in his work on grief he accepted that *pair bonds*—the relationships of spouses and, presumably, of other committed couples—also were forms of attachment. These two bonds are now regularly assumed to be attachments (see, e.g., Field, Gao, & Paderna, 2005; M. S. Stroebe, Schut, & Stroebe, 2005). The bond that links parents to their children, on the other hand, is sometimes assumed to be something different, a caretaking bond, because it is concerned with the security of the other rather than of the self (Main, 1999, p. 203). However, one could argue that this bond also uses the attachment emotional system, but with mental representations that link the self with the provision of security and the other with its need (Weiss, 2001; see also Mason & Mendoza, 1998).

Bowlby (1980) believed that given loss of an attachment figure, acceptance of that loss was necessary to amelioration of grief (p. 18). Yet loss of an attachment figure often seems beyond full acceptance, if that means there is a time when memory does not again trigger some elements of grief. Observation suggests that even in bereaved people who seem to have fully regained effective functioning the emotions associated with attachments can be elicited years after the death of the attachment figures—on anniversaries of the death, for example. Indeed, it has been argued that the persistence of bonds to lost figures may sustain effective functioning in the bereaved person instead of being an impediment to its return (see chap. 6, this volume; Klass, Silverman, & Nickman, 1996; Klass & Walter, 2001).

Observations of children whose parents have died and parents whose children have died support the idea that in these losses the maintenance of a continuing bond to the lost figure can be strengthening. It may be, however, that the nature of the relationship is important: In a study of people whose husbands or wives had died 5 years earlier, there was no connection between the intensity of the bereaved person's memory of the lost figure and the extent to which his or her grief had subsided (Field, Gal-Oz, & Bonanno, 2003; see also Field, Nichols, Holen, & Horowitz, 1999). It seems established that under some circumstances continuing bonds are reliably sustaining, but it is uncertain exactly what those circumstances are (for a discussion of competing views, see Walter, 1999, pp. 103–113).

An implication of the idea of a persisting bond is that the bereaved person maintains a continuing mental representation of the lost figure. Archer (1999, p. 7; see also chap. 3, this volume) listed alternative phrasings of the concept of continuing representation, including *working models* (Bowlby, 1969, 1973), *schemas* (Horowitz, 1990; Horowitz, Bonanno, & Holen, 1993; Janoff-Bulman, 1989, 1993), and *assumptive worlds* (Parkes, 1971). Recent advances in the study of brain functioning in memory suggest the neural mechanisms that might underlie such mental representations. A study of a small sample of people who had been bereaved approximately 8 months earlier found that presentation of a reminder of the lost figure activated regions in their brains that earlier work had shown to be associated with affect, cognition, imagery, and memory (Gundel, O'Connor, Littrell, Fort, & Lane, 2003). To produce a sense of a continuing relationship with an absent other, connections of these kinds would be directed to the frontal lobes, whose task it would be to construct from them an affectively anchored image of the lost figure. The result would be experienced as a coherent mental representation, although it would have been produced by a complex process of association and construction.

Maintaining a Meaningful World

Just as it seems obvious that grief implies persisting investment in a lost figure, so too does it seem obvious that the loss of a spouse damages, and perhaps destroys, the underlying assumptions of the bereaved person's life. A second theoretical approach to the nature of grief proposes that it is the impact on the bereaved person of this disruption of underlying assumptions that gives rise to much of the phenomena of grief. The bereaved person's world, in emotionally critical ways, has become fundamentally different.

There is strong empirical support for the belief that the disruption of someone's life situation gives rise to severe psychological and social stress and that this stress in turn increases the person's risk for depression. Furthermore, it is not so much the objective disturbance that matters as it is the meaning the person gives to the disturbance. The impact of the disruption seems especially severe when the disruption has occurred without warning, so that the suddenly bereaved person can have had no opportunity for preparation or, afterward, any assurance that disaster will not again strike unexpectedly (Parkes & Weiss, 1983).

The view of grief as a response to a disruption of the subjective representation of the world has the great merit of bringing within the same explanatory framework the distress produced by bereavement, loss of a home, loss of a job, and loss of a cherished image of oneself (Marris, 1974). Although responses to a home, job, and view of oneself regularly give rise to states that may justifiably be described as grief, they are difficult to incorporate into the view that grief is produced only by the severance of bonds. It can seem a stretch to talk about an affectional bond or attachment (in the Bowlby sense) to a home or a job. In these instances, it seems preferable to talk about the loss of the fundamental yet taken-for-granted aspects of one's life.

On the other hand, there are problems in the proposal that grief is a consequence of disruption in the griever's subjective representation of the world. Is it any disruption at all that is grief producing, or only negative disruptions? Would winning a lottery, followed by major changes in the assumptions underlying the winner's functioning, produce grief? Specification of the kinds of disruption that lead to grief seems needed—but then something more than the simple disruption of the fundamental understandings of one's life would have to be invoked.

In addition, although grief appears to be a complex affective state, an emphasis on meaningfulness and perceived reality seems to give cognition and perception primacy over affect in explanation of grief. This is particularly the case when this outlook is used to describe how grief is resolved or to propose interventions that might foster its resolution. Thus, Neimeyer, Prigerson, and Davies (2002) wrote, "Bereavement . . . prompts us to 'relearn the self' and 'relearn the world' in the wake of loss" (p. 239). Although it may be the case that cognitive change begins a process that leads to emotional change, emotion here seems secondary to cognition.

Perhaps the best assessment of the present state of this approach to the explanation of grief is that although disruption of taken-for-granted understandings of reality does seem to play a role in grief, exactly what kinds of disruption reliably give rise to grief (because it is evident that not all do), and how they are linked to the affective injury that seems essential to bereavement, still need to be determined.

Loss of Relational Supports

Another apparent aspect of bereavement, in addition to its testimony to the persistence of an affective bond and its obvious disruption of the underlying assumptions of the bereaved person's life, is its removal of relational supports for the bereaved person's functioning. The loss of a marital partner deprives the bereaved person of support for the rhythms of life; for social participation; and for examination and modification of perceptions, thoughts, and feelings. The loss of a child, even though it does not deprive the bereaved parent of a supportive figure, may interfere with the parent's self-regulation by causing the parent to question his or her own capability, trustworthiness, and meaningfulness (see also chap. 18, this volume). The loss of a parent may deprive the adult child of the reassurance provided by awareness of an accessible loving figure (see also chap. 19, this volume).

Myron Hofer has given much attention to the role of maternal presence in the regulation of the functioning of infants. Extrapolating from that work, he proposed that the despair state of grief among the conjugally bereaved can be seen as an expression of dysregulation resulting from the absence of the marital partner (Hofer, 1984). The loss of that partner, in his view, deprives the bereaved person of a relationship that established times for sleep and for meals and that helped him or her maintain a satisfactory social life and a satisfactory sense of self: "Habitual tasks, attention, concentration, sleep, food intake, and mood become fragmented. These changes are most accurately characterized as a widespread dysregulation of functional systems" (Hofer, 1996, p. 578).

Because marital partners provide each other with another view of the minutiae of life, the absence of a marital partner can produce dysregulation of assessments of oneself and others. Without a life partner whose reactions, even without conversation, communicate agreement or disagreement with one's own, and who, in discussion, corroborates or disputes one's perceptions, it becomes easier to misread and misjudge and to be convinced of the validity of one's unquestioned misassessments.

Both loneliness and social isolation can be risks for people whose spouse has died. Loneliness is a risk because of the loss of a primary attachment figure; social isolation also is a risk, because bereavement may foster a desire to withdraw from friends and family who do not experience the loss in the same way. Having lost their life partners, the bereaved become at risk of also losing their place in their social communities (see chap. 20, this volume; W. Stroebe, Stroebe, & Abakoumkin, 1996; Wenger & Burholt, 2004).

Some among the bereaved are able to call on family and on old and new friends to help them reestablish their lives. Friends and family may provide them with people to talk to, some of whom may also provide more material help. Although it may not be the case that the more social support the better, it does seem, on the basis of personal accounts (e.g., Lewis, 1961), that some minimum level of social support is needed by the bereaved. Still, the questions of just how much help is needed, of what sort, and how it may best be provided, although they have been examined at length, seem still to lack entirely adequate answers.

A COMPARISON OF THE THEORIES OF GRIEF

All three approaches to explaining grief take the postloss affective states of agitation and distress as their primary concern. For the approaches that focus on meaning and dysregulation, the postloss affective states are their only concern. Attachment theory, in Bowlby's (1969, 1973, 1980) development draws attention to the possibility that there may be an initial shock associated with recognition of loss. Attachment theory (see chap. 5, this volume) also does well in explaining why grief should sometimes show itself as anxious searching and sometimes as withdrawn despair.

The concern with meaning does well with the wide range of losses that can give rise to grief. It also treats as a critical issue, and not just one more expression of confusion, the need of the bereaved to make sense of what has happened to them, and it satisfactorily explains the cognitive component in bereaved people's efforts to regain the ability to care about current and future life.

The emphasis on regulation and support helps explain some of the specific symptoms associated with grieving: sleep difficulties, changes in appetite, social withdrawal, loss of self-confidence. Also, it contributes to informal and formal programs of intervention by suggesting ways others can be helpful, although this aspect of the theory awaits further development.

The three approaches to explanation of grief, taken together, span the distance from the strongly subjective to the strongly objective. The focus on the meaning of the bereavement is concerned entirely with the way the bereaved person grasps the external world. At the other extreme, the focus on dysregulation is concerned primarily with changes in the bereaved person's functioning. The approach that focuses on the interruption of security-sustaining bonds may stand midway in that it deals both with the more nearly subjective experience of bonding and with its behavioral expression.

In his pioneering work, *Widows and Their Families*, Marris (1958) had no theory other than psychoanalytic speculation to guide him in his efforts to understand the deep grief regularly reported to him by young widows. There now are good theories about how grief is linked to the nature of the relationship that was lost, to that relationship's meaning for the bereaved person, and to the ways in which the relationship may have served regulatory functions. Investigators have not yet integrated these theories; neither do they fully understand the mental and emotional processes that may underlie them. However, if we have not achieved full understanding of grief in the 50 years since Marris's report, we have nevertheless made a great deal of progress.

REFERENCES

American Psychiatric Association. (1994). *Diagnostic and statistical manual of mental disorders* (4th ed.). Washington, DC: Author.

Archer, J. (1999). *The nature of grief: The evolution and psychology of reactions to loss.* London: Routledge.

Bonanno, G. A. (2001). Grief and emotion: A social–functional perspective. In M. S. Stroebe, R. O. Hansson, W. Stroebe, & H. Schut (Eds.), *Handbook of bereavement research: Consequences, coping, and care* (pp. 493–516). Washington, DC: American Psychological Association.

Bonanno, G. A., & Kaltman, S. (2001). The varieties of grief experience. *Clinical Psychology Review, 21,* 705 734.

Bonanno, G. A., Keltner, D., Holen, A., & Horowitz, M. J. (1995). When avoiding unpleasant emotions might not be such a bad thing: Verbal–autonomic response dissociation and midlife conjugal bereavement. *Journal of Personality and Social Psychology, 69,* 975–989.

Bonanno, G. A., Wortman, C. B., & Lehman, D. R. (2002). Resilience to loss and chronic grief: A prospective study from preloss to 18-months postloss. *Journal of Personality and Social Psychology, 83,* 1150–1164.

Bowlby, J. (1961). Processes of mourning. *International Journal of Psychoanalysis, 42,* 317–340.

Bowlby, J. (1969). *Attachment.* New York: Basic Books.

Bowlby, J. (1973). *Separation: Anxiety and anger.* New York: Basic Books.

Bowlby, J. (1980). *Loss: Sadness and depression.* New York: Basic Books.

Bowlby, J., & Parkes, C. M. (1970). Separation and loss within the family. In E. J. Anthony & C. Koupernik (Eds.), *International yearbook of child psychiatry and allied professions: Vol. 3. The child in his family* (pp. 197–216). New York: Wiley.

Darwin, C. (with Introduction, Afterword, and Commentary by P. Ekman). (1998). *The expression of the emotions in man and animals* (3rd ed.). New York: Philosophical Library. (Original work published 1872)

Ekman, P. (1999). Basic emotions. In T. Dalgleish & M. Power (Eds.), *Handbook of cognition and emotion* (pp. 45–60). Sussex, England: Wiley.

Ekman, P., Sorenson, E. R., & Friesen, W. V. (1969, April 4). Pan-cultural elements in facial displays of emotion. *Science, 164,* 86–88.

Field, N. P., Gal-Oz, E., & Bonanno, G. A. (2003). Continuing bonds and adjustment at 5 years after the death of a spouse. *Journal of Consulting and Clinical Psychology, 71,* 110–117.

Field, N. P., Gao, B., & Paderna, L. (2005). Continuing bonds in bereavement: An attachment theory based perspective. *Death Studies, 29,* 277–299.

Field, N. P., Nichols, C., Holen, A., & Horowitz, M. J. (1999). The relation of continuing attachment to adjustment in conjugal bereavement. *Journal of Consulting and Clinical Psychology, 67,* 212–218.

Fraley, E. C., & Shaver, P. (1999). Loss and bereavement: Attachment theories and recent controversies concerning "grief work" and the nature of detachment. In J. Cassidy & P. R. Shaver (Eds.), *Handbook of attachment: Theory, research and clinical applications* (pp. 735–759). New York: Guilford Press.

Goodkin, K., Baldewicz, T. T., Blaney, N. T., Asthana, D., Kumar, M., Shapshak, P., et al. (2001). Physiological effects of bereavement and bereavement support group interventions. In M. S. Stroebe, R. O. Hansson, W. Stroebe, & H. Schut (Eds.), *Handbook of bereavement research: Consequences, coping, and care* (pp. 671–703). Washington, DC: American Psychological Association.

Goodkin, K., Lee, D., Frasca, A., Molina, R., Zheng, W., O'Mellan, S., et al. (2005). Complicated bereavement: A commentary on its state of evolution. *Omega: The Journal of Death and Dying, 52,* 99–105.

Gundel, H., O'Connor, M.-F., Littrell, L., Fort, C., & Lane, R. D. (2003). Functional neuroanatomy of grief: An fMRI Study. *American Journal of Psychiatry, 160,* 1946–1953.

Hempel, C. G. (1963). Typological methods in the social sciences. In M. Natanson (Ed.), *Philosophy of the social sciences* (pp. 210–230). New York: Random House.

Hofer, M. A. (1984). Relationships as regulators: A psychobiologic perspective on bereavement. *Psychosomatic Medicine, 46,* 183–197.

Hofer, M. A. (1996). On the nature and consequences of early loss. *Psychosomatic Medicine, 58,* 570–581.

Horowitz, M. J. (1990). A model of mourning: Change in schemas of self and other. *Journal of the American Psychoanalytic Association, 38,* 297–324.

Horowitz, M. J. (2005). Meditating on complicated grief disorder as a diagnosis. *Omega: The Journal of Death and Dying, 52,* 87–89.

Horowitz, M. J., Bonanno, G. A., & Holen, A. (1993). Pathological grief: Diagnosis and explanation. *Psychosomatic Medicine, 55,* 260–273.

Horowitz, M. J., Siege, B., Holen, A., Bonanno, G. A., Milbrath, C., & Stinson, C. (1997). Diagnostic criteria for complicated grief disorder. *American Journal of Psychiatry, 154,* 904–910.

Janoff-Bulman, R. (1989). Assumptive worlds and the stress of traumatic events: Applications of the schema construct. *Social Cognition, 7,* 113–136.

Janoff-Bulman, R. (1993). *Shattered assumptions: Towards a new psychology of trauma.* New York: Free Press.

Klass, D., Silverman, P. R., & Nickman, S. L. (Eds.). (1996). *Continuing bonds: New understandings of grief*. Washington, DC: Taylor & Francis.

Klass, D., & Walter, T. (2001). Processes of grieving: How bonds are continued. In M. S. Stroebe, R. O. Hansson, W. Stroebe, & H. Schut (Eds.), *Handbook of bereavement research: Consequences, coping, and care* (pp. 431–448). Washington, DC: American Psychological Association.

Lehman, D. R., Wortman, C. B., & Williams, A. F. (1987). Long-term effects of losing a spouse or child in a motor vehicle crash. *Journal of Personality and Social Psychology, 52,* 218–231.

Lewis, C. S. (1961). *A grief observed*. New York: Seabury Press.

Main, M. (1999). Attachment theory: Eighteen points with suggestions for future studies. In J. Cassidy & P. R. Shaver (Eds.), *Handbook of attachment: Theory, research and clinical applications* (pp. 845–887). New York: Guilford Press.

Malkinson, R., & Bar-Tur, L. (2005). Long term bereavement processes of older parents: The three phases of grief. *Omega: The Journal of Death and Dying, 50,* 103–129.

Marris, P. (1958). *Widows and their families*. London: Routledge & Kegan Paul.

Marris, P. (1974). *Loss and change*. London: Routledge & Kegan Paul.

Mason, W. A., & Mendoza, S. P. (1998). Generic aspects of primate attachments: Parents, offspring and mates. *Psychoneuroendocrinology, 23,* 765–778.

Neimeyer, R. A., Prigerson, H. G., & Davies, B. (2002). Mourning and meaning. *American Behavioral Scientist, 46,* 235–251.

Osterweis, M., Solomon, F., & Green, M. (Eds.). (1984). *Bereavement: Reactions, consequences, and care*. Washington, DC: National Academy Press.

Parkes, C. M. (1970). "Seeking" and "finding" a lost object: Evidence from recent studies of the reaction to bereavement. *Social Science & Medicine, 4,* 187–201.

Parkes, C. M. (1971). Psychosocial transitions: A field for study. *Social Science & Medicine, 5,* 101–115.

Parkes, C. M. (1991). Attachment, bonding, and psychiatric problems after bereavement in adult life. In C. M. Parkes, J. Stevenson-Hinds, & P. Marris (Eds.), *Attachment across the life cycle* (268–292). New York: Routledge.

Parkes, C. M. (2005). *Love and loss: The roots of grief and its complications*. New York: Routledge.

Parkes, C. M. (Ed.). (2005–2006). Complicated grief [Special issue]. *Omega: The Journal of Death and Dying, 52*(1).

Parkes, C. M., & Weiss, R. S. (1983). *Recovery from bereavement*. New York: Basic Books.

Prigerson, H. G., & Jacobs, S. C. (2001). Traumatic grief as a distinct disorder: A rationale, consensus criteria, and a preliminary empirical test. In M. S. Stroebe, R. O. Hansson, W. Stroebe, & H. Schut (Eds.), *Handbook of bereavement research: Consequences, coping, and care* (pp. 613–637). Washington, DC: American Psychological Association.

Russell, J. A. (1994). Is there universal recognition of emotion from facial expression? A review of the cross-cultural studies. *Psychological Bulletin, 115,* 102–141.

Shear, K., Frank, E., Houck, P. R., & Reynolds, C. F. (2005). Treatment of complicated grief: A randomized controlled trial. *Journal of the American Medical Association, 293,* 2601–2607.

Shuchter, S., & Zisook, S. (1993). The course of normal grief. In M. S. Stroebe, W. Stroebe, & R. O. Hansson (Eds.), *Handbook of bereavement: Theory, research and intervention* (pp. 23–43). Cambridge, England: Cambridge University Press.

Stroebe, M. S., Hansson, R. O., Stroebe, W., & Schut, H. (2001). Introduction: Concepts and issues in contemporary research on bereavement. In M. S. Stroebe, R. O. Hansson, W. Stroebe, & H. Schut (Eds.), *Handbook of bereavement research: Consequences, coping, and care* (pp. 3–22). Washington, DC: American Psychological Association.

Stroebe, M. S., Schut, H., & Stroebe, W. (2005). Attachment in coping with bereavement: A theoretical integration. *Review of General Psychology, 9,* 48–66.

Stroebe, W., Schut, H., & Stroebe, M. (2005). Grief work, disclosure and counseling: Do they help the bereaved? *Clinical Psychology Review, 20,* 57–75.

Stroebe, W., Stroebe, M. S., & Abakoumkin, G. (1996). The role of loneliness and social support in adjustment to loss: A test of attachment versus stress theory. *Journal of Personality and Social Psychology, 70,* 1241–1249.

Walter, T. (1999). *On bereavement: The culture of grief.* Buckingham, England: Open University Press.

Weiss, R. S. (2001). Grief, bonds, and relationships. In M. S. Stroebe, R. O. Hansson, W. Stroebe, & H. Schut (Eds.), *Handbook of bereavement research: Consequences, coping, and care* (pp. 47–62). Washington, DC: American Psychological Association.

Wenger, G. C., & Burholt, V. (2004). Changes in levels of social isolation and loneliness among older people in a rural area: A twenty-year longitudinal study. *Canadian Journal on Aging, 23,* 115–127.

Wortman, C. B., Silver, R. C., & Kessler, R. C. (1993). The meaning of loss and adjustment to bereavement. In M. S. Stroebe, W. Stroebe, & R. O. Hansson (Eds.), *Handbook of bereavement: Theory, research and intervention* (pp. 349–366). Cambridge, England: Cambridge University Press.

3

THEORIES OF GRIEF: PAST, PRESENT, AND FUTURE PERSPECTIVES

JOHN ARCHER

Although Darwin did not put forward a theory of grief, his observations of the facial expressions associated with grieving, and their existence in animals (Darwin, 1872/1904), laid the basis for the later development of the theme that the origins of human grief are to be found in the animal world and can be understood in terms of natural selection. Most historical accounts of theoretical ideas about grief begin with Freud's (1917/1957) *Mourning and Melancholia*, according to which grief has a specific function: to detach thoughts and feelings from the dead person so that the bereaved person can move on with his or her life. This can be achieved only through an active process, later termed *grief work*, whereby the attachment to the dead person is given up through continued confrontation of memories and thoughts associated with the loss. Freud also speculated that pathological grief arose from either avoidance of grief work or conflicting feelings about the deceased. Freud's views, both of the nature of the grief process and of its pathological features, have influenced theory and practice up to the present.

Writing at about the same time as Freud, Shand (1914, 1920) set out what he referred to as the *laws of sorrow*. These concerned individual variations in the grief process, changes over time, the importance of social support, and the additional distress caused by sudden death. Of particular importance was Shand's statement that although expressing thoughts and feelings and disclosing them to others is associated with benefits, expressing negative emotions is associated with more intense grief. Although such a distinction has not been made in writings about grief work, recent empirical studies (e.g., Bonanno & Keltner, 1997; Bonanno, Papa, Lalande, Zhang, & Noll, 2005) have indeed shown that the expression of negative emotions earlier in the grief process is associated with a poorer later outcome, providing support for at least part of Shand's distinction. Although they did not constitute a coherent theory of grief, Shand's laws of sorrow covered a broader range of features of grief than Freud's (1917/1957) account did. They would have provided a more sound basis for empirical research. Instead, they were lost to subsequent researchers and practitioners.

Although some interesting studies were carried out in the 1950s (see Archer, 1999), the most enduring theoretical contribution is Bowlby's (1961, 1973, 1980). He applied attachment theory to separation reactions and to grief, linking these together in a coherent biological framework. Bowlby restated the origins of grief in the animal world, he suggested how grief could have arisen by natural selection, he showed the importance of the attachment bond for understanding subsequent grieving, and he showed how grief reactions developed from the separation reactions of children. Despite his evolutionary and ethological emphasis, Bowlby's theorizing originated in his psychoanalytic training, and so he retained a number of key ideas, such as the importance of grief work and the nature and origins of pathological forms of grief, from Freud's writings. Parkes (1972a) extended Bowlby's writings on grief to encompass some pioneering empirical studies.

Until the 1980s, theoretical treatments of grief were largely the domain of practitioners working within a psychoanalytical framework. Many of their established concepts had not been subject to critical scrutiny or empirical testing. This occurred later, when empirically based psychologists became interested in grief. Shackleton (1984) examined the main theories of grief available at the time and found them lacking both logical coherence and evidential basis. Wortman and Silver (1989) referred to "the myths of coping with loss," such as the belief that if bereaved people do not show distress or depression, this indicates delayed grief; that recovery always occurs, given time; and that grief work is always necessary for the resolution of grief.

Stroebe (1992–1993) developed one of these themes in a critical assessment of grief work theory that had been central to many writings about grief since Freud (1917/1957) first proposed it. Stroebe first indicated the problems involved in defining the concept, and in separating it from rumination and yearning, both of which are viewed as hindering progress, and from finding meaning, which may involve negative attributions. Stroebe's analysis of grief work was accompanied by the first empirical investigation of the concept (Stroebe & Stroebe, 1991), which led the way to a number of other studies of the processes underlying the resolution of grief. Associated with these has been the introduction of theory from different areas of psychology, such as cognitive stress, trauma, and attachment (Bonanno & Kaltman, 1999; Janoff-Bulman, 1993; Stroebe, Schut, & Stroebe, 2005), as well as evolutionary principles (Archer, 1999, 2001b).

Following from the influence of Freud's (1917/1957) grief work theory, the resolution of grief has been the central issue for both theory and practice over the last 15 years. Of the other considerations that are set out in Bowlby's (1961, 1973, 1980) biologically based account of grief, its resolution is but one component of a comprehensive theory of grief (Archer, 2001a). Such a theory would include the following six aspects, which are covered in the remainder of this chapter: (a) the evolutionary origins of grief, in terms of similar processes in other species, and its adaptive significance; (b) how differences in grief following the loss of different types of relationships can be understood using evolutionary principles; (c) the mechanism that triggers the process of grief, which involves attachment theory and cognitive theories; (d) how these frameworks can help understanding of variations in grief according to the context of the loss; (e) the resolution of grief; and (f) how differences in attachment styles may underlie some individual differences in grief.

EVOLUTIONARY ORIGINS OF GRIEF

The background to any explanation of the origins of grief in evolutionary history is that it is a universal human reaction to loss, occurring throughout human history and across different cultures (Archer, 1999, 2001b). Moreover, as Darwin (1872/1904) noted, grieflike processes occur among social birds and mammals. Bowlby (1961), Pollock (1961), and Averill (1968) have drawn attention to the occurrence of grief in animals, and both Bowlby (1980) and Parkes (1972a) have sought to answer the fundamental question of its evolutionary function: Why have grieving individuals, who are distressed and distracted from the daily problems of survival, not been replaced by those that instantly forget their dead mate or young and engage more effectively in survival tasks?

Looked at in these terms, the existence of grief is a puzzle, and there have been some unconvincing attempts to explain it in terms of a direct advantage (see Archer, 1999). The origin and maintenance of grief can be better understood through Bowlby's (1969) attachment theory (see also chap. 5, this volume). *Attachment* is the process of forming emotional bonds to significant others; it was originally studied in the context of the child-to-parent bond (Bowlby, 1958, 1969) but has since been extended to cover all biologically important relationships (involving kinship, parental units, and allies). The process involves a motivational system with the overall goal of maintaining attachment. Behavior controlled by this system is therefore functional in that it maintains proximity with the attachment figure or (in humans) maintains contact with them in other ways (e.g., writing or phoning). Temporary separations induce a strong emotional reaction and the motivation to regain contact: Reunion behavior, such as hugging the loved one, provides reassurance that the bond is maintained. Separation reactions, therefore, are indicative of strong motivations to regain contact with an attachment figure. They are common to humans and nonhumans, to adults and to children. Thus, a core reaction—termed *separation distress*—occurs whenever an animal, child, or adult human is separated from its attachment figure.

Bowlby (1973, 1980) argued that although separation reactions are clearly adaptive for maintaining attachment bonds by ensuring that the individual does not form a new relationship whenever the attachment figure is absent, grief reactions are not. They represent the inevitable consequence of these reactions occurring when no reunion is possible. Because separation is far more common than death, and the mechanisms are not flexible enough to have two reactions, grief is viewed as a cost of the overall adaptive separation reaction. If we add to this the consideration that until relatively late in human evolution, there was probably no clear understanding of the permanence of death (Archer, 1999, 2001b), it becomes clear that seeking an adaptive explanation to grief in isolation from the separation reaction is misguided.

Although this attachment-based view would seem to explain the evolutionary origins of grief, Nesse (2000) put forward an alternative, arguing that grief does have direct adaptive benefits. He regarded grief as a special state that evolved to cope with the loss of a loved one by changing goals; signaling to others; and reassessing priorities, plans, and relationships. Grief is viewed as a necessary reaction to a social loss, whose function is to aid resolution, a view that can be seen as an extension of grief work theory. As will become apparent when I discuss the evidence relating to this theory, there is little empirical support for this position.

INDIVIDUAL DIFFERENCES IN GRIEF FROM AN EVOLUTIONARY PERSPECTIVE

Several additional evolutionary principles have been applied to understanding individual differences in grief. Underlying all of these is the assumption, derived from the principle of natural selection, that close relationships have arisen as a consequence of mechanisms that aided our ancestors' survival or reproductive chances or those of their close relatives. It is as a result of these past selection pressures that attachments are formed most readily to offspring, parents, and other close relatives; to those who are good prospects as long-term mates; and to those who are reliable allies. In the case of relatives, the principle of the *coefficient of relatedness* (Wright, 1922) is a measure of the extent to which two individuals share genes that are rare in the population as a whole. Three studies have found more intense grief for the loss of a mono-zygotic than a dizygotic twin, corresponding with coefficients of relatedness of 1.0 and .5, respectively (Segal & Ream, 1998; Segal, Welson, Bouchard, & Gitlin, 1995). Segal and Bouchard (1993) also found that monozygotic twins showed more intense grief after the loss of a co-twin than after the loss of a spouse. A comparison of the grief reported by these twins for other rela-tives with coefficients of relatedness of .5 with those of .25 showed a large dif-ference between them (Archer, 2001b), as did another comparison of the grief estimated by bereaved parents for themselves and for more distant rela-tives, such as aunts and uncles (Archer, 2001b).

These associations between grief and the coefficient of relatedness may be mediated by closeness of attachment, which is likely to follow the degree of relatedness and to be especially pronounced in the case of twins (Tancredy & Fraley, 2006). The influence of kinship would then be an indirect effect of variables such as longer exposure (and therefore greater attachment) to closer kin. Thus, the introduction of the evolutionary principle would not have added anything to an analysis in terms of attachment. Indeed, the two are difficult to separate, and they would have to be investigated by studying cases in which the coefficient of relatedness was different but the degree of coresidence was similar, as in the cases of stepchildren.

A second evolutionary principle that has been applied to the study of grief is *reproductive value* (Fisher, 1930), which is the expected contribution of a close relative (usually offspring) to an individual's fitness. It is typically low at the beginning of life, because of high infant and childhood mortality, and increases to an optimum at the beginning of reproductive life, after which it declines. The prediction derived from this principle is that parents' grief for their offspring will steadily increase from conception to young adulthood and then gradually decline. In a study of perinatal grief, Toedter, Lasker, and Alhadeff (1988) found a correlation of .47 between grief and age within this limited age range, thus indicating an increase in grief on the ascending part of the reproductive value curve. In a study of bereaved couples whose off-spring had died at various ages, Wijngaards-de-Meij et al. (2005) measured grief and depression at 6, 13, and 20 months after the death. As expected, both measures decreased over time. As predicted by the principle of repro-ductive value, there was a curvilinear relationship between grief and the child's age at the time of death: Grief increased until 17 years and decreased thereafter. These findings, and a study of people who rated the expected grief for losses at different ages (Crawford, Salter, & Jang, 1989), suggest that grief following the loss of an offspring corresponds with the reproductive value of the deceased.

THE IMMEDIATE CAUSE OF THE GRIEF REACTION

In addition to providing a plausible framework for considering the evolutionary origin of grief, Bowlby's (1961, 1973, 1980) attachment theory also has implications for the causal mechanisms underlying grief, that is, what triggers it. From this viewpoint, grief is clearly a deficit reaction set in motion by separation from an attachment figure, and this is generated by an integrated behavioral system that incorporates a clear representation of the attachment figure together with the goal of maintaining proximity to it. When the outside world no longer contains the attachment figure, a deficit-driven reaction is set in motion.

Klinger (1975) viewed the process that initiated grief as applying more generally than to the loss of an attachment figure. Every time an expected rewarding event fails to occur, there is a miniature grief reaction, which entails anger and distress followed by increased vigor, goal-related behavior, and inactivity (or giving up). Grief is therefore regarded as one example of a general process whereby an animal becomes disengaged from situations that are no longer reinforcing. Thus, minor disappointments, such as a jammed photocopier or a disrupted journey, are miniature grief experiences that are soon forgotten.

The implications of Klinger's (1975) theory are that grief is a series of reactions whose function is to gain access to the source of an incentive. Strong emotions are generated, and these motivate the animal to seek the incentive; if unsuccessful, a more depressive reaction occurs, and this serves to disengage the individual from that particular incentive. There clearly are parallels between responses to frustrating events and grief reactions. As C. S. Lewis (1961) noted, grief "comes from the frustration of so many impulses that have become habitual" (p. 39). Is grief therefore merely the sum of the many individual frustrations that occur when an attachment figure is lost? In a way it is, but it differs in one crucial respect from a series of unconnected frustrating events: In the case of grief, all the frustrated impulses are centered on the lost loved one, providing constant reminders of the loss and generating thoughts that return the bereaved person back to the reality of his or her loss. According to the attachment view, the notion of a central organizing principle linking individual separation reactions together is explicit, involving an internal model of the attachment figure rather than being a series of disconnected responses, as Klinger suggested.

Cognitive theories of the origin of grief can be regarded as largely complementing attachment theory, but with a different emphasis. This is centered on the nature of the internal representations involved, termed *internal working models* by Bowlby (1969, 1973). In seeking to understand how grieflike reactions can occur to other types of loss, such as a home or limb, Parkes (1971) elaborated the nature of these internal models in terms of the concept of *assumptive worlds*, the sum of people's expectations and assumptions about the world in which they live. These would include not only attachment figures and the person's relationships but also other aspects of the person's habitual world, such as possessions, assumptions about the self, and the person's cherished beliefs and expectations about the future. Whenever there is a sudden change corresponding to large parts of one's assumptive world, a deficit-driven, grief-like reaction occurs. The assumptive-world framework broadens the grief response so that a range of negative life events, such as job loss (Archer & Rhodes, 1993, 1995) or a loss of a body part or function (Parkes, 1972b), can be seen in a light similar to bereavement.

Coming from a different theoretical background, that of trauma theory, Horowitz (1976, 1988) and Janoff-Bulman (1989, 1993) also have emphasized the internal models that are shattered by a traumatic life change. They referred to these as *schemata*, although Janoff-Bulman (1989) also used the term *assumptive worlds*. *Schemata* are internal models of important parts of an individual's personal world, not only the person's attachments to people, places, and ways of life but also his or her basic assumptions—for example, that the world in which he or she lives is predictable and safe. When outside events are discrepant from these basic assumptions, traumatic stress reactions occur. In the context of bereavement, they are most likely to be apparent when this follows a homicide, an accident, or a disaster. In addition to widening our understanding of the context of grief, the concept of assumptive worlds also shifts the emphasis from general descriptions of the typical grief process to an acknowledgment of individual variability, arising from the relative importance people attach to different areas of their lives and from the context in which the loss has occurred. In the next section, I consider how cognitive theories of the generation of grief can help understanding of contextual influences on grief.

CONTEXTUAL INFLUENCES ON THE GRIEF PROCESS

Cognitive theories of the generation of grief can take us some way toward understanding the two main contextual variations that have been studied in relation to grief: (a) the degree of forewarning and (b) the trauma surrounding the death. Regarding the former, there is some evidence that grief is more intense in cases in which there has been no forewarning of the death than when there has (e.g., Parkes & Weiss, 1983), although there are also null results (see Bonanno & Kaltman, 1999). These findings would be expected from the perspective that forewarning may facilitate changes in the person's assumptive world before the death has occurred. On the other hand, a sudden death would involve a large change in the person's outside world and would therefore produce a greater discrepancy between this and his or her assumptive world.

When the death is both sudden and involves traumatic circumstances—for example, if it is the result of an accident, a suicide, or murder—then there is a discrepancy not only with assumptions about the personal world but also with basic assumptions about the outside world, for example, that it is safe and trustworthy (Janoff-Bulman, 1993). In such cases, concepts derived from trauma theory are applicable to bereavement. On the basis of Freud's (1914/1958) writings about reactions to traumatic events, Horowitz (1976) described two basic reactions to a traumatic event: (a) a compulsive tendency to repeat the experience and (b) attempts to avoid and suppress its memory. These tend to alternate with one another and to be out of the person's control. This is the essence of posttraumatic stress disorder (PTSD). In terms of the cognitive processes involved, Horowitz argued that the trauma produces discrepant information that cannot be integrated into schemata and is therefore stored in what he called *active memory*. Attempts to integrate the highly discrepant information are unsuccessful and produce cycles of intrusion and denial. PTSD reactions have been found in a number of studies on traumatic forms of bereavement, such as bereavement following homicide (e.g., Masters, Friedman, & Getzel, 1988). Among a sample of parents bereaved through a violent death, finding meaning in such circumstances was associated with lower mental distress and better physical health but with only a smaller (and nonsignificant) lowering in PTSD measures (Murphy, Johnson, & Lohan, 2003; see chap. 18, this volume).

EMPIRICAL ASSESSMENT OF GRIEF WORK THEORY

As indicated in the first section of this chapter, much of the recent research on grief has been concerned with reexamining long-established notions about the resolution of grief, in particular the concept of grief work. It is clear that bereaved people typically progress from a distressed state, with disruption of everyday activities and a high negative affect, to an effective level of everyday function, with lower levels of distress. For example, among a study of widows in San Diego, California, the percentages of participants who showed tearfulness were 73% at 2 months, 35% at 13 months, and 17% at 49 months (Shuchter, 1986). Grief work theory holds that this apparent resolution can be achieved only through an active process of confronting thoughts and feelings associated with the loss.

In the first study to test this, Stroebe and Stroebe (1991) assessed grief work by the degree to which bereaved men and women confronted or suppressed grief. An example of confrontation is "I think about him/her a lot," and an example of suppression is "I avoid anything that would be too painful a reminder." These measures formed predictors in a longitudinal study, with depression and acceptance of the loss being the outcome measures. Overall, men's depression levels were lower than women's at the first time of measurement (4 to 7 months after the loss), and they declined over the next two measurement times (at 14 and 24 months). Women's depression levels declined only a little over these 2 years. The central question posed in the study was whether grief work at 4 to 7 months (or at 14 months) predicted subsequent improvement in the two measures. The answer was that it did for the widowers (who showed an overall decline in depression) but not for the widows (whose depression levels changed little).

The explanation given at the time was that men have a greater need to engage in grief work because they tend not to confront their negative feelings and thoughts as much as women do (Stroebe & Stroebe, 1991). Although this is consistent with other evidence (Bonanno et al., 2005; Pennebaker, Zech, & Rimé, 2001; Schut, Stroebe, van den Bout, & de Keijser, 1997), there are several reasons why it is unlikely to be the explanation in the original study. First, men and women differed little in the grief work measures that were associated with recovery. Therefore, the assumption that these reflect different coping styles in men and women would be difficult to sustain. Second, only two of the six items measuring grief work were associated with improvement for men, and the different measures were not closely associated. Other studies (e.g., Videka-Sherman, 1982; Wegner & Zanakos, 1994) have suggested that suppression and distraction, which were combined on the grief work scale, are likely to have different consequences, with distraction being more effective.

Bonanno et al. (2005) showed that measures of the deliberate avoidance of grief were unrelated to measures of grief processing, again indicating that the two should not be combined. They found that an index of initial grief processing predicted more rather than less long-term distress, regardless of the initial level of distress, in a sample from the United States (but it had no influence in a sample from China). What is perhaps even more inexplicable from a grief-work perspective is the finding that a measure of grief avoidance (which was unrelated to grief processing) also predicted greater long-term distress in the American sample.

The issue of whether disclosing to others feelings and thoughts about a loss or another traumatic event can be beneficial to the resolution of grief and to subsequent mental and physical health is one that has yielded conflicting findings. In a retrospective study, Pennebaker and O'Heeron (1984) found that the more spouses of suicide and accident victims said that they discussed the death with friends, the fewer health problems and less rumination about the loss they reported. However, when Range, Kovac, and Marion (2000) asked bereaved people either to write about a loss or about a trivial topic, they found no difference in measures of recovery over time between these two conditions, either immediately after the writing or 6 weeks later. Writing about previously undisclosed emotional topics in this way is a method that has been found to produce benefits in health in a number of studies, which I discuss shortly.

Stroebe, Stroebe, Schut, Zech, and van den Bout (2002) investigated whether spontaneous disclosure of emotions (measured by a five-item scale) predicted subsequent adjustment following bereavement among a sample of 128 widows and widowers. As expected, both disclosure and distress declined over the study period, from 4 to 25 months after the death, and there was individual consistency in these measures over time. Level of disclosure at 4 months was unrelated to subsequent distress, therefore showing no indication that it aided the resolution of grief. A second study assessed whether induced disclosure (as used by Range et al., 2000) would improve adjustment among a sample of bereaved people. Participants wrote in a diary either about their deepest emotions or about problems due to the loss, or both, or they did not write anything. Stroebe et al. measured depression and anxiety, the degree of intrusive thoughts, and avoidance of loss-related thoughts. They found that the writing conditions made no difference to subsequent adjustment assessed by these measures, and there was no impact of the suddenness of the loss, the degree of disclosure, or the need to disclose that the person expressed.

Two studies have measured the avoidance or expression of emotions more directly, as opposed to being disclosed to others or put in written form. The first study (Bonanno, Keltner, Holen, & Horowitz, 1995) assessed the extent to which people avoided negative emotions by the degree of mismatch between their autonomic arousal and reported emotional state. Thus, people with high heart rates and low reported negative emotion were inferred to have a high degree of avoidance of their emotional state. Such individuals, measured at 6 months after their loss, had fewer signs of grief and fewer somatic symptoms when assessed 8 months later, compared with those with a lesser disparity between their heart rates and their self-reports. Contrary to what would be expected from grief work theory, this study seems to indicate that avoidance of acknowledging one's underlying emotional state is an effective way of coping with grief.

In the second study, Bonanno and Keltner (1997) observed facial expressions of members of groups of bereaved people 6 months after their loss and assessed their grief, health, and well-being at 14 and 25 months. The expression of negative emotions (e.g., anger, contempt, and fear) at 6 months was associated with more severe grief at 15 and 25 months. This is to be expected because people who are more distressed earlier on tend to be more distressed later (Bonanno, 2004; Wortman & Silver, 1989). However, this still occurred when the participants' initial self-reported distress was controlled, indicating that their relative recovery was poorer than that of participants whose expressions showed a lesser degree of negative emotions. Consistent with this, positive expressions (laughs and smiles) at 6 months were associated with better adjustment later. This study therefore found that more positive and fewer negative emotional expressions early on were associated with a better outcome later. This may be due to a causal connection, or it could be that those individuals have a personality or coping style that shows itself in their facial expressions early on and in better outcomes later.

Thus far there seems to be little evidence that disclosure of emotions to others leads to better adjustment following bereavement. Showing overt negative emotions is associated with a poorer outcome, both in absolute terms and relative to initial levels of distress. Furthermore, avoidance of one's underlying emotional state may actually help subsequent adjustment. Nevertheless, when considering disclosure in relation to grief work, we need to acknowledge the wider background to this topic, because a number of studies, beginning with Pennebaker and Beall's (1986), have indicated that writing about emotional topics is associated with better physical health and improved psychological well-being (Pennebaker, 1997; Pennebaker et al., 2001; Sloan, Marx, & Epstein, 2005).

Pennebaker, Mayne, and Francis (1997) analyzed participants' writings in six of their studies to assess the hypothesis that it is the change in thinking patterns over time, the increased level of insight, that is responsible for subsequent health benefits. They found that changes in thinking patterns, assessed by an increase in the level of insight or the use of causal words, predicted subsequent greater improvement in health. They also measured expressed negative emotions and found that these did not predict improvement and indeed may have been associated with a detriment to health. Pennebaker et al. suggested that cognitive reframing of a negative life event is necessary for disclosure to have an impact on physiological regulation and health. Thus, finding meaning in the event is crucial. Spoken or written language aids this reorganization and reassimilation, but simply expressing the emotion does not, and disclosure by itself would not necessarily do so. Pennebaker et al. also measured cognitive change in the interview transcripts of men who had lost partners to AIDS and found that these measures did predict distress at 1 year postbereavement.

An earlier study (McIntosh, Silver, & Wortman, 1993), of a sample of parents bereaved by sudden infant death syndrome, used a self-report measure of *cognitive processing,* the extent to which parents engaged in attempts to work through their loss and to purposely think and talk about the baby and his or her death. At first (at 3 months after the death), the higher the level of cognitive processing, the greater was the reported distress. However, when the initial level of well-being was controlled, higher initial levels of cognitive processing predicted slightly less distress at 18 months after the loss. This provides some support for Pennebaker et al.'s (1997) emphasis on cognitive processing, although finding meaning in the loss was not measured in this study.

A further study of parents bereaved by sudden infant death syndrome (Lepore, Ragan, & Jones, 2000) measured the extent to which they talked about their intrusive thoughts and how they viewed the social surroundings restraining their doing so. If the perceived social constraints were high, then more intrusive thoughts at 3 weeks after the loss predicted greater depression, both at the time and 15 months later. If the perceived social constraints were low, then intrusive thoughts at 3 weeks predicted less depression at 18 months. Thus, intrusive thoughts kept to oneself predicted a poor outcome, whereas intrusive thoughts shared with others predicted a better outcome. An explanation in terms of Pennebaker et al.'s (1997) framework would be that social constraints inhibit someone talking about his or her loss, thus interfering with cognitive processing of the loss and preventing effective cognitive restructuring, leading to higher levels of depression. However, sharing thoughts and feelings about the loss to sympathetic others could foster new and supportive relationships, which in turn generate a greater sense of well-being. In contrast, unhappy thoughts kept to oneself generate a sense of isolation. This alternative explanation would not necessarily involve cognitive restructuring.

One study that directly assessed the meaning people found in coming to terms with their loss was conducted by Davis, Nolen-Hoeksema, and Larson (1998). They argued that previous studies had conflated making sense of the loss and deriving benefit from it, so they constructed scales to measure these two forms of meaning. In a sample of mainly middle-aged adults who had lost a spouse, parent, or other family member, they found that making sense was greater among participants who held religious beliefs and in cases when the deceased was older, whereas finding benefit was associated with dispositional optimism. Higher levels of both measures predicted lower distress at 6 months after the loss, but deriving benefit was more strongly related to later adjustment. Although this study seems to provide clear evidence that finding meaning is associated with better adjustment, it may be (as mentioned in relation to Bonanno & Keltner's [1997] study) that people who hold religious beliefs or are dispositional optimists cope better with negative life events.

Where does this evidence leave us in terms of the theory of grief work? There is some evidence for changes consistent with this view, but it is restricted to the following three: (a) specific measures involving either purposely engaging in thinking about the loss, or changes in the pattern of thinking; (b) a link with being able to talk about intrusive thoughts, which could be a secondary consequence of the social support involved; and (c) cases in which finding meaning was measured in terms of making sense of the loss or finding benefit from it, although there is an alternative explanation for this in terms of individual differences. Overall, therefore, the grief work hypothesis has not been well supported by these empirical studies, but it might still operate in the form of cognitive restructuring, as outlined by Pennebaker and his colleagues (e.g., Pennebaker et al., 1997, 2001).

FILLING THE THEORETICAL GAP

Bonanno and Kaltman (1999) referred to a "theoretical vacuum" left as a result of the accumulation of evidence that challenged grief work theory. They elaborated other psychological perspectives that might be applied to grief to fill this gap. One was the *cognitive stress perspective,* which involves an emphasis on cognitive appraisal of a stressful event and the subsequent use of coping strategies that seek to counter the effects of the stress in various ways. Such strategies may operate to avoid or regulate the impact of the loss, to seek to change the meaning it holds for them, or to alter their environment so as to avoid or counter its most distressing effects. There is no prior assumption (as in the case of grief work theory) that any one of these is necessarily the most effective. An avoidant coping style could be effective in some cases. Bonanno and Kaltman also noted that one implication of the attachment perspective was that there could be a reorganization of the attachment bond to take account of the death, instead of the gradual and painful withdrawal envisaged by grief work theory (see also Klass & Walter, 2001; Stroebe et al., 2005). Another perspective, the *social–functional approach* to emotion, can be applied to grief in terms of emphasizing the adaptive role of positive emotional expression and the maladaptive role of negative emotional expression. Last, the *trauma perspective,* mentioned in relation to the cause of the grief reaction, would view grief as involving a set of reactions similar to those that follow other major negative life events. Here the emphasis is on the way that such events challenge established beliefs people have about their personal world.

Bonanno and Kaltman (1999) sought to integrate these different perspectives to fill the gap left by the grief work perspective. However, their application was wider than the resolution of grief and included processes involved in the generation of grief and contextual variables (discussed in previous sections of this chapter) as well as individual differences. Their main alternative to grief work theory of the resolution of grief involved cognitive restructuring, which took account of the reorganization of attachment bonds, and some aspects of the cognitive stress perspective. However, it was not a well-developed alternative theory, and it probably could have benefited from a closer link with Pennebaker's (1997) concept of reframing of thoughts.

A more systematic application of the cognitive stress perspective is the dual-process model (DPM) of Stroebe and Schut (1999). They argued that emphasis on grief work (or on cognitive restructuring) concerns only one form of coping with bereavement, referred to as *loss oriented,* to distinguish it from *restoration-focused* coping, which involves coping with the loss by turning attention away from it and engaging in new tasks and relationships. These are not merely alternative coping styles that different people use, although there are individual differences; they also occur within the same person as alternating (or oscillating) processes. Both are important for the eventual resolution of grief. Avoidance and mitigation allow the individual to operate in the world and to rebuild his or her life, whereas confronting the loss internally allows restructuring of the mental representations of the lost relationship. Oscillation between the two enables a balanced recovery to occur. Like grief work theory, and Pennebaker's (1997) cognitive restructuring, the DPM is a functional model, concerned with processes that aid resolution.

In a previous discussion of the DPM (Archer, 1999), I raised the issue of whether forming a new relationship (an extreme restoration-oriented strategy) can shorten the process of grief. In some (collectivist) cultures, the widow is provided with new sexual partner or is obliged to marry the husband's brother, if he is available, and this may occur within days or weeks of the death. In Shuchter's (1986) longitudinal study, carried out in California, 19% of the participants were cohabiting or married 10 months after bereavement, a figure that rose to 30% at 19 months. Reported interest in dating was high throughout the study period (1 to 22 months after the loss), and the participants who reported that they still enjoyed sex numbered between 40% and 70% throughout the study period. Several studies have found more well-being and less distress in people who have remarried than those who have not. Although it is likely that those who remarry were less distressed and more cheerful before meeting their new partners, a longitudinal study (Burks, Lund, Gregg, & Bluhm, 1988) found a progressively greater increase in adjustment over time in bereaved people who remarried, compared with those who had not.

Although the empirical evidence on which to base a theory of the resolution of grief is much more advanced than it was 15 years ago, there is still no comprehensive evidence-based theory to account for the way in which people move from initial high levels of distress to levels similar to those before the loss. The DPM sets out one possibility, but this has yet to be comprehensively tested. Theories involving cognitive restructuring or cognitive reframing have received mixed support and are perhaps most similar to grief work theory, although Pennebaker's (1997) theory is more precise in terms of specifying the process that is involved.

INDIVIDUAL DIFFERENCES IN GRIEF FROM AN ATTACHMENT PERSPECTIVE

Once it is recognized that there is no single process through which all bereaved people must necessarily go in order to resolve their grief, the sources of individual variations in the grief process become particularly important. Bowlby's (1961, 1973, 1980) attachment framework has been used to generate testable hypotheses about such individual differences in grief. In this context, it is the style of attachment, rather than the process of forming and breaking attachment bonds, that is the important issue. The three original attachment styles, transferred to adults by Hazan and Shaver (1987; see also chap. 5, this volume) on the basis of studies of the infant-to-parent bond (Ainsworth, Blehar, Waters, & Wall, 1978), are (a) secure, (b) anxious–ambivalent (or preoccupied), and (c) anxious–avoidant. The preoccupied style of attachment is similar to the concept of dependency, which was linked to more intense prolonged grief by Bowlby (1980), in his analysis of atypical grief, and in several studies (e.g., Parkes & Weiss, 1983; Prigerson, Shear, Bierhals, et al., 1997; Prigerson, Shear, Frank, et al., 1997) that have used assessments of dependency given after the death. The anxious–avoidant style corresponds to Bowlby's (1980) description of a pattern involving an absence of overt grieving, which he believed would produce later problems in accordance with the grief work view. However, such a pattern of delayed grief has not been shown in any empirical study (Bonanno, 2004).

The three-category model of adult attachment style was developed into a four-category model by Bartholomew and Horowitz (1991), who distinguished between two types of anxious–avoidant attachment: (a) fearful–avoidant and (b) dismissing–avoidant. These were originally conceived of in terms of two orthogonal dimensions—valuing the self and valuing the other (Griffin & Bartholomew, 1994)—but they have since been characterized as high or low attachment-related avoidance and high or low anxiety about attachment (Fraley & Shaver, 2000).

Fraley and Bonanno (2004; see also chap. 14, this volume) used ratings of anxiety, depression, grief, and PTSD from structured clinical interviews at 4 and 18 months after bereavement to assess how both the level and change over time differed among the four attachment styles (measured 2 weeks before the first assessment period). People with the dismissing–avoidant style showed signs of resilience in the face of the loss, similar to people with a secure attachment, with low levels of anxiety, depression, grief, and PTSD at both 4 and 18 months after the loss. In contrast, people with a fearful–avoidant style showed higher levels of all four measures at both times. People with a preoccupied style were similar to the fearful category for anxiety and depression but tended to show levels of grief and PTSD that were lower than those of people in the fearful category but still at levels higher than those of people in the two resilient categories. It is clear that the two avoidant styles showed very different patterns of grieving: Whereas dismissing individuals are relatively little affected by the loss, individuals with a fearful style are much affected by the loss. The essential difference was where the two groups were on the dimension of anxiety about attachment: People with high anxiety levels were most affected by the loss. Such people, Fraley and Bonanno suggested, particularly needed reassurance, comfort, and contact with their partners when they were alive and are strongly affected by not being able to have these needs met after the death.

THE RELATIONS BETWEEN PRACTICE, RESEARCH, AND THEORY

Although the resolution of grief is only one aspect of a comprehensive theory of grief, it has been the central concern in theories of grief, from the time of Freud to the present. If grief work theory is correct, then certain interventions would, if followed, facilitate people's recovery. Grieving people would be advised to follow procedures designed to promote confrontation and disclosure, and to provide them with insight and meaning into their loss, and they would be advised to regard as counterproductive avoiding thinking about the loss or distracting themselves with other activities. Research would be best restricted to finding out exactly which aspect of the various activities that have been described as grief work are the most effective for adjustment.

The empirical evidence has largely been unsupportive of the simple grief work position. Nevertheless, in some cases, cognitive restructuring and finding meaning in the loss have been associated with benefits, but it seems that *cognitive restructuring* has to be defined in a precise way. It is not simply the extent to which the person thinks and talks about the deceased (Bonanno et al., 2005), or the person's degree of emotional expression (Bonanno & Keltner, 1997); it has to be characterized in terms of the level of insight or meaning involved (Pennebaker et al., 1997). This view is consistent with studies that have reported an association between finding meaning and lower levels of grief (Davis et al., 1998; Murphy et al., 2003). However, when Davis, Wortman, Lehman, and Silver (2000) examined the empirical evidence for three core beliefs about the role of meaning in coming to terms with loss, they found little support for these. Thus, people were not necessarily motivated to find meaning for their loss; neither did most people find such meaning over time, and the extent to which they did or did not find meaning was unrelated to recovery.

Some of the puzzling and contradictory findings are likely to be understood by moving from attempts to find a single theory of the resolution of grief to the study of individual and contextual variability, as outlined in earlier sections of this chapter. The application of attachment theory to the grief process, described in the previous section, is a particularly important development because it shows that the way people related to the deceased has a crucial bearing on how they respond to their loss. One interesting theoretical development is the integration of attachment style with the DPM. Stroebe et al. (2005) suggested that securely attached people will be better able to move from loss-oriented to restoration-oriented coping, and vice versa, thus showing greater flexibility. Those with a preoccupied style are likely to focus on loss-oriented coping and to be unable to move away from this. People with an avoidant style are likely to focus on restoration and to avoid overt grief. This pattern has recently been viewed as resilience in the face of a loss (Davis et al., 2000; Fraley & Bonanno, 2004). Stroebe et al. also suggested that people with a fearful–avoidant (or disorganized) attachment style are likely to experience problems with their grieving: Such individuals were viewed as showing a pattern typically found in response to traumatic events, with little control over moving from loss to restoration-oriented processes. Support for this view came from Fraley and Bonanno's (2004) study, both in terms of the high levels of distress and elevated levels of PTSD measures in this group. It is clear that such recent research on attachment styles and their relation to ways of coping has the potential to transform the way practitioners deal with bereaved people. Rather than holding the view that people must necessarily engage in grief work, practitioners could offer instead a range of interventions tailored to individual characteristics and circumstances.

REFERENCES

Ainsworth, M. D. S., Blehar, M. C., Waters, E., & Wall, S. (1978). *Patterns of attachment: A psychological study of the strange situation*. Hillsdale, NJ: Erlbaum.

Archer, J. (1999). *The nature of grief*. London: Routledge.

Archer, J. (2001a). Broad and narrow perspectives in grief theory: Comment on Bonanno and Kaltman (1999). *Psychological Bulletin, 127*, 554–560.

Archer, J. (2001b). Grief from an evolutionary perspective. In M. S. Stroebe, W. Stroebe, R. O. Hansson, & H. Schut (Eds.), *Handbook of bereavement research: Consequences, coping, and care* (pp. 263–283). Washington, DC: American Psychological Association.

Archer, J., & Rhodes, V. (1993). The grief process and job loss: A cross sectional study. *British Journal of Psychology, 84*, 395–410.

Archer, J., & Rhodes, V. (1995). A longitudinal study of job loss in relation to the grief process. *Journal of Community and Applied Social Psychology, 5*, 183–188.

Averill, J. R. (1968). Grief: Its nature and significance. *Psychological Bulletin, 70*, 721–748.

Bartholomew, K., & Horowitz, L. M. (1991). Attachment styles among young adults: A test of a four-category model. *Journal of Personality and Social Psychology, 61*, 226–244.

Bonanno, G. A. (2004). Loss, trauma and human resilience: Have we underestimated the human capacity to thrive after extremely aversive events? *American Psychologist, 59*, 20–28.

Bonanno, G. A., & Kaltman, S. (1999). Toward an integrative perspective on bereavement. *Psychological Bulletin, 125*, 760–776.

Bonanno, G. A., & Keltner, D. (1997). Facial expression of emotion and the course of conjugal bereavement. *Journal of Abnormal Psychology, 106*, 126–137.

Bonanno, G. A., Keltner, D., Holen, A., & Horowitz, M. J. (1995). When avoiding unpleasant emotions might not be such a bad thing: Verbal-autonomic response dissociation and midlife conjugal bereavement. *Journal of Personality and Social Psychology, 69*, 975–989.

Bonanno, G. A., Papa, A., Lalande, K., Zhang, N., & Noll, J. G. (2005). Grief processing and deliberate grief avoidance: A prospective comparison of bereaved spouses and parents in the United States and the People's Republic of China. *Journal of Consulting and Clinical Psychology, 73*, 86–98.

Bowlby, J. (1958). The nature of the child's tie to his mother. *International Journal of Psychoanalysis, 39*, 350–373.

Bowlby, J. (1961). Processes of mourning. *International Journal of Psychoanalysis, 42*, 317–340.

Bowlby, J. (1969). *Attachment and loss: Vol. 1. Attachment*. London: Hogarth Press & Institute of Psychoanalysis.

Bowlby, J. (1973). *Attachment and loss: Vol. 2. Separation: Anxiety and anger*. London: Hogarth Press & Institute of Psychoanalysis.

Bowlby, J. (1980). *Attachment and loss: Vol. 3. Loss: Sadness and depression*. London: Hogarth Press & Institute of Psychoanalysis.

Burks, V. K., Lund, D. A., Gregg, C. H., & Bluhm, H. P. (1988). Bereavement and remarriage for older adults. *Death Studies, 12*, 51–60.

Crawford, C. B., Salter, B. E., & Jang, K. L. (1989). Human grief: Is its intensity related to the reproductive value of the deceased? *Ethology and Sociobiology, 10*, 297–307.

Darwin, C. (1904). *The expression of the emotions in man and animals*. London: Murray. (Original work published 1872)

Davis, C. G., Nolen-Hoeksema, S., & Larson, J. (1998). Making sense of loss and benefiting from the experience: Two construals of meaning. *Journal of Personality and Social Psychology, 75*, 561–574.

Davis, C. G., Wortman, C. B., Lehman, D. R., & Silver, R. C. (2000). Searching for meaning in loss: Are clinical assumptions correct? *Death Studies, 24*, 497–540.

Fisher, R. A. (1930). *The genetical theory of natural selection*. Oxford, England: Clarendon Press.

Fraley, R. C., & Bonanno, G. A. (2004). Attachment and loss: A test of three competing models on the association between attachment-related avoidance and adaptation to bereavement. *Personality and Social Psychology Bulletin, 30*, 878–890.

Fraley, R. C., & Shaver, P. R. (2000). Adult romantic attachment: Theoretical developments, emerging controversies, and unanswered questions. *Review of General Psychology, 4*, 132–154.

Freud, S. (1957). Mourning and melancholia. In J. Strachey (Ed. & Trans.), *The standard edition of the complete psychological works of Sigmund Freud* (Vol. 14, pp. 239–260). London: Hogarth Press & Institute of Psychoanalysis. (Original work published 1917)

Freud, S. (1958). Remembering, repeating and working through. In J. Strachey (Ed. & Trans.), *The standard edition of the complete psychological works of Sigmund Freud*

(Vol. 12, pp. 147–156). London: Hogarth Press & Institute of Psychoanalysis. (Original work published 1914)

Griffin, D., & Bartholomew, K. (1994). Models of the self and other: Fundamental dimensions underlying measures of adult attachment. *Journal of Personality and Social Psychology, 67*, 430–445.

Hazan, C., & Shaver, P. R. (1987). Romantic love conceptualized as an attachment process. *Journal of Personality and Social Psychology, 52*, 511–524.

Horowitz, M. J. (1976). *Stress response syndrome*. New York: Jason Aronson.

Horowitz, M. J. (1988). *Introduction to psychodymanics: A new synthesis*. New York: Basic Books.

Janoff-Bulman, R. (1989). Assumptive worlds and the stress of traumatic events: Applications of the schema construct. *Social Cognition, 7*, 113–136.

Janoff-Bulman, R. (1993). *Shattered assumptions: Towards a new psychology of trauma*. New York: Free Press.

Klass, D., & Walter, T. (2001). Process of grieving: How bonds are continued. In M. S. Stroebe, W. Stroebe, R. O. Hanson, & H. Schut (Eds.), *Handbook of bereavement research: Consequences, coping, and care* (pp. 431–448). Washington, DC: American Psychological Association.

Klinger, E. (1975). Consequences of commitment to and disengagement from incentives. *Psychological Review, 82*, 1–25.

Lepore, S. J., Ragan, J. D., & Jones, S. (2000). Talking facilitates cognitive–emotional processes of adaptation to an acute stressor. *Journal of Personality and Social Psychology, 78*, 499–508.

Lewis, C. S. (1961). *A grief observed*. London: Faber & Faber.

Masters, R., Friedman, L. N., & Getzel, G. (1988). Helping families of homicide victims: A multidimensional approach. *Journal of Traumatic Stress, 1*, 109–125.

McIntosh, D. N., Silver, R. C., & Wortman, C. B. (1993). Religion's role in adjustment to a negative life event: Coping with the loss of a child. *Journal of Personality and Social Psychology, 65*, 812–821.

Murphy, A. A., Johnson, L. C., & Lohan, J. (2003). Finding meaning in a child's violent death: A five-year prospective analysis of parents' personal narratives and empirical data. *Death Studies, 27*, 381–404.

Nesse, R. (2000). Is grief really maladaptive? [Review of the book *The Nature of Grief: The Evolution and Psychology of Reactions to Loss*]. *Evolution and Human Behavior, 21*, 59–61.

Parkes, C. M. (1971). Psychosocial transitions: A field for study. *Social Science & Medicine, 5*, 101–115.

Parkes, C. M. (1972a). *Bereavement: Studies of grief in adult life*. New York: Tavistock.

Parkes, C. M. (1972b). Components of the reaction to loss of a limb, spouse or home. *Journal of Psychosomatic Research, 16*, 343–349.

Parkes, C. M., & Weiss, R. S. (1983). *Recovery from bereavement*. New York: Basic Books.

Pennebaker, J. W. (1997). Writing about emotional experiences as a therapeutic process. *Psychological Science, 8,* 162–166.

Pennebaker, J. W., & Beall, S. K. (1986). Confronting a traumatic event: Toward an understanding of inhibition and disease. *Journal of Abnormal Psychology, 95,* 274–281.

Pennebaker, J. W., Mayne, T. J., & Francis, M. E. (1997). Linguistic predictors of adaptive bereavement. *Journal of Personality and Social Psychology, 72,* 863–871.

Pennebaker, J. W., & O'Heeron, R. C. (1984). Confiding in others and illness rate among spouses of suicide and accidental-death victims. *Journal of Abnormal Psychology, 93,* 473–476.

Pennebaker, J. W., Zech, E., & Rimé, B. (2001). Disclosing and sharing emotion: Psychological, social and health consequences. In M. S. Stroebe, W. Stroebe, R. O. Hansson, & H. Schut (Eds.), *Handbook of bereavement research: Consequences, coping, and care* (pp. 517–543). Washington, DC: American Psychological Association.

Pollock, G. H. (1961). Mourning and adaptation. *International Journal of Psychoanalysis, 42,* 341–361.

Prigerson, H. G., Shear, M. K., Bierhals, A. J., Pilkonis, P. A., Wolfson, L., Hall, M., et al. (1997). Case histories of complicated grief. *Omega: The Journal of Death and Dying, 35,* 9–24.

Prigerson, H. G., Shear, M. K., Frank, E., Beery, L. C., Silberman, R., Prigerson, J., & Reynolds, C. F., III (1997). Traumatic grief: A case of loss-induced trauma. *American Journal of Psychiatry, 154,* 1003–1009.

Range, L. M., Kovac, S. H., & Marion, M. S. (2000). Does writing about the bereavement lessen grief following sudden, unintentional death? *Death Studies, 24,* 115–134.

Schut, H. A. W., Stroebe, M. S., van den Bout, J., & de Keijser, J. (1997). Intervention for the bereaved: Gender differences in the efficacy of two counselling programmes. *British Journal of Clinical Psychology, 36,* 63–72.

Segal, N. L., & Bouchard, T. J. (1993). Grief intensity following the loss of a twin and other relatives: Test of kinship hypotheses. *Human Biology, 65,* 87–105.

Segal, N. L., & Ream, S. L. (1998). Decreases in grief intensity for deceased twin and non-twin relatives: An evolutionary perspective. *Personality and Individual Differences, 25,* 317–325.

Segal, N. L., Welson, S. M., Bouchard, T. J., & Gitlin, D. G. (1995). Comparative grief experiences of bereaved twins and other bereaved relatives. *Personality and Individual Differences, 18,* 525–534.

Shackleton, C. H. (1984). The psychology of grief: A review. *Advances in Behavior Research and Therapy, 6,* 153–205.

Shand, A. F. (1914). *The foundations of character*. London: Macmillan.

Shand, A. F. (1920). *The foundations of character* (2nd ed.). London: Macmillan.

Shuchter, S. R. (1986). *Dimensions of grief: Adjusting to the death of a spouse*. San Francisco: Jossey-Bass.

Sloan, D. M., Marx, B. P., & Epstein, E. M. (2005). Further examination of the exposure model underlying the efficacy of written emotional disclosure. *Journal of Consulting and Clinical Psychology, 73*, 549–554.

Stroebe, M. (1992–1993). Coping with bereavement: A review of the grief work hypothesis. *Omega: The Journal of Death and Dying, 26*, 19–42.

Stroebe, M. S., & Schut, H. A. W. (1999). The dual process model of coping with bereavement: Rationale and description. *Death Studies, 23*, 197–224.

Stroebe, M., Schut, H., & Stroebe, W. (2005). Attachment in coping with bereavement: A theoretical integration. *Review of General Psychology, 9*, 48–66.

Stroebe, M., & Stroebe, W. (1991). Does "grief work" work? *Journal of Consulting and Clinical Psychology, 59*, 479–482.

Stroebe, M., Stroebe, W., Schut, H., Zech, E., & van den Bout, J. (2002). Does disclosure of emotions facilitate recovery from bereavement? Evidence from two prospective studies. *Journal of Consulting and Clinical Psychology, 70*, 169–178.

Tancredy, C. M., & Fraley, R. C. (2006). The nature of adult twin relationships: An attachment-theoretical perspective. *Journal of Personality and Social Psychology, 90*, 78–93.

Toedter, L. J., Lasker, J. N., & Alhadeff, J. M. (1988). The Perinatal Grief Scale: Development and initial evaluation. *American Journal of Orthopsychiatry, 58*, 435–449.

Videka-Sherman, L. (1982). Coping with death of a child: A study over time. *American Journal of Orthopsychiatry, 52*, 688–698.

Wegner, D. M., & Zanakos, S. (1994). Chronic thought suppression. *Journal of Personality, 62*, 615–640.

Wijngaards-de-Meij, L., Stroebe, M. S., Schut, H., Stroebe, W., van den Bout, J., & van der Heijden, P. (2005). Couples at risk following the death of their child: Predictors of grief versus depression. *Journal of Consulting and Clinical Psychology, 73*, 617–623.

Wortman, C. B., & Silver, R. C. (1989). The myths of coping with loss. *Journal of Consulting and Clinical Psychology, 57*, 349–357.

Wright, S. (1922). Coefficients of inbreeding and relationship. *American Naturalist, 56*, 330–338.

4

GRIEVING IN CONTEMPORARY SOCIETY

ROBERT KASTENBAUM

The young woman in Alexander McCall Smith's (2005) novel was startled.

> Her wise and worldly new friend had been born "Right here? In this build-ing?" Domenica nodded. "In those days people were born in places where people lived. Astonishing, but true. I came into this world, would you believe it, in this very room. Precisely sixty-one years ago next Friday. . . . That's my father there." (Smith, 2005, p. 68)

Continuity was less startling in years gone by. People lived in settled neighborhoods that had lives of their own. The significant people in their lives were close at hand. Local stores were operated by the same families that had served their parents and grandparents. When children entered a classroom for the first time, their teachers remembered the quirks of their older brothers and sisters. Daughters were to become new editions of their mothers. Farmers' children grew into farmers; youthful miners descended into the same pits where their fathers had performed sunless labors. Few people traveled to distant places to learn how others live.

Channelization accompanied continuity. People associated with their "own kind" for the most part. Casual and work-oriented interactions were condoned, but the more intimate zones of experience were off limits for people who did not share one's own national origins, religion, or race. Everybody married "from the neighborhood." Parental reins tightened as schoolboys and schoolgirls started to morph into adolescents: The prospect of mixed marriages was a common fear for guardians of all kinds of traditions.

Nevertheless, continuity between generations and obedience to ethnic boundaries always admitted to exceptions and was vulnerable to sociotechnological shift. Radio, for example, brought an intoxicating variety of people, events, and music into our homes. The automobile spurred us to explore beyond neighborhood confines, as did both economic depression and boom times. New perspectives on life emerged in the United States as veterans returned from military service in other lands and contacts with other people. Education widened a knowledge and attitude gap between generations, and media ascendancy became a more pervasive force. Family ties competed with the lure of a larger and more exciting life. Everything was moving faster, and big was becoming bigger. Rural areas would maintain tradition longer, but the expansion of highways, communication technology, and corporate power was altering the conditions of life almost everywhere.

Back to Domenica's apartment: "That's my father there" referred to a photograph. The man himself had vanished into frigid North Atlantic waters when his convoy was attacked in World War II. The circumstances of this bereavement could not but leave an enduring mark on the young girl. There would be the keen sense of loss and abandonment that alerts the vigilance–survival system. Young Domenica would have been working hard to comprehend the death but with limited experience and only partially developed cognitive skills. Her mother's grief would also have been a salient part of her life. There would have been no body in a casket, no burial, no palpable way of establishing closure. Father still had to be somewhere, and so he was: as a photograph in a room that meant home. In her eventful life, Domenica would venture to distant places, accept challenges, deepen and refine her character, and know both the joys and sorrows of love. Now it was time to return to the memory space where sorrow and comfort abided, where perhaps her life would end in the bed of its origin.

Domenica's friend Pat, at age 20, was enthralled but confused by this encounter with a life course so different from her own. Unfocused, throbbing with impulses and desires, Pat tried one thing, and then another. That a woman could know who she was, where she belonged, and what she was capable of doing! The depth of love and grief that is possible within a patterned life of meaning was not yet for her. Domenica represents a fading social order in which the course of life and the observances of death were fairly expectable. The wrong kind of death—a young husband and father lost in war—ripped the fabric of expectations.

How meaningful is a death that does not occur within an established pattern of meaning? And what if death itself becomes the pattern? What kind of grief and mourning are possible when reckless and random death not only escapes but dissolves meaning? A mother holding the body of her dead child is a searing, perhaps definitive image of grief. What if the transition from life to death should lose its impact of immediacy and instead become another cork floating in a confused sea of mediated experiences? In short, how might patterns of grieving and mourning change as we move deeper into the 21st century and beyond? I begin this chapter by locating grief within both the individual and the societal death system with a bias toward converting assumptions into questions. Grieving is seen as a significant interaction among individual experiences, circumstances, and social forces. Next, I discuss how changing circumstances of dying can influence the ways in which people grieve, as illustrated by a review of dominant modes of death from the past to the present. The reader is then prepared to consider the powerful phenomenon of grieving not only for one's personal bereavement but also for the loss of the world as it had been experienced and understood. I conclude the chapter with still another question that will have to find its answer elsewhere: Is grieving functional?

IS THERE ANYTHING NEW ABOUT CONTEMPORARY GRIEF?

The mission to develop a 21st-century perspective could lure us into overemphasizing differences from the past. Alternatively, we might start with the assumption that grief cannot change in a significant way because it is intrinsic to the human condition. Mourning practices vary, but grief remains grief. These alternatives deserve careful consideration rather than a hasty conclusion.

The Death System

There is reason to think that changes have been taking place in the circumstances of life and, therefore, possibly also of dying, death, and grief. In pursuing this line of inquiry I use a concept known as the *death system*: "The interpersonal, sociophysical, and symbolic network through which society mediates the individual's relationship to death" (Kastenbaum, 2007, p. 111). All societies have a death system with the basic functions of warning and prediction, prevention, caring for the dying, disposing of the dead, social consolidation after death, making sense of death, and killing. Components that enter into death-related processes include people, places, times, objects, and symbols. The death system is pervasive and dynamic. Some connections of social process with death are evident at the surface, such as when public health regulations lead to the removal of asbestos from school buildings to protect children from possible life-threatening illness. Other connections are characterized by less transparency and more ambiguity, such as when a medical school accepts cadaver donations for training physicians and covertly arranges to sell them for military or corporate experiments. One body might serve the prevention function by helping car designers produce safer vehicles, another might help weapon specialists to devise more lethal land mines.

Disposing of the dead, social consolidation after death, and making sense of death are the functions that bear most obviously on grief. However, grief can also be discerned in the other functions as well. For example, people who have experienced the Holocaust, ethnic cleansing, natural disaster, traumatic illness, or accident might become so active in warning, predicting, and prevention that they annoy those who are engrossed in the routines of daily life. By contrast, a bereaved parent might be less attentive to the children's safety; a depressed widowed senior might not prepare meals or take medications. Grief can also be released in violence, such as when victims seek revenge. Grief-become-rage has been a reliable source of intergroup violence through the centuries. The death system approach encourages close attention to the many ways in which social institutions and processes influence how we understand and cope with mortality. Life and death are not kept in separate boxes.

How, when, and where we die are demonstrably linked with the conditions of life. Might this connection also encompass grieving? One of history's many examples occurred during the tumultuous 16th- and 17th-century conflict between the established Catholic regime and the contending Protestant Reformation in the United Kingdom. At times, it was dangerous to be a Protestant; at other times, it was dangerous to be a Catholic. During Queen Elizabeth's long reign, it was the Catholics who had to keep their heads down. Funeral ritual became a test case, because praying for the dead had been ruled illegal (Gittings, 1984; Greenblatt, 2001, 2004). Banished were the flickering of the candles, the tolling of the bells, the alms distributed in the name of the dead, the family lamenting, the neighbors crossing themselves and praying by the side of the corpse, and the priests reciting Masses to ease the soul's passage. The dead became nonpersons, and traditional mourners became enemies of church and state. Catholics of England were not only deprived of public support but also subjected to feelings of guilt and foreboding for having failed to do what was right for the deceased. What solace and salvation could they expect when their turn came?

Grieving is more than a dependent variable; it is more usefully regarded within a contextual and interactive perspective. Consider, for example, the surge of interest in *spiritism* (also known as *spiritualism*) in times of war and other mass deaths. One such surge occurred when fathers, husbands, brothers, and sons perished in World War I (Hazelgrove, 2000). Many bereaved people sought comfort in nontraditional belief groups that promised communication with the dead. Mainstream religion found itself subject to desertion from grieving individuals at the same time that challenges were mounting from science and technology. The resulting threat to established religion had a ripple effect on the stability of other societal institutions. Furthermore, the grief of even one individual can influence society. For example, the impact of his mother's early death remained with Darwin through his adult years and stimulated his fascination with life forms and the survival of species (Browne, 2002; Colp, 1975). In his last years, Darwin studied worms as agents of renewal, passing the earth through themselves.

Grief or Grieving?

How would we know if not only circumstances but also grief itself were undergoing transformation? This question prompts us to reconsider how we think of grief. Doka (2003) defined *grief* as "a type of stress reaction, a highly personal and subjective response to a real, perceived, or anticipated loss" (p. 350). Stroebe, Hansson, Stroebe, and Schut (2001) defined it as "a primarily emotional (affective) reaction to the loss of a loved one through death. It incorporates diverse psychological (cognitive, social–behavioral) and physical (physiological–somatic manifestations)" (p. 6). Both definitions regard grief as a multilevel configuration of responses to loss. The anthropological, clinical, and research literature supports this organismic and holistic approach. What Greek mourners have called *ponos*, the pain of grief (Danforth & Tsiaras, 1982), is a salient feature. Studies repeatedly have found that cognitive processes, behavior patterns, interpersonal relationships, and physiological functioning can all be affected adversely by the trauma of loss and the altered conditions of life without the loved one.

As the preceding definitions imply, individual experiences and expressions of grief are not uniform (Rosenblatt & Barner, 2006). One person has frequent episodes of sobbing and weeping; another keeps tight control over emotional expression. One speaks in a scattered and fragmented way, another hardly speaks at all, whereas still another is trapped in obsessive review (Parkes, 2001). This person seeks the comfort of companionship; that person withdraws from relationships. Bereavement leads to outbursts of rage for one person but to a sunken, apologetic state accompanied by low self-esteem in another. Here is a bereaved person who barely attends to the activities of daily life; there is another bereaved person who has become embedded in a rigorous work schedule (Rosen, 1998). Physical symptoms become the focus of one person's response (Hall & Irwin, 2001), whereas another is tortured by a search for meaning and seems oblivious to what is happening somatically (Holland, Currier, & Neimeyer, 2006).

The individual variation in what can be termed *grief profiles* at any particular time makes it difficult to evaluate possible changes with time and circumstance. What is the key dimension: physical distress, interpersonal functioning, cognitive performance? What evidence supports a uniform hierarchy of grief component salience? Furthermore, the closer we come to the experiential core of grief, the less we can rely on orthodox objectivistic measures.

Pain is perhaps the most telling example. Attempts to assess pain associated with medical conditions have proven to be a challenging enterprise (e.g., Turk & Melzack, 1992). Pain itself has been analyzed as multidimensional, although in practice it is often simplified to the single dimension of intensity. The pain of grief is even more difficult to assess, providing more leeway for observers to bring their own variability to the task. People also differ in how they express their "real" pain or their "grief" pain. Comparing one person's report of pain (or sorrow, or joy) with another's is a shaky proposition both philosophically and methodologically. Nevertheless, grief is sometimes operationalized as a simple variable that can be plugged into a time series analysis with the assumption that our understanding will therefore be advanced.

Consider setting aside the construction of *grief* as a noun and regarding *grieving* as a verb, a process. The reification of grief too often surrenders to abstraction and standardization and away from the actual ways in which an individual or a society is responding to loss. The project of reconstructing the concept of *complicated grief*, for example, has taken on a life of its own because of its diagnostic applications (Goodkin et al., 2005–2006; Prigerson & Maciejewski, 2005–2006). Focusing on a type of grief as a pathological entity might clarify discussion and classification; however, constructing grief as an isolated noun–thing–entity also increases the distance between theory and lived experience.

Let us go back to the starting question: Is there something new about contemporary grieving? The shape of grieving has much to do with the circumstances of dying, so that is the next concern I address.

DYING AS CONTEXT FOR GRIEVING

Bereavement is "the objective situation of having lost someone significant" (Stroebe et al., 2001, p. 6). The focus is not on death in general but on the loss of a particular person who has died in particular circumstances.

Who Dies? Who Grieves?

Why is it always cloudy and damp when one visits an old graveyard? Old graveyards provide a mute answer to another question: Who dies? The answer is: mostly the young and the very young. Family gravesites often include markers for perished children, who far outnumber the adults. The available statistical evidence supports this impression. In the 1700s, for example, life expectancy at birth was approximately 35 years (Gee, 2003). Surviving infancy was a chancy thing. Few families escaped loss. The bereaved person was most likely to be an adult; the deceased an infant, child, or youth. Bereavement was expectable, the occasions many.

Women were at high risk during and soon after their pregnancies. A culture historian concluded that it was fear of death rather than emotional inhibitions that interfered with enjoyment of sexual activity (Gay, 1993). Husbands became widowers; children lost their mothers. In developed nations today, the average life expectancy floats a little above the biblical 3 score and 10. Infants and children are now expected to grow into long-lived adults. Women, once so vulnerable to birth-related hazards, now outlive men. Nevertheless, there is at least one significant way in which the "who dies?" question could be answered today as it would have been in the past: The poor die. The poor die younger, and the poor die in more miserable circumstances.

What About Grieving?

In the past, people were bereaved earlier and more often than is the norm today. Grieving shadowed a society's public and private lives. In turn, society was tasked with the responsibility for regulating the expression of grief. Ernst Becker (1973) proposed in *The Denial of Death* that societal institutions serve primarily to hold individual death anxiety in check. However, one might add that the death system has the additional function of maintaining equilibrium between grieving and withdrawal. A society's viability could be endangered if the bereaved find no consolation or fail to perform their communal obligations. As part of this balancing act, provisions often were made for diverting the grieving response into other channels. Events that provided outlets for emotional release offered temporary relief from tension and affirmed group solidarity. Another reliable strategy was the construction of "others" as available targets for violence. The private hell of grieving could be vented through blooded rage.

It is probable that grieving is shaped differently in high- and low-mortality societies. Fatalism might dull the edge of acute suffering. Also, the anxiety–apprehension component of grieving becomes increasingly salient when the mortality rate is elevated. Sorrow and rumination would compete with concern about one's own survival. One might soon share the fate of the family member who died of the bubonic plague or the friend who fell to cholera. Grieving in such circumstances might therefore have more a quality of apprehension about one's personal future as distinguished from engrossment in the lost relationship.

One might also expect differences between crowded urban and sparsely populated rural areas, and between settled communities and corridors of migration and invasion. Gender-specific roles throughout life provide another pattern of grieving, as in, for example, folk cultures in which women bear responsibility for ritual lamenting while men remain silent. The pain of personal loss would meld with role expectations, perhaps enhancing the power of women as they command the sacred space between living and dead.

The relationship between life course and grieving is not yet well understood; however, what children make of death and loss can influence their adult attitudes, expectations, and relationships. The shadow of death that has accompanied them through the years might be dealt with in various ways and subtly influence many aspects of their lives. Today as well as in the past, the shape, intensity, and expression of the grieving response might differ between people in the mainstream of developed nations and those who have experienced only a context of high risk and frequent bereavement.

MODES OF DYING AND THE SHAPE OF GRIEVING

How we die is almost certain to affect the grieving process. Suicide, for example, has been construed as criminal, weakness, madness, heroic, and rational. Each of these constructions had its implications for grieving and mourning. Within mainstream Christian tradition, suicide has long been reviled as sinful (Alvarez, 1970; Kastenbaum, 2007; Murray, 1998, 2000). The taint of suicide distorted the family's normal grieving process. In the past, family property was sometimes subject to confiscation, reducing the survivors to poverty. The communal finger of shame also pointed at them. Families tried to avoid the stigma by concealing the suicide, which became a tension-producing secret over several generations. Physicians today sometimes are still faced with the choice between certifying suicide or easing a bereaved family by naming a more acceptable cause of death.

The response to a suicide in the family can also take a lethal form, such as when a child or younger sibling takes this action as a model for what one should do when life seems overwhelming or hopeless. The reluctance to discuss this tainted mode of dying can contribute to the survivors' isolation and withdrawal from potential interpersonal support.

I now consider a broader range of interactions between modes of dying and grieving. Links between some salient modes of dying and their implications for images of death are identified in Table 4.1. The Black Death produced symptoms horrifying both to victims and observers. Its impact rocked all social institutions (Calvi, 1989; Geary, 1994; Herlihy, 1997). The macabre image of death reigned supreme, a hideous and merciless stalker. The anxiety component of grieving understandably became elevated. In *Histories of a Plague Year*, Calvi (1989) described the desperation of families attempting to cope with a bubonic infection within the household, coupled with the fear that other members would become infected and that authorities would board up and quarantine the home.

Another source of torment struck at the core of morale and worldview. There were too many dead and too few able-bodied living to perform dignified and effective body disposal operations. Those who did undertake this task

TABLE 4.1

Modes of Dying and the Images of Death They Have Encouraged

Condition	Markers	Signifiers
The Black Death	Agony, disfiguration, partial decomposition while still alive, putrefaction.	Human vanity and pride, punished and abandoned by God.
Syphilis	Facial disfiguration, dementia, moral degradation.	Wages of sin.
Tuberculosis	Death steals our breath; blood flows from our bodies, which increasingly become skeletonized.	Curse of the cities and factories but also a romantic exit for beautiful, brilliant, doomed youth.
Live burial	Imagined and occasionally actual fate of some who have fainted, seized, or otherwise lost consciousness.	Terror of life in death.
Cancer	Pain, anxiety, body damage and distortion.	Insidious attack by an enemy from within.
Persistent vegetative state	Profound helplessness, inability to think or act on one's own behalf.	Terror of death in life.
AIDS	Symptoms and stigma of many of the earlier forms of catastrophic dying— blood- and body-fluid related, disfiguration, dementia, skeletonization, respiratory distress, plus linkage with taboo sexuality.	Death encompasses the most frightening experiences and outcomes that have ever haunted the imagination.
Alzheimer's disease	Slow, progressive loss of self-identity and cognition, but with the long-term persistence of the physical shell.	Death as oblivion, emphasized by fading of the spirit while the body remains palpable.

Note. From *Death, Society, and Human Experience* (9th ed., p. 96), by R. Kastenbaum, 2007, Boston: Allyn & Bacon. Copyright ©2007 by Pearson Education. Reprinted by permission of the publisher.

were aware of their heightened risks. The community was traumatized by heaped corpses, mass burials, and the pervasive odor of decomposition. Family members despaired because they were failing their obligations to the deceased. The departing soul, always in peril, might be refused salvation because the rites of final passage had been omitted. In turn, the survivors' own salvation was also jeopardized. Grieving during the plague years had an eschatological component that might be difficult to comprehend from a 21st-century worldview.

The frenzy and ferment of this time were well described by Tuchman (1978). One striking feature was the outbreak of violence toward self and others, inflamed by religious beliefs raging within desperate minds. It is likely that the bereavement overload and overstressed grieving response contributed significantly to this violence (Kastenbaum, 2004). Much remains to be learned about the transformation of grieving into rage. Identification with the aggressor is a related strategy of desperation in times of mass death. The apprehensive griever switches allegiance to the winning side: death.

The arrival of syphilis in Europe, with its vivid symptomatology, was interpreted by the religious establishment as the wages of sin. Grieving the death of a syphilis victim was complicated by the shame that person had brought on him- or herself and community. Hidden, and for that reason even more painful, was a mother's grieving for her stillborn baby—dead of the syphilis her husband had contracted with another woman.

In its terminal phase of tuberculosis, death seemed almost visible, with the skeleton barely concealed under the skin. As with the bubonic plague, tuberculosis complicated the grieving process through anxiety that inhibited interactions with the victim. It took some doing to sit by the bedside of a person with a highly contagious disease who was coughing and spitting up blood and pieces of lung tissue. The specter of tuberculosis heightened anxiety about the end of life, increased ambivalence about being with the terminally ill, and burdened grieving with guilt about not having done enough.

Live burial occurred most frequently in the imagination (served up liberally by the new genre of horror stories). Fear of live burial had been a fringe concern at least as early as the 17th century but became a specialty of the 19th century and faded only reluctantly with the advance of medical technology. *Complicated* is perhaps an insufficient term to characterize the grieving process when there was suspicion that the coffin had been closed on a living person. Grieving could not easily resolve when the basic question of "dead or alive" remained in doubt.

Cancer has become a more common cause of death as life expectancy has increased and other scourges have been brought under control. Contagion is not an issue, but the course of terminal cancer in another can be perceived as a possible rehearsal for one's self, and so grieving combines concern for "thee" and "me." Also, the extended struggle with cancer can generate a dialectic between hope and acceptance–resignation. The prospect for surviving cancer can fluctuate as various treatments are tried and as the condition becomes either more or less aggressive. Throughout the ordeal, families become vulnerable to what might be called *habituated grieving*. The edge and intensity of the grieving process are worn down by daily repetition. There is a parallel to the vigilance system through which we respond to threat signals. Prolonged vigilance becomes exhausting. Family and friends who have experienced the patient's long struggle with cancer might have very little psychic energy left when the struggle comes to its end. It had been their struggle, too, and the more obvious signs of grieving might become attenuated.

The persistent vegetative state is the current, updated version of live burial. Fear of lingering on the borderlands of life and death was a prime motivation for the establishment of informed consent and advance directives. Grieving is complicated by ambiguity. Is this a dead person in a living body, or a living person in a dead body? Is there a chance for recovery? Can this person feel hunger, thirst, and pain? When and how should we grieve? The tension of uncertainty sometimes converts the delayed grieving response into anger against those who interpret the situation differently.

AIDS brought something of the raw anxiety and horror associated with the Black Death into contemporary society when it first appeared with devastating symptoms and inadequately understood contagion risks. There were also resonances with syphilis as a sexually transmitted and hence shameful disease, all the more so because of its early association with homosexual promiscuity. In recent years, society has become more accepting of HIV/AIDS victims, and so-called "normal" grieving is replacing the earlier conflicted and judgmental response.

The incidence of Alzheimer's disease has increased along with longevity. Families confront the sorrow and burden of caring while experiencing anxiety about their own possible fate. Habituated grieving can develop over the lengthy course of the condition. The family grieving process is influenced by cognitive dissonance: The stricken family member is both present and absent. The nature of the relationship between family members and the patient is subject to ambiguity and change. People who see a family member vanish into the oblivion of his or her dissolving memory often fear that they might be seeing their own future selves. It is not unusual to hear a family member quietly say, "That will be me." This self-referential perspective can increase the difficulties in understanding and caring for the fading person.

Modes of dying do have implications for the ways in which we experience the grieving process. The patterns of grieving in society might differ markedly over time as some modes of dying become less common and others become more common.

HOW DOES ONE GRIEVE FOR LOST WORLDS?

Domenica's father had died more than half a century ago, but his absence remained present to her (Smith, 2005). Although active in contemporary life, she continued to experience a lost-world theme. Place had been a connector both between generations and between one's own youth and adulthood. Now, however, for society in general, place had given way to flux. "Home" was not where most people were born, where they died, where the family sat down regularly to meals together, or where issues were shared and addressed. There were increasing odds that home and neighborhood had morphed into something different and impersonal. The functions and perhaps even the experience of grieving could be altered if the lost-world theme becomes increasingly prevalent. I next look briefly at personal and public spheres.

On the Loss of Personal Worlds

Loss experiences become more probable as people move into the later years of the life course. It seems to me that more can be at stake than the response to a specific bereavement: Privately, perhaps unrecognized by others, there is the feeling that all of the world has been lost.

A woman I will call Amelia Longbridge was one of the loners in a large geriatric facility. Because she was not a troublemaker, Amelia was nearly invisible. I became acquainted with her while extending my studies of personal time perspective to senior adults (Kastenbaum, 1977). Amelia was "the last leaf on the tree," as she described herself once she overcame her reluctance to share her memory treasure with a stranger. It was Amelia and nobody else who remembered her grandparents, parents, and siblings, not to mention the one-eyed cat that lived in the barn but that she would let sneak into the house. The sorrow of repeated bereavements had settled into her character and was no longer a source of perceived distress. But that whole world—gone! Amelia felt weighted with the responsibility for keeping the lost world alive in her own memory. I wondered if she felt like a museum curator. "Or a librarian," she replied. "I was a librarian."

Amelia's lost world did not exist for others, but it was not dead to itself. She recaptured a feeling of anticipation as she described events that were about to happen back then—*past futures*, they might be called. Amelia could see few traces of the vanished world around her and knew nobody who could help her validate its existence. Grieving for a lost world might be more common than we realize in a mass society that rapidly sheds the skins of its past. "What is the worst of it?" I asked Amelia. "That it's all gone. No—that it's all gone and nobody knows it once was."

The other lost-world theme to be mentioned here has been the subject of lament for untold centuries. Legions of poets have despaired the transience of "youth's magic horn." Shakespeare (1601/1984) urged, "Then come and kiss me, sweet-and-twenty, Youth's a stuff will not endure" (p. 523) He was a late arrival to this theme, which already had been voiced by maidens of the Chou period (1000–600 BC), one of whom advised, "The plum tree drops its fruit . . . All you men who court me, I ask you to speak up!" (Watson, 1984, p. 21). Gene modification research has plucked the baton from ancient alchemy in the attempt to stop the clock or rejuvenate people who are already feeling their accumulated years. Commercial interests, physical trainers, and cosmetic surgeons have been feasting on the baby boomers' resolve not to lose the precious world of youth. Anxiety might spark with the first wrinkle or gray hair, but efforts to mask or overcome signs of aging can delay the development of a complete grieving response. Nevertheless, some people do divide their lives into the lost world of youth and the drab aftermath known as adulthood. As one octogenarian put it, "I had my prospects. Had my fun. And then—nothing ever after."

Currently, anxiety about leaving one's youth behind seems to be diminishing, because the middle adult years are now associated with continued health and vigor and the later adult years have become less of an unknown territory. The attitude that people can do almost anything at almost any age is weakening stereotypes. Furthermore, long-lived adults now are more likely to have age peers available with enough shared generational memories to reduce the need for grieving for the loss of a private world (Kastenbaum, 1995).

On the Loss of the Shared World

Annihilation of the shared world has been prophesied throughout much of history, as exemplified by the Book of Revelation. With remarkable serenity, some native peoples of Australia and the United States have incorporated into their worldviews the belief that even the everlasting mountains and the gods will pass away, as will all of creation (Kastenbaum, 2004). Past generations have encountered diseases of such virulence and natural disasters of such proportions that it seemed as if annihilation were on the way. In our own times, humankind has assumed a key role in the large-scale destruction of life and habitat. In the following sections, I briefly consider a few ongoing or emerging loss-of-the-world scenarios with implications for grieving.

Violence, Memory, and Grieving

The ongoing Darfur (Sudan) genocide demonstrates that large-scale violence did not end with the 20th century and its staggering toll of death and destruction (Rummel, 1997). I focus here on two examples: (a) Germany after World War II and (b) Russia after the Stalinist purges preceding that war.

Sebald (2003) noticed what did *not* happen in Germany after World War II. Where was the grieving? The memory? The sorrow? The anger? More than 1 million tons of bombs had fallen on German towns and cities. Approximately 600,000 civilians were casualties of these raids, and an estimated 3.5 million homes were destroyed. Much of the normal world had been reduced to rubble. There was a puzzling disconnect between the magnitude of the loss and its imprint on society a few years later: "It seems to have left scarcely a trace of pain behind in the collective consciousness. It has been largely obliterated from the retrospective understanding of those affected" (Sebald, 2003, p. 4).

People walked through the ruins as though nothing had happened. How could survivors disconnect themselves not only from the past but also from the rubble of the present?

Sebald (2003) had an answer to offer: Energies were devoted to

> the now legendary and in some respects genuinely admirable reconstruction of the country after the devastation . . . [that] prohibited any backward view . . . through the sheer amount of labour required and the creation of a new, faceless reality, pointing the population exclusively toward the future and enjoining on it silence about the past. (pp. 6–7)

This societal response to massive loss resonates with the "digging into work" pattern shown by some individuals after personal bereavement (e.g., Parkes, 2001). The hard work of environmental reconstruction provided battered Germany an opportunity for purposeful action with visible results in a shared enterprise. This is not often an option for the individual bereaved person.

Difficult questions remain. How much of the response noted by Sebald (2003) was related to complex and unresolved feelings about the war? The same level of devastation caused by natural catastrophes might have resulted in a different response. What is the spiritual cost of disconnecting from the past to reduce the trauma of loss? What are the consequences for a nation with a history of celebrating its history? Can there be a future again or only a series of drifting "presents"? Memory and expectation are at the core of human experience. Disconnecting from the past might energize the present but have unsettling and unpredictable consequences for the future.

Russia entered the 20th century already painfully acquainted with excess death in comparison with most other European countries. Hardship and disease accounted for much of the high mortality rate, but "judicial murder" also took a significant toll. The Czarist regime executed hundreds, sometimes thousands, of people each day. Suicide was also prevalent, often related to disenfranchisement, poverty, and Durkheim's (1951) seldom-applied category of fatalism. Multiple bereavement was common, and grieving was a way of life. War-related casualties were enormous, with soldiers sacrificed in human wave attacks or left to perish because of inadequate supplies. Nevertheless, Stalin's Soviet Union outperformed all other causes of death. At least 11 million Russian peasants were massacred or starved to death in a "reform" campaign between 1929 and 1932. At least half a million other citizens were exterminated as "dissidents" in 1937–1938, this time including military officers and other people of achievement. As Soviet secrets continue to leak, the actual death tolls are being revised upward.

Catherine Merridale (2002) took on the challenge of examining the Soviet "night of stone" in her book of the same title within the context of her subtitle, *Death and Memory in Twentieth-Century Russia*. There is a striking similarity with Sebald's (2003) observations in Germany:

> Hard work became the commonest and most effective means of recreating a person's sense of self . . . and silencing intrusive ghosts and questions . . . when I asked how they coped with painful memories [I was told], "We had too much else to think about." The solution worked, at least in part, because it was so perfectly tailored to the socialist collective ethos. (p. 121)

Vodka helped, too.

There were also important differences, not the least of which was the totalitarian structure that had dominated from Czarist times through the Soviet regime. Strenuous attempts were made to eradicate private grieving and public mourning. Comrade workers were told they should devote themselves to joyful collective labors here on earth and not dwell on fallen individuals and the fate of their souls. This manifesto evokes the image of a windowless vehicle—the present moment—moving along an assembly line from nowhere to nowhere. The state eventually backed off from this extreme position (partially because Soviet leaders themselves craved mourning and memorialization). The impulse to remember, grieve, and mourn might not always overcome the agendas and machinations of a power establishment. Germany and Russia demonstrated that grieving can be regarded as dissidence and therefore be subject to all the influences that the leaders of a controlled, media-saturated culture can bring to bear.

Grieving for Everyone and Everything?

Up to this point, I have mostly considered loss of the past to particular individuals or societies. I shift now to the probable loss of the future for everybody and everything. There is little within bereavement studies or the larger field of thanatology to provide guidance. Perhaps, though, I can take stock of what little is known and can be observed.

Religious ideology has been the primary source of end-of-days prophecies, usually with more fervor than grieving. Today, it is science that offers dysphoric visions. The local scenarios predict the degradation of our planet as a life support system with accelerating extinction of species. The cosmic scenarios insist that the universe itself is a blip in space–time that will eventually go out of business: Whatever it becomes will be neither congenial nor comprehensible. One searches in vain for a current theory of any repute that forecasts a thriving universe full of life, coherence, and "things."

That grieving in advance for everyone and everything seems far-fetched probably indicates more about the limited scope of our mundane cognitions than it does about objective reality. It is fair to ask whether we should start grieving for loss of all that is and could be. A prior question, though is whether we can grieve for total loss of future and its retro-effect on the past and memory. Both questions are probably far beyond us at present, but the phenomena are already evident.

The media dutifully remind us each day of the disasters that are befalling people throughout the world. Often, these are people we have never seen in places we have never lived. How much and how often can we "realize" (Weisman, 1974) the existence of these remote people, and how can we feel compassion and loss at their deaths (see also chaps. 12 and 22, this volume)? Anthropologists have often remarked on the group dynamics that maintain strict boundaries between "us" and "them," with the latter being less than human and their deaths of negligible concern. To the extent that the world is becoming a global village, does this mean that we will expand our sense of relationship (with its potential for an expanded range of grieving), or that we will stiffen the boundaries so we can avoid the pain of compassion with so wide a world of distress?

Next, we could explore attitudes toward species that are known to be endangered or have already become extinct. This would not be a simple project. Some people hunt, some people grieve for their animal companions, and some people do both. The extent to which grieving for the death of animals is accepted or disenfranchised varies with social mores that in turn are influenced by beliefs regarding the place of humans among other life forms. Furthermore, the role of human agency in the extinction of species has continued to accelerate. For many years now, human activity has been most responsible directly or indirectly for the disappearance of species (Hallam, 2005). Perhaps an increasing sense of guilt would engage, or perhaps it would suppress, the grieving response.

The link of grieving to action is not yet well understood. The extinction issue offers the opportunity to explore the dynamics that operate between grieving and acting. Grieving forms around a loss the way that biological processes attempt to protect and heal a wound. This past orientation could isolate the grieving person from discovering options to deal with the future. However, human nature seldom can be encompassed by a simple proposition. The pain of loss might instead spur us on to prevent further losses. Many organizations provide information and suggestions for at least slowing the rate of species extinction, but this does not yet seem to be a priority for the public at large or political decision makers. The march of species extinction continues, and we still do not understand what role, if any, might be played by compassion and grieving.

A larger question looms: At what point, if any, will the prospect of total extinction of life in a vanishing universe register on our thoughts and feelings? At present, there is little indication that this cosmic-sized version of anticipatory grieving is being experienced. It is also possible that inertia, the illusion of continuity, and a spectrum of denial-type strategies (Kastenbaum, 2007) will protect us from ever doing so. Amelia Longbridge and many other individuals have been keenly aware of their private lost worlds and have devoted themselves to the memory work of grieving. Perhaps, however, the passing of the universe will not be grieved either in prospect or retrospect. The bottom line is that we simply do not know how individuals and society will respond to the mega-loss of existing and possible worlds.

IN CONCLUSION: IS GRIEVING FUNCTIONAL?

John Archer (2001; see also chap. 3, this volume) has proposed that grieving has an adaptive function. This assertion seems counterintuitive. Grieving tends to reduce coping skills through its absorption of energy and attention. Nevertheless, Archer has made a thought-provoking case for the survival function of grieving in animals as well as humans. Emphasis is given to the distress signal that is evoked by separation as well as bereavement. Natural selection favors the survival of individuals (animals or humans) that have strong social bonds. Grief is a "by-product of mechanisms, whose primary function it is to maintain social relationships" (Archer, 2001, p. 269).

How does this evolutionary perspective apply to the changing circumstances of life and death? Consider some of the following differences and their possible implications for the function of grieving:

- Attachment theory and research most often focus on mother–infant interaction. Does grieving have the same survival function in societies with increasing proportions of long-lived people?
- Isolation and loneliness have increased with mobility, the withering of neighborhoods, and other manifestations of accelerating change in mass society (Putnam, 2001). Many people do not have familiar and caring others to receive distress signals. How adaptive is grieving among strangers?
- Is it possible that grief work will more often make use of a split-self strategy in which the forlorn, despairing victim of loss is comforted by the internalized "other"? ("I must be my own comforter because there are none who respond to my distress signals.")
- Still another possibility is that more people will attach themselves to whatever seems more durable than the ruins of human relationships—for example, religion, patriotism, or material goods.

These observations only begin the list of possible changes in the nature and function of grieving as the conditions of life and death continue to twist into new shapes.

REFERENCES

Alvarez, A. (1970). *The savage god*. New York: Random House.

Archer, J. (2001). Grief from an evolutionary perspective. In M. S. Stroebe, R. O. Hansson, W. Stroebe, & H. Schut (Eds.), *Handbook of bereavement research: Consequences, coping, and care* (pp. 263–284). Washington, DC: American Psychological Association.

Becker, E. (1973). *The denial of death*. New York: Free Press.

Browne, J. (2002). *Charles Darwin*. New York: Knopf.

Calvi, G. (1989). *Histories of a plague year*. Berkeley: University of California Press.

Colp, R. J. (1975). The evolution of Charles Darwin's thoughts about death. *Journal of Thanatology, 3*, 191–206.

Danforth, L. M., & Tsiaras, A. (1982). *The death rituals of rural Greece*. Princeton, NJ: Princeton University Press.

Doka, K. J. (2003). Grief, acute. In R. Kastenbaum (Ed.), *Macmillan encyclopedia of death and dying* (Vol. 1, pp. 350–352). New York: Macmillan.

Durkheim, E. (1951). *Suicide*. New York: Free Press.

Feifel, H. (Ed.). (1959). *The meaning of death*. New York: McGraw-Hill.

Gay, P. (1993). *Education of the senses: The bourgeois experience. Vol. 1: Victoria to Freud*. New York: Norton.

Geary, P. J. (1994). *Living with the dead in the Middle Ages*. Ithaca, NY: Cornell University Press.

Gee, E. (2003). Life expectancy. In R. Kastenbaum (Ed.), *Macmillan encyclopedia of death and dying* (Vol. 2, pp. 526–533). New York: Macmillan.

Gittings, C. (1984). *Death, burial, and the individual in early modern England*. London: Croom Helm.

Goodkin, K., Lee, D., Molina, R., Zheng, W., Frasca, A., O'Melian, S., et al. (2005–2006). Complicated bereavement: Disease state or state of being? *Omega: The Journal of Death and Dying, 52*, 21–36.

Greenblatt, S. (2001). *Hamlet in Purgatory*. Princeton, NJ: Princeton University Press.

Greenblatt, S. (2004). *Will in the world: How Shakespeare became Shakespeare*. New York: Norton.

Hall, M., & Irwin, M. (2001). Physiological indices of functioning in bereavement. In M. S. Stroebe, R. O. Hansson, W. Stroebe, & H. Schut (Eds.), *Handbook of bereavement research: Consequences, coping, and care* (pp. 473–492). Washington, DC: American Psychological Association.

Hallam, T. (2005). *Catastrophes and lesser calamities: The causes of mass extinction*. New York: Oxford University Press.

Hazelgrove, J. (2000). *Spiritualism and British society between the wars*. Manchester, England: Manchester University Press.

Herlihy, D. (1997). *The Black Death and the transformation of the West*. Cambridge, MA: Harvard University Press.

Holland, J. M., Currier, J. M., & Neimeyer, R. A. (2006). Meaning reconstruction in the first two years of bereavement: The role of sense-making and benefit finding. *Omega, 53,* 175–192.

Kastenbaum, R. (1977). Memories of tomorrow: On the interpenetrations of time in later life. In B. S. Gorman & A. E. Wessman (Eds.), *The personal experience of time* (pp. 194–214). New York: Plenum Press.

Kastenbaum, R. (1995). *Dorian, graying: Is youth the only thing worth having?* Amityville, NY: Baywood.

Kastenbaum, R. (2004). *On our way: The final passage through life and death.* Berkeley: University of California Press.

Kastenbaum, R. (2007). *Death, society, and human experience* (9th ed.). Boston: Allyn & Bacon.

Merridale, C. (2002). *Night of stone.* New York: Penguin.

Murray, A. (1998). *Suicide in the Middle Ages: Vol. 1. The violent against themselves.* Oxford, England: Oxford University Press.

Murray, A. (2000). *Suicide in the Middle Ages: Vol. 2. The curse on self-murder.* Oxford, England: Oxford University Press.

Parkes, C. M. (2001). *Bereavement* (3rd ed.). New York: International Universities Press.

Prigerson, H. G., & Maciejewski, P. K. (2005–2006). A call for sound empirical testing and evaluation of criteria for complicated grief proposed for *DSM–V. Omega: The Journal of Death and Dying, 52,* 9–20.

Putnam, R. D. (2001). *Bowling alone.* New York: Simon & Schuster.

Rosen, E. J. (1998). *Families facing death.* San Francisco: Jossey-Bass.

Rosenblatt, P. C., & Barner, J. R. (2006). The dance of closeness–distance in couple relationships after the death of a parent. *Omega: The Journal of Death and Dying, 53,* 277–294.

Rummel, R. J. (1997). *Statistics of democide: Genocide and mass murder since 1901.* Charlottesville: University of Virginia Press.

Shakespeare, W. (1984). Twelfth night. In A. L. Rowse (Ed.), *The annotated Shakespeare* (pp. 502–557). New York: Crown. (Original work published 1601)

Sebald, W. G. (2003). *On the natural history of destruction.* New York: Penguin.

Smith, A. M. (2005). *44 Scotland Street.* New York: Anchor.

Stroebe, M. S., Hansson, R. O., Stroebe, W., & Schut, H. (2001). Introduction: Concepts and issues in contemporary research on bereavement. In M. S. Stroebe, R. O. Hansson, W. Stroebe, & H. Schut (Eds.), *Handbook of bereavement research: Consequences, coping, and care* (pp. 3–22). Washington, DC: American Psychological Association.

Tuchman, B. W. (1978). *A distant mirror: The calamitous 14th century.* New York: Knopf.

Turk, D. C., & Melzack, R. (Eds.). (1992). *Handbook of pain assessment.* New York: Guilford Press.

Watson, B. (Ed. & Trans.). (1984). *Anon: The plum tree drops its fruit.* New York: Columbia University Press.

Weisman, A. D. (1974). *The realization of death.* New York: Jason Aronson.

5

AN ATTACHMENT PERSPECTIVE ON BEREAVEMENT

MARIO MIKULINCER AND PHILLIP R. SHAVER

She can't bring herself to throw away a wafer-thin alarm clock [her deceased husband] gave her that stopped working the year before he died . . . She can't eat, can't sleep, can't think without remembering, can't remember without hurting, and for six long months can't even dream. . . . She understands, for the first time, "the power in the image of the rivers, the Styx, the Lethe, the cloaked ferryman with his pole," the burning raft of grief. No matter where she hides, the vortex finds her. (Leonard, 2005, reviewing Joan Didion's *The Year of Magical Thinking* [2005])

In an account of his 34-year-old wife's death from breast cancer, the memoirist David Collins summarized with poignant precision the rationale underlying his feeling that "I wanted to die too—so I could be with her." Explaining "so freshly present she seemed [that] I had this thought: *I could follow her*." He adds, "I just wanted to go after her, not let her get away. I wanted to find her again. Hadn't I found her once [before]?" (Gilbert, 2006, p. 3)

What is it about suddenly losing a husband of 40 years that drives a woman as coolly analytic and articulate as Joan Didion "crazy" for months? This brilliant agnostic writer, known for her precise, unsentimental observations of the modern world—labeled "a pretty cool customer" by an orderly at the New York hospital where her husband was declared dead—kept his shoes in their closet for months so he would have something to wear "because he would need shoes if he were to return" (Didion, p. 37). Anyone who has lived through a similar "year of magical thinking" knows these reactions are irrational but has persisted in them nevertheless. For the bereaved, the formerly solid door separating life from death—"this world" from "the netherworld"— suddenly becomes so thin, so ephemeral, that a previously rational adult feels he could float right through to the place where his dead lover now lives, ready to embrace him or her again.

Ever since John Bowlby (1980) published *Loss: Sadness and Depression*, attachment theory has been used to illuminate grief. Throughout his famous trilogy on attachment and loss, Bowlby (1969, 1973, 1980) shed new light on human beings' deep emotional bonds with "attachment figures" and their powerful emotional reactions to separation and loss: disbelief, horror, angry protest, and despair (see also chaps. 2 and 3, this volume). These reactions have now been studied in empirical detail by developmental psychologists specializing in childhood attachments and by social and clinical psychologists specializing in romantic and marital relationships. Besides explaining attachment and grief within a single theoretical framework, Bowlby provided a preliminary theoretical account of individual differences in reactions to separation and loss and in functional and dysfunctional forms of loss-related anger, anxiety, and sadness. He had noticed in his clinical work that grief is experienced and processed somewhat differently by people who are secure, anxious, or avoidant in their attachments.

On the basis of the evidence gathered to date concerning attachment and loss, we (Mikulincer & Shaver, 2003; Shaver & Mikulincer, 2002) have extended Bowlby's ideas to create a contemporary psychodynamic model of what he called the *attachment behavioral system* in adulthood (Bowlby, 1982). Hypotheses based on this model have been tested in diverse correlational and experimental studies, and we and our colleagues are beginning to conduct neuroscientific studies as well (Gillath, Bunge, Shaver, Wendelken, & Mikulincer, 2005). In this chapter, we use our model as a framework for conceptualizing the psychodynamic processes involved in normative and pathological grief. The chapter is intended to update and improve on earlier accounts stemming from our line of research (e.g., Fraley & Shaver, 1999; Shaver & Tancredy, 2001). Our previous chapters on bereavement have reviewed selected theoretical arguments and controversies but were not organized around our model, and of course they did not include the research evidence amassed since they were written.

We begin with a brief summary of Bowlby's theory, focusing on his postulation of an innate attachment behavioral system. We then describe the normative features and individual-difference variants of the system's functioning, distinguishing between attachment security and two forms of insecurity: (a) hyperactivation of the attachment system (*anxious attachment*) and (b) deactivation of the system (*avoidant attachment*). Next, we consider how the attachment system reacts to important relationship losses and how a secure person adjusts to loss. Finally, we deal with the roles of anxious and avoidant attachment in pathological grief reactions. This chapter is partly theoretical, because theory motivates and organizes the research literature. However, we also cover many examples of recent research because there is better evidence than ever before, based on experiments and on clinical observations, for some of the psychodynamic processes Bowlby discussed.

BASIC CONCEPTS IN ATTACHMENT THEORY AND RESEARCH

One of the core tenets of attachment theory (Bowlby, 1969, 1973, 1980, 1982) is that human beings, like many of their primate and mammalian relatives, are born with an innate psychobiological system (the attachment behavioral system) that motivates them to seek proximity to significant others (attachment figures) in times of need as a way of protecting themselves from threats and alleviating distress. Over time, human infants and young children become emotionally attached to their primary attachment figures, and once this happens they show a clear preference for these figures, exhibit fear or wariness of strangers, become distressed when separated from a primary attachment figure, and can be fully soothed and calmed only by the physical and emotional availability of this figure or another major attachment figure in times of need. Although Bowlby thought the attachment system was most important early in life, he also claimed that it is active over the entire life span and is manifest in thoughts and behaviors related to proximity seeking in times of need (Bowlby, 1988). Moreover, people of all ages are capable of forming attachment bonds (becoming emotionally attached to another person, using such a person as a stronger and wiser attachment figure—i.e., as a safe haven and secure base in times of need—and feeling distress on separation from or loss of this person) with a variety of close relationship partners, including siblings, friends, and romantic partners. They form what Bowlby (1969, 1982) called a person's "hierarchy of attachment figures." Because he focused mostly on mother–infant relationships, and in a time when mothers were clearly the primary attachment figures for young children, he believed in what he called *monotropy*—the idea that most children have a single primary attachment figure at the top of the hierarchy and that no one can fully replace that figure when a child is highly distressed. Although these days a child in a modern industrial–digital society is likely to have multiple caregivers, it seems safe to say that most young children still view their mother as their attachment figure nonpareil. However, this does not mean that the father, grandparents, older siblings, and familiar day care workers are not also very important attachment figures in many families and many settings.

According to Bowlby (1969, 1982), the attachment behavioral system is activated by perceived threats and dangers, which cause a frightened person to seek proximity to protective others. The attainment of proximity and protection results in feelings of relief and a sense of security—a sense that the world is a generally safe place, that attachment figures are helpful when called on, and that it is possible to explore the environment curiously and confidently and to engage rewardingly with other people. Bowlby (1988) viewed the sense of attachment security as crucial for maintaining emotional stability; developing a solid and authentic sense of self-worth; and forming mutually satisfying, long-lasting close relationships. Moreover, optimal functioning of the attachment system facilitates relaxed and confident engagement in nonattachment activities, which Bowlby attributed to other behavioral systems, such as exploration, affiliation, and caregiving.

In addition to mapping universal aspects and functions of the attachment behavioral system, Bowlby (1973) described important individual differences in attachment-system functioning. He viewed these differences as largely derived from reactions of attachment figures to a child's attachment behavior (e.g., proximity seeking, attempting to use attachment figures as a safe haven and secure base) and from internalization of these reactions in attachment working models of self and others (i.e., complex mental representations, with associated emotional and behavioral tendencies). Interactions with attachment figures who are available and supportive in times of need facilitate optimal development of the attachment system, promote a sense of safety and security, and allow people to rely more confidently on proximity seeking as a distress regulation strategy and on attachment figures as a source of protection and comfort. In contrast, when a person's attachment figures are not reliably available and supportive, a sense of security is not attained, and strategies of affect regulation other than proximity seeking (secondary attachment strategies, characterized by avoidance and anxiety) are developed.

Empirical tests of Bowlby's ideas in studies of adults have generally focused on a person's attachment style—the systematic pattern of relational expectations, emotions, and behaviors that results from internalization of a particular history of attachment experiences (Fraley & Shaver, 2000). Research, beginning with Ainsworth, Blehar, Waters, and Wall (1978) and continuing through recent studies by social and personality psychologists (reviewed by Shaver & Mikulincer, 2002), indicates that individual differences in attachment style can be measured with self-report scales tapping two orthogonal dimensions: (a) attachment-related anxiety and (b) avoidance (Brennan, Clark, & Shaver, 1998). A person's position on the avoidance (or avoidant attachment) dimension indicates the extent to which he or she distrusts relationship partners' goodwill and strives to maintain behavioral independence and emotional distance from others. A person's position on the anxiety (or anxious attachment) dimension indicates the degree to which he or she worries that a partner will not be available and supportive in times of need. People who score low on both dimensions are said to be secure, securely attached, or to have a secure attachment style. People who score high on both dimensions are said to be "fearfully avoidant" (Bartholomew & Horowitz, 1991).

On the basis of an extensive literature review, we (Mikulincer & Shaver, 2003, 2007a) proposed a three-phase model of attachment-system activation and dynamics in adulthood. Following Bowlby (1969, 1982), we assumed that relatively continuous monitoring of experiences and environmental events results in attachment-system activation when a potential or actual threat is detected. Once the attachment system is activated, an affirmative answer to the question "Is an attachment figure available and likely to be responsive to my needs?" results in a sense of security and facilitates the application of security-based strategies of affect regulation (Shaver & Mikulincer, 2002). These strategies are aimed at alleviating distress; maintaining comfortable, supportive intimate relationships; and increasing personal adjustment. They consist of optimistic beliefs about distress management, trust in others' goodwill, and a sense of self-efficacy about dealing with threats. They also consist of constructive coping strategies: acknowledgment and display of distress without personal disorganization, support seeking, and problem solving. These are the main notable characteristics of securely attached individuals.

Perceived unavailability of an attachment figure results in attachment insecurity, which forces a decision about the viability of proximity seeking as a protective strategy. When proximity seeking is appraised as likely to be successful, assuming that sufficient effort is expended, a person tends to make very energetic, insistent attempts to attain proximity, love, and support. These intense efforts are called *hyperactivating strategies* (Cassidy & Kobak, 1988) because they involve strong activation of the attachment system until an attachment figure is perceived to be available and willing to provide safety and security. Hyperactivating strategies include insistent attempts to elicit a partner's involvement, care, and support through clinging and controlling responses; hypervigilance to a relationship partner's positive and negative behaviors (e.g., approval, acceptance, rejection, disinterest, criticism), and intense protest and distress in response to minimal signs of a partner's disapproval or rejection (Shaver & Hazan, 1993). These maneuvers result in overdependence on relationship partners as a source of protection and serious doubts about one's value and lovability as well as the capacity to deal with life's demands and threats alone (Mikulincer & Shaver, 2003). These aspects of attachment-system hyperactivation account for many of the empirically documented characteristics of people who score high on attachment-anxiety scales (Mikulincer & Shaver, 2003, 2007a).

Appraising proximity seeking as unlikely to alleviate distress, and perhaps even as likely to exacerbate distress, results in inhibition of the support seeking and determination to handle distress alone, which is often accomplished by suppression of feelings and grandiose self-enhancement. These approaches to affect regulation are called *deactivating strategies* (Cassidy & Kobak, 1988) because their primary goal is to keep the attachment system deactivated so as to avoid the frustration and anguish that comes from repeated instances of attachment-figure insensitivity or unavailability. These strategies involve denial of attachment needs; avoidance of emotional involvement in and dependence on close relationships; suppression of attachment-related thoughts; and adoption of a highly self-reliant stance, which Bowlby (1973) called *compulsive self-reliance*. They also involve dismissal of threat-related cues and suppression of threat-related thoughts, because perceiving oneself as vulnerable to threats can automatically reactivate a deactivated attachment system. These aspects of deactivation are characteristic of people who score high on measures of avoidant attachment (Mikulincer & Shaver, 2003, 2007a).

AN ATTACHMENT PERSPECTIVE ON LOSS AND BEREAVEMENT

According to attachment theory, the loss of an attachment figure is a devastating event that triggers intense and pervasive distress (which Bowlby [1969, 1982] called *separation distress*), because the person cannot imagine regaining a sense of security, support, protection, and love without this person's availability and responsiveness. Bowlby's (1969, 1982) initial ideas about separation distress were inspired by observations reported by Burlingham and Freud (1944) and filmed by Robertson and Bowlby (1952), who noticed that infants and young children who were separated from their primary caregivers for extended periods passed through a predictable series of states, which Bowlby originally called *protest*, *despair*, and *detachment*. In infancy, the initial response to separation from an attachment figure is protest: The child very actively resists separation by crying, calling, searching, and clinging in an attempt to regain contact. These reactions are marked by anxiety and anger and seem to be generally adaptive reactions aimed at preventing the loss of a major source of protection and comfort or successfully altering the temporarily frightening behavior of an unavailable or inattentive caregiver (Bowlby, 1969, 1982). Intense protest reactions often cause an attachment figure, who sees that the infant is inconsolably distressed, feels wronged, and refuses to calm down, to restore proximity. (Most experienced parents remember all too well what it was like to leave their young child alone with an unfamiliar relative or babysitter the first few times.)

If protest fails to restore proximity, as is obviously the case following the death of an attachment figure, then these vigorous reactions eventually wane, and anxiety and anger give way to pervasive despair, including depressed mood, pained expressions, decreased appetite, and disturbed sleep. Bowlby (1969, 1980) viewed this despair phase of prolonged separation or permanent loss as resulting from the failure of protest to induce a desired change in an attachment figure's behavior and restore a sense of security. Robertson and Bowlby (1952) noted, in their films of children separated from primary attachment figures during prolonged hospitalizations, that despair usually subsides over time and gives way to a third phase of separation distress, which Bowlby (1969, 1982) initially called *detachment*. This phase is marked by apparent recovery and gradual renewal of interest in other activities and new relationship partners. However, there were many indications that detachment is not a neutral termination of the attachment bond but instead reflects defensive suppression of emotions and thoughts related to the missing attachment figure. Bowlby (1980) noted that reunion with a lost attachment figure can evoke strong reactions, including crying, physically following the attachment figure, and anger intermingled with excessive vigilance and anxious clinging.

Bowlby (1979, 1980) viewed adult romantic, or *pair bond*, relationships as the major attachment bonds in adulthood (see also Shaver, Hazan, & Bradshaw, 1988) and assumed that adults who lose or are separated from their long-term romantic partner will undergo a series of reactions similar to those observed in infants (see also Fraley & Shaver, 1999; Parkes & Weiss, 1983; Vormbrock, 1993; Weiss, 1993). These reactions appear mainly if people have already formed full-blown attachments with the romantic partner and consider him or her to be their primary attachment figure and major safe haven and secure base (Hazan & Zeifman, 1999). Like infants, adults react with strong protest, panic, anger, calling, and yearning for reunion. When a loss is prolonged or permanent, the protest phase often includes preoccupation with the missing person, pervasive distress, and lack of interest in other activities. When a person fully realizes that his or her partner will not return, despair and disorganization can ensue, accompanied by sleeping and eating disturbances, social withdrawal, intense sorrow, and loneliness that cannot be alleviated by the presence of others (Weiss, 1993).

There is extensive evidence in bereavement research for the power and pervasiveness of this despair phase (for reviews, see M. Stroebe, Hansson, Stroebe, & Schut, 2001). This research clearly indicates that the death of a close relationship partner is one of the most painful, emotionally engaging, and preoccupying events one can experience, and it typically elicits extreme mixtures of distress, sorrow, loneliness, pining, anxiety, anger, and guilt. It typically includes painful longing for the deceased (e.g., Parkes, 1985; Raphael, 1983; Zisook, Shuchter, Sledge, Paulus, & Judd, 1994). The distress can be so intense and pervasive that it disrupts psychological functioning for an extended period of time (Didion [2005] famously called her 1st year of bereavement the "year of magical thinking" because she noticed how close to being crazy she seemed following the sudden unexpected death of her husband).

It can sometimes result in depressive disorders, posttraumatic stress disorder, and health impairments (e.g., Futterman, Gallagher, Thompson, & Lovett, 1990; Murphy et al., 1999; Zisook et al., 1994; see also chap. 8, this volume). Cross-cultural research also attests that, despite variations in mourning rituals and expressions of grief across cultures, the death of a close relationship partner elicits profound distress everywhere in the world (e.g., W. Stroebe & Stroebe, 1987).

In the case of adult bereavement, Bowlby (1980) preferred to call the final phase of separation distress *reorganization* rather than *detachment* because adults often transfer their proximity seeking and search for a safe haven and secure base (which Ainsworth, 1991, called *attachment functions*) at least partly to new relationship partners without removing the lost partner from the hierarchy of attachment figures. According to Bowlby (1980), adults do not need to defensively detach from a lost attachment figure and suppress all feelings, thoughts, or memories of the deceased. Rather, they can rearrange their representations of self and the deceased so that he or she can continue to serve as a symbolic source of protection, comfort, and love while life with other people continues, perhaps on new foundations. Of course, religious beliefs and practices as well as the establishment of memorials of all kinds can aid this process of continuing a relationship while reorganizing one's life and attachment hierarchy.

According to Bowlby (1980), reorganization is the optimal psychological resolution of attachment-figure loss. It involves two major psychological tasks: (a) accepting the death of the attachment figure, returning to mundane activities, and forming new attachment bonds; and (b) maintaining some kind of symbolic attachment to the deceased and integrating the lost relationship within a new reality. These tasks require an editing of the hierarchy of attachment figures in a process that resembles the replacement of parents by peers as primary attachment figures during adolescence and early adulthood (e.g., Hazan & Zeifman, 1999; Weiss, 1982, 1991). As in the adolescent–young adult transition, reorganization following a major loss involves gradually replacing the deceased with other relationship partners so that actual proximity seeking can be targeted to these real partners, who then become major providers of protection, security, and comfort. Moreover, just as adolescents and young adults typically keep their parents as "attachment figures in reserve" (Weiss, 1982; see also chaps. 2 and 6, this volume), bereaved adults can transform the functions of the deceased partner so that he or she gradually becomes a symbolic rather than a physically present source of security. Psychologically successful mourners can integrate elements of their identity that were related to the lost relationship into a new reality, maintain a symbolic bond to the deceased while adjusting to real circumstances, and restore and even enhance their sense of security and well-being on the basis of both the continuing attachment bond with the deceased and new attachment bonds with living companions.

It is interesting that attachment reorganization involves some degree of both hyperactivating and deactivating strategies (normal parts of temporary insecurity that have typically been viewed in the attachment literature as secondary attachment strategies that can become permanent forms of poor adjustment). By driving people to experience the deep pain of loss, repeatedly reactivate memories of the deceased alongside realizations that the person is gone, and yearn for his or her proximity and love, attachment-system hyperactivation allows mourners to explore the meaning and significance of their lost relationships and find ways of maintaining reorganized, mainly symbolic bonds with loved partners. When this form of hyperactivation is not overwhelming, paralyzing, or disorganizing, it allows bereaved people to productively incorporate the past into the present without splitting off important segments of broken attachments related to their personal and social identities.

Deactivating strategies can also contribute productively to the reorganization process by enabling momentary detachment from the deceased and inhibition or suppression of painful feelings and thoughts. While effectively using a certain degree of avoidance and denial, bereaved people can manage funerals, clean out their closets, begin to create and explore their new reality, return to mundane activities, and recognize that lost relationships continue to have meaning and that life provides new opportunities following a loss. When deactivation is targeted mainly on thoughts of the deceased rather than on shutting down all forms of proximity seeking and social involvement, the formation of new attachment bonds and the adaptive transfer of attachment functions can be facilitated.

Without some degree of attachment-system hyperactivation, the bereaved person would not be able to consider and experience all aspects of his or her new situation and find new meanings and functions for the lost attachment figure. This is the process that Freud (1917/1957) discussed in terms of *hypercathexis* and *decathexis* of mental representations of a deceased loved one, which was his way of talking about the intensely emotional evocation of memories of the deceased and then defusing some of the feelings associated with them. Similarly, without some degree of attachment-system deactivation (targeted on the lost figure), a bereaved person might remain stuck in memories and feelings related to the lost relationship and be unable to cope with new circumstances. Attachment reorganization requires activation of both kinds of secondary strategies in dynamic alteration—a process that M. Stroebe and Schut (1999) called *oscillation*. According to M. Stroebe, Schut, and Stroebe (2005),

> oscillation occurs in the short term (transient fluctuations in the course of any particular day) as well as across the passage of time, because adaptation to bereavement is a matter of slowly and painfully exploring and

discovering what has been lost and what remains: what must be avoided
or relinquished versus what can be retained, created, and built on. (p. 52)

With the successful reorganization of the attachment system, this oscillation
is reduced, and a person begins to feel safe and protected by images of the
deceased loved one as well as by continuing and new relationship partners.

Bowlby's (1980) perspective on the bereavement process is significantly
different from two alternative conceptions of attachment and bereavement:
(a) Freud's (1917/1957) notion of decathexis of lost object representations,
which is more similar to detachment than to reorganization; and (b) Klass,
Silverman, and Nickman's (1996) emphasis on continuing bonds with the
deceased (see also chap. 6, this volume). Freud's view was overly emphatic
about complete detachment, and Klass et al.'s view was insufficiently attentive
to the importance of reorganization. According to Bowlby (1980), adjustment
to loss involves the rearrangement and perhaps retuning of emotional invest-
ments rather than complete detachment from the deceased. It involves a transformation of the bond with the deceased and a concomitant, often gradual,
establishment of new partners as primary attachment figures. Fraley and Shaver
(1999) quoted several passages from Bowlby's (1980) main book about loss and
grief to show that he clearly understood the dialectical interplay between continuing, although reorganized, symbolic bonds with a lost attachment figure and
a shift toward reliance on others, including new security providers.

Bowlby's (1980) reasoning fits well with the various dual-process models
of bereavement (e.g., Rando, 1992; Rubin, 1991; M. Stroebe & Schut, 1999).
For example, M. Stroebe and Schut (1999) viewed adjustment to loss as a
dynamic oscillation between loss orientation and restoration orientation.
Loss orientation is conceptually similar to attachment-system hyperactivation,
which is in turn similar in some ways to Freud's notion of hypercathexis and
includes yearning, rumination, separation distress, and reappraisal of the meaning and implications of the loss. Restoration orientation accomplishes the same
functions as attachment-system deactivation—attending to life changes, doing
new things, distracting oneself from grief, denying or suppressing grief, and
forming new relationships. In this model, oscillation between these two orientations brings about a gradual reorganization of life and mind, such that the
deceased is integrated into one's identity and the bereaved individual expands
the functions of other relationships, establishes new relationships, and finds
new meanings in life. Didion's (2005) book provides a good example: Although
she focused on her year of magical thinking (i.e., the uncharacteristic "crazi-
ness" that engulfed her following her husband's death), she also demonstrated
her gradual healing, evidenced by the book itself, which displays enormous
intelligence, delicate balance (including well-placed, self-directed humor),
and an almost miraculously beautiful prose style—and won the National
Book Award. She was able to ruminate about her long and deep relationships

with her writer husband and their daughter, reorganize the structure of her life, and create a work of art that reviewer John Leonard (2005), writing in the *New York Review of Books*, said he could not imagine getting through the rest of his life and dying without!

Despite the persuasive logic of Bowlby's ideas about coping with and adjusting to loss, and despite their echoes in other models of bereavement, no systematic longitudinal research has been conducted on hyperactivation–deactivation oscillations and their implications for mental health and adjustment. Most of the research has focused on attachment-style differences in coping and adjusting to loss (which we discuss later in this chapter), but there is growing evidence for the claim that both hyperactivation and deactivation are important to grief resolution. For example, Schut, Stroebe, de Keijser, and van den Bout (1997) found that men who habitually avoided confronting their grief benefited from counseling that encouraged them to deal with neglected aspects of their loss. These researchers also found that women who habitually dwelled on the emotional meaning and deep personal implications of the loss benefited from counseling that focused on learning how to deal with everyday activities.

In a longitudinal study of grief reactions following the death of a spouse, Shuchter and Zisook (1993) found that widows and widowers adapted to the new reality without relinquishing their symbolic attachments to the deceased 2, 7, and 13 months after the loss. According to Shuchter and Zisook, mourners maintained this bond by transforming

> what had been a relationship operating on several levels of actual, symbolic, internalized, and imagined relatedness to one in which the actual (living and breathing) relationship has been lost, but the other forms remain or may even develop in more elaborate forms. (p. 34)

These symbolic forms included experiencing comfort because the spouse was in heaven, experiencing the spouse's presence in daily life and dreams, talking with the spouse regularly, or keeping the deceased's belongings (as Joan Didion did with her deceased husband's alarm clock and shoes). Conceptually similar findings were reported by Roberto and Stanis (1994) in a study of older women's reactions to the death of close friends.

These examples call attention to the need for new longitudinal studies using sophisticated assessment techniques and analytic strategies to track attachment reorganization and the adaptive oscillation between secondary attachment strategies. Such studies should build on what is already known about attachment-style differences in emotion regulation more generally (Shaver & Mikulincer, 2007) and should seek a deeper understanding of how these individual differences affect reorganization and the oscillation between hyperactivating and deactivating regulation strategies. We deal with relevant theoretical issues in the following section.

ATTACHMENT INSECURITIES AND
DISORDERED PATTERNS OF MOURNING

Beyond describing the normative processes of bereavement and coping with the loss of a close relationship partner, Bowlby (1980) proposed a framework for conceptualizing disordered patterns of mourning. His analysis of these atypical forms suggests that secondary attachment strategies, which are normally involved in attachment reorganization, can sometimes complicate grief; that is, they can have both adaptive and maladaptive consequences. As when they occur in early child–parent relationships, these strategies are initially adaptive, but if the oscillation between hyperactivating and deactivating strategies during bereavement fails to help with attachment reorganization and fails to restore a person's sense of security, continued reliance on secondary attachment strategies may hinder effective coping and resolution of the loss or reorganization of working models of self and the world. This is what attachment researchers who use the Adult Attachment Interview (George, Kaplan, & Main, 1996) to assess "state of mind with respect to attachment" call "unresolved or disorganized" attachment, which has been associated with a number of serious clinical outcomes (see reviews by Hesse, 1999, and Lyons-Ruth & Jacobvitz, 1999).

The effectiveness of oscillation between hyperactivation and deactivation depends mainly on two things: the extent to which (a) the deceased was a source of security and (b) continuing or new relationship partners are willing and able to provide security and comfort. When the lost figure was unavailable and rejecting while alive, hyperactivation can overwhelm the bereaved person with distress and ambivalence, and little comfort can be found in imagined relations with the deceased. Moreover, encountering new relationship partners who are emotionally distant and unresponsive to one's bids for proximity and comfort can prevent the transfer of attachment functions to these partners and block the formation of a new security-enhancing attachment bond. In both cases, reorganization may fail if continued hyperactivation interferes with the effort to reconstruct a meaning for the lost relationship and the symbolic continuation of the disrupted attachment bond. In a parallel way, but with different effects, attachment-system deactivation can be overgeneralized and become a pervasive barrier to acknowledging attachment needs and engaging in attachment behavior.

Bowlby (1980) also suggested that attachment reorganization depends on the ways a person's attachment system has become organized over the course of development—the eventually dispositional pattern of attachment that we and researchers in our line of attachment research call *attachment style*. Bowlby observed that adults who possess negative models of self and others, and who suffer from chronic attachment insecurities, often have special difficulties when grieving. Anxiously attached individuals, who are unwilling or unable to maintain a normal degree of autonomy and handle many life tasks on their own, find it hard to deactivate or inhibit painful feelings, thoughts, and memories related to a deceased partner, which makes the deactivation side of the normative oscillation between secondary strategies impossible. Avoidant individuals, who regularly suppress attachment-related thoughts and feelings and cognitively distance themselves from all sources of distress, even when they are not grieving, are unwilling or unable to experience thoughts, feelings, and memories related to a deceased partner, which makes it difficult to create meaning from the loss. In both cases, attachment-related worries and defenses may interfere with adaptive oscillation between hyperactivation and deactivation, rigidify and overgeneralize the use of one secondary strategy at the expense of the other, and thereby complicate the grief process.

In contrast, attachment security, which can be either general and dispositional or rooted in the lost relationship, facilitates the reorganization of working models of self and partner and makes adjustment to loss more likely. Securely attached people can recall and think about a lost partner without extreme difficulty, can acknowledge feelings of love and grief, and can discuss the loss coherently in the same way they are able, in the Adult Attachment Interview (Hesse, 1999), to discuss good and bad memories of their childhood relationships with parents (Shaver & Tancredy, 2001). Moreover, their constructive coping strategies allow them to experience and express grief, anger, and distress without feeling overwhelmed by these emotions and without total disruption of their normal functioning (M. Stroebe et al., 2005). In addition, secure individuals' positive models of others allow them to continue to think positively about the deceased, and their positive models of self allow them to cope with the loss and begin to form new relationships. They can therefore invest emotionally in new partners and activities without totally severing their previous emotional bonds.

Reasoning along these lines, Bowlby (1980) suggested that attachment insecurities contribute to two major forms of disordered mourning: (a) "chronic mourning" and (b) "prolonged absence of conscious grieving" (p. 138). Chronic mourning is characterized by overwhelming anxiety and sadness, prolonged difficulty in reestablishing normal functioning, rumination on the missing partner, and maintenance of intense attachment to the deceased partner for years after the loss. In contrast, prolonged absence of grief is characterized by lack of overt expressions of sadness, anger, or distress; detachment from the missing partner; and continuation of normal life without major disruptions. Most clinicians agree with Bowlby's conceptualization of these two forms of disordered mourning, although they tend to label the absence of grief *delayed grief, inhibited mourning,* or *absent mourning* (see M. Stroebe et al., 2001). According to Bowlby, whereas attachment anxiety and pervasive attachment-system hyperactivation underlie chronic mourning, attachment avoidance and the defensive denial of attachment needs and bonds explain the absence of grief.

ANXIOUS ATTACHMENT AND CHRONIC MOURNING

Even when their attachment figures are alive, anxiously attached people are preoccupied with their availability and responsiveness, likely to make intrusive demands for greater closeness, prone to jealousy, quick to cry, and eager for love and reassurance (Mikulincer & Shaver, 2003; Shaver, Schachner, & Mikulincer, 2005). Anxiously attached people often blame themselves for not having sufficient resources and skills to gain a partner's attention and affection, and they invest heavily in their relationships and become highly dependent on their partners (e.g., Alonso-Arbiol, Shaver, & Yárnoz, 2002). It is not surprising, therefore, that when they lose a primary attachment figure they are likely to experience intense anxiety, anger, and sorrow; yearn inconsolably for the lost partner; fail to accept the loss; and have difficulty establishing a new life structure. These are some of the core features of chronic mourning.

Another characteristic of chronic mourning is that the bereaved person is frequently reminded of the deceased by diverse stimuli and situations that unintentionally trigger thoughts, feelings, and memories of the deceased and he or she is unable to effectively manage these intrusive and disruptive mental processes (Boelen, van den Hout, & van den Bout, 2006; Lichtenthal, Cruess, & Prigerson, 2004). This inability to control the flow of intrusive feelings of grief can overwhelm a person and prevent calm exploration of new possibilities for meanings in life and a reorganization of working models related to attachment. What is important to realize, from a scientific standpoint, is that these tendencies of anxiously attached people are present in milder form even without bereavement.

In an experimental study of emotional memories, Mikulincer and Orbach (1995) asked participants to recall early childhood experiences of anger, sadness, anxiety, or happiness and interpreted the memory retrieval latencies as indicators of cognitive accessibility or inaccessibility. Participants also rated the intensity of focal and nonfocal emotions in each recalled event (i.e., the emotion they were asked to target vs. other emotions that might also be aroused). In the memory task, anxiously attached individuals had the quickest access to targeted memories. Moreover, whereas secure people took more time to retrieve negative than positive emotional memories, anxious people took longer to retrieve positive than negative memories. In the emotion rating task, secure individuals rated focal emotions (e.g., sadness when they had been instructed to retrieve a sad memory) as much more intense than nonfocal emotions (e.g., anger when instructed to retrieve a sad memory). In contrast, anxious individuals reported intense focal and nonfocal emotions when asked to remember examples of anxiety, sadness, and anger. Negative emotional memories seemed to spread like wildfire throughout their memory systems, and this did not depend on thoughts about loss or grief in particular.

Roisman, Tsai, and Chiang (2004) reported related findings concerning people's facial expressions during the Adult Attachment Interview. Whereas securely attached individuals' facial expressions were highly congruent with the valence of the childhood events they were describing, anxiously attached individuals exhibited marked discrepancies between the quality of the childhood experiences they described and their facial expressions (e.g., facial expressions of sadness or anger were noticeable while they were speaking about neutral or positive childhood experiences). According to Roisman et al., these discrepancies reflect anxious individuals' confusion and emotional dysregulation when they are asked to talk about emotional experiences. We believe that this is the same kind of confusion and disorganization that occur when anxiously attached mourners are bombarded with intrusive images, thoughts, feelings, and memories about the deceased, although it is likely to be even more intense during bereavement.

In two experiments examining the link between negative moods and cognitive processing, Pereg and Mikulincer (2004) further documented anxiously attached people's lack of control of the spread of activation among distress-eliciting thoughts. In two studies, participants were assigned to a negative mood condition (reading an article about a car accident) or a control condition (reading about how to construct and use a hobby kit), and then incidental recall or causal attributions were assessed. Whereas the induction of a negative mood, compared with a control condition, influenced secure participants to recall more positive information and to attribute a negative event to less global and less stable causes (the pattern of cognitive processing that Forgas, 1995, called *mood incongruent*), participants who scored higher on attachment anxiety reacted to an induced negative mood with heightened recall of negative information and a tendency to attribute a negative event to more global and stable causes. This mood-congruent pattern of cognition favors the spread of negative feelings throughout memory and heightens access to distressing thoughts. In the case of bereaved people, this pattern of emotion regulation makes it difficult to manage intrusive memories of the deceased.

Another feature of chronic mourning is the pervasive presence of negative beliefs about the self, one's life, and the future, such as "I am worthless without my beloved," "My life is meaningless after the loss," and "The future is hopeless" (e.g., Boelen, van den Bout, & van den Hout, 2003; Neimeyer, Prigerson, & Davies, 2002). These negative beliefs contribute to the development of depression (Beck, 1972), disrupt psychological functioning even when they fall short of depression, and strengthen a mourner's inclination to dwell on the loss and long for the comfort and meaning once provided by the deceased (Boelen et al., 2003). According to Foa and Rothbaum (1998), these negative beliefs can be particularly resistant to change when the loss confirms negative views of the self, hopeless beliefs, and catastrophic cognitions that were present before the loss. This is more likely to be the case when a person was already anxiously attached, possessed negative views of self, exaggerated even fairly minor threats, held pessimistic beliefs about managing distress, and attributed threatening events to uncontrollable causes and pervasive personal inadequacies (for extensive reviews, see Mikulincer & Shaver, 2003, 2007a; Shaver & Mikulincer, 2007).

AVOIDANT ATTACHMENT AND THE ABSENCE OF GRIEF

Avoidant people try to deny attachment needs, suppress attachment-related thoughts and emotions, and inhibit unwanted urges to seek proximity or support (Mikulincer & Shaver, 2003). This kind of person, whom Bowlby (1969, 1982) called "compulsively self-reliant," values independence to the point of avoiding deep emotional interdependence even with long-term mates. After the loss of an attachment figure, such a person is likely to use well-established defenses to inhibit anxiety and sadness, downplay the importance of the loss, and try to steer clear of thoughts and memories focused on the deceased. This is what Bowlby (1980) meant by the "absence of grief." He considered this to be a defensive reaction involving redirection of attention away from painful thoughts and feelings ("defensive exclusion") and the segregation or dissociation of memories of the deceased that nevertheless continued to influence emotions and behaviors without the individual's awareness of their existence or effects.

Bowlby (1980) thought the prolonged absence of grief could eventually lead to difficulties in mental and physical health, perhaps especially when subsequent losses are experienced. He thought that people who fail to mourn would have difficulties integrating losses meaningfully into their working models and personal narratives. (This is precisely the phenomenon that gets a person classified as "unresolved with respect to losses or traumas" in the Adult Attachment Interview; Hesse, 1999.) Because a bereaved person is likely to have engaged in many daily activities with the now-deceased partner, each of these activities or the places where they occurred becomes an unwanted reminder of the loss and a further source of either distress or need to suppress thoughts and feelings. According to Fraley and Shaver (1999), "Repeated activation of inexplicable and partially suppressed negative emotions may eventually have a negative impact on psychological well-being or physical health" (p. 743). Bowlby (1990) provided a fascinating and detailed example of these negative consequences of suppressed grief in his final book, *Charles Darwin: A New Life*, in which he connected Darwin's suppression of grief following the death of his mother when he was 8 years old (a suppression demanded by his avoidant father) and the emergence of "hyperventilation syndrome" (persistent gastric pains and heart palpitations) during adulthood.

Of course, the negative emotional and physical sequelae of an absence of grieving are most likely to emerge when the mourner was deeply attached to the lost partner and the partner was the individual's only safe haven and secure base. If an avoidant person was able to avoid proximity seeking, deep interdependence, and extensive attachment to a partner while he or she was alive, then the bereaved person may experience less anxiety and sadness following the loss even without strenuous suppression or mental segregation. In such cases, the absence of grieving may reflect a real absence of distress (relative to that experienced by other bereaved individuals) rather than a defensive reaction to the pain of a meaningful loss. Compatible with this idea is evidence that many people who show few signs of grief shortly after the loss of a partner do not exhibit heightened distress or maladjustment months or years later (for a review, see Bonanno, 2001). It may be difficult, in particular cases, to tell the difference between successful but very active suppression, on the one hand, and a true absence of anything to suppress, on the other hand. For several years, our own research was unclear about the existence of this difference. Now, however, Bowlby's (1980) ideas about avoidant people's defensive suppression of memories, thoughts, and feelings concerning separations and losses have been well supported in a series of experiments conducted in our laboratories.

Using Wegner's (1994) thought-suppression paradigm, Fraley and Shaver (1997) asked participants to write about whatever thoughts and feelings they were experiencing while being allowed to think about anything except thoughts about their mate leaving them for someone else. (All of the participants were involved in long-term couple relationships.) In one study, the ability to suppress these thoughts was assessed by the number of times they appeared in participants' stream of consciousness following the suppression effort (during what Wegner [1994] called the *rebound* period). In another study, this ability was assessed by the level of physiological arousal (skin conductance) during the suppression task: The lower the arousal, the greater the presumed ability to suppress the troubling thoughts. The results indicated that avoidant attachment was associated with both less frequent thoughts of loss following the suppression task and lower skin conductance during the task, suggesting that avoidant defenses block unwanted thoughts and prevent the emotional arousal they might otherwise cause. A recent functional magnetic resonance imaging study (Gillath et al., 2005) shows that these avoidant defenses are also evident in patterns of brain activation and deactivation when people are attempting to suppress thoughts about breakups and losses.

While probing further into the regulatory mechanisms underlying avoidant defenses, Fraley, Garner, and Shaver (2000) asked whether they function in a preemptive manner—for example, by directing attention away from, or encoding in a shallow way, attachment-related information—or in a "postemptive" manner (repressing material that has already been encoded).

Participants listened to a genuinely emotional interview about the loss of a close relationship partner and were later asked to recall details of the interview, either soon after hearing them (Study 1) or at various delays, ranging from half an hour to 21 days (Study 2). An analysis of forgetting curves plotted over time revealed two things: (a) Avoidant people initially encoded less information about the interview, and (b) people with different attachment styles forgot encoded information at the same rate. Thus, avoidant defenses sometimes act preemptively, by blocking threatening material from awareness before it is fully encoded.

However, although these studies imply that avoidant defenses are effective in suppressing memories and thoughts concerning separation and loss, Mikulincer, Dolev, and Shaver (2004) recently found that avoidant people can nevertheless be disturbed by the unwanted resurgence of suppressed thoughts (a phenomenon Freud called "the return of the repressed"; Freud, 1926/1959). In one study, participants were asked to think about a painful relationship breakup and were either instructed or not instructed to suppress thoughts about this separation. Mikulincer et al. then examined the rebound of the suppressed separation-related thoughts under conditions of low or high cognitive load, which enabled them to determine whether avoidant defenses are capable of inhibiting the postsuppression rebound effect even when other cognitive demands draw on limited psychological resources. The implicit activation of previously suppressed thoughts was assessed by measuring the extent to which they influenced performance on a Stroop color naming task. Participants performed a Stroop task under low or high cognitive load (holding a one- or seven-digit number in mind), and the researchers assessed color naming reaction times for separation-related words. (Longer latency times imply greater activation of the verbal content printed in color.)

In a second study, Mikulincer et al. (2004) examined possible consequences of failed suppression efforts on avoidant individuals' self-concepts: If high cognitive load impairs the effectiveness of avoidant defenses, then it may render an avoidant person defenseless against reactivation of doubts about his or her lovability and sense of personal worth (core doubts resulting from a history of relationships with unavailable and rejecting partners). To examine this possibility, Mikulincer et al. asked study participants to recall either a painful breakup with a romantic partner or a more neutral experience (being at a drugstore) and to perform a 5-minute stream-of-consciousness task. In this task, participants were either instructed or not instructed to suppress thoughts about the just-recalled episode. All participants then performed the Stroop color naming task while at the same time carrying out a relatively easy or demanding cognitive task. The main dependent variables were color naming reaction times for participant-specific negative self-traits and positive self-traits taken from lists supplied by the participants in a previous research session weeks before.

The results clearly showed that avoidant attachment was associated in the control condition with the prevention of unwanted reactivation of previously suppressed thoughts about a painful separation (Mikulincer et al., 2004). Under conditions of low cognitive load, avoidant people were able to suppress thoughts related to the breakup, and they evinced lower accessibility of such thoughts and higher accessibility of positive self-representations following suppression. However, the effectiveness of avoidant defenses was significantly impaired when a high cognitive load taxed the mental resources needed to maintain thought suppression. Under conditions of high cognitive load, avoidant people exhibited greater automatic activation of thoughts of separation and negative self-traits following suppression. In other words, their defenses collapsed when mental resources were too scarce to maintain them, and this collapse was associated with a spread of activation from unwanted attachment-related thoughts to formerly suppressed negative self-representations. This is the kind of psychodynamic phenomenon, central to Bowlby's (1980) theory, that research psychologists have often thought could not be empirically demonstrated (Shaver & Mikulincer, 2002).

Overall, the findings imply that under strain, an avoidant mind, accustomed to attachment-system deactivation, is less able to exclude loss-related information from awareness and to segregate or dissociate painful memories. In line with Bowlby's (1980) analysis of absence of grieving, avoidant individuals' attempts to suppress or repress unacceptable or unmanageable thoughts and feelings concerning a loss fail to eliminate the distress, and the suppressed material can resurface in experience and action when high cognitive (or, we assume, emotional) demands are encountered. This vulnerability resembles one that Wenzlaff, Rude, Taylor, Stultz, and Sweatt (2001) documented in the case of individuals at risk for depression:

> High levels of thought suppression may indicate that the individual has not resolved the negative patterns of thinking that contributed to the previous depressive episode. These patterns of negative thinking are apt to become evident when stress undermines mental control efforts. (pp. 448–449)

EMPIRICAL EVIDENCE ON ATTACHMENT-STYLE DIFFERENCES IN ADJUSTMENT TO LOSS

Beyond providing experimental evidence concerning patterns of coping with loss-related thoughts and memories, few studies have directly examined attachment-style differences in adjustment to the loss of a close relationship partner. The major findings of those few studies generally support the idea that secure attachment facilitates emotional adjustment during bereavement. For example, van Doorn, Kasl, Beery, Jacobs, and Prigerson (1998) interviewed adults while they were caring for their terminally ill spouses and found that global attachment security in romantic relationships and specific attachment security in the marriage were both associated with less intense grief reactions to the critical illness of their spouse. Similarly, Fraley and Bonanno (2004) found that people classified as securely attached 4 months after the loss of a spouse reported relatively low levels of bereavement-related anxiety, grief, depression, and posttraumatic distress 4 and 18 months after the loss. Conceptually similar findings have been reported by Wayment and Vierthaler (2002) and Waskowic and Chartier (2003).

There is also evidence of anxiously attached people's complicated grief reactions (Field & Sundin, 2001; Fraley & Bonanno, 2004; Wayment & Vierthaler, 2002). For example, Field and Sundin (2001) found that anxious attachment, assessed 10 months after the death of a spouse, predicted higher levels of psychological distress 14, 25, and 60 months after the loss. With regard to attachment avoidance, studies have generally found no significant association between this attachment dimension and depression, grief, or distress (Field & Sundin, 2001; Fraley & Bonanno, 2004; Wayment & Vierthaler, 2002). However, Wayment and Vierthaler (2002) found that avoidance was associated with higher levels of somatic symptoms, implying that avoidant defenses might block conscious access to anxiety and depression but without suspending the more subtle and less conscious somatic reactions to loss. (These results are similar to ones obtained by Berant, Mikulincer, & Florian [2001] and Mikulincer, Florian, & Weller [1993] in studies of other severe stressors, such as giving birth to a child with a serious heart defect and coping with war.) In addition, Fraley and Bonanno (2004) found that the combination of avoidance and attachment anxiety (the pattern that Bartholomew & Horowitz [1991] called *fearful avoidance*) produced the highest levels of anxiety, depression, grief, trauma-related symptoms, and alcohol consumption following the death of one's spouse.

There is also evidence concerning attachment-style differences in continuing attachment to and detachment from a lost partner. Field and Sundin (2001), for example, found that more avoidant people reported more negative thoughts about their lost spouse 14 months after the loss, perhaps reflecting a distancing, derogating attitude toward the deceased (something commonly found in studies of avoidant attachment and relationship dissatisfaction). In contrast, attachment anxiety was associated with more positive thoughts about the lost spouse, probably reflecting a continuing emotional investment in an idealized figure. This kind of idealization was also evident in Nager and de Vries's (2004) content analysis of memorial Web sites created by adult daughters for their deceased mothers. Comments about missing the deceased and idealized descriptions of mothers (e.g., "You were the most beautiful, strongest, determined, smartest, fascinating woman in the world") were more frequently found on Web sites created by anxiously attached daughters (according to a self-report measure) than in those created by secure or avoidant daughters. Using the Continuing Bonds Scale (Grund, 1998), Waskowic and Chartier (2003) found that secure people maintained an adaptive attitude toward a lost partner; although they scored lower than their insecure counterparts on rumination about and preoccupation with a lost spouse, they still scored higher on positive reminiscences about and symbolic exchanges with the deceased.

CONCLUDING REMARKS

Although it would take more space than we have available to spell out the details of Bowlby's (1980) theory of attachment and loss and to provide the extensive and still-growing evidence for it, we hope we have provided enough examples of recent studies to entice the reader to delve deeper into the recent literature. Bowlby's ideas were rooted in his experience as a psychoanalyst, but they were made more concrete and verifiable than previous psychoanalytic theories thanks to his heavy and detailed reliance on the research literature of his time. Today, we have additional research methods contributed by social cognition researchers, psychophysiologists, and cognitive neuroscientists—methods that have proven valuable in our own studies of anxious and avoidant defenses and the benefits of experimentally enhanced attachment security (e.g., Mikulincer & Shaver, 2005, 2007b, 2007c). It will be some time before these studies are extended and integrated with appropriate longitudinal studies of bereavement, but we remain confident that many of Bowlby's key ideas and insights will continue to be relevant to understanding and coping with grief. Every person who lives very long will, unfortunately, have several opportunities to experience years of magical thinking and occasions for standing at death's door. There is no way to live without these experiences, and life would be less engaging if there were, but understanding the evolutionary–biological and psychological processes involved can make these experiences less foreign and baffling, for both clinicians and ordinary educated adults.

REFERENCES

Ainsworth, M. D. S. (1991). Attachment and other affectional bonds across the life cycle. In C. M. Parkes, J. Stevenson-Hinde, & P. Marris (Eds.), *Attachment across the life cycle* (pp. 33–51). New York: Routledge.

Ainsworth, M. D. S., Blehar, M. C., Waters, E., & Wall, S. (1978). *Patterns of attachment: Assessed in the strange situation and at home.* Hillsdale, NJ: Erlbaum.

Alonso-Arbiol, I., Shaver, P. R., & Yárnoz, S. (2002). Insecure attachment, gender roles, and interpersonal dependency in the Basque country. *Personal Relationships, 9,* 479–490.

Bartholomew, K., & Horowitz, L. M. (1991). Attachment styles among young adults: A test of a four-category model. *Journal of Personality and Social Psychology, 61,* 226–244.

Beck, A. T. (1972). *Depression: Causes and treatment.* Philadelphia: University of Pennsylvania Press.

Berant, E., Mikulincer, M., & Florian, V. (2001). Attachment style and mental health: A one-year follow-up study of mothers of infants with congenital heart disease. *Personality and Social Psychology Bulletin, 8,* 956–968.

Boelen, P. A., van den Bout, J., & van den Hout, M. A. (2003). The role of cognitive variables in psychological functioning after the death of a first degree relative. *Behavior Research and Therapy, 41,* 1123–1136.

Boelen, P. A., van den Hout, M. A., & van den Bout, J. (2006). A cognitive–behavioral conceptualization of complicated grief. *Clinical Psychology: Science and Practice, 13,* 109–128.

Bonanno, G. (2001). Grief and emotion: A social–functional perspective. In M. Stroebe, W. Stroebe, R. O. Hansson, & H. A. W. Schut (Eds.), *Handbook of bereavement research: Consequences, coping, and care* (pp. 493–515). Washington, DC: American Psychological Association.

Bowlby, J. (1969). *Attachment and loss: Vol. 1. Attachment.* New York: Basic Books.

Bowlby, J. (1973). *Attachment and loss: Vol. 2. Separation: Anxiety and anger.* New York: Basic Books.

Bowlby, J. (1979). *The making and breaking of affectional bonds.* London: Tavistock.

Bowlby, J. (1980). *Attachment and loss: Vol. 3. Sadness and depression.* New York: Basic Books.

Bowlby, J. (1982). *Attachment and loss: Vol. 1. Attachment* (2nd ed.). New York: Basic Books.

Bowlby, J. (1988). *A secure base: Clinical applications of attachment theory.* London: Routledge.

Bowlby, J. (1990). *Charles Darwin: A new life.* New York: Norton.

Brennan, K. A., Clark, C. L., & Shaver, P. R. (1998). Self-report measurement of adult romantic attachment: An integrative overview. In J. A. Simpson & W. S. Rholes (Eds.), *Attachment theory and close relationships* (pp. 46–76). New York: Guilford Press.

Burlingham, D., & Freud, A. (1944). *Infants without families.* London: Allen & Unwin.

Cassidy, J., & Kobak, R. R. (1988). Avoidance and its relationship with other defensive processes. In J. Belsky & T. Nezworski (Eds.), *Clinical implications of attachment* (pp. 300–323). Hillsdale, NJ: Erlbaum.

Didion, J. (2005). *The year of magical thinking.* New York: Knopf.

Field, N. P., & Sundin, E. C. (2001). Attachment style in adjustment to conjugal bereavement. *Journal of Social and Personal Relationships, 18,* 347–361.

Foa, E. B., & Rothbaum, B. O. (1998). *Treating the trauma of rape: Cognitive–behavior therapy for PTSD.* New York: Guilford Press.

Forgas, J. P. (1995). Mood and judgment: The affect infusion model (AIM). *Psychological Bulletin, 117,* 39–66.

Fraley, R., & Bonanno, G. A. (2004). Attachment and loss: A test of three competing models on the association between attachment-related avoidance and adaptation to bereavement. *Personality and Social Psychology Bulletin, 30,* 878–890.

Fraley, R. C., Garner, J. P., & Shaver, P. R. (2000). Adult attachment and the defensive regulation of attention and memory: Examining the role of preemptive and postemptive defensive processes. *Journal of Personality and Social Psychology, 79,* 816–826.

Fraley, R. C., & Shaver, P. R. (1997). Adult attachment and the suppression of unwanted thoughts. *Journal of Personality and Social Psychology, 73,* 1080–1091.

Fraley, R. C., & Shaver, P. R. (1999). Loss and bereavement: Attachment theory and recent controversies concerning grief work and the nature of detachment. In J. Cassidy & P. R. Shaver (Eds.), *Handbook of attachment: Theory, research, and clinical applications* (pp. 735–759). New York: Guilford Press.

Fraley, R. C., & Shaver, P. R. (2000). Adult romantic attachment: Theoretical developments, emerging controversies, and unanswered questions. *Review of General Psychology, 4,* 132–154.

Freud, S. (1957). Mourning and melancholia. In J. Strachey (Ed. & Trans.), *The standard edition of the complete psychological works of Sigmund Freud* (Vol. 14, pp. 237–260). New York: Basic Books. (Original work published 1917)

Freud, S. (1959). Inhibitions, symptoms, and anxiety. In J. Strachey (Ed. & Trans.), *The standard edition of the complete psychological works of Sigmund Freud* (Vol. 20, pp. 75–175). London: Hogarth Press. (Original work published 1926)

Futterman, A., Gallagher, D., Thompson, L. W., & Lovett, S. (1990). Retrospective assessment of marital adjustment and depression during the first 2 years of spousal bereavement. *Psychology and Aging, 5,* 273–280.

George, C., Kaplan, N., & Main, M. (1996). *Adult Attachment Interview* (3rd ed.). Unpublished manuscript, University of California, Berkeley.

Gilbert, S. M. (2006). *Death's door: Modern dying and the ways we grieve.* New York: Norton.

Gillath, O., Bunge, S. A., Shaver, P. R., Wendelken, C., & Mikulincer, M. (2005). Attachment-style differences in the ability to suppress negative thoughts: Exploring the neural correlates. *Neuroimage, 28,* 835–847.

Grund, D. (1998). *Positive attachment to the deceased and death anxiety.* Unpublished honors thesis, University of Saskatchewan, Saskatoon, Saskatchewan, Canada.

Hazan, C., & Zeifman, D. (1999). Pair-bonds as attachments: Evaluating the evidence. In J. Cassidy & P. R. Shaver (Eds.), *Handbook of attachment: Theory, research, and clinical applications* (pp. 336–354). New York: Guilford Press.

Hesse, E. (1999). The Adult Attachment Interview: Historical and current perspectives. In J. Cassidy & P. R. Shaver (Eds.), *Handbook of attachment: Theory, research, and clinical applications* (pp. 395–433). New York: Guilford Press.

Klass, D., Silverman, P., & Nickman, S. (Eds.). (1996). *Continuing bonds: New understandings of grief*. Washington, DC: Taylor & Francis.

Leonard, J. (2005). The black album [Review of the book *The year of magical thinking*]. *New York Review of Books, 52*(16). Retrieved December 12, 2007, from http://www.nybooks.com/articles/18352

Lichtenthal, W. G., Cruess, D. G., & Prigerson, H. G. (2004). A case for establishing complicated grief as a distinct mental disorder in *DSM–V*. *Clinical Psychology Review, 24*, 637–662.

Lyons-Ruth, K., & Jacobvitz, D. (1999). Attachment disorganization: Unresolved loss, relational violence, and lapses in behavioral and attentional strategies. In J. Cassidy & P. R. Shaver (Eds.), *Handbook of attachment: Theory, research, and clinical applications* (pp. 520–554). New York: Guilford Press.

Mikulincer, M., Dolev, T., & Shaver, P. R. (2004). Attachment-related strategies during thought-suppression: Ironic rebounds and vulnerable self-representations. *Journal of Personality and Social Psychology, 87*, 940–956.

Mikulincer, M., Florian, V., & Weller, A. (1993). Attachment styles, coping strategies, and posttraumatic psychological distress: The impact of the Gulf war in Israel. *Journal of Personality and Social Psychology, 64*, 817–826.

Mikulincer, M., & Orbach, I. (1995). Attachment styles and repressive defensiveness: The accessibility and architecture of affective memories. *Journal of Personality and Social Psychology, 68*, 917–925.

Mikulincer, M., & Shaver, P. R. (2003). The attachment behavioral system in adulthood: Activation, psychodynamics, and interpersonal processes. In M. P. Zanna (Ed.), *Advances in experimental social psychology* (Vol. 35, pp. 53–152). New York: Academic Press.

Mikulincer, M., & Shaver, P. R. (2005). Mental representations of attachment security: Theoretical foundation for a positive social psychology. In M. W. Baldwin (Ed.), *Interpersonal cognition* (pp. 233–266). New York: Guilford Press.

Mikulincer, M., & Shaver, P. R. (2007a). *Attachment in adulthood: Structure, dynamics, and change*. New York: Guilford Press.

Mikulincer, M., & Shaver, P. R. (2007b). Boosting attachment security to promote mental health, prosocial values, and inter-group tolerance. *Psychological Inquiry, 18*, 139–156.

Mikulincer, M., & Shaver, P. R. (2007c). Reflections on security dynamics: Core constructs, psychological mechanisms, relational contexts, and the need for an integrative theory. *Psychological Inquiry, 18*, 197–209.

Murphy, S. A., Braun, T., Tillery, L., Cain, K. C., Johnson, L. C., & Beaton, R. B. (1999). PTSD among bereaved parents following the violent deaths of their 12-

to 28-year-old children: A longitudinal prospective analysis. *Journal of Traumatic Stress, 12,* 273–291.

Nager, E. A., & de Vries, B. (2004). Memorializing on the World Wide Web: Patterns of grief and attachment in adult daughters of deceased mothers. *Omega, 49,* 43–56.

Neimeyer, R. A., Prigerson, H. G., & Davies, B. (2002). Mourning and meaning. *American Behavioral Scientist, 46,* 235–241.

Parkes, C. M. (1985). Bereavement. *British Journal of Psychiatry, 146,* 11–17.

Parkes, C. M., & Weiss, R. S. (1983). *Recovery from bereavement.* New York: Basic Books.

Pereg, D., & Mikulincer, M. (2004). Attachment style and the regulation of negative affect: Exploring individual differences in mood congruency effects on memory and judgment. *Personality and Social Psychology Bulletin, 30,* 67–80.

Rando, T. A. (1992). The increased prevalence of complicated mourning: The onslaught is just beginning. *Omega, 26,* 43–60.

Raphael, B. (1983). *The anatomy of bereavement.* New York: Basic Books.

Roberto, K. A., & Stanis, P. I. (1994). Reactions of older women to the death of their close friends. *Omega, 29,* 17–28.

Robertson, J., & Bowlby, J. (1952). Responses of young children to separation from their mothers. *Courrier of the International Children's Center, 2,* 131–140.

Roisman, G. I., Tsai, J. L., & Chiang, K. H. S. (2004). The emotional integration of childhood experience: Physiological, facial expressive, and self-reported emotional response during the Adult Attachment Interview. *Developmental Psychology, 40,* 776–789.

Rubin, S. S. (1991). Adult child loss and the two-track model of bereavement. *Omega, 24,* 183–202.

Schut, H. A. W., Stroebe, M., de Keijser, J., & van den Bout, J. (1997). Intervention for the bereaved: Gender differences in the efficacy of grief counseling. *British Journal of Clinical Psychology, 36,* 63–72.

Shaver, P. R., & Hazan, C. (1993). Adult romantic attachment: Theory and evidence. In D. Perlman & W. Jones (Eds.), *Advances in personal relationships* (Vol. 4, pp. 29–70). London: Jessica Kingsley.

Shaver, P. R., Hazan, C., & Bradshaw, D. (1988). Love as attachment: The integration of three behavioral systems. In R. J. Sternberg & M. Barnes (Eds.), *The psychology of love* (pp. 68–99). New Haven, CT: Yale University Press.

Shaver, P. R., & Mikulincer, M. (2002). Attachment-related psychodynamics. *Attachment and Human Development, 4,* 133–161.

Shaver, P. R., & Mikulincer, M. (2007). Adult attachment strategies and the regulation of emotion. In J. J. Gross (Ed.), *Handbook of emotion regulation* (pp. 446–465). New York: Guilford Press.

Shaver, P. R., Schachner, D. A., & Mikulincer, M. (2005). Attachment style, excessive reassurance seeking, relationship processes, and depression. *Personality and Social Psychology Bulletin, 31,* 1–17.

Shaver, P. R., & Tancredy, C. M. (2001). Emotion, attachment, and bereavement: A conceptual commentary. In M. Stroebe, R. O. Hansson, W. Stroebe, & H. Schut (Eds.), *Handbook of bereavement research: Consequences, coping, and care* (pp. 63–88). Washington, DC: American Psychological Association.

Shuchter, S. R., & Zisook, S. (1993). The course of normal grief. In M. Stroebe, W. Stroebe, & R. O. Hansson (Eds.), *Handbook of bereavement: Theory, research, and intervention* (pp. 23–43). New York: Cambridge University Press.

Stroebe, M., Hansson, R. O., Stroebe, W., & Schut, H. (Eds.). (2001). *Handbook of bereavement research: Consequences, coping, and care*. Washington, DC: American Psychological Association.

Stroebe, M., & Schut, H. A. W. (1999). The dual process model of coping with bereavement: Rationale and description. *Death Studies, 23*, 1–28.

Stroebe, M., Schut, H. A. W., & Stroebe, W. (2005). Attachment in coping with bereavement: A theoretical integration. *Review of General Psychology, 9*, 48–66.

Stroebe, W., & Stroebe, M. (1987). *Bereavement and health: The psychological and physical consequences of partner loss*. New York: Cambridge University Press.

van Doorn, C., Kasl, S. V., Beery, L. C., Jacobs, S. C., & Prigerson, H. G. (1998). The influence of marital quality and attachment styles on traumatic grief and depressive symptoms. *Journal of Nervous and Mental Disease, 186*, 566–573.

Vormbrock, J. (1993). Attachment theory as applied to wartime and job-related marital separation. *Psychological Bulletin, 114*, 122–144.

Waskowic, T. D., & Chartier, B. M. (2003). Attachment and the experience of grief following the loss of a spouse. *Omega: The Journal of Death and Dying, 47*, 77–91.

Wayment, H. A., & Vierthaler, J. (2002). Attachment style and bereavement reactions. *Journal of Loss and Trauma, 7*, 129–149.

Wegner, D. M. (1994). Ironic processes of mental control. *Psychological Review, 101*, 34–52.

Weiss, R. S. (1982). Attachment in adult life. In C. M. Parkes & J. Stevenson-Hinde (Eds.), *The place of attachment in human behavior* (pp. 171–184). New York: Basic Books.

Weiss, R. S. (1991). The attachment bond in childhood and adulthood. In C. M. Parkes, J. Stevenson-Hinde, & P. Marris (Eds.), *Attachment across the life cycle* (pp. 66–76). London: Tavistock/Routledge.

Weiss, R. S. (1993). Loss and recovery. In M. S. Stroebe, W. Stroebe, & R. O. Hansson (Eds.), *Handbook of bereavement* (pp. 271–284). New York: Cambridge University Press.

Wenzlaff, R. M., Rude, S. S., Taylor, C. J., Stultz, C. H., & Sweatt, R. A. (2001). Beneath the veil of thought suppression: Attentional bias and depression risk. *Cognition & Emotion, 15*, 435–452.

Zisook, S., Shuchter, S. R., Sledge, P. A., Paulus, M. P., & Judd, L. W. (1994). The spectrum of depressive phenomena after spousal bereavement. *Journal of Clinical Psychiatry, 55*, 29–36.

6

WHETHER TO RELINQUISH OR MAINTAIN A BOND WITH THE DECEASED

NIGEL P. FIELD

There is increasing recognition in the bereavement literature that the bereaved often maintain their attachment with the deceased and that this is an integral part of successful adaptation to the death of a loved one (Attig, 2000; Klass, Silverman, & Nickman, 1996; Klass & Walter, 2001). Proponents of what has come to be known as the *continuing bonds* (CB) perspective on adaptation to mourning have made an important contribution in promoting greater awareness among practitioners working with the bereaved on the value of interventions that go beyond an exclusive focus on disengagement from the deceased in seeking to foster a healthy CB as a central treatment goal (Neimeyer, 2001). The CB literature has also contributed to a better understanding of historical and cultural influences that may underlie the undue emphasis in the earlier bereavement literature on separation and individuation in adapting to the loss of a loved one when observed from a broader historic–cultural viewpoint as a product of Western individualist values (Goss & Klass, 2005; Stroebe, Gergen, Gergen, & Stroebe, 1992).

The CB literature, however, has been criticized for its global treatment of CB as invariably adaptive and for disregarding conditions under which it may be maladaptive (Field, Gao, & Paderna, 2005; Fraley & Shaver, 1999; see also chap. 5, this volume). This unidimensional way of conceptualizing

CB obscures its likely complex relation to grief outcome. For example, does a focus on fond memories or the use of the deceased as a valued reference point or ideal have the same implications for adjustment as more dissociative-like sense of presence CB expressions? Is time since the death a significant factor in determining whether CB indicates successful adjustment? Such questions are overlooked if one assumes that CB is invariably adaptive.

As I elaborate later, this unidimensional treatment of CB may have contributed to a tendency among CB proponents to misrepresent as "relinquishment theorists" a number of prominent bereavement theorists who consider the relationship between CB and adaptation to be complex. In effect, there appears to be a tendency among CB proponents to equate any reference to assertion that the bereaved must relinquish some aspect of the bond as adherence to wholesale relinquishment. This unidimensional way of conceptualizing CB may stem from a tendency of CB proponents to conflate relinquishing the bond to the deceased with grief work. In this chapter, I argue that the two need to be distinguished to facilitate an understanding of the full complexity of the relationship between CB and bereavement-related adaptation.

I propose that a more constructive approach toward determining the adaptiveness of CB is to attempt to identify what can be continued and what needs to be relinquished in contrast to simply whether to continue or to relinquish the bond. This perspective entails conceptualizing CB as multidimensional, regarding the endpoint of grief work not as detachment but as involving reconstruction of the relationship with the deceased. I believe that this will be a more fruitful way of clarifying the function of CB and inspiring systematic research toward investigating the conditions under which CB is adaptive or maladaptive.

DISTINGUISHING GRIEF WORK FROM DETACHMENT

The perspective that the bereaved must relinquish their attachment to the deceased in adjusting to bereavement originated from Freud's (1917/1957) classic work *Mourning and Melancholia*, in which he regarded the task of mourning as requiring the withdrawal of *libido*, or psychic energy linked with the sexual instinct, from the representations of the deceased loved one. The "work of mourning," or *grief work*, is the mechanism through which the bereaved person relinquishes his or her bond with the deceased. This entails repeatedly confronting the discrepancy between the wish to continue to invest libido in the deceased as an object of instinctual gratification and the awareness that it is no longer possible to do so because the other is dead. Through repeated exposure to such frustrated attempts, the bereaved individual gradually accepts the reality of no longer being able to gratify his or her instinctual aim with the deceased—and eventually de-invests, or *decathects*, his or her libido from the deceased, thus freeing it up for investment in other relationships.

It is important to distinguish between grief work, the mechanism by which decathexis occurs, and the endpoint of mourning involving detachment. In the Freudian perspective on object relatedness, attachment ties to others are secondary to drive gratification. In other words, there is no intrinsic attachment orientation toward others apart from their function in satisfying more primary drives (Eagle, 1987; Greenberg & Mitchell, 1983). Thus, the bond with the other, at least in principle, is more expendable, or more fluid, within a Freudian framework than it is in the case of contemporary object relational psychoanalytic and attachment approaches. The latter emphasize relatedness as a fundamental orientation in its own right separate from the sexual and aggressive drives (Greenberg & Mitchell, 1983).

Given the emphasis of the Freudian perspective on drive gratification, it follows that the purpose of mourning is to decathect libido from the deceased, who can no longer serve as an object for drive satisfaction, and to redirect it toward a suitable substitute. It also follows that complicated grief is understood in terms of failure to decathect, given its status as a limited energy resource that cannot be invested in others if not freed from the deceased. On the other hand, given their primary emphasis on the function of the other as a source of security and trust as opposed to a means for drive gratification, object relations and attachment theorists regard attachment ties as less easily substitutable relative to the Freudian perspective (Juri & Marrone, 2003). Consequently, interpersonal loss is inherently more problematic within this framework, and there should be a greater impetus here toward finding a means to preserve the bond as opposed to relinquishing it. As I elaborate later in this chapter, the goal of grief work from an object relations and attachment perspective does not involve detachment per se; rather, the goal involves a reorganization of the relationship with the deceased that accommodates the reality of the ending of the physical relationship.

In line with the Freudian perspective, there is a tendency among CB proponents to equate grief work with detachment. In fact, CB has been cited as evidence against a grief work perspective on mourning (Silverman & Klass, 1996; Stroebe et al., 1992). There is much controversy in the empirical bereavement literature regarding the role of grief work in adaptation to bereavement (for critical perspectives on grief work, see Bonanno & Kaltman, 1999; Wortman & Silver, 1989). Although a full discussion of this is not possible here, I believe that research cited as evidence against the value of grief work is based on an overly narrow definition of what is meant by the term, such as equating it with rumination (Nolen-Hoeksema, 2001), continued search for meaning in the loss (Davis, Wortman, Lehman, & Silver, 2000), or expression of negative emotion when focusing on the past relationship (Bonanno & Keltner, 1997).

These ways of operationalizing grief work fail to appreciate the complex set of cognitive–affective processes that constitute working through the grief. In the psychoanalytic literature, the concept of working through was introduced to address the problem of how, despite receiving insight into conflicted aims that are presumed to underlie symptoms through a correct interpretation, this would not necessarily be translated into a change in behavior among psychotherapy patients (Fialkow & Muslin, 1987). It is the means by which insight is translated into action that defines *working through*. This requires the therapist to repeatedly bring to the patient's awareness how his or her dynamic issues get played out across different experiential contexts. The translation of insight into action gradually generalizes across situations through such repetition. Concerning bereavement, such working through entails repeated entry into awareness that the other is dead in the context of expectations, plans, hopes, and goals connected with the attachment. This leads to a gradual revision in the latter in light of the new life situation.

Central to working through at the information-processing level is a process of matching new information with preestablished mental schemas and a gradual revising of these schemata to accommodate the discrepant information (Horowitz, 1986). In the context of bereavement, this involves an active reconstructive process toward revising mental schemata of the relationship with the deceased to bring them into accord with the new life situation through repeated exposure to the discrepant information in the service of integration (Horowitz, 1991). Although repeated confrontation with reminders of the loss at times may evoke painful emotion, and this may serve as an important motivator of schematic change, it is not necessary to assume that this active revision process is invariably accompanied by expression of strong emotion. In fact, there may be a misplaced emphasis in the clinical bereavement literature on the importance of emotional expression in grief work. It may be less a question of overt grief expression and more a question of whether the bereaved engages in excessive avoidance of thoughts pertaining to the death and its implications that are appraised as too threatening to contemplate that defines failure to engage in grief work. Consistent with this, cognitive behavior therapy approaches involving interventions that counteract avoidance through imagery and in vivo exposure to reminders of the death have been shown to be effective in the treatment of complicated grief (Shear, Frank, Houck, & Reynolds, 2005).

WHAT NEEDS TO BE RELINQUISHED AND WHAT CAN BE CONTINUED?

Recognizing that the goal of grief work is not tantamount to detachment, it is then possible to shift from a unidimensional focus on whether to relinquish or continue a bond to a more nuanced perspective addressing what needs to be relinquished and what can be continued. Major adjustments are required in adapting to the death of a significant other; one of these involves a change in the nature of the relationship with the deceased. Furthermore, such adjustment takes time that entails a period of disequilibrium in the process of constructing a new life. In referring to mourning as a *psychosocial transition*, Parkes (1988) addressed how the loss of a loved one, such as the death of a spouse, requires the bereaved to readjust his or her assumptive world in coming to terms with the death:

> The death of a spouse invalidates assumptions that penetrate many aspects of life, from the moment of rising to going to sleep in an empty bed. Habits of action (setting the table for two) and thought ("I must ask my husband about that") must be revised if the survivor is to live as a widow. (p. 56)

Grief work is the means through which such revision takes place. This psychosocial transition involves both deconstruction and reconstruction. *Deconstruction* requires accommodation of expectancies, beliefs, and goals linked with the attachment to the deceased, including the relinquishment of the attachment as it was, in line with the new life situation. *Reconstruction* involves the construction of a new meaningful life that can include a new relationship with the deceased based on acceptance that the bond is an exclusively internal connection.

Therese Rando's (1993) phase model perspective on adaptation to bereavement as presented in her comprehensive volume *Treatment of Complicated Mourning* captures this process of deconstruction and reconstruction in successful adaptation to bereavement that encompasses both relinquishing and continuing aspects of attachment to the deceased. Her work is a good example of a prominent bereavement theorist who has been categorized as a relinquishment theorist (e.g., Silverman & Klass, 1996; Stroebe & Schut, 2005).

In incorporating both relinquishment and CB facets into her phasic model of mourning, Rando (1993) nicely articulated the complexity of CB to adjustment. In the *confrontation* phase, which occurs at an early point after the death, the bereaved must emotionally confront the death and relinquish the goal of maintaining the relationship with the deceased as it existed prior to the loss:

> All the needs, feelings, thoughts, memories, behavior and interaction patterns, hopes, wishes, fantasies, dreams, assumptions, expectation, and beliefs—and feelings associated with them—must be revived and re-experienced, if not in actuality, then in memory. In this way, the emotional charge of each is defused a little each time, and the affect accompanying it lessens in intensity. This causes the ties to loosen. (Rando, 1993, p. 50)

The process of working through described in this passage is similar to Freud's (1917/1957) description of grief work. In fact, it would be easy to equate Rando's position with that of Freud as a relinquishment theorist if one did not look beyond her confrontation phase.

Rando (1993) identified the development of a new relationship with the deceased as part of the final, *accommodation* phase of mourning. She regards the development of a healthy new relationship with the deceased as opposed to relinquishing the attachment as a component of successful adaptation. The central issue here is one of determining what an appropriate connection is, as opposed to whether to maintain a bond. Rando believes that a healthy relationship with the deceased is determined on the basis of two conditions. The first condition requires fully recognizing that the person is dead and the implications; the second condition is that the bond must not interfere with moving forward into a new life. It is not a question of whether a bond should simply be maintained or relinquished.

Rando (1993) identified a number of CB expressions frequently discussed in the bereavement literature that satisfy these two conditions. The use of the deceased as a reference point in decision making is an example of a healthy CB expression. It is considered healthy when a widow imagines how her deceased husband might have acted in a particular situation and uses this as an important source of information in deciding how she will respond. This is fully compatible with an orientation toward autonomy and independence that is required in successfully adjusting to the loss of her husband. If, however, the widow feels compelled to do things identically to how she imagines her husband would want her to act if he were living, thus allowing him to maintain power over her in the present despite the fact that he is dead, then this would no longer be adaptive. She has not met both conditions of a healthy CB. First, she has failed to recognize that her husband no longer has control over her; she has not recognized the implications of the death. Second, by abiding by the same conditions that existed when her husband was alive, she has not moved forward (Rando, 1993).

The legacy of the deceased is another widely discussed expression in the CB literature that Rando (1993) identified as healthy. This may involve awareness of the continuing positive influence of the deceased on the bereaved individual's current life through an internalization of what had been gained in the past relationship, including identification with the deceased person's values and ideals. Such an expression can be fully consistent with an acknowledgment of the reality of the death that helps the individual maintain continuity with the past in the context of moving into a new life.

Rando (1993) identified CB as an evolving relationship, as opposed to one that is fixed in the past. For example, someone who lost a parent in childhood may exhibit age-appropriate changes in his or her representation of the deceased in accord with his or her changing life situation. This may include a new appreciation for the deceased parent's positive influence at a later point in development, such as when the bereaved person becomes a parent. Again, this reconstructive memory perspective on CB articulated by Rando can be fully consistent with accepting the reality of the loss and does not need to interfere with the bereaved person's entry into a new life.

Rando's (1993) treatment of CB indicates that to classify her as a relinquishment theorist who regards detachment as the goal of mourning would be to misrepresent her. Her position on CB is consistent with psychoanalytic perspectives that emphasize internalization as a means for maintaining a bond with the deceased. For example, the contemporary ego psychoanalytic theorist Vaillant (1993) emphasized how individuals assimilate those whom they have loved through identification:

> With identification, we assimilate a person's real strengths and become our strength. We can also acknowledge the person's faults and leave those faults behind. . . . Identification enhances our capacity to gain self-esteem. Always, the aim of identification is to continue a relationship with another person by transferring the relationship from the outer to the inner world. (p. 352)

Identification as described here involves enrichment of the self through an inner connection with the deceased that at the same time respects a clear boundary between this inner relationship and the outer relationship that existed prior to the loss. In effect, it constitutes a healthy attachment that fully accepts the reality of the loss.

AN ATTACHMENT-THEORY-BASED PERSPECTIVE ON CONTINUING BONDS

Normative Changes in the Continuing Bond

My colleagues and I introduced an attachment-theory-based perspective on CB that is consistent with Rando (1993) in that it identifies CB as integral to successful adaptation to bereavement. It also is capable of distinguishing adaptive from maladaptive variants of CB expression (Field et al., 2005). Like Rando, Bowlby has been identified as a relinquishment theorist (e.g., Silverman & Klass, 1996). Again, a more accurate account of his perspective on CB is that he regards it as a question not of whether to relinquish or continue a bond but of the nature of the bond that distinguishes healthy from maladaptive adjustment to bereavement.

Bowlby (1980) identified healthy mourning as occurring when an individual accepts "both that a change has occurred in his external world and that he is required to make corresponding changes in his internal, representational world and to *reorganize* [italics added], and perhaps reorient, his attachment behavior accordingly" (p. 18). Noteworthy here is his focus on reorganization and not detachment as the outcome of successful adaptation to bereavement.

Reorganization toward full acknowledgment of the permanence of the loss is a gradual and emotionally painful process. According to attachment theory, individuals possess an innate goal-corrected behavioral system to seek physical proximity to an individual who helps reinstate a sense of safety in situations of perceived danger (Bowlby, 1969). The attachment system is activated in the context of separation, including separation through the death of a loved one. Because this behavioral system does not distinguish separation from loss, in regarding loss as a temporary condition it treats death as reversible early on in the course of bereavement.

Search-related behavior that is commonly reported in the early period following the death reflects this attachment–system-based goal of attempting to recover the deceased. Hallucinations and illusions of the deceased and the urge to visit places formerly frequented by the deceased reflect this (Bowlby, 1980; Parkes, 1998). Maintaining the deceased's possessions exactly as they were prior to the death also may reveal the expectation and hope that he or she will return. These CB expressions reflect a working model of attachment to the deceased that as yet has not assimilated the reality of the death. Bowlby (1980) emphasized that these expressions are understandable early on after a death as a natural response to separation and thus should not be interpreted as pathological.

Because these searching attempts to find the deceased are met with failure, they are disorganizing in that they no longer are effective strategies for regaining physical proximity in the changed environment, the way they were prior to the death (Main, Goldwyn, & Hesse, 2002). Repeated failed attempts to reestablish physical proximity to the deceased lead to a gradual revising of the working model of attachment to the deceased in order to accommodate the reality of the permanence of the physical separation. This revision process is contingent on the bereaved person's ability to endure the emotional pain of recognizing the irrevocability of the loss. In other words, the bereaved must engage in grief work in a similar fashion to that described by Freud (1917/1957). Termination of search behavior in having accepted the impossibility of finding the deceased is therefore an essential requirement in successful adaptation to bereavement.

Even though the goal of reestablishing physical proximity to the deceased needs to be surrendered, this is not the same as saying that the bereaved must relinquish the attachment. Through internalization it is possible to establish proximity to the deceased at the mental representational level, or *psychological proximity*, while fully accepting the irrevocability of the loss (Field et al., 2005). This is shown in the continued use of the attachment system functions of *safe haven* and *secure base* in the relationship with the deceased, despite the impossibility of regaining physical proximity. For example, the bereaved can make use of the deceased as a safe haven in evoking an internal image of his or her comforting presence when under duress. Similarly, the deceased can function as a secure base in serving as an important reference point when making important autonomy-promoting decisions. Because safe haven and secure base are functional criteria that define an attachment bond, their effective continued use after the death indicates how CB is integral to healthy adjustment to bereavement (Field et al., 2005).

The Continuing Bond in Unresolved Loss

Bowlby (1980) believed that under certain conditions, such as the death of a parent in childhood or a violent death, and for individuals who are anxiously attached, the death can be so emotionally overwhelming that grief work is blocked. This is an extreme form of avoidance in which the implications of the death are defensively excluded from experience (Bowlby, 1973). In effect, thoughts and feelings related to the loss may become dissociated, or split off, thus operating as *segregated systems* (Bowlby, 1980, p. 345). Bowlby's concept of segregated systems was inspired by Hilgard's (1973) neodissociative perspective on multiple executive processing systems to explain information processing outside of awareness during hypnosis. In line with Hilgard, Bowlby proposed that individuals are best characterized as possessing multiple self systems and that the extent to which these self systems are integrated into an overarching executive organization differs from person to person. To the degree that such systems have restricted communication with one another, they are understood as segregated.

The involvement of segregated systems may account for how the bereaved may oscillate between a brief, keen sense of the deceased as permanently gone in one state of mind and in another state of mind has a sense of the deceased's presence in a way that indicates a failure to acknowledge the reality of the death. It can also explain the defensive use of a given state to exclude aspects of experience linked to a different self system, such as in using CB to exclude the painful reality of the loss from awareness.

The more recent attachment literature on disorganized attachment following loss, or *unresolved loss*, identifies such integration failure indicative of segregated systems (Hesse, Main, Abrams, & Rifkin, 2003). This has implications for understanding the maladaptive use of CB expressions (for a more in-depth discussion, see Field, 2006b). An individual is classified as having unresolved loss if he or she shows marked lapses in reasoning or incoherencies in discourse when discussing previous losses in the Adult Attachment Interview (AAI; Main et al., 2002). The AAI is an extensive semistructured interview that inquires about the respondent's relationships with his or her parents and other attachment figures when growing up and their effect on later years. It also inquires about previous traumas and losses. A prominent discourse marker of a lapse in reasoning when discussing prior losses involves a statement that implies disbelief that the other is dead. This type of lapse in reasoning involves a failure to recognize that what is stated cannot be true in the external world—namely, that a person cannot be both dead and alive at the same time (Main, 1991). In the context of bereavement, it is reflected in the failure to distinguish the past versus present relationship with the deceased and failure to acknowledge the permanence of the physical separation.

An example of a lapse in reasoning indicative of disbelief that the other is dead was provided by Turton, Hughes, Fonagy, and Fainman (2004) in their study of unresolved loss after stillbirth. The following statement made by one of the mothers who had lost her child through stillbirth 3 years previously was enough to classify her as having unresolved loss: "I used to go to the cemetery every day because I felt that if I didn't then she would feel like I didn't care about her any more. But she knows we're getting married on her birthday" (Turton et al., 2004, p. 246). This statement implies that the baby is still alive with needs that must be attended to and thus denotes failure to register the reality of the loss. This example also reflects a lapse in metacognitive monitoring in failing to appreciate the contradiction between a segregated mental representation of her child as conscious with her dominant executive function knowledge that her child is dead (Main, 1991). To the degree that such CB expressions serve as a defense against the emotional pain of the loss that interferes with the grief work task of achieving a unified working model of the attachment that fully accommodates the death, they can be said to be maladaptive.

The empirical findings in the AAI literature on the negative consequences of unresolved loss have focused on its intergenerational effects. Although this research has not directly addressed the relationship between unresolved loss and complicated grief symptoms, the findings on the intergenerational effects of unresolved loss nevertheless provide indirect support for its maladaptive psychological consequences. Because CB expressions that indicate disbelief that the other is dead, such as the example just provided in Turton et al.'s (2004) study of grief after stillbirth, are a prominent indicator of unresolved loss, the AAI empirical literature on unresolved loss has important implications for understanding maladaptive CB. There is evidence, replicated across a number of studies, that mothers with unresolved loss assessed in the AAI are more likely to have a young child with disorganized attachment (van IJzendoorn, 1995). Disorganized attachment, as expressed at the behavioral level in the 1- to 2-year-old child, is shown in the child's behavior on reunion with the mother in the Strange Situation procedure (Ainsworth, Blehar, Waters, & Wall, 1978). Here, the mother is separated from her child for a few minutes, and the child's behavior is examined over the period from when the mother leaves the room to when she is reunited with her child. When the mothers reentered the room, some children showed bizarre behavior toward them that indicated an approach–avoidance conflict, such as freezing, appearing dazed, or rapidly shifting between moving toward and moving away from the mothers (Main & Solomon, 1990). In effect, these children appeared to lack a coherent strategy for responding to their attachment figures under the attachment system activating condition of prior separation from their mothers.

There is mounting evidence that mothers with unresolved loss exhibit momentary "frightened and frightening" behavior toward their children when interacting with them in free-play situations (for a review, see Hesse et al., 2003). It is believed that activation of traumatic memories from past losses, evoked when interacting with the child, may lead to brief episodes of dissociative behavior in the mother that is frightening to the child. The child is thus placed in an unresolvable dilemma because the mother is both the source of fear as well as the attachment figure whom the child turns to for protection when afraid. In effect, the child is left with no coherent attachment strategy, which is considered an explanation for his or her disorganized behavior in the Strange Situation procedure. Because disorganized attachment in early childhood is predictive of later psychological problems, including maladaptive controlling behavior toward the parent in middle childhood (George & Solomon, 1996) and dissociation at age 16 (Carlson, 1998), these findings highlight the potential long-term psychological consequences of unresolved loss through its detrimental impact on the quality of parents' caregiving.

IMPLICATIONS OF UNRESOLVED LOSS FOR ASSESSING MALADAPTIVE CONTINUING BOND EXPRESSIONS

The attachment literature on unresolved loss has important implications for defining maladaptive CB on the basis of disbelief that the other is dead. This literature suggests that the failure to maintain a clear boundary between the living and dead, such that the experience of CB is segregated from the knowledge that the other is dead, is the key factor in determining whether a CB expression indicates unresolved loss.

It follows from this perspective that the relationship between CB and adaptation to bereavement is complex. Early after the death, search-related CB expressions that indicate failure to acknowledge the reality of the loss are assumed to be relatively common and not necessarily maladaptive. However, in the normative course of bereavement there should be a noteworthy reduction over time in the use of such expressions as a consequence of working through the loss. Therefore, the continued use of search-related CB expressions well after the death indicates failure in reorganization and therefore should be associated with indexes of maladaptive adjustment. On the other hand, CB expressions more indicative of internalization should be related to successful adaptation. In effect, type of CB expression should be an important factor in distinguishing adaptive versus maladaptive CB at a later point after the death.

With regard to the normative course of CB, no systematic longitudinal research has assessed reduction in search-related CB expressions over time. Research on search-related CB expressions has been largely devoted to examining the incidence of experiencing the deceased's presence without directly focusing on the frequency of such experiences as a function of time since the death. Across a number of studies, a significant percentage of bereaved have reported having experienced a sense of the deceased's presence at some point after the death (Haraldsson, 1988–1989). However, because in many cases these sensing experiences occurred years before the research was conducted, memory bias effects are of serious concern in drawing conclusions on the basis of these results. Furthermore, given the phrasing of the question in which participants were typically asked whether they had experienced a sense of the deceased's presence, with no clarification offered by the investigator as to what was meant by this, it is ambiguous as to whether search-related hallucinatory experiences versus a more memory-based subjective sense of the other was being assessed.

As part of an in-progress research project toward developing and validating a comprehensive CB self-report measure, in a preliminary analysis I have obtained some support for a reduction in search-related CB expressions as a function of time since the death. This measure assesses the extent to which the bereaved have experienced each of a broad range of CB expressions during the past month. This measure was recently administered to a large sample of undergraduate students who had lost someone through death during the previous 5 years. Controlling for the strength of the attachment in the previous relationship with the deceased, those who had lost someone within the previous 6 months reported significantly greater use of searching–phase-related CB expressions involving illusions (e.g., "Even if only momentarily, I have mistaken other sounds for the deceased's voice, footsteps, or movement") and hallucinations (e.g., "I actually saw the deceased stand before me") than for those in which the loss occurred more than 6 months previously. On the other hand, time was not a significant factor in the extent of use of CB expressions that were more indicative of reorganization involving the legacy of the deceased (e.g., "I thought about the positive influence of the deceased on who I am today"). Thus, a significant interaction was found between time since the death and type of CB expression. Given that the items assessing illusions and hallucinations used in this study are less ambiguously related to the searching phase relative to the sense of presence items used in previous research, these results provide initial support for the multidimensional nature of CB with respect to the normative course of their expression.

In future work on the normative course of CB expression it will be important to use a longitudinal design involving multiple waves of data collection beginning at a point early after the death. Because CB expressions associated with the searching phase may be short lived and scarce after the first month or two following the death, it would be essential to assess the bereaved individual early after the death to identify the presence of and changes over time in these CB expressions. Multiple waves of data collection would provide a means for conducting growth curve analyses assessing the trajectory of change for different types of CB expression.

Although search-related CB expressions may be relatively common early in bereavement and not a sign of maladaptive functioning, their presence later after the death may indicate poor adjustment. It therefore follows that at some point after the death, the type of CB expression may be an important indicator of whether the bereaved has adapted successfully to the loss. My colleagues and I found preliminary support for this (Field, Nichols, Holen, & Horowitz, 1999). Specifically, greater use of CB expressions assumed to be more closely aligned with an attempt to regain physical proximity, involving excessive use of special possessions of the deceased for comfort or failure to sort through his or her possessions at 7 months postloss predicted more severe concurrent grief and less of a decrease in grief-specific symptoms over 25 months postloss. In contrast, a CB expression assumed to be more characteristic of the ability to maintain a bond through psychological proximity, involving comfort through fond memories, was not predictive of poor adjustment. More recently, however, Boelen, Stroebe, Schut, and Zijerveld (2006) failed to replicate this. They found that comfort through memories was also predictive of less of a reduction in grief over time. This may reflect the fact that excessive involvement in any form of CB expression at a later point after the death may be maladaptive such that extent of involvement apart from type of involvement may be important in its own right (Field, Gal-Oz, & Bonanno, 2003).

In future research, it will be important to use a more comprehensive set of CB expressions that include those associated with the searching phase, including hallucinations and illusions, and those that are congruent with reorganization. These measures ideally would be administered in repeated waves of data collection from early after the death along with repeated measures of adjustment. This type of longitudinal design would provide a means for identifying possible causal relationships between these two sets of variables via path analytic methods and thereby determine whether certain CB expressions are simply correlates of bereavement-related symptoms or in fact moderate changes in symptoms over time.

Although type of CB expression may be a factor in identifying CB expressions that indicate unresolved loss, a more in-depth assessment may be needed beyond simply determining whether the bereaved individual makes use of a given CB expression. For example, the sense of the deceased as a comforting presence who is always there in the background involves a more internalized memory-based sense of the other that is consistent with the full appreciation that the other is dead. If the bereaved individual has metacognitive awareness of the sense of presence as a subjective state as opposed to an external reality independent of his or her subjectivity, it is not segregated in that a clear boundary is maintained between the living and dead. On the other hand, a more concrete or literal sense of the deceased's presence at a point well after the death, such as hallucinations of the deceased that indicate dissociation, would be evidence for unresolved loss.

Similarly, continued involvement with the deceased's possessions may or may not indicate unresolved loss. Certainly, maintaining the deceased's possessions exactly as when alive at a point well after the death suggests an underlying fantasy of his or her continuing existence and eventual return. Bowlby (1980, p. 151) provided a clinical case example to illustrate this involving a woman treated for anxiety and depression precipitated by the death over a year before of her elderly father following an unsuccessful medical procedure. She continued to insist that his place not be redecorated given her belief that the hospital had mistaken the identity of the man who died and that her father was still alive and would eventually return. Her awareness of the tenuousness of her belief was shown in the fact that she did not share it with others, knowing that they would laugh at her. Keeping these beliefs about the deceased private insulated her from revising such ideas in light of the kind of questioning response that she would be likely to receive from her family and others. In effect, such refusal to disclose served as a defense against the full realization of the reality of her father's death. Thus, the death remained unintegrated through the defensive use of the deceased's possessions as an attempt to maintain a CB via the fantasy of regaining physical proximity to the deceased. This is very different from simply keeping a few keepsakes of the deceased in memory of him or her.

It is important to take into account the bereaved person's religious and cultural beliefs regarding life after death in determining whether a given CB expression indicates unresolved loss (see also chaps. 7, 10, and 16, this volume). Belief in the continuing existence of the deceased's spirit and expectation of being eventually reunited with the deceased in heaven would not be considered evidence for unresolved loss as long as a boundary is maintained between the relationship with the deceased as it existed prior to the loss and as currently maintained. For example, in the Japanese ancestor worship ritual a clear line is drawn between the land of the living and land of the dead. During the ritual, the bereaved steps into the land of the dead in evoking the deceased's presence by positioning him- or herself at the home altar, clapping hands, and lighting candles (Goss & Klass, 2005). At the close of the ritual, the bereaved bows out and steps back into the world of the living.

A study conducted by Yamamoto, Okonogi, Iwasaki, and Yoshimura (1969) identifying the importance of ancestor worship in the mourning process among Japanese widows nicely illustrates this distinction between a CB that recognizes this boundary between the living and dead and a CB expression that does not. These widows reported a sense of connection with their husbands during the ritual and found it helpful in coping with their loss. This culturally prescribed deliberative ritual enactment entails a clear boundary between stepping into and out of the worlds of the dead and the living, respectively. This is in marked contrast to other experiences reported by the same widows involving unbidden illusions of their deceased husbands' voices or footsteps, or brief searching attempts to regain physical proximity to them, such as in one widow's going to the streetcar stop at the time her husband previously returned from work as if to meet him. These latter CB expressions are more clearly segregated, or dissociated, in representing search attempts implying that the husband is still alive. Because these widows had lost their husbands within the previous 3 months, and given the fact that the deaths were unexpected, it is not surprising that they were unresolved in their grief at this early point after the death. These CB expressions indicative of unresolved loss presumably will recede in the next few months, whereas the same will not hold true for the widows' continuing involvement in the ancestor ritual.

FUTURE DIRECTIONS

The lapse in reasoning involving disbelief that the other is dead is only one among a number of criteria that are used to classify unresolved loss in the AAI. Although this type of lapse in reasoning is a prominent marker for unresolved loss, the extent to which this criterion contributes to the findings in the literature on unresolved loss is not known. Therefore, no definitive conclusions can be drawn as to the implications of these findings on unresolved loss for the maladaptive nature of CB expressions indicating disbelief that the other is dead.

The challenge, then, is how to develop a CB measure that is capable of identifying CB expressions that indicate failure to integrate the loss from those that are integral to successful adaptation. This may entail going beyond the use of standard self-report measures that typically simply ask about the extent of use of a given CB expression without further enquiry. I have recently developed an interview-based CB measure that attempts to accomplish this (Field, 2006a). This measure is informed by the work in the attachment literature on the lapse in reasoning implying disbelief that the other is dead as an important indicator of unresolved loss. For example, in assessing the sense of the deceased's presence, one item asks, "In the past month, did you ever have a sense of [deceased's] presence—the sense that s/he knew what you were doing, watched you, or even guided you as if invisibly present?" Thus, beyond simply determining how often the bereaved experienced the deceased's presence during the previous month, additional information is sought to distinguish whether the experience is characterized as more of a subjective or inner sense of the deceased as opposed to experiencing him or her as an external conscious being. The respondent is asked to first describe his or her experience. This provides a basis for content-analyzing the discourse in terms of whether the sense of presence is identified more as an inner sense of the other that is more akin to internalization or as a more paranormal experience of the deceased. He or she is then asked,

> Would you describe this as occurring at a specific location and time— such as sensing his/her presence in the bedroom, at a particular restaurant, or while watching a TV program—or is it more a general sense of him/her as always there in the background?

If the sense of presence of the deceased is more externalized, then this is more likely to be experienced as occurring at a specific place and time. Further questions include "Did you believe s/he was aware of you?" and "Did these experiences involve actually seeing, hearing, feeling, or smelling [deceased]? If so, which sensory modes were involved?" The aim is to obtain sufficient information on the nature of the sense of presence experience to be able to identify whether it implies disbelief that the other is dead, which indicates unresolved loss, in a way that is not possible when simply relying on a single-item measure, which has typically been the case in previous research.

This CB (Field, 2006a) measure is currently being used in a study comparing widows with and without a diagnosis of complicated grief who lost their husband between 1 and 2 years previously. This study thus involves an in-depth investigation of the nature of CB expression in persons with clinically significant levels of grief-specific symptoms. The aim is to highlight the aforementioned complex relationship between CB and adjustment to bereavement. The AAI is also being administered to the same group of women to determine whether those with complicated grief are more likely to be classified as having unresolved loss and to assess the relationship between unresolved loss as identified in the AAI and that identified via the interview-based CB measure.

CONCLUSIONS

There has been a tendency among proponents of the CB perspective on bereavement to oversimplify its relation to adjustment and to misrepresent and summarily categorize as relinquishment theorists those such as Rando (1993) and Bowlby (1980), who have underscored its complex relation to adjustment. This may at stem at least in part from a tendency to conflate grief work with a relinquishment of the bond in failing to distinguish grief work as a mechanism for integrating the death from its goal, which need not necessarily entail relinquishing the bond. In contrast to the Freudian perspective, in which object ties are regarded as secondary to drive expression and therefore more substitutable when no longer available to serve as an object for gratification, object relational psychoanalytic approaches and attachment perspectives that emphasize the fundamental relatedness of human beings are more oriented toward preserving as opposed to relinquishing attachment following the death of a significant other. Therefore, in the latter approaches the emphasis is on reorganization rather than detachment as the main goal of grief work. Through internalization, it is possible to maintain a bond with the deceased that at the same time fully acknowledges the ending of the physical bond as it existed prior to the death. CB expressions that indicate internalization are therefore seen as integral to successful adaptation to bereavement. On the other hand, CB expressions that fail to acknowledge the reality of the loss are maladaptive in that they constitute defensive efforts that interfere with grief work. Indirect support for the maladaptive consequences of the latter is shown in the findings in the attachment literature on the detrimental impact of unresolved loss on caregiving that results in disorganized attachment in the child. Because the focus of the AAI literature on unresolved loss has been on its transgenerational effects, with no attempt to examine its relation to a descriptive diagnosis of complicated grief, it will be important for future work to address this; specifically, it will be important to introduce a CB measure that is capable of assessing CB expressions that indicate failure to acknowledge the reality of the death and to demonstrate their relation to complicated grief while also showing that CB expressions that are integrated with full appreciation of the permanence of the loss are associated with successful mourning. In a recent review of the literature, Stroebe and Schut (2005) pointed out how methodological limitations in the existing empirical literature on CB preclude any clear conclusions as to its adaptiveness. In particular, they noted how the results of existing CB studies do not provide a basis for determining whether CB is simply a facet or correlate of grief symptoms or whether in fact it plays a causal role in adjustment to bereavement. In this context, Stroebe and Schut advocated the use of longitudinal research designs that are capable of assessing the directionality of the relationship between CB and measures of adjustment. However, as I have attempted to elucidate in this chapter, beyond the use of appropriate research designs it is essential to define and operationalize CB in a way that captures the complexity of its relation to bereavement-related adaptation. It is only in doing so that it will be possible to gain a full understanding of the function of CB in adjustment to the death of a loved one.

REFERENCES

Ainsworth, M. D. S., Blehar, M. C., Waters, E., & Wall, S. (1978). *Patterns of attachment: A psychological study of the Strange Situation.* Hillsdale, NJ: Erlbaum.

Attig, T. (2000). *The heart of grief*. New York: Oxford University Press.

Boelen, P. A., Stroebe, M. S., Schut, H. A. W., & Zijerveld, A. M. (2006). Continuing bonds and grief: A prospective analysis. *Death Studies, 30*, 767–776.

Bonanno, G. A., & Kaltman, S. (1999). Toward an integrative perspective on bereavement. *Psychological Bulletin, 125*, 760–776.

Bonanno, G. A., & Keltner, D. (1997). Facial expressions of emotion and the course of conjugal bereavement. *Journal of Abnormal Psychology, 106*, 126–137.

Bowlby, J. (1969). *Attachment and loss: Vol. 1. Attachment*. New York: Basic Books.

Bowlby, J. (1973). *Attachment and loss: Vol. 2. Separation: Anxiety and anger*. New York: Basic Books.

Bowlby, J. (1980). *Attachment and loss: Vol. 3. Loss: Sadness and depression*. New York: Basic Books.

Carlson, F. A. (1998). A prospective longitudinal study of disorganized/disorientated attachment. *Child Development, 69*, 1107–1128.

Davis, C. G., Wortman, C. B., Lehman, D. R., & Silver, R. C. (2000). Searching for meaning in loss: Are clinical assumptions correct? *Death Studies, 24*, 497–540.

Eagle, M. N. (1987). *Recent developments in psychoanalysis*. Cambridge, MA: Harvard University Press.

Fialkow, N. J., & Muslin, H. L. (1987). Working through: A cornerstone of psychotherapy. *American Journal of Psychotherapy, 41*, 443–452.

Field, N. P. (2006a). *Continuing Bonds Interview*. Unpublished measure.

Field, N. P. (2006b). Unresolved loss and the continuing bond to the deceased. *Death Studies, 30*, 739–756.

Field, N. P., Gal-Oz, E., & Bonanno, G. A. (2003). Continuing bonds and adjustment at 5 years after the death of a spouse. *Journal of Consulting and Clinical Psychology, 71*, 1–8.

Field, N. P., Gao, B., & Paderna, L. (2005). Continuing bonds in bereavement: An attachment theory based perspective. *Death Studies, 29*, 1–23.

Field, N. P., Nichols, C., Holen, A., & Horowitz, M. J. (1999). The relation of continuing attachment to adjustment in conjugal bereavement. *Journal of Consulting and Clinical Psychology, 67*, 212–218.

Fraley, R. C., & Shaver, P. R. (1999). Loss and bereavement: Bowlby's theory and recent controversies concerning grief work and the nature of detachment. In J. Cassidy & R. R. Shaver (Eds.), *Handbook of attachment theory and research* (pp. 735–759). New York: Guilford Press.

Freud, S. (1957). Mourning and melancholia. In J. Strachey (Ed. & Trans.), *The standard edition of the complete psychological works of Sigmund Freud* (pp. 152–170). London: Hogarth Press. (Original work published 1917)

George, C., & Solomon, J. (1996). Representational models of relationships: Links between caregiving and attachment. *Infant Mental Health Journal, 17*, 198–216.

Goss, R. E., & Klass, D. (2005). *Dead but not lost: Grief narratives in religious traditions*. New York: Altamira Press.

Greenberg, J. R., & Mitchell, S. A. (1983). *Object relations in psychoanalytic theory*. Cambridge, MA: Harvard University Press.

Haraldsson, E. (1988–1989). Survey of claimed encounters with the dead. *Omega: The Journal of Death and Dying, 19*, 103–113.

Hesse, E., Main, M., Abrams, K., & Rifkin, A. (2003). Unresolved states regarding loss or abuse can have "second-generation" effects: Disorganization, role inversion, and frightening ideation in the offspring of traumatized, non-maltreating parents. In M. Solomon & D. Siegel (Eds.), *Healing trauma: Attachment, mind, body, and brain* (pp. 57–106). New York: Norton.

Hilgard, E. (1973). A neodissociation interpretation of pain reduction in hypnosis. *Psychological Review, 80*, 396–411.

Horowitz, M. J., (1986). *Stress response syndromes*. Northvale, NJ: Jason Aronson.

Horowitz, M. J. (1991). Person schemas. In M. J. Horowitz (Ed.), *Person schemas and maladaptive interpersonal patterns* (pp. 13–31). Chicago: University of Chicago Press.

Juri, L. J., & Marrone, M. (2003). Attachment and bereavement. In M. Cortina & M. Marrone (Eds.), *Attachment theory and the psychoanalytic process* (pp. 242–267). London: Whurr.

Klass, D., Silverman, P., & Nickman, S. L. (Eds.). (1996). *Continuing bonds: New understandings of grief*. Washington, DC: Taylor & Francis.

Klass, D., & Walter, T. (2001). Processes of grieving: How bonds are continued. In M. Stroebe, R. Hansson, W. Stroebe, & H. Schut (Eds.), *Handbook of bereavement research: Consequences, coping, and care* (pp. 431–448). Washington, DC: American Psychological Association.

Main, M. (1991). Metacognitive knowledge, metacognitive monitoring, and singular (coherent) vs. multiple (incoherent) models of attachment: Findings and directions for future research. In C. M. Parkes, J. Stevenson-Hinde, & P. Marris (Eds.), *Attachment across the life cycle* (pp. 127–159). London: Tavistock/Routledge.

Main, M., Goldwyn, R., & Hesse, E. (2002). *Adult attachment scoring and classification systems* (Version 7). Unpublished manual.

Main, M., & Solomon, J. (1990). Procedures for identifying infants as disorganized/disoriented during the Ainsworth Strange Situation. In M. T. Greenberg, D. Cicchetti, & E. M. Cummings (Eds.), *Attachment in the preschool years* (pp. 121–160). Chicago: University of Chicago Press.

Neimeyer, R. A. (2001). Reauthoring life narratives: Grief therapy as meaning reconstruction. *Israel Journal of Psychiatry and Related Sciences, 38*, 171–183.

Nolen-Hoeksema, S. (2001). Ruminative coping and adjustment to bereavement. In M. Stroebe, R. Hansson, W. Stroebe, & H. Schut (Eds.), *Handbook of bereavement research: Consequences, coping, and care* (pp. 545–562). Washington, DC: American Psychological Association.

Parkes, C. M. (1988). Bereavement as a psychosocial transition: Processes of adaptation to change. *Journal of Social Issues, 44*, 53–65.

Parkes, C. M. (1998). *Bereavement: Studies of grief in adult life* (3rd ed.). Harmondsworth, England: Pelican Books.

Rando, T. A. (1993). *Treatment of complicated grief*. Champaign, IL: Research Press.

Shear, K., Frank, E., Houck, P. R., & Reynolds, C. F. (2005). Treatment of complicated grief: A randomized controlled trial. *JAMA, 293*, 2601–2608.

Silverman, P. R., & Klass, D. (1996). Introduction: What's the problem? In D. Klass, P. R. Silverman, & S. Nickman (Eds.), *Continuing bonds: New understandings of grief* (pp. 3–27). Washington, DC: Taylor & Francis.

Stroebe, M., Gergen, M., Gergen, K., & Stroebe, W. (1992). Broken hearts or broken bonds? *American Psychologist, 47*, 1205–1212.

Stroebe, M., & Schut, H. (2005). To continue or relinquish bonds: A review of consequences for the bereaved. *Death Studies, 29*, 477–494.

Turton, P., Hughes, P., Fonagy, P., & Fainman, D. (2004). An investigation into the possible overlap between PTSD and unresolved responses following stillbirth: An absence of linkage with only unresolved status predicting infant disorganization. *Attachment and Human Development, 6*, 241–253.

Vaillant, G. E. (1993). *The wisdom of the ego*. Cambridge, MA: Harvard University Press.

van IJzendoorn, M. H. (1995). Adult attachment representations, parental responsiveness, and infant attachment: A meta-analysis on the predictive validity of the Adult Attachment Interview. *Psychological Bulletin, 117*, 387–403.

Wortman, C. B., & Silver, R. C. (1989). The myths of coping with loss. *Journal of Consulting and Clinical Psychology, 57*, 349–357.

Yamamoto, J., Okonogi, K., Iwasaki, T., & Yoshimura, S. (1969). Mourning in Japan. *American Journal of Psychiatry, 125*, 1661–65.

7

THE MEASUREMENT OF GRIEF: PSYCHOMETRIC CONSIDERATIONS IN THE ASSESSMENT OF REACTIONS TO BEREAVEMENT

ROBERT A. NEIMEYER, NANCY S. HOGAN, AND ANNA LAURIE

When Chantay's cousin, Demarcus, was shot and killed one night on a street in the "wrong part of town," some people in her family regarded the event as sadly inevitable. For the past few years he had been spending more and more time with a bad crowd, getting into drugs and trouble with the law and drifting farther away from family, despite his mother's attempt to hold on to the "good boy" she had raised. Perhaps because she had been brought up in the same tight extended family with Demarcus, Chantay's grief following the traumatic phone call informing her of his death was acute—at an emotional level, she felt like she had lost a brother. Although the family and African American community pulled together at the time of the funeral, Chantay found herself struggling with the unreal sense of the loss in the months that followed as the family adopted a code of silence about the death. Likewise, she struggled with the perception that she, as the oldest daughter, needed to be strong and not disclose her personal distress or the terrifying images of the shooting that so often came at night. What was more confusing was that Chantay's White college roommate kept encouraging her to open up about her feelings, in contradiction to her community's unspoken rule not to share family business with outsiders. For Chantay, however, the religious platitudes she received from family when she did raise the issue of Demarcus's death were unsatisfying, although she did find some genuine solace in prayer.

At age 64, Sau-Chu was stricken with both grief and guilt when her husband died after a prolonged struggle with cancer. Her guilt stemmed from what she viewed as the ultimate cause of his death—her insistence that they purchase a surprisingly affordable and spacious apartment near a hillside cemetery in their crowded city of Hong Kong, an "unlucky" location that disrupted the feng shui of their new home, into which they had moved only a few months before he grew ill. Sau-Chu's gnawing remorse was compounded by her failure to be by her husband's hospital bed at the moment of his death, despite her diligent attendance for many nights before. On seeing him when called in by hospital staff, Sau-Chu was further pained to see his half-open mouth—a clear sign that he had died with important words unspoken, perhaps because she had not been there to hear them. As a result, she was not surprised that he refused to "visit" her through making an appearance in her home or in her dreams on the 7th day following his death, giving further evidence of his accusation of her for her failure as a wife. Barred, like other traditional Chinese widows, from family celebrations (birthdays, wedding parties) for the 1st year of her bereavement because of the bad luck she would presumably bring, Sau-Chu spent a good deal of time ruminating on her loss. It was not until her husband appeared in the form of a "patient cockroach" on the small altar she had prepared for him beneath his picture in the living room that she felt she was able to speak to him about her distress and her love for him and begin to feel consoled in her grief.

How adequately do existing research tools capture the important nuances of grief responses like those of Chantay and Sau-Chu, which represent their unique attempts to adapt to traumatic loss and widowhood, respectively? How much could conventional grief assessment instruments reveal about these two women's sources of possible complication and resilience for a counselor attempting to help them respond adaptively to their respective losses, if they were to reach out to the new bereavement services being developed for their communities? How well would these scales measure the most relevant outcomes of their therapies to provide evidence of their efficacy? Even more broadly, how valid and reliable are existing instruments for measuring the grief responses of the different cultural groups to which they could be applied? As has been recently emphasized in deliberations on evidence-based practice in psychology, "developing well normed measures that clinicians can use to quantify their diagnostic judgments, measure therapeutic progress over time, and assess the therapeutic process" (American Psychological Association, 2005, p. 14) is a crucial scientific and practical priority, as is understanding the cultural context of the patient and adapting services accordingly (American Psychological Association, 2005; see also chaps. 4 and 10, this volume). Thus, in this chapter we provide a brief review of several relatively established measures, building on a more extensive consideration of these scales; the appropriateness of using standard inventories targeting depression, anxiety, or general distress in the bereaved; and the role of qualitative research in elucidating bereavement responses that was published earlier (Neimeyer & Hogan, 2001). We then note several newly published scales and summarize evidence of their validity and reliability. Finally, we offer a few comments on how such measures are only now beginning to be adapted for use in various cultural and subcultural settings and the extent to which the assessment of adaptation to bereavement has moved toward greater psychometric rigor and sensitivity in recent years.

GENERAL-PURPOSE GRIEF SCALES

Literally dozens of measures of adaptation to loss have been proposed by various investigators, ranging from a few informal face-valid questions for use in a particular study to elaborate multidimensional scales comprising hundreds of items. Most focus on prominent grief-related symptomatology, including separation distress; disruption of social relationships; or incapacity to function in important life roles, such as in work or family settings. On occasion, however, they measure different constructs that are not reducible to grief per se, such as worrisome symptoms associated with other psychiatric disorders, or even positive adaptations to loss, such as personal growth. Whatever the content focus, each yields a measure of the frequency or intensity of certain responses to bereavement, as framed by the scale's author. As such, they are potentially useful in identifying particular vulnerabilities or (more rarely) strengths displayed by a given respondent, in making comparisons over time or across groups of bereaved persons and in evaluating the efficacy of grief therapy. They are, however, less sensitive than qualitative research in elucidating unique meanings and experiences that characterize particular bereaved individuals or groups (Neimeyer & Hogan, 2001). In this chapter, we consider 12 scales with sufficient psychometric backing to warrant continued research. Half of them represent general-purpose instruments for studying the grieving processes of most bereaved populations, and half are designed to shed light on particular processes or unique groups of mourners. For each measure we review, we consider issues pertaining to its design, format and scaling, and advantages and limitations, tabulating data on its internal consistency; test–retest reliability; convergent and discriminant validity; construct validity; and, where available, factorial validity. Finally, we note translations that facilitate the application of each scale to different cultural settings, and we briefly note 3 scales now in development that could contribute to the assessment of bereavement in the near future, in both research and clinical contexts.

Texas Revised Inventory of Grief

Instrument Description

The Texas Revised Inventory of Grief (TRIG; Faschingbauer, 1981) was designed to assess grief as a present emotion of longing, as an adjustment to a past life event with several stages, as a medical psychology outcome, and as a personal experience. As is true for most grief scales, its items were rationally developed on the basis of the literature on normative and atypical grief reactions. The TRIG includes subscales focusing on Past Behavior (8 items) and Present Feelings (13 items) whose items consist of simple declarative statements (e.g., "I found it hard to sleep after the person died"; "I can't avoid thinking about the person who died") to which the respondent replies on a 5-point Likert scale that ranges from *completely true* to *completely false*. Because Part I of the TRIG by definition should be invariant if respondents accurately report their reactions at the time of the death, Part II is the primary measure used in studies of changing grief symptomatology over time. Psychometric data for the TRIG and subsequent scales appear in Table 7.1. Versions of the scale are available in Hebrew, French, Dutch, Croatian, and Spanish.

Advantages and Limitations

The TRIG has the advantage of widespread adoption as a function of its 25-year history, which permits users to compare scores with numerous published studies. However, it is also fraught with disadvantages. Some investigators have criticized the TRIG for problems with item redundancy; extensive overlap with measures of depression; omission of more threatening symptoms associated with guilt, bitterness, and performance disruption; and the assumption that a comparison of scores on Parts I and II yields information on the respondent's progress through bereavement (Burnett, Middleton, Raphael, & Martinek, 1997; Hansson, Carpenter, & Fairchild, 1993; Prigerson et al., 1995). Despite these psychometric problems, the TRIG remains a commonly used instrument in the literature.

Grief Experience Inventory

Instrument Description

With 135 items, the Grief Experience Inventory (GEI; Sanders, Mauger, & Strong, 1985) is one of the longest bereavement instruments in widespread use, its content being derived from a review of the literature and informal observations of grieving persons. Items are phrased as simple sentences (e.g., "I feel restless"; "Looking at photographs of the deceased is too painful") to which the respondent answers "true" or "false." Following the style of

TABLE 7.1

Psychometric Properties of Best Established General-Purpose Measures of Grief

Criterion	Internal consistency (Cronbach's alpha)	Test–retest reliability	Convergent and discriminant validity[a]	Construct validity	Factorial validity
Texas Revised Inventory of Grief (TRIG; Pt. I: Past Behaviors)	.77–.87 (Faschingbauer, 1981), .78–.89 (Longman, 1993).				Exploratory factor analysis, with retention of items loading .40 (Faschingbauer, 1981).
TRIG (Pt. II: Present Feelings)	.69–.89 (Faschingbauer, 1981), .90–.93 (Longman, 1993).		.87 with Inventory of Complicated Grief (Prigerson et al., 1995).	Higher grief for intimate than for nonintimate relationships (Faschingbauer, 1981; Gilbar & Dagan, 1995).	Exploratory factor analysis, with retention of items loading .40 (Faschingbauer, 1981).
Grief Experience Inventory (GEI)	.34–.59 for validity scales, .52 to .84 for clinic.al scales (Sanders et al., 1985).	.53–.61 for validity scales, .71–.87 for clinical scales over 9 weeks; much lower over 18 months (Sanders et al., 1985).	.3–.5 with Minnesota Multiphasic Personality Inventory scales (Sanders et al., 1985).	Clinical scales discriminate between bereaved and non-bereaved groups and are higher for bereaved parents than spouses (Sanders et al., 1985). Clinical scores are higher for respondents indicating greater "trouble" with the death (Gamino et al., 1998).	Items grouped rationally, not empirically; factor analysis suggests three factors, with dominant one measuring depression (Sanders et al., 1985).

(continued)

TABLE 7.1

Psychometric Properties of Best Established General-Purpose Measures of Grief (*Continued*)

Criterion	Internal consistency (Cronbach's alpha)	Test–retest reliability	Convergent and discriminant validity[a]	Construct validity	Factorial validity
Core Bereavement Items	.91 (Burnett et al., 1997).		Not reported, although the larger set of items from which the Core Bereavement Items derived correlate with anxiety and depression (Byrne & Raphael, 1997).	Discriminates between bereaved parents > bereaved spouses > bereaved adult children; scores higher for unexpected than expected deaths; scores diminish over time (Middleton et al., 1998).	Items grouped by rational/empirical strategy into subscales reflecting images and thoughts, acute separation, and grief, but these scales are highly intercorrelated (Burnett et al., 1997).
Inventory of Complicated Grief (ICG)	.94 (Prigerson et al., 1995), .95 (Currier et al., 2006).	.80 over 6 months of bereavement (Prigerson et al., 1995).	.87 with TRIG Part II, but the ICG better discriminates good from poor outcome; .67 with depression (Prigerson et al., 1995).	ICG is associated with lower quality of life (Prigerson et al., 1995); predicts global functioning, mood, sleep quality, self-esteem 18 months after spousal loss (Prigerson et al., 1995).	ICG was refined through use of principal-components analysis combined with TETRAD II to produce a pure measure of complicated grief (Prigerson et al., 1995).
Hogan Grief Reaction Checklist (HGRC)	Consistent alphas demonstrated since development of measure. Representative values: Despair, .89; Detachment, .87; Disorganization,	.56–.85 over a 4-week interval with 65 undergraduate students who had experienced the death of a loved one (Hogan et al., 2001).	Positive correlations between HRGC grief process subscales and TRIG, GEI, and Impact of Events Scale (IES). Correlations higher with similar variables (e.g., HGRC Despair and GEI	Confirmatory factor analysis revealed good fit of model to data $\chi^2(155, N = 209) = 313.26$, SRMR = 0.05, CFI = .94. R^2 values range from .53 to .83. Discriminates groups by cause of death, time since death, and adaptive and maladaptive	Exploratory factor analysis from 586 bereaved adults revealed six subscales (Hogan et al., 2001). Confirmatory factor analysis revealed good fit of model to data with 209 bereaved parents (Hogan & Schmidt, 2002).

Measure				
	.84; Panic Behavior, .90; Blame and Anger, .79; Personal Growth, .82 (Hogan et al., 2001).		Despair, .60); higher correlations (.33–.46) with TRIG Present than TRIG Past (.13–.33). Higher correlations of grief process variables with IES Intrusion (.31–.62) than with IES Avoidance (.20–.30). Grief outcome variable (Personal Growth) negatively correlated with GEI subscales (–.19, Death Anxiety to –.50, Despair), TRIG (–.13, Present, –.39, Past), and IES (–.44 Intrusion, –.19 Avoidance; Hogan et al., 2001).	grief (Hogan & Schmidt, 2002).
Grief Evaluation Measure	.92 for Experiences subscale, .97 for Problems subscale (Jordan et al., 2005).	.97 for Experiences subscale, .88 for Problems subscale (Jordan et al., 2005).	Experiences subscale: .82 with ICG, .54–.65 with Impact of Event Scale—Revised (IES–R), .57–.76 with Treatment Outcome Package. Problems subscale: .74 with ICG, .72–.76 with IES–R, .78–.92 with TOP (Jordan et al., 2005).	Experiences and Problems subscales were predictive of ITG scores at 1 year ($r =$ .67/.68; Jordan et al., 2005). Good predictive validity for mourner adjustment 1 year after initial assessment (Jordan et al., 2005).

Note. Blank cells indicate that data were not reported for that category. SRMR = standardized root-mean-square residual; CFI = comparative fit index.
[a] *Convergent validity* refers to correlations with established measures of grief symptoms; *discriminant validity* refers to freedom from social desirability confounds.

the Minnesota Multiphasic Personality Inventory—2 (Butcher, Dahlstrom, Graham, Tellegen, & Kaemmer, 1989), items are clustered into three validity scales (Denial, Atypical Response, and Social Desirability) and nine rationally derived clinical scales (Despair, Anger/Hostility, Guilt, Social Isolation, Loss of Control, Rumination, Depersonalization, Somatization, and Death Anxiety). The GEI is available in Spanish as well as the original English.

Advantages and Limitations

Although the GEI assesses a broad range of grief responses, it does so unsystematically. In addition to the difficulties with factor structure and internal consistency, the GEI has been criticized for its true–false item formatting, extensive redundancy, and occasional use of the past tense, all of which reduce the instrument's sensitivity to changes in grief intensity over time (Burnett et al., 1997; Lev & McCorkle, 1993). Equally problematic is that responses of probable high relevance to grief (e.g., items bearing on sadness over the loss, missing the lost person, or crying at reminders; Burnett et al., 1997) are altogether missing. Nonetheless, the GEI continues to be used in both research and clinical settings.

Core Bereavement Items

Instrument Description

The brief Core Bereavement Items (CBI) scale represents a distillation of the Bereavement Phenomenology Questionnaire, whose 76 items were drawn from the literature by Burnett et al. (1997) to "provide a basis for the detailed description of the evolution of the overall bereavement response" (p. 52). The CBI contains 17 questions referring to commonly occurring symptoms (e.g., "Do you experience images of events surrounding 'x''s death?"; "Do you find yourself missing 'x'?"), which the respondent is instructed to answer on a 4-point scale of frequency. Japanese and Bosnian versions of the instrument are also available.

Advantages and Limitations

One possible advantage of the CBI is its explicit focus on common responses to loss that are likely to occur with some frequency in many cultural groups. Further validational work on the scale is needed, however, a point that is acknowledged by its authors (Burnett et al., 1997). Little is currently known about the CBI's relationship to broad-band scales of distress, its convergence with other measures of grieving, or its stability over even brief periods of time. In addition, its focus on core bereavement phenomena makes it best suited to the study of "normal" grief responses, rather than the more complicated or debilitating courses assessed by other instruments.

Inventory of Complicated Grief

Instrument Description

The Inventory of Complicated Grief (ICG) was constructed by Prigerson et al. (1995) to measure "symptoms of grief [that] form a unified component of emotional distress that is clearly distinguishable from the symptoms of depression and anxiety" (p. 66). Its revised and expanded form, the ICG–R, consists of 37 statements (e.g., "I have lost my sense of security or safety since the death of _____"; "I feel like the future holds no meaning or purpose without _____"), which the respondent endorses using a 5-point scale to reflect his or her experience over the past month (Prigerson & Jacobs, 2001). The ICG–R yields both a continuous score and a dichotomous complicated grief diagnosis, which has been found to have a sensitivity of .93 and a specificity of .93 in the detection of interview-determined complicated grief (Barry, Kasl, & Prigerson, 2002) using criteria being developed for inclusion in the fifth edition of the *Diagnostic and Statistical Manual of Mental Disorders* (Prigerson & Maciejewski, 2006). The ICG–R is the most extensively translated grief scale in current use, with versions in a dozen languages, including Spanish, French, Japanese, Dutch, and Arabic.

Advantages and Limitations

A great deal of research using the ICG has appeared over the past 7 years, providing considerable evidence supporting its validity and reliability. However, it is worth emphasizing that the ICG was designed to focus on symptoms that are pathognomic for a diagnosis of complicated grief or prolonged grief disorder and associated with adverse health and mental health outcomes.[1] As such, it underrepresents symptoms of normal grief and shares with all of the previous scales a concentration on bereavement-related distress rather than resilience. Therefore, it is best used in studies or assessment contexts in which problematic adaptation to loss is the focal concern. Moreover, its concentration on distinctive symptoms of complicated grief as a response to disrupted attachment (e.g., yearning, disbelief about the death, detachment from others)

---

[1]The nomenclature of problematic grief is evolving. The American Psychiatric Association's working group for formulating criteria for this diagnosis has been advocating moving from use of the term *complicated grief* toward the use of *prolonged grief disorder* to emphasize more strongly the role of chronicity of debilitating symptoms of grief, many of which would be normative if experienced in a more transitory fashion in the early months of loss. However, the ICG is likely to retain its current title in view of its long history of use in the literature.

means that it intentionally disregards other potentially worrisome symptoms (e.g., depressed mood, guilt, avoidance of traumatic stimuli) associated with other psychiatric disorders, a point acknowledged by the authors (see also chap. 8, this volume).

Hogan Grief Reaction Checklist

Instrument Description

The Hogan Grief Reaction Checklist (HGRC; Hogan, Greenfield, & Schmidt, 2001) is a 61-item questionnaire designed to assess the multidimensional nature of the bereavement process. Items were empirically developed through a qualitative analysis of bereaved adults' grief narratives and written texts and are phrased as declarative statements (e.g., "I ache with loneliness"; "I reached a turning point where I began to let go of some of my grief") that respondents endorse on a 5-point scale to describe their feelings over the past 2 weeks. The 61 items factor into six empirically derived subscales (Despair, 13 items; Detachment, 8 items; Disorganization, 8 items; Panic Behavior, 14 items; Blame and Anger, 7 items; and Personal Growth, 11 items). The HGRC has been translated into Spanish, Italian, Finnish, Turkish, French, and German.

Advantages and Limitations

The HGRC's validity and reliability are well documented. It has the additional distinction of assessing possible adaptive as well as maladaptive responses to loss with the inclusion of the Personal Growth factor. Although the HGRC subscales were developed to be treated as separate variables, researchers have successfully combined the five grief subscales (Despair, Detachment, Disorganization, Panic Behavior, and Blame and Anger) to form a composite of grief variable (Gamino, Sewell, & Easterling, 2000).

Grief Evaluation Measure

Instrument Description

The Grief Evaluation Measure (GEM; Jordan, Baker, Matteis, Rosenthal, & Ware, 2005) is a recently developed self-report scale used to assess an individual's risk of complicated mourning. It is unique in its intent to provide a comprehensive evaluation of clinically significant risk factors associated with complicated mourning trajectories, and it spans six sections: Section 1, sociodemographic information; Section 2, clinically relevant background factors (e.g., history of loss or major psychiatric disorder); Section 3, prior relationships and coping styles; Section 4, circumstances of the death (e.g., its cause, the respondent's level of involvement); Section 5, experiences since the death (e.g., psychological reactions, disruption of the assumptive world); and Section 6, subsequent problems (e.g., suicidal ideation, sleep disturbance). In addition, there is a free-response (i.e., open-ended) item for additional details and comments. The 58 items that comprise the centrally important "Experiences" portion (Section 5) have a broader focus than most symptom-oriented grief instruments, including statements such as "The professionals with whom I have dealt around the death . . . have not been helpful to me" and "I am doing a good job of learning how to live in the world without my loved one," with which the respondent indicates agreement on a 6-point scale. Psychometric data are available for this section and the 33-item "Problems" portion (Section 6), each of which can be administered separately from the entire GEM.

Advantages and Limitations

For a new measure, the two core sections (5 and 6) of the GEM have impressive reliability and predictive validity, in addition to convergence with established measures of clinical complication. Moreover, the nearly comprehensive scope of the instrument, combined with the opportunities it affords for narrative elaboration by the respondent, could provide a wealth of data for clinical users. However, this same breadth and depth could also make the GEM unwieldy for research applications or as a brief screening measure, suggesting the value of further research to identify critical red flag items that might constitute a more streamlined scale.

Comments on General-Purpose Grief Scales

By any account, the past decade has seen a great deal of progress in the development of measures to assess adaptation to bereavement. Only 15 years ago, researchers and clinicians faced a Hobson's choice: to measure a survivor's grief poorly, or not at all. Because extant grief scales were psychometrically problematic, many users defaulted to the alternative of assessing a cognate set of symptoms—often focusing on depression—using the validated psychological measures available for this purpose (Neimeyer & Hogan, 2001). Now, however, clinicians and researchers have available several potential scales, some of which focus on what is unique to bereavement (Prigerson & Maciejewski, 2006) and others that offer a multimodal measurement of both struggle and growth in the aftermath of loss (Hogan et al., 2001; Jordan et al., 2005). It is also encouraging that the translation of several of these scales has given an impetus for research in other cultures outside the dominant English-speaking world in which most research has been conducted. More work is needed, however, to demonstrate that such measures perform differently than widely used measures of depression and other psychiatric symptomatology as well as to develop scales that permit the distinctive testing of processes posited by leading-edge grief theories, a point to which we return later in this chapter.

SPECIALIZED GRIEF SCALES

Broadly speaking, the development of specialized grief scales has been driven by a focus on the experience of distinctive subgroups of the bereaved that is based on the type of loss suffered (e.g., perinatal or suicide bereavement); the relationship to the deceased (e.g., adolescent siblings); or, more recently, dimensions of grieving that go beyond psychological symptomatology. This level of specialization permits researchers and therapists to assess unique features of loss (e.g., survivor guilt, stigmatization) that fall outside the purview of most general scales. An overview of these instruments is provided in Table 7.2.

Perinatal Grief Scale

Instrument Description

The Perinatal Grief Scale (PGS; Toedter, Lasker, & Alhadeff, 1988) was devised by selecting items from the literature on grief in general and perinatal loss in particular. It was constructed to represent the potentially unique reactions of women and their partners who had experienced spontaneous abortion (i.e., miscarriage), ectopic pregnancies, fetal death, and neonatal loss. The original version of the PGS consisted of 84 rationally constructed items in the form of simple statements (e.g., "I find it hard to make decisions since the baby died") to which the respondent replies on a 5-point Likert scale that ranges from *strongly agree* to *strongly disagree*. Further psychometric refinement of the scale reduced it to three 11-item subscales assessing Active Grief, Difficulty Coping, and Despair (Potvin, Lasker, & Toedter, 1989; Toedter et al., 1988).

Advantages and Limitations

The unique content and economy of the abbreviated PGS, coupled with its apparent reliability and validity, make it the instrument of choice for measuring reactions that could be distinctive to this kind of loss (e.g., maternal guilt, stigmatization as a bereaved parent). Moreover, extensive research in northern Europe using Dutch and German translations of the scale has begun to clarify both commonalities and differences in perinatal grief across cultures (Toedter, Lasker, & Janssen, 2001). However, its focus on psychological complications leaves unaddressed other potentially salient dimensions of perinatal

TABLE 7.2

Psychometric Properties of Best Established Specialized Grief Scales

Criterion	Internal consistency (Cronbach's alpha)	Test–retest reliability	Convergent and discriminant validity[a]	Construct validity	Factorial validity
Perinatal Grief Scale (PGS)	Good alphas for nine theoretical subscales (Stinson et al., 1992), but it is preferable to interpret empirically established subscales of the abbreviated form: Active grief, .88–.93; Difficulty coping, .70–.97; Despair, .85–.91; total PGS .92–.96 (Toedter et al., 2001), .92–.96 subscales (average): .92 for active grief, .89 for difficulty coping (Toedter et al., 2001).	.59–.66 over 1 year for brief form (Potvin et al., 1989); .59–.66 (Toedter et al., 2001).	.73 with Symptom Checklist 90 depression (Toedter et al., 1988); unspecified correlations with trauma (Hunfeld et al., 1993) and personal inadequacy (Hunfeld, Wladimiroff, & Passchier, 1997). .68–.89 for rationally derived subscales; .97 overall (Barrett & Scott, 1989). .70–.87 for empirical subscales (Bailley et al., 2000).	PGS associated with longer gestation, poorer ratings of mental and physical health (Hunfeld et al., 1993; Toedter et al., 2001).	Exploratory factor analysis established three subscales for short and longer forms (Potvin et al., 1989; Toedter et al., 1988).

(continued)

TABLE 7.2

Psychometric Properties of Best Established Specialized Grief Scales (*Continued*)

Criterion	Internal consistency (Cronbach's alpha)	Test–retest reliability	Convergent and discriminant validity[a]	Construct validity	Factorial validity
Hogan Sibling Inventory of Bereavement (HSIB)	.90–.95 for Grief subscale, .88–.90 for Personal Growth (Blankenship, 1990; Hogan & Greenfield, 1991), .85–.93 for HSIB total completed by siblings, mothers and fathers, .77 for grief and .62 for abbreviated version (Hogan & Balk, 1990).		Discriminates time since death (Hogan & Greenfield, 1991).	Higher HSIB scores were associated with poorer adolescent self-concept (Hogan & Greenfield, 1991).	Exploratory factor analysis identified 24-item Grief factor and a 22-item Personal Growth factor (Hogan & DeSantis, 1996).
Grief Experience Questionnaire	.68–.89 for rationally derived subscales, .97 overall (Barrett & Scott, 1989); .70–.87 for empirical subscales (Bailley et al., 2000).			Differentiates suicidally bereaved from those suffering accidental, unexpected natural, and expected natural losses (Barrett & Scott, 1989).	Principal-components analysis identified eight factors: Abandonment/ Rejection, Stigmatization, Search for Explanation, Guilt, Somatic Reactions, Personal Responsibility, Self-Destructive Orientation, & Shame and Embarrassment (Bailley et al., 2000).

Continuing Bonds Scale	Good alpha of .87 (Field et al., 2003).	At 5 years postloss, continuing bonds positively correlated to ratings of satisfaction with relationship and negatively related to degree of blame in a role-played conversation with deceased (Field et al., 2003).	Principal-components analysis yielded one factor that included all 11 items (Neimeyer et al., 2006).
Marwit–Meuser Caregiver Grief Inventory, long (MM-CGI) and short forms (MM-CGI-SF)	.90–.96 for three factors and total grief score in long form (Marwit & Meuser, 2002); .80–.83 for three factors in MM-CGI-SF (Marwit & Meuser, 2005); .89 for Factor 1 subscale (Ho et al., 2002).	.86 with Anticipatory Grief Scale, .87 with the Beck Depression Inventory, .78 with Caregiver Strain Index, .83 with GDS, .78 with Perceived Social Support—Family Questionnaire, and .93 with Well-Being Scale—Basic Needs (Marwit & Meuser, 2002). Correlations between MM-CGI-SF and standardized measures used in study consistent were with MM-CGI (Marwit & Meuser, 2005).	Principal-components analysis yielded three factors in MM-CGI: Personal Sacrifice Burden, Heartfelt Sadness and Longing, and Worry and Felt Isolation (Marwit & Meuser, 2002). Factors 1, 2, and 3 of MM-CGI-SF correlate at .915, .925, and .928, respectively, with MM-CGI (Marwit & Meuser, 2005).

(continued)

TABLE 7.2

Psychometric Properties of Best Established Specialized Grief Scales (*Continued*)

Criterion	Internal consistency (Cronbach's alpha)	Test–retest reliability	Convergent and discriminant validity[a]	Construct validity	Factorial validity
Chinese Grief Reaction Assessment Form				Higher scores associated with women and individuals experiencing unanticipated death of a significant other (Ho et al., 2002).	Principal-components analysis identified three factors: Factor 1 reflected symptomatology of bereaved individuals; Factor 2 contained items on memory, coping ability, and overall distress levels (Ho et al., 2002).

Note. Empty cells indicate data were not reported.

[a]*Convergent validity* refers to correlations with established measures of grief symptoms; *discriminant validity* refers to freedom from social desirability confounds.

grief, such as the strong and ongoing efforts of bereaved parents to maintain an attachment bond to their infants, which has been underscored by qualitative researchers (Klass, 1999).

Hogan Sibling Inventory of Bereavement

Instrument Description

The Hogan Sibling Inventory of Bereavement (HSIB; Hogan & Greenfield, 1991) is unusual not only in its focus on the loss of brothers and sisters during childhood or adolescence but also in its method of item development. Like the more general HGRC described earlier, the HSIB was developed by analyzing conversations of the bereaved—in this case, children and adolescents—to ensure that it reflected issues of relevance to this population. The inventory comprises 46 items, which begin with the stem "Since my brother or sister died . . ." and then concludes with a variety of personal reactions (e.g., "I am uncomfortable when having fun"; "I have grown up faster than my friends"). The respondent is asked to give a rating that ranges from 1 (*does not describe me at all*) to 5 (*describes me very well*). Items load on two factors: (a) a 24-item Grief factor, which encompasses such areas as physical effects and desire for reunion with the sibling; and (b) a 22-item Personal Growth factor, which assesses such outcomes as increased resilience and ability to give and receive help (Hogan & DeSantis, 1996). The HSIB is also available in Finnish and Norwegian translations.

Advantages and Limitations

Because the HSIB was derived from the responses of bereaved children as well as adolescents, investigators might well find it attractive as a measure for preteen children. However, to date the instrument has been used only with adolescents (aged 13–18). Thus, its appropriateness for younger children remains to be established, especially in view of the sophisticated content (e.g., loss of control, changed priorities) of some items.

Grief Experience Questionnaire

Instrument Description

The Grief Experience Questionnaire (Barrett & Scott, 1989) is notable for its focus on reactions characteristic of suicide bereavement, such as disgrace or guilt. The scale is made up of 55 items, each of which begins with a common stem. The stems have alternative sentence endings that are rated on 5-point Likert scales that range from *never* to *almost always*. An example is "Since the death of [this person], how often did you: Feel like others may have blamed you for the death?"

Advantages and Limitations

In its more defensible factor-analyzed form (Bailley, Dunham, & Kral, 2000), the Grief Experience Questionnaire no longer has a separate subscale that assesses general grief reactions, making it potentially an inappropriate choice for the assessment of normative grieving. On the other hand, the instrument probably has wider applicability than to suicide bereavement per se, because items would seem to be equally pertinent to a range of potentially stigmatizing deaths, such as death from AIDS, drug overdose, and so on.

Continuing Bonds Scale

Instrument Description

Unlike more symptom-oriented inventories, the Continuing Bonds Scale (CBS; Field, Gal-Oz, & Bonanno, 2003) concentrates not on bereavement-related problems but on one particular dimension intrinsic to grieving, namely, the extent to which the bereaved person feels the lost loved one remains a part of his or her life. Its focus on the maintenance or relinquishment of connection to the deceased is therefore broadly consonant with an attachment theory perspective on grief (Field, Gao, & Paderna, 2005). The CBS consists of 11 rationally derived items, such as "I seek out things to remind me of _____" and "I have inner conversations with my spouse where I turn to him or her for comfort or advice," which the respondent rates using a Likert-type scale that ranges from 1 (*not true at all*) to 5 (*very true*). A principal-components analysis suggests that these items load on a single factor, which assesses the strength of the ongoing relationship to the deceased (Neimeyer, Baldwin, & Gillies, 2006).

Advantages and Limitations

The unique focus of the CBS on basic processes of grieving that go beyond the stress of bereavement per se could help round out the attention given to symptoms, complications, and personal growth that characterizes other instruments. However, it is premature to conclude that a high level of continuing bond with the deceased is intrinsically either beneficial or detrimental, insofar as research on its relationship to bereavement adaptation is clearly in its infancy (Stroebe & Schut, 2005).

Marwit–Meuser Caregiver Grief Inventory

Instrument Description

The Marwit–Meuser Caregiver Grief Inventory (MM-CGI) is unique in that it focuses on grief over an ongoing loss with no clear endpoint, namely, that of a caregiver to a family member experiencing progressive dementia (Marwit & Meuser, 2005). In this sense, it would seem to concentrate on *chronic sorrow*, a normal form of grieving for an "abnormal" loss (Roos, 2002). Item content reflects themes generated by focus groups of spouses and adult children of dementia patients, ultimately winnowed through principal-components analysis to a 50-item scale containing three interpretable factors: (a) Personal Sacrifice Burden, (b) Heartfelt Sadness and Longing, and (c) Worry and Felt Isolation. A second round of distillation of the measure with an expanded sample permitted the authors to identify the six items that loaded the highest on each factor to comprise a short form of the scale with 18 items, making it more amenable to screening and self-scoring. In both versions of the scale, item format involves respondents rating responses such as "It hurts to put him/her to bed at night and know that he/she is 'gone'," and "I feel I am losing my freedom," which are endorsed on a 5-point scale of agreement.

Advantages and Limitations

The MM-CGI provides the best available assessment of the unique losses that attend providing care for a loved one whose cognitive presence is being compromised by a progressive neurological condition such as Alzheimer's disease. Especially in its efficient short form, the measure could permit screening of caregivers in need of additional support services to prevent burnout, or to help demonstrate the efficacy of intervention programs to render their grief more bearable. Although only one item specifically mentions dementia, suggesting that a modest adaptation of the scale might make it relevant to other caregiving contexts (e.g., for family members with amyotrophic lateral sclerosis, chronic mental illness, or autism), such extension should be done cautiously to demonstrate the scale's validity with other populations.

Grief Reaction Assessment Form

Instrument Description

The Grief Reaction Assessment Form (GRAF; Ho, Chow, Chan, & Tsui, 2002) represents a novel, if preliminary, contribution to assessment methods, insofar as it is one of the rare scales to originate outside of North America. The original form of this scale consisted of 21 items, most of which were drawn from the Western literature on grief, which were then translated into Cantonese for widows and widowers seeking assistance at an innovative bereavement support program in Hong Kong. The initial pool of 21 items focused on memories of the deceased, coping, social and behavioral problems in bereavement, and especially negative emotions following the loss. However, factor analysis of the instrument suggested two factors, of which only one, broadly defined as Grief Symptomatology, was interpretable. Several of the 16 items on the reduced scale are more somatic in character than those on many Western grief measures (e.g., "Numbness or tingling in parts of the body"), although others are explicitly psychological (e.g., "I feel isolated and lonely"). Each is rated on a 10-point scale for its accuracy in describing personal reactions over the past week.

Advantages and Limitations

The GRAF appears to offer a useful description of the grief symptomatology of Hong Kong Chinese, and it has the benefit of brevity. In addition, it is striking that its most strongly endorsed item is "I do not want to abandon him/her," suggesting the importance of a continuing bond with the deceased in traditional Chinese culture. However, this suggests the possible utility of developing more culturally sensitive instruments grounded in a systematic qualitative study of various cultural groups—in this case, Hong Kong Chinese—rather than presuming the relevance of Western grief concepts such as those that shaped most items on the measure.

Comments on Specialized Grief Scales

Relative to even a few years ago (Neimeyer & Hogan, 2001), the assessment of grief processes has advanced substantially, adding to the repertory of omnibus scales a growing number of instruments targeting particular losses and populations. Although some of these scales are of recent construction and hence have accrued only preliminary psychometric support (e.g., the CBS or GEM), others are well established (e.g., the PGS and HSIB). Moreover, germinal attempts to construct culturally sensitive measures, such as the GRAF, offer the prospect of tailoring assessment to the diverse contexts that shape grief and morning in a multicultural world (Irish, Lundquist, & Nelsen, 1993). The result is likely to be a more adequate depiction of the nuances of particular losses and culturally shaped experiences, as in the case studies of Chantay and Sau-Chu with which this chapter opened.

However, the reader should bear in mind that this possibility of increased precision comes at a price, namely in terms of a sacrifice in generality made possible through the use of more global grief measures. For example, a well-constructed general measure might well prove preferable for cross-cultural comparisons, for which a scale that focused on culturally specific symptoms or responses could be inappropriate. Likewise, by definition an instrument designed to assess grief after a specific loss (e.g., of a child) could not be used to compare the impact of losses of different types (e.g., of a spouse or sibling). Finally, to the extent that specialized scales focus on a single dimension (e.g., one's continuing relationship to the deceased), they should not be used to assess the full spectrum of grief responses. However, used judiciously to supplement rather than substitute for more general measures, the growing armamentarium of specialized scales should contribute to the refinement of grief assessment in the future.

FUTURE HORIZONS

Several promising grief scales are under development or just entering the literature, with preliminary psychometric data supporting their eventual use in clinical and research settings. The first of these is the Inventory of Daily Widowed Life (Caserta & Lund, 2007), a 22-item scale that measures features of the dual-process model of coping with bereavement (Stroebe & Schut, 1999), with its twin focus on processes of both (a) loss accommodation and (b) restoration of adaptive social functioning. Initial data support the coherence and validity of subscales assessing these two dimensions of grief adaptation, although further refinements of the scale to assess subtle features of the dual-process model are indicated. A second measure with strong psychometric properties is the Grief and Meaning Reconstruction Inventory (GMRI; Gillies & Neimeyer, 2007). The GMRI stems from a conception of grieving as a process that entails the reaffirmation or reconstruction of a world of meaning that has been challenged by loss (Neimeyer, 2001, 2005). As such, the GMRI accords with a growing body of research that links bereavement adaptation with survivors' success in assimilating the loss into their existing systems of practical, secular, or spiritual meaning, or, alternatively, accommodating these systems to find new significance and orientation in the loss and in the lives they must now lead (Gillies & Neimeyer, 2006). Preliminary analyses support the validity and reliability of the GMRI's five factors: (a) Continuing Bonds, (b) Personal Growth, (c) Sense of Peace, (d) Emptiness and Meaninglessness, and (e) Valuing Life. A third scale, under development by Rubin and his colleagues, is the Two Track Bereavement Questionnaire, reflecting the theory that survivors progress along two parallel paths in bereavement adaptation, one that concerns their biopsychosocial functioning and a second one that concentrates on the reorganization of their relationship to the deceased (Rubin, 1999; see also chap. 9, this volume). The 70 items in the scale assess both factors, as well as traumatic responses to loss, broadly defined. Preliminary principal-components analyses are promising in supporting the scale's structure, and validational work on the measure is currently underway. Last, the Response to Loss Scale is being constructed by Schneider to operationalize his transformative model of grieving (Schneider, 1984), with an exhaustive 523 items measuring normal grief. Schneider's model postulates three areas of focus—(a) what is lost, (b) what remains, and (c) what is possible—each of which assesses various dimensions of adaptation.

The most significant analyses to date have concentrated on the Response to Loss Scale's discriminant validity in differentiating grief from depression. These next-generation scales share the distinction of being grounded in contemporary models of grief, thus opening the prospect that future grief research could permit more trenchant testing of major theories of bereavement and their clinical implications.

BEYOND THE QUESTIONNAIRE

What are the unique advantages of quantitative approaches to the assessment of grief, considered as a whole? Such scales have several legitimate uses, including fine-grained measurement of grief responses in different groups of bereaved persons, diagnosis of populations potentially at risk for complicated courses of bereavement, and the tracking of attenuation or intensification of grief symptoms over time or in response to treatment. Moreover, the ability of these quantitative approaches to assess grief intensity as a continuous variable permits investigators to identify predictors of postbereavement functioning, such as the nature of the attachment to the deceased, preexisting mental health risk factors in the bereaved person, and so on. In addition, with the advent of newer specialized scales and theory-guided measures, clinicians and researchers are in a better position than they were even a few years ago to refine theory in light of empirical data and assess factors specific to a given loss or process of adaptation, including various dimensions of growth through grief that transcend a struggle with symptomatology.

These many strengths notwithstanding, we believe that standardized questionnaires also have intrinsic limitations that leave room for the creative application of alternative methods. Among the most important of these are instruments that are anchored in qualitative research, which encompasses a broad range of techniques for study design, data collection, analysis, and interpretation (Lincoln & Guba, 1985). Space constraints preclude a thorough discussion of the place of such methods in elucidating adaptation to bereavement of the kind that is available elsewhere (Carverhill, 2002; Center for the Advancement of Health, 2004; Neimeyer & Hogan, 2001). Qualitative research is especially valuable in generating theory where little good theory exists; in revealing how people make meaning of events; and in moving toward a deeper understanding of a particular phenomenon, rather than a nomothetic set of causal inferences presumed to generalize across different cultures and settings. Qualitative research also can be used to ensure the content validity of quantitative measures. We concentrate here on two new studies that demonstrate how qualitative analysis is well suited to extend work based on conventional questionnaires and to investigate the role of culture in grief, as illustrated in the case studies of Chantay and Sau-Chu with which this chapter opened.

African American Grief

Recent research using quantitative measures has begun to elucidate distinctive features of grief among African Americans, with particular emphasis on issues of identity change, interpersonal dimensions of the loss, and continuing attachments with the deceased (Laurie & Neimeyer, in press). A large sample of bereaved young people (940 Caucasians and 641 African Americans) completed the ICG–R, the CBS, and questions regarding the circumstances surrounding their loss. The results revealed that relative to their Caucasian peers, African Americans experienced more frequent bereavement by homicide; maintenance of a stronger continuing bond with the deceased; greater grief for the loss of extended kin beyond the immediate family; and a sense of support in their grief, despite their tendency to talk less with others about the loss or seek professional support for it. Thus, use of existing measures in combination with questions concerning features of the loss offers a partial sketch of the distinctive pattern of challenge and resilience displayed by bereaved African American young adults as a cultural group. Research drawing on qualitative methods usefully extends this picture.

In a recent book-length treatment of African American grieving, Rosenblatt and Wallace (2005) drew on grounded theory analysis to offer additional insight into how African Americans experience bereavement (see also chap. 10, this volume). For example, themes emerging from in-depth interviews suggested that like Chantay, introduced at the beginning of this chapter, African Americans tend to rely on religion as they make sense of loss; may have a need to be "strong" during bereavement and reticent in discussing their grief, especially outside the family; and seek a continued bond with the deceased that includes the expectation that they will be reunited in heaven. Moreover, although the authors were careful not to overemphasize differences from other cultural groups, it was noteworthy that informants viewed their grief as different than that displayed by White Americans, seeing it as more honest and more expressive of emotion during the funeral service itself. They also saw themselves as being more supportive of each other in times of bereavement.

The most striking theme permeating the narratives of the African American participants was racism, both as a cause of death and in the lives of the deceased. For example, one participant, Franklin, described the racist assignment to hazardous military duty as contributing to the deaths of men in his community. Although his stepfather survived the Vietnam War, Franklin questioned the rate at which African Americans were killed: "Who were the ones that were . . . filling up the body bags in outrageous numbers? Black folk. Who were the ones who had all of this hazardous duty crap . . . ? It was black folk" (Rosenblatt & Wallace, 2005, p. 9). The authors acknowledged that the experience of racism for African Americans is almost inextricable from grief;

it is interwoven in the lives and pasts of the participants of this study as it is in the larger culture. To discuss African American grief, argued Rosenblatt and Wallace (2005), is to touch on racism on many levels: "African Americans who are grieving a death are, at the same time, dealing with grief connected to racist oppression experienced by [the] self, the deceased, the family and all African Americans both recently and in the past" (p. 168). To the extent that such factors as religious-based coping with loss (Wortmann & Park, in press) and complications arising from racism are neglected by standardized grief measures, qualitative research can play an especially useful role in elucidating the experience of specific cultural groups.

Grief Among Hong Kong Chinese

Studies that have used quantitative grief measures, such as the GRAF (Ho et al., 2002) and standard scales of anxiety and depression (Chow, Chan, & Ho, 2007), have begun to clarify the universal and culturally specific ways in which Chinese experience loss and share their bereavement reactions with others. However, the case study of Sau-Chu at the beginning of this chapter suggests several further dimensions of private grieving and public mourning that standardized measures tend to miss, ranging from her attributions for the cause of her husband's death to the experiences that exacerbated or relieved her distress over the course of bereavement. In contrast, an intensive quali- tative study by Chan et al. (2005) of the therapy transcripts of 52 bereaved Hong Kong Chinese provides a framework of understanding within which such responses are entirely comprehensible. The blend of Taoist, Confucian, and Buddhist concepts that characterizes Chinese culture provides a unique framework for both making sense of loss and for appropriate action in its after- math, especially for traditional Chinese. For example, participants in Chan et al.'s study, although they readily understood the explicit, physical cause of death, frequently found deeper meaning in their loved one's dying by view- ing it as resulting from karma. As one widow expressed it,

> My husband is a good person who did a lot of charitable work. He died young probably because of the bad deeds he did in the life before this life. I'm sure he had just finished paying his debt and will lead a good life next time. (Chan et al., 2005, p. 930)

Alternatively, others explained the death as a result of "fate clashes" in which the life of the deceased collided with that of the bereaved, and the stronger one won. A host of such factors, ranging from the loved one dying with open eyes (and, therefore, "unwillingly") to patterns of "visitation" of the loved one's ghost after death, had the power to complicate grief or assuage pain. An example of the latter was the protest of one wife, who lamented,

All along, I thought I was the most important person in the eyes of my husband. . . . Yet, I was so angry to know that my husband appeared in the dream of his sister! Why did he go to her place and not mine? . . . He was cheating me all along! He cared for his sister rather than me! (Chan et al., 2005, p. 939)

In general, great weight was placed on the nature of the continuing bond with the deceased, with various ritual practices reinforcing or undermining it. Although recent developments in grief assessment—with appropriate translation—move toward greater adequacy in tracing such culturally relevant processes, it is clear that there will always be a role for qualitative studies in revealing the richness and diversity of human responses to loss.

CONCLUSION

Relative to only a few years ago (Neimeyer & Hogan, 2001), great strides have been made in the assessment of grief, particularly in the construction and validation of an impressive armamentarium of quantitative scales for measuring grief as a profound biopsychosocial response to the loss of a major attachment bond (Bowlby, 1980). Thus, although good scientific and clinical reasons exist for assessing a broad band of potential responses to bereavement (e.g., depressive, anxious, or posttraumatic symptoms), so too are there ample reasons (and resources) to assess processes unique to grieving. Efforts to strengthen the validity and reliability of existing scales are certainly indicated, as is their application in diverse communities. Moreover, the tailoring of new instruments to unique features of underrepresented losses or grief processes should be encouraged. However, as psychometrically validated scales for mapping grief are developed—ideally on the basis of sophisticated qualitative studies—there is reason to expect that their more widespread adoption will yield a clearer picture of the human encounter with death and loss, in all of its psychological, existential, social, and cultural complexity.

REFERENCES

American Psychological Association. (2005). *Report of the 2005 Presidential Task Force on Evidence-Based Practice*. Retrieved April 3, 2006, from http://www.apa.org/practice/ebpreport.pdf

Bailley, S. E., Dunham, K. T., & Kral, M. J. (2000). Factor structure of the Grief Experience Questionnaire and its sensitivity to suicide bereavement. *Death Studies, 24*, 721–738.

Barrett, T. W., & Scott, T. B. (1989). Development of the Grief Experience Questionnaire. *Suicide and Life-Threatening Behavior, 19*, 201–215.

Barry, L. C., Kasl, S. V., & Prigerson, H. G. (2002). Psychiatric disorders among bereaved persons: The role of perceived circumstances of death and preparedness for death. *American Journal of Geriatric Psychiatry, 10*, 447–457.

Beck, A. T., Ward, C. H., Mendelson, M., Mock, J., & Erbaugh, J. (1961). An inventory for measuring depression. *Archives of General Psychiatry, 4*, 561–571

Berg-Weger, M., McGartland Rubio, D., & Steiger Tebb, S. (2000). The Caregiver Well-Being Scale revisited. *Health & Social Work, 25*, 255–263.

Blankenship, M. (1990). *Adolescent sibling bereavement: Family factors associated with adjustment to loss*. Unpublished master's thesis, Bowling Green State University, Bowling Green, OH.

Bowlby, J. (1980). *Attachment and loss* (Vol. 3). New York: Basic Books.

Burnett, P., Middleton, W., Raphael, B., & Martinek, N. (1997). Measuring core bereavement phenomena. *Psychological Medicine, 27*, 49–57.

Butcher, J. N., Dahlstrom, W. G., Graham, J. R., Tellegen, A., & Kaemmer, B. (1989). *Minnesota Multiphasic Personality Inventory—2*. Minneapolis: University of Minnesota Press.

Byrne, G., & Raphael, B. (1997). The psychological symptoms of conjugal bereavement in elderly men over the first 13 months. *International Journal of Geriatric Psychiatry, 12*, 241–251.

Carverhill, P. A. (Ed.). (2002). Qualitative research in thanatology [Special issue]. *Death Studies, 26*(3).

Caserta, M. S., & Lund, D. A. (2007). Toward the development of an Inventory of Daily Widowed Life (IDWL). *Death Studies, 6*, 505–535.

Center for the Advancement of Health. (2004). Report on bereavement and grief research. *Death Studies, 28*, 489–575.

Chan, C. L. W., Chow, A., Ho, S., Tsui, Y., Tin, A., Koo, B., et al. (2005). The experience of Chinese bereaved persons: A preliminary study of meaning making and continuing bonds. *Death Studies, 29*, 923–947.

Chow, A., Chan, C. L. W., & Ho, S. (2007). Social sharing of bereavement experience by Chinese bereaved persons in Hong Kong. *Death Studies, 31*, 601–618.

Currier, J., Holland, J., & Neimeyer, R. A. (2006). Sense making, grief and the experience of violent loss: Toward a mediational model. *Death Studies, 30*, 403–428.

Derogatis, L. R., & Cleary, P. A. (1977). Confirmation of the dimensional structure of the SCL-90: A study in construct validation. *Journal of Clinical Psychology, 33*, 981–989.

Faschingbauer, T. R. (1981). *Texas Revised Inventory of Grief manual*. Houston, TX: Honeycomb.

Field, N. P., Gal-Oz, E., & Bonanno, G. A. (2003). Continuing bonds and adjustment at 5 years after the death of a spouse. *Journal of Consulting and Clinical Psychology, 71*, 110–117.

Field, N. P., Gao, B., & Paderna, L. (2005). Continuing bonds in bereavement: An attachment theory based perspective. *Death Studies, 29*, 277–299.

Gamino, L. A., Sewell, K. W., & Easterling, L. W. (1998). Scott & White Grief Study: An empirical test of predictors of intensified mourning. *Death Studies, 22,* 333–355.

Gamino, L. A., Sewell, K. W., & Easterling, L. A. (2000). Scott & White Grief Study—Phase 2: Toward an adaptive model of grief. *Death Studies, 24,* 633–660.

Gilbar, O., & Dagan, A. (1995). Coping with loss: Differences between widows and widowers of deceased cancer patients. *Omega, 331,* 207–220.

Gillies, J., & Neimeyer, R. A. (2006). Loss, grief and the search for significance. *Journal of Constructivist Psychology, 19,* 31–65.

Gillies, J., & Neimeyer, R. A. (2007). *Development and validation of the Grief and Meaning Reconstruction Inventory.* Manuscript in preparation, University of Memphis, Memphis, TN.

Hansson, R. O., Carpenter, B. N., & Fairchild, S. K. (1993). Measurement issues in bereavement. In M. S. Stroebe, W. Stroebe, & R. O. Hansson (Eds.), *Handbook of bereavement* (pp. 62–74). Cambridge, England: Cambridge University Press.

Ho, S., Chow, A., Chan, C. L. W., & Tsui, Y. (2002). The assessment of grief among Hong Kong Chinese: A preliminary report. *Death Studies, 26,* 91–98.

Hogan, N. S., & Balk, D. E. (1990). Adolescent reactions to sibling death: Perceptions of mothers, fathers, and teenagers. *Nursing Research, 39,* 103–106.

Hogan, N. S., & DeSantis, L. (1996). Basic constructs of a theory of adolescent sibling bereavement. In D. Klass, P. R. Silverman, & S. L. Nickman (Eds.), *Continuing bonds* (pp. 235–255). Philadelphia: Taylor & Francis.

Hogan, N. S., & Greenfield, D. B. (1991). Adolescent sibling bereavement symptomatology in a large community sample. *Journal of Adolescent Research, 6,* 97–112.

Hogan, N. S., Greenfield, D. B., & Schmidt, L. A. (2001). Development and validation of the Hogan Grief Reactions Checklist. *Death Studies, 25,* 1–32.

Hogan, N. S., & Schmidt, L. A. (2002). Testing the grief to personal growth model using structural equation modeling. *Death Studies, 26,* 615–634.

Horowitz, M., Wilner, N., & Alvarez, W. (1979) Impact of Event Scale: A measure of subjective stress. *Psychosomatic Medicine, 41,* 43–65.

Hunfeld, J., Wladimiroff, J., & Passchier, J. (1997). Prediction and course of grief four years after perinatal loss due to congenital abnormalities: A follow-up study. *British Journal of Medical Psychology, 70,* 85–91.

Hunfeld, J. A. M., Wladimiroff, J. W., Passchier, J., Uniken-Venema, M., Frets, P. G., & Verhage, F. (1993). Reliability and validity of the Perinatal Grief Scale for women who experienced late pregnancy loss. *British Journal of Medical Psychology, 66,* 295–298.

Irish, D., Lundquist, K., & Nelsen, V. (Eds.). (1993). *Ethnic variations in dying, death, and grief.* Washington, DC: Taylor & Francis.

Jordan, J. R., Baker, J., Matteis, M., Rosenthal, S., & Ware, E. S. (2005). The Grief Evaluation Measure (GEM): An initial validation study. *Death Studies, 29,* 301–332.

Klass, D. (1999). *The spiritual lives of bereaved parents*. Philadelphia: Brunner/Mazel.

Kraus, D. R., Seligman, D., & Jordan, J. R. (2005). Validation of a behavioral health treatment outcome and assessment tool designed for practice research networks and other naturalistic settings: The treatment outcome package. *Journal of Clinical Psychology, 61*, 315–322.

Laurie, A., & Neimeyer, R. A. (in press). African Americans in bereavement: Grief as a function of ethnicity. *Omega: The Journal of Death and Dying*.

Lev, E., & McCorkle, R. (1993). A shortened version of an instrument measuring bereavement. *International Journal of Nursing Studies, 30*, 213–226.

Lincoln, Y. S., & Guba, E. G. (1985). *Naturalistic inquiry*. Newbury Park, CA: Sage.

Longman, A. J. (1993). Effectiveness of a hospice community bereavement program. *Omega, 27*, 165–175.

Marwit, S. J., & Meuser, T. M. (2002). Development and initial validation of an inventory to assess grief in caregivers of persons with Alzheimer's disease. *The Gerontologist, 42*, 751–765.

Marwit, S. J., & Meuser, T. M. (2005). Development of a short form inventory to assess grief in caregivers of dementia patients. *Death Studies, 29*, 191–205.

Middleton, W., Raphael, B., Burnett, P., & Martinek, N. (1998). A longitudinal study comparing bereavement phenomena in recently bereaved spouses, adult children and parents. *Australian and New Zealand Journal of Psychiatry, 32*, 235–241.

Neimeyer, R. A. (Ed.). (2001). *Meaning reconstruction and the experience of loss*. Washington, DC: American Psychological Association.

Neimeyer, R. A. (2005). Widowhood, grief and the quest for meaning: A narrative perspective on resilience. In D. Carr, R. M. Nesse, & C. B. Wortman (Eds.), *Late life widowhood in the United States* (pp. 227–252). New York: Springer Publishing Company.

Neimeyer, R. A., Baldwin, S. A., & Gillies, J. (2006). Continuing bonds and reconstructing meaning: Mitigating complications in bereavement. *Death Studies, 30*, 715–738.

Neimeyer, R. A., & Hogan, N. (2001). Quantitative or qualitative? Measurement issues in the study of grief. In M. S. Stroebe, R. O. Hansson, W. Stroebe, & H. Schut (Eds.), *Handbook of bereavement research: Consequences, coping, and care* (pp. 89–118). Washington, DC: American Psychological Association.

Potvin, L., Lasker, J., & Toedter, L. (1989). Measuring grief: A short version of the Perinatal Grief Scale. *Journal of Psychopathology and Behavioral Assessment, 11*, 29–45.

Prigerson, H. G., & Jacobs, S. C. (2001). Traumatic grief as a distinct disorder: A rationale, consensus criteria, and a preliminary empirical test. In M. S. Stroebe, R. O. Hansson, W. Stroebe, & H. Schut (Eds.), *Handbook of bereavement research: Consequences, coping, and care* (pp. 614–646). Washington, DC: American Psychological Association.

Prigerson, H. G., & Maciejewski, P. K. (2006). A call for sound empirical testing and evaluation of criteria for complicated grief proposed by the *DSM-V*. *Omega: The Journal of Death and Dying, 52*, 9–19.

Prigerson, H. G., Maciejewski, P., Newson, J., Reynolds, C. F., Bierhals, A. J., Miller, M., et al. (1995). Inventory of Complicated Grief: A scale to measure maladaptive symptoms of loss. *Psychiatry Research, 59,* 65–79.

Procidano, M. E., & Heller, K. (1983). Measures of perceived social support from friends and from family: Three validation studies. *American Journal of Community Psychology, 11,* 1–24.

Robinson, B. C. (1983). Validation of a Caregiver Strain Index. *Journal of Gerontology, 38,* 344–348.

Roos, S. (2002). *Chronic sorrow.* New York: Brunner Routledge.

Rosenblatt, P., & Wallace, B. (2005). *African American grief.* New York: Routledge.

Rubin, S. (1999). The two-track model of bereavement. *Death Studies, 23,* 681–714.

Sanders, C. M., Mauger, P. A., & Strong, P. N. (1985). *A manual for the Grief Experience Inventory.* Blowing Rock, NC: Center for the Study of Separation and Loss.

Schneider, J. (1984). *Stress, loss and grief.* Baltimore: University Park Press.

Spirtes, P., Scheines, R., Meek, C., & Glymour, C. (1994). TETRAD II: Tools for causal modeling [Computer software]. Carnegie Mellon University, Pittsburgh, PA.

Stinson, K. M., Lasher, J. N., Lohman, J., & Toedter, L. J. (1992). Parents' grief following pregnancy loss: A comparison of mothers and fathers. *Family Relations, 41,* 218–223.

Stroebe, M., & Schut, H. (1999). The dual process model of coping with bereavement: Rationale and description. *Death Studies, 23,* 197–224.

Stroebe, M., & Schut, H. (2005). To continue or relinquish bonds: A review of consequences for the bereaved. *Death Studies, 29,* 477–494.

Theut, S. K., Jordan, L., Ross, L. A., & Deutsch, M. D. (1991). Caregiver's anticipatory grief in dementia: A pilot study. *International Journal of Aging and Human Development, 33,* 113–118.

Toedter, L. J., Lasker, J. N., & Alhadeff, J. M. (1988). The Perinatal Grief Scale: Development and initial validation. *American Journal of Orthopsychiatry, 58,* 435–449.

Toedter, L. J., Lasker, J. N., & Janssen, H. (2001). International comparison of studies using the Perinatal Grief Scale. *Death Studies, 25,* 205–228.

Wortmann, J. H., & Park, C. L. (in press). Religion and spirituality in adjustment following bereavement: An integrative review. *Death Studies.*

III

CONTEMPORARY SOCIETAL
AND PRACTICE CONCERNS

8

A CASE FOR INCLUSION OF PROLONGED GRIEF DISORDER IN *DSM–V*

HOLLY G. PRIGERSON, LAUREN C. VANDERWERKER,
AND PAUL K. MACIEJEWSKI

Although grief in response to loss is a normal, inevitable part of life, psychiatrists (Freud, 1917/1957; Lindemann, 1944), psychologists (Marwit, 1991), oncologists (Penson, Green, Chabner, & Lynch, 2002), social workers (Lacey, 2005), geriatricians (Berezin, 1970), nurses (Dunne, 2004), and family members and friends of bereaved individuals (Swarte, van der Lee, van der Bom, van den Bout, & Heintz, 2003) have all recognized that grief may, in certain instances, be acutely distressing and functionally impairing. The National Institute of Mental Health (http://www.nimh.nih.gov/), the National Cancer Institute (http://www.cancer.gov/cancertopics/pdq/supportivecare/bereavement/patient/page8), and the U.S. military (http://www.ncptsd.va.gov/facts/disasters/fs_grief_disaster.html) all offer definitions

This research was supported in part by National Institute of Mental Health Grants MH56529 and MH63892 (both to Holly G. Prigerson) and National Cancer Institute Grant CA106370 (to Holly G. Prigerson); a Fetzer Religion at the End-of-Life Grant (to Holly G. Prigerson); an American Foundation for Suicide Prevention grant (to Lauren C. Vanderwerker and Holly G. Prigerson); National Institute of Neurological Disorders and Stroke Grant NS044316 (to Paul K. Maciejewski); and a grant from the Center for Psycho-Oncology and Palliative Care Research, Dana Farber Cancer Institute (to Holly G. Prigerson and Lauren C. Vanderwerker).

and recommendations for bereaved survivors who may have what is called *complicated grief*.

Nevertheless, in the fourth edition of the *Diagnostic and Statistical Manual of Mental Disorders* (*DSM–IV*; American Psychiatric Association, 1994), bereavement is most frequently cited as a potential exclusion criterion for mental disorders (e.g., major depressive disorder [MDD], adjustment disorder) and is not considered a form of mental illness in its own right. In *DSM–IV*, bereavement is classified among "conditions or problems . . . related to . . . mental disorders" (i.e., a V code). A single paragraph in *DSM–IV* is devoted to bereavement. It focuses exclusively on symptoms of depression (e.g., psychomotor retardation, feelings of worthlessness, excessive guilt, thoughts of death) subsequent to the loss of a significant other, and it guides clinicians to diagnose bereaved individuals with MDD if they experience the specified depressive symptoms 2 months or longer after the loss. Criteria for diagnosing severe, prolonged, maladaptive grief remain conspicuously absent from *DSM–IV*. Its guidelines on bereavement are at odds with substantial evidence that symptoms apart from those of depression, those we refer to as *prolonged grief disorder*, constitute a separate pathological form of bereavement-related psychic distress.

To clarify terminology, we now use the term *prolonged grief disorder* (PGD) to refer to this bereavement-specific syndrome. Although the renaming may be unsettling to researchers and clinicians who have become accustomed to the term *complicated grief*, it is justified on the grounds that it provides greater clarity in defining this disorder. The term *traumatic grief* resulted in confusion with *posttraumatic stress disorder* (PTSD), and *pathological grief* seemed pejorative. *Complicated* is defined as "difficult to analyze, understand, explain" (see http://dictionary.reference.com/browse/complicated) and therefore is an inaccurate descriptor given that we have attempted to clarify the features of this bereavement-specific form of distress. The term *prolonged* better captures the nature of the disorder; that is, it constitutes a persistently elevated set of specific symptoms of grief identified in bereaved individuals with significant difficulties adjusting to the loss. The use of the word *prolonged* should not imply that duration is the only indicator of the pathological nature of grief. Another problem with the term *complicated grief* is that it could be confused with *complicated bereavement*—a term used in *DSM–IV* to refer to symptoms of major depression secondary to bereavement. Designation of the term PGD permits recognition of other psychiatric complications that may also follow from a significant interpersonal loss, with PGD, MDD, generalized anxiety disorder (GAD), and PTSD all possible and perhaps co-occurring mental disorders. For these reasons, we refer to this form of mental disturbance secondary to a significant interpersonal loss as PGD.

There exists a sizable and growing body of evidence indicating that PGD symptomatology meets the *DSM–IV* definition of a mental disorder—that is, it constitutes "a clinically significant behavioral or psychological syndrome or pattern that occurs in an individual and that is associated with present distress or disability" (American Psychiatric Association, 1994, p. xxi). As we describe in this chapter, PGD is distinct from other disorders currently found in *DSM–IV* (e.g., MDD, PTSD). Thus, many cases of clinically significant distress among bereaved persons would be missed by the sole reliance on the disorders currently included in *DSM–IV*. The omission of PGD from the diagnostic nomenclature inhibits the ability of clinicians to diagnose and treat the many bereaved individuals who will develop PGD (see chap. 9, this volume).

The absence of PGD from the *DSM* affects a substantial number of people. There are approximately 2.5 million deaths per year in the United States (Hoyert, Kung, & Smith, 2005). With an estimated 4 survivors per death and using an estimated 11% prevalence rate of PGD following deaths from natural causes (Barry, Kasl, & Prigerson, 2001; Latham & Prigerson, 2004), there would be approximately 1.1 million annual cases of PGD in the United States alone. This figure does not include deaths occurring in other countries or higher rates that likely would follow exposure to disasters and other traumatic forms of death or follow the death of a child. Consequently, the ability to detect and ameliorate acute distress and disability associated with bereavement should become and, for some national organizations (National Institute of Mental Health, National Cancer Institute, and the U.S. military) has become, recognized as a public health concern. The number of people likely to be affected by this disorder—and by *affected* we mean not only the bereaved survivor who meets criteria for PGD but also the individuals with whom this person lives and the organizations and people with whom this person works—highlights the broader public interest in *DSM–V*'s inclusion of PGD.

In this chapter, we summarize the research that demonstrates that PGD constitutes a distinct mental disorder worthy of inclusion in the *DSM*. We begin with a description of the normal course of grief and contrast this with the symptom course in the case of PGD. We then summarize results indicating PGD's distinctive phenomenology; describe the compromise criteria set for PGD; and review evidence of the specific risk factors, outcomes, and response to treatment associated with PGD. In light of the evidence in support of PGD as a separate mental disorder, there is a need for explicit and agreed-on (standardized) criteria so it can be reliably and validly diagnosed. Standardized criteria would enable clinicians to detect, treat, and receive reimbursement for the treatment of PGD and enable researchers to investigate the prevalence, risk factors, outcomes, neurobiology, prevention, and treatment of this disorder. We conclude the chapter with a description of our efforts to standardize a criteria set for PGD proposed for inclusion in *DSM–V*.

EVIDENCE THAT PROLONGED GRIEF DISORDER CONSTITUTES A DISTINCT MENTAL DISORDER

Studies of PGD show that it fulfills Robins and Guze's (1970) requirements for establishing the validity of a mental disorder—that is, its phenomenology, etiology and correlates, outcomes, clinical course, and response to treatment are distinct from those of other *DSM–IV* disorders. Before describing how PGD distinguishes itself from other mental disorders, however, there is a need to distinguish PGD from "normal" (average) grief. The characterization of typical grief will enable us to show how PGD deviates from the normative response to the death of a significant other.

Normal Grieving

Approximately 80% to 90% of bereaved individuals experience normal grief (Barry et al., 2001; Latham & Prigerson, 2004; Prigerson, 2004). Although normal grief can be very painful and disruptive, most bereaved survivors overcome the initial sense of disbelief and gradually come to accept the loss as a reality. The vast majority of bereaved people are eventually able to move on with their lives and proceed with their daily functions and activities. Most people are able to adjust to the loss over time in a more or less adaptive way.

What does the normal, or average, resolution of grief look like? Over the years, the stage theory of grief resolution (see top panel of Figure 8.1) described for dying patients by Kübler-Ross (1969) and for adjustment to bereavement by Bowlby (1961) and Parkes (1972) has had enormous appeal and acceptance among bereavement experts and laypersons (Parkes & Weiss, 1983; see also chaps. 2, 3, and 5, this volume). Although the stage theory of grief resolution has never been tested explicitly, there has been wide acceptance of the notion that normal grief involves an orderly progression through the following stages: disbelief or shock; separation distress or yearning; angry protest; depressed mood or despair; and ultimate acceptance of or recovery from the loss (Bowlby, 1961; National Cancer Institute, n.d.). The bottom panel of Figure 8.1 illustrates the average pattern of resolution of each of these five grief stage indicators in a sample of bereaved community-based participants in the Yale Bereavement Study ($N = 281$).

In Figure 8.1, yearning, rather than disbelief, is the most frequently endorsed initial reaction, with yearning remaining the most frequent negative symptom of grief throughout the study observation period. It should be noted that shock and other immediate reactions to the death prior to 2 months predated the initial bereavement assessment, and thus the results pertain only to the 2- through 24-months postloss period, so it is possible that disbelief may have peaked prior to 2 months postloss. Disbelief, depressed

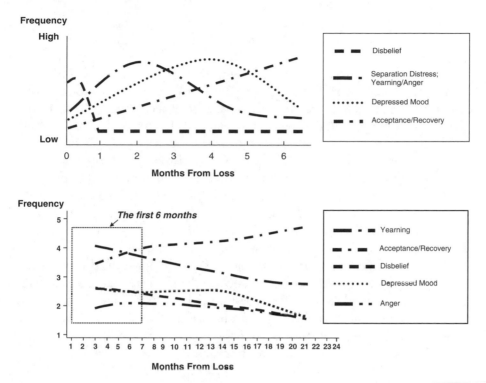

Figure 8.1. Hypothesized resolution of grief model and observed changes in grief symptomatology over time from loss. Top panel: Hypothesized grief resolution. "Separation distress" refers to what is often described as the stage of anger in grief literature. Yearning is conceptualized here as an operationalization of separation distress. Bottom panel: Unadjusted mean grief resolution scores. Bottom panel: "Frequency" refers to 1 = less than once a month; 2 = monthly; 3 = weekly; 4 = daily; 5 = several times a day, except for indicator of "depressed mood." In the bottom panel, all of the lines start from 2 months after loss and end at 24 months. From *Pathologic Grief: Maladaptation to Loss* (p. 17), by S. Jacobs, 1993, Washington, DC: American Psychiatric Press. Copyright 1993 by American Psychiatric Press. Adapted with permission.

mood, and yearning decline gradually over time from 2 to 24 months post-loss, whereas anger levels remain stably low throughout the observation period. Over time, acceptance of the loss increases and reveals a pattern inverse to changes in disbelief and yearning. These results suggest that grief intensity tends to decline gradually over time from loss and that acceptance of the death increases as time progresses from the death. This pattern was consistently observed in subsequent analyses that adjusted for significant confounding influences (Zhang, el-Jawahri, & Prigerson, 2006) and analyses that removed participants who met criteria for PGD and survivors of unnatural deaths (Maciejewski, Zhang, Block, & Prigerson, 2007). However, in analyses that rescaled these indicators to determine and to compare when each of the five grief indicators peaked, the sequence of stages proposed by Bowlby (1961) and Parkes (1972) and displayed in Jacobs (1993) was observed, and all occurred within the first 6 months postloss (Maciejewski et al., 2007).

During the initial months following the loss, many of the signs and symptoms of normal grief are similar to those of PGD, yet by 6 months post-loss, most bereaved individuals reach some sense of acceptance, see the future as holding some potential for satisfying relationships and endeavors, are able to engage in productive work, and enjoy leisure activities (Prigerson, 2004). By 6 months postloss, the majority of bereaved individuals are capable of finding some meaning and purpose in their lives, maintaining connections with others, and developing new relationships. The bereaved person's self-esteem and sense of competence have not been adversely affected by the loss. Most bereaved individuals ultimately appear able to adapt to their loss, and bereavement is generally not a cause for clinical concern.

For a significant minority of bereaved persons, however, this is not the case. Bereaved survivors who experience well-recognized adjustment diffi-culties, such as suicidal thoughts and gestures, MDD, or PTSD, and those who maintain chronically high levels of a specific set of symptoms of PGD for more than 6 months after the loss are a cause for clinical concern. In the following sections, we describe PGD reactions in greater detail.

Descriptive Features of Prolonged Grief Disorder

In contrast to bereaved survivors who experience normal grief, those with PGD are essentially stuck in a state of chronic mourning (Prigerson, 2004). Much of the mental anguish stems from a psychological protest against the reality of the loss and a general reluctance to make adaptations to life in the absence of the loved one. PGD is characterized by an intense longing and yearning for the person who died. Survivors who meet criteria for PGD feel bitter over the loss and wish desperately that their life could revert back to the time when they were together with their deceased loved one. Without the deceased person, the bereaved survivor with PGD feels empty and has little hope that he or she will find fulfillment in the future. Such persons are often preoccupied by their sorrow and regrets concerning the loss. Their ruminations and inability to concentrate on things aside from their loss, the sense of feeling disconnected from people with whom they pre-viously had felt close prior to the death, exacerbate the sense of alienation and social isolation. Recurrent, intrusive, and distressing thoughts about the absence of the deceased make it difficult for persons with PGD to move beyond an acute state of mourning and live in the present. People with PGD feel that life lacks meaning and purpose without the deceased, and they find it extremely difficult to move on with their lives by forming other interper-sonal relationships and engaging in potentially rewarding activities. People with PGD feel that a part of themselves died along with the deceased loved one, that they are "hollow" and that their sense of identity is confused or lost without the deceased person. They are convinced that the rest of their lives will be empty, dissatisfying, and spent missing the deceased. It is no wonder that PGD, over and above confounding influences such as MDD, has repeatedly been shown to heighten risk for suicidal thoughts and behaviors (Latham & Prigerson, 2004; Prigerson, Bridge, et al., 1999; Prigerson et al., 1997, 2007).

Proposed Prolonged Grief Disorder Criteria for the Fifth Edition of the *Diagnostic and Statistical Manual of Mental Disorders*

On the basis of analyses that we describe at the end of this chapter, we derived a diagnostic algorithm for PGD. The criteria were reviewed and critiqued by colleagues to produce a compromise criteria set that specifies that the reaction has to follow the loss of a significant other (Criterion A: Bereavement) and that the bereaved person must experience at least one of the following three symptoms daily or to an intense or disruptive degree: (a) intrusive thoughts related to the deceased, (b) intense pangs of separation distress, or (c) distressingly strong yearnings for that which was lost (Criterion B: Separation Distress). The bereaved person must have five of the following nine symptoms daily or to an intense or disruptive degree: (a) confusion about one's role in life or a diminished sense of self (e.g., feeling that a part of oneself has died); (b) difficulty accepting the loss; (c) avoidance of reminders of the reality of the loss; (d) an inability to trust others since the loss; (e) bitterness or anger related to the loss; (f) difficulty moving on with life (e.g., making new friends, pursuing interests); (g) numbness (absence of emotion) since the loss; (h) feeling that life is unfulfilling, empty, and meaningless since the loss; and (i) feeling stunned, dazed, or shocked by the loss (Criterion C: Cognitive, Emotional, and Behavioral Symptoms). Duration of at least 6 months from the onset of separation distress (Criterion D: Duration) and the preceding symptomatic disturbance must cause clinically significant distress or impairment in social, occupational, or other important areas of functioning (e.g., domestic responsibilities). Further requirements stipulate that the disturbance is not due to the physiological effects of a substance or a general medical condition and that the symptoms could not be better accounted for by MDD, GAD, or PTSD.

How Soon After a Loss Can a Diagnosis of Prolonged Grief Disorder Be Made, and What Types of Losses May Trigger Its Onset?

The criteria for PGD proposed for inclusion in *DSM–V* specify that the particular symptomatic distress must persist for at least 6 consecutive months, regardless of when those 6 months occur in relation to the loss. Hence, chronic and delayed subtypes of grief could both fit within this conceptualization of PGD, as long as the chronicity and delay each include at least 6 months of symptomatic distress. More commonly, however, people diagnosed with PGD do not experience delays in the onset of symptoms postloss. It is much more often the case among those struggling with PGD that their grief has been intense and unrelenting since the death. Although the criteria we propose here were tested for bereavement, because grief is a response to the loss of something cherished, the criteria may well apply to other significant losses apart from death (e.g., divorce, loss of pets, terminal illness). Future research will need to validate the performance of the proposed criteria with respect to these other types of losses.

Why Wait 6 Months to Diagnose Prolonged Grief Disorder?

Both prior studies (Prigerson et al., 1997; Prigerson, Frank, et al., 1995) and the results from our *DSM–V* field trial, which we describe at the end of this chapter, have shown that PGD symptoms at 6 months predict more negative outcomes at 13 to 23 months postloss than those assessed earlier. As stated previously, many of the symptoms of PGD are very similar to the symptoms first experienced by bereaved persons who have normal grief during the initial months following their loss. However, in the case of normal grief, these symptoms subside over time. Because of the similarities in the manifestation of early normal grief and PGD, it is important to be conservative in diagnosing PGD to avoid diagnosing bereaved people whose grief is likely to resolve naturally with time; in other words, it is important to reduce the likelihood of false positive diagnoses of PGD that would occur if bereaved persons were diagnosed before 6 months postloss. Requiring the symptomatic distress to last longer than 6 months minimizes Type I error and ensures a higher rate of true positive cases of PGD. It is noteworthy that in analyses that compared mean grief scores among bereaved persons diagnosed with PGD and not diagnosed with PGD at 6 months postloss and beyond, those diagnosed with PGD revealed persistently high levels of grief that did not drop to the level of those without PGD throughout the study observation period. In addition, the empirical examination of the phase theory of grief found that each of the five grief indicators had peaked by 6 months postloss, suggesting further that much of normal intense grief is experienced within the first 6 months. Thus, the PGD diagnosis after 6 months postloss identified a group of bereaved individuals who would remain persistently grief stricken. Given the greater predictive validity, low false positive rate, and chronicity of grief associated with a 6-month postloss diagnosis, and the more conservative requirement that the symptomatic distress endure for 6 months, we propose a duration of 6 months as the temporal criterion for diagnosing PGD.

Prolonged Grief Disorder and Other Mental Disorders
Subsequent to Bereavement

The focus here on PGD is not intended to imply that this disorder is the only, or even the primary, complication that may follow from bereavement. Other psychiatric disorders, such as MDD or PTSD, may develop in response to the loss of a significant other. For example, Zisook and Shuchter (1991) reported that 24% of their sample met criteria for depressive episodes, and 10% met criteria for PTSD, at 2 months postloss. Barry et al. (2001) found, in the first 122 participants who enrolled in the Yale Bereavement Study, that at 4 months postloss the rates of MDD, PTSD, and PGD were 9.0%, 5.7%, and 10.7%, respectively.

Although PGD often co-occurs with other mental disorders in the context of bereavement, studies have shown that PGD symptoms form a coherent cluster that is distinct from bereavement-related depressive and anxiety symptom clusters (Boelen, van den Bout, & de Keijser, 2003; Prigerson et al., 1996, 1997; Prigerson, Frank, et al., 1995; Prigerson, Maciejewski, et al., 1995). Symptoms of depressed mood, psychomotor retardation, and damaged self-esteem are all depressive symptoms, whereas symptoms of yearning, disbelief about the death, a feeling that life is empty and unfulfilling without the deceased, difficulty moving on/a sense of feeling stuck, feeling emotionally numb, and feeling bitter about the death are all specific indicators of PGD (Boelen, van den Bout, & de Keijser, 2003; Prigerson et al., 1996, 1997; Prigerson, Frank, et al., 1995; Prigerson, Maciejewski, et al., 1995). In contrasting PTSD and PGD (Prigerson et al., 2000), we note that avoidance of threatening stimuli is not a salient feature of PGD following a natural death. With PGD there is an avoidance of reminders of the loss as being real, difficulty accepting the loss, and an avoidance of moving on in life without the deceased, not a phobic avoidance of reminders of the traumatic event. Generally speaking, fears of violent physical harm to self or significant others, and the hypervigilance and hyperarousal triggered by a sense of impending attack, play a more salient role for trauma victims than they do for people with PGD that occurs in response to naturally occurring deaths. Also, the unique core PGD symptoms of separation distress, such as longing and pining for the deceased, are not criteria for PTSD or MDD; neither do they appear in any other disorder descriptions in *DSM–IV*. In an analysis of the Yale Bereavement Study sample, Barry et al. (2001) reported rates of diagnostic agreement between PGD and MDD ($\Phi = 0.36$) and PGD and PTSD ($\Phi = 0.26$) that suggest only modest diagnostic overlap. Taken together, these findings demonstrate that although PGD is frequently comorbid with other psychiatric disorders, many cases of PGD would be missed by reliance on only the psychiatric disorders currently found in *DSM–IV*.

Risk Factors for Prolonged Grief Disorder

Risk factors specific to PGD suggest that insults to secure attachment are central to the disorder's etiology. Risk factors include childhood abuse and serious neglect (Silverman, Johnson, & Prigerson, 2001); childhood separation anxiety (Vanderwerker, Jacobs, Parkes, & Prigerson, 2006); close kinship relationship to the deceased (e.g., parents are the most adversely affected adults; Cleiren, Diekstra, Kerkhof, & van der Wal, 1994; van Doorn, Kasl, Beery, Jacobs, & Prigerson, 1998); insecure attachment styles and marital closeness, support, and dependency (Carr et al., 2000; Johnson, Vanderwerker, Bornstein, Zhang, & Prigerson, 2006; van Doorn et al., 1998); controlling parents in childhood (Johnson, Zhang, Greer, & Prigerson, 2007); and, in parental bereavement, the number of remaining children (Wijngaards-de Meij et al., 2005). In a recent study of 346 bereaved older adults, African American bereaved respondents were nearly 5 times more likely than White respondents to meet criteria for PGD (odds ratio = 4.9, 95% confidence interval: 1.3, 18.4; Goldsmith, Morrison, Vanderwerker, & Prigerson, in press). Advance preparation for the loss (Barry et al., 2001), as well as having a good social support network (Vanderwerker & Prigerson, 2004), has been associated with a lower risk of PGD. Taken together, these results suggest that bereaved persons with attachment difficulties, and those who feel unprepared before the death and unsupported after it, are at heightened risk of PGD. Interventions to promote secure alternative attachments to others and emotional reengagement are needed to address the detachment and disengagement that are symptomatic of PGD.

Outcomes of Prolonged Grief Disorder

Although bereavement itself has been shown to pose an elevated risk for a variety of negative physical, mental, and social outcomes, and death (Bornstein, Clayton, Halikas, Maurice, & Robins, 1973; Bruce, Kim, Leaf, & Jacobs, 1990; Kaprio, Koskenvuo, & Rita, 1987; Lund, Dimond, & Caserta, 1985; Schaefer, Quesenberry, & Wi, 1995), studies have found that PGD among the bereaved is associated with heightened risk of physical and mental impairments. Among bereaved individuals, those with PGD have been identified as a subgroup at heightened risk of enduring distress and dysfunction. For example, PGD, after the effects of depressive and anxiety symptoms are taken into account, has been associated with an increased risk of cancer, hypertension, cardiac events, and suicidal ideation (Latham & Prigerson, 2004; Prigerson, Bridge, et al., 1999; Prigerson et al., 1997). This indicates that PGD has incremental validity. It has been associated with disability; functional impairments (social, family, and occupational dysfunction); depressive symptoms; hospitalization; adverse health behaviors, such as increased alcohol and cigarette consumption; and reduced quality of life (e.g., Latham & Prigerson, 2004; Ott, 2003; Prigerson, Bridge, et al., 1999; Prigerson et al., 1997; Prigerson, Frank, et al., 1995; Prigerson, Maciejewski, et al., 1995; Simon et al., 2005).

Prolonged Grief Disorder: Treatment-Specific Response

The distress, adverse health behaviors, and health impairments associated with PGD imply the need for health care professionals to attend specifically to symptoms of PGD. Research has demonstrated the efficacy of nortriptyline and interpersonal psychotherapy for the reduction of bereavement-related depression, but these treatments have not proven effective for the reduction of grief symptomatology (Pasternak et al., 1991; Reynolds et al., 1999). These results provide further support for the notion that symptoms of grief are distinct from those of depression and suggest that additional research is needed to demonstrate the efficacy of pharmacotherapy for the reduction of symptoms of grief per se. To date, there have been no randomized controlled trials of pharmacotherapies for the reduction of grief symptom severity. Open trials of selective serotonin reuptake inhibitors have been conducted and suggest the promise of these and similar agents for the reduction of PGD symptom severity (Zygmont et al., 1998), but randomized placebo-controlled trials are needed before more definitive conclusions can be drawn about their efficacy for the amelioration of PGD symptomatology.

With respect to psychotherapeutic interventions designed for acutely distressed bereaved individuals, Shear, Frank, Houck, and Reynolds (2005) published a randomized controlled trial of a manualized psychotherapy developed specifically for PGD symptoms: Complicated Grief Treatment (hereafter CG Treatment). Shear et al. compared the newly developed therapy with interpersonal psychotherapy among patients from a university-based psychiatric research clinic and a satellite clinic in a low-income African American community. Participants who met the criteria for CG (formerly known as *complicated grief*; see the explanation of the justification of the change in terminology we give at the beginning of this chapter) were randomly assigned to receive interpersonal psychotherapy ($N = 46$) or CG Treatment ($N = 49$); both were administered in 16 sessions during an average interval of 19 weeks per participant. Treatment response was defined either as an independent evaluator-rated Clinical Global Improvement score of 1 or 2 or as time to a 20-point or better improvement in the self-reported Inventory of Complicated Grief (ICG; Prigerson, Frank, et al., 1995). The results indicated that both treatments significantly reduced PGD symptoms, but the response rate was much greater for CG Treatment (51%) than for interpersonal psychotherapy (28%, $p = .02$), and the time to response was shorter for

CG Treatment ($p = .02$). This randomized controlled trial of a psychotherapy for CG provides a solid evidence base for guiding clinical intervention with bereaved persons with this newly defined disorder, although further testing is needed for symptoms of PGD explicitly. Other online interventions for PGD are in development and are expected to prove promising for the reduction of grief-specific distress.

A MOVEMENT TOWARD STANDARDIZED CRITERIA FOR PROLONGED GRIEF DISORDER

To summarize, laypersons and health care professionals have recognized the need for PGD criteria in the large number of people likely to develop this disorder; research has repeatedly demonstrated that the symptoms of PGD are distinctive, associated with substantial distress and disability; and the only randomized controlled trial that significantly reduced symptoms of PGD was one designed specifically to target these symptoms. Still, DSM–IV does not acknowledge that grief may be a distinct mental disorder, and there has been reluctance voiced among bereavement scholars concerning the potential risks of a PGD diagnosis and the need for more evidence in support of a proposed criteria set for such a disorder (Hogan, Worden, & Schmidt, 2003–2004; chap. 9, this volume; Stroebe & Schut, 2005; Stroebe, Schut, & Finkenauer, 2001; Stroebe et al., 2000).

Several objections have been raised about the inclusion of PGD in the DSM. Stroebe et al. (2000, 2001; Stroebe & Schut, 2005) have expressed apprehension about the potential for bereaved individuals diagnosed with PGD to be stigmatized by the classification of their reaction as a mental disorder. Their additional concerns and recommendations relate to

> the definition of pathological grief, the distinction of pathological from normal grief and its relationship with other disorders, and the lack of agreement among scientists about criteria for pathological grief. Further research needs to focus on delineation of syndromes that comprise "pathological grief," and on derivation of acceptable, valid, diagnostic criteria. (Stroebe & Schut, 2005, p. 57)

Earlier in this chapter, we presented our consensus criteria set for PGD that we propose for inclusion in DSM–V (Prigerson et al., 2007), and we have shown how the symptoms of PGD differ from normal grief and from other mental disorders common in bereavement. Next, we address further the topics of normal versus pathological grief and stigmatization, and we present the results of our efforts to build a consensus among scientists by gaining independent expert endorsement of a clinician-informed and empirically derived algorithm for diagnosing PGD with proven reliability and validity (Prigerson et al., 2007).

Concerns About Pathologizing a Normal Reaction to Loss

Stroebe et al. (2001) expressed concern about "creating a new *DSM* category for grief, because an essentially normal (although harrowing) reaction to the death of a significant person will become placed in the realm of psychopathologies" (p. 198). As we noted earlier in this chapter, only a small minority of bereaved individuals (e.g., 11%) develop PGD, thereby indicating that the response is not the norm. Also, research participants who meet criteria for PGD have been shown to be at heightened risk for serious adverse outcomes (e.g., suicidality, high blood pressure, increased smoking and alcohol consumption, functional impairment, and emotional distress; e.g., Latham & Prigerson, 2004; Ott, 2003; Prigerson, Bridge, et al., 1999; Prigerson et al., 1997; Prigerson, Frank, et al., 1995; Prigerson, Maciejewski, et al., 1995; Simon et al., 2005). Thus, PGD is neither normal nor benign but rather represents a pathological response meeting the distress and impairment criteria as much as, and adjusting for, other mental disorders. The argument of pathologizing a normal reaction would have to be applied to all psychiatric illnesses, such as MDD or bipolar disorder. It would deny that somewhere along the continuum of psychological symptom severity (e.g., depressive or anxiety-related symptoms, suicidality) the response is no longer within a normal range (statistically or otherwise) but instead is severe and of clinical concern. The issues concerning the psychopathologizing of grief are not specific to grief and appear to be a more general indictment of potential abuses inherent in psychiatry and the *DSM*.

Second, the concern that a PGD diagnosis would prove stigmatizing has been raised in the absence of data. In our *DSM–V* field trial, we added questions that were answered by 135 community-based bereaved respondents an average of 19 months after the death of a significant other. The responses indicated that 87.5% of those who met criteria for PGD said that a diagnosis would make them relieved to know that they were not going crazy, 93.8% said that they would be relieved to know that they had a recognizable problem, and 100% said that the diagnosis would help their family members to understand better what they were experiencing. On the basis of these preliminary results it appears that people diagnosed with PGD think that the diagnosis would enhance others' ability to comprehend their suffering. Additional research conducted on significant others of those diagnosed with and/or treated for PGD is needed to determine whether family and friends withdraw support or develop a greater appreciation and understanding of the severity of the illness, how and why it manifests itself, and the bereaved person's need for help in adjusting to the loss.

An Effort to Build a Consensus

The remaining obstacle to the inclusion of PGD in the *DSM* has been the lack of agreement among clinicians and scientists about diagnostic criteria for PGD. Despite evidence supporting the validity of PGD as a distinct mental disorder, the field has not to date settled on explicit and consensually derived criteria for PGD. Psychiatrists such as Freud (1917/1957), Lindemann (1944), Bowlby (1980), Parkes and Weiss (1983), Raphael (1994), Horowitz et al. (1997), and Jacobs (1993) have noted the suffering imposed by intense, chronic mourning, and symptoms and diagnostic algorithms for pathological grief have been proposed. Because independent investigators have identified largely the same set of pathological grief symptoms, such efforts provide independent validation and demonstrate clinical agreement and understanding of the distinct symptomatic distress and impairment associated with intense, chronic grief. Nevertheless, prior to the most recent study (Prigerson et al., 2007), which we describe shortly, explicit and agreed-on (i.e., standardized) criteria had not been field-tested in non–treatment-seeking community-based respondents, or approved by independent bereavement experts. Here we describe the process by which we derived the proposed diagnostic criteria for PGD and achieved consensus via compromise and collaboration with Mardi Horowitz, the leading proponent of an alternative diagnostic algorithm for PGD.

As a first step toward the development of explicit and agreed-on criteria for PGD, we and our colleagues (Prigerson, Shear, et al., 1999) convened a group of clinical and scientific experts in bereavement, mood and anxiety disorders, and psychiatric nosology to review the evidence justifying the development of criteria for PGD (details of the consensus conference are provided in Prigerson & Jacobs, 2001). Following the panel's conclusion that the evidence merited the development of criteria for PGD, the panel formulated a consensually agreed-on criteria set. Using the most relevant, though incomplete, data available at the time, a preliminary testing of the consensus criteria yielded results that supported their sensitivity and specificity (Prigerson & Jacobs, 2001).

Next, we conducted a field trial to evaluate the performance of the proposed consensus criteria for PGD (Prigerson et al., 2007). We revised the ICG (Prigerson, Frank, et al., 1995) to facilitate the assessment of symptoms identified by the consensus panel. We then obtained data to assess the symptoms, correlates, and consequences of PGD from an inception cohort of 317 community-based bereaved respondents from in-person interviews conducted, on average, at 6.2 ($SD = 6.9$), 10.8 ($SD = 5.9$), and 19.7 ($SD = 5.8$) months postloss. Before conducting the analysis, we restructured the data such that assessments were grouped into more uniform time periods: 0 to 6 months, 6 to 12 months, and 12 to 24 months postloss. We then conducted a series of focused analyses designed to produce, in the end, an efficient, robust, evidence-based *DSM*-style diagnostic algorithm (i.e., presentation with at least X actual symptoms from a specific list of Y possible symptoms) for PGD.

To start, we wanted to evaluate the level of information and robustness of all ICG—Rater Administered Structured Clinical Interview (ICG–RA;

Prigerson & Jacobs, 2001) symptoms assessed through interviews conducted by trained interviews (trained to standards acceptable to Selby Jacobs, MD; Prigerson et al., 2007). All symptoms considered for inclusion in the proposed criteria for PGD would be informative and uniformly applicable to individuals independent of factors such as age, sex, and time from loss. We used two techniques—(a) item information function (IIF) analysis and (b) differential item functioning (DIF) analysis—each within the framework of item response theory (IRT), to evaluate the suitability of ICG–RA symptoms.

In the IIF analysis, we identified and subsequently removed symptoms that contributed less than 20% of the information contributed by the most informative symptom (Prigerson et al., 2007). DIF analyses were then conducted to derive a set of symptoms that would be uniformly applicable to individuals independent of age, sex, and kinship relationship to the deceased. Biased items were removed from further consideration. On the basis of the results of these IIF and DIF analyses, the following 12 informative, unbiased ICG–RA symptoms were retained for consideration in a diagnostic algorithm: (a) yearning; (b) avoidance of reminders of the deceased; (c) disbelief or trouble accepting the death; (d) a perception that life is empty or meaningless without the deceased; (e) feelings of bitterness or anger; (f) emotional numbness or detachment from others; (g) feeling stunned, dazed, or shocked; (h) feeling part of oneself died along with the deceased; (i) difficulty trusting others; (j) difficulty moving on with life; (k) feeling on edge or jumpy; and (l) survivor guilt.

In the absence of an established, standard method for diagnosing PGD, we needed to develop a criterion standard for "case-ness" of PGD by which we could evaluate the performance of alternative DSM-style diagnostic algorithms for PGD. We trained raters to an acceptable standard (i.e., $\kappa \geq .90$ agreement between Holly G. Prigerson and the rater) for the diagnosis of PGD (Prigerson et al., 2007). We then had these trained raters evaluate whether the participant, in the rater's expert opinion, represented a present case of PGD. This rater determination of "case-ness" of PGD had the advantage of reflecting experienced clinical judgment but was also, at times, inconsistent with the IRT model scores for the underlying grief attribute (i.e., some participants with high scores were not considered to meet criteria for PGD, and vice versa). We wanted our criterion standard to not only be informed by clinical judgment but also be a function of PGD symptom severity.

Toward this end, we used scores from an IRT model for PGD based on the most informative, unbiased ICG–RA symptoms determined in our prior IIF and DIF IRT analyses as an effective means for ordering bereaved individuals in terms of symptom severity (Prigerson et al., 2007). We then maximized agreement between rater diagnoses and diagnoses made by a range of minimum-threshold grief attribute assessments of "case-ness" of PGD. Having an IRT model PGD score above this minimum-threshold value became our criterion standard for PGD.

We considered each of the ICG–RA symptoms retained after our IIF and DIF IRT analyses a candidate symptom for inclusion in a *DSM*-style diagnostic algorithm for PGD (Prigerson et al., 2007). On the basis of a consensus opinion of an expert panel (Prigerson, Shear, et al., 1999) we included yearning as a mandatory symptom. However, in our analyses we would consider that the remaining ICG–RA symptoms could be present or absent (i.e., if they had a severity of at least 4 on a 5-point response format) in any combination.

We sought to ascertain the number and combination of the remaining symptoms in addition to yearning that would yield the most efficient (i.e., optimum balance between sensitive and specific) diagnosis for PGD with respect to our criterion standard (Prigerson et al., 2007). We used *combinatorics* (Abramowitz & Stegun, 1972), the branch of mathematics that studies the number of different ways of arranging sets, to enumerate sets of symptoms that might be considered the basis of *DSM*-style algorithms for PGD. A total of 4,785 *DSM*-style algorithms for prolonged grief were enumerated and subsequently evaluated with respect to the criterion standard.

The optimal, most efficient diagnostic algorithm included yearning and at least five of the following nine symptoms: (a) avoidance of reminders of the deceased; (b) disbelief or trouble accepting the death; (c) a perception that life is empty or meaningless without the deceased; (d) feelings of bitterness or anger related to the loss; (e) emotional numbness; (f) feeling stunned, dazed, or shocked; (g) feeling part of oneself died along with the deceased; (h) difficulty trusting others; and (i) difficulty moving on with life (Prigerson et al., 2007). Sensitivity, specificity, and positive and negative predictive values were all above .94. The optimal algorithm displayed convergent validity with respect to a previously proposed diagnostic algorithm for prolonged grief, the rater diagnosis of prolonged grief, the criterion standard, and discriminant validity with respect to other mood and anxiety disorders.

Next, the predictive validity of the optimal *DSM*-style diagnostic algorithm for PGD with respect to subsequent *DSM* mental disorders (MDD, PTSD, or GAD), disturbed sleep, suicidal ideation, functional disability, and poor quality of life was evaluated (Prigerson et al., 2007). Relative risks for these outcomes associated with PGD diagnoses assessed 0 to 6 months and 7 to 12 months postloss were assessed separately in two groups: (a) those who did not and (b) those who did concurrently meet *DSM* criteria for MDD, PTSD, or GAD. Among those not concurrently meeting *DSM* criteria for MDD, PTSD, or GAD, PGD diagnoses assessed 0 to 6 months postloss were significantly associated with psychiatric diagnoses (MDD, PTSD, or GAD); disturbed sleep, suicidal ideation, and poor quality of life 7 to 12 months postloss; and suicidal ideation 13 to 24 months postloss, and diagnoses of PGD assessed 7 to 12 months postloss were significantly associated with psychiatric diagnoses (MDD, PTSD, or GAD) and suicidal ideation, functional disability, and low quality of life 13 to 24 months postloss. Among persons concurrently meeting

DSM criteria for MDD, PTSD, or GAD, PGD diagnoses 0 to 6 months post-loss were significantly associated with psychiatric diagnoses (MDD, PTSD, or GAD) at 7 to 12 months and 13 to 24 months postloss, and PGD diagnoses 7 to 12 months postloss were significantly associated with psychiatric diagnoses (MDD, PTSD, or GAD) at 13 to 24 months postloss.

As final steps toward building a consensus, we asked a group of leading authorities in bereavement research and clinical care,[1] most of whom were not involved in the DSM–V field trial, to review the evidence just presented and to offer their feedback (Prigerson et al., 2007). We requested an international community of clinicians, researchers, organizations, and potential PGD sufferers, all of whom had directly expressed to us an interest in the proposed criteria for PGD (e.g., members of the International Society for Traumatic Stress Studies Special Interest Group on Traumatic Loss and PGD, the DSM–V PGD work group, and others who contacted the authors about the criteria) to critique the methods and results described in this chapter. We incorporated comments and collaborated with Mardi Horowitz's group, and together we formulated and tested the diagnostic criteria for PGD proposed for DSM–V described earlier. The results for the compromise PGD criteria are entirely consistent with the results reported in this chapter and are reported elsewhere (Prigerson et al., 2007). They show that over half of the participants who met criteria for another assessed DSM–IV disorder did not meet criteria for PGD and would have been missed. Moreover, among the participants who met the compromise criteria for PGD but did not meet criteria for the other DSM–IV disorders (i.e., MDD, GAD, PTSD), the PGD diagnosis at 7 to 12 months postloss significantly predicted any DSM–IV disorder, suicidal ideation, functional impairment, and poor quality of life at 13 to 24 months postloss (Prigerson et al., 2007).

A PROPOSAL TO INCLUDE PROLONGED GRIEF DISORDER IN THE FIFTH EDITION OF THE *DIAGNOSTIC AND STATISTICAL MANUAL OF MENTAL DISORDERS*

In this chapter, we have summarized the evidence that PGD constitutes a distinct mental disorder and our efforts to develop a standardized, clinically informed, evidence-based, DSM-style diagnostic algorithm for PGD. The criteria proposed here for PGD were initially formulated by a consensus panel of experts and then field-tested using established, scientifically sound techniques

---

[1]The bereavement panel reviewing the prolonged grief disorder proposed for inclusion in DSM-V included Holly G. Prigerson, Mardi J. Horowitz, Mihaela Aslan, Selby C. Jacobs, Colin M. Parkes, Beverley Raphael, Camille Wortman, Karl Goodkin, Robert Neimeyer, George Bonanno, Susan D. Block, David W. Kissane, Stephen J. Marwit, Paul Boelen, Andreas Maercker, Brett Litz, Jeffrey G. Johnson, Michael B. First, and Paul K. Maciejewski.

applied to a community-based sample of recently bereaved individuals. The empirical results were then reviewed and ultimately approved by a separate set of both clinical researchers who have studied bereavement extensively, those who met the proposed criteria for PGD, and experts in psychiatric nosology. Thus, the proposed criteria set for PGD has factored in clinical insights and experience from an international panel of bereaved individuals and bereavement experts, were evidence based and analyzed with objective statistical methods, and approved by an independent set of individuals affected personally and/or professionally by this mental disorder and the leading proponent of an alternative diagnostic algorithm for PGD (Horowitz et al., 1997).

As a culmination of this effort, we are now poised to propose a refined consensus criteria set for PGD for inclusion in *DSM–V*. We have produced a diagnostic algorithm for PGD that is the synthesis of clinical consensus, client response, objectively gathered data, and evidence. The methods used to refine this criteria set over years of study are as clinically informed and rigorously tested on relevant data as those used for disorders currently found in *DSM–IV*. Lay and professional organizations and people have recognized the clinical utility of diagnostic criteria for PGD. The time has come for the *DSM* to acknowledge the need for diagnostic criteria for PGD, to review the evidence amassed, and to consider seriously the inclusion of criteria for PGD that have resulted from this and related efforts.

REFERENCES

Abramowitz, M., & Stegun, I. A. (1972). Combinatorial analysis. In M. Abramowitz & I. A. Stegun (Eds.), *Handbook of mathematical functions with formulas, graphs, and mathematical tables* (pp. 821–827). New York: Dover.

American Psychiatric Association. (1994). *Diagnostic and statistical manual of mental disorders* (4th ed.). Washington, DC: Author.

Barry, L. C., Kasl, S. V., & Prigerson, H. G. (2001). Psychiatric disorders among bereaved persons: The role of perceived circumstances of death and preparedness for death. *American Journal of Geriatric Psychiatry, 10,* 447–457.

Berezin, M. A. (1970). The psychiatrist and the geriatric patient: Partial grief in family members and others who care for the elderly patient. *Journal of Geriatric Psychiatry, 4,* 53–70.

Boelen, P. A., van den Bout, J., & de Keijser, J. (2003). Traumatic grief as a disorder distinct from bereavement-related depression and anxiety: A replication study with bereaved mental health care patients. *American Journal of Psychiatry, 160,* 1229–1241.

Bornstein, P. E., Clayton, P. J., Halikas, J. A., Maurice, W. L., & Robins, E. (1973). The depression of widowhood after 13 months. *British Journal of Psychiatry, 122,* 561–566.

Bowlby, J. (1961). Processes of mourning. *International Journal of Psychoanalysis, 42,* 317–340.

Bowlby, J. (1980). *Attachment and loss: Vol. 3. Loss: Sadness and depression.* New York: Basic Books.

Bruce, M. L., Kim, K., Leaf, P. J., & Jacobs, S. C. (1990). Depressive episodes and dysphoria resulting from conjugal bereavement in a prospective community sample. *American Journal of Psychiatry, 147,* 608–611.

Carr, D., House, J. S., Kessler, R. C., Nesse, R. M., Sonnega, J., & Wortman, C. (2000). Marital quality and psychological adjustment to widowhood among older adults: A longitudinal analysis. *Journals of Gerontology Series B: Psychological Sciences and Social Sciences, 55,* S197–S207.

Cleiren, M., Diekstra, R. F., Kerkhof, A. J., & van der Wal, J. (1994). Mode of death and kinship in bereavement: Focusing on "who" rather than "how." *Crisis, 15,* 22–36.

Dunne, K. (2004). Grief and its manifestations. *Nursing Standard, 18,* 45–51.

Freud, S. (1957). Mourning and melancholia. In J. Strachey (Ed. & Trans.), *The complete psychological works of Sigmund Freud* (pp. 152–170). London: Hogarth Press. (Original work published 1917)

Goldsmith, B., Morrison, R. S., Vanderwerker, L. C., & Prigerson, H. G. (in press). Elevated rates of complicated grief in African Americans. *Death Studies.*

Hogan, N. S., Worden, J. W., & Schmidt, L. A. (2003–2004). An empirical study of the proposed complicated grief disorder criteria. *Omega: The Journal of Death and Dying, 48,* 263–277.

Horowitz, M. J., Siegel, B., Holen, A., Bonanno, G. A., Milbrath, C., & Stinson, C. H. (1997). Diagnostic criteria for complicated grief disorder. *American Journal of Psychiatry, 154,* 904–910.

Hoyert, D. L., Kung, H.-C., & Smith, B. L. (2005, February 28). *Deaths: Preliminary data for 2003* (National Vital Statistics Reports, Vol. 53, No. 15). Hyattsville, MD: National Center for Health Statistics. Retrieved December 4, 2007, from http://www.cdc.gov/nchs/data/nvsr/nvsr53/nvsr53_15.pdf

Jacobs, S. (1993). *Pathologic grief: Maladaptation to loss.* Washington, DC: American Psychiatric Press.

Johnson, J. G., Vanderwerker, L. C., Bornstein, R. F., Zhang, B., & Prigerson, H. G. (2006). Development and validation of an instrument for the assessment of dependency among bereaved persons. *Journal of Psychopathology and Behavioral Assessment, 28,* 1–10. doi: 10.1007/s10862-005-9016-3, http://dx.doi.org/10.1007/s10862-005-9016-3

Johnson, J. G., Zhang, B., Greer, J. A., & Prigerson, H. G. (2007). Parental control, partner dependency and complicated grief among widowed adults in the community. *Journal of Nervous and Mental Disease, 195,* 26–30.

Kaprio, J., Koskenvuo, M., & Rita, H. (1987). Mortality after bereavement: A prospective study of 95,647 widowed persons. *American Journal of Public Health, 77,* 283–287.

Kübler-Ross, E. (1969). *On death and dying.* New York: Macmillan.

Lacey, D. (2005). Nursing home social worker skills and end-of-life planning. *Social Work Health Care, 40,* 19–40.

Latham, A. E., & Prigerson, H. G. (2004). Suicidality and bereavement: Complicated grief as psychiatric disorder presenting greatest risk for suicidality. *Suicide and Life-Threatening Behavior, 34,* 350–362.

Lindemann, E. (1944). Symptomatology and management of acute grief. *American Journal of Psychiatry, 101,* 141–148.

Lund, D., Dimond, M., & Caserta, M. S. (1985). Identifying elderly with coping difficulties 2 years after bereavement. *Omega: The Journal of Death and Dying, 16,* 213–224.

Maciejewski, P. K., Zhang, B., Block, S. D., & Prigerson, H. G. (2007). An empirical testing of the stage theory of grief resolution. *Journal of the American Medical Association, 297,* 716–723.

Marwit, S. J. (1991). *DSM–III–R,* grief reactions, and a call for revision. *Professional Psychology: Research and Practice, 22,* 75–79.

National Cancer Institute. (n.d.). *Loss, grief, and bereavement (PDQ®).* Retrieved December 4, 2007, from http://www.nci.nih.gov/cancertopics/pdq/supportive-care/bereavement/Patient/page6

Ott, C. H. (2003). The impact of complicated grief on mental and physical health at various points in the bereavement process. *Death Studies, 27,* 249–272.

Parkes, C. (1972). *Bereavement: Studies in grief in adult life.* London: Tavistock.

Parkes, C. M., & Weiss, R. S. (1983). *Recovery from bereavement.* Northvale, NJ: Jason Aronson.

Pasternak, R. E., Reynolds, C. F., Schlernitzauer, M., Hoch, C. C., Buysse, D. J., Houck, P. R., & Perel, J. M. (1991). Acute open-trial nortriptyline therapy of bereavement-related depression in late life. *Journal of Clinical Psychiatry, 52,* 307–310.

Penson, R. T., Green, K. M., Chabner, B. A., & Lynch, T. J. (2002). When does the responsibility of our care end: Bereavement. *The Oncologist, 7,* 251–258.

Prigerson, H. G. (2004). Complicated grief: When the path of adjustment leads to a dead-end. *Bereavement Care, 23,* 38–40.

Prigerson, H. G., Bierhals, A. J., Kasl, S. V., Reynolds, C. F., Shear, M. K., Day, N., et al. (1997). Traumatic grief as a risk factor for mental and physical morbidity. *American Journal of Psychiatry, 154,* 616–623.

Prigerson, H. G., Bierhals, A. J., Kasl, S. V., Reynolds, C. F., Shear, M. K., Newsom, J. T., & Jacobs, S. (1996). Complicated grief as a disorder distinct from bereavement-related depression and anxiety: A replication study. *American Journal of Psychiatry, 153,* 1484–1486.

Prigerson, H. G., Bridge, J., Maciejewski, P. K., Beery, L. C., Rosenheck, R. A., Jacobs, S. C., et al. (1999). Influence of traumatic grief on suicidal ideation among young adults. *American Journal of Psychiatry, 156,* 1994–1995.

Prigerson, H. G., Frank, E., Kasl, S. V., Reynolds, C. F., Anderson, B., Zubenko, G. S., et al. (1995). Complicated grief and bereavement-related depression as distinct disorders: Preliminary empirical validation in elderly bereaved spouses. *American Journal of Psychiatry, 152,* 22–30.

Prigerson, H. G., Horowitz, M. J., Jacobs, S. C., Aslan, M., Parkes, C. M., Raphael, B., et al. (2007). *Field trial of consensus criteria for PGD proposed for* DSM–V. Manuscript submitted for publication.

Prigerson, H. G., & Jacobs, S. C. (2001). Traumatic grief as a distinct disorder: A rationale, consensus criteria, and preliminary empirical test. In M. S. Stroebe, R. O. Hansson, W. Stroebe, & H. Schut (Eds.), *Handbook of bereavement research: Consequences, coping, and care* (pp. 613–645). Washington, DC: American Psychological Association.

Prigerson, H. G., Maciejewski, P. K., Reynolds, C. F., Bierhals, A. J., Newsom, J. T., Fasiczka, A., et al. (1995). Inventory of Complicated Grief: A scale to measure maladaptive symptoms of loss. *Psychiatry Research, 59,* 65–79.

Prigerson, H. G., Shear, M. K., Jacobs, S. C., Kasl, S. V., Maciejewski, P. K., Silverman, G. K., et al. (2000). Grief and its relationship to PTSD. In D. Nutt & J. R. T. Davidson (Eds.), *Post traumatic stress disorders: Diagnosis, management and treatment* (pp. 163–186). New York: Martin Dunitz.

Prigerson, H. G., Shear, M. K., Jacobs, S. C., Reynolds, C. F., Maciejewski, P. K., Davidson, J. R. T., et al. (1999). Consensus criteria for traumatic grief: A preliminary empirical test. *British Journal of Psychiatry, 174,* 67–73.

Raphael, B. (1994). *The anatomy of bereavement: A handbook for the caring professions.* New York: Jason Aronson.

Reynolds, C. F., Miller, M. D., Pasternak, R. E., Frank, E., Perel, J. M., Cornes, C., et al. (1999). Treatment of bereavement-related major depressive episodes in later life: A controlled study of acute and continuation treatment with nortriptyline and interpersonal psychotherapy. *American Journal of Psychiatry, 156,* 202–208.

Robins, L., & Guze, S. B. (1970). Establishment of diagnostic validity in psychiatric illness: Its application to schizophrenia. *American Journal of Psychiatry, 126,* 983–987.

Schaefer, C., Quesenberry, C. P., & Wi, S. (1995). Mortality following conjugal bereavement and the effects of a shared environment. *American Journal of Epidemiology, 141,* 1142–1152.

Shear, M. K., Frank, E., Houck, P., & Reynolds, C. F. (2005). Treatment of complicated grief: A randomized controlled trial. *Journal of the American Medical Association, 293,* 2601–2659.

Silverman, G. K., Johnson, J. G., & Prigerson, H. G. (2001). Preliminary explorations of the effects of prior trauma and loss on risk of psychiatric disorders in recently widowed people. *Israel Journal of Psychiatry and Related Sciences, 38,* 202–215.

Simon, N. M., Pollack, M. H., Fischmann, D., Perlman, C. A., Muriel, A. C., Moore, C. W., et al. (2005). Complicated grief and its correlates in patients with bipolar disorder. *Journal of Clinical Psychiatry, 66,* 1105–1110.

Stroebe, M., & Schut, H. (2005). Complicated grief: A conceptual analysis of the field. *Omega, 52,* 53–70.

Stroebe, M., Schut, H., & Finkenauer, C. (2001). The traumatization of grief: A conceptual framework for understanding the trauma–bereavement interface. *Israel Journal of Psychiatry and Related Sciences, 38,* 185–201.

Stroebe, M., van Son, M., Stroebe, W., Kleber, R., Schut, H., & van den Bout, J. (2000). On the classification and diagnosis of pathological grief. *Clinical Psychology Review, 20,* 57–75.

Swarte, N. B., van der Lee, M. L., van der Bom, J. G., van den Bout, J., & Heintz, A. P. (2003). Effects of euthanasia on the bereaved family and friends: A cross sectional study. *British Medical Journal, 327,* 189–192.

Vanderwerker, L. C., Jacobs, S. C., Parkes, C. M., & Prigerson, H. G. (2006). An exploration of association between separation anxiety in childhood and complicated grief in late-life. *Journal of Nervous and Mental Disease, 194,* 121–123.

Vanderwerker, L. C., & Prigerson, H. G. (2004). Social support and technological connectedness as protective factors in bereavement. *Journal of Loss and Trauma, 9,* 45–57.

van Doorn, C., Kasl, S. V., Beery, L. C., Jacobs, S. C., & Prigerson, H. G. (1998). The influence of marital quality and attachment styles on traumatic grief and depressive symptoms. *Journal of Nervous and Mental Disease, 186,* 566–573.

Wijngaards-de Meij, L., Stroebe, M., Schut, H., Stroebe, W., van den Bout, J., van der Heijden, P., & Dijkstra, I. (2005). Couples at risk following the death of their child: Predictors of grief versus depression. *Journal of Consulting and Clinical Psychology, 73,* 617–623.

Zhang, B., el-Jawahri, A., & Prigerson, H. G. (2006). Update on bereavement research: Evidence-based guidelines for the diagnosis and treatment of complicated bereavement. *Journal of Palliative Medicine, 9,* 1188–1203.

Zisook, S., & Shuchter, S. R. (1991). Depression through the first year after the death of a spouse. *American Journal of Psychiatry, 148,* 1346–1352.

Zygmont, M., Prigerson, H. G., Houck, P. R., Miller, M. D., Shear, M. K., Jacobs, S., & Reynolds, C. F. (1998). A post hoc comparison of paroxetine and nortriptyline for symptoms of traumatic grief. *Journal of Clinical Psychiatry, 59,* 241–255.

9

CLINICAL ASPECTS OF A *DSM* COMPLICATED GRIEF DIAGNOSIS: CHALLENGES, DILEMMAS, AND OPPORTUNITIES

SIMON SHIMSHON RUBIN, RUTH MALKINSON,
AND ELIEZER WITZTUM

The death of a significant loved one is a painful but inevitable fact of life. On the basis of clinical and research literature, the inclusion of a complicated grief (CG) category in diagnostic nomenclatures has much to recommend it, yet, as we try to show in this chapter, a significant gap separates the clinical spectrum of complications of bereavement from current proposals advanced to conform to the requirements of the *Diagnostic and Statistical Manual of Mental Disorders* (*DSM*; e.g., 4th ed., *DSM–IV*; American Psychiatric Association, 1994). We favor a diagnostic spectrum addressing bereavement in the *DSM*. Nevertheless, we question whether the emphasis placed on identifying individuals who are suffering from particularly pronounced complications of bereavement may not exclude too many cases of bereavement complication in some cases while being overinclusive in others. Furthermore, although we support the identification of bereavement complications among the population of people who have lost significant loved ones, we remain acutely aware that these developments can be accompanied by a variety of potentially negative implications whose impact cannot be fully perceived at this time. Because grief is a ubiquitous experience, and because all humankind encounters loss and experiences grief and mourning, identifying some degrees and areas of grief as problematic with a medical diagnosis will almost certainly generate public attention and controversy, as is already the case in the professional community (Parkes, 2006). Some of this undoubtedly will present an opportunity for education about grief and loss, and we welcome that. Predicting how a diagnosis that focuses on the complications of grief will affect the natural ecology and supports available to the bereaved is a risky business; how such a diagnosis may affect the nonmedical therapies is a question of no less importance. As clinicians and researchers, we believe it necessary to develop valid, sensitive, and relevant categories to classify the responses of bereavement. Whether the mobilization of natural supports and public awareness of bereavement will be helped or hindered by any moves toward these diagnostic categories, however, is something we should all consider on the way to the next *DSM*.

We open this chapter with a consideration of two challenges: (a) how not to do harm in our movement toward a classification designed to assist the bereaved and (b) how to include in our formulations the nuances of the relationship to the one who died. We then turn to three dilemmas: (a) how to integrate lessons learned from the evolution of the posttraumatic stress disorder (PTSD) diagnosis into a *DSM* diagnosis for CG; (b) how to address the trauma–bereavement interface, as presented in three case vignettes; and (c) how to formulate relational terms (particularly the problematic aspects of the representation of interpersonal relationships) into a symptomatic phenomenological approach. For the last of these we use two recent proposal summaries to convey our view and to consider variations on how to work with these proposals for CG (as well as the alternative, prolonged grief disorder) advanced by Prigerson, Horowitz, and their colleagues (Parkes, 2006; chap. 8, this volume). We conclude with a consideration of the opportunities that follow naturally from the material considered in this chapter.

THE CHALLENGES

Classification

The loss of a significant other is a multidimensional experience with significant variation in people's responses. Considerable evidence exists that bereavement can be facilitated by social support and personal resources, and the majority of the bereaved do not require professional intervention (Kyrouz, Humphreys, & Loomis, 2002; Malkinson, Rubin, & Witztum, 2000, 2005). A considerable body of opinion and research also indicates that sometimes bereavement can be overwhelming, with the bereaved unable to return to adequate functioning in their lives without professional assistance. Estimates of problems in processing grief and bereavement range from 15% to 20% prevalence (Bonanno, Wortman, & Nesse, 2004; Prigerson et al., 1995). There is evidence that some bereaved individuals benefit from professional interventions by counselors and mental health personnel (Jordan & Neimeyer, 2003; Schut, Stroebe, van den Bout, & Terheggen, 2001).

Categorizing various trajectories of loss and showing how they unfold over time require decisions about how to view these responses with an eye to diagnosis. How soon after a loss should difficulty be identified, and how long must difficulty be present for a diagnosis to be made? If one chooses to emphasize the most extreme and problematic responses that persist, then a longer time period will be chosen, and this may leave many suffering people outside the diagnosis. (This sometimes is referred to as a *Type II error*, although it is actually a conscious choice and not an error.) If a shorter time period is chosen, then many self-reparative people may be included as a by-product of the wish to minimize suffering and maximize early intervention. A recent special issue of the *Omega: The Journal of Death and Dying* critically addressed considerations of the proposed criteria for a CG diagnosis (Parkes, 2006; Prigerson & Maciejewski, 2006). Conceptual, clinical, research, and social considerations were among the issues addressed as the strengths, weaknesses, merits, and drawbacks of the diagnostic category were debated. We return to the proposed criteria of that issue in a later section of this chapter.

Many factors affect a person's response to bereavement and expose people to varying degrees of risk for more protracted, problematic, or atypical presentations of grief. Many clinicians confronted with a bereaved individual or family typically take into account the identity of the bereaved, the identity of the deceased, the circumstances of the loss, and the culture (Witztum, Malkinson, & Rubin, 2001). The bereaved person's strengths, the nature of his or her support systems, and his or her individual makeup are considered in decisions on the necessity of intervention or follow-up.

How might the addition of CG as a diagnostic criterion affect the multiple sources of social support, service delivery, and the bereaved person's understanding of what he or she is going through? If strong responses to bereavement become medicalized, then the natural support systems that nonprofessional people can provide each other may not fully blossom, and individuals whose bereavements are painful but not sufficiently problematic to receive professional attention may be lost in the shuffle.

The addition of a CG diagnosis or spectrum could lead to improved services for people in need, or it could direct attention away from indigenous supports and natural healing of loss. Identifying some bereavements as problematic goes against the idea that disruption because of loss is to be expected as normative for a time (Engel, 1961; Freud, 1917/1957). A century of clinical and research literature, however, documents the consistency of dysfunctions following bereavement.

Retaining respect for individual and familial resilience is important. Similarly, the community-based supports and the self-help frameworks that provide so much assistance to the bereaved have an important role to play (Malkinson & Geron, 2006; Silverman, 1986). Yet classifying the complications of bereavement, some of which may be endemic to certain losses, is preferable to not looking for them. In this we follow Rando (1993), who pointed out risks and vulnerability present in complications of bereavement.

The challenge of ensuring that the diagnosis of CG will be rigorous yet sufficiently relevant to many forms of bereavement difficulties is large. To retain sensitivity to the variations in bereavement difficulties, to be attuned to the complexity of the potential pathways for adjustment and maladjustment, and not to overemphasize a model stressing pathology are all aspects of the challenge. Above all, the importance of not doing harm, as a by-product of the wish to do good, is an issue for practical consideration as decisions are made on the diagnoses of grief and bereavement.

Relationship

For someone to be properly classified with a diagnosis of CG, a degree of complication or dysfunction must be present that meet the agreed criteria. When arguing for inclusion in the *DSM*, one wonders the extent to which the dysfunction is, at its root, bound up with the bereavement or merely triggered by it. Dysfunction associated with a bereavement diagnosis, of course, should not be sufficiently subsumed under the classification of other disorders already present in the current *DSM* classification system. Determining whether bereavement is a precipitating cause of disorder—say, in provoking a depressive episode that responds to medication or some form of psychotherapy—or whether it is a fundamental sustaining cause, as when depression continues only so long as the bereavement itself is not confronted by a specific intervention, is a matter for research. In the latter case, however, it would be logical to tailor some treatments, or aspects of treatments, specifically to the factors unique to loss. The research evidence available so far suggests the latter scenario is correct in some cases of bereavement dysfunction (Shear, Frank, Houck, & Reynolds, 2005).

The multidimensional complexity of response to loss and bereavement poses a challenge for the diagnosis of CG and for mourning. The adequacy and breadth of the bereaved's biopsychosocial functioning are important in assessment, but this axis alone is insufficient for gauging the impact of death on a significant other. The ongoing relationship to the deceased is a central and parallel axis for measuring the bereavement response over time. Addressing these twin domains of functioning and relationship is significant from the vantage points of theory, empirical findings, diagnostic implications, and intervention strategies. Repeated attention to this has emerged in the literature. The *two-track model of bereavement* was formulated and developed to keep this double perspective at the heart of bereavement work (Malkinson, Rubin, & Witztum, 2006; Rubin, 1981, 1984, 1993, 1999; Rubin, Malkinson, & Witztum,

2000). The *dual-process model of bereavement* (Stroebe & Schut, 1999) has focused on the oscillating coping processes directed to the bereaved's restorative connection with the world on the one hand and the relationship with the deceased on the other. As for current CG proposals for the *DSM*, we believe there is a need to emphasize further and specify issues related to the relationship.

The significance, nature, and organization of the postloss relationship to the memories and mental representations of the deceased are neither easy to grasp nor easy to measure. This relationship is intuitively and intellectually appealing and confusing at the same time. How can one have a relationship with someone who has died? Yet we know that simply not seeing or not talking to someone for a time does not alter the fact that that person is important to us and to our psychological well-being. Interpersonal loss often pummels the psychological and mental organization of the bereaved's relationship with the deceased, just as loss by death works to remove the deceased from mutual physical interaction with the world of the living. Memories of the other person, and of the relationship with him or her (including the way the memories are structured and the degree to which they are available), are involved. It is appropriate to examine the types, degree, and nature of the affects aroused following loss. Discovery of what the bereaved has "lost" following the death (Freud, 1917/1957), as well as what aspects of the relationship and connection with the deceased remain, are embedded in the narrative story of the relationship and the self.

Assessing the perception of and relation to the deceased is a rich domain (Field, 2006; Klass, 2006; Stroebe, Gergen, Gergen, & Stroebe, 1993; Stroebe & Schut, 2005). It is not identical to addressing the bereaved person's degree of yearning or progress in accepting the reality of the death. The challenge is to consider fundamental aspects of the organization of the cognitive–emotional map of the deceased and the relationship to him or her (Rubin, 1999). Memories of the deceased may be minimal, reasonably accessible, or intrusive (Horowitz et al., 1997). They may cause distress and discomfort or contribute to a sense of well-being and support (Main, 1991). If both biopsychosocial function and the nature of the ongoing relationship with the deceased are assessed in the diagnosis of CG, then the potential for a unique bereavement focus is enhanced. Focusing on dysfunction alone as manifest in the behavioral realm misses the heart of bereavement and misses the opportunity to focus attention on what bereavement is: response to interpersonal loss. Addressing the heightened pining for the bereaved in the context of a relationship still leaves unexplored much variation in relational factors associated with the bereavement response.

It is difficult, but not impossible, to assess the nature of the psychological relationship in a screening or brief self-report measure. Learning what the bereaved individual thinks, remembers, and feels about the deceased has been considered in combinations of quantitative and qualitative research (Field,

2006; Horowitz et al., 1984; Klass, Silverman, & Nickman, 1996; Main, 1991; Rubin, 1992, 1999; Saldinger, Porterfield, & Cain, 2004; Silverman, Baker, Cait, & Boerner, 2003). A description of the cognitive–emotional organization of the relationship must also address function and dysfunction for it to interest users of the *DSM*. In the absence of sensitive and robust indicators of the nature of the relationship to the deceased, yearning has emerged as a prominent and overt marker of relationship, as have strong periods of emotion (Parkes, 2006). What holds untapped promise for understanding complications of grief, however, is a focused evaluation of the nature of the relationship postloss. In addition to yearning and strong emotion, there are implications for various relational constructions that include process, structure, and content. The what, when, degree, and narrative tied up in the bereaved's thoughts can be facilitative or deleterious for him or her. Therapy often focuses on just these issues. Research on the activation of the attachment network and the relationship to significant others has documented the network of behavioral and cognitive–affective connections that are involved in relationships from the viewpoint of content and process (chap. 5, this volume; Malkinson & Rubin, 2007; Malkinson & Witztum, 2007; Mikulincer & Shaver, 2003; Rubin, 1984).

Loss can affect many domains of biopsychosocial functioning. A range of categories exists, involving cognitive, emotional, interpersonal, and somatic features. They include the ability to maintain individual homeostasis of self-esteem, management of investment in life tasks, management of significant interpersonal relationships within and outside the family, and the wherewithal to adopt a worldview and meaning structure that can contain the shock of loss and the changes that ensue (Attig, 1996; Bowlby, 1969, 1973, 1980; Neimeyer, 2001; Neimeyer, Keese, & Fortner, 2000; Rubin, 1999; Stroebe & Schut, 1999).

The current proposal for a CG diagnostic category concentrates on a subset of problems and dysfunctions that follow loss. Taking into account how the bereaved individual's psychological relationship to the deceased continues is a significant challenge for any classification of bereavement dysfunction. We are concerned that without greater specificity in this domain a number of conceptualizations and interventions may make strategies for the suppression of this relationship central to adaptive bereavement. This would go against much of what we have learned about continuing bonds and their adaptive nature for the bereaved.

THE DILEMMAS

Lessons From Posttraumatic Stress Disorder

The decisions made in response to three dilemmas will affect the evolution and uses of the CG diagnosis. The first dilemma is whether and how to apply relevant lessons from PTSD to the spectrum of responses associated with disorder following loss. On the face of it, the similarities between PTSD as a *DSM* syndrome and the proposed criteria for CG make this a relevant comparison. PTSD is unusual among *DSM* syndromes in that the diagnostic criteria specify an etiologic event: exposure to a traumatic stressor. Regardless of the symptoms present, unless a person has been exposed to a qualifying stressor, the diagnosis cannot be made. The proposed diagnosis of CG parallels the diagnosis of PTSD in that without the event of loss this diagnosis cannot be made.

If the criteria are approved for inclusion in *DSM–V*, then CG will be the second syndrome besides PTSD that specifies exposure to an external event. In its first *DSM* inclusion, PTSD was classified as outside the range of usual human experience, and this was changed later (Brom & Kleber, 2000). An event resulting from direct or indirect exposure is a probable cause of the development of a disorder; more specifically, in the case of PTSD it is not the presence of symptoms per se but the exposure to trauma as a stressor that evokes the intense fear, helplessness, or horror that qualifies the diagnosis based on the nature of the symptom picture (McNally, 2003).

In its original formulation, the PTSD concept originated from Kardiner's (1941) descriptions of traumatic neurosis, and when it was made into a diagnostic criterion it was based not only on empirical data but also on a conceptual structure: "The intent here was to offer an objective measure of trauma sufficient to cause PTSD and to bracket that class of traumatic events from other stressful experiences and PTSD from other responses to stress" (Breslau, 2002, p. 34). Also, "distinguishing traumatic stressors from other serious but more common life stressors (e.g., bereavement, chronic illness, job loss, marital conflict, and motor vehicle crash) implied that the valence of the stressor would overwhelm the adaptive capacities of most people" (Lasiu & Hegadoren, 2006, p. 73).

A major concern was related to the observation that individuals who do not meet the full set of diagnostic criteria for PTSD may suffer from clinically significant symptoms; consequently, the concept of *partial PTSD* (PPTSD), sometimes called *subthreshold PTSD*, was introduced to describe subsyndromal forms of PTSD (Breslau, Lucia, & Davis, 2004). Among the first to observe and comment on complications in the diagnosis were Stein, Walker, Hazen, and Forde (1997), who pointed out that "among the unresolved questions in the diagnosis and classification of PTSD is the taxonomic status and clinical importance of subsyndromal or subthreshold variants"; that is, some individuals exhibit only part of the symptoms, so they are not eligible for a full PTSD diagnosis but "a partial PTSD" (p. 1114).

The prevalence of PPTSD among Vietnam War veterans and survivors of sexual abuse and other forms of trauma is quite high. Factors that increase the risk for PPTSD risk include being female (Stein et al., 1997). Adult age also appears to be a risk factor; for age, the picture is more equivocal and may depend also on culture and the type of the trauma (McMillen, North, & Smith,

2000). The main concern is that in too many cases a person's symptoms may fall short of meeting full diagnostic criteria for PTSD yet still reflect problems in the assimilation of the experience. Stein et al. (1997) noted that unlike PTSD, subthreshold presentations for depression and social phobia have been recognized in the *DSM*.

Although the debate regarding the various definitions of PTSD continues, the issue is relevant for consideration of the proposed CG criteria. For example, the observation that the frequency of PPTSD is similar to or even greater than the frequency of full PTSD should give us all pause (Stein et al., 1997), yet, in spite of the reported high prevalence of PPTSD, it was not accepted for inclusion in *DSM–IV* (American Psychiatric Association, 1994).

An additional but related controversy is that of delayed onset and its potential parallels to CG. Delayed-onset PTSD seems to deviate from the commonly observed trajectory of posttraumatic morbidity. After experiencing trauma, most survivors experience acute posttraumatic symptomatology, which in a minority does not remit and subsequently develops into PTSD. In contrast, according to *DSM–IV*, delayed-onset PTSD does not develop until at least 6 months post-trauma (American Psychiatric Association, 1994), with onset potentially delayed for years. Reports of delayed onset of PTSD as long as 30 years after the alleged precipitating event raise many questions about the nature and mechanisms of PTSD. Longitudinal studies of motor vehicle accidents have provided estimates of delayed-onset PTSD ranging from 4% to 20%, with most finding rates below 7% (Bryant & Harvey, 2002; Mayou, Bryant, & Duthie, 1993). Although overall rates of delayed-onset PTSD are low, the proportion of PTSD cases that are delayed can be as high as 18% (Bryant & Harvey, 2002).

Several explanations have been proposed for delayed-onset PTSD. A number of empirical studies have noted that individuals who are eventually diagnosed with the condition have reported subsyndromal levels of PTSD at initial assessments. Results of these studies suggest that delayed-onset PTSD cases fail to meet the full criteria for PTSD initially but subsequently satisfy them because their condition deteriorates to the point of meeting the diagnostic threshold. Also, there is evidence that many cases of delayed-onset PTSD had elevated levels of PTSD symptoms during the acute period. This may mean that a number of cases of so-called delayed-onset PTSD may in fact represent delayed identification rather than delayed onset. Other studies have found that people who developed delayed-onset PTSD experienced more persistent stressors after the trauma, which may also contribute to PTSD development (Blanchard & Hickling, 2004).

What might these findings imply for the proposed CG diagnostic criteria? Like PTSD, CG is proposed to become a unique diagnostic criterion in *DSM–V*, specifying an etiologic event, namely, exposure to a bereavement. The category will probably encounter problems similar to those linked to the

PTSD diagnosis in the areas of subthreshold, variations due to risk factor, and the nature of the stressors involved. Of particular concern are the following four issues: (a) the different rates of response and recovery for different types of loss (loss of spouse, parental loss, child loss, loss of meaningful others, etc.; Rando, 1993; Raphael, 1983; Rubin & Malkinson, 2001), (b) the heterogeneity of response due to variation in the nature of postloss stressors (economic, social, familial, etc.), (c) how time elapsed since the loss may interact with delayed onset of CG, and (d) ambiguity about whether someone has partial or full CG. The dilemma here is whether to introduce CG with criteria that are sufficiently stringent to identify an extreme and nonresolving response to loss, with all that this entails, or to introduce more flexible criteria allowing inclusion of more of the spectrum of problem responses. A middle ground may yet be found.

Trauma and Bereavement

The second dilemma revolves around how to address the overlap between the domains of stress and trauma that carry implications for diagnosis and intervention. There is a considerable diversity among researchers and clinicians with regard to definitions of CG and its location as a separate domain of a diagnostic criteria or one that overlaps with trauma (Stroebe & Schut, 2006). We present three cases with varying components of traumatic loss. Each reflects a different facet of complication following loss. Each, however, can be conceptualized from either a trauma or loss perspective alone, although a combined perspective is the most appropriate.

The first case is that of a married army reservist who was called up to active combat duty. He developed symptoms following involvement in a car bomb attack in which two army buddies were killed while he alone survived. He subsequently developed a variety of symptoms, including depression, somatic complaints involving paralysis of his leg, and nightmares. He was diagnosed initially as suffering from acute anxiety and later from conversion reaction and PTSD following exposure to life threat. The treatment protocol followed the formulation regarding PTSD. Treatment did not yield significant improvement, however, and in discussion with the client it became clear that he experienced significant guilt at having survived and was in psychological conflict within himself. He felt he had "ignored" the death of his fallen fellows, and he did not accept that he should be living a normal life when they were dead. When the treatment focus was shifted from trauma symptoms to the relationship, a significant change took place in his depression, somatic complaints, energy level, and overall state of mind. Helping the client mark, memorialize, honor, and pay tribute to his fallen comrades allowed significant improvement, which had not taken place without that focus. A fuller presentation of the case, formulation, and treatment can be found elsewhere (Daie & Witztum,

1991; Rubin, Malkinson, & Witztum, 2003). In this case the involvement of bereavement would be easy to miss because the symptom picture was consistent with acute stress and other features related to conversion and PTSD; evidence of longing for the deceased was absent, and no formal kinship relationship existed in terms of traditional family. Although the duration of the problem and the degree of dysfunction in such a case might meet criteria for a CG diagnosis, in the absence of a fuller psychological exploration of the relationship cases such as these typically would not be understood as problematic grief responses. As a result, the ultimately helpful intervention that focused on the relationship would not have been considered.

The second case is of a man who lost his wife and child during childbirth. As part of his lawsuit, he asked for compensatory damages for his problematic grief, and he was evaluated. The father of three small children, he had remarried within the 1st year of his wife's death and showed no evidence of dysfunction or symptoms in somatic function, anxiety, depressed mood, or other negative outcome. His low score on the Index of Traumatic Grief was commensurate with this picture of absence of symptoms of difficulty (Prigerson & Jacobs, 2001). The absence of symptoms coincided with what has been termed by some clinicians an *absence of grief* (Deutsch, 1937). In the context of a spousal kinship relationship, the absence of yearning and the absence of symptoms excluded this man from a diagnosis of grief-related problems. However, were one to consider the extent to which the psychological relationship with his deceased wife was cognitively and emotionally accessible to him in some degree, one could make some additional determinations. Difficulties may be encountered later in any number of areas; for example, how does the cognitive affective relationship with the deceased wife influence this man's relationship with his current wife? What are the consequences of this approach for the picture and history of their biological mother transmitted to the children? In these areas, current difficulties might be anticipated. The later development of physical consequences cannot be ruled out, given what appears to be the strong defense this man uses to distance the loss of his former wife. CG classifications emphasizing only yearning or longing for the deceased miss what a broader set of markers can balance. By the inclusion of the parameter of avoidance of stimuli (memories, thoughts, associations, places, pictures, etc.) that are connected to the loss and the relationship to the deceased, broader net is cast to locate difficulties in response to loss. We might parenthetically add that the literature on variations in trajectories of grief and in mourning patterns gives rise to important questions as to exactly what variations in the cognitive and emotional organization and reorganization of relationships, as well as what symptom picture one should look for after a loss (Bonanno, 2004; chap. 14, this volume; Wortman & Silver, 2001).

The last case illustration is that of a woman who lost her husband in a terror-related incident. She too did not experience strong yearning or particularly strong feelings of connection to her spouse. Nine months after her loss, her response to it involved anxiety and depression, along with some symptoms characteristic of PPTSD. She received a provisional diagnosis of difficulties adjusting to loss. Treatment progressed in two phases. The first phase took more than a year and was directed toward symptom management of anxiety, relearning the world, and learning to trust and become reinvolved in her life. The second phase focused on the spousal relationship, addressing the ambivalence, the woman's relief at his death, and the guilt engendered by this relief. Although the initial treatment work had resulted in significant easing of symptoms, the second phase was critical to bringing about a fundamental shift in her freedom to reclaim her husband's memory and ultimately to reclaim aspects of herself (Malkinson, 2001, 2003, 2007). This case dovetails with reports in the literature that have addressed ambivalence in relationships following loss (Bowlby, 1980; Freud, 1917/1957; Raphael, 1983).

The three cases we have just described illustrate a portion of the mixtures of relational and traumatic features present in loss (Jacobs, 1999; Witztum et al., 2001, 2005). Whether to begin to address these combinations in the proposed diagnostic formulation or to concentrate on dysfunction primarily bound up with the wish to be with the deceased is a dilemma yet to be resolved.

Relationship to the Deceased and the *Diagnostic and Statistical Manual of Mental Disorders*

The third and final dilemma we raise is how to formulate relational features in the symptomatic phenomenological approach of the *DSM*. To demonstrate this, we examine criteria proposed by Holly Prigerson and her colleagues and by Mardi Horowitz and his colleagues, with the intent to consider how the CG diagnostic proposals may be improved. The recent proposals for CG, which have been the focus of discussion, were considered recently in a special issue of *Omega: The Journal of Death and Dying* (Parkes, 2006); they were generated by Horowitz and his colleagues and Prigerson her and colleagues, respectively. We now consider each in turn.

We add the following to what is addressed in the Exhibit 9.1. We consider first Prigerson and Maciejewski's (2006) proposal, which has four components. Developing a rubric for the classification of disorders following loss and the closely linked corollary, prescribing when these disorders or complications of loss deserve professional attention, will remain controversial. It may well be most clinically efficacious to have a bereavement reaction category identifying individuals whose loss is sufficiently problematic, painful, and/or overwhelming to be the focus of professional attention. This can proceed by the inclusion of a bereavement category that need not imply that the loss response itself requires professional intervention.

EXHIBIT 9.1
Evaluation of Proposed Criteria for Complicated Grief—2006

Criterion A: Chronic and disruptive yearning, pining, longing for the deceased.
Basic features: In complicated bereavement, the focus is on the experience of longing for the deceased. This longing is intense, prolonged, disruptive, and distressing. This criterion is directly connected to the client's relationship to the deceased
and stresses the basic wish to be with the deceased.

Suggestion for further development: Complications of the relationship may include
disruptions in which something other than yearning is present. Thoughts of the
deceased accompanied by distressing emotions may include anxiety, negative
thoughts, feelings of guilt, rage, or pronounced sadness. The mental organization
of the deceased might be skewed. The deceased may be remembered in a problematic fashion: highly idealized, devalued, constricted, placard-like, and/or confusing. Longing may be denied, and the relationship's importance in the present
may be minimized.

**Criterion B: Four of the following eight remaining symptoms are experienced
at least several times a day, or to a degree intense enough to be distressing and disruptive: (1) trouble accepting the death, (2) inability to trust
others since the death, (3) excessive bitterness over the death, (4) feelings
of uneasiness about moving on with life, (5) feelings of numbness being
detached, (6) feeling that life is empty or meaningless without the deceased, (7) feeling that one has a bleak future, (8) feeling agitated.**
Basic features: Four domains are addressed: (a) cognitive and emotional degree
of acceptance of death (Items 1 and 3); (b) an extreme degree of social dysfunction (Items 2 and 5); (c) ability to invest in life and meaning (Items 4, 6,
and 7); (d) agitation, anxiety, lack of calmness (Item 8). These items sample
important domains of coping with life's demands indicative of significant dysfunction. The shift from the earlier formulation of "marked or extreme" (Parkes,
2006) adds flexibility and allows ways to include dysfunction that may reside in
other areas, for example, difficulty in ability to parent children or to invest in
partner relationships. Similarly, problems in connecting to previously meaningful personal values and/or spirituality can be subsumed in these criteria under
Item 4 and/or 6.

Suggestion for further development: Additional features associated with trauma—
images related to the death and or the deceased that are experienced as intrusive,
or are avoided, are relevant here (see Exhibit 9.2).

**Criterion C: The symptom disturbance causes marked and persistent dys-
function in social, occupational, or other important domains.**
Basic features: Significant dysfunction is present—with the thesis that these are
related to the loss. Ultimately, how Criteria A and B combine to produce C will
have implications for the spectrum of complicated grief disorders.

Criterion D: The symptom disturbance must last at least 6 months.
Basic feature: This replaces the previous 2-month criterion and uses an extended
time that will minimize the number of people who qualify for the diagnosis.

Suggestion for further development: Although for many bereaved individuals
this extended time frame will allow for self-reparative and social support
processes to operate, for some this is too long a wait. A sliding criterion might
fit better, particularly because this time frame need not begin with the loss
event itself.

Note. Text in boldface type indicates criteria according to Prigerson and Maciejewski (2006).

In other words, if the proposed diagnostic category can adequately pin-point the bereaved individual's experience of loss as the central issue, then it allows a focus on loss and the response to it. This leaves room for alternative pathways for amelioration, and thus some of the controversy may become moot. Such a category would address the pain and need of the bereaved without the implication that it will necessarily remain an ongoing problem without medical or professional intervention. Thus, bereavement can remain associated with loss of a significant other and retain a perspective specific to that class of event. To make the *DSM* criteria so stringent that almost all would agree that the response is pathological will leave out too many individuals who would benefit from being understood as having difficulty responding to loss. Allowing for a spectrum classification that serves as an umbrella classification suitable for the inclusion of various degrees of difficulty in response to loss should allow for greater flexibility. We return to this point shortly.

We now consider the criteria of Horowitz et al. (1997; see Exhibit 9.2). The Horowitz group proposal (Horowitz et al., 1997) vividly transmits the sense of difficulty adjusting to loss by including responses manifest in intrusion, avoidance, and problem functioning. These do not progress toward resolution, assimilation, or accommodation. Both relational material and how the individual functions are present in this formulation.

Flexibility with an eye to clinical needs may be the best way to proceed. Horowitz's (2006) suggestion to combine self-report measures with clinician interviews adds flexibility with an eye to encompassing clinical needs and may yield the best solution for the integration of the two proposals: "The reasons for clinician judgment is that professionals can assess degrees of coping and defense, which are issues as important in diagnosis as emotional–relational contents such as rage, pining and yearning, and a sense of personal apathy and emptiness" (Horowitz, 2006, pp. 87–88). The manner in which the bereaved individual's processing of the loss and his or her relationship to the deceased and the difficulties manifest in the bereaved person's life following loss are at the heart of both proposals. Of Prigerson and Maciejewski's (2006) and Horowitz et al.'s (1997) proposals, the latter is more inclusive with regard to the relational aspects of difficulty, but we believe still more needs to be done in this area. Overall, the fact that discussions about the diagnostic criteria are continuing bodes well for ongoing advances in the proposed CG category.

OPPORTUNITIES AND CONCLUDING REMARKS

CG is proposed as a diagnostic category to classify bereaved persons who have notable dysfunction related to processing the loss. Distressing pre-occupation with the loss is generally significant. In recent years, it has become clear that the range of responses to loss is more varied and that not all bereaved

EXHIBIT 9.2
Evaluation of Proposed Criteria for Complicated Grief—1997

Criterion A: Event criterion/prolonged response criterion. Bereavement (loss of a spouse, other relative, or intimate partner) at least 14 months ago (12 months is avoided because of possible intense turbulence from an anniversary reaction).

Basic feature: The key feature is loss of significant kinship to bereavement that has not subsided significantly within the time frame.

Suggestions for further development: A more flexible identification of both kinship and time frame might better serve the range of persons in need.

Criterion B: Signs and symptoms; in the last months, the client experiences three of any of the following seven symptoms (grouped into intrusive symptoms, avoidance symptoms, and functioning/failure to adapt) with a severity that interferes with daily functioning.

Intrusive symptoms: (1) unbidden memories or intrusive fantasies related to the lost relationship, (2) strong spells or pangs of severe emotion related to the lost relationship, (3) distressingly strong yearning or wishes that the deceased were there.

Basic features: The relational issues are at the forefront and are indicative of problems because of their intrusive nature, the strength of the emotions, or the strength of the yearning.

Suggestions for further development: The process is emphasized rather than the content. It would be important to consider the psychological organization of the relationship cognitively as well as affectively. In addition, some of the imagery may consist of images of the death, particularly in cases where trauma and bereavement are intertwined.

Avoidance symptoms: (4) Feelings of being far too much alone or personally empty and (5) excessively staying away from people, places, or activities that remind the client of the deceased.

Basic features: Item 5 communicates that the deceased is not being integrated into the bereaved's life adequately. Item 4 may be associated with the bereaved being emotionally distant from the bereaved, but this is not clear.

Suggestions for further development: The nature of what in the organization of the loss and the relationship to the deceased is being avoided (cognitively and affectively) could be further clarified.

Functioning/failure to adapt: (6) unusual level of sleep disturbance and (7) loss of interest in work, social, caretaking, or recreational activities to a maladaptive degree.

Basic features: Significant difficulties in functioning, including sleep difficulties and the inability to invest in life tasks, must be present.

Suggestions for further development: There are many additional areas of functioning, which appear singly or together. These include medical and somatic difficulties, anxiety, depression, problems with self-esteem, a decline in the ability to manage the demands of work (not loss of interest), substance abuse, and problems in maintaining a coherent worldview as well as the activities mentioned for inclusion earlier. A more flexible categorization would be helpful.

Note. Text in boldface type indicates criteria according to Horowitz et al. (1997).

people experience strong and continued distress (Bonanno, 2004). There are also indications that some bereaved individuals (e.g., those whose loss was due to violent death) are more likely to respond in ways that manifest elements associated with trauma (Rynearson, 2001, 2006).

Current efforts to specify a diagnostic category encompassing the complications of bereavement provide an opportunity to balance clinical considerations, social responsibility, and the requirements of nosological classification schema (Beutler & Malik, 2002; Lichtenthal, Cruess, & Prigerson, 2004). These efforts also provide an opportunity to include a variety of aspects of the relational bond into considerations of successful and problematic responses to loss. The momentum generated by these discussions and considerations provide the energy required to overcome inertia and reconfigure how bereavement is understood in both its uncomplicated and complicated states.

The dilemmas we cited earlier can be seen as potential opportunities to be grasped responsibly. In line with our view that complications in bereavement represent a spectrum of responses, current proposals might better address this spectrum because of their implications. Extending the framework of CG by means of the inclusion of bereavement reaction as the focus of professional attention, alongside a more full-blown diagnosis of CG, would group the complications of bereavement together and emphasize the continuum of disorder and suffering that are present. At this time, the mix of trauma and bereavement elements blended into many losses represents an opportunity to be clearer about the relationship of trauma and bereavement and how they interact. The proposals and scientific evidence put forward by Prigerson, Horowitz, and colleagues are central to the rationale for a CG category. We have the opportunity to integrate, rework, and extend these proposals to meet the challenges we have outlined. If the field can respond to the challenges and dilemmas we have raised, these issues may well be considered opportunities to determine how best to assist the bereaved (Horowitz, 2006). Advances in the field have the potential to assist professionals working clinically with the bereaved as well as those pursuing research on postloss outcomes. As we in the field consider the diagnostic category of CG, the bereaved and the public at large can benefit greatly from the attention to loss, its normal course, and the spectrum of difficulties that may follow in its wake.

REFERENCES

American Psychiatric Association. (1994). *Diagnostic and statistical manual of mental disorders* (4th ed.). Washington, DC: Author.

Attig, T. (1996). *How we grieve: Relearning the world.* New York: Oxford University Press.

Beutler, L. E., & Malik, M. L. (2002). *Rethinking the DSM: A psychological perspective.* Washington, DC: American Psychological Association.

Blanchard, E. B., & Hickling, E. (2004). *After the crash: Psychological assessment and treatment of survivors of motor vehicle accidents* (2nd ed.). Washington, DC: American Psychological Association.

Bonanno, G. A. (2004). Loss, trauma, and human resilience: Have we underestimated the human capacity to thrive after extremely aversive events? *American Psychologist, 59*, 20–28.

Bonanno, G. A., Wortman, C. B., & Nesse, R. M. (2004). Prospective patterns of resilience and maladjustment during widowhood. *Psychology and Aging, 19*, 260–271.

Bowlby, J. (1969). *Attachment and loss: Vol. 1. Attachment.* London: Hogarth Press & Institute of Psychoanalysis.

Bowlby, J. (1973). *Attachment and loss: Vol. 2. Separation: Anxiety and anger.* London: Hogarth Press & Institute of Psychoanalysis.

Bowlby, J. (1980). *Attachment and loss: Vol. 3. Loss: Sadness and depression.* London: Hogarth Press & Institute of Psychoanalysis.

Breslau, N. (2002). Gender differences in trauma and posttraumatic stress disorder. *Journal of Gender Specific Medicine, 5*, 34–40.

Breslau, N., Lucia, V. C., & Davis, G. C. (2004). Partial PTSD versus full PTSD: An empirical examination of associated impairment. *Psychological Medicine, 34*, 1205–1214.

Brom, D., & Kleber, R. (2000). On coping with trauma and coping with grief: Similarities and differences. In R. Malkinson, S. Rubin, & E. Witztum (Eds.), *Traumatic and nontraumatic loss and bereavement: Clinical theory and practice* (pp. 41–66). Madison, CT: Psychosocial Press.

Bryant, R. A., & Harvey, A. G. (2002). Delayed-onset posttraumatic stress disorder: A prospective evaluation. *Australian and New Zealand Journal of Psychiatry, 36*, 205–209.

Daie, N., & Witztum, E. (1991). Short term strategic treatment in traumatic conversion reactions. *American Journal of Psychotherapy, 45*, 335–347.

Deutsch, H. (1937). Absence of grief. *Psychoanalytic Quarterly, 6*, 12–22.

Engel, G. L. (1961). Is grief a disease? *Psychosomatic Medicine, 23*, 18–22.

Field, N. (2006). Unresolved grief and continuing bonds: An attachment perspective. *Death Studies, 30*, 739–756.

Freud, S. (1957). Mourning and melancholia. In J. Strachey (Ed. & Trans.), *Standard edition of the complete psychological works of Sigmund Freud* (pp. 152–170). London: Hogarth Press. (Original work published 1917)

Horowitz, M. (2006). Meditating on complicated grief disorder as a diagnosis. *Omega: The Journal of Death and Dying, 52*, 67–69.

Horowitz, M. J., Siegel, B., Holen, A., Bonanno, G. A., Milbrath, C., & Stinson, C. H. (1997). Diagnostic criteria for complicated grief disorder. *American Journal of Psychiatry, 154*, 904–910.

Horowitz, M. J., Weiss, D., Kaltreider, N., Krupnick, J., Wilner, N., Marmar, C., & DeWitt, K. (1984). Reactions to the death of a parent: Results from patients and field subjects. *Journal of Nervous and Mental Disease, 172*, 383–392.

Jacobs, S. (1999). *Traumatic grief: Diagnosis, treatment, and prevention*. Philadelphia: Brunner/Mazel.

Jordan, J., & Neimeyer, R. (2003). Does grief counseling work? *Death Studies, 27,* 765–786.

Kardiner, A. (1941). *The traumatic neuroses of war*. New York: Hoeber.

Klass, D. (2006). Continuing conversations about continuing bonds. *Death Studies, 30,* 843–859.

Klass, D., Silverman, P. R., & Nickman, S. L. (Eds.). (1996). *Continuing bonds: New understandings of grief*. Washington, DC: Taylor & Francis.

Kyrouz, E. M., Humphreys, K., & Loomis, C. (2002). A review of the research on the effectiveness of self-help mutual aid groups. In B. J. White & E. J. Madara (Eds.), *American Self-Help Group Clearinghouse self-help group sourcebook* (7th ed., pp. 71–86). Denville, NJ: American Self-Help Group Clearinghouse.

Lasiu, G. C., & Hegadoren, K. M. (2006). Posttraumatic stress disorder Part II: Development of the construct within the North American psychiatric taxonomy. *Perspectives in Psychiatric Care, 42,* 73–81.

Lichtenthal, W. G., Cruess, D. G., & Prigerson, H. G. (2004). A case for establishing complicated grief as a distinct mental disorder in DSM–V. *Clinical Psychology Review, 24,* 637–662.

Main, M. (1991). Metacognitive knowledge, metacognitive monitoring and singular (coherent) vs. multiple (incoherent) models of attachment: Findings and directions for future research. In C. M. Parkes, J. Stevenson-Hinde, & P. Marris (Eds.), *Attachment across the life cycle* (pp. 127–159). London: Tavistock.

Malkinson, R. (2001). Cognitive behavioral therapy of grief: A review and application. *Research on Social Work Practice, 11,* 671–698.

Malkinson, R. (2003). Battling the Black Sea despair: Cross-cultural consultation following an air disaster. *Journal of Loss and Trauma, 8,* 99–113.

Malkinson, R. (2007). *Cognitive grief therapy: Constructing a rational meaning to life following loss*. New York: Norton.

Malkinson, R., & Geron, Y. (2006). Intervention continuity in posttraffic fatality: From notifying families of the loss to establishing a self-help group. In E. K. Rynearson (Ed.), *Violent death: Resilience and intervention beyond the crisis* (pp. 217–232). New York: Routledge.

Malkinson, R., & Rubin, S. (2007). The two-track model of bereavement: A balanced model. In R. Malkinson (Ed.), *Cognitive grief therapy: Constructing a rational meaning to life following loss* (pp. 23–43). New York: Norton.

Malkinson, R., Rubin, S., & Witztum, E. (Eds.). (2000). *Traumatic and non-traumatic loss and bereavement: Clinical theory and practice*. Madison, CT: Psychosocial Press.

Malkinson, R., Rubin, S., & Witztum, E. (2005). Terror, trauma, and bereavement: Implications for theory and therapy. In Y. Danieli, D. Brom, & J. Stills (Eds.),

The trauma of terrorism: Shared knowledge and shared care, an international handbook (pp. 467–477). New York: Haworth Press.

Malkinson, R., Rubin, S., & Witztum, E. (2006). Therapeutic issues and the relationship to the deceased: Working clinically with the two-track model of bereavement. *Death Studies, 30,* 797–816.

Malkinson, R., & Witztum, E. (2007). Cognitive intervention with complicated grief: Letter writing as a leave-taking ritual in search of a meaning. In R. Malkinson (Ed.), *Cognitive grief therapy: Constructing a rational meaning to life following loss* (pp. 154–175). New York: Norton.

Mayou, R. A., Bryant, B., & Duthie, R. (1993). Psychiatric consequences of road traffic accidents. *British Medical Journal, 30,* 647–651.

McMillen, J. C., North, C. S., & Smith, E. M. (2000). What parts of PTSD are normal: Intrusion, avoidance, or arousal? Data from the Northridge, California, earthquake. *Journal of Traumatic Stress, 13,* 57–75.

McNally, R. J. (2003). Progress and controversy in the study of posttraumatic stress disorder. *Annual Review of Psychology, 54,* 229–252.

Mikulincer, M., & Shaver, P. R. (2003). The attachment behavioral system in adulthood: Activation, psychodynamics, and interpersonal processes. In M. P. Zanna (Ed.), *Advances in experimental social psychology* (Vol. 35, pp. 53–152). San Diego, CA: Academic Press.

Neimeyer, R. (Ed.). (2001). *Meaning reconstruction and the experience of loss.* Washington, DC: American Psychological Association.

Neimeyer, R., Keese, B. V., & Fortner, B. (2000). Loss and meaning reconstruction: Propositions and procedures. In R. Malkinson, S. Rubin, & E. Witztum (Eds.), *Traumatic and nontraumatic loss and bereavement: Clinical theory and practice* (pp. 197–230). Madison, CT: Psychosocial Press.

Parkes, C. M. (Ed.). (2006). Complicated grief [Special issue]. *Omega: The Journal of Death and Dying, 52*(1).

Prigerson, H. G., Frank, E., Kasl, S. V., Reynolds, C. F., III, Anderson, B., Zubenko, G. S., et al. (1995). Complicated grief and bereavement-related depression as distinct disorders: Preliminary empirical validation in elderly bereaved spouses. *American Journal of Psychiatry, 152,* 22–30.

Prigerson, H. G., & Jacobs, S. C. (2001). Traumatic grief as a distinct disorder: A rationale, consensus criteria, and a preliminary empirical test. In M. S. Stroebe, R. O. Hansson, W. Stroebe, & H. Schut (Eds.), *Handbook of bereavement research: Consequences, coping, and care* (pp. 613–645). Washington, DC: American Psychological Association.

Prigerson, H., & Maciejewski, P. (2006). A call for sound empirical testing and evaluation of criteria for complicated grief proposed by the *DSM–V*. *Omega: The Journal of Death and Dying, 51,* 9–20.

Rando, T. A. (1993). *Treatment of complicated mourning.* Champaign, IL: Research Press.

Raphael, B. (1983). *The anatomy of bereavement.* New York: Basic Books.

Rubin, S. (1981). A two-track model of bereavement: Theory and research. *American Journal of Orthopsychiatry, 51,* 101–109.

Rubin, S. (1984). Mourning distinct from melancholia. *British Journal of Medical Psychology, 57,* 339–345.

Rubin, S. (1992). Adult child loss and the two-track model of bereavement. *Omega: The Journal of Death and Dying, 24,* 183–202.

Rubin, S. (1993). The death of a child is forever: The life course impact of child loss. In M. S. Stroebe, W. Stroebe, & R. O. Hansson (Eds.), *Handbook of bereavement: Theory, research and intervention* (pp. 285–299). Cambridge, England: Cambridge University Press.

Rubin, S. (1999). The two-track model of bereavement: Overview, retrospect and prospect. *Death Studies, 23,* 681–714.

Rubin, S., & Malkinson, R. (2001). Parental response to child loss across the life-cycle: Clinical and research perspectives. In M. Stroebe, R. Hansson, W. Stroebe, & H. Schut (Eds.), *Handbook of bereavement research: Consequences, coping, and care* (pp. 219–240). Washington, DC: American Psychological Association.

Rubin, S., Malkinson, R., & Witztum, E. (2000). An overview of the field of loss. In R. Malkinson, S. Rubin, & E. Witztum (Eds.), *Traumatic and nontraumatic loss and bereavement* (pp. 5–40). Madison, CT: Psychosocial Press.

Rubin, S., Malkinson, R., & Witztum, E. (2003). Trauma and bereavement: Conceptual and clinical issues revolving around relationships. *Death Studies, 27,* 667–690.

Rynearson, E. K. (2001). *Retelling violent death.* Philadelphia: Taylor & Francis.

Rynearson, E. K. (Ed.). (2006). *Violent death.* New York: Routledge.

Saldinger, A., Porterfield, K., & Cain, A. (2004). Meeting the needs of parentally bereaved children. *Psychiatry, 67,* 331–352.

Schut, H., Stroebe, M. S., van den Bout, J., & Terheggen, M. (2001). The efficacy of bereavement interventions: Determining who benefits. In M. S. Stroebe, R. O. Hansson, W. Stroebe, & H. Schut (Eds.), *Handbook of bereavement research: Consequences, coping, and care* (pp. 705–738). Washington, DC: American Psychological Association.

Shear, K., Frank, E., Houck, P., & Reynolds, C. F. (2005). Treatment of complicated grief: A randomized controlled trial. *Journal of the American Medical Association, 293,* 2601–2608.

Silverman, P. R. (1986). *Widow to widow.* New York: Springer Publishing Company.

Silverman, P. R., Baker, J., Cait, C. A., & Boerner, K. (2003). The effects of negative legacies on children's adjustment after parental death. *Omega: The Journal of Death and Dying, 64,* 359–376.

Stein, M. B., Walker, J. R., Hazen, A. L., & Forde, D. R. (1997). Full and partial post-traumatic stress disorder: Findings from a community survey. *American Journal of Psychiatry, 154,* 1114–1119.

Stroebe, M., Gergen, M., Gergen, K., & Stroebe, W. (1993). Broken hearts or broken bonds: Love and death in historical perspective. *American Psychologist, 47*, 1205–1212.

Stroebe, M. S., & Schut, H. W. (1999). The dual process model of coping with bereavement: Rationale and description. *Death Studies, 23*, 197–224.

Stroebe, M., & Schut, H. (2005). To continue or relinquish bonds: A review of consequences for the bereaved. *Death Studies, 29*, 477–494.

Stroebe, M., & Schut, H. (2006). Complicated grief: A conceptual analysis of the field. *Omega: The Journal of Death and Dying, 52*, 51–70.

Witztum, E., Malkinson, R., & Rubin, S. (2001). Death, bereavement and traumatic loss in Israel: A historical and cultural perspective. *Israel Journal of Psychiatry, 38*, 157–170.

Witztum, E., Malkinson, R., & Rubin, S. (2005). Traumatic grief and bereavement resulting from terrorism: Israeli and American perspectives. In S. C. Heilman (Ed.), *Death, bereavement, and mourning* (pp. 105–120). New York: Transaction Books.

Wortman, C. B., & Silver, R. C. (2001). The myths of coping with loss revisited. In M. S. Stroebe, R. O. Hansson, W. Stroebe, & H. Schut (Eds.), *Handbook of bereavement research: Consequences, coping and care* (pp. 405–429). Washington, DC: American Psychological Association.

10

GRIEF ACROSS CULTURES: A REVIEW AND RESEARCH AGENDA

PAUL C. ROSENBLATT

Everything written and everything known about grief through study and personal experience is saturated with cultural perspectives, concepts, and beliefs. No knowledge about grief is culture free. Many of us who study grief are immersed in a single culture, and so it is not difficult for us to assume that our culture (our language, concepts, culturally based views of human nature, and culturally saturated lived experience) defines what is true about all humans. As good scholars and practitioners we try to develop research, theory, and practical knowledge about what we presume is true of all people but, because we are embedded in the realities of the culture we know best, we may well be oblivious to the cultural saturation of our knowledge and the many ways that such saturation makes us ill fit to understand, or even pay attention to, the grieving of people from cultures different from our own.

On the other hand, even as the bereavement field, like other fields devoted to understanding human beings, continues to develop a substantial literature that is oblivious to culture (an argument made by Currer, 2001), it also is developing a substantial literature about the connections of culture and grief (see, e.g., Goss & Klass, 2004; Rosenblatt, 2001; Rosenblatt & Wallace, 2005a, 2005b; Rosenblatt, Walsh, & Jackson, 1976; Shapiro,

1996). The primary message of this culturally sensitive literature is that culture creates, influences, shapes, limits, and defines grieving, sometimes profoundly.

Understanding the complex entanglement between culture and grieving is a first step toward theorizing about grief in a culturally attuned way and in providing support to culturally diverse grieving people. Beyond that, it can be theoretically of great importance to understand what the cultural differences are. Such differences can tell us much about human plasticity; about important variations in human relationships and meanings related to grieving; and the awesome ways in which grieving from culture to culture is embedded in fully functioning, ongoing systems that make sense in their own terms even if they are stupefyingly nonsensical from the perspective of one's own culture.

LITERATURE REVIEW

There are substantial differences across cultures in how, when, and possibly whether grief is expressed, felt, communicated, and understood. Cultures differ in the ways people grieve for various kinds of deaths, and they differ in how deaths are classified. For example, one culture may treat a miscarriage as a death to be grieved, whereas another may ignore it. One culture may give special attention to a death in warfare, whereas another may see it as no different from other deaths. In fact, every topic discussed in this volume (death, grief, gender, feelings, emotion, culture, cognition, society, evidence, religion, trauma, family, etc.) is culturally constructed and could be validly and usefully understood in ways that are alien to the Western culture version of modern psychology (Rosenblatt, 2001). Making sense of the many cultural variations in grieving and in meanings of what one takes as givens is important from the viewpoint of understanding grief, providing grief support and services to diverse others, and making sense of our own grieving (Stroebe & Schut, 1998).

A *culture* is a social construction. One might frame it as a construction that encompasses language, beliefs, practices, social patterns, history, identity, something like a religion, and so on. However, it is also important to remember that many cultures encompass a great deal of variation in language spoken and language fluency, in beliefs, practices, social patterns, religion, and so on. Cultures are fluid, ever changing, filled with contradictions and ambiguities, and often entangled in blurry and complicated ways with other cultures. Thus, knowing that someone is, say, culturally Zulu from South Africa, one still needs to know whether this person's religion comprises traditional Zulu ancestor beliefs or something she understands as Christian; whether she lives in the Zulu homeland of KwaZulu Natal or one of the great cities of South Africa; and whether Zulu, English, Sotho, or some other language is the language of her everyday life and thought. In fact, any simple statement about how people in a given culture grieve is probably so simplistic as to be unhelpful to a person trying to help or support someone from that culture who is grieving (Rosenblatt, 1993, 1997). Moreover, to understand how an individual from a culture is functioning in bereavement, one needs not only to understand her culture but also to examine the fit between how she is grieving and what her culture appears to ask of bereaved people (Shapiro, 1996). The issue of fit is partly about how much knowing a person's culture or cultures tells about the cultural patterning and resources of the person's grief, but it also tells one how much, and in what ways, the person's grief is policed by others (Walter, 1999), pushed along some paths and denied access to other paths.

There are many steps on the way toward deep and thorough cultural sensitivity and awareness. Among those steps are writings that characterize great religions of the world (Gunaratnam, 1997). Knowing "the" Muslim, Buddhist, and so on view of death and grieving can be a helpful source of hunches and potential insights about someone's grieving, but followers of the great religions are enormously diverse culturally and in their interpretations of and adherence to their religion (Al-Adawi, Burjorjee, & Al-Issa, 1997; chap. 16, this volume; Klass, 1999; Wikan, 1988). Another step that might on occasion be useful but is no substitute for deep cultural sensitivity is what may be called a *fact summary*, which in one page or chapter provides a brief, broad overview of a culture. Treating such brief statements as though they necessarily are accurate or necessarily apply to the diversity of people to whom they are said to apply would be a mistake that substitutes stereotypes for genuine understanding (Gunaratnam, 1997). It may actually be better to start in total ignorance of someone's cultural background and try to be genuinely open, curious, and free of assumptions (Gunaratnam, 1997).

Another step on the path toward greater cultural sensitivity, but one that falls short of actually getting there, is what Klass (1999) called a *multicultural* perspective, which presumes that human grief everywhere has a core of similarity. As Klass characterized the multicultural literature, there has not been an openness to challenging the presumption of universality of a core to grieving, so there is no documentation, just a claim based on untested, undocumented faith. At the same time, this presumption makes it more difficult to recognize how different grief is from one culture to another and to challenge the concepts of grief that underlie the multicultural perspective.

Different Realities in Different Cultures

One way to begin to grasp the challenge in knowing and understanding how grief varies cross-culturally is to recognize that people in different cultures may have divergent realities. Even the most fundamental matter in trying to understand grief—the meaning of death, for example—may vary widely from culture to culture.

The Meaning of Death

In the United States, the time of death is generally considered to be the point at which a person stops breathing. In other cultures, the time of death may be quite different. For example, in Oman, some people who stop breathing are considered not dead but temporarily removed from the present as a result of a sorcerer's action (Al-Adawi et al., 1997). Even after burial and the end of formal mourning, people may still believe it is possible that the dead person will be brought to life by something that neutralizes the sorcery. In such cases, the initial meaning of death is not an end but a victimization that temporarily removes one from the living. On the other hand, there are cultures—for example, the Matsigenka of Peru—in which someone may be considered dead before cessation of breathing (Shepard, 2002).

From another angle, one aspect of the meaning given to a death has to do with the multiple losses that come with it. These multiple losses vary enormously from culture to culture, so the meanings of a death must also vary. Even losses that seem the same between two cultures—for example, economic losses or losses of a planned-for future—may seem similar only when worded in abstract terms. When we get down to specifics, there are many cultures in which the multiple losses that come with a death are far outside the experience of most who write about grief. For example, a young Arapesh man grieving the death of his father may talk about losing the mentoring he needed to become effective, the loss of help his father would have given him in obtaining a wife, and the strength a young man is able to draw out of his father (Leavitt, 1995). (Putting these ideas into English obscures how alien the Arapesh world of help, obtaining a wife, and acquiring strength is to Western culture.)

In many cultures, deaths are classified as "good" or "not good" (Abramovitch, 2000; chap. 4, this volume). However, what is considered good and what is not may vary immensely from culture to culture. For example, a good death in one culture may be death as a religious martyr, whereas in another culture a good death may be death in extreme old age, surrounded by children and grandchildren.

An important part of the grieving of quite a few adults in many societies is to develop a narrative about the person who died, how the death came about, what the death means, what the bereaved person's relationship is with the deceased, and what has happened as a result of the death (Riches & Dawson, 1996; Rosenblatt, 2000). Across cultures, such narratives deal with an enormous diversity of realities, and those realities are often built around cultural scripts or discourses that are widely known and that provide key ingredients or patterns as grieving people work at making sense of a death (Seale, 1998). For example, in a culture in which sorcery is often seen as a cause of death, a grieving person's narrative may talk about who killed the deceased through sorcery, why the deceased was a target, and how the sorcery was carried out (Brison, 1992). African Americans' grief narratives may often deal with racism in the life of the deceased and as one of the causes of the death (Rosenblatt & Wallace, 2005a, 2005b). However, a narrative at any given time may not be what it will be later on. For example, the narrative of a Japanese mother grieving the cancer death of her child will change as the mother's sense of the location of the child changes, as her relationship with the child changes, and as her relationship with the remains of the child changes (Saiki-Craighill, 2001).

Cultures vary widely in explanations for death, and often several explanations are available for a particular category of death. Sometimes more than one explanation is put forward for a particular death, and these may or may not seem logically consistent to a cultural outsider. Consider Hmong immigrants in Australia making sense of child and maternal death (Rice, 2000). Among explanations that make cultural sense are that the woman carried too heavy a physical load, that she behaved badly toward her parents, that her labor in childbirth was too long and difficult, that the life aura of the mother and baby were imbalanced, or that the mother had a chance encounter with a malevolent spirit. In the first case, the heavy lifting is thought to distress the baby and may cause it to die. In the second case, behaving badly toward a parent may cause the spirit of a deceased parent to return to take the daughter's life.

The Spirit of the Deceased

Many people in most cultures think that a person who died continues to exist in some form (Rosenblatt et al., 1976) and that the deceased maintains contact, at least for awhile, with the living. In some societies, people typically welcome this; in others, they fear it. There is great variety in whether and how the living and dead are thought to be in contact with each other and in what exactly *contact* means. For example, deceased relatives may come to the Toraja of Indonesia in their dreams, and those dreams may be welcomed as a portent of coming prosperity (Hollan, 1995; Wellenkamp, 1991). Taiwanese widows (Hsu, Kahn, & Hsu, 2002) believe in the reality of the ghost of a deceased husband and in the possibility that the ghost could be a watchful and helpful presence or could cause serious trouble as the ghost tries to clear up unfinished business. One could consider this similarity of belief in the continuity of the deceased in spiritual form as a sign of basic human processes across cultures (Klass, 1996; Rosenblatt et al., 1976). However, the emphasis on similarity submerges the details of difference that are likely to have enormous impact on the grief process. There may be a world of difference in the grief process when in one case the spirit of the deceased is a benevolent, watchful presence versus when the spirit is disgusting, terrifying, and dangerous; when the spirit portends good things to come versus when it is a distant god with little or no interest in the living; when the spirit becomes a larger-than-life hero who will return to earth to help his family versus being reincarnated in the next child born in the community. Such differences may have a great impact on grieving; however, it may be that the grief process and the nature of the spirits' actions are related to some underlying factor. Goss and Klass (2004, p. 5) suggested that perhaps the spirits of the dead are much more likely to be benevolent in societies where people have a great deal of freedom to choose their social bonds, for example, where marriages are not arranged and where adults have the freedom to be close to or distant from parents.

The Nature of Grief

Cultures differ greatly in how grief is expressed. For example, bereaved people in some cultures often somaticize grief, so that a grieving person often feels physically ill (Abu-Lughod, 1985; Fabrega & Nutini, 1994; Prince, 1993). Cultures also differ greatly in who grieves, how they grieve, and how much they grieve. In some cultures, the dead, and not the living, are thought to grieve the most (e.g., among the Matsigenka of Peru; Shepard, 2002), and then it is the reactions of the living to the grief of the dead that greatly influence what goes on after the death.

Cultures differ greatly in the extent to which grief involves remembering or forgetting the deceased. Among the Achuar, a Jivaro cultural group of eastern Ecuador, bereaved people exert considerable effort to forget the dead (Taylor, 1993), including their names, individuality, and deeds, distancing the connections they had with them in life. The process is facilitated by the postdeath transformation of the image of the deceased to a troublesome, vengeful, or murderous entity. The dead are seen as intensely lonely and as not wanting to separate from the living, and survivors fear the connection the deceased might want with them. Immediately after a death, Achuar people will feel and express something that could be glossed in English as *grief*—with women wailing and appearing to be distraught and nostalgic and men appearing in public to be enraged and perhaps wailing implicitly or in private. Soon after, a series of rituals is held to reduce the connection of the living with the dead. Women, however, are more likely to continue to wail for the deceased and treat the deceased as still kin, whereas men will deny their relationship with the deceased. Both genders, but particularly men, will distance the deceased by using only a generalized pronoun in speaking about or addressing the deceased and by working at imagining the deceased as decomposing rather than as the person he or she was when alive. Soon, the name of the deceased is recycled by being given to a newborn.

Some cultures have ideas about something like *grief pathology*, grief that in some way has gone wrong (Rosenblatt, 1997). These notions may be quite different from such pathology as defined in the West (Shapiro, 1996). A culture may have a sense, for example, that grieving that goes on too long or not long enough, that is too expressive of feeling or not expressive enough, is a problem. To illustrate, a grieving Balinese person who is visibly sad or upset is seen by other Balinese as vulnerable in many ways, and they may try to cheer the person up (Wikan, 1990). For the Balinese, visible sorrow is pathological because of the trouble it may bring. The Toraja worry about a person who does not cry immediately after a death or who grieves too much, for too long (Wellenkamp, 1988). A bereaved Toraja who lacks emotional equanimity is perceived by other Toraja as at great risk of physical and mental difficulties, punishment from the ancestors, and vengeful behavior from others who take offense at what the person does while he or she is in an intensely emotional state (Hollan, 1992). However, what is grief pathology in one culture may be appropriate in another. For example, a mother in Cairo, Egypt, who was close to catatonic with grief for years after a child died would not be seen as deviant there (Wikan, 1988). In many African American communities, bereaved people often grieve much more intensely at a funeral than is common for European Americans (Rosenblatt & Wallace, 2005a). On the other hand, Taiwanese widows are discouraged from crying in front of the body of a recently deceased husband (Hsu et al., 2002), although later on they are free to cry and may do so quite intensely. Thus, from a cross-cultural perspective it is risky to take the concepts of grief pathology from one culture and apply them to people from cultures in which grief is conceptualized differently (see also chap. 7, this volume).

Cultures differ in how they categorize what in English would be defined as *grief*. In English, grief is an emotion. Emotion theorists have different ways of defining emotions, but for the sake of argument let us say an *emotion* in English is a feeling with a verbal label and some sort of cognition attached. Other cultures may think of grief differently. For example, in some cultures grief is thought of as *feeling–thought,* an inseparable binding of feeling and thought (Lutz, 1985; Wikan, 1990). The distinction is subtle but, I think, real. Future research could examine the feeling–thought idea and other conceptions of grief across cultures to understand human plasticity and the grief of people in cultures that conceive of grief in those ways.

There is also the issue of what exists in various cultures in the emotional space that in the English language is expressed with the term *grief*, a word that highlights sorrow and sadness. In some cultures, that emotional space is inhabited by something else—for example, the desire for revenge or to exact restitution (see Bagilishya, 2000, who wrote about Rwanda)—or emotional emptiness.

Across cultures, there are enough seemingly different and unique "feeling terms" that describe what people experience after a loss that it might be useful to explore what these differences imply about grief. A comparative study might explore what underlies such diversity in grieving as, for example, *lalomweiu* and *fago* among Ifaluk people in the Pacific (Lutz, 1985); the combination of sadness and anger, of grief and indignation, that demands compensation among the Kaluli of New Guinea (Schieffelin, 1985); and grief expression in Iran (Good, Good, & Moradi, 1985), which includes feelings of duty, the moral rightness of anger at being victimized, and identification with the kin of religious martyrs.

Cultural Context and Grief

Every culture provides a set of contexts for grieving, situations and experiences that profoundly affect the living and that often are a major source of how deaths come about. By this I mean contexts such as poverty, warfare, and racial discrimination. These contexts, which of course are filtered through cultural meanings and conceptions, can have an enormous impact on grieving (see also chap. 4, this volume). For example, governments are often directly or indirectly responsible for many deaths. These include the deaths of political opponents; people forced to live in dangerous or unhealthy locations; people who because of political decisions by others are denied adequate food, police protection, health care, or housing; people forced to work at dangerous jobs; and people forced into a migration that can be life threatening. Grieving a death caused by a government can be risky. For example, people in Latin America grieving for relatives who have been "disappeared" or murdered during times of political violence typically have to refrain from communicating their thoughts and feelings about the disappearance or death to others (e.g., Hollander, 1997; Zur, 1998). Self-censorship in grieving might well give the grief powerful elements of emotional control, distance from others, fear, and unreality, as well as a possibly very difficult, large disjunction between what the grieving person does in private versus in public.

To consider another example, genocide may also provide a context that has an enormous impact on grieving. For example, during the genocide in Rwanda, hundreds of thousands of the dead did not receive proper funeral rituals. According to Rwandan beliefs (Bagilishya, 2000), when proper funeral and mourning practices are not followed, misfortunes arise. Knowing that this will happen, a Rwandan grieving for loved ones killed in the genocide will experience not only grief for each relative lost but also emotions linked to the loss of a way of life and an ongoing family as well as feelings about the consequences of the failure of the proper rituals to have been followed.

Cultural Variation in Mourning and Grief

The distinction is often drawn between *mourning* (cultural practices observed by people connected in certain ways to a person who has died) and *grief* (feelings and thoughts of people who have experienced a loss that are not part of mourning). This distinction once made sense to me, but I think now it is a blurry one. Perhaps it is never possible to know whether grieving or an expression of grief is unconnected to mourning. Perhaps most, if not all, mourning practices are tinged by grieving. Perhaps grieving reflects the demands of mourning, particularly when mourning necessitates major changes in everyday life (cf. Stroebe & Schut, 1998). Those caveats aside, it is clear that many cultures have certain mourning practices that seem to limit and shape when, how, and how long people grieve. In the following sections, I discuss the common practices of marking and isolating the bereaved.

In some cultures, bereaved people in certain categories (e.g., children of the deceased, widows) are marked in some way that sets them off from others in the community—for example, their heads are shaved, or they wear special clothing (Rosenblatt et al., 1976). In some cultures, bereaved people in certain categories are isolated from most or all other people (Rosenblatt et al., 1976). The cultural meanings of these ritual activities vary widely from society to society. Among the Zulu of South Africa (Rosenblatt & Nkosi, 2007), widows typically are marked by wearing special black clothing for 1 year and are relatively isolated from others (e.g., they are not supposed to interact directly with others, or to attend various social events, and they are required to sit behind others rather than with or in front of them). These mourning activities of Zulu widows express respect for the deceased husband, show that they are proper Zulu women, and protect others from the bad fortune that widows are believed to radiate. Also, other Zulus may fear that a Zulu widow is a witch, so they are strongly motivated to keep their distance from her. A widow's grief is quite likely shaped by marking and isolation, which reduce her contact with people who might be supportive and reduce her opportunities to talk about the death. This means she has relatively little opportunity to develop grief narratives through conversing with others. At the same time, the marking and isolation give the widow more time to feel, to think, to reflect, to live the grief rather than having it be buried under the demands of high levels of interaction with others.

In some cultures, grief centers in important ways on the remains of the deceased. For Bosnian Muslims (Pollack, 2003), a failure to carry out certain rituals involving the remains of loved ones means one cannot move on in the mourning process, perhaps cannot even accept that the loved one is dead. Without those rituals, the soul of the deceased cannot move on to heaven (Pollack, 2003). Engaging in the proper rituals might also symbolize (to the world, to other Bosnians, to Serbs, to politicians) various political messages, including the horror and insanity of massacres that killed so many Bosnian Muslims and of what has transpired in Bosnia since then (Pollack, 2003).

The Search for Grief Universals and Differences

From a positivist perspective, looking for universals in bereavement is a noble activity. The search for universals can help us recognize what is present in all (or most, or some) of humanity. It can help us see what is basic to human biology, social relationships, and culture and to feel the hopefulness that comes with thinking that there is a common foundation for understanding one another. We can know, for example, that in societies all over the world many people are obviously upset by the death of someone close to them, and the upset may continue long after the death. Also all over the world, deaths bring many losses—not just the loss of the person but the loss of planned futures, the deceased's economic contributions and companionship, shared memories, and much else. If one looks for universals, one may find them. On the other hand, from a postmodern perspective (e.g., Kvale, 1996; Rosenau, 1992), looking for universals is rather pointless. If we look for universals, we will mislead ourselves about the nature of knowledge and will miss all the extremely useful information that is bound up in the specifics, details, contradictions, and variability and the narratives that are different from place to place, time to time, context to context, person to person.

Related to the crucial importance of difference is that there are enormous, and as yet not well studied, challenges in translating bereavement feeling terms from one language to another. A frustration is that some terms do not translate, or translate poorly, from one language and culture to another. For example, Lutz (1985) wrote about the terms *lalomweiu* and *fago*, part of the vocabulary of grief in Ifaluk, a Pacific atoll society. It is possible to render a rough English language approximation of the terms, but that rough translation does not capture linguistic, cultural, emotional, and historical context or the full meaning of the terms. In fact, even when terms appear on the surface to translate well there can be such differences in context and connotations that the appearance of similarity is almost meaningless. For example, widows in the United States and Zulu widows in South Africa may both speak of feeling angry about the death of their husband, but the U.S. widow may feel angry about suspected medical malpractice or the loss of a planned future, whereas the Zulu widow may feel angry about the witchcraft that killed her husband, the grinding poverty with which she is left to cope on her own, or the burdens of observing year-long widowhood mourning practices (Rosenblatt & Nkosi, 2007).

To consider another example, Hsu and Kahn (1998–1999), writing about Taiwanese widows, listed activities engaged in by some of the Taiwanese widows they interviewed. Some widows dealt with feelings of loss, guilt, unfinished business, or continuing obligations to their deceased husband by "doing something for him"—perhaps chanting at a mass Buddhist ritual, paying for a ritual, or providing continuing financial support to the husband's mother. One could draw similarities between these feelings and activities and what one might commonly observe in widows in the United States. However, to interpret those things that way is to be oblivious to differences that might be substantial between Taiwanese and U.S. cultures. For example, the feelings that translate from Chinese into *loss, guilt, unfinished business,* or *continuing obligation* may be quite different in Taiwan than they are in the United States. The activities, although superficially alike, may be quite different in what they require of the widow and what they mean. Hsu and Kahn, alert to the possible differences, wrote that "there were important cultural and linguistic differences in interpreting emotional terminology. As with many other languages, intended meanings were frequently hidden by surface terms that made use of proverbs, idioms, and other forms of metaphor" (p. 275). They discussed the rich cultural context of Chinese widow obligations, the Chinese concept of self, cultural rules about being reticent about feelings and not expressing certain feelings directly, Chinese concepts of harmony, and Chinese conceptions of being a good wife. So someone in the United States might say, "What Taiwanese widows do sounds familiar," but the more one understands about meanings and context (and I have simplified what Hsu and Kahn wrote), the more one understands that the equivalence might be superficial and the underlying differences profound, great, and of the utmost importance.

RESEARCH AGENDA

Researchers in the field of grief and mourning need to give the highest priority to rich studies of grief in diverse cultures. Such research would include data on indigenous terms, concepts, relationships, theories, beliefs, understandings, philosophies, values, and local practices. To be usefully informative about culture, those studies would examine what is in those cultures, the understandings, ways of talking, and so on, rather than exploring how their practices fit into and mesh with universalistic theory and research findings. Research is needed that is free to come to new conceptions and understandings of grief. Such research would certainly be a strong basis of practice, if practice is appropriate with people from the culture in which the research was conducted (see Almeida, 2004; see also chap. 7, this volume). This type of research also would develop alternative theories that might better fit the culture under study and could conceivably challenge researchers and practitioners in the United States and other countries who are working with more or less shared understandings of grief to look at grief in new ways (see Currer, 2001).

The research almost certainly would not fit dominant models for studying grief represented in this volume. For example, research in some other cultures might focus on lamentation (Wilce, 1999) or other forms of grief expression and communication that are not common in the cultures in which bereavement is usually studied. Also, the research in other cultures may focus on changing forms of grieving or diversity in forms of grieving as the culture changes. Some of those changes may come from the influence of Christian or Muslim missionaries (Wilce, 1999), although even in those cases we must be alert to the enormous diversity of local practice and belief associated with various worldwide religions (see, e.g., Wikan's [1988] discussion of Islam). We must also be alert to the possibility that the changes themselves are sources of grieving as people grieve a lost way of life (see, e.g., Prince [1993], who discussed the Cree of northern Quebec). Researchers also should realize that it is possible for adopted beliefs and practices surrounding bereavement to coexist with those from the culture's past (Adams, 1993; Crain, 1991; Rosenblatt & Nkosi, 2007).

Such cross-cultural research would certainly look at how grief is linked to other aspects of culture. Wikan (1988), writing about grief in Egypt and Bali, made a strong case for looking at cultural conceptions of health and sanity; that is, how people grieve or do not grieve is linked to what is considered good for their health and what is considered sane.

Research that is sensitive to culture must also be sensitive at a methodological level. One cannot presume that the methods one would use in studying bereavement in cultures where psychology has flourished would be appropriate in other cultures. Every aspect of research might have to fit the cultural setting. For example, it is much more challenging to conduct interviews in a culture in which a direct question or a follow-up question may be considered rude (Rosenblatt & Nkosi, 2007). In fact, it may even be difficult to recruit people to talk about bereavement. Hsu, Tseng, Banks, and Kuo (2004) needed 2½ years to recruit 20 women informants in a study of Taiwanese grieving after stillbirth. Most women they contacted refused to participate, saying they did not want to cry again or did not want to bring bad luck into their lives or would be going against how other family members felt about how to deal with the tragedy if they gave an interview. In some cultures, an older person would never reveal his or her emotions to an interviewer who was the age of his or her children (Bagilishya, 2000). In research on Zulu widows by Rosenblatt and Nkosi (2007), many people in the communities where the study was conducted thought it was an insane pursuit of bad luck to talk with widows, who carried bad luck with them and were possibly witches. Of course, the questions asked of people cannot be based on universalist assumptions that the terms used in research interviews in one culture (e.g., *grief*) are meaningful in, or even translatable into, the language of, another. In some cultures crucial aspects of people's thoughts and communication about the aftermath of a death might not be statements of feeling or memory but something else— for example, proverbs, tales, parables, and culturally meaningful nonverbal gestures (Bagilishya, 2000).

The results of this proposed research might challenge Western understanding of the emotions of grief. For example, in the metaphors for grief in Tagalog (a dominant language in the Philippines), grief is talked about as an intense pressure erupting from the chest or as a hard feeling, like tears of stone (Palmer, Bennett, & Stacey, 1999).

Culturally sensitive grief studies could eventually lead to a typology in which most or even all cultural variations in grieving would seem to fall into a limited range, perhaps of what Klass (1999, p. 165) called "archetypical scripts." In that way of thinking, there are cross-cultural differences in patterns that recur; perhaps among them would be feelings connected to a belief that a death has been caused by a malevolent force and that calls for vengeance. Klass (1999), however, asserted that "death . . . can be regarded as a universal arouser of something called grief" (p. 165), although which deaths would produce which reactions would depend on interpretive schemes provided by culture. The scheme might include interpretations of death (e.g., as polluting or dangerous) and of matters related to who died or individual mourners, for example, gender, emotional control, or death through illness. Similarly, Stroebe and Schut (1998, 1999) have offered a dual-process model that addresses cultural differences in loss-oriented versus restoration-oriented approaches to dealing with a death. Their model also assumes that grief is universal, although cultures differ markedly in the context, rules, expectations, and so on that they provide for grieving people.

For grief research and theory to advance, they must be informed by cross-cultural information and perspectives. To be effectively cross-cultural, grief studies must be freed from a "science" that assumes all cultures and all humans can be understood on the basis of principles, concepts, categories, and processes that make sense in English and a few European languages. It must move to a science in which not everyone can be measured on everything, in which measurement is always a matter of great skepticism, and in which contradiction and difference count for a lot. Grief studies can advance if they are freed from *ethnocentrism*, the assumption that what makes sense in one culture makes sense in all. Ethnocentrism may lead to generalizations about or idealizations of all cultures or of "primitive" cultures (Walter, 1994–1995). It also may lead to the belief that the psychology, sociology, and thanatology developed in one culture offers the best or even the only way of understanding people in other cultures. The reality is that with a genuinely open perspective on culture, everything is open to question—what is grief, what are standards for human and family functioning, what is "normal," and how it is we know what we know. Otherwise, grief is policed (Walter, 1999) not only at the level of the local community or culture but also limited, controlled, and shaped by researchers who study, write about, and attempt to help others deal with loss.

REFERENCES

Abramovitch, H. H. (2000). "Good death" and "bad death": Therapeutic implications of cultural conceptions of death and bereavement. In R. Malkinson, S. S.

Rubin, & E. Witztum (Eds.), *Traumatic and nontraumatic loss and bereavement: Clinical theory and practice* (pp. 255–272). Madison, CT: Psychosocial Press.

Abu-Lughod, L. (1985). Honor and the sentiments of loss in a Bedouin society. *American Ethnologist, 12,* 245–261.

Adams, K. M. (1993). The discourse of souls in Tana Toraja Indonesia: Indigenous notions and Christian conceptions. *Ethnology, 32,* 55–68.

Al-Adawi, S., Burjorjee, R., & Al-Issa, I. (1997). *Mu-ghayeb:* A culture-specific response to bereavement in Oman. *International Journal of Social Psychiatry, 43,* 144–151.

Almeida, R. (2004). *The politics of mourning: Grief management in cross-cultural fiction.* Madison, NJ: Farleigh Dickinson University Press.

Bagilishya, D. (2000). Mourning and recovery from trauma: In Rwanda, tears flow within. *Transcultural Psychiatry, 37,* 337–353.

Brison, K. J. (1992). *Just talk: Gossip, meetings, and power in a Papua New Guinea village.* Berkeley: University of California Press.

Crain, M. M. (1991). Poetics and politics in the Ecuadorean Andes: Women's narratives of death and devil possession. *American Ethnologist, 18,* 67–89.

Currer, C. (2001). Is grief an illness? Issues of theory in relation to cultural diversity and the grieving process. In J. Hockey, J. Katz, & N. Small (Eds.), *Grief, mourning and death ritual* (pp. 49–60). Philadelphia: Open University Press.

Fabrega, H., Jr., & Nutini, H. (1994). Tlaxcalan constructions of acute grief. *Culture, Medicine, and Psychiatry, 18,* 405–431.

Good, B. J., Good, M. D., & Moradi, R. (1985). The interpretation of Iranian depressive illness and dysphoric affect. In A. Kleinman & B. J. Good (Eds.), *Culture and depression: Studies in the anthropology and cross-cultural psychiatry of affect and disorder* (pp. 369–428). Berkeley: University of California Press.

Goss, R. E., & Klass, D. (2004). *Dead but not lost: Grief narratives in religious traditions.* Walnut Creek, CA: AltaMira.

Gunaratnam, Y. (1997). Culture is not enough: A critique of multi-culturalism in palliative care. In D. Field, J. Hockey, & N. Small (Eds.), *Death, gender and ethnicity* (pp. 166–186). New York: Routledge.

Hollan, D. (1992). Emotion work and value of emotional equanimity among the Toraja. *Ethnology, 31,* 45–56.

Hollan, D. (1995). To the afterworld and back: Mourning and dreams of the dead among the Toraja. *Ethos, 23,* 424–436.

Hollander, N. C. (1997). *Love in a time of hate: Liberation psychology in Latin America.* New Brunswick, NJ: Rutgers University Press.

Hsu, M.-T., & Kahn, D. L. (1998–1999). Coping strategies of Taiwanese widows adapting to loss. *Omega, 28,* 269–288.

Hsu, M.-T., Kahn, D. L., & Hsu, M. (2002). A single leaf orchid: Meaning of a husband's death for Taiwanese widows. *Ethos, 30,* 306–326.

Hsu, M.-T., Tseng, Y.-F., Banks, J. M., & Kuo, L.-L. (2004). Interpretations of stillbirth. *Journal of Advanced Nursing, 47,* 408–416.

Klass, D. (1996). Ancestor worship in Japan: Dependence and the resolution of grief. *Omega: The Journal of Death and Dying, 33*, 279–302.

Klass, D. (1999). Developing a cross-cultural model of grief: The state of the field. *Omega: The Journal of Death and Dying, 39*, 153–176.

Kvale, S. (1996). *InterViews: An introduction to qualitative research interviewing.* Thousand Oaks, CA: Sage.

Leavitt, S. C. (1995). Seeking gifts from the dead: Long-term mourning in Bumbita Arapesh cargo narrative. *Ethos, 23*, 453–473.

Lutz, C. (1985). Depression and the translation of emotional worlds. In A. Kleinman & B. J. Good (Eds.), *Culture and depression: Studies in the anthropology and cross-cultural psychiatry of affect and disorder* (pp. 63–100). Berkeley: University of California Press.

Palmer, G. B., Bennett, H., & Stacey, L. (1999). Bursting with grief, erupting with shame: A conceptual and grammatical analysis of emotion-tropes in Tagalog. In G. B. Palmer & D. J. Occhi (Eds.), *Languages of sentiment: Cultural constructions of emotional substrates* (pp. 171–200). Amsterdam: John Benjamins.

Pollack, C. E. (2003). Intentions of burial: Mourning, politics, and memorials following the massacre at Srebrenica. *Death Studies, 27*, 125–142.

Prince, R. H. (1993). Psychiatry among the James Bay Cree: A focus on pathological grief reactions. *Transcultural Psychiatric Research Review, 30*, 3–50.

Rice, P. L. (2000). Death in birth: The cultural construction of stillbirth, neonatal death, and maternal death among Hmong women in Australia. *Omega: The Journal of Death and Dying, 41*, 39–57.

Riches, G., & Dawson, P. (1996). "An intimate loneliness": Evaluating the impact of a child's death on parental self-identity and marital relationships. *Journal of Family Therapy, 18*, 1–22.

Rosenau, M. P. (1992). *Postmodernism and the social sciences.* Princeton, NJ: Princeton University Press.

Rosenblatt, P. C. (1993). Cross-cultural variation in the experience, expression, and understanding of grief. In D. P. Irish, K. F. Lundy, & V. J. Nelsen (Eds.), *Ethnic variations in dying, death, and grief: Diversity in universality* (pp. 13–19). Washington, DC: Taylor & Francis.

Rosenblatt, P. C. (1997). Grief in small scale societies. In C. M. Parkes, P. Laungani, & B. Young (Eds.), *Death and bereavement across cultures* (pp. 27–51). London: Routledge.

Rosenblatt, P. C. (2000). *Parent grief: Narratives of loss and relationship.* Philadelphia: Brunner/Mazel.

Rosenblatt, P. C. (2001). A social constructionist perspective on cultural differences in grief. In M. S. Stroebe, R. O. Hansson, W. Stroebe, & H. Schut (Eds.), *Handbook of bereavement research: Consequences, coping, and care* (pp. 285–300). Washington, DC: American Psychological Association.

Rosenblatt, P. C., & Nkosi, B. C. (2007). South African Zulu widows in a time of poverty and social change. *Death Studies, 31*, 67–85.

Rosenblatt, P. C., & Wallace, B. R. (2005a). *African American grief*. New York: Brunner-Routledge.

Rosenblatt, P. C., & Wallace, B. R. (2005b). Narratives of grieving African-Americans about racism in the lives of deceased family members. *Death Studies, 29*, 217–235.

Rosenblatt, P. C., Walsh, R. P., & Jackson, D. A. (1976). *Grief and mourning in cross-cultural perspective*. New Haven, CT: Human Relations Area Files Press.

Saiki-Craighill, S. (2001). The grieving process of Japanese mothers who have lost a child to cancer: Part II. Establishing a new relationship from the memories. *Journal of Pediatric Oncology Nursing, 18*, 268–275.

Schieffelin, E. L. (1985). The cultural analysis of depressive affect. In A. Kleinman & B. J. Good (Eds.), *Culture and depression: Studies in the anthropology and cross-cultural psychiatry of affect and disorder* (pp. 429–490). Berkeley: University of California Press.

Seale, C. (1998). *Constructing death: The sociology of dying and bereavement*. New York: Cambridge University Press.

Shapiro, E. (1996). Family bereavement and cultural diversity: A social developmental perspective. *Family Process, 35*, 313–332.

Shepard, G. H., Jr. (2002). Three days for weeping: Dreams, emotions, and death in the Peruvian Amazon. *Medical Anthropology Quarterly, 16*, 200–229.

Stroebe, M., & Schut, H. (1998). Culture and grief. *Bereavement Care, 17*(1), 7–11.

Stroebe, M., & Schut, H. (1999). The dual process model of coping with bereavement: Rationale and description. *Death Studies, 23*, 197–224.

Taylor, A. C. (1993). Remembering to forget: Identity, mourning and memory among the Jivaro. *Man, 28*, 653–678.

Walter, T. (1994–1995). Natural death and the noble savage. *Omega: The Journal of Death and Dying, 30*, 237–248.

Walter, T. (1999). *On bereavement: The culture of grief*. Philadelphia: Open University Press.

Wellenkamp, J. C. (1988). Notions of grief and catharsis among the Toraja. *American Ethnologist, 15*, 486–500.

Wellenkamp, J. C. (1991). Fallen leaves: Death and grieving in Toraja. In D. R. Counts & D. A. Counts (Eds.), *Coping with the final tragedy* (pp. 113–134). Amityville, NY: Baywood.

Wikan, U. (1988). Bereavement and loss in two Muslim communities: Egypt and Bali compared. *Social Science & Medicine, 27*, 451–460.

Wikan, U. (1990). *Managing turbulent hearts: A Balinese formula for living*. Chicago: University of Chicago Press.

Wilce, J. M., Jr. (1999). Transforming laments: Performativity and rationalization as linguistic ideologies. In G. B. Palmer & D. J. Occhi (Eds.), *Languages of sentiment: Cultural constructions of emotional substrates* (pp. 39–63). Amsterdam: John Benjamins.

Zur, J. N. (1998). *Violent memories: Mayan war widows in Guatemala*. Boulder, CO: Westview Press.

11

DISENFRANCHISED GRIEF IN HISTORICAL AND CULTURAL PERSPECTIVE

KENNETH J. DOKA

Every concept has a biography or a history of how that concept was born, developed, and matured. The concept of disenfranchised grief began in a graduate seminar on aging that I was teaching early in the 1980s. As we were exploring widowhood in later life, one of my students, a middle-aged woman, remarked: "If you think widows have it rough, you ought to see what happens when your ex-spouse dies." I was intrigued by her comment, and I asked her if she would share her experiences. She did. She had been divorced. Two years after her divorce, her ex-husband died of cancer. The divorce had been angry and painful; she had caught him having an affair with a neighbor whom she had viewed as a friend. She spoke of the awkward experiences in visiting her ex-husband at the hospital and attending his subsequent funeral. The woman found little support as she struggled with her ambivalence and grief in the aftermath of that death. They had been divorced, her friends and family surmised, so why would she feel grief? Some friends even ventured that it was a sweet revenge. She noted that she had to take vacation days to attend the funeral because her workplace bereavement policies offered leave only for present spouses—not past ones.

Although it was compelling enough in itself, her narrative resonated with me for another reason. I had been asked to present a paper at a Foundation of

Thanatology Conference in New York on "Unsanctioned and Unrecognized Grief." I had been casting about for an idea. I now had one.

As I researched the loss of an ex-spouse, I found a number of items of interest. First, although intensity of reactions varied, all individuals in the small samples I found did experience some form of grief reaction. Second, all noted that the lack of social support for their losses—both the divorce and the subsequent death—was a complicating factor in their ability to adapt to the loss.

After completing that paper, I decided to continue researching losses that were unacknowledged and unrecognized by others. I reasoned that if a lover in an extramarital affair dies, the grief of the surviving lover might well be unrecognized or unacknowledged. Because it was difficult to locate a large enough sample, I decided to expand the research into individuals, heterosexual or homosexual, who had any significant dyadic relationship outside of marriage. This included couples living together, couples dating but not cohabiting, and even engaged people whose partners had died. Again, the results were similar. As the individuals recounted their stories, they noted that they had suffered a significant loss but, as one gay man mentioned, "had no right to grieve." As I emphasized that latter point in my presentation, participants at the conference shared with me their own stories about losses where they had "no right to grieve." I realized there that I had touched a common chord in these very different situations of loss, and in 1985 I presented a conceptual paper on what I called *disenfranchised grief*.

In that paper (Doka, 1985b), I defined disenfranchised grief as grief that results when a person experiences a significant loss and the resultant grief is not openly acknowledged, socially validated, or publicly mourned. In short, although the individual is experiencing a grief reaction, there is no social recognition that the person has a right to grieve or a claim for social sympathy or support.

THE DISENFRANCHISEMENT OF GRIEF

The concept of disenfranchised grief integrates psychological, biological, and sociological perspectives on grief and loss. Since the middle of the 20th century, considerable research has examined psychological, biological, and physiological responses to loss (see, e.g., Bowlby, 1980; Lindemann, 1944; Parkes & Weiss, 1983). This research has demonstrated the myriad affective, physical, cognitive, behavioral, and spiritual ways grief is manifested.

The social aspect of grief often is neglected, however. Although an individual may have an intense and multifaceted reaction to loss, that loss and the ensuing responses may be unacknowledged by surrounding others or the society at large. Although the individual grieves, others do not acknowledge that he or she has a right to grieve. Such persons are not offered the "rights" or the "grieving role," such as a claim to social sympathy and support or compensations such as time off from work or diminishment of social responsibilities.

To understand the social aspect of grief, it is important to remember that every society has norms that govern not only behavior but also affect and cognition. Hochschild (1979), for example, wrote of "feeling rules" or norms that govern what individuals are supposed to feel in a given situation (see also chap. 4, this volume). Statements such as "I know I should not feel guilty" or "I have every right to feel angry" bear testimony to the reality of these feeling rules. These statements justify feelings on the basis of shared understandings or what feelings are to be expected in a given social context. Similarly, there are "thinking rules" that govern how one is supposed to think in a given situation. Again, statements such as "How can you think like that?" imply that an individual's cognitions are outside a society's range of acceptability or understanding of logic and reason. Similarly, there are "spiritual rules." These rules tell people what to believe. For example, in some religions one might be expected to believe that expressions of grief are inappropriate because the deceased has entered a wonderful afterlife.

As part of these rules, every society has norms that frame grieving. These norms include not only expected behaviors but also feeling, thinking, and spiritual rules. These grieving rules govern what losses one grieves, how one grieves them, who legitimately can grieve the loss, and how and to whom others respond with sympathy and support. These norms exist not only as *folkways*, or informally expected behaviors, but also as *laws*, meaning that these norms may carry sanctions. For example, these norms are evidenced in company policies that extend bereavement leave to certain individuals as well as regulations and laws that define what family member or other person has control of the deceased's body or funeral rituals. In the United States and many other Western societies, these grieving rules emphasize that family members have a right to grieve the deaths of other family members. When a family member dies, one is allowed and expected to grieve, often in a specified way. Family members then are accorded rights such as time off from work, diminished social responsibilities, and social support.

Yet human beings exist in *intimate networks*, associations that include both kin and non-kin. Individuals experience a range of losses that are not death related. Divorce, or the relinquishment of a child in adoption or foster care, is an example of non–death-related loss that can arouse grief. In addition, humans form attachments with a wide range of individuals—friends, coworkers, clergy, coaches, therapists, physicians and other health care workers, clients, and patients, to name just a few. Human attachments go beyond relationships even with other humans. We form attachments to celebrities, even if we have never met them (see chap. 12, this volume). We bond with animal companions. Even possessions can take on great significance and meaning in our lives. One of the most profound cases of grief I ever encountered was a woman who lost Christmas ornaments collected over a period of 400 years, family heirlooms, in the Red River Floods in North Dakota in the mid 1990s.

In such situations, the personal experience of grief is discordant with the society's grieving rules. The person experiences a loss, but others do not recognize that grief. The person's losses may fall outside of a society's grieving rules and may be disenfranchised to a degree. However, the central question—why is grief disenfranchised?—remains. Why are only deaths of family members accorded social recognition and support?

There are probably a number of reasons for this. First and foremost, in most Western societies, the family is the primary unit of social organization. Hence, kin ties have clear acknowledgment in norms and laws. Although most individuals actually live their lives in the intimate networks mentioned previously, only kin have legal standing.

Kamerman (1993) described a latent function of these grieving rules. They strengthen the traditional family by denying recognition of other relationships, outside of the family, especially socially unsanctioned relationships, such as lovers or unmarried partners, that might weaken the primacy of family relationship. Kamerman also suggested that perhaps there is a limited reservoir of social support. If the circle of grievers or the circumstances of grief were enlarged, then less support might be available to the immediate family survivors of a death.

Another principle of contemporary Western societies has been *rationality*. That is, beyond the family, organizations such as businesses attempt to organize work policies in fair, functional, and rational ways, and grieving roles reflect that. As Kamerman (1993) observed, to extend grieving roles to nondeath situations or to non-kin would create organizational burdens. Organizations would be forced to define *levels of friendship* or *types of loss*. They might be required to broaden the concept of bereavement leave, at considerable cost. Acknowledging the death of kin alone makes organizational sense. It recognizes the grief of kin when a family member dies, at least symbolically. Limiting the acknowledgment of loss to family members avoids confusion and potential abuse, affirming a single rational standard. This keeps organizations from having to assess, from an individual standpoint, whether this loss or relationship is entitled to recognition. These policies reflect and project societal recognition and support, again reaffirming and sanctioning familial relationship.

They also point to another significant factor: the relationship of grieving rules to ritual. As an interpsychic process, *mourning* refers to the ways that grief is socially acknowledged, for example, accepted behaviors, such as mourning dress, that signify that an individual has experienced a loss. Rituals that connote loss are critical to mourning. These rituals allow structure and support to the expression of grief. For example, Durkheim (1915) claimed that "mourning is not a natural movement of private feelings; it is a duty imposed by the group. One weeps, not simply because he is sad, but because he is forced to weep" (p. 443).

Durkheim, in justifying the critical importance of social norms, exaggerated. Yet he did contribute a central point: Social expectations frame the experience of grief.

Pine (1989) stressed the critical role that funerals have in enfranchising grief. The funeral becomes the vehicle by which grief is acknowledged and sanctioned and the locale where support is extended. The primacy of a family at the funeral reaffirms that these survivors have experienced a loss and that their subsequent grief needs sanction, acknowledgment, and support. The rite of the funeral publicly testifies to and affirms the right to grieve.

Of course, other factors influence grieving rules and thereby affect disenfranchisement. For example, the culture of counseling (see T. Martin & Doka, 1999; Sue & Sue, 1999) emphasizes affect. Persons who grieve in other ways may be accorded less than full recognition or support for their grief. Societies, too, may consider certain types of death as punitive, anxiety provoking, or embarrassing, and thus withhold full support (Doka, 1989; Rando, 1993; see chap. 10, this volume).

D. Martin (2005) developed this further in his analysis of the role of blame in offering support to parents whose children were murdered. Martin noted that grief was legitimated only when the lives of victims were considered beyond reproach. When the victim was seen as engaging in activities that were criminal or self-destructive, social support and sympathy were withheld. Often this is connected to an individual victim or mourner's status within the social structure. In cases of individuals of lower income, there was often an attribution of blame, such as that the individual had little reason to be where, or with whom, he or she was. In such cases, police often took a highly inquisitive, rather than supportive, stance with families as they notified the family about the death. Think as well, for example, of someone who dies of lung cancer. Often, the first question asked is whether the deceased individual smoked. Implicit in this question is a possible assumption that such a person bears responsibility for his or her illness.

Naturally, in a diverse society even losses disenfranchised by society as a whole may be acknowledged within a smaller subculture. For example, the death of a gay lover in many societies may not be fully recognized by family or coworkers, but the grieving lover may be recognized and supported within the gay community (Eyetsemitan, 1998). Then, too, grieving rules can differ among subcultural groups, whether defined by class, ethnicity, or another organizing factor (see Doka & Davidson, 1998; Eyetsemitan, 1998). Thus, subcultures may mitigate the sense of disenfranchisement. Two implications follow.

The first implication is that grieving rules differ between cultures. What is disenfranchised in one culture may be supported in another. For example, in some cultures, gay relationships are highly proscribed. In other cultures, such as those of the Netherlands, Canada, or some states in the United States, homosexual marriages or domestic partnerships are fully legal. Obviously, differential levels of social support can be expected in these distinct societies at the death of a gay partner.

Cultural norms may affect the process of grieving in other ways as well. In some cultures, certain ways of grieving may be understood as valid expressions of grief, whereas in other cultures the same behaviors may be disdained as excessive or inappropriate. Similarly, certain types of relationships might be acknowledged in some cultures but ignored in others. In Italian and Hispanic cultures, godparents are accorded great importance. Whether family or non-family members are selected, they are recognized as having a significant role in the life of a godchild. Should one's godchild or godparent die, grief would be expected. In other Christian cultures, such a role may have only symbolic importance, one primarily limited to the time of the godchild's baptism. In other cultures, with different faith systems, such relationships may not even exist. These are just some examples of how grieving rules differ across cultures, redefining for every culture what types of losses are in fact disenfranchised (see also chap. 10, this volume).

Cultures, of course, change. Eyetsemitan (1998) noted that these grieving rules may change over time. Younger cohorts, for example, may be more supportive than older people of the loss of a partner in an unmarried cohabiting couple; they may also be more supportive than their older counterparts of losses within a homosexual relationship. In the United States, there has been a growing awareness of certain losses, such as perinatal loss (at least for the mother), that is now evidenced by the appearance of greeting cards that console mothers for such a loss. Similarly, other cards have recently appeared acknowledging other losses as well, such as the loss of a pet.

The second implication is that there is recognition of degrees of support. In most Western societies, when friends, coworkers, colleagues, neighbors, or even celebrities and political and cultural leaders die, individuals may be expected both to show a display of grief and even possibly engage in mourning behaviors—attending the funeral, sending flowers or a contribution, and otherwise supporting the family. However, they are not accorded the full rights given to family grievers, such as an extended leave, diminished social responsibility, and extensive social sympathy and support. In fact, they may be expected to convey support to the family. The nature of disenfranchised grief is that the attachment to the deceased and the grief experienced by non-kin may not be accorded commensurate recognition and support by the larger society.

The discussion so far has emphasized the sociological aspects of disenfranchised grief yet, as Kauffman (2002) stressed, there is an intrapsychic dimension to disenfranchised grief as well. These societal grieving rules are internalized. The rules become standards by which we assess and judge the legitimacy of our own grief reactions. Thus, disenfranchisement is not only imposed by the society but also can be self-initiated, such as when shame and guilt over one's own attachments and subsequent grief may define a particular grief reaction as inappropriate or unworthy and the griever thus disenfranchises his or her own reactions to the loss.

Neimeyer and Jordan (2002) contributed a term that integrates the societal and intrapsychic dimensions of disenfranchised grief while offering a clinically important concept for assessing and treating this grief. To Neimeyer and Jordan (2002), the essential issue in disenfranchised grief is *empathic failure*, defined as "the failure of one part of the system to understand the meaning and experience of another" (p. 96). Here there is a failure to understand any given individual's personal experience or meaning construct of a particular loss and therefore a failure to render sufficient sympathy and support.

Empathic failure can take place at a very basic level—the interface between self-experience and self-interpretation. This would refer to Kauffman's (2002) intrapsychic dimension of disenfranchised grief. Neimeyer and Jordan (2002) offered the example of a mother of a child with significant disabilities who struggles with the intense ambivalent emotions that frame her grief reaction to her son's death. Empathic failure can occur at the level of family and intimate network as persons in the immediate surround fail to acknowledge and support another's grief. It also can take place within the larger community, where there is little recognition or validation of support. It can even involve a sense of spiritual alienation whereby an individual mourner feels separated from his or her own sense of spirituality or divinity as he or she copes with loss. The role of counselors, then, is to analyze and counter this empathic failure.

The sources and reasons for disenfranchised grief, then, are diverse and multifaceted. Yet, the results are the same: An individual experiences a loss that is not socially sanctioned, publicly acknowledged, or openly mourned.

TYPOLOGIES OF DISENFRANCHISED GRIEF

Which losses are disenfranchised? In my 1989 book *Disenfranchised Grief: Recognizing Hidden Sorrow* (Doka, 1989), I suggested three broad categories of loss and implied a fourth. These categories were developed inductively and clinically; that is, certain types of cases suggested a series of broad categories. In 1989, I proposed the following.

The Relationship Is Not Recognized

As stated earlier, in U.S. society most attention is placed on kin-based relationships and roles. Grief may be disenfranchised in situations in which the relationship between the bereaved and deceased is not based on recognizable kin ties. Here the closeness of other non-kin relationships may simply not be understood or appreciated. For example, Folta and Deck (1976) noted that

> while all of these studies tell us that grief is a normal phenomenon, the intensity of which corresponds to the closeness of the relationship, they fail to take this (i.e., friendship) into account. The underlying assumption is that closeness of relationships exists only among spouses and/or immediate kin. (p. 239)

The roles of lovers, friends, neighbors, foster parents, colleagues, in-laws, stepparents and stepchildren, caregivers, counselors, coworkers, and roommates (e.g., in nursing homes) may be long lasting and intensely interactive, but even though these relationships are recognized, mourners may not have full opportunity to publicly grieve a loss. At most, they might be expected to support and assist family members. This is especially true for formal or professional caregivers. As Moss, Moss, Rubinstein, and Black (2003) noted, many nursing homes view the facility in an almost familial way, but despite the strong metaphors of family that are often used, staff members' grief when a resident died was in many ways disenfranchised.

Research has added nuances to the study of relationships that are disenfranchised. For example, places such as prisons can disenfranchise even socially legitimated relationships. Both Ferszt (2002) and Olson and McEwen (2004) have found that grief is often disenfranchised in the prison system when a loved one dies on the outside. Even if the role is acknowledged as significant (e.g., a parent), participation in rituals may be inhibited and sympathy withheld partially out of security concerns and because the prisoner may not be regarded as worthy of support (see D. Martin, 2005). Both studies (Ferszt, 2002, and Olson & McEwen, 2004) found the concept of disenfranchised grief to be a useful interpretive tool.

There has been little research on the effects of newer technologies, such as the Internet, on the experience of grief (see chap. 12, this volume). Although thanatologists have explored the role of the Internet in grief education and support (see chap. 26, this volume; T. Martin & Doka, 1999), the effect of the Internet on grief has been largely ignored. Yet many individuals maintain extensive contacts on the Internet, interacting with a range of individuals, developing Web-based friendships and sharing intimacies. In such cases, the only indication of a loss may be unanswered e-mail or a cryptic "host unknown." The Internet is likely to spawn grief as well as to inform and support grievers.

There also are relationships that may not be publicly recognized or socially sanctioned. For example, some nontraditional relationships, such as extramarital affairs, have, at least in many cultures, tenuous public acceptance and limited legal standing and face negative sanction within the larger community. Individuals involved in such relationships are touched by grief when the relationship is terminated by the death of the partner. Others in their world, such as children, may also experience a grief that cannot be acknowledged or socially supported.

Even persons whose relationships existed primarily in the past may experience grief. Ex-spouses, past lovers, or former friends may have limited contact, or they may even engage in interaction in the present. Yet the death of that significant other can still cause a grief reaction because it brings finality to that earlier loss, ending any remaining contact or fantasy of reconciliation or reinvolvement. The grief over the death of an ex-spouse may be experienced not only by the surviving spouse but also by others in the family system, such as surviving children or even ex-in-laws. They too may mourn the loss of what once was and what might have been. For example, in one case, a 12-year-old child of an unwed mother, who had never even been acknowledged or seen by the father, still mourned the death of his father because it ended any possibility of a future liaison. However, although loss is experienced, society as a whole may not perceive that the loss of a past relationship could or should cause reaction.

The Loss Is Not Acknowledged

In other cases, the loss is not socially defined as significant. For example, some people may not perceive the loss of an animal as a cause for intense grief. Nevertheless, research (e.g., Kay, Nieburg, Kutscher, Grey, & Fudin, 1984) has shown strong ties between pets and humans and profound reactions to loss.

In some cases, the reality of the loss itself is not socially validated. Thanatologists have long recognized that significant losses can occur even when the object of the loss remains physically alive. Sudnow (1967) for example, discussed *social death*, in which the person is alive but is treated as if dead. Examples may include persons who are institutionalized or comatose. Similarly, *psychological death* has been defined as conditions in which the person lacks a consciousness of existence (Kalish, 1966), such as someone who is brain dead. One can also speak of *psychosocial death*, in which the persona of someone has changed so significantly, through mental illness, organic brain syndromes, or even significant personal transformation (e.g., through addiction, religious conversion, Alzheimer's disease and related dementias), that significant others perceive the person as he or she previously existed as dead (Doka, 1985a). In all of these cases, spouses and others may experience a profound sense of loss, but that loss cannot be publicly acknowledged because the person is still biologically alive.

Rando (2000), in her exemplary work on anticipatory mourning, explored the range of losses that persons experience and mourn in life-threatening illness. Rando made the point that individuals do not simply mourn the fact that they or someone they love has a terminal disease and will one day die. Although that is part of their grief, they mourn as well all the losses experienced along the way. I remember one friend whose husband died of amyotrophic lateral sclerosis, a motor neuron disease. She told me once that even worse than the death was the loss of his ability to speak. She grieved their inability to communicate, to discuss the affairs of life—once such a vital part of their relationship. In the same way, the secondary losses that follow a death, such as changes in lifestyle of other relationships, may also be mourned.

In the years since this concept of disenfranchised grief was proffered, the category of unacknowledged loss has generated much of the research that has focused on disenfranchised grief. Studies have applied the concept of disen-franchised grief to the reactions of the loss of romantic relationships in ado-lescence (Kaczmarek & Backlund, 1991) and young adults (Robak & Weitzman, 1995); grief responses to reproductive (Gray & Lassance, 2003) and perinatal losses (Hazen, 2003); and reactions to the experiences of incest (Dwyer & Miller, 1996), disability (Sapey, 2004), job loss (Leana & Feldman, 1992), or growing up in a dysfunctional family (Zupanick, 1994). In addition, the concept has been applied to the grief process of cultural reentry (Lester, 2000). It has even been used to understand the effects of the Great Irish Hunger (1846–1852) as a cultural grief reaction experienced by the descendents of that Irish dias-pora (Peck, 2000). Berra et al. (1993) documented how the loss of a religious identity due to changes in belief created a sense of grief in many respondents. Yet much of this research has been primarily descriptive, documenting a type of loss and using the term *disenfranchised grief* in a descriptive way by explain-ing that many persons who identified this loss experienced limited social sup-port. With the exception of Corr (1998), Eyetsemitan (1998), and Kamerman (1993), little work has offered critical analysis that either challenged or expanded the concept.

The Griever Is Excluded

There are situations in which the characteristics of the bereaved in effect disenfranchise their grief. Here the person is not socially defined as capable of grief; therefore, there is little or no social recognition of his or her sense of loss or need to mourn. Despite evidence to the contrary, others typically perceive both the old and the very young as having little comprehension of, or reaction to, the death of a significant other. Often, then, both young children and older adults are excluded from both discussions and rituals (Raphael, 1983).

Similarly, persons with intellectual disabilities may also be disenfranchised in grief. Although persons with intellectual disabilities are able to understand the concept of death (Lipe-Goodson & Goebel, 1983) and, in fact, experience grief (Edgerton, Bollinger, & Herr, 1984), others may not recognize or know how to manage the grief of a person with intellectual or other mental disabilities (Clements, Focht-New, & Faulkner, 2004; McEvoy & Smith, 2005). Over time, two additional categories were added, described in the sections that follow.

Circumstances of the Death

In my 1989 book (Doka, 1989), I suggested that certain circumstances surrounding the death might disenfranchise grief. The nature of the death may constrain the solicitation of the bereaved for support as well as limit the support extended by others. For example, many survivors of a suicide loss often feel a sense of stigma, believing that others may negatively judge the family because of the suicide. Similarly, the stigma of AIDS may lead survivors of an AIDS-related loss to be circumspect in sharing the loss with others (see Doka, 1993). Here, survivors may fear the responses of others including isolation, judgment, or a morbid curiosity.

Rando (1993) further developed this idea. She asserted that deaths that provoke anxiety (e.g., suicide, mutilating loss, the death of a child) or embarrassment (e.g., death from autoerotic asphyxiation or homicides, especially those that incur media notoriety or involve other family members) are likely to cause disenfranchised grief. Other circumstances that minimize support may be those in which support is withheld punitively (e.g., when an individual is executed) or where the deceased is otherwise devalued (e.g., the death of an alcoholic).

The Ways an Individual Grieves

The way an individual grieves also can contribute to disenfranchisement. T. Martin and Doka (1999) suggested that there are different styles of grieving. Some individuals grieve in a more intuitive way, experiencing and expressing grief as deep feeling. Those who are more instrumental experience and express grief reactions in a way that is more physical, cognitive, or behavioral. The counseling community tends to disenfranchise instrumental grievers because counselors often place a high value on affective response (see T. Martin & Doka, 1999; Sue & Sue, 1999). The larger community disenfranchises instrumental grievers early in the grieving process, when affective displays are expected, and intuitive grievers later in the grieving process, when affective responses are considered less appropriate (T. Martin & Doka, 1999). Certain cultural modes of expressing grief, such as stoicism or wailing, may fall beyond the grieving rules of a given society and thus can be disenfranchising (Doka & Davidson, 1998).

Alternate Typologies

These examples and categories are meant to illustrate the many ways grief may be disenfranchised. They are not exhaustive; neither are they exclusive. An individual's grief may be disenfranchised for a number of these reasons. For example, a foster parent experiencing the death of a HIV-positive foster child may see grief disenfranchised because the foster parent relationship may not be validated and the disease stigmatized within his or her community.

Also, of course, this particular taxonomy draws on examples attuned to contemporary Western culture. In other cultures, the relationships not recognized, losses not acknowledged, grievers excluded, circumstances under which an individual dies, or how a person grieves—all the factors that disenfranchise grief—may differ.

Neither is this the only taxonomy of disenfranchised grief. Corr (1998) offered another way to categorize disenfranchised grief. Corr approached classification deductively, asking "What is disenfranchised in grief?" He concluded that the state of bereavement, the experience of grief, and the process of mourning can all be disenfranchised.

These taxonomies assist in understanding two facets of disenfranchised grief: They (a) further contribute to an analysis of the reasons why grief is disenfranchised and (b) delineate the types of losses and situations that can create disenfranchisement, thus furthering application and research.

DISENFRANCHISED GRIEF AS A COMPLICATING FACTOR

Disenfranchised grief has been identified as a complicating factor in bereavement (see Rando, 1993). The problem of disenfranchised grief can be expressed in a paradox: The nature of disenfranchised grief creates additional problems for grief, while removing or minimizing sources of support.

Disenfranchised grief may exacerbate the problem of bereavement in a number of ways. First, the situations that often result in disenfranchised grief tend to intensify emotional reactions. Although each of the situations described is in its own way unique, the literature uniformly reports how each of these disenfranchising circumstances can intensify feelings of anger, guilt, or powerlessness (see, e.g., Doka, 1985a, 1986, 1987; Geis, Fuller, & Rush, 1986; Kelly, 1977; Miller & Roll, 1985; Peppers & Knapp, 1980).

Second, both ambivalent relationships and concurrent crises have been identified in the literature as conditions that complicate grief (Rando, 1993; Raphael, 1983; Worden, 1982). These conditions can often exist in many types of disenfranchised grief. For example, studies have indicated the ambivalence that can exist in cases of abortion (Raphael, 1983), among ex-spouses (Doka, 1986; Scott, 1985), among significant others in nontraditional roles (Doka, 1987; Horn, 1979), and among families of individuals with Alzheimer's disease (Doka, 1985a). Similarly, the literature documents the many kinds of concurrent crises that can trouble the disenfranchised griever. For example, in cases of cohabiting couples, either heterosexual or homosexual, studies have often found that survivors may experience legal and financial problems regarding inheritance, ownership, credit, or leases (e.g., Doka, 1987; Horn, 1979; Kimmel, 1978, 1979). Likewise, the death of a parent may leave a person with a mental disability not only bereaved but also bereft of a viable support system (Edgerton et al., 1984).

Disenfranchised grief is complicated, and many of the factors that facilitate mourning are not present. In death-related losses, the bereaved may be excluded from an active role in caring for the dying. Funeral rituals, normally helpful in resolving grief, may not help here. In some cases, the bereaved may be excluded from attendance. In other cases, they may have no role in planning those rituals or in deciding whether even to have them. Or in cases of divorce, separation or psychosocial death, rituals may be lacking altogether.

In addition, the nature of the disenfranchised grief precludes social support. Often there is no recognized role in which mourners can assert the right to mourn and thus receive such support. Grief may have to remain private. Although the bereaved may have experienced an intense loss, they may not be given time off from work, have the opportunity to verbalize the loss, or receive the expressions of sympathy and support characteristic of a death. Even traditional sources of solace, such as religion, are unavailable to those whose relationships (e.g., extramarital, cohabiting, homosexual, divorced) or acts (e.g., abortion) may be condemned within that faith tradition.

COUNSELING DISENFRANCHISED GRIEVERS

The complications often experienced by the person disenfranchised in his or her grief reinforce Neimeyer and Jordan's (2002) concept of empathic failure. Their approach to counseling persons who are experiencing disenfranchised grief is to begin by assessing this empathic failure. Among the questions they suggested therapists consider are queries that attempt to assess where empathic disconnection occurs. How much does an individual contribute to his or her own disenfranchisement? Does an individual isolate him- or herself or shroud a loss in secrecy or deception, thereby minimizing support? Do the norms and values of the individual's family or community censure certain behaviors or relationships limiting support? Does an individual's spirituality create a sense of spiritual alienation? Does disenfranchisement seem to occur at any particular time in the mourning process; for example, do many mourners experience a sense of support early in the grieving process that dissipates over time? The concept of disenfranchised grief should not be reduced to a typology. Neimeyer and Jordan emphasized that the clinical importance of the concept is that it offers the clinician a lens through which to understand the support that a client does or does not receive from others as he or she copes with grief.

Once an assessment is made, empathic failure can be countered. Sometimes, the very naming of the grief as disenfranchised has power, breaking the silence around the loss and offering a sense of legitimacy (Kuhn, 2002). As Neimeyer and Jordan (2002) stressed, disenfranchised grief is grief—the techniques that one would use in counseling persons who are grieving can be applied here. Evidence indicates that support groups are a useful strategy (Olson & McEwen, 2004; Pesek, 2002). Because rituals are often unavailable or limited in meaning to persons experiencing disenfranchised grief, I have suggested the value of using therapeutic rituals within the counseling process (Doka, 2002). The very act of counseling is valued because it offers support and validation that might not be provided elsewhere.

IMPLICATIONS AND CONCLUSION

Despite the shortage of critical and analytical research on and attention given to the issue of disenfranchised grief, it remains a significant and growing issue. Millions of individuals are involved in losses in which grief is effectively disenfranchised. There are estimates that 3% of men and 2% to 3% of women are exclusively homosexual, with similar percentages having mixed homosexual and heterosexual encounters (Gagnon, 1977). Approximately 1 million abortions are performed each year; even though many of the women involved may not experience grief reactions, some are clearly at risk. As individuals continue to live longer, more will suffer from severe forms of chronic brain dysfunctions. As the persons with developmental disabilities live longer, they too will experience the grief of parental and sibling loss. In short, the proportion of disenfranchised grievers in the general population will rise rapidly in the future.

It is likely that bereavement counselors will have increased exposure to cases of disenfranchised grief. In fact, the very nature of disenfranchised grief and the unavailability of informal support make it likely that those who experience such losses will seek formal supports. Professionals in the field of death education also need to consider the many kinds of relationships and subsequent losses that people can experience.

In many ways, the work on disenfranchised grief has been part of a larger challenge to the ways that we understand loss. It certainly has led to an increased sensitivity to the many situations and circumstances that create loss and evoke grief. Yet there is a danger here that it may broaden the concept of loss so widely that grief is trivialized and support lessened. This is Kamerman's (1993) caution: How can we offer support to every person affected by each circumstance of loss?

Many years ago, I spoke at a conference about disenfranchised grief. After the presentation, I met an old childhood friend, now a clinician. He had moved in his early adolescence, and we had had no contact since that time. He jokingly reminded me of an incident in which his baseball glove had been stolen. He remembered that I had stayed and sympathized with him over his loss. "I was," he claimed, "your first case of disenfranchised grief."

As the myriad circumstances of loss become more recognized, there is a pressing need for research that really describes the particular and unique responses to different types of losses; compares reactions, outcomes, and problems associated with these losses; assesses possible interventions; and describes the critical variables that affect each loss. One clear benefit of the concept of disenfranchised grief has been a heuristic value that has, in fact, encouraged research on many situations of loss or has evaluated the viability of the concept of disenfranchised grief for understanding different types of loss (chap. 21, this volume; Dwyer & Miller, 1996; Ferszt, 2002; Hazen, 2003; Kaczmarek & Backlund, 1991; Lester, 2000; Moss et al., 2003; Olson & McEwen, 2004; Peck, 2000; Robak & Weitzman, 1995; Sapey, 2004; Thornton & Zanich, 2002; Zupanick, 1994). However, as mentioned earlier, more research is clearly needed. This research needs to go beyond simply describing the experiences of varied losses that seem to engender reactions typified as disenfranchised grief. Instead, this research should provide a base on which to assess the ways grief reactions vary among different types of losses regarding the intensity of reactions as well as the process and outcomes of grief. Such research will expand our understanding of grief and avoid trivializing loss and, most critically, it will offer a background to acknowledge, assist, and enfranchise the disenfranchised.

REFERENCES

Berra, D. M., Carlson, E., Maize, M., Murphy, W., O'Neal, B., Sarver, R., & Zinner, E. S. (1993). The dark night of the spirit: Grief following a loss in religious identity. In K. Doka (with J. Morgan) (Eds.), *Death and spirituality* (pp. 291–308). Amityville, NY: Baywood.

Bowlby, J. (1980). *Attachment and loss: Vol. 3. Sadness and depression.* New York: Basic Books.

Clements, P. T., Focht-New, G., & Faulkner, M. (2004). Grief in the shadows: Exploring loss and bereavement in people with developmental disabilities. *Issues in Mental Health Nursing, 25*, 799–808.

Corr, C. (1998). Enhancing the concept of disenfranchised grief. *Omega: The Journal of Death and Dying, 38*, 1–20.

Doka, K. (1985a, March). *Crypto-death and real grief.* In A. Kutscher (Chair), symposium conducted at the Foundation of Thanatology, New York.

Doka, K. J. (1985b, April). *Disenfranchised grief.* In *Death education*, symposium conducted at the Foundation of Thanatology, New York.

Doka, K. (1986). Loss upon loss: Death after divorce. *Death Studies, 10*, 441–449.

Doka, K. (1987). Silent sorrow: Grief and the loss of significant others. *Death Studies, 11*, 455–469.

Doka, K. (1989). *Disenfranchised grief: Recognizing hidden sorrow.* Lexington, MA: Lexington Books.

Doka, K. (1993). *AIDS, fear and society: Challenging the dreaded disease.* Washington, DC: Taylor & Francis.

Doka, K. (2002). The role of ritual in the treatment of disenfranchised grief. In K. Doka (Ed.), *Disenfranchised grief: New directions, challenges and strategies for practice* (pp. 135–148). Champaign, IL: Research Press.

Doka, K., & Davidson, J. (1998). *Living with grief: Who we are, and how we grieve.* Washington, DC: Hospice Foundation of America.

Durkheim, E. (1915). *The elementary forms of religious life.* New York: Free Press.

Dwyer, J., & Miller, R. (1996). Disenfranchised grief after incest: The experience of victims/daughters/mothers/wives. *Australian and New Zealand Journal of Family Therapy, 17,* 137–146.

Edgerton, R. B., Bollinger, M., & Herr, B. (1984). The cloak of competence: After two decades. *American Journal of Mental Deficiency, 88,* 345–351.

Eyetsemitan, F. (1998). Stifled grief in the workplace. *Death Studies, 22,* 469–479.

Ferszt, G. (2002). Grief experiences of women in prison following the death of a loved one. *Illness, Crisis & Loss, 10,* 242–254.

Folta, J., & Deck, G. (1976). Grief, the funeral and the friend. In V. Pine, A. H. Kutscher, D. Peretz, R. C. Slater, R. DeBellis, A. I. Volk, & D. J. Cherico (Eds.), *Acute grief and the funeral* (pp. 231–240). Springfield, IL: Charles C Thomas.

Gagnon, J. (1977). *Human sexuality.* Glenview, IL: Scott, Foresman.

Geis, S., Fuller, R., & Rush, J. (1986). Lovers of AIDS victims: Psychosocial stresses and counseling needs. *Death Studies, 10,* 43–54.

Gray, K., & Lassance, A. (2003). *Grieving reproductive loss: The healing process.* Amityville, NY: Baywood.

Hazen, M. (2003). Societal and workplace responses to perinatal loss: Disenfranchised grief or healing connections. *Human Relations, 56,* 147–168.

Hochschild, A. R. (1979). Emotion work, feeling rules and social support. *American Journal of Sociology, 85,* 551–573.

Horn, R. (1979). Life can be a soap opera. In I. Gerber, A. Weiner, A. Kutscher, D. Battin, A. Arkin, & I. Goldberg (Eds.), *Perspectives on bereavement* (pp. 118–123). New York: Arno Press.

Kaczmarek, M., & Backlund, B. (1991). Disenfranchised grief: The loss of an adolescent romantic relationship. *Adolescence, 26,* 253–259.

Kalish, R. (1966). A continuum of subjectively perceived death. *The Gerontologist, 6,* 73–76.

Kamerman, J. (1993). Latent function of enfranchising the disenfranchised griever. *Death Studies, 17,* 281–287.

Kauffman, J. (2002). The psychology of disenfranchised grief: Liberation, shame and self-disenfranchisement. In K. Doka (Ed.), *Disenfranchised grief: New directions, challenges and strategies for practice* (pp. 61–78). Champaign, IL: Research Press.

Kay, W. J., Nieburg, H., Kutscher, A., Grey, R., & Fudin, C. (1984). *Pet loss and human bereavement.* New York: Arno Press.

Kelly, J. (1977). The aging male homosexual: Myth and reality. *The Gerontologist, 17,* 328–332.

Kimmel, D. (1978). Adult development and aging: A gay perspective. *Journal of Social Issues, 34*, 113–131.

Kimmel, D. (1979). Life history interview of aging gay men. *International Journal of Aging and Human Development, 10,* 237–248.

Kuhn, D. (2002). A pastoral counselor looks at silence as a factor in disenfranchised grief. In K. Doka (Ed.), *Disenfranchised grief: New directions, challenges, and strategies for practice* (pp. 119–126). Champaign, IL: Research Press.

Leana, C., & Feldman, D. (1992). *Coping with job loss: How individuals, organizations and communities respond to layoffs.* Lexington, MA: Lexington Books.

Lester, J. (2000). Strangers in their own land: Culture loss, disenfranchised grief, and re-entry adjustment. *Dissertation Abstracts International: Section B: The Sciences and Engineering, 61* (9-B), 4992. (UMI No. 9985178)

Lindemann, E. (1944). Symptomatology and management of acute grief. *American Journal of Psychiatry, 101,* 141–149.

Lipe-Goodson, P. S., & Goebel, B. I. (1983). Perception of age and death in mentally retarded adults. *Mental Retardation, 21,* 68–75.

Martin, D. (2005). Acute loss and the social construction of blame. *Illness, Crisis & Loss, 13,* 149–168.

Martin, T., & Doka, K. (1999). *Men don't cry, women do: Transcending gender stereotypes of grief.* Philadelphia: Brunner/Mazel.

McEvoy, J., & Smith, E. (2005). Families' perceptions of the grieving process and concept of death in individuals with intellectual disabilities. *British Journal of Developmental Disabilities, 51*(100, Pt. 1), 17–25.

Miller, L., & Roll, S. (1985). A case study in failure: On doing everything right in suicide prevention. *Death Studies, 9,* 483–492.

Moss, M., Moss, S., Rubinstein, R., & Black, H. (2003). The metaphor of family in staff communication about dying and death. *Journals of Gerontology Series B: Psychological and Social Sciences, 58,* S290–S296.

Neimeyer, R., & Jordan, J. (2002). Disenfranchisement as empathic failure: Grief therapy and the co-construction of meaning. In K. Doka (Ed.), *Disenfranchised grief: New directions, challenges and strategies for practice* (pp. 95–118). Champaign, IL: Research Press.

Olson, M., & McEwen, M. (2004). Grief counseling groups in a medium-security prison. *Journal for Specialists in Group Work, 29,* 225–236.

Parkes, C. M., & Weiss, R. (1983). *Recovery from bereavement.* New York: Basic Books.

Peck, D. (2000). Silent hunger: The psychological impact of the great Irish hunger: An Gorta Mor (1845–1852). *Dissertation Abstracts International: Section B: The Sciences and Engineering, 61* (5-B), 2819. (UMI No. 9974823)

Peppers, L., & Knapp, R. (1980). *Motherhood and mourning.* New York: Praeger.

Pesek, E. M. (2002). The role of support groups in disenfranchised grief. In K. Doka (Ed.), *Disenfranchised grief: New directions, challenges and strategies for practice* (pp. 127–134). Champaign, IL: Research Press.

Pine, V. (1989). Death, loss and disenfranchised grief. In K. Doka (Ed.), *Disenfranchised grief: Recognizing hidden sorrow* (pp. 13–24). Lexington, MA: Lexington Books.

Rando, T. A. (1993). *Treatment of complicated mourning.* Champaign, IL: Research Press.

Rando, T. A. (2000). *Clinical dimensions of anticipatory mourning.* Champaign, IL: Research Press.

Raphael, B. (1983). *The anatomy of bereavement.* New York: Basic Books.

Robak, R., & Weitzman, S. (1995). Grieving the loss of romantic relationships in young adults: An empirical study of disenfranchised grief. *Omega: The Journal of Death and Dying, 30,* 269–281.

Sapey, B. (2004). Impairment, disability, and loss: Reassessing the rejection of loss. *Illness, Crisis & Loss, 12,* 90–101.

Scott, S. (1985, April). *Grief reactions to the death of a divorced spouse.* Paper presented at the Seventh Annual Meeting of the Forum for Death Education and Counseling, Philadelphia.

Sudnow, D. (1967). *Passing on: The social organization of dying.* Englewood Cliffs, NJ: Prentice Hall.

Sue, D. W., & Sue, D. (1999). *Counseling the culturally different* (3rd ed.). New York: Wiley.

Thornton, G., & Zanich, M. L. (2002). An empirical assessment of disenfranchised grief: 1989–2000. In K. Doka (Ed.), *Disenfranchised grief: New directions, challenges and strategies for practice* (pp. 79–90). Champaign, IL: Research Press.

Worden, W. (1982). *Grief counseling and grief therapy.* New York: Springer Publishing Company.

Zupanick, C. (1994). Adult children of dysfunctional families: Treatment from a disenfranchised grief perspective. *Death Studies, 18,* 183–195.

12

THE NEW PUBLIC MOURNING

TONY WALTER

Grieving for no one I know,
I awaken at 3 a.m.
sobbing;
the air
laden
with the sadness of multitudes. (Linenthal, 2001, p. 109)

This poem was one of thousands that poured into the mayor's and governor's offices following the April 19, 1995, bombing of the Alfred P. Murrah Federal Building in Oklahoma City, Oklahoma, in which 168 people died, including several children in a day care center (Linenthal, 2001). Does this grief, and the mailed poem it inspired, represent a postmodern form of human connection, in which strangers who know of each other only through the news media nevertheless connect? This seemed to be the intention of a sizable collage, pinned to the railings of Kensington Palace, the London home of Diana, Princess of Wales, after her death. It was addressed to her two children, then ages 15 and 12:

> Dear Prince William, Prince Harry
>   Texas, USA is here to give you our love and prayers. You mother will always be our Princess! And will forever be there by your side to guide you, encourage you and love you!

Or do such messages, such sentiments, even such middle-of-the-night tears, represent "recreational grief," "grief lite"—a lightweight, undemanding image of connection, a pseudocommunity that is increasingly replacing the face-to-face connections of family, church, and neighborhood, as ephemeral as the television images that spawn it (West, 2004)? An electronic discussion group following the death of Diana took up the debate:

> Personal is when my grandmother dies, not when some play of light and shadow disappears.
>
> Diana told me of her dreams and disappointments—and despair; my grandmother never did. So for whom should I really mourn? (Sofoulis, 1997, p. 14)

The debate can even be internal to the individual. After Diana's death, many who mourned her came to question after a few days why they had mourned someone they had never met (Walter, 1999c).

Academics ask similar questions; anthropologists and psychologists have debated the roots of emotion for 100 years. Durkheim (1915) saw the positive functions of mourners gathering together: "When someone dies, the group to which he belongs feels itself lessened and, to react against this loss, it assembles. . . . Collective sentiments are renewed which then lead men to seek one another and to assemble together" (p. 339). When the group to which the deceased belongs is an entire city or nation, then the assembly will be that much bigger. For Durkheim, mourning was inherently social and was a major source of social integration. Such anthropological functionalism was rejected by post-Marxist cultural theorist Merrin (1999): "Compared with grief felt towards someone we have lost, this communal hysteria must have appeared unconvincing, even offensive. . . . [Diana's] funeral was a non-event—a media event: a scripted, televised, public performance" (pp. 49, 53). Merrin reflected here a view, increasingly popular in many, but not all, Western democracies, that privileges private grief over social mourning.

I argue in this chapter that in many Western countries two kinds of social mourning lost legitimacy in the 20th century: (a) Although private grief for an intimate remains legitimate, its social expression came to be severely constrained, and (b) public mourning for people whom you do not know, unless sanctioned by the state (e.g., the war dead, astronauts, victims of the 9/11 terrorist attacks), came to be seen as inauthentic. The history of this is key to understanding both the recent revival of public mourning and its critics. In the following sections, I assess media, cultural, political, and psychological explanations of public mourning before sketching clinical and policy issues (see also chap. 4, this volume).

TRADITIONAL MOURNING

In 1912, in London, eight Boy Scouts drowned on an outing down the River Thames; as the bodies were brought back in a special naval vessel, flags were flown at half-mast, all work in the London docks stopped, and a crowd of nearly 1 million watched (Morrison, 2005).

In the 1960s, John was 15 when his father died in Lancashire, England. He and his sister had separate bedrooms, but—without needing to discuss the decision—they slept in the same room as their mother for the next few days.

After September 11, 2001, when hijackers flew planes into the World Trade Center's Twin Towers and the Pentagon, newspapers depicted suburban front lawns flying the stars and stripes. The message was: Several thousand are dead, but America lives on and will not be defeated.

This Durkheimian assembling, this huddling together, this displaying of flags and other group totems, seems almost instinctual, yet if it is instinctual then why, in most traditional and in some modern societies, is it required, with rituals specified and nonattenders sanctioned (Wouters, 2002)? The reason may be because public mourning plays various social functions identified by historians and anthropologists. It may affirm the values of society (Taylor, 1983; Wolffe, 2000); the legitimacy of religion or a secular state; or family or patriarchal relationships, with women often being expected, or even required, to mourn more than men (Morley, 1971).

In a thought-provoking book, Holst-Warhaft (2000) modified the Durkheimian perspective. She showed how the passion of grief can be the cue not for stabilizing but for transforming society. Grief is one of the most powerful emotions that humans feel; it can carry one to the edge of madness. In many societies, it was indulged, performed, and shaped into song and lament (see, e.g., Danforth, 1982). However, throughout history, authority figures in church and state have feared grief's passion, banning songs, laments, and wakes, making mourning a dull business and turning the energy of grief into depression. This provides another clue as to why the apparent instinct to assemble is socially controlled. Holst-Warhaft's point is that the passions of assembly and its collective effervescence can be subversive, and so have to be controlled by the guardians of state, religion, and patriarchy. In Victorian Britain, the Church of England suppressed popular funeral songs (Gammon, 1988). Islam's proscriptions for mourning are in tension in many parts of the world with Muslims' actual practice (Campo, 2006). Thus, public mourning throughout history has come in two forms—folk and official—which may coexist or may conflict.

THE 20TH CENTURY: PRIVATE GRIEF

In Western societies, from the 19th century on, the control of public mourning, the requirement to be seen as grieving in particular ways and to mourn one's superiors, came under challenge, for two reasons. The first reason is that the romantic movement (Ariès, 1981) celebrated conjugal and parental love. If grief is the price we pay for love, then a culture that celebrates love over property and patriarchy must also deal with personal grief. Once people began to marry and to have children for love, they inevitably also grieved for love. The Victorian period in Europe saw a peak of required mourning and religious hope, but these were increasingly in tension with the unique, private pain felt for a unique relationship. It was the latter that eventually won out in the 20th century, in both clinical psychology and in popular culture (Stroebe, Gergen, Gergen, & Stroebe, 1992). People now grieve as hard and as long as they want, not as hard and long as social convention dictates.

The second, and related, reason came with modern notions of individual liberty. The upper class women who questioned Victorian required mourning in England were the same women supporting the suffragette movement (Taylor, 1983). If women were to be independent individuals in their own right, free to grieve or not grieve, then grief needed to be private, because public grief could be observed, inspected, and controlled. Hence the 20th-century notion developed of grief as a private, inner emotional process that cannot easily be inferred from outward behavior (Walter, 1999b). Mourners in the Western societies most affected by individualism (such as Britain, North America, and Australia) eventually came to be guided no longer by the social dictates of Victorian mourning but by the inner "grief process" of 20th-century psychology and the notion that grief reflects the mourner's unique attachment to the deceased.

THE 20TH CENTURY: PUBLIC MOURNING

Before taking the story further, I must note the exceptions. There are major national, as well as class, ethnic, and religious, variations in public mourning (see also chap. 10, this volume). A litmus test I pose to my students is, "Have you ever been to the funeral of someone you never met?" The English students look horrified and answer "Of course not!" (One or two may have accompanied their best friend to a grandparent's funeral, but this usually was motivated by personal care, not social requirement.) Irish and Japanese students answer "Naturally, yes." In Ireland and Japan, the wake for an elderly person may attract hundreds of mourners. In Japan, a worker may be expected to attend his boss' mother's funeral to demonstrate loyalty to his boss and to the firm. Mourning in England affirms one's connections as a nuclear family; in Japan, it affirms much wider affiliations. Attendance at wakes in Japan and Ireland is how social connections are affirmed; loyalty to social superiors is displayed, and there is pressure to be seen in attendance.

In a number of societies, especially Eastern countries, where ancestors are venerated, and in Catholic countries, where the dead are prayed for, public memorials for the dead are common. At Japan's annual O'bon festival, the spirits of the dead are called back to earth to commune for a day with the living before being sent back to the other world. Private remembrance and public assembly go hand in hand. Mexico's famous Day of the Dead operates on similar principles.

Even in countries with little or no influence from Catholicism or ancestor veneration, the war dead have been remembered at ritual places and times that balance private mourning and public remembrance, for example, Britain's Remembrance Sunday and London's Cenotaph memorial (Cannadine, 1981; King, 1998); ANZAC (Australian and New Zealand Army Corps) Day and Australia's National Memorial in Canberra; Amsterdam's Anne Frank House and Holocaust memorials in several countries; America's Memorial Day (Warner, 1959); and the Vietnam Veterans Memorial in Washington, DC. In many Western countries, public mourning came to be limited to the state's sacred dead (Goss & Klass, 2005); otherwise, 20th-century grief in most northwest European and English-speaking countries has been predominantly private, and it has generally been deemed unseemly to mourn people one did not personally know.

THE NEW PUBLIC MOURNING

For some people, and for the news media, there is now ambivalence and even approval for mourning people one never knew in life. Even in countries such as England and Holland, where 20th-century private grief had had its strongest hold, the late 20th century witnessed a proliferation of high-profile public mourning for new categories of deceased. Popular opinion or the media now catapult many more into the superleague of the sacred dead. In addition to war remembrance (which currently is undergoing a revival in the United Kingdom; Walter, 2001) and mourning for public figures, such as glamorous princesses, heads of state, or popes, whose status derives from the state (or, in the Pope's case, the Roman Catholic Church), there are now two new kinds of public mourning. First, some who mourn people they knew personally are publicizing their own grief, for example, in Internet cemeteries (Sofka, 1997), and after a violent death by means of roadside shrines and campaigns against drunk driving. Second, public mourning for people one did not know personally—notably celebrities, professional athletes, and victims of high-profile tragedies—has become common.

The new public mourning (NPM) has two temporal components (Grider, 2006). First are the spontaneous shrines (Reid, 2003; Santino, 2006), comprising items such as flowers, notes, and soft toys that are vulnerable to the weather and typically last for the period from death to the burial or shortly after. There may also be an organized silence or (e.g., in Holland) a silent march a few days after the death or deaths (Post, Grimes, Nugteren, Pettersson, & Zondag, 2003). Second are permanent memorials and annual commemorations. I focus mainly on the first component of NPM, although I also sketch some implications for the second component. At each stage, for every person who participates directly there may be many more watching at home on television (which raises the question whether the at-home viewer's mourning is public or private).

Modernity in general, and individualism in particular, have eroded required traditional life cycle rituals. This need not mean the end of rituals; rather, there seems to be a renaissance of rituals (Grimes, 2000; Post et al., 2003), but these are optional, a matter of choice, and not socially required (Wouters, 2002). In her study of roadside memorials, Everett (2002) argued that the lack of codified rituals in the United States has not left people lost (as some thanatologists have suggested) but has opened up cultural space in which people can fashion their own rituals. This cultural space has two components: (a) time and (b) place.

Regarding time, the period after a death is liminal, with normal hierarchical relationships held in abeyance (Turner, 1977). This opens the possibility for ordinary citizens to create rites in public spaces that would ordinarily be impossible (e.g., Walter, 1991). Regarding place, during the liminal period certain places may be coopted by public action that ordinarily would be controlled by the other groups; after Princess Diana's death, for example, in some English towns mourners left flowers and messages at the town war memorial, to the dismay of veterans, who felt they owned the memorials (Walter, 2001). Cemeteries often have strict rules regarding the articles that may be left at graves, opening hours, and the wording on gravestones; by moving into the street, public mourners reclaim public space.

This happens with roadside shrines to young people who died in automobile accidents. A number of these shrines are constructed by the deceased's young friends. Whereas the cemetery is adult space, controlled by officialdom, the street is where young people hang out; by constructing a roadside memorial they are free to express themselves and to reclaim the street not only from authority but also, perhaps, symbolically from death (Clark & Cheshire, 2004; Everett, 2002).

On the gravestone, as in newspaper "in memoriam" columns, private feelings are published. The roadside memorial extends this tradition, as do the memorial murals found in Hispanic areas in many North American cities (Cooper & Sciorra, 1994) and the memorial decals that adorn the rear windows of young Hispanics' automobiles in California (Engel, 2005). Like the Internet cemetery—free of the constraints of newspaper editors and cemetery managers—the road is a free space, not quite Foucault's (1984) heterotopia but something like it (St. John, 2000), where private feeling and public communication can interact in new ways.

At least, that is the hope; in practice, roadside shrines are often a source of conflict. Although they often bring the deceased's friends and family together, they alienate some drivers, who do not wish to be reminded of their mortality; also, highway authorities may remove them against the wishes of the people who created and maintain them (Everett, 2002; Excell, 2004; Post et al.,

2003). The memorials proliferating on Scottish mountain summits have led to similar conflict (Jones, 2005). This struggle over control typically emerges once the liminal period is over.

What, though, has caused the proliferation and transformation of public mourning? I address this question in the following section.

EXPLANATIONS FOR THE NEW PUBLIC MOURNING

Media Explanations

On the deaths of King George VI (1952) and former Prime Minister Winston Churchill (1965), there were fears that television would reduce the numbers attending the funeral procession (Wolffe, 2000). More recently, however, the concern has been the opposite: that the news media, especially television, create a public response to celebrity deaths quite out of proportion to any authentic grief.

In media research it is much easier to analyze the message or text itself than to ascertain its effects. Whether violence on television makes child viewers more violent, for example, is notoriously difficult to ascertain. Therefore, one must proceed with caution before concluding that the media cause public mourning. There are three possible processes: that the news media (a) create events (in this case, public mourning), (b) amplify existing events, and/or (c) simply report events. Any or all of these processes can occur, depending on the particular death being mourned. One must be careful before jumping to conclusions. The media's hand in creating a mourning event is likely to be precisely where it is least visible: less—as often supposed (e.g., Merrin, 1999)—in the mourning for Diana, more—as rarely suspected—in Britain's revived formal 2-minute November 11th silence for its war dead (Walter, 2001).

How accurate and selective are news reports of public mourning? After Diana died, few who came to pay respects were in tears, and even fewer cried aloud; instead, there was silence and a pensive calm. Yet television cameras focused on the one person in tears, cutting away to an apparently large crowd, giving the impression of thousands in tears (Kitzinger, 1998). The media proclaimed a new, emotional Britain.

Behavior and Perceptions

On the basis of the Mass Observation archive of written feelings and experiences following Diana's death, gathered from a panel of 249 ordinary Britons, Thomas (2002) showed that the news media were more effective in changing perceptions than behavior. The media provided wall-to-wall coverage of crowds laying flowers and queuing to sign books of condolence, yet—unlike Swedes after the *Estonia* disaster (Post et al., 2003)—only a minority of Britons, probably no more than 10%, actually participated in acts of public mourning; the majority chose to act differently from what the media portrayed "the people" as doing. One year later, the media predicted that several thousand people would come to London for the first anniversary of Diana's death, but only 300 came. Behavior is not so easily manipulated.

The media did, however, manipulate perceptions of what everyone else was doing. The members of the Mass Observation panel, like the population at large, knew few if any friends, family, or neighbors who had engaged in a public act of mourning for Diana, yet in the week after her death virtually all of them believed media images that the whole nation was mourning. They discounted personal observation and believed the televised images. Furthermore, they believed the selective media portrayal of a new, emotional Britain, even though any of them who had actually engaged in any public mourning were aware of the lack of tears and the crowds' mood of quiet calm.

Because most people keep quiet about personal views they perceive to be unpopular, a spiral of silence evolved: Believing themselves to be in a small minority, the majority of Britons kept quiet about their views. The result, Thomas (2002) showed, was a sense of alienation from an apparently united, newly emotional Britain. It is indeed worrying, and potentially dangerous, if the majority keep silent because they have been manipulated into thinking they are a tiny and unfashionable minority. Only in the weeks after Diana's funeral did dissident views emerge, producing a revisionist account in which many Britons now criticize the "mass hysteria" of that week. Hysteria was the only explanation they could find for a nation that in an instant had supposedly changed its character. This is the image that remains: a critical rather than a positive image, but still a false image, an image of an entire nation spending a week in tears.

Even scholars reproduce this false image. In her otherwise-excellent book, Holst-Warhaft (2000) wrote: "As the British people poured into central London and wept and hugged one another before the cameras, they seemed to surprise even themselves by their frank display of emotion" (p. 160). Researchers need to remain skeptical of media images, and their research needs to be based on carefully compiled statistics, observation, interview, and autobiography.

Status and Mourning

In one sense, nothing remarkable is happening in the NPM. Anthropologist Robert Hertz (1907/1960), in his seminal 1907 essay on collective representations of death, observed,

> In one and the same society the emotion aroused by death varies extremely in intensity according to the social status of the deceased. . . . At the death of a chief, or a man of high rank, a true panic sweeps over the

group. . . . On the contrary the death of a stranger, a slave or a child will go almost unnoticed; it will arouse no emotion, occasion no ritual. (p. 76)

Hertz's rule—that the size and intensity of mourning relate to the deceased's status and engagement in social relationships—has not changed. What has changed is who has high status: Children now have higher status than elderly people, and (in a reversal of Victorian customs) children's deaths are mourned accordingly; the "chief," the "man of high rank," is now the media celebrity, the sports star and the movie actor. These people, all known to the public through the mass media, receive the mass mourning, the panic that sweeps over the group, that in tribal societies was reserved for the chief, and whereas once "the death of a stranger, a slave, a child" went "almost unnoticed," now it is precisely the deaths of children, the vulnerable, and the victim that have the potential to generate mass mourning. In the Oklahoma City bombing, it was the inclusion among the dead of children in day care that for millions led to the most anguish (Linenthal, 2001). What leads most to Hertz's group panic is when children are murdered while in the care of trusted others (e.g., in the cases of the Dunblane primary school in Dunblane, Scotland; Columbine High School in Littleton, Colorado; the Murrah Federal Building in Oklahoma City, Oklahoma; and the school hostage crisis in Beslan, Russia).

So yes, the media create the celebrities and the victims that are the subject of public mourning, but this is simply a postmodern, global variation on Hertz's (1907/1960) rule. Is it any less authentic than the mourning of the tribesman for his chief?

It is, however, a matter of judgment whether these new foci for public mourning are seen as reflecting a democratic society in which everyone, even (perhaps especially) the vulnerable, has rights, including the right to be mourned, or a decadent society in which victimhood is valued more than heroism, the vulnerability of the young is valued more than the wisdom of the elderly, and celebrity is valued more than merit (Anderson & Mullen, 1998).

Cultural Explanations

There are a number of possible cultural explanations for the NPM. I outline some of them here.

The Diana Effect

Many British journalists today assume that mass public mourning started with the death of Diana in 1997; however, there was public mourning, similar in nature and even scale, for a number of disasters in the late 1980s, notably the Hillsborough soccer stadium disaster of 1989 (Walter, 1991). Earlier than this, flowers were laid in London where policewoman Yvonne Fletcher was shot dead during the 1984 Iranian embassy siege and outside Elvis Presley's home after his death in 1977; also, the tree in suburban London where pop singer Marc Bolan was killed in 1977 became a shrine. The daily transformation of the Vietnam Veterans Memorial into a folk shrine began with the memorial's completion in 1982 (Grider, 2006). In Sweden, the 1986 assassination of Olaf Palme was the catalyst for later spontaneous shrines. Indeed, since the early 19th century there have periodically been deaths that have rocked nations (Wolffe, 2000). As an explanation of the NPM, the so-called "Diana effect" is unhistorical and wrong.

Global Awareness

Another popular explanation is that as people travel more and see more of other cultures through the media and the Internet, so too do customs travel between countries. After Diana's death, many commented on the "Mediterranean" nature of some of the shrines, which some criticized as un-English (Excell, 2004). It is possible that mourners have adopted practices from other countries, but there are many things they do not adopt. Young Britons on vacation, for example, pick up some customs (e.g., Thai cuisine, Greek music) but not others (e.g., Thai politeness, Greek secondary burial). So travel, by itself, is far from a full explanation.

This raises an intriguing question about public mourning. In a global society of travel, television, and the Internet, why do some forms of the NPM (e.g., 1-minute silences, flowers, teddy bears, poems) travel from one country to another whereas others (e.g., the Dutch silent march) do not? Why do roadside memorials in secular Australia typically feature crosses but the ones in secular England do not (Excell, 2004)? Why (until the death of George Best in 2005) did English soccer crowds stand in silence to mark a player's death whereas Scottish and European soccer crowds cheered? Do roadside crosses in Texas derive from Mexican immigrants or would they have developed without Mexican immigrants (Everett, 2002)? Public mourning is both global and culturally specific, and deciphering the relation between the two is not easy (Post et al., 2003).

The Expressive Revolution

If, and it is a big if, public mourning in some countries represents a new emotional expressiveness, this shift could be explained in terms of the expressive revolution (Martin, 1981) that arguably has affected the Baby Boom generation. Especially in Western Europe, 60 years of peace and 50 years of affluence have provided the leisure and relative rarity of death for mourners to cope through talk, not least about their feelings, replacing the 1914–1950 culture of silent stoicism when people just had to get on with life because there was a war to fight or poverty to endure (Walter, 1999b). In Stroebe and Schut's (1999) dual-process terminology, late 20th-century culture has to some extent elevated emotion-focused coping over task-focused coping. Critics, though, deplore this elevation of feeling, image, and spontaneity over reason, reality, and restraint (O'Hear, 1998).

Gender

Just as in most Western societies women grieve more expressively than men (Stroebe, 1998), and in many traditional cultures women do the lamenting (e.g., Danforth, 1982), so too in the NPM are women typically more in evidence than men. In accordance with Simonds and Rothman (1992), one may argue that women's grief in the 19th and even much of the 20th century was kept out of sight of the public world dominated by men, first behind veils and social exclusion and then hidden in the inner recesses of private grief. The women's movement, however, has now enabled not only women, but also their emotionality, to move into the public sphere. This was particularly evident in the mourning for Diana, who in life had introduced female hugs and tears into public view (Walter, 1999c). Against this (and the previous) argument is my earlier observation that public mourning in many Western societies is not, *contra* media images, particularly emotional. In Diana's case, it may have been rather that women more than men follow with intense interest stories of love, sex, emotions, self-disclosure, and personal growth and so were more fascinated by Diana, in death as in life (Sofoulis, 1997). Public mourning may be specific to the deceased's particular identity.

Insecurity in a Safe World

In late modern societies, most infants live to adulthood, and most adults live to old age. Thus, any realization that some "people who are not old and who are not engaging in risky behaviour are dying suddenly, unexpectedly, violently, and sometimes en masse results in tremendous personal insecurity and cultural uncertainty" (Haney, Leimer, & Lowery, 1997, p. 160). When workers in the World Trade Center, or citizens attending to routine matters in a federal building, or children in a primary school, or tourists on an Indonesian beach are suddenly overwhelmed by terrorism or by natural forces, people's sense of security in modernity is threatened (Walter, 2006). This, according to Haney et al. (1997), is the cause of spontaneous memorialization and public mourning. It is a variant on Beck's (1992) more general thesis that the safer the modern world becomes, the more obsessed and worried its citizens become about risks to that safety. This arguably has reached its height in Sweden, a law-abiding country of safe Volvos and a highly effective welfare state, a country that prides itself on being the safest on earth: When Swedish premier Olaf Palme was assassinated in 1986 and when the *Estonia* ferry sank in 1994, the reaction of

Swedes was disbelief that such things could happen in their country (Post et al., 2003, chap. 4).

Political Explanations

Throughout history, public mourning has been politically motivated or controlled. The death of a leader is the most likely occasion for a power struggle over the succession, so the leader's family or dynasty has an interest in affirming its legitimate dominance over the subject group, affirmed first through elaborate funeral rites and memorials (Childe, 1945) and second through controlling the stories about the dead (Goss & Klass, 2005). In societies that are less than democratic (Watson & Rawski, 1988), attendance at the leader's funeral may be orchestrated, examples being Kim Il Sung (North Korea), Mao Tse-tung (China), and Josip Broz Tito (Yugoslavia). In democracies, funerals do not have quite so much work of this nature to do, but—especially in conflict situations— they retain a significant political role. After Diana's death, frantic activity behind the scenes ensured the institution of the British monarchy was secured. During the troubles in Northern Ireland, people attended funerals en masse, to support "their" side. In an unprecedented move, the 2005 funeral of Belfast-born soccer star George Best took place in the Stormont parliament building: Why was an alcoholic former soccer player getting, in all but name, a state funeral? Best, a sporting hero to both Protestant and Catholic communities, was being promoted by government and media as a symbol of postconflict Northern Irish unity. (The public attendance for the funeral procession was far less than predicted, indicating again limits to the ability of politicians and media to manipulate behavior.)

The power of grief (Holst-Warhaft, 2000) motivates some lobbying groups. In France, a campaign by La Ligue Contre La Violence Routière (League Against Roadway Violence) instituted the erection of full-scale silhouettes or dummies, black with red seeping through the head, where motorists have died (Morrison, 2005). The formation of the groups Mothers Against Drunk Driving (MADD, in the United States) and RoadPeace (in the United Kingdom) was motivated by parents' anger at the needless deaths of their children; these groups negotiate with the authorities for deaths to be marked permanently by memorials that have the double function, personal and political, of memorializing the dead and warning the living to drive better. The American AIDS quilt, in surface area possibly the largest memorial in history, had a similar double function: (a) memorializing the dead and (b) fighting for AIDS awareness and gay rights (Hawkins, 1995). Even those not bereaved may be driven by anger; in Holland, spontaneous memorials to the beating to death of a woman thought to be homeless became a focus for protest against mindless violence (Stengs, 2003). Santino (2006, p. 13) argued that spontaneous shrines, by personalizing a social problem (violence, drunk driving, an out-of-touch monarchy), have the power to effect change. If soldiers can kill because they are trained to depersonalize the enemy, spontaneous shrines work the opposite way, by repersonalizing statistics. "You don't think drunk driving is a problem? My daughter was killed—here, at this spot—because of it."

Psychological Explanations

Conspicuous Compassion

An explanation and criticism of public mourning articulated by some popular writers in Britain points to a desire to be noticed by people whose identity has been fractured by loss of community, a look-at-me grief that aims to show others how deeply caring they are (O'Hear, 1998; West, 2004). These writers, however, assume rather than empirically research mourners' motivations. When mourners take photographs of each other at the shrine, is this because they wish to show themselves as caring, because they wish to document their presence at what they perceive to be a world event, or is there another motive? Without research, we do not know. An alternative hypothesis is that, compared with the truly conspicuous mourning of a traditional Irish or modern Japanese wake, no one monitors whether you engage in the NPM, and there are no sanctions should you fail to attend—after Diana's death, there was as much criticism of mourners as of nonmourners.

Vicarious Grief

Bereavement counselors often claim that public mourners are working through an unresolved previous grief. This is doubtless true for some individuals, as indeed it is for some people at any funeral. Public mourning can trigger the reworking of a previous grief; the reworking, however, does not explain public mourning any more than it explains why we hold funerals. Vicarious grief is often a consequence of public mourning, but consequences are not the same as causes.

There is, however, a more sophisticated argument that may have explanatory power. The objects of public mourning are either private individuals, such as disaster or murder victims, about whose lives we know little, or they are celebrities whose lives the media have supersaturated with stories, identities, and meanings. In either case, mourners are free to project onto the deceased any one of a number of identities, so their death can easily stand in for the one the subconscious wishes to mourn (Brennan, 2001). It is intriguing that the reverse argument has also been made: We know celebrities and soap opera characters better than our own families, and therefore we grieve for them more deeply (Boycott, 2005). Each argument can account for the mass scale of public mourning for characters whom mourners have not met but whom they imagine they know well; each can also account for the emotional intensity of public mourning (although unfortunately this intensity is often more a media construct than reality, so the argument explains too much). Each argument—like others discussed earlier—remains at the level of hypothesis, requiring empirical research.

Which Explanation Is Best?

How can we assess these explanations? First, many writers mistake the media image of public mourning for the reality. Explanations generally require a much better empirical base, although a start in documentation has been made by ethnographers such as Everett (2002), Grider (2006), Post et al. (2003), Linenthal (2001), Santino (2006), and myself (Walter, 1999a). Second, a comprehensive explanation requires some combination of the psychological and the social (Brennan, 2001). Psychological explanations can explain why particular individuals participate in public mourning, but by themselves they cannot explain why large numbers of people have shifted their behavior. Social and historical explanations can explain such shifts but are in danger of neglecting the emotional, nonrational, or even subconscious elements in public mourning. Third, although there are elements in common, different instances of public mourning may require different explanations. A roadside memorial erected by MADD is not the same as the response of Columbine High School students to the murder of their schoolmates or the public response to 9/11, and the artifacts left at each site reflect the unique circumstances of both the deaths and the bereaved community (Grider, 2006). Mourning for a single national leader is not the same as mourning within a community after a localized disaster in which many have died. Public mourning is as diverse as influenza: There are various manifestations and causes, but they are given one label.

That said, I suggest the two most powerful explanations for the NPM. The first is Hertz's (1907/1960) analysis of public mourning for high-status individuals, modified for modern conditions in which status is defined in new, more democratic, and highly mediated ways. No longer can the aristocracy, or even the modern state, have a monopoly on defining who deserves public mourning. Nevertheless, when public mourning is not state approved, charges of inauthenticity are more likely to be made against people who mourn individuals they had never known. The second most powerful explanation, Santino's (2006) analysis, makes sense of the many spontaneous shrines that are clearly intended to initiate political change.

CLINICAL IMPLICATIONS

I now sketch clinical implications for three groups: (a) the deceased's intimates who cannot grieve entirely in private because of the public nature of the death, (b) nonintimates who join or witness the public mourning, and (c) witnesses to the death.

The Bereaved

Do the deceased's intimates find the interest of millions of others a help or a hindrance? Either can occur. Sheila Ravenscroft, widow of British disc jockey and radio show host John Peel, wrote,

> In the weeks that followed, the e-mails and correspondence flooded in. People who had never even met John sent flowers and letters. . . . Graffiti appeared. . . . The children and I were taken aback by the response from the public and the media. We drew from them an enormous amount of comfort. . . . Wherever we looked, people were mourning John. We knew the tributes weren't for our benefit. . . . Knowing other people out there were sharing our sadness helped tremendously. (Ravenscroft, 2005, p. 23)

In today's geographically mobile and long-lived society, with home and work separated, children moving away, and parents moving away on retirement, mourners are typically surrounded by people who did not know the deceased (Walter, 1999b). When my mother died at age 92, few of my neighbors and none of my workmates had met her; they could offer their condolences, but they did not share my sorrow; much more helpful were statements from the few who could say that they too missed her. Peel's widow and children, however, found themselves embraced by a nation acting rather like a traditional village, with millions who knew John and in their own way missed him. That is what his widow found to be a support.

However, mourning in private, given this public attention, can be problematic. The murder in 2002 of two English 10-year-olds, Holly Wells and Jessica Chapman, was international as well as national news; their parents, it was reported in many newspapers (e.g., Boycott, 2005), were disturbed by the "grief tourists" descending on their small village of Soham, and the vicar appealed for outsiders to keep away. The widow of a dissident member of a British government was disturbed that his funeral was hijacked by the political party, which—with a slim majority and a by-election pending—needed to put on a good show of solidarity; thus, the funeral reflected the party's values, not his. The parents of young people killed on roadways are usually comforted by shrines erected by others at the site, but they may have to battle with the public authorities for the shrines' continuance (Everett, 2002). Even in traditional societies, social expectations may conflict with the emotional needs of the bereaved (Cannadine, 1981; Hill, 1977). The experiences of the bereaved today at the center of public mourning encompass both the pluses and minuses of mourning in traditional villages (sometimes literally overwhelming support, or alienation), experiences very different from the ordinary urban bereaved (who may experience lack of support and isolation).

Some bereaved people, especially those who have lost children, become professional campaigners (Riches & Dawson, 1996; Rock, 1998). Counselors can be concerned that such people get stuck in anger or that their grief becomes prolonged. This may, however, be a price campaigners choose to pay for using their anger to shape a better society for future generations (Holst-Warhaft, 2000); at least the campaigning gives the death meaning. Campaigning mourners may need support to bear this price, not be "therapied" out of their anger.

In automobile fatalities in which one car has driven into another, with parties in each vehicle killed, the ensuing shrine is typically to the memory of the "innocent" dead (Everett, 2002)—just as war memorials are to "our" dead, not "theirs." This may comfort the family and friends of the innocent party, but what of the equally bereaved family and friends of the guilty party? Their deceased has been deliberately omitted from the shrine and the attendant public mourning and may be publicly vilified.

The Public Mourners

What about people who did not personally know the deceased but who engage in public mourning? It is possible their mourning reflects a previous unresolved grief for which support may be needed. It is also possible they are suffering not grief but a degree of trauma (Shevlin, Davies, Walker, & Ramkalawan, 1999), with the death raising particular fears or insecurities—not only for adults but also for children, who begin to realize that the world is not as safe a place as they had been led to believe. Children may exaggerate the nature of the risk (believing that each new picture of the same devastation represents another earthquake or terrorist bomb), or they may not take it seriously enough, mistaking news pictures for fiction. Ronald Grimes (Post et al., 2003) described how he created a household ritual to make 9/11 real for his children.

Witnesses

Witnesses to violent death also need to be considered. A neighbor who witnesses a road traffic accident in front of her house may come to detest the spontaneous shrine that reminds her of the trauma every time she steps outside. Even a permanent memorial, erected by MADD, RoadPeace, or La Ligue Contre La Violence Routière to remind motorists of their vulnerability may not be what traumatized witnesses need to see.

I end this section with a caveat. However much the NPM may help or hinder the psychosocial adaptation that is the concern of clinicians, this is perhaps not the touchstone by which the NPM should be judged by society at large. As with funerals, the explicit purpose of the NPM is not personal adaptation but public honoring of the dead (Post et al., 2003).

POLICY IMPLICATIONS

As this last example hints, public mourning raises issues of public policy. Several of these issues concern the managed evolution of spontaneous public mourning into permanent public memorialization—which itself does not preclude mourning: War memorials, for example, can trigger mourning decades later. If public mourning is often swayed by the media, public memorialization often results from decisions by local or national government or its officials.

Spontaneous Shrines

After Diana's death, 10,000 tons of flowers were estimated to have been left outside Kensington and Buckingham Palaces (Jack, 1997); how were the authorities to dispose of these in a way that the public would deem respectful? In this particular case, they were composted. More tricky are memorials at the site of death itself, because site and shrine may continue to be considered sacred, at least to the bereaved, if not to a wider public. How should highway authorities deal with roadside shrines, especially if they consider them a danger that distracts motorists' concentration and encourages pedestrians to loiter at a proven danger spot? The value of spontaneous shrines, especially for teenagers, is that the bereaved have constructed them themselves; the removal of a shrine and its replacement by an official plaque may be tidier and safer, but it steals from the youngsters their way of mourning. Mementoes left at the Vietnam Veterans Memorial in Washington, DC, are removed daily and archived; this strategy could be appropriate in a few other cases, if only temporarily, but is neither appropriate nor affordable for most authorities.

Memorializing Evil

How should the site of a highly public murder be managed? How may public mourning be prevented from evolving into ghoulish rather than respectful remembrance? If there is a danger the existing building could become a shrine to evil, encouraging ghoulish tourism, should it be torn down? If so, what should be erected in its place? When the site is also valuable real estate, as at Ground Zero, the site of the former World Trade Center, the issues are compounded. Examples include Ford's Theatre, in Washington, DC, where Abraham Lincoln was assassinated in 1865, and the parking lot at Kent State University in Ohio where protesting students were shot by National Guardsmen in 1970. After President John F. Kennedy was assassinated in Dallas in 1963, people were unsure of what to do with the Texas School Book Depository Building, from which the fatal shots were fired. Should they tear it down and then regret it or preserve it and be called tasteless? The building was eventually purchased by the county in 1977, and the room from which the shots were fired later became a museum to the event, run by the Dallas County Historical Foundation (Sellars & Walter, 1993).

The terraced (or row) house in Gloucester, England, in which Fred and Rose West murdered and hid the remains of 10 young females, including their own daughter, raised similar problems. After their 1995 trial, the house was demolished and a park was created in its place: The gap in the row of houses is clearly visible, so tourists have no trouble identifying the site, but the house of evil has itself been destroyed.

Memorializing Conflict

With these murders and assassinations, there was widespread agreement in American and British society as to the evil nature of the deed. The evolution of public mourning into public memorialization can be even more problematic when society cannot agree on the meaning, or meaninglessness, of the deaths. Civil war, like road deaths, raises the question of whether both sides can be memorialized together, even long after the conflict. The Gettysburg battlefield cemetery has succeeded in memorializing the dead of both sides of the American Civil War (Sellars, 1986), as has Memorial Day (Warner, 1959). Ben-Ze'ev and Ben-Ari (1996), however, described the attempt to create a museum of coexistence in Jerusalem where the narratives of two or more groups marked by confrontation are set out side by side. Given its location and management by Israelis, however, the museum failed. The design of the Vietnam Veterans Memorial was fraught with political and aesthetic conflict: Were the American dead heroes of a just war or victims of an unjust one? What aesthetic could memorialize such conflicting memories and such convoluted grief (Howett, 1985)? However, the memorial's initially controversial design has proved startlingly successful, enabling visitors of all persuasions to mourn and to remember (Sellars & Walter, 1993).

CONCLUSION

In this chapter, I have not covered public mourning in non-Western and in nondemocratic societies. I have argued that in Western societies, where the mass media and ideas of freedom, individuality, and personal choice are well developed, an NPM has developed, with the following features.

First, the NPM is not entirely manufactured by the media. Media coverage is selective and can mislead scholars and commentators as well as the mass of viewers.

Second, mourning people you have not met rarely has the characteristics of grief for an intimate as outlined by 20th-century grief psychology. Public mourning is short lived; mourners continue their everyday lives with no empty space in the marital bed or at the dining room table, and there is no psychosocial adjustment to make—although there may be temporary shock or even a degree of trauma.

Third, the NPM is in some ways comparable to the public mourning that has followed the death of high-status individuals throughout human history: It is a social, and sometimes a political, as much as an emotional phenomenon. Status is typically conferred by a global media or national politics rather than by feudal hierarchy; also, the NPM differs from traditional public mourning in three ways:

1. Whereas in traditional, feudal, patriarchal, and totalitarian societies, subjects have been required to mourn their social superiors, the NPM is entirely optional. No one is required to mourn.
2. Because mourning is no longer a required duty, the NPM may express personal feeling. In a reflection of the new informalization of public life, mourners need not wear formal black: Whether for pope, princess, or murdered child, the crowds come dressed as they choose. Clothing, like the new mourning itself, expresses personal feeling, not social requirement.
3. Nonmourners today may be required to keep their doubts to themselves in the liminal period before burial, but after the deceased is decently buried they may voice criticism of those who mourned. Consequently, the new public mourners may find themselves criticized by friends, family, or the press. For critics to dismiss mourners' feelings and behavior as inauthentic, not genuine, or recreational, however, is to misidentify the phenomenon, to see it as grief rather than mourning. Such charges of inauthenticity ignore how most human societies through history have mourned and privilege a norm of private grief that is specific to the 20th-century modern West, especially northwest Europe. These charges reveal how taken-for-granted and historically unreflexive this norm has become, both in lay consciousness and in clinical lore. They tell us more about the hegemony of private grief than anything about the NPM.

REFERENCES

Anderson, D., & Mullen, P. (1998). *Faking it: The sentimentalisation of modern society.* London: Social Affairs Unit.

Ariès, P. (1981). *The hour of our death.* London: Allen Lane.

Beck, U. (1992). *Risk society.* London: Sage.

Ben-Ze'ev, E., & Ben-Ari, E. (1996). Imposing politics: Failed attempts at creating a museum of co-existence in Jerusalem. *Anthropology Today, 12,* 7–13.

Boycott, R. (2005, August 27). Mourning sickness. (London). *Daily Mail.*

Brennan, M. (2001). Towards a sociology of (public) mourning? *Sociology, 35,* 205–212.

Campo, J. (2006). Muslim ways of death: Between the prescribed and the performed. In K. Garces-Foley (Ed.), *Death and religion in a changing world* (pp. 147–177). Armonk, NY: M. E. Sharpe.

Cannadine, D. (1981). War and death, grief and mourning in modern Britain. In J. Whaley (Ed.), *Mirrors of mortality* (pp. 187–242). London: Europa.

Childe, V. G. (1945). Directional changes in funerary practice during 50,000 years. *Man, 45,* 13–19.

Clark, J., & Cheshire, A. (2004). RIP by the roadside: A comparative study of roadside memorials in New South Wales and Texas. *Omega: The Journal of Death and Dying, 48,* 203–222.

Cooper, M., & Sciorra, J. (1994). *R.I.P.: Memorial wall art.* New York: Henry Holt.

Danforth, L. (1982). *The death rituals of rural Greece.* Princeton, NJ: Princeton University Press.

Durkheim, E. (1915). *The elementary forms of the religious life.* London: Unwin.

Engel, A. (2005, December 11). In the rear window, tributes to the dead. *New York Times.* Retrieved December 8, 2007, from http://www.nytimes.com/2005/12/11/fashion/sundaystyles/11DECALS.html

Everett, H. (2002). *Roadside crosses in contemporary memorial culture.* Denton: University of North Texas Press.

Excell, G. (2004). *Roadside memorials in the UK: Private grief made public.* Unpublished master's thesis, University of Reading, Reading, England.

Foucault, M. (1984, October). Of other spaces. *Diacritics, 16*(1), 22–27.

Gammon, V. (1988). Singing and popular funeral practices in the eighteenth and nineteenth centuries. *Folk Music Journal, 5,* 412–447.

Goss, R. E., & Klass, D. (2005). *Dead but not lost: Grief narratives in religious traditions.* Walnut Creek, CA: AltaMira.

Grider, S. (2006). Spontaneous shrines and public memorialization. In K. Garces-Foley (Ed.), *Death and religion in a changing world* (pp. 246–264). Armonk, NY: M. E. Sharpe.

Grimes, R. (2000). *Deeply into the bone: Re-inventing rites of passage.* Berkeley: University of California Press.

Haney, C. A., Leimer, C., & Lowery, J. (1997). Spontaneous memorialization: Violent death and emerging mourning ritual. *Omega: The Journal of Death and Dying, 35,* 159–171.

Hawkins, P. (1995). Naming names: The art of memory and the NAMES Project AIDS quilt. *Critical Inquiry, 19,* 752–779.

Hertz, R. (1960). *Death and the right hand.* London: Cohen & West. (Original work published 1907)

Hill, S. (1977). *In the springtime of the year.* London: Penguin.

Holst-Warhaft, G. (2000). *The cue for passion: Grief and its political uses.* Cambridge, MA: Harvard University Press.

Howett, C. W. (1985). The Vietnam Veterans Memorial: Public art and politics. *Landscape, 28*, 1–9.

Jack, I. (1997). Those who felt differently. *Granta, 60*, 9–35.

Jones, G. (2005, September). Mountain memorials. *The Scottish Mountaineer, 28*. Retrieved December 8, 2007, from http://www.mountaineering-scotland.org.uk/access/memorials.html

King, A. (1998). *Memorials of the Great War in Britain: The symbolism and politics of remembrance*. Oxford, England: Berg.

Kitzinger, J. (1998). Image. *Screen, 39*, 73–79.

Linenthal, E. (2001). *The unfinished bombing: Oklahoma City in American memory*. New York: Oxford University Press.

Martin, B. (1981). *A sociology of contemporary cultural change*. Oxford, England: Blackwell.

Merrin, W. (1999). The death of Diana and the media. *Mortality, 4*, 41–62.

Morley, J. (1971). *Death, heaven & the Victorians*. London: Studio Vista.

Morrison, B. (2005, November 3). Saying it with flowers. *Guardian*. Retrieved December 8, 2007, from http://www.guardian.co.uk/britain/article/0,,1607218,00.html

O'Hear, A. (1998). Diana, queen of hearts: Sentimentality personified and canonised. In D. Anderson & P. Mullen (Eds.), *Faking it: The sentimentalisation of modern society* (pp. 181–190). London: Social Affairs Unit.

Post, P., Grimes, R., Nugteren, A., Pettersson, P., & Zondag, H. (2003). *Disaster ritual: Explorations of an emerging ritual repertoire*. Leuven, Belgium: Peeters.

Ravenscroft, S. (2005, October 11). Life without John (London). *Daily Telegraph*, p. 23.

Reid, J. K. (2003). Impromptu memorials to the dead. In C. Bryant (Ed.), *Handbook of death and dying* (pp. 712–720). Thousand Oaks, CA: Sage.

Riches, G., & Dawson, P. (1996). Communities of feeling: The culture of bereaved parents. *Mortality, 1*, 143–161.

Rock, P. (1998). *After homicide: Practical and political responses to bereavement*. Oxford, England: Clarendon Press.

Santino, J. (Ed.). (2006). *Spontaneous shrines and the public memorialization of death*. Basingstoke, England: Palgrave Macmillan.

Sellars, R. W. (1986). Vigil of silence: The Civil War memorials. *History News, 41*, 19–23.

Sellars, R. W., & Walter, T. (1993). From Custer to Kent State: Heroes, martyrs and the evolution of popular shrines in the USA. In I. Reader & T. Walter (Eds.), *Pilgrimage in popular culture* (pp. 179–200). Basingstoke, England: Macmillan.

Shevlin, M., Davies, M., Walker, S., & Ramkalawan, T. (1999). A nation under stress: The psychological impact of Diana's death. In T. Walter (Ed.), *The mourning for Diana* (pp. 89–96). Oxford, England: Berg.

Simonds, W., & Rothman, B. K. (1992). *Centuries of solace: Expressions of maternal grief in popular literature*. Philadelphia: Temple University Press.

Sofka, C. (1997). Social support "internetworks," caskets for sale, and more: Thanatology and the information superhighway. *Death Studies, 21,* 553–574.

Sofoulis, Z. (1997). Icon, referent, trajectory, world. In Re: Public (Ed.), *Planet Diana: Cultural studies and global mourning* (pp. 13–18). Kingswood, New South Wales: University of Western Sydney, Research Centre in Intercommunal Studies.

Stengs, I. (2003). Ephemeral memorials against "senseless violence." *Etnofoor, 16,* 26–40.

St. John, G. (2000). *Alternative cultural heterotopia.* Unpublished doctoral dissertation, LaTrobe University, Melbourne, Australia. Retrieved December 8, 2007, from http://www.confest.org/thesis/oneach.html

Stroebe, M. (1998). New directions in bereavement research: Exploration of gender differences. *Palliative Medicine, 12,* 5–12.

Stroebe, M., Gergen, M., Gergen, K., & Stroebe, W. (1992). Broken hearts or broken bonds: Love and death in historical perspective. *American Psychologist, 47,* 1205–1212.

Stroebe, M., & Schut, H. (1999). The dual process model of coping with bereavement. *Death Studies, 23,* 197–224.

Taylor, L. (1983). *Mourning dress: A costume and social history.* London: Allen & Unwin.

Thomas, J. (2002). *Diana's mourning: A people's history.* Cardiff: University of Wales Press.

Turner, V. (1977). *The ritual process.* Ithaca, NY: Cornell University Press.

Walter, T. (1991). The mourning after Hillsborough. *Sociological Review, 39,* 599–625.

Walter, T. (1996) A new model of grief: Bereavement and biography. *Mortality, 1,* 7–25.

Walter, T. (Ed.). (1999a). *The mourning for Diana.* Oxford, England: Berg.

Walter, T. (1999b). *On bereavement: The culture of grief.* Philadelphia: Taylor & Francis.

Walter, T. (1999c). The questions people asked. In T. Walter (Ed.), *The mourning for Diana* (pp. 19–47). Oxford, England: Berg.

Walter, T. (2001). From cathedral to supermarket: Mourning, silence and solidarity. *Sociological Review, 49,* 494–511.

Walter, T. (2006). Disaster, modernity, and the media. In K. Garces-Foley (Ed.), *Death and religion in a changing world* (pp. 265–282). Armonk, NY: M. E. Sharpe.

Warner, W. L. (1959). *The living and the dead: A study of the symbolic life of Americans.* New Haven, CT: Yale University Press.

Watson, J. L., & Rawski, E. S. (1988). *Death ritual in late imperial and modern China.* Berkeley: University of California Press.

West, P. (2004). *Conspicuous compassion: When sometimes it really is cruel to be kind.* London: Civitas.

Wolffe, J. (2000). *Great deaths: Grieving, religion, and nationhood in Victorian and Edwardian Britain.* Oxford, England: Oxford University Press.

Wouters, C. (2002). The quest for new rituals in dying and mourning. *Body & Society, 8,* 1–27.

IV

PATTERNS AND CONSEQUENCES OF GRIEF: PHENOMENA AND MANIFESTATIONS

13

CAREGIVING AND BEREAVEMENT

RICHARD SCHULZ, KATHRIN BOERNER, AND RANDY S. HEBERT

Of the approximately 2.4 million deaths that occur in the United States each year, nearly 70% are the result of chronic conditions such as heart disease, cancer, stroke, and respiratory diseases. Even in developing countries, where diarrhea and pneumonia were once the leading causes of death, chronic disease now accounts for the majority of deaths (Reddy, 2002; World Health Organization, 2004). The worldwide shift to chronic-disease mortality has important implications for both formal and informal (i.e., family members) health care providers. In both developed and developing countries, the capacity of the formal health care system to provide care and support to individuals with chronic disease and disability is highly constrained, resulting in increased demands on family members to fill this role.

The large majority of these deaths occur among older persons suffering from one or more disabling conditions that compromise their ability to function independently prior to death (see also chap. 20, this volume). As a result,

Preparation of this chapter was supported in part by National Institute of Nursing Research Grants NR08272 and NR09573; National Institute on Aging Grants AG15321 and AG026010; National Institute of Mental Health Grant MH071944; National Center on Minority Health and Health Disparities Grant MD000207; National Heart, Lung, and Blood Institute Grant H076858; and National Science Foundation Grant EEEC-0540856.

cal death is preceded by an extended period of time during which one
ore family members provide health and support services to their disabled
ive. The purpose of this chapter is to review the existing research on the
ects of bereavement when it is preceded by chronic illness, disability, and
caregiving. The underlying premise of our approach to bereavement is that
the effects of bereavement are context dependent, and the nature of the caregiving experience is likely to play an important role in shaping an individual's response to bereavement. Specific topics we address in this chapter
include the following:

- What are the prevalence and nature of bereavement in a
  caregiving context?
- What are the psychiatric and physical morbidity effects of
  bereavement after caregiving?
- What is the relation between caregiving experience and bereavement outcomes?
- How do forewarning, preparedness, and anticipatory grief affect
  postdeath adjustment? What avenues of intervention and treatment are suggested by this review?

PREVALENCE OF BEREAVEMENT IN A CAREGIVING CONTEXT

The definition and boundaries of what is meant by the term *caregiving*
often vary depending on the purpose for which such definitions are used (Schulz
et al., 1997; Stone, 1991). Providing help to a family member with a chronic
illness or disability is not very different from the tasks and activities that characterize interactions among families and close friends without the presence of
illness or disability. Thus, a wife who provides care to her husband with
Alzheimer's disease by preparing his meals may be engaging in an activity she
would normally do for a husband without cognitive impairment. However, if a
wife also helps bathe and dress her husband with cognitive impairment, few
would question whether caregiving is taking place. The difference is that providing assistance with bathing and dressing, or assisting with complex medical
routines, clearly represents "extraordinary" care and exceeds the bounds of what
is normative or usual. Similarly, parents caring for a child with a chronic illness
may need to assist with daily medical routines (e.g., insulin injections or chest
physical therapy) that are time consuming and difficult and are done in addition to normal parenting responsibilities (Quittner, Opipari, Regoli, Jacobsen,
& Eigen, 1992). Extraordinary care involves significant expenditure of time and
energy, often for months or years, requires one to perform tasks that may be
physically demanding and unpleasant, and frequently disrupts the caregiver's
other family and social roles. The intensity and type of care provided vary

widely. At one extreme, caregivers may help intermittently a few hours per week; at the other extreme, caregivers may provide personal care for more than 40 hours per week and be on call 24 hours a day.

No matter how one defines *caregiving*, its prevalence is undeniably high. Proponents of a broadly inclusive approach might argue that a caregiver is needed for every person with health-related mobility and self-care limitations that make it difficult to take care of personal needs, such as dressing, bathing, and moving around the home. Current estimates indicate that 4% of the non-institutionalized U.S. population under age 55 meets these criteria. Beyond age 55, the proportion of persons with mobility and/or self-care limitations increases dramatically; nearly 60% of the population falls into this category after age 85 (see statistics from the National Center for Health Statistics available in table format at http://www.cdc.gov/nchs/agingact.htm). Overall, it is estimated that nearly 40 million Americans, or 15% of noninstitutional-ized individuals, have a disability that results in activity limitations, and nearly 12 million (4.6%) have major activity limitations, meaning that they are unable to attend school, work or keep house, or care for themselves (Kraus, Stoddard, & Gilmartin, 1996). Assuming these individuals need fam-ily caregiving support to survive in the community, this number provides a lower boundary for the number of individuals involved in long-term caregiv-ing in the United States. The upper boundary is reflected in a recent national survey on caregiving that indicates that more than 44 million adults in the United States are involved in caregiving annually (National Alliance for Caregiving & the AARP, 2004). This number may even be higher in devel-oping countries because of a higher prevalence of some chronic diseases (e.g., the millions afflicted with AIDS on the African continent). There may also be more of a need for family caregiving because of lesser access to or avail-ability of appropriate health care (e.g., viable treatment options and formal caregiving services).

Although there are no exact data on the number of caregivers who see their patients through to the end of life, it is safe to assume that the majority of caregivers fall into this category (Emanuel et al., 1999). We make this assump-tion on the basis of the facts that most individuals die of chronic disease and that few individuals are placed in long-term care facilities for extended time periods prior to death. Recent data on end-of-life caregivers collected through a national needs assessment of individuals enrolled in hospices in the United States (Salmon et al., 2003) show that caregivers were, on average, 62 years old, primarily female (77%), and caring for a spouse (50%) or parent (29%) and that they provided an average of 87 hours of care per week for an average of 7 months. As would be expected from a hospice sample, the primary diagnosis of the care receivers was cancer (59%). Profiles of bereaved caregivers for other patient populations vary in predictable ways. For example, compared with care-givers of cancer patients, caregivers of patients with dementia tend to be older and provide care for much longer periods of time, typically years, before the patient dies. In general, disease attributes have a strong influence on the duration and intensity of the caregiving experience prior to death (Ory, Hoffman, Yee, Tennstedt, & Schulz, 1999).

COURSE OF BEREAVEMENT AFTER CAREGIVING

At least three types of hypothesis have been proposed to predict the effects of bereavement after caregiving (Bass, Bowman, & Noelker, 1991; Park & Folkman, 1997; Schulz, Newsom, Fleissner, deCamp, & Nieboer, 1997). A *cumulative stress perspective* or "wear and tear" hypothesis would argue that the combined effects of caregiving stress and death deplete coping resources, resulting in negative bereavement outcomes. The *stress reduction perspective* makes the opposite prediction, arguing that death causes a significant decline in caregiving stressors and patient suffering, resulting in more positive bereavement outcomes relative to noncaregiving groups. The third hypothesis is that because death is more likely to be anticipated in a caregiving context, much of the grief work occurs before as opposed to after death. This would predict a trade-off between pre- and postbereavement effects; that is, anticipatory bereavement intensifies the caregiving experience but alleviates or reduces distress after death. Because bereavement is a time-dependent dynamic process, testing these alternative hypotheses would require greater specificity about the time course of bereavement effects after death. For example, it may be that in the short run, caregivers exhibit cumulative stress effects in response to death but that in the long run, they show stress reduction effects. Without specific predictions regarding the timing of bereavement outcomes, it would be difficult to know whether this pattern of findings supports the cumulative stress hypothesis or the stress reduction hypothesis.

In a previous review of the literature on bereavement after caregiving, Schulz, Newsom, Fleissner, et al. (1997) concluded that caregivers experienced relatively little difficulty in adjusting to the loss of their relatives. They found some evidence for short-term negative affects associated with the death of the care recipient but also evidence for positive outcomes, including feelings of relief from overload and work strain and increased quality of life. A number of mechanisms were identified to account for these findings. First, the death of the care recipient often brings with it an end to the patient's suffering as well as an end to demanding caregiving tasks. Second, the fact that death in many cases occurs after a period of disability and decline enables the caregiver to grieve prior to the death, as well as pragmatically prepare for the death and its aftermath. Third, the need for caregiving is likely to mobilize a familial support system to aid and provide relief to the caregiver. Thus, when death occurs the support system is already in place, and roles for individual members of the support system have been defined and are ready to be implemented. The combined effect of these multiple mechanisms is to attenuate the impact of the loss and promote adaptive postloss functioning.

These conclusions primarily were based on cross-sectional and retrospective studies of bereaved caregivers. Since then, the literature has been enriched with numerous prospective studies as well as more focused and ambitious retrospective studies of bereavement in a caregiving context (see Table 13.1 for a list and description of studies published since 1997). One of the advantages of the recent literature on bereavement is that it allows us to describe both the general effects of bereavement after caregiving as well as the time course of bereavement responses.

A number of researchers have reported improvement in mental health from pre- to postloss time points in the short term (i.e., within 6 months of the death). Chentsova-Dutton et al. (2002) found stability in depression up to the first 2 months postdeath but then declines afterward, at 2 to 13 months. These results are similar to those reported by Schulz et al. (2003) and Ferrario, Cardillo, Vicario, and Balzarini (2004), who found significant declines in depression up to the first 3 months after death, as did Grant et al. (2002), who reported reduced Hamilton depression scores and physical symptoms up to 6 months after death. Two qualitative retrospective studies further support this conclusion (Almberg, Grafstrom, & Winblad, 2000; Koop & Strang, 2003), noting that the majority of caregivers reported relief after death (Almberg et al., 2000) as well as feelings of accomplishment, improved family relationships, and satisfaction with the care they provided (Koop & Strang, 2003). A possible limitation of these findings is that they are all based on deaths related to either dementia or cancer, which are characterized by high levels of caregiving demand and involvement prior to death.

There are few exceptions to the general pattern of short-term improvement. For example, Schulz et al. (2001) reported stable depression scores predeath to 6 months postdeath among highly strained caregivers. In a study of AIDS caregivers, Park and Folkman (1997) found stability of support resources pre- to postdeath on indicators such as social support and religious activities. However, in a subsequent report from this study, Bonanno, Moskowitz, Papa, and Folkman (2005) found initial short-term improvement in depression scores up to 4 months postloss, even across different grief trajectory groups.

In the medium term (i.e., 6 months to 1 year postbereavement), Chentsova-Dutton et al. (2002) found further declines in depression, as did Schulz et al. (2003) and Li (2005). Only Ferrario et al. (2004) reported increases in depression from 3 to 12 months.

Although relatively few studies have followed bereaved caregivers for longer than 1 year, those that did have reported further declines in depression (Aneshensel, Botticello, & Yamamoto-Mitani, 2004; Li, 2005). Li (2005) reported declines up to 4 years after death, whereas Aneshensel et al. (2004)

TABLE 13.1
Recent Studies on Caregiving and Bereavement

Authors	Description of study	Time course of bereavement	Predictors of bereavement outcomes
Almberg et al. (2000)	Retrospective qualitative study of 30 caregivers of patients with dementia within 6 months after death.	Almost all reported predeath grief; 11 reported grief after death; 18 reported relief for person who died and/or relief from caregiving responsibilities.	Prebereavement: Feeling exhausted and having a breakdown during caregiving (higher burden) was associated with negative thoughts and guilt postdeath; positive appraisals of caregiving were associated with greater relief after death.
Aneshensel et al. (2004)	Prospective study of caregivers ($n = 291$) of patients with dementia; prebereavement baseline assessment and up to 5 annual postbereavement follow-ups were conducted. Multivariate models were tested to characterize the bereavement response over time.	Overall, the majority of participants showed stability or decline pre- to postbereavement. Caregivers with few or no depressive symptoms (64%) maintained this level throughout follow-up; highly depressed caregivers (8%) remained distressed throughout; temporarily depressed caregivers (18%) showed a decline at end of 1st year.	Prebereavement: Prior depressive symptoms and role overload were associated with depression. Postbereavement: Grief was associated with depression. Stable predictors: Being female, low self-esteem, and low socio-emotional support were associated with more depression.
Barry et al. (2002)	Retrospective study of 122 older bereaved persons who had lost a spouse, assessed 4 and 9 months after death.	Percentages of participants with complicated grief, major depressive disorder, and posttraumatic stress disorder at 4 and 9 months were 11 and 8, 9 and 6, and 6 and 3, respectively.	Prebereavement: Not being prepared was associated with complicated grief at baseline (4 months post-loss) and follow-up (9 months post-loss).

Bernard and Guarnaccia (2003)	Prospective study of 213 breast cancer patients and husband ($n = 126$) and daughter ($n = 87$) caregivers assessed at multiple close intervals prior to death and 90 days after death.	Prebereavement: Husbands—prior anxiety, depression, emotional strain, and health strain were associated with worse bereavement adjustment. Daughters—no effects. Stable predictors: Age was associated with better adjustment.
Boerner et al. (2004)	Prospective study of caregivers ($n = 217$) of patients with dementia, assessed 16 weeks prior to death and 15 weeks after death. Multivariate models were used to predict grief and depression after death.	See Schulz et al. (2003). Prebereavement: Prior depression, caregiving benefit, and poor health were associated with depression. Prior depression caregiving benefit was associated with grief as measured with the Texas Revised Inventory of Grief (TRIG; Faschingbauer, 1981). Postbereavement: Time since death was negatively associated with depression. Stable characteristics: Spouses reported higher grief.
Bonanno et al. (2005)	Prospective study of caregiving partners of men with AIDS ($n = 56$), assessed up to 8 months prebereavement and up to 8 months postbereavement. A subsample HIV+ bereaved caregivers ($n = 34$) was compared with nonbereaved, noncaregiving HIV+ group ($n = 45$).	27% showed no elevated depression levels at any point (CES–D < 16); 25% exhibited elevated levels only after the death; another 25% had elevated depression levels before and after; and 9% had elevated levels before, but no longer after the death. Prebereavement: No significant effect for caregiver HIV status. HIV+ caregivers had higher average depression levels than the comparison group.

(continued)

TABLE 13.1
Recent Studies on Caregiving and Bereavement (*Continued*)

Authors	Description of study	Time course of bereavement	Predictors of bereavement outcomes
Brazil et al. (2002)	Retrospective study of caregivers of terminally ill patients who died ($n = 151$) 294 days prior to assessment. Multivariate modeling of bereavement outcomes was tested.	SF-12 Mental Health postbereavement was significantly lower than population norm; SF-12 Physical Health was significantly higher than population norm.	Prebereavement predictors: Family members who reported caregiving as a major disruption in usual activities had lower physical health. Insufficient family support during caregiving was linked to poor mental health. Patient dying at home associated with better mental health. Stable predictors: Age of caregiver recipient and poor mental health were associated with poorer physical health.
Chentsova-Dutton et al. (2002)	Prospective study of 48 caregivers of hospice patients assessed shortly before death and 2, 7, and 13 months after death.	Hamilton depression scores did not change predeath to 2 months postdeath but declined significantly from 2 to 13 months postdeath. Some components of grief scores (TRIG—present feelings) declined over time.	
Christakis and Iwashyna (2003)	Matched retrospective cohort study of couples where decedent did ($n = 30,838$) or did not ($n = 30,838$) use hospice care. Multivariate models of 18-month mortality in surviving spouse were tested.		Prebereavement: Wives and husbands were less likely to die when decedent used hospice (4.9% vs. 5.4% and 13.2% vs. 13.9%, respectively).

Ferrario et al. (2004)	Prospective study of 111 caregivers of home-treated terminal cancer patients; baseline assessment followed by postdeath assessments at 3, 6, and 12 months ($n = 93$) after death. Multivariate modeling was used to predict maladjusted bereavement.	Prebereavement: Emotional burden was associated with maladjusted bereavement. Stable predictors: Age and being a spouse were associated with maladjustment.
Grant et al. (2002)	Prospective study of 119 caregivers of patients with dementia, assessed at 6-month intervals for 18 months; four groups were identified: (a) continuing caregivers ($n = 38$), (b) caregivers who placed patient in hospice ($n = 28$), (c) hospice placement followed by death ($n = 27$), and (d) death at home ($n = 26$).	Significant decrease in anxiety after death; initial decrease (3 months) and then increase in depression (12 months). Hospice placement and death were associated with improvement in depression (Hamilton scores) and physical symptoms compared with continuing caregivers and control participants.
Hebert et al. (2006)	Prospective study of caregivers ($n = 217$) of patients with dementia; repeated assessments within 6 months after death, 7 to 12 months after death, and 13 to 18 months after death. Multivariate models characterizing the role of preparedness for death (asked after death) were used as a predictor of bereavement outcomes.	See Schulz et al. (2003). Prebereavement: Not being prepared for death was associated with depression, complicated grief, and anxiety.

(continued)

TABLE 13.1
Recent Studies on Caregiving and Bereavement (Continued)

Authors	Description of study	Time course of bereavement	Predictors of bereavement outcomes
Koop and Strang (2003)	Retrospective qualitative study of 15 bereaved caregivers of cancer patients assessed twice, 5 and 12 months after death.	Positive bereavement outcomes predominated (feelings of accomplishment, improved family relationships, and satisfaction with care provided); some negative responses also were reported (haunting images, feelings of failure).	
Kurtz et al. (1997)	Prospective study of 114 caregivers of cancer patients surveyed 3 months before and 3 months after death. Multivariate modeling was used to predict postbereavement depression (CES–D).		Prebereavement: Prior depression and lower support from friends were associated with post-bereavement depression. Stable: Optimism was associated with lower depression.
Li (2005)	Prospective study of wife and daughter caregivers ($n = 157$); four measurement points at approximately 18-month intervals describing sample from 4 years prior to death to 4 years after death.	Overall, depression trajectory showed an increase as death approached and a decrease over the 4-year follow-up after death.	Prebereavement: High overload/burden and high problematic behaviors were associated with depression. Postbereavement stable predictors: Low income and being a spouse.
Park and Folkman (1997)	Prospective study of partners of men with AIDS 3 months and 1 month prior to death and 2 weeks, 1, 3, 5, and 7 months after death.	No changes in resources (support, religious activities, optimism) pre- to postbereavement.	
Seltzer and Li (2000)	Prospective study assessing effects of bereavement on wife ($n = 34$) and daughter ($n = 65$) caregivers compared with continuing caregivers; two assessments 3 years apart. Multivariate modeling was used to predict changes in well-being.	Increased level of social participation, participation in leisure activities, feelings of personal growth, and mastery. Pre-to-post bereavement was noted among wives only. There was no change in depression pre- to postdeath and no change in continuing caregiving wives.	

Study	Description	Findings
Schulz et al. (2001)	Prospective study of spouse caregivers and control participants ($n = 129$) assessed 1 year prior to and approximately 1 year after death.	No change in depression and improved self-care was observed for strained caregivers; increased depression, increased antidepressant medication use, and weight loss were observed among noncaregivers.
Schulz et al. (2003)	Prospective study of caregivers ($n = 217$) of patients with dementia, assessed 16 weeks prior to death and 15 weeks after death. Multivariate models were tested to characterize the nature of end-of-life dementia care and time course of bereavement.	Depression briefly spiked at time of death and declined significantly within 3 months; at 1 year post-death depression was near normative levels.
Schulz et al. (2006)	Prospective study of caregivers ($n = 217$) of patients with dementia, assessed 16 weeks prior to death and 15 weeks after death. Multivariate models were used to predict complicated grief.	20% of the sample met criteria for complicated grief 15 weeks after death; 15% met the criteria 9 to 15 months after death. Prebereavement: Prior depression, burden, caregiving benefit, patient's level of cognitive impairment, and being in the control condition of the intervention study were associated with complicated grief. Postbereavement: Longer time since death and lower postloss depression were associated with lower rates of complicated grief.

Note. CES–D = Center for Epidemiologic Studies Depression Scale (Radloff, 1977); SF-12 = SF-12 Health Survey (Ware, Kosinski, & Keller, 1996).

found declines in depression between the 1st and 2nd year after death and stability thereafter. Overall, these studies show short, medium, and longer term improvement among bereaved caregivers.

Despite these generally positive postbereavement trends, it is important to note that there are distinct individual trajectories that provide a richer and more detailed account of bereavement after caregiving. For example, in their study of AIDS caregivers, Bonanno et al. (2005) identified four trajectory groups based on data from 8 months preloss to 8 months postloss. Caregivers were categorized as resilient (27%) if they did not show elevated depression levels (Center for Epidemiologic Studies Depression Scale score [Radloff, 1977] < 16) at any point and as having a grief reaction if elevated depression levels emerged only after the loss (25%). Caregivers who exhibited elevated depression levels before the loss could be divided into those who remained distressed (chronic depression, 25%) and those who improved (9%).

Four distinctive clusters of depressive symptoms over time were also identified in a study of caregivers of patients with Alzheimer's disease (Aneshensel et al., 2004). The largest group, referred to as *repeatedly symptomatic*, (64%) comprised individuals who reported symptoms regularly but infrequently throughout the 5-year follow-up period. A second group (*temporarily distressed*, 18%) experienced improved emotional well-being over time. The remaining two groups had consistently high (*repeatedly distressed*, 8%) or nonexistent (*repeatedly asymptomatic*, 11%) depressive symptom levels throughout the bereavement period. These studies indicate that the average trajectory of increasing depression prior to death and decreasing symptoms over time after bereavement comprises distinct subgroups. Factors such as problematic behaviors of the care recipient prior to death, caregiver overload, income, and relationship (e.g., being a spouse) tend to moderate the trajectory. We examine these issues in greater detail in the next section, in our discussion of predictors of the bereavement response in caregivers.

The overwhelming conclusion derived from the studies just mentioned is that caregivers as a group exhibit no evidence of increased distress associated with bereavement and that many show improvement over time postbereavement. Although most of the studies mentioned earlier did not include a noncaregiving control group, there is evidence for a pattern of stability or improvement in bereavement outcomes among bereaved caregivers as compared with increases in negative outcomes that were found for their noncaregiving counterparts (Schulz et al., 2001). However, it is important to remember that caregiving, especially near the end of life, is a highly stressful experience; thus, caregivers as a group enter the bereavement experience with higher levels of distress than most noncaregivers. In addition, although the normative bereavement response of caregivers leans toward the positive side, there clearly exist subgroups of individuals who exhibit high levels of distress postbereavement. From a clinical perspective, it is important to characterize this subgroup and determine whether there are features of the caregiving experience that uniquely contribute to problematic bereavement outcomes.

PREDICTORS OF BEREAVEMENT OUTCOMES AMONG CAREGIVERS

Like other bereaved populations, caregivers exhibit considerable variability in response to the death of their relatives. Understanding this variability and the role of caregiving factors as predictors of bereavement outcomes is critical to developing effective interventions for this group. To address this issue, we distinguish among three types of predictors of depression and grief outcomes among caregivers: (a) variables associated with the caregiving experience prior to death; (b) factors associated with depression and grief assessed postbereavement; and (c) stable attributes of individuals, such as sociodemographic characteristics, linked to bereavement outcomes. The rationale for making this distinction is that the three types of predictors provide different opportunities for intervention. Identifying which caregiving factors contribute to poor bereavement outcomes may provide important leads about interventions that could be delivered during caregiving. Likewise, postbereavement factors linked to poor bereavement response may help identify intervention options that can be delivered after death. Finally, it is important to differentiate stable predictors from others because they typically reflect factors that are not amenable to intervention (e.g., gender, age, relationship), although they may help identify individuals at high risk of negative outcomes. These patterns of association for recently completed studies involving caregiving and bereavement are summarized in column 3 of Table 13.1.

The most common finding across multiple studies is that prebereavement levels of mental distress, such as depression and anxiety, are predictive of postbereavement adjustment. A related finding is that high levels of burden, feeling exhausted and overloaded, lack of support, and experiencing role strain is associated with negative postbereavement outcomes (see Table 13.1). Increased burden may also partially explain the higher mortality rate observed among caregivers of terminal patients who do not use hospice services compared with those who do (Christakis & Iwashyna, 2003). Variables associated with the challenges of caregiving are likely to be linked both directly and indirectly, through depression and anxiety, to postbereavement distress.

One of the intriguing findings to emerge from the recent caregiving literature is that individuals who report more benefit from caregiving are also likely to exhibit higher rates of depression, grief, and complicated grief (e.g., Boerner, Schulz, & Horowitz, 2004). *Caregiver benefit*—the extent to which caregivers find meaning, value, and importance in their role—is viewed as a positive aspect of caregiving. One possible explanation for the relationship between caregiving benefit and postbereavement distress is that death deprives caregivers of an important and meaningful role. Another possibility is that finding benefit in caregiving is associated with the quality of relationship between caregiver and patient; caregivers who find benefit in caregiving may feel closer to the patient and consequently suffer a greater loss when the patient dies.

Two studies have reported that not being prepared for the patient's death was associated with higher levels of depression and grief (Barry, Kasl, & Prigerson, 2002; Hebert, Dang, & Schulz, 2006). Despite providing high-intensity care, often for years, many bereaved caregivers perceive themselves as unprepared for the death (Hebert et al., 2006). These individuals typically report more symptoms of depression and anxiety, are more likely to be clinically depressed, and have more complicated grief symptoms. Although worthy of future study, these findings should be viewed cautiously, because questions of preparedness were asked after, as opposed to before, death and may therefore be influenced by the emotional response to death rather than vice versa. In addition, these studies do not provide deep insight into what it means to be prepared, because this construct is typically assessed with a single question asking the respondent whether he or she was prepared for the death.

The findings regarding postbereavement factors associated with bereavement outcomes are limited. Several studies have shown that negative outcomes tend to be associated with each other; thus, persons who are depressed also exhibit more symptoms of grief, and physical health is associated with mental health. In addition, as noted earlier, time since death is associated with decreases in negative symptomatology.

Two demographic characteristics—being female and being a spouse—are examples of stable factors associated with higher levels of distress postdeath. Two studies have reported that age is associated with greater distress postdeath (Brazil, Bedard, & Willison, 2002; Ferrario et al., 2004), and one (Bernard & Guarnaccia, 2003) reported the reverse. Low levels of self-esteem and socioemotional support and lower income are also associated with more negative bereavement outcomes, suggesting that depleted levels of psychological, social, and financial resources makes coping with the sequelae of death more difficult.

FOREWARNING, PREPAREDNESS, AND ANTICIPATORY GRIEF

The majority of studies on caregiving and bereavement are based on patient populations such as those with dementia or terminal cancer, for whom death is highly probable within some fixed time interval. Therefore, it would be reasonable to assume that caregivers are forewarned of the death and have the opportunity to prepare for it. This should in turn facilitate adjustment to death (Lindemann, 1944). However, the relationship between death forewarning and psychological adjustment is inconclusive. Studies have suggested that sudden spousal death is associated with worse psychological adjustment (Farberow, Gallagher-Thompson, Gilewski, & Thompson, 1992). Others have shown the opposite, that the greater the forewarning, the worse the psychological outcomes (Gerber, Rusalem, Hannon, Battin, & Arkin, 1975). Finally, some studies have shown no relationship or a mixed relationship (McGloshen & O'Bryant, 1988).

Multiple factors may contribute to these discrepancies. First, in most studies the investigators rather than survivors specify whether the death was anticipated (Bowling & Cartwright, 1982; Sanders, 1982–1983). Thus, if death is preceded by a long period of illness, then it is judged to have been anticipated (O'Bryant, 1990–1991); alternatively, if the death occurred suddenly, as a result of violent causes, such as suicide or homicide, it is viewed as unanticipated (Rynearson & McCreery, 1993). These assumptions may not be valid, because many deaths among older adults that are classified as sudden or unanticipated are in fact anticipated and viewed as timely by the survivors (Neugarten & Hagestad, 1976). Similarly, deaths that a researcher might view as predictable and certain are not necessarily viewed that way by family members. In one study, 20% of the relatives of hospice cancer patients did not think that death was a certainty as late as 1 to 2 weeks before their loved one's death (Houts, Lipton, Harvey, Simmonds, & Bartholomew, 1989). Teno et al. (2004) interviewed caregivers from a national probability sample of 1,578 decedents and found that approximately 23% of respondents reported that death was "extremely" unexpected.

A second source of confusion in this literature concerns the meaning of an *anticipated death*. Some researchers would claim that the mere fact that a death is predictable should facilitate postdeath adjustment, whereas others imply that only when a predictable death results in preparatory psychological and practical adjustments does it facilitate adaptation to the death. In other words, knowing that death is imminent is not the same as being prepared for it. Advancing research in this area would require studies that prospectively assess whether a death is anticipated from the survivors' perspective as well as an assessment of strategies and behaviors used to prepare for the death. To our knowledge, such studies currently do not exist.

There are, however, two small literatures relevant to this issue. One deals with research on preparedness for death, and the other focuses on anticipatory grief. Two recent studies have shown that caregivers who report a personal sense of preparedness for the death are better adjusted after the death. Barry et al. (2002) asked bereaved caregivers of hospice patients, "How prepared did you feel for the death?" Lack of preparedness was associated with complicated grief 4 months and 9 months after the death and with major depressive disorder 9 months after the death. Another study showed similar effects: Caregivers of patients enrolled in hospice for fewer than 4 days were almost nine times more likely to be depressed (Kris et al., 2006). Hebert et al. (2006) reported similar findings in a sample of recently bereaved caregivers of patients with dementia and further showed that African Americans, caregivers with less education, those with less income, and those with more depressive symptoms were more likely to perceive themselves as "not at all" prepared for the death. In contrast, the amount of pain the care recipient was in prior to death was positively associated with preparedness. Despite having provided care to their relatives with dementia for a median of 3 years, 23% of caregivers reported that they were "not at all" prepared for the death (Hebert et al., 2006).

As noted earlier, these findings should be viewed cautiously, because the question on preparedness was asked after the death occurred. A second limitation of these data is that a single question on preparedness tells little about what it means to be prepared. It could mean that the caregivers understood and accepted the prognosis of the patient, that they engaged in advance care planning, dealt with conflict surrounding the death, resolved spiritual issues, and so on. Future research will need to unravel what it means to be prepared for death and develop interventions for enhancing individuals' sense of being prepared.

Research on anticipatory grief among caregivers may also shed light on the effects of prebereavement preparation. Several researchers have administered grief scales to caregivers while they were caring for their relatives in order to characterize the nature of the grief response prior to death, describe its correlates, and compare it with postdeath grief responses (Gilliland & Fleming, 1998; Meuser & Marwit, 2001; Walker & Pomeroy, 1997). Predeath grief is positively associated with other measures of psychological distress; is equivalent in intensity and breadth to postdeath grief, at least among caregivers of patients with dementia; and exhibits a pattern of correlates similar to those observed for depression in caregivers. Unfortunately, these studies did not reassess caregivers after death to determine whether predeath grief responses were related to postdeath effects.

CONCLUSION AND FUTURE DIRECTIONS

Most deaths are the result of chronic conditions that occur in middle and old age, and family members are often intensively involved in providing care to their relative prior to death. Given this reality, our goal in this chapter has been to show that caregiving and bereavement experiences are closely intertwined and that understanding either requires a comprehensive assessment of the interrelations between them.

Hundreds of studies carried out in the past 20 years have documented the negative health effects of caregiving, showing that caregivers are at increased risk of psychiatric and physical morbidity. The challenges of caregiving become even more extreme as the care recipient nears death. When the death does occur, the caregiver enters bereavement already compromised by high levels of depression and anxiety and sometimes physical exhaustion. Even with these vulnerabilities, caregivers, for the most part, adapt well to the death. Psychiatric symptomatology typically improves, and caregivers are able to effectively reengage in activities that may have lapsed while they were caregiving.

Despite this generally positive picture of caregiver adaptation to bereavement, a minority of caregivers exhibit adverse bereavement outcomes in the form of high levels of depression and complicated grief. Finding benefit in the caregiving role; as well as not feeling prepared for the death; along with traditional predictors, such as prebereavement anxiety and depression, were all associated with negative postbereavement outcomes. These findings provide important leads about opportunities for bereavement interventions. Although empirical support for the efficacy of interventions to enhance adaptation to bereavement is mixed at best (Schut & Stroebe, 2005; Shear, Frank, Houck, & Reynolds, 2005), researchers have generally not tested preventive approaches in which interventions are delivered prior to death. Caregiving interventions designed to treat caregiver burden and depression have been shown to decrease the risk of complicated grief after death (Schulz, Boerner, Shear, Zhang, & Gitlin, 2006). These findings, along with research on the role of preparedness in coping with bereavement, suggest that interventions designed to treat prebereavement distress and prepare the caregiver for the eventuality of death may be particularly effective in reducing adverse postbereavement outcomes. This type of research should receive high priority.

A related research theme identified in this chapter is the need to better understand what it means to *anticipate*, *expect*, or *prepare for* death. Existing research suggests these constructs are important correlates of bereavement outcomes; however, the fact that they are typically assessed after death and with single questions raises issues of interpretation. For example, feeling prepared may be a consequence, as opposed to a cause, of effective bereavement adaptation when it is assessed after death. A single question assessing preparedness tells one little about underlying behavioral aspects of this construct.

One of the strengths of the existing caregiving studies is that researchers have assessed anticipatory grief as a component of the caregiving experience, showing that it has many of the same features as postdeath grief. What is missing from this literature are data showing how anticipatory grief affects bereavement adaptation. A better understanding of the role of anticipating and preparing for death may yield new opportunities for interventions that simultaneously facilitate adjustment to caregiving before death and adjustment to death afterward.

This chapter has focused on normative death experiences of caregivers, and the conclusions we draw can be generalized to middle-aged children caring for their parents or to older spouses caring for husbands or wives. However, because the bulk of research on caregiving and bereavement has been conducted in the United States, our analysis is limited to U.S. study populations. Moreover, not included in our analysis are nontraditional caregivers, such as parents caring for young children who ultimately die, or even adolescent children caring for disabled parents. Because of the unique features characterizing each of these situations, we advise caution in applying the conclusions reported here to these populations.

REFERENCES

Almberg, B. E., Grafstrom, M., & Winblad, B. (2000). Caregivers of relatives with dementia: Experiences encompassing social support and bereavement. *Aging and Mental Health, 4*, 82–89.

Aneshensel, C. S., Botticello, A. L., & Yamamoto-Mitani, N. (2004). When caregiving ends: The course of depressive symptoms after bereavement. *Journal of Health and Social Behavior, 45*, 422–440.

Barry, L. C., Kasl, S. V., & Prigerson, H. G. (2002). Psychiatric disorders among bereaved persons: The role of perceived circumstances of death and preparedness for death. *American Journal of Geriatric Psychiatry, 10*, 447–457.

Bass, D. M., Bowman, K., & Noelker, L. S. (1991). The influence of caregiving and bereavement support on adjusting to an older relative's death. *The Gerontologist, 31*, 32–42.

Bernard, L. L., & Guarnaccia, C. A. (2003). Two models of caregiver strain and bereavement adjustment: A comparison of husband and daughter caregivers of breast cancer hospice patients. *The Gerontologist, 43*, 808–816.

Boerner, K., Schulz, R., & Horowitz, A. (2004). Positive aspects of caregiving and adaptation to bereavement. *Psychology and Aging, 19*, 668–675.

Bonanno, G. A., Moskowitz, J. T., Papa, A., & Folkman, S. (2005). Resilience to loss in bereaved spouses, bereaved parents, and bereaved gay men. *Journal of Personality and Social Psychology, 88*, 827–843.

Bowling, A., & Cartwright, A. (1982). *Life after death: A study of the elderly widowed.* London: Tavistock.

Brazil, K., Bedard, M., & Willison, K. (2002). Correlates of health status for family caregiving in bereavement. *Journal of Palliative Medicine, 5*, 849–855.

Chentsova-Dutton, Y., Shuchter, S., Hutchin, S., Strause, L., Burns, K., Dunn, L., et al. (2002). Depression and grief reactions in hospice caregivers: From predeath to 1 year afterwards. *Journal of Affective Disorders, 69*, 53–60.

Christakis, N. A., & Iwashyna, T. J. (2003). The health impact of health care on families: A matched cohort study of hospice use by decedents and mortality outcomes in surviving, widowed spouses. *Social Science & Medicine, 57*, 465–475.

Emanuel, E. J., Fairclough, D. L., Slutsman, J., Alpert, H., Baldwin, D., & Emanuel, L. L. (1999). Assistance from family members, friends, paid care givers, and volunteers in the care of terminally ill patients. *New England Journal of Medicine, 341,* 956–963.

Farberow, N. L., Gallagher-Thompson, D., Gilewski, M., & Thompson, L. (1992). Changes in grief and mental health of bereaved spouses of older suicides. *Journals of Gerontology, 47,* P357–P366.

Faschingbauer, T. R. (1981). *Texas Revised Inventory of Grief manual.* Houston, TX: Honeycomb.

Ferrario, S. R., Cardillo, V., Vicario, F., & Balzarini, E. (2004). Advanced cancer at home: Caregiving and bereavement. *Palliative Medicine, 18,* 129–136.

Gerber, I., Rusalem, R., Hannon, N., Battin, D., & Arkin, A. (1975). Anticipatory grief and aged widows and widowers. *Journals of Gerontology, 30,* 225–229.

Gilliland, G., & Fleming, S. (1998). A comparison of spousal anticipatory grief and conventional grief. *Death Studies, 22,* 541–569.

Grant, I., Adler, K. A., Patterson, T. L., Dimsdale, J. E., Ziegler, M. G., & Irwin, M. R. (2002). Health consequences of Alzheimer's caregiving transitions: Effects of placement and bereavement. *Psychosomatic Medicine, 64,* 477–486.

Hebert, R. S., Dang, Q., & Schulz, R. (2006). Preparedness for the death of a loved one and mental health in bereaved caregivers of dementia patients: Findings from the REACH study. *Journal of Palliative Medicine, 9,* 1164–1171.

Houts, P. S., Lipton, A., Harvey, H. A., Simmonds, M. A., & Bartholomew, M. J. (1989). Predictors of grief among spouses of deceased cancer patients. *Journal of Psychosocial Oncology, 7,* 113–126.

Koop, P. M., & Strang, V. R. (2003). The bereavement experience following home-based family caregiving for persons with advanced cancer. *Clinical Nursing Research, 12,* 127–144.

Kraus, L., Stoddard, S., & Gilmartin, D. (1996). *Chartbook on disability in the U.S.* Washington, DC: U.S. National Institute on Disability and Rehabilitation Research.

Kris, A. E., Cherlin, E. J., Prigerson, H., Carlson, M. D. A., Johnson-Hurzeler, R., Kasl, S. V., & Bradley, E. H. (2006). Length of hospice enrollment and subsequent depression in family caregivers: 13-month follow-up study. *American Journal of Geriatric Psychiatry, 14,* 264–269.

Kurtz, M. E., Kurtz, J. C., Given, C. W., & Given, B. (1997). Predictors of post-bereavement depressive symptomatology among family caregivers of cancer patients. *Support Care Cancer, 5,* 53–60.

Li, L. W. (2005). From caregiving to bereavement: Trajectories of depressive symptoms among wife and daughter caregivers. *Journals of Gerontology, 60B,* P190–P198.

Lindemann, E. (1944). Symptomatology and management of acute grief. *American Journal of Psychiatry, 151,* 155–160.

McGloshen, T. H., & O'Bryant, S. L. (1988). The psychological well-being of older, recent widows. *Psychology of Women, 12,* 99–116.

Meuser, T. M., & Marwit, S. J. (2001). A comprehensive, stage-sensitive model of grief in dementia caregiving. *The Gerontologist, 41*, 658–670.

National Alliance for Caregiving & the AARP. (2004, April). *Caregiving in the U.S.* Washington, DC: National Alliance for Caregiving.

Neugarten, B., & Hagestad, G. O. (1976). Age and the life course. In G. Binstock & E. Shanas (Eds.), *Handbook of aging and the social sciences* (pp. 33–55). New York: Van Nostrand Reinhold.

O'Bryant, S. L. (1990–1991). Forewarning of husband's death: Does it make a difference for older widows? *Omega: The Journal of Death and Dying, 22*, 227–239.

Ory, M. G., Hoffman, R. R., III, Yee, J. L., Tennstedt, S., & Schulz, R. (1999). Prevalence and impact of caregiving: A detailed comparison between dementia and non-dementia caregivers. *The Gerontologist, 39*, 177–185.

Park, C. L., & Folkman, S. (1997). Stability and change in psychosocial resources during caregiving and bereavement in partners of men with AIDS. *Journal of Personality, 65*, 421–447.

Quittner, A. L., Opipari, L. C., Regoli, M. J., Jacobsen, J., & Eigen, H. (1992). The impact of caregiving and role strain on family life: Comparison between mothers of children with cystic fibrosis and matched controls. *Rehabilitation Psychology, 37*, 275–290.

Radloff, L. (1977). The CES–D scale: A self-report depression scale for research in the general population. *Applied Psychological Measurement, 1*, 385–401.

Reddy, S. K. (2002). Cardiovascular diseases in the developing countries: Dimensions, determinants, dynamics and directions for public health action. *Public Health Nutrition, 5*, 231–237.

Rynearson, E. K., & McCreery, J. M. (1993). Bereavement after homicide: A synergism of trauma and loss. *American Journal of Psychiatry, 150*, 258–261.

Salmon J. R., Deming, A. M., Kwak, J., Acquaviva, K. D., Brandt, K., & Egan, K. (2003). *Caregiving at life's end: The national needs assessment and implications for hospice practice.* Clearwater, FL: Hospice Institute of the Florida Suncoast.

Sanders, C. M. (1982–1983). Effects of sudden vs. chronic illness on bereavement outcome. *Omega: The Journal of Death and Dying, 13*, 227–241.

Schulz, R., Beach, S. R., Lind, B., Martire, L. M., Zdaniuk, B., Hirsch, C., et al. (2001). Involvement in caregiving and adjustment to death of a spouse: Findings from the Caregiver Health Effects Study. *Journal of the American Medical Association, 285*, 3123–3129.

Schulz, R., Boerner, K., Shear, K., Zhang, S., & Gitlin, L. N. (2006). Predictors of complicated grief among dementia caregivers: A prospective study of bereavement. *American Journal of Geriatric Psychiatry, 14*, 650–658.

Schulz, R., Mendelsohn, A. B., Haley, W. E., Mahoney, D., Allen, R. S., Zhang, S., et al. (2003). End of life care and the effects of bereavement on family caregivers of persons with dementia. *New England Journal of Medicine, 349*, 1936–1942.

Schulz, R., Newsom, J. T., Fleissner, K., deCamp, A. R., & Nieboer, A. P. (1997). The effects of bereavement after family caregiving. *Aging and Mental Health, 1*, 269–282.

Schulz, R., Newsom, J., Mittelmark, M., Burton, L., Hirsch, C., & Jackson, S. (1997). Health effects of caregiving: The Caregiver Health Effects Study. An ancillary study of the Cardiovascular Health Study. *Annals of Behavioral Medicine, 19,* 110–116.

Schut, H., & Stroebe, M. S. (2005). Interventions to enhance adaptation to bereavement. *Journal of Palliative Medicine, 8,* S140–S147.

Seltzer, M. M., & Li, L. W. (2000). The dynamics of caregiving: Transitions during a three-year prospective study. *The Gerontologist, 40,* 165–178.

Shear, K., Frank, E., Houck, P. R., & Reynolds, C. F., III (2005). Treatment of complicated grief: A randomized controlled trial. *Journal of the American Medical Association, 293,* 2601–2608.

Stone, R. (1991). Defining family caregivers of the elderly: Implications for research and public policy. *The Gerontologist, 31,* 724–725.

Teno, J. M., Clarridge, B. R., Casey, V., Welch, L. C., Wetle, T., Shield, R., et al. (2004). Family perspectives on end-of-life care at the last place of care. *Journal of the American Medical Association, 291,* 88–93.

Walker, R. J., & Pomeroy, E. C. (1997). The impact of anticipatory grief on caregivers of persons with Alzheimer's disease. *Home Health Care Services Quarterly, 16,* 55–76.

Ware, J. E., Kosinski, M., & Keller, S. D. (1996). A 12-item short-form health survey: Construction of scales and preliminary tests of reliability and validity. *Medical Care, 34,* 200–233.

World Health Organization. (2004, April 1). *Cancer control, report of the Secretariat, WHO executive board, 114th session, provisional agenda item 4.1, EB114/3.* Retrieved November 23, 2005, from http://www.who.int/gb/ebwha.pdf-files/EB114/B114_3en.pdf

14

TRAJECTORIES OF GRIEVING

GEORGE A. BONANNO, KATHRIN BOERNER,
AND CAMILLE B. WORTMAN

The death of a close relative or friend is almost always painful and disturbing. Yet, it has become increasingly obvious that not everybody reacts to such losses in the same way. A small subset of bereaved individuals, usually 10% to 15%, suffer chronic distress and depression for years after the loss. Others experience acute distress and depression from which they recover only gradually over a period of 1 or 2 years. However, many and sometimes the majority of bereaved individuals exhibit only short-lived grief reactions and manage to maintain a relatively stable trajectory of healthy functioning or resilience throughout bereavement (Bonanno, 2004; Bonanno & Kaltman, 2001). Understanding these divergent patterns and the factors that predict their occurrence has become an important area of bereavement inquiry. In this chapter, we briefly discuss the historical background on the subject and then review several recent studies of bereavement outcome trajectories. We focus on findings from prospective studies that challenge traditional ideas about bereavement. These studies illustrate the importance of examining the full spectrum of bereavement outcome patterns.

A BRIEF LOOK AT THE HISTORICAL BACKGROUND

The earliest taxonomies of individual differences in grief reaction were based primarily on clinical observation or on data sets based on psychiatric samples. It is not surprising that the earliest models of bereavement outcome focused primarily on the distinction between normal and abnormal or pathological forms of grieving. Using these models, bereavement scholars pondered the question of what constitutes a normal grief course. They also focused attention on the possible role played by avoidant or defensive processes in delaying the onset of grief.

One of the earliest comparative descriptions of normal and pathological forms of grieving came from Parkes's (1965) groundbreaking study of bereaved psychiatric patients. Parkes distinguished three types of pathological grief reaction: (a) *chronic grief*, (b) *inhibited grief*, and (c) *delayed grief*. Bowlby (1980) later echoed Parkes's taxonomy to propose "disordered forms of mourning" that could be arrayed along a single conceptual dimension. Anchoring one end of the continuum was *chronic mourning*. At the other end, Bowlby placed the *prolonged absence of conscious grieving* (p. 138). He maintained that individuals who show an absence of conscious grieving "may appear to be coping splendidly" (p. 153) but are often tense and short tempered, with tears just below the surface. Bowlby believed that physical symptoms, such as headaches and heart palpitations, were also common in this group. He indicated that sooner or later many people who consciously avoid grieving become depressed, often in response to a subsequent, more minor loss.

On the basis of the evidence available at the time, Raphael (1983) also proposed a number of "morbid or pathological patterns of grief" (p. 59). These included chronic, unresolved grief reactions as well as the absence of grief, in which "the grieving affects or mourning process may be totally absent, partially suppressed, or inhibited" (p. 60). Like Bowlby (1980), she noted that some bereaved people seem to cope remarkably well and often carry on as if nothing had happened. Although she acknowledged that such responses "may be seen as evidence of strength and coping by many" (p. 205), she too argued that in most cases they were actually markers of psychopathology.

In 1984, the Institute of Medicine released a report summarizing the state-of-the-art knowledge about bereavement. The report concluded that the death of a loved one produced a "near universal occurrence of intense emotional distress . . . with features similar in nature and intensity to those of clinical depression" (Osterweis, Solomon, & Green, 1984, p. 18). The report also concluded that absent grief was a pathological form of mourning that "represents some form of personality pathology" and that "persons who show no evidence of having begun grieving" should receive "professional help" (Osterweis et al., 1984, p. 65). Several years later, Middleton, Moylan, Raphael, Burnett, and Martinek (1993) surveyed an international sample of researchers, theorists, and clinicians working in the field of bereavement. A compelling majority of these experts endorsed the idea that absent grief was a pathological grief reaction that usually stemmed from denial or inhibition of the normal grief reaction. This response was almost always viewed as maladaptive in the long run.

Is this really the case, however? When people experience relatively mild or short-lived grief reactions, should this be considered atypical or pathological? In 1989, Wortman and Silver noted that there was no convincing empirical evidence to support this assertion. More recently, Bonanno and colleagues (e.g., Bonanno, 2004, 2005; Bonanno, Znoj, Siddique, & Horowitz, 1999) have argued that many bereaved people show a clear resilience in the face of loss. At the other end of the spectrum, one might also question whether psychopathology observed during bereavement should always be interpreted as an abnormal grief reaction. Might not at least some of the chronic dysfunction be attributed to an enduring emotional disturbance that predates the loss?

THE CRUCIAL IMPORTANCE OF PROSPECTIVE RESEARCH

The most straightforward way to examine these questions and to adjudicate among these various perspectives is to conduct prospective research using community-based samples. This involves identifying a relatively large sample of respondents who are not anticipating a pending loss well before the death of a loved one, and then following those who have suffered a loss for an extended period of time during bereavement. Studies of this nature are rare, for obvious reasons. A design of this type is both expensive and time consuming; however, there are two reasons why this type of prospective approach is crucial.

The first reason is that it is not possible to detect some grief trajectories without accurate information about preloss functioning. For example, at least some individuals who experience depression, or what appears to be grief-related pathology following the loss, may have been depressed prior to the loss. As we discuss in more detail later in this chapter, such individuals may be more accurately viewed as suffering from chronic depression rather than chronic grief. Still another possibility, only recently considered in the bereavement literature, is that some people might actually experience improvements in their psychological well-being after the death. This possibility contrasts markedly with the traditional view that loss typically involves prolonged suffering and distress. However, there are almost certainly circumstances in which the death of a loved one will come as a relief. For example, it may mark the end of a long and arduous period of suffering or exposure to chronic stress (Bodnar & Kiecolt-Glaser, 1994; A. Horowitz, 1985; Schulz et al., 2003; Wheaton, 1990). In such circumstances, a person may have experienced heightened distress or depression prior to the loss and then marked improvement after the death. Although people who show this pattern may be indistinguishable from other resilient bereaved people following the loss, it would be important to distinguish among these groups and explore the ways in which they may differ.

A second reason is that without prospective data, it is difficult to adjudicate among competing views about why bereaved people may not evidence pronounced grief. Moreover, the absence of prospective data complicates efforts to identify the factors that might explain divergent reactions to loss. We noted earlier that bereavement theorists have historically viewed the absence of pronounced grief reactions as a relatively rare and pathological form of inhibited grieving. Such a reaction has traditionally been regarded as indicative of denial or inhibition. The alternative is that such reactions indicate resilience on the part of the bereaved survivor. However, it is difficult to tease these explanations apart after the loss has occurred.

A number of studies have documented that mild or absent grief reactions are not rare but tend to occur as often as, and sometimes more often than, any other response to loss (for reviews, see Bonanno, 2004, 2005; Bonanno & Kaltman, 1999, 2001; Wortman & Boerner, 2006; Wortman & Silver, 2001). Also, several studies have directly examined the question of whether mild grief reactions eventually might give way to delayed grief. To date, however, convincing evidence of delayed grief has not been reported. For example, Middleton, Burnett, Raphael, and Martinek (1996) interviewed bereaved spouses, bereaved adult children, and bereaved parents about their grief experiences at repeated intervals beginning within 1 month of the loss and extending to 13 months postloss. Despite their conviction that delayed grief was a genuine clinical phenomenon, Middleton et al. concluded that "no evidence was found for the pattern of response which might be expected for delayed grief" (p. 169). A similar conclusion was apparent in an even longer term study conducted by Bonanno and Field (2001). Conjugally bereaved individuals were assessed over a 5-year period using multiple outcome measures. Although a few cases of delayed grief were observed, these were captured only on isolated measures, suggesting random measurement error. None of the participants evidenced delayed symptom elevations consistently across the different outcome measures, and when a psychometrically more reliable, weighted composite measure was used, not a single participant evidenced delayed grief.

In sum, past research indicates that minimal or absent grief reactions are very prevalent, whereas delayed grief reactions are quite rare. Despite these findings, however, the view that absent grief portends subsequent difficulties is still prevalent among clinicians (see Wortman & Boerner, 2006, for a review).

The only convincing way to adjudicate among these views is to conduct prospective bereavement research beginning well before the loss has occurred and continuing for several months following the loss. The absence of grief has been regarded as an indication that the person was never that attached to the deceased (e.g., M. J. Horowitz, 1990), perhaps because of a general tendency to remain emotionally cold or distant. Alternatively, people who fail to evidence pronounced grieving may have been involved in marriages that were unsatisfying or characterized by a high degree of conflict (M. J. Horowitz, 1990; Rando, 1993), thus obviating the need for grief (Raphael, 1983). In contrast, if mild grief reactions reflect a genuine resilience, then people who show this pattern following the loss should have normal or nonconflictual relationships prior to the loss. These examples illustrate the importance of identifying the different trajectories of functioning from before to after the death of a loved one. Until recently, there was relatively little systematic research using such a design.

THE CHANGING LIVES OF OLDER COUPLES STUDY

In the mid-1980s, a large-scale prospective study on widowhood in late life, called the Changing Lives of Older Couples Study (CLOC), was initiated by Camille Wortman in collaboration with Ronald Kessler and James House. The CLOC team was able to recruit and interview a baseline sample of 1,532 older married people from the Detroit, Michigan, metropolitan area. Participants who lost a spouse during that time were identified using state death records and invited to participate in subsequent interviews at 6 and 18 months after the loss. This procedure resulted in a sample of 205 people who had been interviewed an average of 3 years prior to the death of their spouse and at 6, 18, and 48 months postloss. The study included a thorough and comprehensive preloss assessment of many variables, including the quality of the marriage, social support, personality, and views of the world. After the spouse's death, the investigators repeated many of these assessments. They also made a careful assessment of grief and a number of related constructs, including indications of continuing attachment and indicators of working through the loss (e.g., frequency of thoughts and conversations about the deceased).

Several years ago, we, along with other colleagues (Bonanno et al., 2002) used the CLOC data to identify the most common or prototypical trajectories of adjustment to loss. To do this, we used a method that involved calculating change scores across time. The first step in this approach was to categorize participants as having either low or high levels of baseline depression, or depression prior to the loss based on the normative range of depression scores observed in other studies. The next step involved categorizing change from before the loss to 6 months postloss. A *grief reaction* was defined as an increase in depression from pre- to postloss that exceeds the standard normal range of variation (i.e., the standard deviation) for each group. If a person with a low prebereavement depression score showed only a minor increase in depression following the loss, one that fell within the normal variation (i.e., less than 1 standard deviation), then this person was classified as not having a substantial grief reaction. This approach also allowed us to identify people who had high prebereavement depression and improved by at least 1 standard deviation during bereavement. This same step was then repeated for comparisons between prebereavement and 18-month depression scores.

The next step was to identify the most prevalent patterns or trajectories that emerged from these data. We (Bonanno et al., 2002) classified participants as either changing, staying the same, or improving from prebereavement to 6 months of bereavement and as changing, staying the same, or improving from prebereavement to 18 months of bereavement. Using these categories, we found five distinct trajectories that cover the outcome patterns of most of the participants: (a) *common grief or recovery* (11%, low preloss depression and high postloss depression at 6 months that improved at 18 months), (b) *stable low distress or resilience* (46%, low pre- and postloss depression at 6 and 18 months), (c) *depression followed by improvement* (10%, high preloss depression and low postloss depression at 6 and 18 months), (d) *chronic grief* (16%, low preloss depression and high postloss depression at 6 and 18 months), and (e) *chronic depression* (8%, high preloss depression that persists at 6 and 18 months postloss).

Finally, Bonanno et al. (2002) examined differences across these trajectories for a number of prebereavement predictor variables as well as for a number of variables measured during bereavement, including markers of more grief-specific symptoms (e.g., yearning) and variables indicative of the extent to which participants processed or avoided the loss.

RESILIENCE TO LOSS

The most compelling finding to emerge from this analysis was that more than half of the participants exhibited low depression throughout bereavement (Bonanno et al., 2002). There were in fact two separate trajectories that culminated in a stable low depression response during bereavement. One trajectory seemed to represent a genuine form of resilience. Participants showing this pattern comprised close to half the CLOC sample (46%). They had little or no depression at any point in the study (i.e., both prior to the death of their spouses and at 6 months and 18 months of bereavement), and they exhibited relatively few symptoms of grief during bereavement. The second trajectory resulting in a low depression outcome during bereavement was smaller, comprising 11% of the CLOC sample. These individuals were highly depressed prior to the death of their spouses but had improved to stable low levels of depression at both time points after the spouse's death, and they also exhibited relatively few grief symptoms during bereavement.

Bonanno et al. (2002) also examined several alternative approaches to define the trajectories, and each produced more or less the same basic results. For example, cluster analyses yielded results strikingly similar to the trajectories just reported. Using either a four- or five-cluster solution, a cluster representing stable low depression throughout the study (resilience) was evident in 49% of the sample. We also used an alternative approach to define change over time based on the standard error of measurement (see Devilly & Foa, 2001, for more detail on this approach), and the proportion evidencing resilience was even higher: 58%. Together, these results provide strong convergent support for the robustness of these patterns.

GENUINE RESILIENCE ACROSS TIME

An important issue that could be addressed in the CLOC study was whether people who showed the stable low depression–low grief profile were actually resilient or were perhaps evidencing a more superficial adjustment. These data could also address the possibility that resilience was nothing more than the absence of attachment to the spouse.

One factor that argues against the low depression–low grief profile as a form of superficial adjustment is that so many participants exhibited this pattern. Another important factor was that almost all participants in this group reported having experienced at least some initial suffering and distress in the early months of bereavement. Although data were not available immediately following their loss, the 6-month interviews did include several questions in which bereaved participants were asked to make retrospective assessments of their early reactions to the loss. About 75% of those who showed a resilient outcome trajectory reported experiencing intense yearning (painful waves of missing the spouse) as well as pangs of intense grief in the earliest months of bereavement. Shortly after the death, the painful reality of the loss had occupied the thoughts of virtually all participants, including the resilient people. All but 1 of the respondents who showed the resilient trajectory reported that shortly after the loss, they experienced intrusive thoughts about the loss that they could not get out of their minds. They also indicated that they found themselves *ruminating*, or going over and over what had happened.

A key to how resilient people managed to cope so well with the death of their spouse despite the painful nature of their grief was suggested by several findings from a follow-up study (Bonanno, Wortman, & Nesse, 2004). First, the resilient people were better able than other participants to gain comfort from talking about or thinking about the spouse; for example, they were more likely than other bereaved people to report that thinking about and talking about their deceased spouse made them feel happy or at peace. They also had low scores on avoidance and distraction, suggesting that their lack of distress indicated good adjustment rather than defensive denial. Resilient bereaved people also reported the fewest regrets about their behavior with the spouse or about things they may have done or failed to do when the spouse was still alive. Finally, resilient individuals were less likely to try to make sense of or find meaning in the spouse's death.

These findings indicate that close to half of the bereaved persons in the CLOC sample exhibited what appeared to be a resilient outcome trajectory. They experienced relatively little depression prior to the death of their spouse, and although they evidenced some cognitive and emotional upheaval immediately following the loss, they had relatively little or no depression and few grief symptoms throughout bereavement. Furthermore, compared with other groups, they seemed to be less troubled by the loss, were not preoccupied with the logic or meaning of the death, and were better able to hold on to positive and comforting memories of the spouse.

The fact that the CLOC data included prebereavement assessments meant that it was possible to examine the additional criticism that ostensibly resilient individuals had simply never been strongly attached to their spouses or that they were superficial or cold and unfeeling people. Recall that the initial baseline or prebereavement interviews in the CLOC study were conducted an average of 3 years prior to the spouse's death. This lengthy interval prior to the loss is important because it means that the data were not likely to have been contaminated by the anticipation of the impending death. Another prospective study (Bonanno, Moskowitz, Papa, & Folkman, 2005) had shown that the likelihood of such anticipatory reactions is dramatically reduced when assessments are obtained 8 months or longer before the death occurs. This interval provided a reasonable assurance that the participants' responses generally reflected their normal lives and relationships with their spouses and were relatively unconfounded with anticipatory grief reactions.

Examination of the prebereavement measures showed no evidence that people with stable low depression and low grief were in any way unhealthy or dysfunctional. Prior to the spouse's death, this group did not have conflicted or low-quality marital relations with the spouse; neither were they ambivalent about or excessively dependent on the spouse, They did not evidence extreme scores on any of the personality measures included in the study, such as extraversion or emotional stability.

Of particular importance to the debate about the type of person who would not exhibit a pronounced grief reaction is that the interviewer's ratings of resilient individuals in the prebereavement interviews did not distinguish them from other participants; for example, they were rated about the same as other participants in the degree to which they appeared to be comfortable or socially skillful during the interview and as expressing warmth when interacting with other people.

Finally, the resilient participants scored relatively higher than other participants on several preloss measures, which is suggestive of resilience-promoting factors that would better prepare them for coping with the impeding loss. For example, resilient individuals reported relatively higher levels of instrumental support and scored higher than other participants on questionnaire measures of belief in a just world and acceptance of death.

IMPROVEMENT DURING BEREAVEMENT

As we discussed earlier, there was clear evidence for a second type of resilience during bereavement: a pattern of poor functioning and adjustment prior to the loss followed by markedly improved psychological health after the spouse's death. Although this was a smaller group than the more straightforward resilient group, this pattern nonetheless captured 11% of the sample (13% in the cluster analyses). Furthermore, the improved group maintained relatively low levels of depression and relatively few grief symptoms across several years of bereavement (we discuss further follow-up on this group at 48 months of bereavement later in this chapter).

In contrast to the stable low depression, or genuinely resilient group, the improved participants were highly depressed prior to the loss. They also had the poorest quality marriages compared with all other participants. They made the least positive and most negative evaluations of their spouses and marriages, and they scored higher on a measure of ambivalence toward the spouse in the prebereavement interviews. It is noteworthy that in addition to their marital difficulties, virtually all the participants in this group had been contending with a seriously ill spouse at the time of the prebereavement interviews. This was an elderly sample, and illness among the spouses was not uncommon. However, no other group was so clearly characterized by spousal illness as the improved group.

Given this difficult situation, it should not be surprising that the improved group also showed a relatively unfavorable psychological profile on other prebereavement measures. They scored high on measures of emotional instability (neuroticism), introspection, and perceived personal injustice. The items that comprised the measure of perceived personal injustice included statements such as "When I look back on what has happened to me, I feel cheated," "I don't seem to get what should be coming to me," and "Other people always seem to get the breaks." Despite this conspicuously unfavorable prebereavement profile, the improved group dropped to relatively low levels of depression and reported relatively low levels of grief symptoms during bereavement. Like the resilient group, the improved participants were also relatively less likely to search for meaning in the loss. Given the difficulties they had experienced prior to the death of their spouses, it is tempting to assume that people could improve this much only by relying heavily on denial or distraction during bereavement. However, again like the resilient group, the improved participants had relatively low scores on a set of questionnaire items that tapped the use of avoidance or distraction.

There were also some key differences between the improved and resilient groups. For example, the improved participants reported thinking about and talking about the loss less frequently. In contrast to the resilient group, who reported the greatest ability to gain comfort from thinking about or talking about the spouse during bereavement, the improved group reported the lowest levels of comfort from memories of the spouse. It is noteworthy, however, that the improved group also exhibited marked increases in the ability to find comfort from thinking or talking about the spouse—they were the only group of participants in the CLOC study to do so—and by 18 months of bereavement they had increased so much in this regard that they were no longer distinct from the resilient group on this variable.

Finally, and of particular note, participants in the improved group were fully aware of the remarkable progress they had made. This group scored higher than any other group on a scale designed to measure the perception of pride in coping ability. The scale included questions such as "During the past month, did you feel amazed at your strength?" and "Did you feel proud of how well you were managing?" The improved group was also more likely than other participants in the CLOC study to report becoming more confident and a stronger person as a result of dealing with the loss of their spouses.

RESILIENCE AND IMPROVED FUNCTIONING IN OTHER STUDIES

Several other recent studies provide convergent evidence for the resilience and depressed–improved patterns identified in the CLOC study. In a study of older adult caregivers, for example, 42.5% of the sample of caregivers had low levels of depression both before and after their partners' death (Zhang, Mitchell, Bambauer, Jones, & Prigerson, in press). Caregiver studies have also provided further evidence for the depressed–improved pattern (e.g., Schulz et al., 2003; for a more detailed review, see chap. 13, this volume).

Both of the resilient and depressed–improved patterns were observed in a prospective study of gay men (Bonanno, Moskowitz, et al., 2005) that used data from the University of California San Francisco Coping Project (Folkman, Chesney, & Christopher-Richards, 1994). Not only was this sample considerably younger (mean age 36 years) than the CLOC sample, but it was also composed exclusively of gay men in committed long-term relationships.

Moreover, all of the men who eventually experienced bereavement had been providing care for a partner who was dying of AIDS, and in some cases both partners in the relationship had tested positive for HIV. If that were not stressful enough, the data for this study were originally collected in San Francisco in the late 1980s and early 1990s, before the advent of antiretroviral medication that dramatically prolongs the lives of people with AIDS. Hence, at that time, being HIV positive (HIV+) generally meant that one had relatively little time left to live.

It is not surprising that on the whole, the sample evidenced high levels of depression, with close to half of the bereaved sample showing elevated depression many months before the eventual death of their partners (Bonanno, Moskowitz, et al., 2005). Nonetheless, it was still possible to map changes across time from prebereavement to postbereavement. Of course, the high levels of depression meant that there would be considerably fewer participants showing the stable low depression pattern. In fact, 9% of the sample showed a depressed–improved pattern, and 27% of the sample had stable low depression or resilience from pre- to postloss. This proportion of resilience was lower than in the CLOC Study; however, if one considers that half of the sample was depressed well before the loss, in actuality this means that about half of the sample that was not depressed before the loss was resilient during bereavement. Also, consistent with other studies (Bonanno, 2004), both the resilient and depressed–improved groups had the highest levels of positive affect during bereavement.

A further analysis using the *normative comparison approach* (Kazdin, 2003) also revealed a level of resilience comparable to that observed in other bereavement studies. Simply put, normative comparisons define health and dysfunction in relative terms using the mean and standard deviation for a comparable group of participants or in relation to established norms for the specified outcome measure (e.g., Foa, Zoellner, Feeny, Hembree, & Alvarez-Conrad, 2002). In this case, Bonanno, Moskowitz, et al. (2005) compared the level of depression in bereaved HIV+ caregivers with a matched sample HIV+ gay men who were not bereaved or caregiving. Exactly half of the HIV+ bereaved sample had a level of depression that was not statistically different than the HIV+ nonbereaved sample. In other words, although they were depressed, their depression was not uncharacteristic of men dealing with the stress of being HIV+ at the time of the study.

CHRONIC GRIEF AND CHRONIC DEPRESSION

The use of prospective data makes it possible to explore several important issues about chronic grief reactions. In past studies, it has often been shown that bereaved people with prior depression or other psychopathology were more likely to experience severe grief reactions during bereavement (e.g., Zisook & Shuchter, 1991). Unfortunately, evidence for this association has relied exclusively on retrospective measures of prebereavement depression that were obtained after the loss had already occurred (e.g., Nuss & Zubenko, 1992; Parkes & Weiss, 1983; Zisook & Shuchter, 1991). However, depressed people often show memory biases toward depressive affective states (e.g., Clark & Teasdale, 1982; Elliot & Greene, 1992), overestimating both the number of previous symptoms of depression (Zimmerman & Coryell, 1986) and their intensity (Schrader, Davis, Stefanovic, & Christie, 1990). Thus, bereaved individuals suffering from chronic grief reactions are also likely to overestimate their prior emotional difficulties. In fact, a 5-year study of bereaved people's memory for previous grief following the death of a spouse (Safer, Bonanno, & Field, 2001) readily demonstrated this bias.

An untested alternative explanation for the link between depression during bereavement and prior depression is that some bereaved people had been depressed prior to the loss and simply remained depressed during bereavement. In this case, the symptoms these individuals exhibited during bereavement would be at least partially due to ongoing difficulties rather than representing a specific reaction to the recent loss.

Addressing this question using the CLOC data produced some striking findings. Chronically elevated depressive symptoms during bereavement were evidenced by 23.4% of the sample (Bonanno et al., 2002); however, these participants formed two distinct trajectories. One trajectory, comprising 15.6% of the sample, suggested an unambiguous chronic grief reaction. These participants manifested low levels of depression prior to the loss but then showed elevated depression at 6 and 18 months of bereavement. A second, smaller group, comprising 7.8% of the sample, had markedly elevated depression prior to bereavement and then showed only a slight increase and remained depressed during bereavement. Both groups had higher levels of grief-specific symptoms (e.g., yearning) measured at 6 and 18 months of bereavement compared with all other participants, and they did not differ from each other in their level of grief symptoms. However, as we discuss shortly, additional data suggested that one of these trajectories represented a relative "pure" chronic grief reaction, whereas the other pattern was more representative of a preexisting chronic depression.

Distinguishing these patterns made it possible to address several core assumptions in the bereavement literature. One of the more widely held assumptions, for example, was that chronic grief arises as a result of a dysfunctional or problematic relationship. Chronic grief following the death of a spouse has been linked with conflict in the conjugal relationship (Parkes & Weiss, 1983; Stroebe & Stroebe, 1993) and with intense ambivalence toward the spouse (e.g., Bowlby, 1980; Parkes & Weiss, 1983); however, there is also a well-established link between marital conflict and depression as it occurs more generally, independent of a loss (Beach, Smith, & Fincham, 1994; Weissman, 1987). Thus, it may be that the observed link between previous marital conflict and chronic grief reactions is not so much a product of unresolved grief, as has been traditionally assumed, but rather a manifestation of an ongoing depressive syndrome that predates the loss.

The trajectory results clearly argued in favor of the latter: People who evidenced the pure chronic grief trajectory did not report extremely conflicted marriages and did not evidence exceedingly high levels of ambivalence about the spouse or marriage when these factors were measured prior to the spouse's death. Chronically grieving individuals scored about the same as resilient individuals on these variables. We noted earlier that it was actually the depressed group, followed by improvement group, that had the most conflicted marriages prior to bereavement. The group that showed a chronic depression pattern from pre- to postbereavement also had high levels of marital conflict and ambivalence prior to the loss. In other words, marital conflict was seen primarily in people with elevated prebereavement depression, which by definition was not a characteristic of the chronic grief trajectory. Furthermore, because only some of the people with elevated prebereavement depression remained depressed during bereavement, while others showed improved adjustment during bereavement, marital conflict by itself did not seem to play a causal role in producing grief reactions.

A related assumption, also common in the bereavement literature, is that chronic grief results from excessive dependency (Lopata, 1979; Osterweis et al., 1984; Parkes & Weiss, 1983; Raphael, 1983), either as a general characteristic of the bereaved person's personality (Prigerson et al., 1997; Sable, 1989) or in its more specific form as a primary feature of the lost conjugal relationship, as for example in Raphael's (1983) notion of a "pathological dependence" on the partner (p. 208). However, just as we saw a general association between marital conflict and depression independent of loss, there is also clear evidence for a general association between interpersonal dependency and depressive symptoms independent of loss (Hokanson & Butler, 1992; Stader & Hokanson, 1998). In other words, people who exhibit both elevated depression during bereavement and interpersonal dependency may be struggling with ongoing difficulties that predate the loss.

In this case, the CLOC data were consistent with at least some aspects of traditional bereavement theory. People who evidenced the pure chronic grief reaction had high levels of personal dependency and dependency on the relationship prior to the death of their spouses. Thus, among people who were not depressed prior to the loss, dependency was an important predictor of grief reactions.

A third important finding was that people who were not depressed prior to the loss but then showed chronic grief were more likely than any other group to have had a healthy spouse, and less likely to have provided health care for the spouse, in the years prior to the spouse's death. One might surmise that people in this group would have been less likely to anticipate that their spouse would die in just a few short years. These people also lost a spouse who may have been a more vital companion than respondents in the other conditions.

Together, these findings suggest that during bereavement, the chronic grief group was struggling primarily with the loss of a beloved and vital spouse on whom they were also dependent. In addition, because the spouses of these participants were typically healthy in the years prior to their death, this struggle was most likely exacerbated by a lack of anticipation or psychological preparation for the loss. In contrast, the prebereavement characteristics of people who showed a chronic depression trajectory suggested that whatever negative reactions they might have had to the spouse's death were layered upon an already-considerable number of ongoing psychological difficulties.

The importance of distinguishing *chronic grief* and *chronic depression* was even more evident in Bonanno, Moskowitz, et al.'s (2005) prospective study of bereaved gay men. In this case, because of the highly stressed nature of the sample, the pattern of elevated pre- and postbereavement depression was even more apparent. In fact, fully half of the men in that study who showed clinically elevated depression during bereavement had also shown clinically elevated depression many months prior to bereavement.

FOLLOWING THE CHANGING LIVES OF OLDER COUPLES SAMPLE INTO THE 4TH YEAR OF BEREAVEMENT

Understanding how bereaved people heal in the long term is one of the most important and least well-understood research questions with regard to grief (Jacobs, 1993). Thus, it is vital to determine how bereaved persons across the different outcome trajectories ultimately adjust to their loss. Building on the prior work described earlier, we further extended the five grief trajectories from the CLOC study to 48 months postloss (Boerner, Wortman, & Bonanno, 2005). For these analyses, we used the data of the 92 bereaved elders who had one preloss assessment and three postloss assessments.

One major question of interest was whether the resilient respondents stay resilient and the depressed–improved respondents remain improved in the long term, 4 years after the loss of their spouse. We predicted that the resilient group would continue to do well at 48 months postloss, meaning that they would show neither delayed grief nor evidence a lack of cognitive and emotional involvement with the deceased (Boerner et al., 2005). We also suspected that the depressed–improved group might do less well than the resilient group at 48 months compared with at 18 months because they had previously shown characteristics (e.g., emotional instability in the prebereavement assessments) that might potentially reemerge at a later date. We expected depression to remain low for the group that showed the common grief or recovery pattern because distress levels in this group had already abated by the time of the 18-month follow-up. We further investigated whether chronic grievers and chronically depressed respondents would remain distressed up to 48 months postloss. We expected that although factors such as losing a beloved, healthy spouse may have resulted in more persistent grief, chronic grievers would show at least some improvement from Month 18 to Month 48. In contrast, because the chronically depressed respondents showed a relatively stable pattern of depression that was present even before the loss, it seemed likely that something besides the loss was contributing to their depression. Therefore, we expected that their depression would remain high longer than in the other groups.

The results supported the prediction that respondents in both the resilient group and the common grief group would continue to do well at 48 months postloss and lent some support to our reasoning that the depressed–improved group may develop adjustment problems over time (Boerner et al., 2005). There was no indication of an ongoing pattern of avoiding thinking about the deceased or the loss among either the resilient or the depressed–improved groups. Rather, respondents in these groups appeared to be able to think about the deceased in a way that was comforting rather than upsetting to them. These findings add to the growing body of evidence challenging the notion of delayed grief as a likely consequence of the failure to become intensely distressed following the loss of a loved one. However, the evidence for a continuously positive adjustment was not as consistent for the depressed–improved group compared with the resilient group; in fact, the depressed–improved group had significantly higher levels of both grief symptoms and depression at 48 months postloss than the resilient group. Hence, the possibility of delayed problems among individuals who show improvement following their loved one's death needs to be further explored.

The differential findings regarding the chronic grief group and chronically depressed group also underscore the need to further refine the criteria that are used to identify individuals who may be at risk for long-term problems. The chronic grief group exhibited a clear turn toward better adjustment. They showed significant reductions in both grief symptoms and depression from 18 to 48 months, and at the 48-month point they had significantly less grief and depression than the chronically depressed group. In contrast, the chronically depressed group clearly demonstrated long-term problems, with little indication of improvement between Month 18 and Month 48. This group not only showed the poorest adjustment 4 years after the loss, but they also struggled more than other participants with questions about meaning. Perhaps these respondents were prone to ruminate about their situation (Nolen-Hoeksema, Parker, & Larson, 1994), and searching for meaning of the loss was part of this more general rumination tendency. Alternately, such a tendency may lie at the core of the depression and explain its toxicity.

CONCLUSION

During the past 10 years, researchers have become increasingly aware that there are divergent reactions to loss. In the majority of studies, however, investigators have assessed grief and depression following the loss and aggregated the data across respondents. Although such data provide information about how grief, on average, changes over time, they obscure the full range of grief reactions.

For the past 50 years, clinicians have described a variety of responses to loss. They have identified and discussed several forms of disordered mourning, including absent grief, chronic grief, and delayed grief. However, few efforts have been made to study these responses empirically. It is widely assumed that recovery from a major loss takes time and that there is something wrong with people who show absent grief or who recover too quickly. In our past theoretical and empirical work, we have suggested that absent grief may indicate resilience. Until recently, however, the lack of prospective data has made it difficult to adjudicate among these completing views or to identify the antecedent factors that might help explain divergent reactions to loss. In the research we have described in this chapter, we relied primarily on data from the CLOC Study (for more detailed descriptions, see Bonanno et al., 2002; Carr, Nesse, & Wortman, 2006) as well as several other prospective and comparative studies (e.g., Bonanno, Moskowitz, et al., 2005). These findings present a dramatic challenge to prevailing assumptions about absent and chronic grief and suggest that many of these assumptions may stem at least in part from confusion between these different patterns. In future research it will be important to further clarify the implications of the results presented here. For example, a number of studies have begun to document the prevalence of the resilient outcome pattern among other extremely adverse stressors, such as urban terrorist attacks (Bonanno, Galea, Bucciarelli, & Vhalhov, 2006) and treatment for breast cancer (Deshields, Tibbs, Fan, & Taylor, 2006). Given the prevalence of the resilient pattern among the diverse samples reported in this chapter, it would also be useful to examine resilience in the context of other types of loss, such as divorce or job loss.

It also will be important to learn more about how resilient individuals are able to assimilate major losses (Bonanno, 2004, 2005). Our initial research suggests that worldviews may be important, but more could be learned about how such views are evoked and why they appear to serve a protective function. In our more recent studies we have also begun to examine the social consequences of resilience, asking friends and associates to rate individuals who demonstrate resilience. It would be intriguing to conduct additional studies to explore the social ramifications of a resilient style (e.g., Bonanno, Rennicke, & Dekel, 2005). One important issue concerns whether there may be costs associated with a resilient style in one's intimate relationships. Resilient people have an outlook on life that may make them less vulnerable to outside stressors but also less attentive to others' concerns, which could have a negative impact on close relationships. Resilient people may also receive negative reactions from others if they appear to recover too quickly from a loss. Others may interpret such a reaction as indication of aloofness or indifference, particularly if it occurs shortly after the loss. Alternatively, others may react more favorably to a resilient person because it is easier for them to be with someone who is less distressed.

Findings from the CLOC study, as well as other recent studies, make it clear that the absence of grief is not an appropriate rationale for clinical intervention. Despite statements from several influential clinicians recommending treatment for individuals who fail to evidence grief, this view has received no empirical support from our research or the findings of others.

As a number of investigators have indicated (e.g., Jordan & Neimeyer, 2003; Mancini, Pressman, & Bonanno, 2006), standard clinical interventions for grief have been shown to be surprisingly ineffective. This may be because in the past, researchers have not been aware of the distinction between chronic grief and chronic depression. It is possible that different types of intervention may be effective for individuals with chronic grief versus chronic depression. For example, those with chronic grief may benefit from therapeutic approaches that facilitate insight into the loss and foster the construction of meaning. In contrast, chronically depressed individuals may benefit more from a focus on enduring issues that may be implicated in the depression, including the absence of supportive relationships, poor coping skills, and poor emotional self-regulation. More research is needed to substantiate these claims.

In our judgment, the majority of grief researchers are open to the idea that there are divergent ways of reacting to the death of a loved one and have a keen interest in learning more about the antecedents and consequences of this variability. It would be interesting to learn more about the current prevailing beliefs about the grieving process held by clinicians and laypersons. It has been more than a decade since Middleton et al. (1993) published their important article surveying clinicians about their beliefs concerning grief. At that time, 65% of respondents endorsed the belief that absent grief typically stems from denial or inhibition and that such a response is generally maladaptive in the long run. What results would emerge if such a survey were conducted today? How do physicians, clergy, and other health care providers react when people deviate from what is believed to be normal grief? Many laypersons still believe that people typically show intense distress following the loss and that this distress decreases over time. This suggests that support providers may respond to the bereaved in ways that are unhelpful if they exhibit too much or too little distress. Moreover, the bereaved themselves may find it disturbing when their reactions are different from what they expected, and this could contribute to the distress they are experiencing. Taken together, the findings we have reviewed here suggest that it would be useful to provide information about so-called normal grieving to health care providers, to support providers, and to the bereaved themselves.

REFERENCES

Beach, S. R., Smith, D. A., & Fincham, F. D. (1994). Marital interventions for depression: Empirical foundation and future prospects. *Applied and Preventative Psychology, 3*, 233–250.

Bodnar, J. C., & Kiecolt-Glaser, J. K. (1994). Caregiver depression after bereavement: Chronic stress isn't over when it's over. *Psychology and Aging, 9*, 372–380.

Boerner, K., Wortman, C. B., & Bonanno, G. A. (2005). Resilient or at risk?: A four-year study of older adults who initially showed high or low distress following conjugal loss. *Journal of Gerontology: Psychological Science, 60B*, P67–P73.

Bonanno, G. A. (2004). Loss, trauma, and human resilience: Have we underestimated the human capacity to thrive after extremely aversive events. *American Psychologist, 59*, 20–28.

Bonanno, G. A. (2005). Resilience in the face of potential trauma. *Current Directions in Psychological Science, 14*, 135–138.

Bonanno, G. A., & Field, N. P. (2001). Evaluating the delayed grief hypothesis across 5 years of bereavement. *American Behavioral Scientist, 44*, 798–816.

Bonanno, G. A., Galea, S., Bucciarelli, A., & Vhalhov, D. (2006). Psychological resilience after disaster: New York City in the aftermath of the September 11th terrorist attack. *Psychological Science, 17*, 181–186.

Bonanno, G. A., & Kaltman, S. (1999). Toward an integrative perspective on bereavement. *Psychological Bulletin, 125*, 760–776.

Bonanno, G. A., & Kaltman, S. (2001). The varieties of grief experience. *Clinical Psychology Review, 20*, 1–30.

Bonanno, G. A., Moskowitz, J. T., Papa, A., & Folkman, S. (2005). Resilience to loss in bereaved spouses, bereaved parents, and bereaved gay men. *Journal of Personality and Social Psychology, 88*, 827–843.

Bonanno, G. A., Rennicke, C., & Dekel, S. (2005). Self-enhancement among high-exposure survivors of the September 11th terrorist attack: Resilience or social maladjustment? *Journal of Personality and Social Psychology, 88*, 984–998.

Bonanno, G. A., Wortman, C. B., Lehman, D. R., Tweed, R. G., Haring, M., Sonnega, J., et al. (2002). Resilience to loss and chronic grief: A prospective study from pre-loss to 18 months post-loss. *Journal of Personality and Social Psychology, 83*, 1150–1164.

Bonanno, G. A., Wortman, C. B., & Nesse, R. M. (2004). Prospective patterns of resilience and maladjustment during widowhood. *Psychology and Aging, 19*, 260–271.

Bonanno, G. A., Znoj, H. J., Siddique, H., & Horowitz, M. J. (1999). Verbal-autonomic response dissociation and adaptation to midlife conjugal loss: A follow-up at 25 months. *Cognitive Therapy and Research, 23*, 605–624.

Bowlby, J. (1980). *Attachment and loss: Vol. 3. Sadness and depression.* New York: Basic Books.

Carr, D., Nesse, R., & Wortman, C. B. (2006). Spousal bereavement in late life. New York: Springer Publishing.

Clark, D. M., & Teasdale, J. D. (1982). Diurnal variation in clinical depression and accessibility of positive and negative experiences. *Journal of Abnormal Psychology, 91*, 87–95.

Deshields, T., Tibbs, T., Fan, M. Y., & Taylor, M. (2006). Differences in patterns of depression after treatment for breast cancer. *Psycho-Oncology, 15*, 398–406.

Devilly, G. J., & Foa, E. B. (2001). The investigation of exposure and cognitive therapy: Comment on Tarrier et al. (1999). *Journal of Consulting and Clinical Psychology, 69*, 114–116.

Elliot, C. L., & Greene, B. L. (1992). Clinical depression and implicit memory. *Journal of Abnormal Psychology, 101*, 572–574.

Foa, E. B., Zoellner, L. A., Feeny, N. C., Hembree, E. A., & Alvarez-Conrad, J. (2002). Does imaginal exposure exacerbate PTSD symptoms? *Journal of Consulting and Clinical Psychology, 70*, 1022–1028.

Folkman, S., Chesney, M. A., & Christopher-Richards, A. (1994). Stress and coping in caregiving partners of men with AIDS. *Psychiatric Clinics of North America, 17*, 35–53.

Hokanson, J. E., & Butler, A. C. (1992). Cluster analysis of depressed college students' social behaviors. *Journal of Personality and Social Psychology, 62*, 273–280.

Horowitz, A. (1985). Sons and daughters as caregivers to older parents: Differences in role performance and consequences. *The Gerontologist, 25*, 612–617.

Horowitz, M. J. (1990). A model of mourning: Change in schemas of self and other. *Journal of the American Psychoanalytic Association, 38*, 297–324.

Jacobs, S. (1993). *Pathologic grief: Maladaptation to loss.* Washington, DC: American Psychiatric Press.

Jordan, J. R., & Neimeyer, R. A. (2003). Does grief counseling work? *Death Studies, 27*, 765–786.

Kazdin, A. (2003). *Research design in clinical psychology* (4th ed.). Boston: Allyn & Bacon.

Lopata, H. Z. (1979). *Women as widows: Support systems.* New York: Elsevier.

Mancini, A. D., Pressman, D. L., & Bonanno, G. A. (2006). Clinical interventions with the bereaved. In D. Carr, R. Nesse, & C. B. Wortman (Eds.), *Spousal bereavement in late life* (pp. 255–278). New York: Springer Publishing Company.

Middleton, W., Burnett, P., Raphael, B., & Martinek, N. (1996). The bereavement response: A cluster analysis. *British Journal of Psychiatry, 169,* 167–171.

Middleton, W., Moylan, A., Raphael, B., Burnett, P., & Martinek, N. (1993). An international perspective on bereavement related concepts. *Australian and New Zealand Journal of Psychiatry, 27,* 457–463.

Nolen-Hoeksema, S., Parker, L. E., & Larson, J. (1994). Ruminative coping with depressed mood following loss. *Journal of Personality and Social Psychology, 67,* 92–104.

Nuss, W. S., & Zubenko, G. S. (1992). Correlates of persistent depressive symptoms in widows. *American Journal of Psychiatry, 149,* 346–351.

Osterweis, M., Solomon, F., & Green, F. (Eds.). (1984). *Bereavement: Reactions, consequences, and care.* Washington, DC: National Academy Press.

Parkes, C. M. (1965). Bereavement and mental illness. *British Journal of Medical Psychology, 38,* 1–26.

Parkes, C. M., & Weiss, R. S. (1983). *Recovery from bereavement.* New York: Basic Books.

Prigerson, H. G., Shear, M. K., Bierhals, A. J., Pilkonis, P. A., Wolfson, L., Hall, M., et al. (1997). Case histories of traumatic grief. *Omega: The Journal of Death and Dying, 35,* 9–24.

Rando, T. A. (1993). *Treatment of complicated mourning.* Champaign, IL: Research Press.

Raphael, B. (1983). *The anatomy of bereavement.* New York: Basic Books.

Sable, P. (1989). Attachment, anxiety, and loss of a husband. *American Journal of Orthopsychiatry, 59,* 550–556.

Safer, M. A., Bonanno, G. A., & Field, N. P. (2001). It was never that bad: Biased recall of grief and long-term adjustment to the death of a spouse. *Memory, 9,* 195–204.

Schrader, G., Davis, A., Stefanovic, S., & Christie, P. (1990). The recollection of affect. *Psychological Medicine, 20,* 105–109.

Schulz, R., Mendelsohn, A. B., Haley, W. E., Mahoney, D., Allen, R. S., Zhang, S., et al. (2003). End of life care and the effects of bereavement among family caregivers of persons with dementia. *New England Journal of Medicine, 349,* 1891–1892.

Stader, S. R., & Hokanson, J. E. (1998). Psychosocial antecedents of depressive symptoms: An evaluation using daily experiences methodology. *Journal of Abnormal Psychology, 107,* 17–26.

Stroebe, W., & Stroebe, M. S. (1993). Determinants of adjustment to bereavement in younger widows and widowers. In M. S. Stroebe, W. Stroebe, & R. O. Hansson (Eds.), *Handbook of bereavement* (pp. 208–226). New York: Cambridge University Press.

Weissman, M. M. (1987). Advances in psychiatric epidemiology: Rates and risk for major depression. *American Journal of Public Health, 77,* 445–451.

Wheaton, B. (1990). Life transitions, role histories, and mental health. *American Sociological Review, 55,* 209–223.

Wortman, C. B., & Boerner, K. (2006). Beyond the myths of coping with loss: Prevailing assumptions versus scientific evidence. In H. S. Friedman & R. C. Silver (Eds.), *Foundations of health psychology* (pp. 285–324). Oxford, England: Oxford University Press.

Wortman, C. B., & Silver, R. C. (1989). The myth of coping with loss. *Journal of Consulting and Clinical, 57,* 349–357.

Wortman, C. B., & Silver, R. C. (2001). The myths of coping with loss revisited. In M. S. Stroebe, R. O. Hansson, W. Stroebe, & H. Schut (Eds.), *Handbook of bereavement research: Consequences, coping, and care* (pp. 405–430). Washington, DC: American Psychological Association.

Zhang, B., Mitchell, S. L., Bambauer, K. Z., Jones, R., & Prigerson, H. G. (in press). Depressive symptom trajectories and associated risks among bereaved Alzheimer's disease caregivers. *American Journal of Geriatric Psychiatry.*

Zimmerman, M., & Coryell, W. (1986). Reliability of follow-up assessments of depressed inpatients. *Archives of General Psychology, 43,* 468–470.

Zisook, S., & Shuchter, S. R. (1991). Depression through the first year after the death of a spouse. *American Journal of Psychiatry, 148,* 1346–1352.

15

REDEFINING GOALS AND REDEFINING SELF: A CLOSER LOOK AT POSTTRAUMATIC GROWTH FOLLOWING LOSS

CHRISTOPHER G. DAVIS

The process of adjusting to loss has been conceptualized in many different ways over the past century, and it is telling that most of these conceptualizations emphasize dealing with and ultimately accepting changes to identity and how one understands the world. Bowlby (1961, 1980) conceptualized the diverse reactions of grief within attachment theory, suggesting that the bereaved experience phases of searching, disorganization, and reorganization. Working through grief, according to Bowlby (1980), involves reorganizing one's working models of self and the world after the disorganization brought on by loss.

This theme of loss and reorganization has been noted by a number of other theorists over the years. Parkes (1988, 1998), for instance, has described loss as a psychosocial transition whereby old identities and ways of understanding the world gradually are given up and replaced with new identities and ways of understanding the world. Parkes (1988) suggested that counseling might facilitate adaptation by preparing the bereaved for the transitions they will face.

The concept of changing worldviews also figures prominently in Janoff-Bulman's (1992) *assumptive world theory*. According to Janoff-Bulman, trauma or loss may shatter the fundamental beliefs one holds about oneself, the world, and the relation between self and world. Successful adjustment from this

309

perspective involves revising worldviews so that they may remain somewhat positive, yet incorporate the loss:

> Even years after traumatic life events, survivors' fundamental assumptions are less positive than they had been previctimization. They have been stripped of illusions and they know that tragedy can strike at any time. Yet, their new assumptive worlds, reconstructed over time, are typically not wholly negative and threatening. Instead, they are generally positive, but allow for the real possibility of misfortune. (p. 318)

Neimeyer (2006), taking a constructivist point of view, likewise argued for the importance of rebuilding a sense of self—or "re-storying the self"—following loss. Recognizing that loss often disrupts one's narrative or life story, Neimeyer argued that a significant part of coping with loss involves the process of developing a new coherent and affirming narrative that incorporates the loss experience. Gillies and Neimeyer (2006) recently proposed a model of the readjustment process following loss that gives center stage to the three interrelated cognitive processes of (a) making sense of loss, (b) finding benefits, and (c) integrating changes in identity.

Managing the changes to identity brought on by loss is also a core feature of the restoration orientation process described in Stroebe and Schut's (1999, 2001) *dual-process model*. Stroebe and Schut (1999) described one of these two central processes, *restoration orientation*, as focusing on the "substantial changes that are secondary consequences of loss" (p. 214), including the tasks of reorganizing one's life and developing a new identity.

It is clear that coping with personal loss requires that one manages change, whether that change centers on one's understanding of the world, life, death, one's purpose, or one's roles and relationships. Yet it should be recognized that the fundamental worldviews and self-views referred to by these scholars are generally understood to be conservative and resistant to change (e.g., Epstein, 1973; Greenwald, 1980; Janoff-Bulman, 1992). Greenwald (1980) described the ego as "totalitarian" in the way that it can fabricate or revise personal histories in an effort to maintain coherent and "beneficient" views of self and world. Likewise, Taylor (1983) described how women with cancer attempted to maintain a positive self-image by selectively interpreting information. To the extent that people are highly motivated to maintain a positive self-view and their understanding of the world, it seems reasonable to presume that managing change involves not so much a replacement of one worldview with another or one view of self with another but more likely a gradual morphing of world-views and self-views. Coping with change is understood to involve revising a prior understanding of self, life, death, and purpose because the original understanding no longer fits, feels right, or is attainable. To the extent that one perceives that one is successful in managing the requisite change, one is apt to consider such change as evidence of personal growth.

LOSS, CHANGE, AND PERCEPTIONS OF GROWTH

The changes brought on by loss—particularly loss that is traumatic—are seldom appraised, at least initially, as opportunities to grow. The death of a loved one often threatens a part of one's identity (e.g., people who are bereaved sometimes say that a "part of me has died"); it shakes one's confidence, shatters hopes and dreams, and many times suggests a less benevolent or predictable view of the world. People coping with loss come to doubt long-held beliefs, the meaning of life, and sometimes whether it is worth going on living, and yet dozens of studies in the past 20 years have reported that most bereaved people report positive life changes or personal growth as a result of their experience.[1] As a result of their experience, people frequently report that they have a greater appreciation for life, that they no longer take things for granted, that they are closer to loved ones, and that they are stronger and more self-confident (e.g., Calhoun & Tedeschi, 1989–1990; Davis, Nolen-Hoeksema, & Larson, 1998; Davis, Wohl, & Verberg, 2007; Edmonds & Hooker, 1992; Lehman et al., 1993; Miles & Crandall, 1983; Nadeau, 1998). The meaning of these reports and the processes involved have been hotly debated issues in recent years. To what extent should reports of growth be taken as an indication of successful adaptation to loss and to what extent should they be interpreted as coping? Are they defensive reactions to threatening information, examples of impression management, or clues that one has accepted the loss and processed its meaning? In this chapter, I outline some distinct functions and ways of understanding reports of personal growth and suggest ways of distinguishing between competing models of the processes involved.

PERSPECTIVES ON GROWTH FOLLOWING LOSS

In their model of posttraumatic growth, Tedeschi and Calhoun (2004) proposed that growth emerges as one cognitively processes the meaning of highly stressful (particularly traumatic) experiences. In their model, events that shatter one's assumptive world—which includes one's fundamental and often-implicit beliefs about control, predictability, and the benevolence of others (see Janoff-Bulman, 1992; Parkes, 1971)—motivate a search for meaning. The course of one's life may no longer be perceived as predictable or controllable, or the assumptions one held about the benevolence of others or the role of chance may be ruptured. Many bereaved people ask, "Why him/her?" or "Why should one so young [or generous, kind, or vibrant] be taken?" This search for

---

[1]Research and theory have typically not distinguished among concepts such as personal growth, benefits, and positive life changes (e.g., Tedeschi & Calhoun, 2004), although later in this chapter I suggest that distinctions among these concepts might be helpful.

meaning represents an attempt to accommodate one's assumptive world as one restructures one's understanding of how the world works. According to this model, as one successfully processes the meaning of the loss, one comes to find value in the experience, and this (positive) valuation of one's experience is understood to be posttraumatic growth. In their struggle to understand why the loss happened, and what it means, people may grow in any number of ways; they may develop new perspectives on and appreciation for life, learn that they are capable or self-reliant, acquire an empathic understanding of others, develop stronger or deeper relationships, become more spiritual, and discover new possibilities (e.g., Tedeschi & Calhoun, 1996). The realization of posttraumatic growth appears to be contingent on successful processing of the meaning of the loss or trauma.

Joseph and Linley (2005) described a similar model. According to their *organismic valuing theory of growth*, people who experience trauma are motivated by an inherent drive for completion (Horowitz, 1986) to process the information of their experience, including its images, emotions, and—most important—implications for their worldview and self-view. If the loss information cannot be assimilated into existing knowledge structures (i.e., it does not make sense), then knowledge structures must be accommodated. *Positive accommodations* are regarded in this theory as growth, whereas *negative accommodations* are taken as indications of depression, hopelessness, or helplessness. Joseph and Linley noted that positive accommodations occur when one is "open to the existential issues raised by the event" and described them as cognitive processing of information that "lead[s] to growth as people reevaluate and more fully appreciate their relationships, their strength and resilience, and their philosophy of life" (p. 273), whereas negative accommodations are those that lead to reactions of hopelessness and helplessness.[2] The theory is organismic in the sense it "posits that humans are active, growth-oriented organisms" (p. 269) and, as such, are naturally motivated toward becoming more authentic and accepting of themselves and others. Overcoming adversity is, in this model, a vehicle to the organismic drive toward greater self-acceptance and self-understanding. Failure to grow after adversity therefore implies either that the event was assimilated within existing knowledge structures or that the knowledge structures have been accommodated negatively (e.g., in views that the world is unsafe and unpredictable and that disaster can strike at any time).

Consistent with both the Tedeschi–Calhoun and Joseph–Linley models, some research suggests that loss of a loved one is associated with less positive

---

[2]It is not clear in Joseph and Linley's (2005) model whether positive and negative accommodations can be assessed or defined independently of their outcomes (growth or helplessness–hopelessness). From their description, it seems that a shift from a naively optimistic view of the world toward one that is more realistic would be considered a negative accommodation if it made one feel depressed or a positive accommodation if it made one feel wiser.

world assumptions. Using Janoff-Bulman's (1989) World Assumptions Scale to assess assumptions about the meaningfulness and benevolence of the world, and self-worth, Schwartzberg and Janoff-Bulman (1991) compared college students who had lost a parent within the past 3 years with students who had not experienced death of a parent and found that the bereaved students reported less positive assumptions about the meaningfulness of the world. Boelen, Kip, Voorsluijs, and van den Bout (2004) conducted a similar study and found that bereaved participants reported less positive assumptions about meaningfulness of the world and less self-worth relative to matched control participants. Matthews and Marwit (2003–2004) also used the World Assumptions Scale to compare bereaved parents with nonbereaved parents and found that bereaved parents differed from nonbereaved parents in terms of assumptions about the benevolence of the world. Matthews and Marwit also found meaningful differences in worldviews as a function of cause of death (i.e., homicide vs. accident vs. illness). Although these studies support the view that loss negatively affects worldviews, they have not established whether such worldview threats are associated with personal growth. I am aware of no studies that have assessed whether particular worldview threats are associated with reports of growth; however, numerous studies have established that the perceived severity of stressors is associated positively with reports of growth (e.g., Park, Cohen, & Murch, 1996; Tedeschi & Calhoun, 1996). In a small community sample of Canadian adults interviewed about 6 weeks after the terrorist attacks of September 11, 2001, Davis and Macdonald (2004) found that those who reported the most distress in the first 24 hours following the attacks and the most negative changes at the first interview were most likely to report positive life changes, concurrently and prospectively, 1 year later. These data suggest that significant threats to worldviews may promote the perception of growth.

SOME CHALLENGES TO MODELS OF POSTTRAUMATIC GROWTH

Both the Tedeschi–Calhoun and Joseph–Linley models emphasize that growth is contingent on successful processing of the meaning of the loss. If the loss event does not shatter worldviews or self-views, and if one is not able to accommodate knowledge structures to account for the implications of the loss, then growth will not result. In a prospective study of loss, Davis et al. (1998) examined the extent to which meaning-making (assessed by asking bereaved participants whether they had been able to make sense of their loss) and perceived growth (assessed by asking whether they had found something positive in their experience) related to each other and to adjustment. Although making sense of loss and finding positives independently predicted adjustment, they were not related to each other; that is, people who perceived growth were no more likely to have made sense of their loss than those who had not.

It is important to note that the losses with which participants in Davis et al.'s (1998) study were coping were not unexpected; all were caregivers of loved ones who were terminally ill, and consequently they were not shocked when the death occurred. Although many perceived the death as unfair and some had great difficulty making sense of the loss, most had an explanation for why their loved one had died and appeared to have assimilated the loss into existing knowledge structures. As one (fairly typical) person in this study stated, "It always made sense to me: I mean, he smoked for years; it's perfectly sensible to me" (p. 566). Thus, for some participants, little processing of the meaning of the loss seemed necessary; they did not search for meaning.

In a second study, Davis, Wortman, Lehman, and Silver (2000) showed the importance of distinguishing people who do not search for meaning (and thus presumably have assimilated the loss into existing knowledge structures or worldviews) from those who do search for meaning (and thus presumably are attempting to accommodate worldviews). Using a sample of people who had lost a spouse or child in a motor vehicle accident and a sample of parents coping with the loss of their baby to sudden infant death syndrome, Davis et al. reported that a sizable minority of people coping with these sudden, traumatic losses do not search for meaning and report better than average adjustment. People who were adjusting least well were those who continued to search unsuccessfully for meaning.

This pattern of results was recently replicated by Tolstikova, Fleming, and Chartier (2005). In a sample of 84 bereaved adults, most of whom had lost a loved one in an accident involving a drunk driver, they found that whereas all participants who met criteria for complicated grief (see chap. 8, this volume) were unable to make sense of their loss, most of those who did not meet criteria for complicated grief reported being able to make sense of their loss or had not attempted to make sense of their loss. Although neither Davis et al. (2000) nor Tolstikova et al. examined the relations of searching for meaning and making sense of loss to perceived growth,[3] their studies suggest that even in situations of traumatic loss some bereaved people appear to cope

---

[3]In a recent study by Holland, Currier, and Neimeyer (2007) involving a large and diverse sample (in terms of types of loss with which participants were coping), items similar to those used by Davis et al. (1998) were used to assess making sense of loss and finding positives. Although Holland et al. found a modest positive correlation between sense making and reports of growth, they also found a significant interaction of making sense and finding positives with regard to complicated grief scores. Consistent with the foregoing analysis, participants with the lowest complicated grief scores were those who had an explanation for the loss and did not report positives. Holland et al. noted anecdotally that many in this group interpreted the loss within a religious framework, which one might presume predated the loss. Participants with highest complicated grief scores were those unable to make sense of loss and unable to report any benefits. Michael and Snyder (2005) also assessed sense making and benefit finding in a bereaved sample but did not report the correlation of one with the other.

well with their loss without questioning why. People in this group could be considered to be resilient, and they appear to adjust relatively quickly to loss, perhaps because they possess a worldview that readily assimilates the information of the loss (Bonanno, 2004; Neimeyer, 2005). In general, it appears that making sense of loss is not critical to adjustment, but—consistent with Joseph and Linley's (2005) organismic valuing theory—being unable to make sense of loss appears to be a clear indicator of adjustment difficulties.

The fact that people often perceive growth in the apparent absence of sense-making (as suggested by nil to modest correlations of the two constructs; Davis et al., 1998; Holland et al., 2007) implies either the need to revise models of posttraumatic growth (which suggests that sense-making or schema reconstruction is critical to subsequent growth) or that growth may occur by other means. A number of authors have suggested that sense-making may not be a critical step. For instance, McMillen (2004), in a commentary on Tedeschi and Calhoun's (2004) model of posttraumatic growth, argued that positive changes (or growth) sometimes have nothing to do with seismic disruption of worldviews, noting, for example, that positive changes in relationships can occur as one comes to share personal experiences with, and depend on, others and that changes in goals can lead to the development of new skills and a new sense of personal mastery. Janoff-Bulman (2004), also responding to Tedeschi and Calhoun's model, suggested three models of growth: (a) one centering on changes in self-understanding that emerge from suffering; (b) one centering on changes in worldview, whereby one comes to realize that assumptions about control, the benevolence of others, and order are in need of revision; and (c) one centering on meaning-making, reprioritizing, revaluing life, and spiritual change. These and other authors have suggested that what is commonly understood to be growth may emerge from a number of processes, some of which may have nothing to do with shattered self-views or worldviews.

Wortman (2004), on the other hand, argued that reports of growth might to some extent reflect defensiveness and attempts on the part of the bereaved to convey an impression of good coping. Some previous research suggests that people in a survivor's social network may "pull" for articulations of positive life changes and growth, in part by reacting negatively to expressions of distress and negative life changes (Coyne, Wortman, & Lehman, 1988; Silver, Wortman, & Crofton, 1990). Indeed, Taylor's (1983) *cognitive adaptation theory* suggests that reports of personal growth may represent cognitive defenses or illusions that serve to maintain or shore up self-esteem and a sense of mastery over the event and over one's life more generally. Taylor argued that one can minimize the implications of a severe negative event by imagining worse situations, by construing benefit from the event, by selectively focusing on aspects that make one appear advantaged, or by comparing oneself with less fortunate others. Perhaps some of the perceived benefits (both changes in how one sees oneself and changes in values and attitudes) that the bereaved describe are not so much examples of growth as defensive reactions (see, e.g., Davis & McKearney, 2003; McFarland & Alvaro, 2000; Schwartzberg, 1993) attributable to threats to self-esteem embedded within the loss experience. Implied within the characteristic statements that one is stronger now, has learned that one can cope, or has learned to appreciate the important things in life as a result of going through this experience is the idea that at an earlier time one was weaker, that one suspected that one would be unable to cope, and that one formerly did not appreciate the important things in life—all of which might represent a threat to self-esteem.

UNPACKING GROWTH

Given the conceptual confusion about how growth might occur, and what it might mean, Davis et al. (2007) considered a different approach to understanding growth processes. Whereas previous studies have summed data across a wide range of perceived changes to yield a posttraumatic growth score (or used a single item to assess for any perceived growth), Davis et al. examined the extent to which bereaved individuals reporting various aspects of perceived growth clustered naturally. To map these clusters onto Tedeschi and Calhoun's (2004) model of posttraumatic growth, they also included responses that the bereaved provided with respect to questions about meanings of loss and whether they reported searching for and finding meaning. Before I describe the results of this study, it is important to note that all participants had lost a loved one (father, son, husband, brother) simultaneously in a tragic mine explosion in Canada. The event received overwhelming and sustained media attention, first as a calamity of national significance and subsequently as a possible case of corporate crime, cover-up, and bureaucratic incompetence. Between May 1992, when the explosion happened, and January 1996, the two daily newspapers of the Canadian province in which this event occurred published 1,765 articles about the event and its aftermath (McMullan & Hinze, 1999). The event became the subject of a public inquiry, a number of scholarly and popular books, a film documentary, and a dramatic play. Criminal charges and civil lawsuits were launched against the company and its management, but for a variety of reasons none have been successful. For family members, the event was not only a sudden, unexpected loss of their loved one but also an ongoing saga of shattered beliefs, broken promises, deceit, and exploitation. As one family member noted,

> I might have been able to accept it if he had a car accident, or if he had cancer, or something, and dealt with it, but I'm not happy with it, no, and I probably never will be, because maybe there'll never be justice. I don't have any faith in it anymore. (Davis et al., 2007, p. 709)

Unlike many losses that have been the focus of research, this loss—in addition to being violent and untimely—struck many as senseless, unnecessary, and preventable, and therefore particularly likely to challenge assumptive worlds (Janoff-Bulman, 1992).

Davis et al. (2007) coded the responses of family members of the deceased miners for themes and then assessed the degree to which each individual was similar to others in the study in terms of the themes he or she noted. The resulting similarity matrix was then subjected to a hierarchical clustering program. Of the three profiles (or clusters) derived, one clearly fit the posttraumatic growth model suggested by Tedeschi and Calhoun (2004): People in this cluster tended to report losing a part of themselves, searching for and finding some meaning (typically noting that it was a source of personal growth), and describing positive changes (e.g., gained inner strength, learned about self). As one person stated about her personal changes,

> I worked very hard to get [something positive] . . . I think a lot of that was thinking of him and what he would want me to do . . . and I got a lot of strength from this. . . . I don't think there is anything that I cannot handle, and I don't think that I had that before, and if I did, I don't think that I knew I had that inner strength.

A second cluster comprised people who were searching unsuccessfully to make sense of loss and were perhaps as a consequence unable to perceive positive change or growth, reporting instead only negative changes and shattered assumptions (Davis et al., 2007). When asked how their loss experience affected their philosophy of life, members of this cluster tended to report primarily negative changes. For example, one participant said, "I never thought that anybody could kill somebody and get away with it, so publicly . . . so my view on life has changed drastically" (Davis et al., 2007, pp. 706–707).

The third cluster, however, was perhaps the most interesting. This cluster comprised individuals who reported that they did not search for meaning and reported modest "growth," primarily on dimensions of positive changes in philosophy of life (e.g., "It's made me value life more"; "I try to live each day at a time and try to live it to its best"). It is debatable whether members of this group could be said to have experienced posttraumatic growth, at least as the concept has been described by Tedeschi and Calhoun (2004) or Joseph and Linley (2005). Although these participants described positive changes equivalent to items on common questionnaires designed to assess posttraumatic growth, there was no sense that they had gone through a process of shattered self-view or worldview, searching for meaning, or rewriting their life narrative. Moreover, the sense of growth that they did report was, for the most part, distinct from the sense of growth reported by participants in the first cluster. They indicated that they "appreciate life more" and "live life in the present," but they did not report changes in how they saw or understood themselves or changes in goals, purpose, or identity. Although there is no way of determining whether one set of changes is more substantial than the other, it seems that the changes reported by the first cluster have more to do with a change in self, a personal growth. In contrast, the changes cited by participants in the third cluster seem more to reflect a refinement of a worldview, as suggested by the following statement by a member of this cluster in response to the question about whether he had searched for some meaning: "I'm not a person who thinks there is a reason for everything that happens. I think it was just meant to be and I think maybe it would've been worse if it didn't happen" (Davis et al., 2007, p. 707). These individuals seem to possess a worldview that accepts the fact that bad things will happen, and thus one must focus one's life on living in the present.

In sum, the mine explosion study suggested some people fit a profile that features a seismic disruption of self; a search for purpose or meaning; and a sense that one has changed, matured, or developed significant personal qualities (e.g., strength, empathy, or coping abilities) that they attribute to having to cope with this experience (Davis et al., 2007). This profile is consistent with models that suggest that meaning-making is critical for posttraumatic growth (Joseph & Linley, 2005; Tedeschi & Calhoun, 2004). However, other participants who reported positive changes did not describe key features of these posttraumatic growth models. Not only did members of this group indicate that they did not search for meaning, but they also indicated somewhat different benefits or positive changes. Rather than describing changes in personal qualities, identity, or life purpose, they emphasized changes in attitude or values. Although these changes may be just as real as those reported by the first group, I suspect that they do not reflect a similar process and have different significance for the bereaved themselves. Such changes might not be considered instances of posttraumatic growth.

PARSING GROWTH: DISTINGUISHING AMONG BENEFITS, INSIGHT, AND SUSTAINED POSTTRAUMATIC GROWTH

Davis et al.'s (2007) study suggests that more finely grained analysis of the growth that people report following loss might help to clarify the processes involved. A better understanding of the processes and meaning of growth might be realized by distinguishing different growth profiles. First, on the basis of these findings, Davis and Nolen-Hoeksema (in press) suggested that a distinction be drawn between *personal growth* and *benefits*. Benefits are the common but relatively transient and incidental by-products of experiencing adversity and include such things as improved social relationships, minor or temporary adjustments to values and priorities, and the realization of new possibilities. I consider posttraumatic growth to be distinct from benefits: It denotes the

TABLE 15.1
Profiles of Growth

Growth	(Perceived) benefits	Change in role and purpose	Insight
Longevity	Temporary or transient	Sustained changes in goal-directed behavior	Sustained changes in understanding of self
Quality	May be illusory, maintain self-esteem	Recognizable to others (e.g., more assertive, nurturant)	May not be recognizable to others (e.g., more self-aware)
What it is dependent on	Incidental to loss or adversity	Contingent on disrupted worldview or self-view	Contingent on loss of attachment figure or on suffering
Effort needed to bring it about	Typically passive, does not require effortful processing	Requires effortful processing of meaning	Requires effortful processing of feelings

significant and sustained positive changes in major commitments and life goals. These might include changes brought on by changes in one's roles. For example, becoming the principal breadwinner or caregiver might lead one to become more assertive and self-confident or empathic and nurturing. Such growth might also include changes in life purpose. For instance, going through a loss experience sometimes motivates people to become involved in hospice and palliative care. Some family members of those who died in the mine explosion (Davis et al., 2007) became politically active as a result of their experience, pressuring government to enact stiffer occupational health and safety laws. The critical point is that such changes are reflected in what one does, not merely in how one thinks about things. Thus, one important way of distinguishing significant personal changes from those that are less significant is that the former should be readily apparent in an individual's behavior to the extent that the changes are evident to others in his or her social network. If the change is significant and sustained, then it will be reflected not only in what one does but also in how one describes one's identity and life narrative (e.g., Neimeyer, 2006; Pals & McAdams, 2004; see Table 15.1).[4]

Second, unlike benefits, posttraumatic growth requires active processing of the meaning of a loss and time to set new goals and begin making significant

[4]In some earlier work, my colleagues and I referred to all aspects of perceived change as *perceived benefits* (Davis et al., 1998), implicitly reserving the term *growth* for changes that are significant, validated against some criteria, and sustained. Some of the changes reported by our participants in these earlier studies may be "benefits" as I here define the term, whereas others may have been better described as "growth." Lacking evidence as to the degree to which these changes were significant, validated, and sustained, we opted to call such reported changes *benefits* rather than *growth*.

progress toward those goals. It is not likely to be achieved overnight,[5] and it is not merely attributable to a reappraisal of the situation or of one's past. This focus on goal pursuit is similar to the notion of a *meaningful life* described by Frankl (1955/1986). Frankl asserted that life devoid of meaning results in an existential vacuum, whereas people who perceive meaning in their lives possess a sense of purpose. According to Frankl, people derive meaning by setting and achieving goals and by actively participating in life as opposed to passively witnessing it. Growth, from this perspective, involves resetting and moving toward the achievement of personally meaningful goals.

I argue that whereas the perception of benefits might be something that can occur relatively soon after trauma and arise from a variety of processes, posttraumatic growth—as I define it—is more likely to follow the process outlined by Tedeschi and Calhoun (2004), including a major shakeup of one's worldview or sense of self, significant cognitive processing of the meaning of the loss or trauma, and a new set of goals or commitments that change the meaning and direction of one's life. Such growth is not simply the adoption of a revised set of priorities or a new philosophy of life but also includes engaging in and sustaining behavior directed toward the achievement of new goals.

A third aspect of change that is distinct from benefits and posttraumatic growth is a more subtle, but important, change in how one understands oneself. I refer to this aspect as *gaining insight*. Along these lines, Nerken (1993) argued that an important aspect of growth is the development of a deeper understanding of the reflective (or interpreting) self. For example, as a result of their experience with loss (or other suffering), some people make statements like "I have gotten to know myself better" or "I got in touch with my feelings." Nerken argued that people grow in this sense as they come to depend less on the deceased for self-understanding and more on oneself for knowledge about who one is and of what one is capable: "As the reflective self works with the core self . . . a more effective level of self-relation, self-consultation or simply self-awareness is achieved, what is more commonly known as authenticity" (p. 57). According to Nerken's description of the process (see also Kessler, 1987), this aspect of growth is distinct from the process described by Tedeschi and Calhoun (2004). The focus here is not on shattered worldviews or self-views or on making sense of loss but on introspection brought on by loss of one who helped with self-definition (i.e., people with whom one has an affectional bond).[6] Nerken argued that such growth involves not a change to the core self (who one is) but in how one understands the core.

---

[5]It is acknowledged, however, that some people appear to change dramatically over a short period of time. Miller (2004) described such conversion experiences as *quantum change*. The extent to which such change should be considered examples of posttraumatic growth is unclear.
[6]Some researchers have also argued that such insight comes from the experience of suffering (e.g., Janoff-Bulman, 2004).

SUMMARY AND CONCLUSION

Posttraumatic growth as a concept has come to mean a lot of things. Tedeschi and Calhoun (2004), for example, defined it broadly as "positive psychological change experienced as a result of the struggle with highly challenging life circumstances" (p. 1). As a result, it is has not been possible to develop a coherent and useful understanding of what growth means and how it happens. From theoretical, empirical, and practical points of view, it may be helpful to draw distinctions between the following three concepts: (a) benefits (which I consider to be the more transient and incidental by-products of experiencing adversity, e.g., becoming closer to family members or forming new friendships); (b) changes in roles and purpose that are significant, sustained and observable (e.g., becoming more self-confident as one experiences success in the pursuit of new goals); and (c) increased insight (e.g., learning more about one's strengths and weaknesses; see Table 15.1). Each reflects a different set of processes, and each may have distinct implications for adjustment and well-being. The model of posttraumatic growth described by Tedeschi and Calhoun—one that begins with a trauma that shattered assumptions, includes a process of making sense of loss or schema reconstruction, and ultimately leads to sustained growth—appears to be viable, but it does not account for other aspects of growth or benefit finding. I suggest that the perception of benefits might represent a range of other distinct processes, some of which might be examples of defensiveness or ways of coping with threat and some of which might be examples of capitalizing on new opportunities. A third category, insight, is suggested by Nerken's (1993) analysis of changes in how one understands the self. Increased self-knowledge may be an important outcome, although methods of assessing such change that go beyond self-report remain to be developed. Uncovering the processes involved and the factors that might promote or inhibit such growth are important goals for future research.

Future research should also focus on interactions among these different processes. For instance, the perception of benefit, whether accurate or not, may be an important initial way of responding to psychological threat. Such initial reactions may help foster subsequent growth by helping maintain hope, optimism, and supportive relationships. Along these lines, Seligman, Rashid, and Parks (2006) recently described a series of homework activities for depressed individuals that seem to reduce levels of depression. The homework activities include such things as reflecting on positive aspects and recording daily "blessings." Encouraging such positive reappraisals (or *benefit-reminding*; see Affleck & Tennen, 1996) may lead people to focus less on the negative impact of the loss, including persistently asking "Why me?" or what they might have done to prevent the death and to focus more on restoration-oriented issues, which include the development of new goals and a new identity (Stroebe & Schut, 1999).

To the extent that models of growth and change are going to be useful, it behooves us to demonstrate empirically how growth happens and what it means. Most researchers, clinicians or counselors, and theorists do not have in mind transient or incidental changes when they speak of growth. Therefore, if our primary interest is in sustained positive changes, then greater attention should be devoted to the outwardly observable changes in goals, purpose, and life direction as well as the growth that is more inwardly centered. To be useful, future research will need to better substantiate claims of growth over time and better demonstrate whether and how such changes have an impact on the course of well-being and adjustment. Self-reports of positive changes or growth may be a good starting point, but such reports do not bring us closer to understanding what these reports might mean. It is hard to know whether the statements "becoming closer to one's family" and "appreciating each day" (Davis et al., 1998; Lehman et al., 1993; Tedeschi & Calhoun, 1996) should be taken as temporary or incidental benefit, an insight, or a sustained and observable change in how one relates to others or what one does each day. Teasing apart these aspects will lead to a clearer understanding of what posttraumatic growth is, how it happens, and what it means. Once that is clarified, we will be in a far better position to help people struggling with the personal, social, and psychological changes brought on by loss.

REFERENCES

Affleck, G., & Tennen, H. (1996). Construing benefits from adversity: Adaptational significance and dispositional underpinnings. *Journal of Personality*, 64, 899–922.

Boelen, P. A., Kip, H. J., Voorsluijs, J. J., & van den Bout, J. (2004). Irrational beliefs and basic assumptions in bereaved university students: A comparison study. *Journal of Rational-Emotive and Cognitive Behavioral Therapy*, 22, 111–129.

Bonanno, G. A. (2004). Loss, trauma, and human resilience: Have we underestimated the human capacity to thrive after extremely aversive events? *American Psychologist*, 59, 20–28.

Bowlby, J. (1961). Processes of mourning. *International Journal of Psycho-Analysis*, 42, 317–340.

Bowlby, J. (1980). *Attachment and loss: Vol. 3. Loss: Sadness and depression*. London: Hogarth Press.

Calhoun, L. G., & Tedeschi, R. G. (1989–1990). Positive aspects of critical life problems: Recollections of grief. *Omega: The Journal of Death and Dying*, 20, 265–272.

Coyne, J. C., Wortman, C. B., & Lehman, D. R. (1988). The other side of support: Emotional overinvolvement and miscarried help. In B. H. Gottlieb (Ed.), *Marshaling social support: Formats, processes, and effects* (pp. 305–330). Newbury Park, CA: Sage.

Davis, C. G., & Macdonald, S. L. (2004). Threat appraisals, distress, and the development of positive life changes following September 11th in a Canadian sample. *Cognitive Behavioural Therapy, 33*, 68–78.

Davis, C. G., & McKearney, J. M. (2003). How do people grow from their experience with trauma or loss? *Journal of Social and Clinical Psychology, 22*, 477–492.

Davis, C. G., & Nolen-Hoeksema, S. (in press). Making sense of loss, perceiving benefits, and posttraumatic growth. In S. Lopez & C. R. Snyder (Eds.), *Handbook of positive psychology* (2nd ed.). New York: Oxford University Press.

Davis, C. G., Nolen-Hoeksema, S., & Larson, J. (1998). Making sense of loss and benefiting from the experience: Two construals of meaning. *Journal of Personality and Social Psychology, 75*, 561–574.

Davis, C. G., Wohl, M. J. A., & Verberg, N. (2007). Profiles of posttraumatic growth following an unjust loss. *Death Studies, 31*, 693–712.

Davis, C. G., Wortman, C. B., Lehman, D. R., & Silver, R. C. (2000). Searching for meaning in loss: Are clinical assumptions correct? *Death Studies, 24*, 497–540.

Edmonds, S., & Hooker, K. (1992). Perceived changes in life meaning following bereavement. *Omega: The Journal of Death and Dying, 25*, 307–318.

Epstein, S. (1973). The self-concept revisited: Or a theory of a theory. *American Psychologist, 28*, 404–416.

Frankl, V. (1986). *The doctor and the soul: From psychotherapy to logotherapy* (3rd ed.). New York: Vintage Books. (Original work published 1955)

Gillies, J., & Neimeyer, R. A. (2006). Loss, grief, and the search for significance: Toward a model of meaning reconstruction in bereavement. *Journal of Constructivist Psychology, 19*, 31–65.

Greenwald, A. G. (1980). The totalitarian ego: Fabrication and revision of personal history. *American Psychologist, 35*, 603–618.

Holland, J. M., Currier, J. M., & Neimeyer, R. A. (2007). Meaning reconstruction in the first two years of bereavement: The role of sense-making and benefit-finding. *Death Studies, 31*, 175–191.

Horowitz, M. J. (1986). *Stress response syndromes*. Northville, NJ: Jason Aronson.

Janoff-Bulman, R. (1989). Assumptive worlds and the stress of traumatic events: Applications of the schema construct. *Social Cognition, 7*, 113–136.

Janoff-Bulman, R. (1992). *Shattered assumptions: Towards a new psychology of trauma*. New York: Free Press.

Janoff-Bulman, R. (1999). Rebuilding shattered assumptions after traumatic life events: Coping processes and outcomes. In C. R. Snyder (Ed.), *Coping: The psychology of what works* (pp. 305–322). New York: Oxford University Press.

Janoff-Bulman, R. (2004). Posttraumatic growth: Three explanatory models. *Psychological Inquiry, 15*, 30–34.

Joseph, S., & Linley, P. A. (2005). Positive adjustment to threatening events: An organismic valuing theory of growth through adversity. *Review of General Psychology, 9*, 262–280.

Kessler, B. G. (1987). Bereavement and personal growth. *Journal of Humanistic Psychology, 27*, 228–247.

Lehman, D. R., Davis, C. G., DeLongis, A., Wortman, C. B., Bluck, S., Mandel, D. R., & Ellard, J. H. (1993). Positive and negative life changes following bereavement and their relations to adjustment. *Journal of Social and Clinical Psychology, 12*, 90–112.

Matthews, L. T., & Marwit, S. J. (2003–2004). Examining the assumptive world views of parents bereaved by accident, murder, and illness. *Omega: The Journal of Death and Dying, 48*, 115–136.

McFarland, C., & Alvaro, C. (2000). The impact of motivation on temporal comparisons: Coping with traumatic events by perceiving personal growth. *Journal of Personality and Social Psychology, 79*, 327–343.

McMillen, J. C. (2004). Posttraumatic growth: What's it all about? *Psychological Inquiry, 15*, 48–52.

McMullan, J., & Hinze, S. (1999). Westray: The press, ideology, and corporate crime. In C. McCormick (Ed.), *The Westray chronicles: A case study in corporate crime* (pp. 183–217). Halifax, Nova Scotia, Canada: Fernwood.

Michael, S. T., & Snyder, C. R. (2005). Getting unstuck: The roles of hope, finding meaning, and rumination in adjustment to bereavement among college students. *Death Studies, 29*, 435–458.

Miles, M. S., & Crandall, E. K. B. (1983). The search for meaning and its potential for affecting growth in bereaved parents. *Health Values, 7*, 19–23.

Miller, W. R. (2004). The phenomenon of quantum change. *Journal of Clinical Psychology, 60*, 453–460.

Nadeau, J. W. (1998). *Families making sense of death.* Thousand Oaks, CA: Sage.

Neimeyer, R. A. (2005). Widowhood, grief and the quest for meaning: A narrative perspective on resilience. In D. Carr, R. M. Nesse, & C. B. Wortman (Eds.), *Late life widowhood in the United States* (pp. 227–252). New York: Springer Publishing Company.

Neimeyer, R. A. (2006). Re-storying loss: Fostering growth in the posttraumatic narrative. In L. Calhoun & R. Tedeschi (Eds.), *Handbook of posttraumatic growth: Research and practice* (pp. 68–80). Mahwah, NJ: Erlbaum.

Nerken, I. R. (1993). Grief and the reflective self: Toward a clearer model of loss resolution and growth. *Death Studies, 17*, 1–26.

Pals, J. L., & McAdams, D. P. (2004). The transformed self: A narrative understanding of posttraumatic growth. *Psychological Inquiry, 15*, 65–69.

Park, C. L., Cohen, L. H., & Murch, R. L. (1996). Assessment and prediction of stress-related growth. *Journal of Personality, 64*, 71–105.

Parkes, C. M. (1971). Psycho-social transitions: A field for study. *Social Science & Medicine, 5*, 101–115.

Parkes, C. M. (1988). Bereavement as a psychosocial transition: Processes of adaptation to change. *Journal of Social Issues, 44*(3), 53–65.

Parkes, C. M. (1998). *Bereavement: Studies in grief in adult life* (3rd ed.). Madison, CT: International Universities Press.

Schwartzberg, S. S. (1993). Struggling for meaning: How HIV-positive gay men make sense of AIDS. *Professional Psychology: Research and Practice, 24,* 483–490.

Schwartzberg, S. S., & Janoff-Bulman, R. (1991). Grief and the search for meaning: Exploring the assumptive worlds of bereaved college students. *Journal of Social and Clinical Psychology, 10,* 270–288.

Seligman, M. E. P., Rashid, T., & Parks, A. C. (2006). Positive psychotherapy. *American Psychologist, 61,* 774–788.

Silver, R. C., Wortman, C. B., & Crofton, C. (1990). The role of coping in support provision: The self-presentational dilemma of victims of life crises. In B. R. Sarason, I. G. Sarason, & G. R. Pierce (Eds.), *Social support: An interactional view* (pp. 397–426). New York: Wiley.

Stroebe, M., & Schut, H. (1999). The dual process model of coping with bereavement: Rationale and description. *Death Studies, 23,* 197–224.

Stroebe, M. S., & Schut, H. (2001). Models of coping with bereavement: A review. In M. S. Stroebe, R. O. Hansson, W. Stroebe, & H. Schut (Eds.), *Handbook of bereavement: Consequences, coping, and care* (pp. 375–403). Washington, DC: American Psychological Association.

Taylor, S. E. (1983). Adjustment to threatening events: A theory of cognitive adaptation. *American Psychologist, 38,* 1161–1173.

Tedeschi, R. G., & Calhoun, L. G. (1996). The posttraumatic growth inventory: Measuring the positive legacy of trauma. *Journal of Traumatic Stress, 9,* 455–471.

Tedeschi, R. G., & Calhoun, L. G. (2004). Posttraumatic growth: Conceptual foundations and empirical evidence. *Psychological Inquiry, 15,* 1–18.

Tolstikova, K., Fleming, S., & Chartier, B. (2005). Grief, complicated grief, and trauma: The role of the search for meaning, impaired self-reference, and death anxiety. *Illness, Crisis & Loss, 13,* 293–313.

Wortman, C. B. (2004). Posttraumatic growth: Progress and problems. *Psychological Inquiry, 15,* 81–90.

16

THE ROLE OF RELIGION
IN BEREAVEMENT

JUDITH C. HAYS AND CRISTINA C. HENDRIX

Dying and religion are inextricably entwined in human experience. Theological doctrines of the world's religions prescribe and contextualize the meaning, rituals, and aftermath of human dying. The impulse of many dying patients is to find transcendent meaning in their lives as they draw to a close. In this chapter, we focus on those who survive such losses—the bereaved—and examine the role of religious meaning-making and religious coping strategies among people who are bereaved because of many kinds of losses. We describe the dimensions of religious coping, how religious coping has been measured, and the major findings of outcome studies of religion and bereavement. For example, which dimensions of religiousness help or hinder bereaved persons to explain, accept, and adapt to loss? What are the implications of religious coping for the bereaved of different faith traditions? We conclude the chapter with an examination of the implications of these findings for practitioners and intervention researchers.

Theories of Bereavement

The current discourse on the role of religion in bereavement lies downstream from a number of important theoretical tributaries. Although these are discussed fully elsewhere (Stroebe & Schut, 2001), we describe briefly here several conceptual streams of thought that are germane to a discussion of research in this area. These conceptual themes include theories of grief, coping and stress, trauma, and multitrack models of bereavement.

Two general theories of grief (psychoanalytic and attachment theories) emphasize the degree to which bereaved individuals undertake the work of separation and loss, that is, *grief work*. The notion of grief work has been criticized for lacking clear definition, operational coherence, empirical support, and cultural generalizability (Stroebe & Schut, 2001). Nevertheless, these theories have had a significant impact on understanding how individuals come to terms with the loss of intimate ties.

In the early 1980s, general theories of coping emerged to explain how humans use specific strategies to manage transactions that tax or exceed their resources, and cognitive stress theories expanded the discussion to consider one such set of transactions related to coping with bereavement. Folkman (2001) refined this earlier work to specify the nature of the bereavement stressor, various continua of strategies used by individuals (e.g., confrontation or avoidance of the reality of the loss), and the adaptive and maladaptive outcomes of their strategic choices.

Trauma theorists focused on two issues of particular relevance to a discussion of the role of religion in bereavement. One thread explored how emotional disclosure and social sharing, as may occur in religious congregations, contribute to adaptive coping (Pennebaker, Zech, & Rimé, 2001). A second thread focused on how traumatic events disrupt three metaphysical assumptions relevant to theological discourse: (a) that humans are worthy, (b) that the world is benevolent, and (c) that events in life have meaning (Janoff-Bulman, 1992). Most recently, multitrack models of coping with grief and bereavement have combined elements of psychological (intrapersonal) and social (interpersonal) experience and specified a temporal dimension to coping with grief in order to represent how the strategic choices of bereaved individuals contribute to adaptation or maladaptation over time (Stroebe & Schut, 2001).

Theories of Religious Coping

Developing in tandem with the aforementioned theory streams was the work of Wuthnow, Christiano, and Kuzlowski (1980), who proposed that religion was particularly salient for coping with bereavement by virtue of its emphasis on assigning meaning to life events, both in codified belief and ethical systems and in interpretations of peak experiences. Furthermore, they noted that coping with bereavement was directly related to religious "belonging," that is, participation in congregational worship; vicarious participation via religious radio, television, and private devotions; charitable service; and funerary rituals. Subsequently, Pargament et al. (1988) proposed that when *religious individuals* (defined as those who search for significance in the sacred) face stressful life events such as bereavement, and particularly when they perceive that human resources are inadequate to managing the challenges of the loss, their favored coping strategies include cognitive constructions of the event that are religious in nature. Furthermore, religious individuals seek religious ends as part of the adjustment process and select religious strategies to achieve those ends.

Challenges to Understanding the Role of Religion in Coping With Bereavement

Measurement

Scholars and scientists have faced three primary challenges to understanding the role of religious coping in bereavement. The first challenge has been to refine the operationalization and measurement of religious coping (Hill & Pargament, 2003). Single-item proxy measures for religious coping (e.g., frequency of worship attendance or prayer) and single-item summary measures for religious coping (e.g., whether spirituality religion was "involved" in coping with an event) have yielded to multidimensional measures with sound psychometric properties. Specifically, Pargament and Park (1997) developed a measure of five religious coping strategies, each expressed on a continuum of valence from positive to negative religious coping. These include (a) seeking comfort versus expressing alienation from God (spiritual support vs. discontent); (b) seeking comfort versus expressing alienation from congregation members or clergy (congregational support vs. discontent); (c) redefining the stressor through religion as potentially beneficial versus as punishment from God for the individual's sins (benevolent vs. punishing reframing); (d) seeking control of problem solving either by one's own initiation alone versus in collaboration with God versus passively yielding to God's control (orientation to agency and control as self-directing, collaborative, or deferring); and (e) use of more versus fewer rituals, such as attendance at religious services, death or mourning rituals, or pilgrimages. More parsimonious measures of positive versus negative religious coping styles have been developed from clusters of the strategies just described (Pargament, 1999).

Unfortunately, the most refined measures of religious coping are seldom used in studies of bereavement. Some studies have examined specific theological beliefs, such as belief in an afterlife; for example, "Which comes closest to what you believe—that people stop existing after their death or that there is an afterlife?" (Higgins, 2002, 194). Other studies have used measures that combine behavioral and cognitive dimensions of religiousness, such as the Shepherd Scale, which examines a person's involvement with and knowledge of Christianity (Austin & Lennings, 1993). Open-ended interview questions, such as "What helps you cope with your loss?" and "To what extent do your religious beliefs or activities help you cope with or handle the loss?", also have been used (Pearce et al., 2002, p. 186).

Relationship to the Decedent

A second challenge is that not only do measures of religious coping vary across studies but also that the nature of the bereavement loss being studied differs widely. It is a central tenet of stress and coping theories that the choice of coping strategies is specific to the situation. Thus, the nature of the relationship between decedent and survivor would be expected to affect the religious coping strategies and goals of survivors. Over the past 15 years, studies have focused on religious coping among bereaved spouses (Fry, 2001; Michael, Crowther, Schmid, & Allen, 2003; Robinson, 1995; Rodgers, 2004), bereaved family members and/or close friends (deVries, 1997; Flannelly, Weaver, & Costa, 2004; Krause et al., 2002; Park & Cohen, 1993), bereaved congregation members (Abrums, 2000), survivors following sudden losses (suicide, homicide, accident, heart attack and stroke; Doka, 1996; P. C. Smith, Range, & Ulmer, 1992; Thompson & Vardaman, 1997), bereaved mothers or parents (McIntosh, Silver, & Wortman, 1993; Murphy & Johnson, 2003; Thearle, Vance, Najman, Embelton, & Foster, 1995; Van & Meleis, 2003), bereaved adult children (S. H. Smith, 2002), bereaved partners of AIDS decedents (Oram, Bartholomew, & Landolt, 2004; Richards & Folkman, 1997), and mourners of heterogeneous losses (Gamino, Sewell, & Easterling, 2000; Pearce et al., 2002). A critical mass of findings regarding religious coping with any one type of loss has been difficult to come by.

Variety of Religious Traditions

As described earlier, religious individuals interpret the death of others in religious terms and understand their goals and how to achieve those goals in religious terms. Thus, meaning-making and coping strategies would be expected to differ across religious traditions. A third challenge to understanding the role of religion in bereavement is the wide variation of religious expression and belief both within and between religious traditions and between individuals within each tradition. With the caveat that bereaved individuals are the most reliable source of information about how religion influences their personal bereavement experience, the following issues may be generally informative about the role of religion in the major world religions.

Buddhism emphasizes that death is an inherent and inevitable part of life and, by virtue of Buddhists' belief in rebirth, repeated many times for the same individual (Keown, 2005). With its strong emphasis on compassion and respect for life, Buddhism has been a strong advocate for the hospice care model of palliative and bereavement care in the United States and United Kingdom for more than 30 years. Bereavement-related meanings and practices may be highly individualized because Buddhism teaches followers to attend to their own consciences, informed by "reflection on scripture, custom and tradition, and the opinions of distinguished teachers" (Keown, 2005, p. 952).

Meaning-making and mourning practices among Christians may also vary widely depending on the religious tradition of the survivors. Coping with bereavement may be influenced by where they place themselves on five theological, liturgical, and social continua: (a) whether the role of religion in their lives is metaphysical or cultural, (b) whether they are individually more or less religiously observant, (c) whether their preferred worship is more or less ceremonial, (d) whether they believe that moral tenets are fixed or evolving, and (e) whether their families and social networks are more or less religiously coherent (Engelhardt & Iltis, 2005).

Hindus generally consider that an individual's current life is a transition between a previous life and the next life and that the deceased is either reincarnated, living in heaven with God, or absorbed into an ultimate reality. Depending on whether the family was able to perform specific rituals to assist the dying person before and after the death (i.e., whether the decedent had a "good death"), their sacred obligations to the decedent may continue for many years into the bereavement period (Firth, 2005).

In Islam, religious explanations for a death, especially of a child, are normative and discussed openly (Gatrad, 1994). The extended family network is likely to be central in the provision of support during bereavement, and formal counseling is not often utilized. Prescribed religious behaviors for survivors differ by gender, based on juridical law that is "inherently discursive and pluralistic in its methods of deliberation" (Sachedina, 2005, p. 775).

Jews from Orthodox and Conservative congregations will likely follow the tenets of Jewish laws that prescribe bereavement rituals, as informed by their rabbi's interpretation; Jews from Reformed traditions may describe more individualistic bereavement experiences (Dorff, 2005). Traditional Jewish mourning practices vary depending on the familial relationship between the deceased and the bereaved, time since the death or burial, and the timing of other religious holidays or festivals.

EVIDENCE OF RELIGIOUS COPING STRATEGIES
IN BEREAVEMENT

Only in recent decades have researchers begun to acknowledge and study the role of religion in human bereavement (Marrone, 1999). There is a scarcity of empirical studies that focus specifically on how religious beliefs and behaviors mitigate the effects of human grieving. Early work on religion and human coping sampled college students, healthy populations, or clinical groups (cf. Koenig, Pargament, & Nielsen, 1998; Phillips, Pargament, Lynn, & Crossley, 2004) and was not focused on bereavement per se.

In our review of empirical literature on religious coping and bereavement, we used the following search strategies. We defined *religious coping* as the use of religious–spiritual beliefs or behaviors to prevent or alleviate the negative consequences of bereavement (Koenig, 1998). To be included in the review, a study needs to address the following question: "Do religious–spiritual beliefs or behaviors help a bereaved person to explain, accept, and come to terms with loss?"

We searched the Medline, CINAHL, PsycINFO, and Web of Science databases using the following search strategy: search terms = [(grief/griev* OR bereav* OR widow* OR death OR dying) AND (religi* OR spiritua*) AND (coping OR cope OR psychological adaptation)], matching the search terms to titles, abstracts, key words, and subject headings. (Truncated search terms with wild card symbols were used to broaden the search.) We limited our search to articles published between 1989 and 2005, generating 624 studies. We then excluded studies whose participants were not bereaved, whose primary aim was not to examine religious–spiritual beliefs and behaviors in bereavement, and whose focus was to look at the idiosyncratic religious beliefs and behaviors of only a certain cultural or racial group. This method yielded 25 studies, which are summarized in Table 16.1.

In general, the methodology of the studies was not strong. The majority of studies were cross-sectional, which prevents assessment of adjustment to loss over time. Sample sizes tended to be small, often fewer than 200 respondents. In addition to the vagaries of measures of religious coping, there was great variability in the types and measurement of dependent or outcome variables of interest to researchers. Confounding factors that may have affected the observed associations, such as social support, were not vigilantly controlled. Control groups of nonbereaved respondents were not included in the majority of studies reviewed, which also made interpretation of results more difficult. That the study of religion in bereavement is still in its infancy was evidenced by the number of qualitative studies, whose aim was to explore the relationship between the two concepts of religious coping and bereavement (see, e.g., Golsworthy & Coyle, 1999; Sormanti & August, 1997). One must conclude, therefore, that the relationship of religious coping strategies to bereavement

TABLE 16.1

Characteristics of Studies of Religious Coping and Bereavement, 1989–2005

Topic and study	Study design	Nonbereavement comparison group	Religious coping construct	Outcome construct
Physical well-being				
Krause et al. (2002)	Prospective	Yes	Turned to, consulted, or sought help from deity, belief in afterlife	Hypertension
Pearce et al. (2002)	Longitudinal	No	Religious Coping Index items ($n = 2$)	Basic activities of daily living; any of seven chronic illnesses; inpatient and outpatient care
Richards and Folkman (1997)	Longitudinal	No	Spiritually framed interpretative schema	Nonspecified physical symptoms ($n = 20$)
Psychological well-being				
Abrums (2000)	Qualitative	No	Belief in afterlife, spiritual experiences	Experience of grieving
Austin and Lennings (1993)	Cross-sectional	No	Shepherd Scale (Christian belief)	Beck Depression Inventory; Hopelessness Scale
Azhar and Varma (1995)	Experimental	No	Religious psychotherapy	Hamilton Depression Scale
Bohannon (1991)	Cross-sectional	No	Church attendance	Grief Experience Inventory
Easterling et al. (2000)	Cross-sectional	No	Index of Core Spiritual Experiences	Grief Experience Inventory, Hogan Grief Reactions Checklist
Fry (2001)	Cross-sectional	No	Religious involvement, religious support, Spirituality Assessment Scale	Depressed, anxious, happy mood states; autonomy; self-esteem; role transition
Gamino et al. (2000)	Cross-sectional	No	Intrinsic spirituality	Grief Experience Inventory, Hogan Grief Reactions Checklist
Higgins (2002)	Cross-sectional	No	Belief in afterlife, church attendance	Center for Epidemiologic Studies Depression Scale (CES–D)
McIntosh et al. (1993)	Longitudinal	No	Importance of religion, religious participation	Affect Balance Scale (positive)
Richards and Folkman (1997)	Longitudinal	No	Spiritually framed interpreted schema	Depressive symptoms, morale, anxiety, anger

(continued)

TABLE 16.1

Characteristics of Studies of Religious Coping and Bereavement, 1989–2005 (Continued)

Topic and study	Study design	Nonbereavement comparison group	Religious coping construct	Outcome construct
Rosik (1989)	Cross-sectional	No	Extrinsic–intrinsic religiousness	Geriatric Depression Scale, Texas Inventory of Grief
Sherkat and Reed (1992)	Cross-sectional	No	Church attendance	Depressive symptoms ($n = 18$), self-esteem items ($n = 3$)
Thearle et al. (1995)	Longitudinal	Yes	Church attendance	Anxiety, depression
Thompson and Vardaman (1997)	Cross-sectional	No	Spiritually based coping, religious support, avoidance, pleading, good deeds, discontent	Brief Symptom Inventory, Curlian Mississippi Scale (posttraumatic stress disorder)
Meaning-making				
Abrums (2000)	Qualitative	No	Importance of faith	Religious meaning-making
Batten and Oltjenbruns (1999)	Qualitative	No	Adolescent religious development	Quest for understanding life's meanings
Golsworthy and Coyle (1999)	Qualitative	No	Spiritual beliefs	Structures of meaning
McIntosh et al. (1993)	Longitudinal	No	Importance of religion, religious participation	Finding any meaning
Murphy and Johnson (2003)	Longitudinal	No	Turning to religion	Found meaning in death; physical health, mental distress
S. H. Smith (2002)	Cross-sectional	No	Belief in afterlife	Religious and existential well-being
Adjustment				
Balk (1991)	Cross-sectional	No	Importance of coping value of difficulty believing in religion	Grief reactions

Study	Design		Religion/spirituality measure	Outcome measures
Brown et al. (2004)	Prospective	Yes	Importance of religion, religious service attendance	Grief index, CES–D, anxiety index, subjective well-being; insecurity
Coleman et al. (2002)	Longitudinal	No	Royal Free Interview of Beliefs	Life Attitude Profile, Bereavement Experience Index, Short Form-36, Geriatric Depression Scale, South Hampton Self-Esteem, Sources of Self-Esteem Scale
Easterling et al. (2000)	Cross-sectional	No	Index of Core Spiritual Experiences	Grief Experience Inventory, Hogan Grief Reactions Checklist
Gamino et al. (2000)	Cross-sectional	No	Intrinsic spirituality	Grief Experience Inventory, Hogan Grief Reactions Checklist
McIntosh et al. (1993)	Longitudinal	No	Importance of religion, religious participation	Bradburn Well-Being Scale ($n = 3$ items)
Park and Cohen (1993)	Cross-sectional	No	Religious Coping Activities Scale	Beck Depression Inventory, Impact of Event Scale, personal growth
Richards and Folkman (1997)	Longitudinal	No	Spiritually framed interpretative schema	Ways of coping
P. C. Smith et al. (1992)	Cross-sectional	No	Belief in afterlife	Religious and existential well-being
Walsh et al. (2002)	Prospective	No	Royal Free Interview of Beliefs	Intensity of grief

outcomes as described in the following paragraphs is speculative. Nevertheless, we describe evidence of four categories of outcomes associated with the use of religious coping strategies, both behaviors and beliefs, in bereavement. These outcome categories are (a) physical well-being, (b) psychological well-being, (c) meaning-making, and (d) adjustment.

Bereavement Outcomes of Religious Coping Strategies

Physical Well-Being

Three studies (Krause et al., 2002; Pearce et al., 2002; Richards & Folkman, 1997) examined physical health outcomes following bereavement, with two of these using a quantitative design. In a prospective study of 1,723 Japanese elders (mean age 69 years), hypertension was significantly reduced by 72% among those who reported belief in a good afterlife and who had lost a significant other 3 years previously (Krause et al., 2002). In other words, those who experienced the death of a loved one but who believed in a good afterlife were less likely to report that they had hypertension over time. However, neither private religious practices nor religious coping offset the noxious effects of bereavement on blood pressure. Limitations of the study included self-reported hypertension and the unproven psychometric properties of the measures for religious practices and religious coping.

Two studies suggested that physical well-being may deteriorate among religious persons in the early period of grief but rebound significantly at a later date. In a study of chronic conditions and functional status among recently bereaved family members ($N = 267$), baseline chronic conditions did not differ among those who did and did not use religious coping strategies, but the more disabled bereaved participants did report a higher prevalence of religious coping at baseline (Pearce et al., 2002). Religious coping behavior was operationalized by using two questions from the Religious Coping Index (Koenig et al., 1998): (a) "What helps you cope with the loss?" and (b) "To what extend do your religious beliefs or activities help you cope with or handle the loss?" Four months later, participants with high religious coping scores demonstrated a trend toward less functional disability than those with low religious coping scores, who reported more functional disability over time. The same pattern was exhibited for chronic conditions. Although potential confounders, such as age and functional disability, were systematically controlled, caution in the interpretation of these results is warranted. The use of only two items from the Religious Coping Index may not be sufficient to capture the construct of religious coping, especially negative religious coping, which may influence health and health care utilization. In addition, self-report of health status and health service use creates a potential for bias.

In another study, Richards and Folkman (1997) used content analysis of data in an ongoing study of gay men and their partners to compare caregivers ($N = 68$) whose partners had recently died from AIDS. Bereaved caregivers were categorized according to whether they did or did not make spiritual or religious references in descriptions of their coping (e.g., belief in and experiences of a higher order, spiritual role of a caregiver). Religious copers were more likely than nonreligious copers to report physical symptoms at 2 and 4 weeks after the death. The authors attributed these results to an increased cognitive processing in the early weeks following the death among spiritually inclined participants. In this case, religious schemata may have provided the framework that makes death less threatening and more available for processing, albeit increasing psychological distress and physical symptoms in the short term because of increased attentiveness to the loss. This study included both a prospective design and triangulation of data collection method and analysis, but the inclusion of only gay participants limits its generalizability.

Psychological Well-Being

As with physical health, there is mixed evidence about the buffering influence of religion against psychological distress among the bereaved, particularly on depressive symptoms. Part of the reason for the interpretive dilemma was the inconsistency on how religious coping was measured. When operationalized as a belief in the afterlife, religious coping was generally associated with positive outcomes on mood among the bereaved. For example, a belief in the afterlife was found to have a significant and negative relationship to depressive mood among parents following the death of a child (Higgins, 2002). Similarly, a small qualitative study among African American bereaved congregation members ($N = 9$) suggested that believing in the prospects of seeing the deceased again may be comforting and in turn decrease significantly the distress associated with bereavement (Abrums, 2000).

Interpretation of results regarding psychological well-being becomes problematic when religious coping was measured in some other ways. Both Easterling, Gamino, Sewell, and Stirman (2000) and Sherkat and Reed (1992) found that religious participation and church attendance had no main effect on grief and depression among the bereaved. Among Australian respondents, belief in Christianity's helpfulness for buffering grief rather than the extent of one's knowledge of Christian doctrine was sufficient to moderate the effects of bereavement on depression and hopelessness (Austin & Lennings, 1993). Mixed results in the extant literature may reflect an insensitivity to the variability within groups of religiously involved bereaved respondents. Specifically, widows and widowers who considered religious involvement as a means to an end rather than as intrinsically valuable reported significantly more depression in one study (Rosik, 1989).

A number of studies have shown a positive effect on psychological well-being of religious social support during bereavement. For example, accessibility to religious support for widows and widowers (Fry, 2001) and for family members of homicide victims (Thompson & Vardaman, 1997) as well as more frequent attendance at religious services by those who have experienced the death of a child (Bohannon, 1991; Higgins, 2002; Thearle et al., 1995) were associated with less distress and depressive symptomatology. In addition, when bereaved parents ($N = 124$) were followed postbereavement, those who attended religious services more frequently perceived themselves as having greater levels of social support and reported more positive affect (McIntosh et al., 1993).

These outcomes may be associated with either the subjective perception that sufficient support is available or the instrumental support that is actually afforded by the religious community—either of which may decrease withdrawal and feelings of isolation. Therefore, the main challenge is to isolate the comfort-seeking (or alienation-inducing) religious impulses and behaviors associated with coping per se from other dimensions of social interaction in the context of bereavement loss. Furthermore, religiousness that is oriented more toward gaining support and comfort without an orientation toward valuing faith as its own reward may yield relatively fewer benefits to the bereaved individual who faces the loneliness and discomforts of the loss of a loved one. Participation in religious services, therefore, may be more adaptive only to the extent that it is coupled with higher levels of intrinsic experiential religiousness.

In a randomized clinical intervention (Azhar & Varma, 1995), Islamic religious psychotherapy in addition to an antidepressant were offered to 15 depressed patients who had just lost a loved one, and this group was compared with a control group ($n = 15$) that was offered only an antidepressant. The emphases of the religious psychotherapy included eliciting thoughts and ideas associated with participants' emotions followed by discussions of verses found in the Koran and Hadith and encouraging prayers in the group. Researchers observed a significant improvement in depressive symptoms in the study group compared with the control group on Days 30, 90, and 180 postbereavement (Azhar & Varma, 1995). However, there was also a considerable improvement in depressive symptoms in the control group at all follow-up time points, although at a much slower pace. Further investigation on the value of adding a religious component to the psychotherapy of bereaved individuals is therefore needed.

Meaning-Making

People do not face stressful life events without bringing with them a system of general beliefs and practices that affect how they deal and cope with the situation (Pargament et al., 1992). Religion is frequently part of this general orienting system and is often used to derive meaning or some explanation for the loss of a loved one to give a sense of order and purpose to his or her existence and death (Golsworthy & Coyle, 1999). Religious individuals may be more prepared than less religious persons to impose satisfactory meaning on a negative event such as bereavement. In general, those who search for meaning were observed to experience a greater degree of emotional distress than those who do not (Golsworthy & Coyle, 1999).

When 9 individuals who held Christian beliefs were interviewed after the death of a partner, the importance of religious faith was a primary theme relating to understanding and coping with their loss (Golsworthy & Coyle, 1999). A key element of their religious faith was the nature of their relationship or connection with God, which imbued the person and the event with purpose and meaning. As 1 participant said in a study that explored the grieving experience among deeply religious church members, "No one's life is lived in vain; and thus, even when someone was murdered, there was a purpose and meaning to this—perhaps to awaken someone else" (Abrums, 2000, p. 138). In another study, respondents concluded that their mothers were now in God's hands and that God was now taking better care of their mothers than they could. Such meaning-making assisted 30 African American middle-aged daughters to cope with the deaths of their mothers (S. H. Smith, 2002).

Religion may particularly enhance a parent's ability to transcend the human limitations found in the death of his or her child (Klass, 1999). Religious coping was central to meaning-making among bereaved parents in several studies. In one study, the greater the importance of religion in the parents' lives, the more they reported finding meaning in the loss of their child to sudden infant death syndrome (McIntosh et al., 1993). Use of religious coping strategies, such as seeking God's help and praying more than usual, were significant predictors of finding meaning among parents 5 years after the sudden death of a child by accident, suicide, or homicide (Murphy & Johnson, 2003). In the same study, finding meaning in the sudden deaths of their children was associated with reports of less mental distress and better self-rated health; however, the exact mechanism by which religious coping may have an impact on finding meaning was not clearly elucidated.

Among bereaved adolescents, loss of a sibling can be especially challenging to frameworks of belief in God. In a qualitative study of meaning-making among adolescents who had recently lost a sibling, intensified positive and negative perspectives on a "higher power" emerged. Some found that their religious beliefs increased, and others expressed a new anger at God (Batten & Oltjenbruns, 1999). As 1 teenager said, "I don't care now about sinning and stuff like that . . . I guess it is my way of getting back at God" (Batten & Oltjenbruns, 1999, p. 542). In another retrospective, cross-sectional study of 42 adolescents who had lost siblings and were living in several U.S. cities, researchers reported similar inconclusive results: Grief reactions were similar among teenagers who did and did not report religious coping after the deaths of their siblings (Balk, 1991). These studies suggest that negative meanings may occur with the use of religious coping, most especially when the bereaved person tries to reconcile a belief in God's goodness with the fact of a dreadful event, such as the loss of a loved one. However, as Batten and Oltjenbruns (1999) discussed, studies of the role of religion in bereavement among adolescents should be interpreted with care, because this age group is characterized by emerging cognitive abilities and, during adolescence, religious values and beliefs begin to be clarified, with potentially confounding results.

Adjustment

A number of studies have examined perceived adjustment following bereavement using a variety of ways of measuring adjustment, including lower levels of grief and an improved sense of well-being. Five of these studies included repeated measures over time (Brown, Nesse, House, & Utz, 2004; Coleman, McKiernan, Mills, & Speck, 2002; McIntosh et al., 1993; Richards & Folkman, 1997; Walsh, King, Jones, Tookman, & Blizard, 2002) and therefore were able to examine adaptation over time. In one such study (McIntosh et al., 1993), parents of infants who had died of sudden infant death syndrome showed better adjustment to the loss 18 months later in a cascade of effects that included more importance ascribed to religion and more religious participation, more cognitive processing and short-term distress, more social support, more satisfactory meaning-making about the death, more affect balance, and fewer symptoms of distress. Across these and other studies, respondents who professed stronger religious and spiritual beliefs generally reported more rapid grief resolution and more personal growth than those with weak or no spiritual beliefs (Brown et al., 2004; Coleman et al., 2002; Gamino et al., 2000; Park & Cohen, 1993; Walsh et al., 2002).

Longitudinal findings were consonant with evidence from cross-sectional studies, that is, that respondents perceived that religiousness had contributed positively to adaptation to their losses. For example, bereaved family members simultaneously reported higher levels of spiritual experience (as measured by the Index of Core Spiritual Experience; Kass, Friedman, Leserman, Zuttermeister, & Benson, 1991) with less grief-related affect at 18 months postbereavement (Easterling et al., 2000). Of interest is that church attendance also appears to be associated with more positive grief outcomes, mainly when attendance is coincident with spiritual experience.

Walsh et al. (2002) suggested a possible explanation for the findings that religious beliefs enhance adjustment to the death of a loved one. Most religious–spiritual beliefs contain tenets that explain the course of human existence and what occurs beyond it, and these beliefs may provide an existential framework in which the bereaved may understand one's personal life story and use it to resolve grief more readily. In further support of this hypothesis, a belief in the afterlife was shown to enhance bereavement recovery among 121 bereaved persons whose strong belief in an afterlife was associated with greater recovery from bereavement (P. C. Smith et al., 1992). Those who believed strongly in an afterlife were less likely to avoid thinking about the death, which perhaps enabled them to dedicate more time and energy for recovery and find some meaning in the loss.

As noted earlier in this chapter, conclusions concerning the role of religion in coping with bereavement remain elusive because study designs generally lack rigor. The challenges to researchers in this area, as outlined by Stroebe (2004), are particularly daunting. Only three studies (Brown et al., 2004; Krause et al., 2002; Thearle et al., 1995) have included a comparison group of nonbereaved participants, allowing for a distinction to be made between general effects of religiousness and those related specifically to grief experiences. All of these studies based their analyses on well-characterized population-based samples, specifically, married adults in Detroit (Brown et al., 2004), Japanese elders (Krause et al., 2002), and Australian parents (Thearle et al., 1995). However, the outcome measures likely lacked some validity and reliability because researchers often cherry-picked subsets of items from established scales, thus diminishing the reader's ability to evaluate psychometric properties. In the one of these studies, which focused on a physical health outcome (Krause et al., 2002), hypertension was self-reported, as is typical in population surveys, but this measurement strategy does introduce the potential for error when one study group is stressed by bereavement and the comparison group is not. In none of these studies did the operationalization of religious coping use well-researched religious coping scales. Confounding variables, such as social support and personality, were controlled to various degrees, including being uncontrolled (Thearle et al., 1995), crudely controlled as marital status (Krause et al., 2002), and well controlled (Brown et al., 2004). Although none of these three studies met all of Stroebe's criteria, they provide worthy methodological standards for future researchers interested in physical and psychological health and overall adjustment following bereavement.

With these strengths and limitations in mind, one may draw some tentative and narrowly focused conclusions from these studies. Belief in an afterlife demonstrated a robust protective dose–response effect on hypertension among bereaved Japanese elders (Krause et al., 2002) and represents a potentially valuable protective factor for future attention in cross-cultural studies. In a U.S. urban sample, bereavement strengthened the respondents' subjective belief in the importance of religion in the early months after the death and, in a cascading effect, showed a sustained protective effect on grief feelings until 2 years after the death, with particularly strong buffering effects among initially insecure widows and widowers at the 1-year anniversary of the death (Brown et al., 2004). In this same sample of spouses as well as among Australian parents

(Thearle et al., 1995), bereavement had a nonsignificant effect on church attendance. Overall, far more nuanced and rigorous studies are required before this complex biopsychosocial phenomenon will yield to valid generalizations, even for religious and population subgroups.

Role of Religion in Caring for the Bereaved

Much has been written about the salutary effects of religion in the lives of medically ill patients and their loved ones, especially during the terminal phase of life (for an overview, see Koenig, McCullough, & Larson, 2001; Ano & Vasconcelles, 2005). How relevant findings from these studies can be drawn out to affect the way care is provided to the bereaved is still in evolution. Mainstream mental health practitioners continue to support faith and religious coping for bereaved individuals only infrequently (Koenig, Bearon, Hover, & Travis, 1991) or around the time of death (Feudtner, Haney, & Dimmers, 2003). Three possible reasons exist. First, many psychotherapeutic systems still lack a conceptual framework within which to address religious issues, which may lead to avoidance of issues by practitioners and a lack of knowledge and guidance for work in these areas (Golsworthy & Coyle, 2001). Second, there are a few reports of negative health outcomes associated with religious involvement (for a discussion, see George, Ellison, & Larson, 2002); thus, full commitment to this idea from practitioners is lukewarm. Third, religious beliefs held by patients and their families are often different from those held by practitioners. A study conducted by Koenig et al. (1991) revealed that only 9% of physicians surveyed believed that religious coping was the most important factor enabling individuals to cope, compared with 44% of patients, 56% of families, and 26% of nurses. Many physicians also worry about overstepping ethical boundaries when they use religion in providing care (Koenig, George, & Titus, 2004).

People who have just lost a significant person are at high risk for psychological dysfunction and thus deserve careful attention from care providers. Specifically, the following are individuals who exhibit intense distress shortly after the death: people who experience the loss under traumatic circumstances, spouses with a disordered attachment history and who had a stabilizing relationship with their deceased partner, and people who lose any identity-defining relationship when the loved one dies (Davis, Wortman, Lehman, & Silver, 2000). Furthermore, parents who have experienced the loss of a child are at higher risk for depression over the course of their lifetime than the general population (Higgins, 2002). Evidence shows that if the bereaved are going to talk to any professional person about their bereavement, they will tend to seek out their clergyperson or physician (Davis et al., 2000). In a single experimental study of grieving patients diagnosed with major depressive disorder, the clinical intervention group was offered antidepressant treatment and weekly religious psychotherapy that involved discussion of religious topics and

Scripture and encouragement of prayer. Compared with control participants who were offered medication and traditional psychotherapy, the intervention group reported fewer depressive symptoms at 1, 3, and 6 months (Azhar & Varma, 1995).

Pastoral care providers are important sources of spiritual support for the bereaved in health care settings. However, access to formal pastoral services is often controlled by health care professionals and unfortunately is especially neglected in hospital settings. A recent survey of hospital chaplains revealed that they are being called to visits with patients and families only when death is imminent to provide the spiritual care that could have helped (Feudtner et al., 2003). When viewed as an alternative practice and complementary adjunct to conventional medical care, the role of spiritual and religious providers of care in acute clinical practice remains largely untapped. Conversely, when family physicians were surveyed, the results revealed that more than 76% referred or recommended their dying patients and their families to clergy and pastoral care providers (Daaleman & Frey, 1998). The outcomes of such referrals are unknown because research about this area is virtually nonexistent. However, as Koenig (2002) pointed out, a more pressing question to ask is, "What is the religious community doing now that facilitates dying, death, and bereavement besides conducting funeral services?" (p. 22). Because there is preliminary evidence of the positive role that religion may play during bereavement (as described earlier), the role of pastoral care providers during these stressful times cannot be ignored.

The general implication for counselors working with bereaved spouses is that they must find ways to stimulate personal meaning-making or deepening purpose for life in order to promote psychological well-being (Fry, 2001). Having a ready assessment strategy for gauging the extent of the person's religious beliefs and experience so that counselors can commence with strategies to assist the bereaved person deal with the tragedy may be useful. Bereavement group sessions have been found to be helpful for some individuals; for example, parents who attended a bereavement support group after losing their child were found to be 4 times more likely to find meaning in their loss (Murphy & Johnson, 2003). In another study, couples who lost an infant consistently reported that attending the bereavement group specifically aided in learning how to tolerate the grief and pain of their loss (Reilly-Smorawski, Armstrong, & Catlin, 2002). Group facilitators should be trained to maximize the adaptive function of religious behaviors and beliefs among individual group members as well as to help members with differing beliefs to respect and support each other.

Several strategies that may be helpful in planning how to use religion in caring for the bereaved are include the following:

- Simply asking bereaved individuals whether and how they use religion to help them cope will provide a sense of how they give meaning and understand their grieving.

- Involving a chaplain or clergyperson as an integral part of the health care team will allow religious issues to be addressed promptly.
- Proactive efforts to understand the spiritual worldviews of traditions common among one's patients will help clinicians avoid insensitivity and bias.
- Prescribing one's own religious practices and beliefs is inappropriate in most circumstances.
- Finding out what family members believe about the nature of death and the required rituals that surround it because failure to carry out death rituals contributes to the experience of unresolved loss.

SUMMARY AND RECOMMENDATIONS

The research and treatment community's understanding of the nature and outcomes of religious coping in the bereavement experience is underdeveloped, although significant groundwork has been laid. Urgently needed are larger and prospective studies conceived in the context of a theoretical framework, testable hypotheses, and psychometrically sound measures. Researchers are urged to consider the developmental aspects of research in this area: How does the interaction of religious experience and bereavement differ across the life span, and what is the impact of religious coping on bereavement over time? Demographic trends in Western societies—aging populations, shrinking families, growth of megachurches, and secularization of the culture—coupled with the growth of radical fundamentalism in developing societies suggest period effects that will make such research complex but critical. Regardless of the state of our systematic understanding of religious coping and bereavement, professional service providers will be called on to support families and friends who have sustained a loss in ways that are sensitive and open-minded and to help them find access from whomever they seek out. This challenge underscores the importance of this topic for clinical research and education.

REFERENCES

Abrums, M. (2000). Death and meaning in a storefront church. *Public Health Nursing, 17*, 132–142.

Ano, G. G., & Vasconcelles, E. B. (2005). Religious coping and psychological adjustment to stress: A meta-analysis. *Journal of Clinical Psychology, 61*, 461–480.

Austin, D., & Lennings, C. J. (1993). Grief and religious belief: Does belief moderate depression? *Death Studies, 17*, 487–496.

Azhar, M. Z., & Varma, S. L. (1995). Religious psychotherapy as management of bereavement. *Acta Psychiatrica Scandinavica, 91,* 233–235.

Balk, D. E. (1991). Sibling death, adolescent bereavement, and religion. *Death Studies, 15,* 1–20.

Batten, M., & Oltjenbruns, K. A. (1999). Adolescent sibling bereavement as a catalyst for spiritual development: A model for understanding. *Death Studies, 23,* 529–546.

Bohannon, J. R. (1991). Religiosity related to grief levels of bereaved mothers and fathers. *Omega: The Journal of Death and Dying, 23,* 153–159.

Brown, S. L., Nesse, R. M., House, J. S., & Utz, R. L. (2004). Religion and emotional compensation: Results from a prospective study of widowhood. *Personality and Social Psychology Bulletin, 30,* 1165–1174.

Coleman, P. G., McKiernan, F., Mills, M., & Speck, P. (2002). Spiritual belief and quality of life: The experience of older bereaved spouses. *Quality in Ageing, 3,* 20–26.

Daaleman, T. P., & Frey, B. (1998). Prevalence and patterns of physician referral to clergy and pastoral care providers. *Archives of Family Medicine, 7,* 548–553.

Davis, C. G., Wortman, C. B., Lehman, D. R., & Silver, R. C. (2000). Searching for meaning in loss: Are clinical assumptions correct? *Death Studies, 24,* 497–540.

deVries, B. (1997). Kinship bereavement in later life: Understanding variations in cause, course, and consequence. *Omega: The Journal of Death and Dying, 35,* 141–157.

Doka, K. J. (1996). *Living with grief after sudden loss: Suicide, homicide, accident, heart attack, stroke.* Washington, DC, and Philadelphia: Hospice Foundation of America and Taylor & Francis.

Dorff, E. N. (2005). End-of-life: Jewish perspectives. *The Lancet, 366,* 862–865.

Easterling, L. W., Gamino, L. A., Sewell, K. W., & Stirman, L. S. (2000). Spiritual experience, church attendance, and bereavement. *Journal of Pastoral Care, 54,* 263–275.

Engelhardt, H. T. J., & Iltis, A. S. (2005). End-of-life: The traditional Christian view. *The Lancet, 366,* 1045–1049.

Feudtner, C., Haney, J., & Dimmers, M. A. (2003). Spiritual care needs of hospitalized children and their families: A national survey of pastoral care providers' perceptions. *Pediatrics, 111,* e67–e72.

Firth, S. (2005). End-of-life: A Hindu view. *The Lancet, 366,* 682–686.

Flannelly, K. J., Weaver, A. J., & Costa, K. G. (2004). A systematic review of religion and spirituality in three palliative care journals, 1990–1999. *Journal of Palliative Care, 20,* 50–56.

Folkman, S. (2001). Revised coping theory and the process of bereavement. In M. S. Stroebe, R. O. Hansson, W. Stroebe, & H. Schut (Eds.), *Handbook of bereavement research: Consequences, coping, and care* (pp. 563–584.) Washington, DC: American Psychological Association.

Fry, P. S. (2001). The unique contribution of key existential factors to the prediction of psychological well-being of older adults following spousal loss. *The Gerontologist, 41,* 69–81.

Gamino, L. A., Sewell, K. W., & Easterling, L. W. (2000). Scott and White Grief Study—Phase 2: Toward an adaptive model of grief. *Death Studies, 24*, 633–660.

Gatrad, A. R. (1994). Muslim customs surrounding death, bereavement, postmortem examinations, and organ transplants. *British Medical Journal, 309*, 521–523.

George, L. K., Ellison, C. G., & Larson, D. B. (2002). Explaining the relationships between religious involvement and health. *Psychological Inquiry, 13*, 190–200.

Golsworthy, R., & Coyle, A. (1999). Spiritual beliefs and the search for meaning among older adults following partner loss. *Mortality, 4*, 21–40.

Golsworthy, R., & Coyle, A. (2001). Practitioners' accounts of religious and spiritual dimension in bereavement therapy. *Counselling Psychology Quarterly, 14*, 183–202.

Higgins, M. P. (2002). Parental bereavement and religious factors. *Omega: The Journal of Death and Dying, 45*, 187–207.

Hill, P. C., & Pargament, K. I. (2003). Advances in the conceptualization and measurement of religion and spirituality: Implications for physical and mental health research. *American Psychologist, 58*, 64–74.

Janoff-Bulman, R. (1992). *Shattered assumptions: Towards a new psychology of trauma.* New York: Free Press.

Kass, J. D., Friedman, R., Leserman, J., Zuttermeister, P. C., & Benson, H. (1991). Health outcomes and a new index of spiritual experiences. *Journal for the Scientific Study of Religion, 30*, 203–211.

Keown, D. (2005). End of life: The Buddhist view. *The Lancet, 366*, 952–955.

Klass, D. (1999). *The spiritual lives of bereaved parents.* Philadelphia: Brunner/Mazel.

Koenig, H. G. (Ed.). (1998). *Handbook of religion and mental health.* San Diego, CA: Academic Press.

Koenig, H. G. (2002). A commentary: The role of religion and spirituality at the end of life. *The Gerontologist, 42*, 20–23.

Koenig, H. G., Bearon, L. B., Hover, M., & Travis, J. L., III. (1991). Religious perspectives of doctors, nurses, patients, and families. *Journal of Pastoral Care, 45*, 254–267.

Koenig, H. G., George, L. K., & Titus, P. (2004). Religion, spirituality, and health in medically ill hospitalized older patients. *Journal of the American Geriatrics Society, 52*, 554–562.

Koenig, H. G., McCullough, M. E., & Larson, D. B. (2001). *Handbook of religion and health.* London: Oxford University Press.

Koenig, H. G., Pargament, K. I., & Nielsen, J. (1998). Religious coping and health status in medically ill hospitalized older adults. *Journal of Nervous and Mental Disease, 186*, 513–521.

Krause, N., Liang, J., Shaw, B. A., Sugisawa, H., Kim, H. K., & Sugihara, Y. (2002). Religion, death of a loved one, and hypertension among older adults in Japan. *Journals of Gerontology Series B: Psychological Sciences and Social Sciences, 57*, S96–S107.

Marrone, R. (1999). Dying, mourning, and spirituality: A psychological perspective. *Death Studies, 23*, 495–519.

McIntosh, D. N., Silver, R. C., & Wortman, C. B. (1993). Religion's role in adjustment to a negative life event: Coping with the loss of a child. *Journal of Personality and Social Psychology, 65*, 812–821.

Michael, S. T., Crowther, M. R., Schmid, B., & Allen, R. S. (2003). Widowhood and spirituality: Coping responses to bereavement. *Journal of Women & Aging, 15*, 145–165.

Murphy, S. A., & Johnson, L. C. (2003). Finding meaning in a child's violent death: A five-year prospective analysis of parents' personal narratives and empirical data. *Death Studies, 27*, 381–404.

Oram, D., Bartholomew, K., & Landolt, M. (2004). Coping with multiple AIDS-related loss among gay men. *Journal of Gay & Lesbian Social Services, 16*, 59–72.

Pargament, K. I. (1999). Religious/spiritual coping. In John E. Fetzer Institute (Ed.), *Multidimensional measurement of religiousness/spirituality for use in health research: A report of the Fetzer Institute/National Institute on Aging Working Group* (pp. 43–56). Kalamazoo, MI: John E. Fetzer Institute.

Pargament, K. I., Kennell, J., Hathaway, W., Grevengoed, N., Newman, J., & Jones, W. (1988). Religion and the problem-solving process: Three styles of coping. *Journal for the Scientific Study of Religion, 27*, 90–104.

Pargament, K. I., Olsen, H., Reilly, B., Falgout, K., Ensing, D. S., & Van Haitsma, K. (1992). God help me (II): The relationship of religious orientations to religious coping with negative life events. *Journal for the Scientific Study of Religion, 31*, 504–513.

Pargament, K. I., & Park, C. L. (1997). In times of stress: The religion–coping connection. In B. Spilka & D. N. McIntosh (Eds.), *The psychology of religion: Theoretical approaches* (pp. 43–53). Boulder, CO: Westview Press.

Park, C. L., & Cohen, L. H. (1993). Religious and nonreligious coping with the death of a friend. *Cognitive Therapy and Research, 17*, 561–577.

Pearce, M. J., Chen, J., Silverman, G. K., Kasl, S. V., Rosenheck, R., & Prigerson, H. G. (2002). Religious coping, health, and health service use among bereaved adults. *International Journal of Psychiatry in Medicine, 32*, 179–199.

Pennebaker, J. W., Zech, E., & Rimé, B. (2001). Disclosing and sharing emotion: Psychological, social, and health consequences. In M. S. Stroebe, R. O. Hansson, W. Stroebe, & H. Schut (Eds.), *Handbook of bereavement research: Consequences, coping, and care* (pp. 517–544). Washington, DC: American Psychological Association.

Phillips, R. E., III, Pargament, K. I., Lynn, Q. K., & Crossley, C. D. (2004). Self-directing religious coping: A deistic god, abandoning god, or no god at all? *Journal for the Scientific Study of Religion, 43*, 409–418.

Reilly-Smorawski, B., Armstrong, A. V., & Catlin, E. A. (2002). Bereavement support for couples following death of a baby: Program development and 14-year exit analysis. *Death Studies, 26*, 21–37.

Richards, T. A., & Folkman, S. (1997). Spiritual aspects of loss at the time of a partner's death from AIDS. *Death Studies, 21*, 527–552.

Robinson, J. H. (1995). Grief responses, coping processes, and social support of widows: Research with Roy's model. *Nursing Science Quarterly, 8*, 158–164.

Rodgers, L. S. (2004). Meaning of bereavement among older African American widows. *Geriatric Nursing, 25*, 10–16.

Rosik, C. H. (1989). The impact of religious orientation in conjugal bereavement among older adults. *International Journal of Aging and Human Development, 28*, 251–260.

Sachedina, A. (2005). End-of-life: The Islamic view. *The Lancet, 366*, 774–779.

Sherkat, D. E., & Reed, M. D. (1992). The effects of religion and social support on self-esteem and depression among the suddenly bereaved. *Social Indicators Research, 26*, 259–275.

Smith, P. C., Range, L. M., & Ulmer, A. (1992). Belief in afterlife as a buffer in suicidal and other bereavement. *Omega: The Journal of Death and Dying, 24*, 217–225.

Smith, S. H. (2002). "Fret no more my child . . . for I'm all over heaven all day": Religious beliefs in the bereavement of African American, middle-aged daughters coping with the death of an elderly mother. *Death Studies, 26*, 309–323.

Sormanti, M., & August, J. (1997). Parental bereavement: Spiritual connections with deceased children. *American Journal of Orthopsychiatry, 67*, 460–469.

Stroebe, M. S. (2004). Religion in coping with bereavement: Confidence of convictions or scientific scrutiny? *International Journal for Psychology of Religion, 14*, 23–36.

Stroebe, M. S., & Schut, H. (2001). Models of coping with bereavement: A review. In M. S. Stroebe, R. O. Hansson, W. Stroebe, & H. Schut (Eds.), *Handbook of bereavement research: Consequences, coping, and care* (pp. 375–403). Washington, DC: American Psychological Association.

Thearle, M. J., Vance, J. C., Najman, J. M., Embelton, G., & Foster, W. J. (1995). Church attendance, religious affiliation and parental responses to sudden infant death, neonatal death and stillbirth. *Omega: The Journal of Death and Dying, 31*, 51–58.

Thompson, M. P., & Vardaman, P. J. (1997). The role of religion in coping with the loss of a family member to homicide. *Journal for the Scientific Study of Religion, 36*, 44–51.

Van, P., & Meleis, A. I. (2003). Coping with grief after involuntary pregnancy loss: Perspectives of African American women. *Journal of Obstetric, Gynecologic, & Neonatal Nursing, 32*, 28–39.

Walsh, K., King, M., Jones, L., Tookman, A., & Blizard, R. (2002). Spiritual beliefs may affect outcome of bereavement: Prospective study. *British Medical Journal, 324*, 1551.

Wuthnow, R., Christiano, K., & Kuzlowski, J. (1980). Religion and bereavement: A conceptual framework. *Journal for the Scientific Study of Religion, 19*, 408–422.

17

BEREAVEMENT AND REACTIONS TO ROMANTIC REJECTION: A PSYCHOBIOLOGICAL PERSPECTIVE

JOHN ARCHER AND HELEN FISHER

The links between grief, which is generally associated with the death of a loved one, and the similar process shown in response to separation from or rejection by a loved one have long been recognized. These links are typically self-evident to biologically oriented researchers and theorists. Perhaps the clearest theoretical framework to link them together is Bowlby's (1958, 1960, 1969) attachment theory. As indicated in other chapters of this volume (e.g., chap. 3), this theory is concerned with "the making and breaking of affectional bonds" (Bowlby, 1979). The "breaking" part is seen to occur through a long and typically painful process of disengagement known as *grief*. From this perspective, grief is only a special case of a wider process that occurs after all forms of separation from a loved one. Some analyses hold that the circumstances leading to grief are wider still, including the loss of nonsocial ties (Parkes, 1971, 1972b). Of course, there is also recognition within attachment theory of differences between separation from (or rejection by) a loved one and the permanent loss through death. Adult humans can usually distinguish these different circumstances, but as Bowlby (1980) suggested, this has not always been the case. The human ancestral environment would have offered instances when a person was missing and it was not clear whether he or she was still alive. A similar situation can occur today in times of war and natural disasters.

Building on Bowlby's evolutionary attachment framework, Archer (1999) argued that the reactions of nonhumans and young children to separation and bereavement will be identical, because they do not understand the permanence of death in the way that adult humans understand it. In humans, a gradual learning about the nature of death occurs (Speece & Brent, 1984), so that adult grief in the context of bereavement can be viewed as having developed from an undifferentiated separation reaction. It will therefore retain many of the features of the generalized separation reaction, along with more specific features associated with the acknowledgment of the permanence of the loss. Similarities have often been noted between many of the reactions shown to separation from or rejection by a loved one and bereavement (Archer, 1999; Bowlby, 1973, 1980; Panksepp, 1998).

Many examples from other times and places illustrate the generality of the mental pain experienced under these circumstances. A 16th-century Aztec Indian left these melancholy words: "Now I know why my father would go out and cry in the dark" (Alarcon, 1992, p. 110). Up the Sepik River in New Guinea, romantically rejected men compose tragic love songs they call *namai*, songs about marriages that might have been (Harrison, 1986). Edna St. Vincent Millay may have expressed the despair of romantic rejection most vividly, writing, "Sweet love, sweet thorn, when lightly to my heart/ I took your thrust, whereby I since am slain,/ And lie disheveled in the grass apart,/ A sodden thing bedrenched by tears and rain" (Millay, 1988, p. 86).

Because romantic love is a cross-culturally universal human experience (Jankowiak & Fischer, 1992), one would expect that when things go wrong, almost no one in the world will escape the feelings of protest, hopelessness, fear, and fury that abandonment can create (Baumeister & Dhavale, 2001). A study of North American college students documented how common such experiences are among young adults in a modern Western nation: Baumeister, Wotman, and Stillwell (1993) found that 93% of participants of both sexes reported that they had been spurned by someone they passionately loved, and 95% said they had rejected someone who was deeply in love with them.

In view of the commonplace nature of feelings of romantic rejection and their similarity to those experienced following bereavement, we present some recent psychobiological research involving the neural mechanisms underlying this state and then compare these findings with those from a preliminary study of bereavement. This research involves the relatively new but widely used technique of *functional magnetic resonance imaging* (fMRI), which allows researchers to observe areas of brain activation when an individual is performing different activities or attending to different stimuli. It involves the use of a magnetic resonance imaging scanner, set up to measure the increased blood flow to the activated areas of the brain on the fMRI scans. The final images from the process show the areas of the brain that were activated by the particular procedure used in the study, for example, looking at an emotion-inducing image or thinking about a loved one. It is important to bear in mind that there is generally activity throughout the brain during these procedures and that studies typically select specific regions of interest.

Similarities between the processes involved following bereavement and romantic rejection raise the possibility that studies of rejection have implications for bereavement. However, romantic rejection may have psychological and social consequences that differ from those associated with bereavement—for example, loss of social networks and often sustained stressful interactions with the abandoning partner.

Although the attachment framework can encompass a wide range of social losses, the motivational systems underlying different types of relationships are different. The classic ethological concept of a *motivational system* or *instinct* (Baerends, 1976; Tinbergen, 1951) distinguishes between the different control systems that underlie different types of biologically important relationships, for example, between a parent and offspring or between *pair-bonds* (committed sexual partners). Similarly, in discussing the social behavior of primates, Harlow and Harlow (1965) referred to different affectional systems that underlie different types of relationships, for example, the infant–mother relationship and the relationship between sexual partners. Despite their differences in motivational control and in ultimate function, these systems all have in common a similar set of responses that are set in motion by situations involving separation and whose function is to regain contact with the lost loved one.

The motivational mechanisms controlling each of these affectional bonds can be elaborated into further component parts. For example, in relation to the sexual affectional system, Fisher (1998) proposed that *Homo sapiens* (and other mammalian and avian species that form pair bonds) have evolved three overlapping brain systems for courtship, mating, and parenting, respectively: (a) the sex drive, (b) attraction, and (c) long-term attachment. The sex drive (*libido* or *lust*) is characterized by the craving for sexual gratification and is often directed toward a range of individuals. In mammals, the sex drive is associated primarily with estrogens and androgens; in humans, androgens, particularly testosterone, are central to sexual desire in both men and women (Sherwin, 1994; van Goozen, Wiegant, Endert, Helmond, & Van de Poll, 1997). fMRI studies of human sexual arousal show that activation in specific areas of the brain is associated with sexual arousal (Arnow et al., 2002; Beauregard, Levesque, & Bourgouin, 2001; Karama et al., 2002; Stoléru et al., 1999). Moreover, the brain mechanisms for the sex drive are overlapping yet distinct from those associated with attraction.

Attraction (and its developed form in humans, known as *romantic love, passionate love, obsessive love,* or *being in love*) is characterized in birds and mammals by increased energy, focused attention on a specific mate, obsessive following, affiliative gestures, possessive "mate guarding," and motivation toward a preferred mating partner (Fisher, 2004; Fisher, Aron, Mashek, Strong, & Brown, 2002a, 2002b). In humans, romantic love is also associated with craving; obsessive thinking; the rearrangement of priorities; emotional and physical dependence; sympathetic nervous system reactions, including sweating and a pounding heart; and an intense motivation to obtain (and retain) a particular mating partner. Recent data (discussed later in this chapter) suggest that this brain system primarily engages subcortical dopaminergic pathways in the reward system of the brain.

Long-term attachment between mates is characterized in birds and mammals by mutual territory defense and/or nest building, mutual feeding and grooming, shared parental chores, and affiliative behaviors (Carter et al., 1997; Lim, Murphy, & Young, 2004; Lim & Young, 2004). Like attachments based on other motivational systems, it also involves maintenance of close proximity and separation anxiety. In humans, long-term attachment, known as *companionate love* (Hatfield, 1988, p. 191), is also associated with feelings of calmness, security, social comfort, and emotional union with a long-term partner. Animal studies suggest that this brain system primarily engages oxytocin and vasopressin in the nucleus accumbens and ventral pallidum, respectively (Lim et al., 2004; Lim & Young, 2004).

Each of these primary brain systems has evolved to play a different role in reproduction (Fisher, 1998, 2004; Fisher et al., 2002b). The sex drive serves to motivate animals to seek coitus with a range of appropriate partners. Romantic love (and its less developed mammalian and avian form, attraction) evolved to motivate individuals to prefer and focus their courtship attention on a specific mating partner, thereby conserving courtship time and energy and facilitating the choice of a long-term partner with features associated with biological fitness. Long-term attachment evolved primarily to motivate individuals to sustain an affiliative connection with this mate at least long enough to complete parental duties.

It would seem that most men and women bereaved by the death of a long-term partner are primarily experiencing disruption of their long-term attachment system, whereas romantically rejected individuals are suffering from disruption of the brain system for romantic love. However, there are exceptions to this generalization. First, some deaths occur relatively early in a couple's relationship, and many apparently stable romantic relationships break up after the couple have spent considerable time together, often because of rejection by one partner. Second, the brain areas underlying initial sexual interest, romantic attraction, and longer term attachment are likely to interact in complex ways to produce the cognitions, emotions, motivations, and behaviors associated with human pair bonding; thus, disruption in any one system is likely to affect the other two related systems (Fisher, 2004; Fisher & Thomson, 2006). Moreover, the brain is likely to use these and other primary systems for multiple purposes. It is therefore possible that rejected men and women and grieving individuals engage similar neural networks to generate and express their similar feelings of protest, anger, despair, and resignation.

In the remainder of this chapter, we explore some current neurological evidence on individuals who are happily in love to support the view that human romantic love is controlled by a basic and powerful mating drive. We then discuss some of the neural correlates of rejection in love and compare these with findings from an fMRI study of bereaved individuals. We have argued earlier in this chapter that grief can be viewed mainly as the response to a severed attachment, whereas a "broken heart" may be the psychobiological response to severed romantic love. We also acknowledge that there will be overlaps between the two processes, for example, if the loved one dies in the romantic phase. Furthermore, both responses may involve similar neural mechanisms, including those underlying the specific aspects of the separation reactions and the grief process, such as anger, anxiety and panic, depression, and despair, because it is likely that these reactions will be common to a range of different types of relationship.

THE BIOLOGY OF ROMANTIC LOVE

Romantic love has been associated with a discrete constellation of emotions, motivations, and behavior (Hatfield & Sprecher, 1986; Liebowitz, 1983; Tennov, 1979). It begins as an individual comes to regard another as special, unique. The lover intensely focuses his or her attention on this preferred individual, aggrandizing the beloved's better traits and overlooking or minimizing his or her flaws. Lovers experience extreme energy. They feel euphoria when things go well and mood swings into despair when things go poorly. When they are apart, they experience *separation anxiety*, a prototype of the grief reaction (Archer, 1999; Bowlby, 1973, 1980). In fact, adversity heightens their passion, in a phenomenon known as the *Romeo and Juliet effect* or *frustration attraction* (Fisher, 2004).

Infatuated men and women also become emotionally and physically dependent on the relationship. Many change their habits and priorities, even their appearance, to win the beloved. Most feel powerful empathy for their amour; in fact, many report they would die for their beloved. Lovers are strongly motivated to win the beloved. A striking property of romantic love is *intrusive thinking*, in which the lover thinks obsessively about the beloved. This is also a feature of grief, although in this case intrusive thoughts are typically associated with distress because they bring the loss to the person's attention. Love-smitten individuals feel intense sexual desire as well as extreme possessiveness, yet their craving for emotional union supersedes their longing for sex. As a result, rejected lovers often go to extraordinary, inappropriate, even dangerous efforts to win back their sweethearts. Often this behavior, termed *stalking*, is unwelcome, distressing, or fear inducing for the one who made the break, and there is now a growing research literature on stalking by an ex-intimate (e.g., Meloy, 1999; Meloy & Fisher, 2005; Sinclair & Frieze, 2000). Many spurned individuals suffer "abandonment rage" and depression as well, culminating in feelings of hopelessness, lethargy, resignation, and despair (Fisher, 2004), reactions that are common to other forms of separation from, or loss of, an attachment figure. Romantic love is involuntary, difficult to control, and often impermanent (Fisher, 2004; Hatfield & Sprecher, 1986; Tennov, 1979).

FUNCTIONAL MAGNETIC RESONANCE IMAGING STUDIES OF ROMANTIC LOVE

The first study using fMRI techniques to investigate the brain activity of people who were in love was conducted by Bartels and Zeki (2000, 2004). Their study involved 6 men and 11 women who reported being "truly, deeply, and madly in love." Brain activation when the participants looked at a photograph of their beloved was compared with brain activation when they looked at photographs of three friends of similar age, sex, and length of friendship. Activity was found in several brain regions, including the posterior cingulate cortex (which is involved in autobiographical memory) and the ventral tegmental area and caudate nucleus.

A subsequent fMRI study conducted by Aron et al. (2005) involved 10 women and 7 men who were specifically chosen as being intensely (and happily) in love. They were recruited by means of a flier beginning with the words "Have you just fallen madly in love?" Participants, whose median age was 21 years, reported being in love for a median of 7 months.

As in Bartels and Zeki's (2000, 2004) study, photographs of the beloved were used because these have been shown to be effective in eliciting feelings of intense romantic love (Mashek, Aron, & Fisher, 2000). The protocol consisted of four tasks presented in an alternating block design. For 30 seconds, participants viewed a photograph of their beloved (positive stimulus); for the next 40 seconds, they performed a countback distraction task, to decrease the carryover effect after they had viewed the positive stimulus; for the next 30 seconds, they viewed a photograph of an emotionally neutral acquaintance (neutral stimulus); and for the final 20 seconds they performed another countback task. The four-part sequence (counterbalanced for order effects) was repeated six times, so the total stimulus protocol was 12 minutes.

Group activation specific to the beloved occurred in several regions, including the right ventral tegmental area (VTA), localized in the region of A10 dopamine cells (Aron et al., 2005). This finding is consistent with findings by Bartels and Zeki (2000, 2004). The VTA is a central region of the mesolimbic pathways in the reward system of the brain (Martin-Soelch et al., 2001; Schultz, 2000) that involves the neurotransmitter dopamine and opioid mechanisms that reduce both physical and social pain (Panksepp, 1998). It is associated with pleasure, general arousal, focused attention, and motivation to pursue and acquire rewards (Delgado, Nystrom, Fissel, Noll, & Fiez, 2000; Elliott, Newman, Longe, & Deakin, 2003; Schultz, 2000). The VTA sends projections to several brain regions, including the caudate nucleus, where (again consistent with Bartels & Zeki's [2000, 2004] findings) group activations were also found, specifically, in the right medial and posterodorsal body (Aron et al., 2005). The caudate plays a role in reward detection and expectation, the representation of goals, and the integration of sensory inputs to prepare for action (e.g., Lauwereyns et al., 2002; Martin-Soelch et al., 2001; Schultz, 2000).

Animal studies have also indicated that regions of the reward system are involved in mate preference, or attraction. When a female, laboratory-raised prairie vole is mated with a male, she forms a distinct preference for him that is associated with a 50% increase of dopamine in the nucleus accumbens, a region of the brain's reward system (Gingrich, Liu, Cascio, Wang, & Insel, 2000). When a dopamine antagonist is injected into the accumbens, the female no longer prefers this partner and begins to prefer the male who is present at the time of the infusion, even if she has not mated with him (Gingrich et al., 2000; Wang et al., 1999). An increase in central dopamine is also associated with mate attraction in female sheep (Fabre-Nys, 1997). In addition to dopamine, opioid mechanisms involving vasopressin are involved in these processes.

These studies suggest that mesolimbic pathways in the reward system of the brain play a role in the pleasurable feelings, focused attention, motivation, and goal-oriented behaviors associated with human romantic love and that this brain system is a developed form of mammalian courtship attraction. The rodent studies also indicate that the neural regions associated with romantic love are distinct from those of the sex drive. Romantic love is likely also to involve activation in other neurotransmitter systems—for example, glutamate in the mesocortical system—because of its role in the release of dopamine in the VTA (Legault & Wise, 1999) and/or its fast signals in the prefrontal cortex regarding reward (Lavin et al., 2005).

These findings suggest that romantic love emanates from brain systems associated with focused attention, intense motivation, and goal-oriented behavior. They support the view that romantic love is a primary mating drive (Fisher, 2004) and can be considered a motivational system designed to enable individuals to build and maintain an intimate relationship with a preferred mating partner (Aron & Aron, 1991; Aron, Paris, & Aron, 1995). From an evolutionary viewpoint, it is necessary for there to be such a mechanism that produces strong initial positive feelings for that specific partner, so that the developing relationship is not subject to disruption whenever the partners are apart (see chap. 3, this volume).

Romantic love shares many of the features of the classic characterization of appetitive motivational systems by ethologists (Baerends, 1976; Bowlby, 1969; Tinbergen, 1951). These are arranged hierarchically, with a top-level goal: In the case of romantic love, this involves continued and maintained contact with the beloved, accompanied by rewarding emotions, such as joy. This top-level goal is tenacious and is not dependent on underlying emotions, which dissipate or change far more rapidly. Like all primary appetitive motivations, romantic love is exceedingly difficult to control, and it is associated with elevated activity of subcortical dopaminergic pathways.

Romantic love would appear to provide a considerably stronger motivation than the sex drive. Few men and women whose sexual advances are rejected go on to kill themselves or someone else, whereas rejected lovers across the world commit suicide or homicide (Meloy & Fisher, 2005); many more become depressed. In a study of 114 Americans who had been romantically rejected in the past 8 weeks, 40% were clinically depressed, and 12% suffered moderate to severe depression (Mearns, 1991). These data suggest that those grieving men and women who have feelings of intense romantic love for their deceased partner are likely to go through profound emotional and physical pain at their loss. Studies of rejection in love also support this hypothesis.

FUNCTIONAL MAGNETIC RESONANCE IMAGING STUDIES OF REJECTION IN LOVE

A second study by Fisher et al. (2005) used fMRI to study 10 women and 5 men who were still very much in love but had recently been rejected by their romantic partner. These participants, whose mean length of time since rejection was 63 days, were recruited by means of a flier that read "Have you just been rejected in love, but can't let go?" The positive–neutral contrast (i.e., the difference between reactions to a photo of the romantic partner and that of an emotionally neutral acquaintance) showed significant effects in the right nucleus accumbens–ventral pallidum–putamen (A-VP-P) region, the lateral orbitofrontal cortex, and the anterior insular–operculum cortex.

Other studies have shown that the first of these, the A-VP-P region, becomes more active as an individual chooses a high-risk investment associated with big gains or big losses (Kuhnen & Knutson, 2005) or anticipates a monetary reward (Zald et al., 2004). This region is also part of the dopaminergic reward system. The second region where activity was found, the lateral orbitofrontal cortex, has been associated with *theory of mind* (Vollm et al., 2005), which involves the tendency to view others as intentional agents like oneself. This brain region is also associated with obsessive–compulsive behaviors (Evans, Lewis, & Iobst, 2004) and controlling anger (Goldstein et al., 2005).

The third region where activity was found, the anterior insular–operculum cortex, has been associated with skin and muscle pain and with anxiety (Schreckenberger et al., 2005).

These results are based on a small sample and therefore should be regarded as preliminary. They suggest that the dopaminergic reward system remains active in recently romantically rejected men and women, but the precise location of activity differs from that of men and women who are happily in love. These results also suggest that neural regions associated with taking risks for big gains or losses, physical pain, obsessive–compulsive behaviors, ruminating on the intentions and actions of the rejecter, evaluating options, and controlling anger all increase their activity when someone is rejected by a beloved.

One should, however, be cautious about these findings because a further fMRI study (Najib, Lorberbaum, Kose, Bohning, & George, 2004) found areas of activation different from those found by Fisher et al. (2005) regarding romantic rejection. Najib et al. (2004) studied 9 women who were "actively grieving" over a recent romantic breakup, and in several regions where Fisher et al. found activations, Najib et al. found deactivations. Among these was decreased activity in parts of the dorsal caudate, a brain region rich in receptor sites for dopamine. Because the participants in Fisher et al.'s study regularly reported anger and hope for reconciliation, whereas those in Najib et al.'s study reported resignation and despair, the differences could reflect two fundamentally different but interconnected neural reactions that underlie the processes of separation. We return to this topic at the end of this chapter.

A FUNCTIONAL MAGNETIC RESONANCE IMAGING STUDY OF BEREAVEMENT

Another group of researchers (Gündel, O'Connor, Littrell, Fort, & Lane, 2003) reported the first fMRI study of bereavement, involving 8 female participants, most of whom had lost a parent during the previous year. As in the studies already described, a photograph (in this case of the deceased) was compared with a matched control photograph (of a stranger). In addition, 15 key words associated with the loss were used as alternative grief-related stimuli; these were compared with 15 matched neutral words. The photographs and words were used as composites, so there were four possible combinations: (a) a grief photograph and a grief word, (b) a grief photograph and a neutral word, (c) a neutral photograph and a grief word, and (d) a neutral photograph and a neutral word. The grief-related photographs and words produced higher values than the neutral ones for both a self-report measure of grief and a measure of autonomic arousal (skin conductance).

A wide variety of brain areas were activated by these grief-evoking stimuli, and the overall pattern has both similarities with and differences from the findings for romantic rejection (Gündel et al., 2003). Three brain areas were activated by both the grief-related photographs and words. One strongly activated region was the posterior cingulate cortex, an area known to be associated with autobiographical memories. This area may therefore represent specific memories about the deceased that are evoked by the stimuli and may represent feelings of grief demanding the person's attention (O'Connor, 2005). The posterior cingulate cortex also was activated in Bartels and Zeki's (2000, 2004) study of romantic love. Another of the areas activated by the grief-evoking photographs, the anterior cingulate cortex, is also linked to attention, but it is also activated when significant events in general happen, so it may not be specific to grief-evoking stimuli. Another area, the insula, is connected with information about the person's bodily state. This was also activated in a study involving social rejection by a group of strangers, generated through a computer game (Eisenberger, Lieberman, & Williams, 2003).

There are some common features in the brain areas activated in Gündel et al.'s (2003) study of bereavement and studies involving romantic and social rejection. However, Gündel et al.'s bereavement study involved a small sample composed mainly of people who had lost a parent, which is a different type of relationship than one involving romantic love. We should therefore expect a number of differences in brain activity to arise from these different types of relationships. fMRI research is only beginning to be studied in both areas (i.e., romantic rejection and bereavement). Future studies may provide a clearer picture of the commonalities and differences arising from different types of relationships (e.g., parent–offspring, romantic partner) and different types of loss (i.e., rejection and bereavement).

ABANDONMENT

Many attempts have been made to order the process of grief and separation into a series of stages or phases, beginning with Bowlby's (1961) account of separation distress in children, elaborated later by Bowlby and Parkes (1970). Although longitudinal studies of grief have shown no evidence for these supposed stages (Archer, 1999), researchers in related areas continue to be attracted to the phase view. Lewis, Amini, and Lannon (2000) divided romantic rejection into two phases, corresponding to the middle two of the four phases of grief (Bowlby & Parkes, 1970) and the first two of Bowlby's (1961) three stages of separation. These were (a) *protest* and (b) *despair or resignation*. Lewis et al. stated that during the initial protest phase, abandoned lovers express intense energy, heightened alertness, and extreme motivation to win back their beloved. This has clear similarities with the reactions to separation among young children and animals (Bowlby, 1960, 1973). The participants in the fMRI study of rejected individuals (Fisher et al., 2005) expressed many of these responses as well as reactions characteristic of the supposed second phase, despair. Many of the participants said they also found it difficult to sleep, several said they had lost weight, and some trembled and others sighed as they discussed their sweethearts during the prescanning interview. All reminisced, fixating on the troubled times, searching for clues of what went wrong, and pondering on how to patch up the partnership. All reported that they thought obsessively about their rejecter. These spurned lovers also took extraordinary measures to reconnect with their rejecting partner, revisiting mutual haunts, phoning, writing, and/or e-mailing. Several pleaded for reconciliation or made dramatic entrances and exits into a beloved's home or place of work. Above all, these rejected people yearned for reunion and fixated on the slightest signs of hope. All of these reactions parallel those that are well-known from studies of separation from an attachment figure among primates and young children and are similar to descriptions of the reactions to the death of a loved one, the grief reaction (Archer, 1999; Parkes, 1972a). The behavioral reactions of the rejected lovers in the fMRI study (Fisher et al., 2005) suggest that the dopaminergic reward system of the nucleus A-VP-P region accompanies reactions that are basic to separation from a loved one that have been known since Darwin's (1872/1904) account of these responses in other mammals. The fMRI findings suggest that the neural mechanism activated following rejection is associated with elevated activity of dopamine, because this neurotransmitter produces heightened alertness, energy, and motivation, traits that abandoned creatures exhibit as they call for help and search for the source of their abandonment: their mother, sibling, or mate.

IDEALIZING THE PARTNER AFTER REJECTION

The results of the fMRI study of rejected lovers (Fisher et al., 2005) may also help explain a common reaction to rejection, which has parallels in individuals who have been abandoned through bereavement (Archer, 1999), in which the rejected lover begins to love the rejecting partner even more passionately (Fisher, 2004). When a reward is delayed, reward-expecting neurons in the brain prolong their activity (Schultz, 2000). This sustained activity in the dopaminergic reward system associated with a delayed reward may intensify the feelings of romantic love (Fisher, 2004).

Viewed in isolation, idealization appears maladaptive: Why should someone feel even more intense passion for a beloved who has rejected him or her? However, this response, which is associated with excessive energy, focused attention, extreme motivation, and pronounced goal-oriented behaviors, can be viewed both in terms of attachment theory (Bowlby, 1973) and in terms of Klinger's (1975) disengagement theory (see also chap. 3, this volume) as useful for regaining a beloved (Fisher, 2004). It is understandable from the general viewpoint that both separation and grief reactions are deficit-driven reactions to loss of a loved one, whose function is reunification. As Bowlby (1980) recognized, separation (where the reactions are adaptive) is far more common than death (where they are not), and it was not possible to evolve separate reactions for the two processes (for further discussion of this point, see Archer, 1999; chap. 3, this volume).

ABANDONMENT RAGE

Anger and aggression are well-known reactions to separation and grief (Archer, 1999), and evidence from both laboratory studies and real world contexts has shown that interpersonal rejection in general leads to anger and aggression (Leary, Twenge, & Quinlivan, 2006). We noted earlier that rejected lovers often experience abandonment rage (Meloy, 1999) and, also as indicated previously, the dopaminergic reward system was activated in the fMRI study of rejected lovers (Fisher et al., 2005). Several brain chemicals are likely to be involved in rage, including Substance P, glutamate, and acetylcholine (Panksepp, 1998). High levels of norepinephrine and low levels of serotonin can generate anger. Low levels of serotonin also contribute to the impulsivity that generally accompanies fury (Panksepp, 1998; Tiihonen et al., 1997). Regardless of the neurotransmitters involved, the primary rage system has pathways to regions in the prefrontal cortex that anticipate rewards (Panksepp, 1998). Animal studies indicate that these reward and rage circuits are closely connected. For example, when a cat is petted, it expresses pleasure; when the stimulation is withdrawn, it will often bite (Panksepp, 1998), which is a response to unfulfilled expectations known as *frustration-induced aggression* (Archer, 1976). The fMRI data on rejected lovers suggest that one of the neural regions associated with the response of abandonment rage, a region of the lateral orbitofrontal cortex, is associated in other studies with controlling anger.

Like idealizing a former partner, abandonment rage, when viewed in isolation, appears maladaptive. It increases the heart rate, raises blood pressure, and suppresses the immune system (Dozier, 2002). However, it again can be viewed as functional in the wider context of frustration-induced aggression (Archer, 1976, 1988) or from attachment theory (Bowlby, 1973, 1980), in which it is part of an integrated series of reactions designed to increase the chances of reunification with a loved one. Whether anger and aggression are functional in the specific context of rejection by a loved one is another matter, for which there is little evidence.

LOVE AND ANGER–RAGE

Abandonment rage and idealization of a partner can operate in tandem. Ellis and Malamuth (2000) explored this phenomenon in a study of 124 dating couples and found that romantic love and what they called "anger/upset" were responses to different kinds of events. The degree of anger and upset oscillates in response to situations that undermine the person's goals, such as a partner's infidelity or lack of emotional commitment. Feelings of romantic love fluctuate instead in response to events that advance the person's goals, such as a partner's social support and happy times in bed together. Hence, Ellis and Malamuth reported that romantic love and anger/upset, although closely linked, are independent systems that can operate simultaneously. They may have several biobehavioral similarities, including focused attention, obsessive thinking, heightened energy, intense passion, motivation, and craving (Fisher, 2004). It would be interesting to have more data on the brain mechanisms underlying the two reactions of abandonment rage and idealization. The fMRI study of rejection in love (Fisher et al., 2005) may indicate some of the neural architecture of this dual-affect system, because it found activity in both the subcortical dopaminergic reward system (associated with romantic love) and activity in the lateral orbitofrontal cortex (associated in other studies with controlling anger). Further evidence is required for whether, within the same individual, activation of each of the two areas occurs at the same time as the different behavioral reactions.

SEPARATION ANXIETY AND THE STRESS RESPONSE

Both bereaved and rejected people also show separation anxiety, a phenomenon known from studies of other mammalian and avian species and of humans from early ages onward. When a bird or mammal mother leaves its infant, the infant becomes profoundly disturbed, showing autonomic activation and making distress calls that are frantic and frequent. When infant rats are separated from their mothers, they emit ceaseless ultrasonic cries (Lewis et al., 2000). Panksepp (1998) speculated that separation anxiety is generated by the panic system in the brain, a complex brain network that makes one feel weak, short of breath, and panicky.

Panic emerges from a region in the periaqueductal Gray (PAG), which lies close to regions that generate physical pain, and activity in this brain region sends signals to many other pathways in the panic system. A neuroimaging study indicated that emotional pain induced by computer-generated social exclusion affects some of the same primary brain regions as does physical pain (Eisenberger et al., 2003), indicating that panic can produce symptoms of pain as well. Exactly which neurotransmitters produce feelings of separation anxiety and panic is not known (Pankseep, 1998). More is known about what quells separation anxiety and panic. Opioids, such as morphine, rapidly soothe the distress calls of abandoned animals. Oxytocin, the hormone associated with social attachment and bonding, also decreases separation-induced distress. This may be why animals tend to stop crying when they are touched: Massage activates oxytocin and opioid receptors. It is likely that several brain systems operate together to create panic or separation anxiety, and this may occur in a range of circumstances involving loss, including both bereavement and romantic rejection.

Both bereavement and romantic rejection involve the *stress response*, a reaction common to many aversive events. The stress response begins in the hypothalamus, where corticotropin-releasing hormone is secreted and travels to the nearby pituitary to initiate the release of adrenocorticotropic hormone. Adrenocorticotropic hormone travels via the bloodstream to the adrenal cortex to synthesize and release the stress hormone cortisol, which then activates a range of brain and bodily systems to counteract stress. Among these is the immune system, which is activated to counteract infection (Campbell, Sedikides, & Bossom, 1994; Smith & Hoklund, 1988). Important for this chapter is that short-term stress also triggers production of dopamine and norepinephrine and suppresses serotonin activity (Nemeroff, 1998; Panksepp, 1998), which probably contributes to feelings of romantic love for the lost partner.

RESIGNATION AND DESPAIR

"I am exhausted by longing," wrote the 8th-century AD Chinese poet Li Po. Loss of a loved one usually triggers deep feelings of sadness, hopelessness, and depression in the human animal, known as the *despair response* (Bowlby, 1960, 1973; Panksepp, 1998). In a study of 114 men and women who had been rejected by a romantic partner within the past 8 weeks, more than 40% were experiencing clinically measurable depression; of these, 12% displayed moderate to severe depression (Mearns, 1991). It has been known for a long time that people can die of a broken heart or grief (Burton, 1651/1938; see also Parkes, Benjamin, & Fitzgerald, 1969). They may expire from heart attacks or strokes caused by their depression (Nemeroff, 1998). This reaction of resignation coupled with despair is well documented in other species, too (Bowlby, 1961; Darwin, 1872/1904). For example, abandoned infant monkeys suck their fingers and toes, clasp themselves, and often curl into a fetal position and rock (Harlow & Harlow, 1962).

The despair response has been associated with several different networks in the mammalian brain (Panksepp, 1998), among them the brain's reward system. As the abandoned partner gradually realizes that the reward will never come, the dopaminergic cells in the midbrain (that became active during the protest reaction) now decrease their activity (Schultz, 2000). This produces lethargy, despondency, and depression (Panksepp, 1998). The stress system also contributes to feelings of despair. As mentioned earlier, short-term stress activates the production of dopamine and norepinephrine and suppresses serotonin, but as the stress wears on it suppresses all of these systems below normal, producing profound depression (Nemeroff, 1998; Panksepp, 1998). These findings suggest that resignation and despair after a loss, whether by romantic rejection or death of a spouse, is associated with reduced activity in subcortical dopaminergic pathways. This finding would be consistent with those of Najib et al. (2004), who found deactivations in several areas following romantic rejection leading to resignation and despair (see the "Functional Magnetic Resonance Imaging Studies of Romantic Love" section earlier in this chapter). These data would be consistent with the position, first found in Darwin's (1872/1904) account of grief and reiterated since (Engel, 1962; Hofer, 1984), that two fundamentally different but interconnected reactions underlie the separation and grief reaction.

Various attempts have been made to explain the evolutionary function of the despair response. In doing so, one should distinguish between the sorrow of abandonment and the depression that can accompany a severe, long-term, internal mental dysfunction, such as bipolar disorder. Our concern here is with the grief that typical men and women feel for a period of time after they have been rejected by someone they adore or after a loved one dies. In Klinger's (1975) disengagement theory, a passive–depressive response enables the animal or person to disengage from a former incentive that controlled his or her behavior. Bowlby (1973, 1980) likewise regarded this despair as a necessary mechanism that enables detachment from the loved one. Researchers have also proposed that this depression motivates the recovering individual to abandon his or her hopeless venture and adopt more successful strategies to achieve reproductive goals (McGuire, Troisi, & Raleigh, 1997). Last, mildly depressed people make clearer assessments of themselves and others (Watson & Andrews, 2002), a valuable trait when someone is trying to adjust or change his or her focus in life.

INDIVIDUAL DIFFERENCES

Current research places considerable emphasis on individual differences in response to bereavement and to traumatic events in general. Bonanno (2004) argued that some individuals remain relatively unaffected by such circumstances, whereas others show prolonged distress and depression, which contrasts with the typical pattern of gradual recovery. Resilience may be mediated by a particular coping style (Bonanno, 2004), by personality characteristics such as dispositional optimism (Davis, Nolen-Hoeksema, & Larson, 1998) or hardiness (Kobassa, 1979), or by a dismissing–avoidant attachment style (Fraley & Bonanno, 2004). In a similar manner, not everyone suffers from romantic rejection or bereavement to the same degree (Downey & Feldman, 1996). How people react to lost love depends on many influences, including their attachment styles. Young men who had either a secure or a dismissing–avoidant attachment style showed less upset after relationship breakup than did those who had an anxious–ambivalent (or preoccupied) attachment style (Hindy & Schwarz, 1994; Keelan, Dion, & Dion, 1994; Simpson, 1990). Similar findings were reported by Fraley and Bonanno (2004) for grief following bereavement (see chap. 3, this volume). Individual differences are also likely in the extent to which alternative partners are available to individuals whose partners have died (Archer, 1999, pp. 125–128).

Men and women also tend to differ in how they handle romantic rejection (Baumeister et al., 1993; Hatfield & Rapson, 1996). Men are 3 to 4 times more likely to commit suicide after being rejected (Hatfield & Rapson, 1996), yet rejected women report more severe feelings of depression (Hatfield & Rapson, 1996; Mearns, 1991) and more chronic strain and rumination after being rejected (Nolen-Hoeksema, Larson, & Grayson, 1999). Women are more likely to talk about their trauma as well, sometimes inadvertently retraumatizing themselves (Hatfield & Rapson, 1996).

Nevertheless, few people avoid the pain of abandonment, either by a rejecting partner or experiencing the death of a mate. "Parting," as Emily Dickinson put it, "is all we know of heaven, and all we need to know of hell" (Dickinson, 1990, p. 49). Regarding romantic rejection, everywhere on earth men and women can recall the bitter details of their distress, even many years after the turmoil has defused (Baumeister & Dhavale, 2001). It is likely that they remember these rejections for important evolutionary reasons: Abandoned men and women have expended precious reproductive time and metabolic energy, and their reproductive future, along with their social alliances and happiness, have been jeopardized. Moreover, those who love, mate, and breed will pass on their genes to succeeding generations, whereas those who lose in love, sex, and reproduction will disproportionately die out. This is the ultimate reason why humans have evolved powerful brain systems to help cope with and to resist romantic rejection.

CONCLUSIONS

In this chapter, we have examined brain imaging studies of romantic love, rejection, and bereavement, which are as yet in their infancy, and we have sought to place them in a wider context of "the making and breaking of affectional bonds," as Bowlby (1979) described the attachment process. Both grief and romantic rejection involve the breaking of bonds, and both set off a deficit-driven reaction, consisting of two processes that researchers have sought to distinguish from the beginning of studies on grief (Darwin, 1872/1904). Brain imaging and other studies suggest that the regions involved in the active protest reaction, consisting of anger, idealization, and separation anxiety, are distinct from those activated in the more passive–depressive response. The former involves increased activity in the dopaminergic reward system, whereas resignation and despair are associated with lower activity in these subcortical dopaminergic pathways. People who are in love but who have not been rejected also show activation in these areas, although the exact location differs. Studies of the brain mechanisms underlying the separation reactions also indicate their relation to areas that control related reactions. For example, separation anxiety may involve activation of a region of the PAG, which lies close to regions that generate physical pain. The PAG is also involved in the panic reaction, which shows many similarities to separation distress.

Although the existing brain imaging studies are limited in scope, their consideration in relation to attachment theory, combined with ethological studies of motivational systems and a consideration of the evolutionary functions of the process of attachment, enable us to identify features that are likely to be common across the different contexts in which a loss or separation from a loved one occurs. We expect that, with time, many more related and integrated brain systems will be found that contribute to a host of types of social loss, including romantic rejection and bereavement.

REFERENCES

Alarcon, F. X. (Ed.). (1992). *Snake poems: An Aztec invocation*. San Francisco: Chronicle Books.

Archer, J. (1976). The organisation of aggression and fear in vertebrates. In P. P. G. Bateson & P. Klopfer (Eds.), *Perspectives in ethology 2* (pp. 231–298). New York: Plenum Press.

Archer, J. (1988). *The behavioural biology of aggression*. Cambridge, England: Cambridge University Press.

Archer, J. (1999). *The nature of grief*. London: Routledge.

Arnow, B. A., Desmond, J. E., Banner, L. L., Glover, G. H., Solomon, A., Polan, M. L., et al. (2002). Brain activation and sexual arousal in healthy, heterosexual males. *Brain, 125*, 1014–1023.

Aron, A., & Aron, E. N. (1991). Love and sexuality. In K. McKinney & S. Sprecher (Eds.), *Sexuality in close relationships* (pp. 25–48). Hillsdale, NJ: Erlbaum.

Aron, A., Fisher, H. E., Mashek, D. J., Strong, G., Li, H. F., & Brown, L. L. (2005). Reward, motivation and emotion systems associated with early-stage intense romantic love: An fMRI study. *Journal of Neurophysiology, 94*, 327–337.

Aron, A., Paris, M., & Aron, E. N. (1995). Falling in love: Prospective studies of self-concept change. *Journal of Personality and Social Psychology, 69*, 1102–1112.

Baerends, G. P. (1976). The functional organization of behaviour. *Animal Behaviour, 24*, 726–738.

Bartels, A., & Zeki, S. (2000). The neural basis of romantic love. *Neuroreport, 11*, 3829–3834.

Bartels, A., & Zeki, S. (2004). The neural correlates of maternal and romantic love. *NeuroImage, 21*, 1155–1166.

Baumeister, R. F., & Dhavale, D. (2001). Two sides of romantic rejection. In M. R. Leary (Ed.), *Interpersonal rejection* (pp. 55–71). New York: Oxford University Press.

Baumeister, R. F., Wotman, S. R., & Stillwell, A. M. (1993). Unrequited love: On heartbreak, anger, guilt, scriptlessness and humiliation. *Journal of Personality and Social Psychology, 64*, 377–394.

Beauregard, M., Levesque, J., & Bourgouin, P. (2001). Neural correlates of conscious self-regulation of emotion. *Journal of Neuroscience, 21*, RC165.

Bonanno, G. A. (2004). Loss, trauma and human resilience: Have we underestimated the human capacity to thrive after extremely aversive events? *American Psychologist, 59*, 20–28.

Bowlby, J. (1958). The nature of the child's tie to his mother. *International Journal of Psychoanalysis, 39*, 350–373.

Bowlby, J. (1960). Separation anxiety. *International Journal of Psychoanalysis, 41*, 89–113.

Bowlby, J. (1961). Processes of mourning. *International Journal of Psychoanalysis, 42*, 317–340.

Bowlby, J. (1969). *Attachment and loss: Vol. 1. Attachment.* London: Hogarth Press and Institute of Psychoanalysis.

Bowlby, J. (1973). *Attachment and loss: Vol. 2. Separation: Anxiety and anger.* London: Hogarth Press and Institute of Psychoanalysis.

Bowlby, J. (1979). *The making and breaking of affectional bonds.* London: Routledge.

Bowlby, J. (1980). *Attachment and loss: Vol. 3. Loss: Sadness and depression.* London: Hogarth Press and Institute of Psychoanalysis.

Bowlby, J., & Parkes, C. M. (1970). Separation and loss within the family. In E. J. Anthony & C. Koupernik (Eds.), *The child and his family* (pp. 187–216). New York: Wiley.

Burton, R. (1938). *The anatomy of melancholy* (6th ed.). New York: Tudor Publishing. (Original work published 1651)

Campbell, W. K., Sedikides, C., & Bossom, J. (1994). Romantic involvement, self-discrepancy, and psychological well-being: A preliminary investigation. *Personal Relationships, 1*, 399–404.

Carter, C. S., DeVries, A. C., Taymans, S. E., Roberts, R. L., Williams, J. R., & Getz, L. L. (1997). Peptides, steroids, and pair bonding. In C. S. Carter, I. I. Lederhendler, & B. Kirkpatrick (Eds.), *Annals of the New York Academy of Sciences: Vol. 807. The integrative neurobiology of affiliation* (pp. 260–272). New York: New York Academy of Sciences.

Darwin, C. (1904). *The expression of the emotions in man and animals*. London: Murray. (Original work published 1872)

Davis, C. G., Nolen-Hoeksema, S., & Larson, J. (1998). Making sense of loss and benefiting from the experience: Two construals of meaning. *Journal of Personality and Social Psychology, 75*, 561–574.

Delgado, M. R., Nystrom, L. E., Fissel, C., Noll, D. C., & Fiez, J. A. (2000) Tracking the hemodynamic responses to reward and punishment in the striatum. *Journal of Neurophysiology, 84*, 3072–3077.

Dickinson, E. (1990). *Selected poems*. New York: Dover.

Downey, G., & Feldman, S. I. (1996). Implications of rejection sensitivity for intimate relationships. *Journal of Personality and Social Psychology, 70*, 1327–1343.

Dozier, R. W. (2002). *Why we hate: Understanding, curbing, and eliminating hate in ourselves and our world*. New York: Contemporary Books.

Eisenberger, N. I., Lieberman, M. D., & Williams, K. D. (2003, October 10). Does rejection hurt? An FMRI study of social exclusion. *Science, 302*, 290–292.

Elliott, R., Newman, J. L., Longe, O. A., & Deakin, J. F. W. (2003). Differential response patterns in the striatum and orbitofrontal cortex to financial reward in humans: A parametric functional magnetic resonance imaging study. *Journal of Neuroscience, 23*, 303–307.

Ellis, B., & Malamuth, N. M. (2000). Love and anger in romantic relationships: A discrete systems model. *Journal of Personality, 68*, 3525–3556.

Engel, G. L. (1962). Anxiety and depression–withdrawal: The primary effects of unpleasure. *International Journal of Psychoanalysis, 43*, 89–97.

Evans, D. W., Lewis, M. D., & Iobst, E. (2004). The role of the orbitofrontal cortex in normally developing compulsive-like behaviors and obsessive–compulsive disorder. *Brain and Cognition, 55*, 220–234.

Fabre-Nys, C. (1997). Male faces and odors evoke differential patterns of neuro-chemical release in the mediobasal hypothalamus of the ewe during estrus: An insight into sexual motivation. *European Journal of Neuroscience, 9*, 1666–1677.

Fisher, H. (1998). Lust, attraction, and attachment in mammalian reproduction. *Human Nature, 9*, 23–52.

Fisher, H. (2004). *Why we love: The nature and chemistry of romantic love*. New York: Henry Holt.

Fisher, H., Aron, A., Mashek, D., Strong, G., Li, H., & Brown, L. L. (2002a). Defining the brain systems of lust, romantic attraction and attachment. *Archives of Sexual Behavior, 31*, 413–419.

Fisher, H., Aron, A., Mashek, D., Strong, G., Li, H., & Brown, L. L. (2002b). The neural mechanisms of mate choice: A hypothesis. *Neuroendocrinology Letters, 23*(Suppl. 4), 92–97.

Fisher, H., Aron, A., Strong, G., Mashek, D. J., Li, H., & Brown, L. L. (2005). *Motivation and emotion systems associated with romantic love following rejection: An fMRI study*. Washington, DC: Society for Neuroscience.

Fisher, H., & Thomson, J. A. (2006). Lust, attraction, attachment: Do the side-effects of serotonin-enhancing antidepressants jeopardize romantic love, marriage and fertility? In S. M. Platek & T. K. Shackelford (Eds.), *Evolutionary cognitive neuroscience* (pp. 285–326). Cambridge, MA: MIT Press.

Fraley, R. C., & Bonanno, G. A. (2004). Attachment and loss: A test of three competing models on the association between attachment-related avoidance and adaptation to bereavement. *Personality and Social Psychology Bulletin, 30,* 878–890.

Gingrich, B., Liu, Y., Cascio, C., Wang, Z., & Insel, T. R. (2000). D2 receptors in the nucleus accumbens are important for social attachment in female prairie voles (*Microtus ochrogaster*). *Behavioral Neuroscience, 114,* 173–183.

Goldstein, R. Z., Alai-Klein, N., Leskovjan, A. C., Fowler, J. S., Wang, G., Gur, R., et al. (2005). Anger and depression in cocaine addiction: Association with the orbitofrontal cortex. *Psychiatry Research, 138,* 13–22.

Gündel, H., O'Connor, M-F., Littrell, L., Fort, C., & Lane, R. D. (2003). Functional neuroanatomy of grief: An fMRI study. *American Journal of Psychiatry, 160,* 1946–1953.

Hammil, S. (Ed.). (1996). *The erotic spirit: An anthology of poems of sensuality, love, and longing.* Boston: Shambhala.

Harlow, H. F. & Harlow, M. K. (1962). Social deprivation in monkeys. *Scientific American, 207,* 136–146.

Harlow, H. F., & Harlow, M. K. (1965). The affectional systems. In A. M. Schrier, H. F. Harlow, & F. Stollnitz (Eds.), *Behavior of non-human primates* (Vol. 2, pp. 287–334). New York: Academic Press.

Harrison, S. (1986). Laments for foiled marriages: Love-songs from a Sepik River village. *Oceania, 56,* 275–288.

Hatfield, E. (1988). Passionate and companionate love. In R. Sternberg & M. Barnes (Eds.), *The psychology of love* (pp. 191–217). New Haven, CT: Yale University Press.

Hatfield, E., & Rapson, R. L. (1996). *Love and sex: Cross-cultural perspectives.* Boston: Allyn & Bacon.

Hatfield, E., & Sprecher, S. (1986). Measuring passionate love in intimate relationships. *Journal of Adolescence, 9,* 383–410.

Hindy, C. G., & Schwarz, J. C. (1994). Anxious romantic attachment in adult relationships. In M. B. Sperling & W. H. Berman (Eds.), *Attachment in adults: Clinical and developmental perspectives* (pp. 179–203). New York: Guilford Press.

Hofer, M. A. (1984). Relationships as regulators: A psychobiological perspective on bereavement. *Psychosomatic Medicine, 46,* 183–197.

Jankowiak, E. R., & Fischer, E. F. (1992). A cross-cultural perspective on romantic love. *Ethnology, 31,* 149–155.

Karama, S., Lecours, A. R., Leroux, J. M., Bourgouin, P., Beaudoin, G., Joubert, S., et al. (2002). Areas of brain activation in males and females during viewing of erotic film excerpts. *Human Brain Mapping, 16*, 1–13.

Keelan, J. P. R., Dion, K. L., & Dion, K. K. (1994). Attachment style and heterosexual relationships among young adults: A short-term panel study. *Journal of Social and Personal Relationships, 11*, 201–214.

Klinger, E. (1975). Consequences of commitment to and disengagement from incentives. *Psychological Review, 82*, 1–25.

Kobassa, S. C. (1979). Stressful life events, personality and health: An enquiry into hardiness. *Journal of Personality and Social Psychology, 37*, 1–11.

Kuhnen, C. M., & Knutson, B. (2005). The neural basis of financial risk taking. *Neuron, 47*, 763–770.

Lauwereyns, J., Takikawa, Y., Kawagoe, R., Kobayashi, S., Koizumi, M., Coe, B., et al. (2002). Feature-based anticipation of cues that predict reward in monkey caudate nucleus. *Neuron, 33*, 463–473.

Lavin, A., Nogueira, L., Lapish, C. C., Wightman, R. M., Phillips, P. E. M., & Seamans, J. K. (2005). Mesocortical dopamine neurons operate in distinct temporal domains using multimodal signaling. *Journal of Neuroscience, 25*, 5013–5023.

Leary, M. R., Twenge, J. M., & Quinlivan, E. (2006). Interpersonal rejection as a determinant of anger and aggression. *Personality and Social Psychology Review, 10*, 111–132.

Legault, M., & Wise, R. A. (1999). Injections of N-methyl-D-aspartate into the ventral hippocampus increase extracellular dopamine in the ventral tegmental area and nucleus accumbens. *Synapse, 31*, 241–249.

Lewis, T., Amini, F., & Lannon, R. (2000). *A general theory of love*. New York: Random House.

Liebowitz, M. R. (1983). *The chemistry of love*. Boston: Little, Brown.

Lim, M. M., Murphy, A. Z., & Young, L. J. (2004). Ventral striato–pallidal oxytocin and vasopressin V1a receptors in the monogamous prairie vole (*Microtus ochrogaster*). *Journal of Comparative Neurology, 468*, 555–570.

Lim, M. M., & Young, L. J. (2004). Vasopressin-dependent neural circuits underlying pair bonding in the monogamous prairie vole (*Microtus ochrogaster*). *Neuroscience, 125*, 35–45.

Martin-Soelch, C., Leenders, K. L., Chevalley, A. F., Missimer, J., Kunig, G., Magyar, S., et al. (2001). Reward mechanisms in the brain and their role in dependence: Evidence from neurophysiological and neuroimaging studies. *Brain Research Reviews, 36*, 139–149.

Mashek, D., Aron, A., & Fisher, H. (2000). Identifying, evoking, and measuring intense feelings of romantic love. *Representative Research in Social Psychology, 24*, 48–55.

McGuire, M. T., Troisi, A., & Raleigh, M. M. (1997). Depression in evolutionary context. In S. Baron-Cohen (Ed.), *The maladaptive mind: Classic readings in evolutionary psychopathology* (pp. 255–282). Hove, England: Psychology Press.

Mearns, J. (1991). Coping with a breakup: Negative mood regulation expectancies and depression following the end of a romantic relationship. *Journal of Personality and Social Psychology, 60,* 327–334.

Meloy, J. R. (1999). Stalking: An old behavior, a new crime. *Forensic Psychiatry, 22,* 85–99.

Meloy, J. R., & Fisher, H. (2005). Some thoughts on the neurobiology of stalking. *Journal of Forensic Sciences, 50,* 1472–1480.

Millay, E. S. V. (1988). *Collected sonnets.* New York: Harper & Row.

Najib, A., Lorberbaum, J., Kose, S., Bohning, D., & George, M. (2004). Regional brain activity in women grieving a romantic relationship breakup. *American Journal of Psychiatry, 161,* 2245–2256.

Nemeroff, C. B. (1998). The neurobiology of depression. *Scientific American, 278,* 42–49.

Nolen-Hoeksema, S., Larson, J., & Grayson, C. (1999). Explaining the gender difference in depressive symptoms. *Journal of Personality and Social Psychology, 77,* 1061–1072.

O'Connor, M-F. (2005). Bereavement and the brain: Invitation to a conversation between bereavement researchers and neuroscientists. *Death Studies, 29,* 905–922.

Panksepp, J. (1998). *Affective neuroscience: The foundations of human and animal emotions.* New York: Oxford University Press.

Parkes, C. M. (1971). Psychosocial transitions: A field for study. *Social Science & Medicine, 5,* 101–115.

Parkes, C. M. (1972a). *Bereavement: Studies of grief in adult life.* New York: Tavistock.

Parkes, C. M. (1972b). Components of the reaction to loss of a limb, spouse or home. *Journal of Psychosomatic Research, 16,* 343–349.

Parkes, C. M., Benjamin, B., & Fitzgerald, R. G. (1969). Broken heart: A statistical study of increased mortality among widowers. *British Medical Journal, 1,* 740–743.

Schreckenberger, M., Siessmeier, T., Viertmann, A., Landvogt, C., Buchholz, H. G., Rolke, R., et al. (2005). The unpleasantness of tonic pain is encoded by the insular cortex. *Neurology, 64,* 1175–1183.

Schultz, W. (2000). Multiple reward signals in the brain. *Nature Reviews. Neuroscience, 1,* 199–207.

Sherwin, B. B. (1994). Sex hormones and psychological functioning in post-menopausal women. *Experimental Gerontology, 29,* 423–430.

Simpson, J. A. (1990). Influence of attachment styles on romantic relationships. *Journal of Personality and Social Psychology, 59,* 971–980.

Sinclair, H. C., & Frieze, I. H. (2000). Initial courtship behaviour and stalking: How should we draw the line? *Violence and Victims, 15,* 23–40.

Smith, D. E., & Hoklund, M. (1988). Love and salutogenesis in late adolescence: A preliminary investigation. *Psychology: A Journal of Human Behavior, 25,* 44–49.

Speece, M. W., & Brent, S. B. (1984). Children's understanding of death: A review of three components of the death concept. *Child Development, 55,* 1671–1686.

Stoléru, S., Grégoire, M, C., Gérard, D., Decety, J., Lafarge, E., Cinotti, L., et al. (1999). Neuroanatomical correlates of visually evoked sexual arousal in human males. *Archives of Sexual Behavior, 28,* 1–21.

Tennov, D. (1979). *Love and limerence: The experience of being in love.* New York: Stein & Day.

Tiihonen, J., Kuikka, J. T., Bergstrom, K. A., Karhu, J., Viinamiki, H., Lehtonen, J., et al. (1997). Single-photon emission tomography imaging of monoamine transporters in impulsive violent behaviour. *European Journal of Nuclear Medicine, 24,* 1253–1260.

Tinbergen, N. (1951). *The study of instinct.* London: Oxford University Press.

van Goozen, S., Wiegant, V. M., Endert, E., Helmond, F. A., & Van de Poll, N. E. (1997). Psychoendocrinological assessment of the menstrual cycle: The relationship between hormones, sexuality, and mood. *Archives of Sexual Behavior, 26,* 359–382.

Vollm, D. A., Taylor, A. N., Richardson, P., Corcoran, R., Stirling, J., McKie, S., et al. (2005). Neuronal correlates of theory of mind and empathy: A functional magnetic resonance imaging study in a nonverbal task. *NeuroImage, 29,* 90–98.

Wang, Z., Yu, G., Cascio, C., Liu, Y., Gingrich, B., & Insel, T. R. (1999). Dopamine D2 receptor-mediated regulation of partner preferences in female prairie voles (*Microtus ochrogaster*): A mechanism for pair bonding? *Behavioral Neuroscience, 113,* 602–611.

Watson, P. J., & Andrews, P. W. (2002). Toward a revised evolutionary adaptationist analysis of depression: The social navigation hypothesis. *Journal of Affective Disorders, 72,* 1–14.

Zald, D. H., Boileau, I., El-Dearedy, W., Gunn, R., McGlone, F., Dichter, G. S., et al. (2004). Dopamine transmission in the human striatum during monetary reward tasks. *Journal of Neuroscience, 24,* 4105–4112.

V

PATTERNS AND CONSEQUENCES OF GRIEF: RELATIONSHIP PERSPECTIVES

18

THE LOSS OF A CHILD: SUDDEN DEATH AND EXTENDED ILLNESS PERSPECTIVES

SHIRLEY A. MURPHY

The primary focus of this chapter is on parents who are bereaved by the sudden, violent deaths of their children, which occur mostly among adolescents and young adults. These deaths are unexpected and untimely and include accident, suicide, and homicide. I begin the chapter with an overview of research findings regarding parental bereavement specific to this subset of deaths (i.e., accident, suicide, and homicide). Then, in an effort to place these deaths into perspective, I summarize the available research findings for parents whose children have died after an extended illness. These deaths are typically neither unexpected nor sudden. The contrasting bereavement trajectories engendered by a child's sudden, violent death versus a death that follows an extended illness provide a context in which to discuss the possibility for determining how the causes of a children's death might influence parents' outcomes. I close the chapter with a discussion of strengths and weaknesses of available data.

The topics discussed in this chapter are based on the premise that the death of a child is more devastating to survivors than the deaths in other kinship relationships—for example, the death of a parent, spouse, or sibling (Middleton, Raphael, Burnett, & Martinek, 1998; Sanders, 1979–1980). Accidents and injuries have been the leading causes of death of young people in many countries, at least in the Western world. In the United States, the incidence of accidental deaths is higher than those in 25 other industrialized nations (Centers for Disease Control and Prevention, 1997; National Center for Health Statistics, 2004). Homicide and suicide are the second and third leading causes of death among 15- to 24-year-olds. Unexpected deaths are thought to be more difficult for survivors to manage than expected deaths. Avery Weisman's (1973) conceptualization of *timely deaths* (when observed survival equals expected survival and is acceptable) versus *untimely deaths* (premature, unexpected, and calamitous) is a preferred distinction, although it is seldom cited in the literature. Cancer is the leading cause of nonaccidental death among children in many countries, including the United States (National Center for Health Statistics, 2004). Evidence suggests that it takes parents many years to come to terms with such a devastating loss. According to James and Johnson (1997), children's deaths by cancer, which are common, are more stressful for parents than deaths that follow other chronic illnesses. Because of this, I focus my later discussion of parental bereavement following children's extended illnesses on cases in which cancer is the cause of death.

THE SUDDEN, VIOLENT DEATH OF A CHILD

When a young person dies violently, the suddenness of the death leaves parents feeling devastated, particularly when harm to the child was intentional, when mutilation occurred, and when parents perceive the death as preventable (Green, 1990; Rando, 1996). Parents have reported relentless intrusive images of the death scene, avoidance of reminders of the child, and hypervigilant distress. Until recently, grief and depression have been the primary outcomes studied. Risk factors that predict parent outcomes have also been studied. These include parents' gender, age, and marital status; self-esteem, coping skills, religiosity, social support, concurrent negative life events, and ability to find meaning in the death; and characteristics of the deceased child, including age, gender, and mode of death (Davis, Wortman, Lehman, & Silver, 2000; Séguin, Lesage, & Kiely, 1995; Stroebe & Schut, 2001). These factors have led to an understanding of some of the parents' needs in a painful transition in which, in contrast to widowhood, no norms are apparent. For example, there is a lack of agreement regarding a formal mourning period and whether and when the parents might have another child.

Parents' marital and social relationships can be affected (Gilbert, 1997; Schwab, 1992; M. P. Thompson, Norris, & Ruback, 1998) by the sudden, violent death of a child. Secondary victimization may result from encounters with the media, the criminal justice system, and naive employers and acquaintances (Amick-McMullan, Kilpatrick, & Resnick, 1991; K. E. Thompson & Range, 1990–1991).

Parents' own deaths have been linked with their children's deaths. Li, Mortensen, and Olsen (2003) showed that mothers bereaved by a child's death from unnatural causes died at significantly higher rates during the first 3 years of bereavement than did mothers in a control group. Specific causes of mother's deaths (i.e., disease or lifestyle factors) were not provided. Fathers whose children had died from unnatural causes were also at higher risk of death but for a shorter time.

In addition to the general findings concerning bereavement by violent death, unique features are associated with each cause of violent death I address in this chapter. For example, most accidental deaths of teenaged children are due to motor vehicle crashes. The child may have engaged in risk-taking behaviors, such as traveling at high speeds, not using restraint systems, and so on (Dryfoos, 1991). Parents frequently blame themselves for not protecting the child regardless of whether they could have done anything differently (Rando, 1996). Deaths from suicide remain highly stigmatized; survivors report intense grief and a lack of support (Jordan, 2001; K. E. Thompson & Range, 1990–1991). Parents bereaved by homicide have reported feelings of outrage, hostility, and revenge and experience symptoms in all three diagnostic clusters of posttraumatic stress disorder (PTSD): (a) reexperiencing of the event, (b) avoidance of reminders, and (c) hypervigilance (Stevens-Guille, 1999; M. P. Thompson et al., 1998).

In summary, findings from previous studies have identified a wide range of negative consequences associated with parents' bereavement following the violent death of a child. However, few studies have used longitudinal, prospective designs; in some cases, samples have been biased by self-selection, and outcome variables are typically unidimensional.

THE PARENT BEREAVEMENT PROJECT

In the 1990s, several colleagues and I conducted a study of parents in two states in the northwest United States who had been bereaved by sudden, violent death. The goal of the study was to extend previous research findings through design and sampling and by addressing multiple outcomes (Murphy, 1997). The purposes of the randomized clinical trial were to test a preventive intervention and to conduct follow-up observations so we could examine change over time in mental and physical health, PTSD symptoms, marital satisfaction, family functioning, and loss accommodation (e.g., acceptance of the death). Before creating the study design, the research team noted that statistically significant differences on outcomes had already been established between bereaved and nonbereaved parents (bereaved parents had poorer mental and physical health ratings).

After receiving institutional approval for protection of human participants, we obtained the names of parents from death certificates of the deceased children so that every bereaved parent we could contact would have an equal chance of being in the study. Over a 3-year period, we enrolled 261 parents (171 mothers and 90 fathers). The sample included 69 married couples and 123 single mothers. Five years later, 173 parents remained in the study, with the same proportions of married couples and single mothers. In this chapter, I present data collected from the 173 retained parents at 4, 12, 24, and 60 months after their children's deaths.

Parents' ages ranged from 32 to 61 years, with 45 years being the average. The sample was 86% Caucasian, which was consistent with the population demographics in the two U.S. states in the 1990s, when the study was undertaken. Study parents' average years of schooling were 13.8, and 65% were employed. Nearly 80% of the parents professed a religious affiliation. Study parents had been married for 18 years on average. The average age of the deceased child was 20 years, and 65% were males. Accidents were the most common cause of death (57.8%), followed by suicide (23.6%), then homicide (9.7%), and then deaths not classified by coroners (8.9%).

The study outcome variables were mental distress, PTSD, marital satisfaction, physical health status, acceptance of death, and finding meaning in the death. Independent variables were coping, self-esteem, and social support. Data were collected by means of questionnaires, parent interviews, and audiotaped transcriptions of group sessions. The findings I present in the next section focus primarily on gender differences and the children's causes of death using the dependent variables just outlined.

Parent Outcomes: Mental Distress, Posttraumatic Stress Disorder, Marital Satisfaction, and Acceptance of the Death

Mental distress (anxiety, cognitive dysfunction, depression, hostility, fear, somatic complaints, thoughts about death, and guilt) was measured by the 53-item Brief Symptom Inventory (BSI; Derogatis, 1992). PTSD symptoms were measured by the 18-item Traumatic Experiences Scale (Murphy, Johnson, Chung, & Beaton, 2003), which is based on criteria from the *Diagnostic and Statistical Manual of Mental Disorders* (3rd ed., revised [DSM–III–R]; American Psychiatric Association, 1987), marital satisfaction was measured by the 10-item Marital Satisfaction subscale of the Dyadic Adjustment Scale (Spanier, 1976), and the acceptance measure was an investigator-developed item.

Symptom constellations of grief—that is, affective and somatic complaints—were measured by the BSI subscales of Somatization, Depression, Anxiety, Hostility, and Phobic Anxiety. According to Amick-McMullan et al. (1991), grief theory does not adequately explain some aspects of violent death bereavement. Survivors of violent death have reported symptom constellations more similar to trauma than to grief, such as intrusive recollections of the death event and attempts to avoid painful stimuli that result in at least temporary functional impairment.

Parent Outcomes by Gender

Within the sample of 173 parents who remained in the study for the 5-year observation period, 115 were mothers and 58 were fathers. Statistically significant gender differences were noted at all study observations for all four outcomes.

Bereaved mothers' scores on mental distress were higher than fathers' scores at all measurement times; however, the two highest BSI subscale scores were the same for both fathers and mothers (Obsessive–Compulsive Cognitive Performance Deficits and Depression). Mothers also scored high on interpersonal sensitivity and anxiety. The steepest decline in scores for mothers was between 4 and 12 months postloss. Fathers' scores on mental distress did not decline significantly until sometime between 2 and 5 years postdeath. In comparison with scores of nonbereaved adults in their same age groups, both study mothers' and fathers' average scores on all BSI subscales were at least twice as high 5 years postdeath (Murphy, Johnson, & Lohan, 2000).

Five years postdeath, 28.0% of the mothers and 12.5% of the fathers continued to meet PTSD diagnostic criteria compared with 9.5% women and 6.3% men in the general U.S. population (Kessler, Sonnega, Bromet, Hughes, & Nelson, 1995). Reexperiencing of symptoms was the most frequently reported; 61% of the mothers and 55% of the fathers reported symptoms in this cluster. Parents' verbatim comments obtained as part of the study data demonstrate the replay of parents' visual and mental imagery: "I can't get past how my child must have struggled with his killer"; "I found him hanging in the basement and could not free him from the rope." Avoidance and hyperarousal symptoms were reported by 48% of the mothers and 38% of the fathers (Murphy, Johnson, Chung, & Beaton, 2003). There were striking differences between parents who met *DSM–III–R* diagnostic criteria for PTSD and those who did not. Parents who met the criteria reported higher rates of mental distress and lower self-esteem, and they used more repressive coping strategies than did parents without PTSD.

Parent Outcomes According to Children's Causes of Death

Does one cause of violent death have more deleterious effects on parents than another? For the past 30 years, the suicide of a significant other has been consistently reported in the nonempirical literature to have the most detrimental effects on family survivors (see review by Jordan, 2001). However, according to Stroebe and Schut (2001), the few empirical studies that have compared the psychological consequences of bereavement because of suicide with those of other types of death have typically failed to find any marked differences in bereavement. The apparent controversy can be resolved by more rigorous study methods and by studying identical outcomes.

In the Parent Bereavement Project (Murphy, 1997), parents' data were grouped for comparison by each of the three causes of their children's deaths (there were 87 sets of parent data in the accident group, 41 in the suicide group, and 35 in the homicide group). The four outcomes examined were the same as for the gender difference analyses: (a) mental distress, (b) PTSD, (c) marital satisfaction, and (d) acceptance of the death. Observations were made at 4, 12, 24, and 60 months postdeath.

Contrary to previously held beliefs, a child's death by suicide did not result in mental distress among parents as profound or long-lasting as when children died by accident or homicide. All three types of violent death bereavement we examined validated the pervasiveness and persistence of negative outcomes; however, parents in the homicide group reported the most negative outcomes. Parents of murdered children showed the highest rates of overall mental distress as measured by the Global Severity Index (GSI) of the BSI compared with the other two groups. The same pattern of results occurred for PTSD: The GSI and PTSD mean scores decreased gradually over time. Parents in the homicide group also reported the lowest levels of marital satisfaction and the least acceptance of the deaths compared with the other two parent groups.

In contrast, parents whose children had died by suicide, compared with the other two groups, reported the lowest mean scores on mental distress and PTSD and the highest mean scores on acceptance of death and marital satisfaction. Several factors could account for these results. First, in hindsight, parents stated that they sometimes had indications of suicide, such as previous attempts; threats of taking one's own life; and the child's chronic depression, mood disorders, and/or substance abuse. One mother put it this way: "My son did not want to die but he could not live in this world." Jordan (2001) wrote that social isolation, stigma, and family disorganization were common experiences for survivors of suicide. These factors were not measured in this study but could be influential nonetheless.

Parents in the accident group reported lower mean scores on the four outcome measures than parents in the homicide group and higher mean scores than parents in the suicide group. These results are surprising. The majority of the children who had died by accident were involved in motor vehicle crashes. Parents told of cars on fire with no way to escape. One might expect that parents' thoughts and images of these death scenarios would lead to PTSD scores as high as those for parents in the homicide group. A statistically significant interaction (Time × Group) was noted only for the acceptance of death (Murphy, Johnson, Wu, Fan, & Lohan, 2003).

Parents' Physical Health and Health Behaviors

Prospective data on health status and health behaviors were collected on the basis of the assumption that parental trauma associated with children's deaths might affect health. No predeath data were available; however, health data were collected over time to examine change in selected health variables.

The initial analysis compared mothers who reported good health with mothers who reported poor health 1 year postloss. The same analyses were undertaken for fathers. Significant differences emerged for both mothers and fathers. Mothers in poor health compared with mothers in excellent health were 11 times more likely to report concurrent emotional distress and 3 times more likely to report trauma symptoms. Fathers in poor health compared with fathers in excellent health were 15 times more likely to report emotional distress and 5 times more likely to report trauma symptoms.

With regard to health protective behaviors (i.e., exercise, eating a healthy diet, not smoking, and moderate alcohol use), at both 4 and 12 months postloss, more than 70% of the mothers and nearly 60% of the fathers reported engaging in two or more of these behaviors each week. The practice of healthy behaviors was significantly associated with fewer stress-related illnesses, days absent from work, and nondiminished productivity at work (Murphy et al., 1999). These data are descriptive; no cause-and-effect inferences can be made.

COPING STRATEGIES IDENTIFIED BY PARENTS DURING THE FIRST 5 YEARS OF BEREAVEMENT

Being bereaved is a global stressor; as such, it is not measurable. To obtain information about specific stressors, parents were asked to list them at each study observation period: 4, 12, 24, and 60 months postloss. At 4 months postloss, parents' highest priority concerns were a profound sense of loss ("I miss her/him"), triggers (i.e., seeing the school bus, seeing their deceased children's friends), self-blame and guilt, dissatisfaction with investigations of the deaths, concerns about other children in the family, physical health concerns (i.e., having no energy), and the inability to sleep and eat. At 12 months postloss, "I miss her/him" was the most frequently listed challenge, followed by questions and concerns about the death itself ("What happened, and why?"), about loss of the future (i.e., "Who will care for me when I am old?"; "I will not have any grandchildren"), about what to do with the child's possessions, and about staying connected with the deceased child (e.g., "What if I forget how his voice sounded?)" At 24 and 60 months postloss, missing the child, staying connected, and anguish over the deaths remained parents' primary concerns. Having parents identify specific stressors does not guarantee that parents will have these concerns in mind as they identify coping strategies they use at each measurement period, but it is one way to attempt to address the global-versus-specific stressor measurement problem.

The examination of coping processes following highly stressful events is important, because cognitive skills can be taught and practiced and can serve as mediators or moderators between stressful events and potentially negative outcomes. However, coping by itself may be insufficient to reduce many negative consequences associated with the violent death of a child. Resources such as adequate income, a sense of mastery, and good health affect both coping efforts and the effectiveness of those efforts (Menaghan, 1983).

Parents' coping strategies were measured by Coping Orientation to Problems Experienced (COPE), a self-administered 53-item questionnaire (Carver, Scheier, & Weintraub, 1989). The data were tested for independence of observations among married couples, social desirability, and gender response set differences (Murphy, Johnson, & Weber, 2002). We then tallied the types of strategies used by gender. Contrary to beliefs about gender socialization, both mothers and fathers used many of the same coping strategies in both the action (problem solving) and affective (talking with others to get help and support) domains. Denial, Behavioral, and Mental Disengagement subscale items of COPE were seldom reported as being used by either mothers or fathers; however, some gender differences did emerge. Mothers selected items on the Turning to Religion Subscale of COPE ("I pray more than usual") more frequently than did fathers. Fathers selected items on the Acceptance subscale of COPE ("I accept the reality of the fact that it happened") more frequently than did mothers.

Hierarchical multiple regression procedures were used to examine the role of resources (i.e., self-esteem and financial status) and their importance along with coping strategies as predictors of parents' mental distress and PTSD. The results of these analyses showed that at 1 and 5 years postdeath, higher self-esteem was a significant predictor of lower mental distress and PTSD. After controlling for self-esteem, active and affective coping strategies predicted less mental distress for fathers but not for mothers. Active and affective coping strategies were not significant predictors of lowered PTSD symptoms for either mothers or fathers. Rather, repressive coping strategies were significant predictors of higher PTSD symptoms for both mothers and fathers at both 1 and 5 years postdeath (Murphy, Johnson, & Lohan, 2003a).

These findings suggest that repressive coping is very damaging because it contributes to high symptom levels of both mental distress and PTSD for both mothers and fathers even 5 years after a child's death. Links among depression, intrusive thoughts and images, and suppressed immune functioning and illness have been shown (Biondi & Picardi, 1996; Cohen & Rodriguez, 1995). Skilled clinicians can use group interaction and role-playing to assist parents in eliminating or reducing the use of coping strategies such as "I admit to myself that

I can't deal with it, and quit trying," and "I refuse to believe that this has happened." Active (e.g., problem solving) and affective (e.g., support seeking) coping strategies did not contribute to lower levels of distress and trauma in mothers like these variables did for fathers. This finding can be interpreted to mean that in some cases, the death of a child is so overwhelming that nothing seems to help. Finally, it appears important that parents maintain high self-esteem over time, which may be difficult for parents to achieve, especially those who blame themselves for the child's death.

Finding Meaning in a Child's Death and Parents' Postdeath Lives

Asking individuals how they have found meaning in negative life events is not new; however, in the Parent Bereavement Project a 5-year perspective on the question was obtained. Janoff-Bulman and Frantz's (1997) constructs of meaning-as-comprehensibility and meaning-as-significance were selected to analyze parents' written responses to questions about finding meaning in their children's deaths and in their own lives. After a traumatic death, the bereaved survivor wants to believe there is something he or she could have done, which minimizes the threat of continued meaninglessness. *Meaning-as-comprehensibility* refers to sense making, that is, a fit within a system of rules or theories. *Meaning-as-significance* refers to whether something is of worth or value, that is, a newly found appreciation of what really matters. These two types of meaning are not dichotomous; rather, they are parts of a process composed of initial terror and disequilibrium followed by self-blame and responsibility for the event that eventually addresses questions of value and significance in daily living, including the reordering of priorities.

The narrative analysis showed that by 12 months postdeath, only 12% of the parents had found meaning in their children's deaths. Parents' responses to the finding-meaning questions early in bereavement reflected the "premeaning" phase described by Janoff-Bulman and Frantz (1997), that is, initial terror, self-blame, and feeling responsible for their children's deaths: "Why couldn't it have been a close call?"; "What really happened? I wish _____ was here to tell us her own story"; "What role and to what degree did I and his father play in his not wanting to live?"

Between 12 and 60 months postdeath, three themes revealed parents' ability to find meaning-as-comprehension. Parents told of establishing rituals and memorials, seeking justice and revenge, and realistic acceptance of the deceased children as they lived their lives. On children's birthdays and other anniversary days, parents lit candles, released balloons, and made gravesite visits. Parents expressed frustration and anger with decisions of the criminal justice system, which seemed to them to provide lenient forms of punishment: "I want [the perpetrator] to stay in prison a long time"; "He will be released soon and may come after us." Many parents were forthcoming about their children's high-risk behaviors (e.g., drug use) as well as chronic health problems associated with their deaths. One father said, "We finally realized that we could do nothing more for her depression."

Five years after their children's deaths, 57% of the parents reported finding meaning-as-significance. Many parents spoke of reordering priorities, learning of their strengths in the face of adversity, and beliefs that the child's suffering had ended. Representative comments on these themes were "Life is to be lived as precious—each day may be your last"; "I was determined to find help. I was not willing to lose another child to suicide"; "He didn't want to hurt me; he just couldn't live in this world"; "I have empathy for other parents struggling with rebellion, drugs, and runaway kids."

Parents who had not found meaning in their children's deaths 5 years afterward made the following comments: "There is no meaning in her rape and murder"; "It was a permanent solution to a temporary problem. I can't fill the hole in my heart that she left"; "I cannot understand it or accept it" (Murphy, Johnson, & Lohan, 2003b).

Next, parents were grouped by whether they had found meaning or not found meaning. Five predictor variables based on published literature were homicide as a child's cause of death and four parent variables: (a) perceived preventability of the death, (b) self-esteem, (c) use of religious coping, and (d) support group attendance. Significant predictors of finding meaning were the use of religious coping strategies and support group attendance.

Parents who found meaning in the deaths of their children reported significantly lower scores on mental distress, higher marital satisfaction, and better physical health than did parents who were unable to find meaning in their children's deaths. The meaning and no-meaning groups were not generated by random selection; therefore, it was not possible to ascertain causality. It may be that finding meaning leads to lower mental distress, higher marital satisfaction, and better physical health. It is also possible that other variables, not measured, caused both sets of variables to change. However, other investigators have also found that parents who found meaning in a child's death had better mental health outcomes than those who had not found meaning (Davis et al., 2000). The temporal relationships between finding meaning and the health and marital satisfaction outcomes were not examined in the Parent Bereavement Project because so few parents found meaning in their children's deaths early in bereavement.

SUDDEN DEATH BEREAVEMENT: SUMMARY

The two important findings from the Parent Bereavement Project were (a) gender differences in mental distress, PTSD, marital satisfaction, acceptance of children's deaths, and coping and (b) differences noted in these same outcome variables when parent data were analyzed by children's causes of death. The gender difference finding is consistent with the published literature, that is, that mothers report more distress than do fathers. Because the study was longitudinal, gender difference data in regard to both symptom severity and differing rates of loss accommodation over time were measured. Gender socialization—mothers' willingness to report feelings and fathers' beliefs that they most "support the family," "be strong," and so on—is likely to have contributed to these findings. Few separations and divorces among married couples were noted in this study. This finding may be attributed to the fact that the average length of time married to the current spouse was 18 years. This finding is inconsistent with the literature suggesting that separation and divorce are common in bereaved couples (Schwab, 1992).

Contrary to some published literature (Jordan, 2001), a child's suicide was reportedly not as devastating for parents, as measured by the outcome variables, as a child's death by homicide or accident. Several factors may account for these findings. First, the outcome variables measured in the Parent Bereavement Project were not the same as those measured in other studies. Second, the study of homicide bereavement is a more recent area of inquiry because of the increases of homicide, particularly in the United States. There have not been as many opportunities to make these comparisons before now.

Mental distress and PTSD symptoms were highly interrelated in the Parent Bereavement Project. This suggests not only measurement overlap but also, more important, that one domain of symptoms cannot be eliminated without addressing the other domain.

The 57% of study parents who found meaning in the deaths of their children 5 years postdeath reported better health and higher levels of marital satisfaction than those who had not found meaning 5 years later. Janoff-Bulman and Frantz (1997) suggested that two meaning-related tasks are addressed by survivors: (a) minimizing the terror of a meaning-less world and (b) maximizing value in their own lives. The meaning findings in the Parent Bereavement Project were consistent with Janoff-Bulman and Frantz's theory.

PARENTS' BEREAVEMENT CHALLENGES FOLLOWING A CHILD'S EXTENDED ILLNESS

Although treatment innovations have led to increased survival rates for children with cancer, cancer remains the leading cause of nonaccidental death in childhood and adolescence in many countries (National Center for Health Statistics, 2004). According to Kazak (2004), "relatively little is known about the natural course of bereavement from the death of a child from cancer" (p. 143). Children's increased survival time is one factor that has apparently influenced a dramatic shift in research away from bereavement and toward illness phases and treatment—for example, remission and relapse, pain control, options for terminal care outside the hospital, and parents' needs for information. More than 350 citations were found in one database for illness processes and family challenges, whereas only a handful of citations were found for parent bereavement following a child's death as a result of cancer.

In addition to the small number of studies available for review, the majority of investigators have used qualitative, cross-sectional study designs, and personal interviews were conducted with small and potentially nonrepresentative samples to obtain data in regard to parents' bereavement experiences. Although few state-of-the-science studies were found, the studies I review next can be useful for hypothesis generation. Some exceptions found in the literature were three longitudinal studies conducted by Birenbaum, Stewart, and Phillips (1996); Martinson and colleagues (Martinson & Cohen, 1988; Martinson, Guang, & Yi-Hua, 1993; Martinson, Lee, & Kim, 2000; Martinson, McClowry, Davies, & Kuhlenkamp, 1994); Saiki-Craighill (2001); and a study that recruited large samples of bereaved and nonbereaved parents by record review (Kreicbergs, Valdimarsdottir, Onelov, Henter, & Steineck, 2004). Finally, several countries are represented in these studies (China, Japan, South Korea, Sweden, Taiwan, and the United States), making the potential for cross-cultural comparisons promising. I present a brief synopsis of these available studies in the following paragraphs.

Gender Differences on Symptoms and Other Outcomes

Birenbaum et al. (1996) examined changes in the health status of 80 parents during the terminal phase of the child's illness and at 2 weeks and 4 and 12 months postdeath. Data were collected using the 63-item Duke–UNC Health Profile (Parkerson et al., 1981). The instrument's four subscales measure physical functional symptoms, emotional health status, social health status, and physical health. Parents' data were not statistically different on the Physical Functional Symptom subscale or the Emotional Health Status subscale compared with a normative sample, or when comparisons were made within the sample to detect change over time. Changes on social and physical health were very small, according to the authors. Mothers and fathers differed on only a few items. The authors did not discuss other gender comparisons.

Martinson and colleagues (Martinson & Cohen, 1988; Martinson et al., 1993, 1994, 2000) conducted studies in the United States, China, South Korea, and Taiwan that involved more than 300 families. The U.S. longitudinal study sample consisted of 48 families. Interviews were conducted with parents 1, 6, 12, and 24 months postdeath and again 5, 7, and 9 years later. The Symptom Checklist 90 (SCL-90; Derogatis, 1977) was administered 2 years postdeath, and only the Depression subscale of the SCL-90 was administered 7 years postdeath. Seven to 9 years later, parents recalled their emotional and physical exhaustion associated with caring for the ill child and feared that cancer would strike them or one of their other children. Although parents stated that the loss required intense family reorganization, there were few divorces, and 7 families had had another child by the time of the follow-up study 7 to 9 years later. Parents also commented on changes in values and priorities in their lives.

Martinson et al. (1993) conducted structured interviews with both parents of 17 families in Guangzhou, China, whose children had died within the past 5 years. Interview topics included a review of the illness, treatment, and death; what happened after the death; the impact on parents, siblings, and other relatives, including both psychosocial and financial aspects and available support; and what advice they would give to other families. Fifteen of the 17 children had died in the hospital, 10 from leukemia. Families were said to be expected by the hospital staff to be present at the hospital at all times. Eleven families remained in the hospital from diagnosis until death without once going home. Treatment was costly; 6 families paid the entire cost themselves, with the remainder obtaining some subsidy. Eight families burned all of the child's belongings and family mementos postdeath; 5 families kept pictures. Mothers were said to have been "worse off," but data to support these comments were not provided by the authors. Parents feared cancer would strike another family member. Few families shared their grief with others because, according to the authors, in China at the time the study was conducted, talking about death was not acceptable. Aspects of this study add to cultural understandings of bereavement, but the small, nonrandom sample interviewed and the time since death and data collection make inferences based on the findings impossible.

Martinson et al. (2000) interviewed 18 families in South Korea, 25 in Taiwan, and 22 in the United States whose children had died from cancer during the past 10 to 15 years. The purposes of the study were to explore family responses to children's deaths and to learn how nurses help families manage bereavement. In Korea, the main caregiver and decision maker was the mother, whereas in Taiwan and the United States, both parents were involved. According to the authors, major impacts of the deaths were grief; varying levels of support, including stigma; finding meaning; and changes in health and attitudes toward life. Grief was accompanied by feelings of guilt, blame, and regret. Of the three samples, Korean mothers expressed the most guilt. Their guilt was attributed to ignorance about the child's condition when he or she was initially sick and to their allowing their children to undergo painful treatment. Parents coped with grief by avoiding any reminders of the deceased child. An unresolved problem for Korean mothers was what to do with time on their hands. As in the Chinese sample (Martinson et al., 1993), parents felt stigmatized and believed cancer is contagious. Changes in family relationships were noted in all three cross-cultural samples. Extensive information was obtained from the personal interviews, and the data were reported and analyzed to allow future comparison studies, including hypothesis testing, to be conducted. Concerns are the retrospective study design and time since loss (10 to 15 years).

Kreicbergs et al. (2004) conducted a study to identify anxiety and depression among bereaved parents 4 to 9 years following a child's death from cancer. A population-based register was used to identify the children. Parents of these children were selected for the years 1992 through 1997, and 449 agreed to participate, an 80% response rate. A sample of 368 children was randomly selected and matched with deceased children on demographic variables. The nonbereaved parent sample, 457, consisted of 69% of parents contacted. Data were obtained by a comprehensive questionnaire that was developed using information obtained from interviews with subsamples of parents. Bereaved parents were at significantly higher levels of risk compared with nonbereaved parents in regard to both anxiety and depression, with higher risk a 4 to 6 years postloss than at 7 to 9 years postloss. Risks for both variables were higher for bereaved mothers than for bereaved fathers and when the child had been age 9 or older. The large samples and a nonbereaved control group were strengths of this study. The retrospective design was a limitation.

Rando (1983) recruited 27 married couples whose children had died of cancer 2 months to 3 years previously. Contacts were made with parents prior to the child's death, but data were not collected until after the deaths. Rando administered the Grief Experiences Inventory (Sanders, 1979–1980) and conducted interviews with the couples. Poor adjustment was found to be higher among parents who had little warning of the child's death (less than 6 months) or too much time prior to death (more than 18 months).

Saiki-Craighill (2001) interviewed 24 Japanese mothers before they joined a support group and again 6 and 12 months later. Qualitative data were also obtained from support group transcriptions. The support group was conducted over a 2-year period. The findings were reported as chronological reflections of the mothers' experiences, for example, the initial numbing of emotions; grieving, including depression and moving out of depression; and, later, recognition of the positive aspects of the child's illness and death experiences on the mothers. Some similarities to Martinson et al.'s (1993) study were that mothers reported guilt for the treatment imposed on their children, felt the deaths were beyond their control, and reported being misread by others (e.g., "I am glad you are doing well"). Mothers could handle these assumptions and comments later, but not early in bereavement.

Finding Meaning and Making Sense of the Deaths: Cross-Cultural Comparisons

Martinson et al.'s (2000) cross-cultural study was the only one that asked questions regarding the meaning of life and death and beliefs about suffering and death. Korean participants' responses were that parents and spouses are buried underground, but children are buried in your heart. In Taiwan, responses to the first question focused on a child's death as "off time," that is, that parents should not have to bury their children. Some parents felt that their children's suffering was so intense they were better off not living.

Parents' Bereavement Health Status Following a Child's Death by Cancer

Birenbaum et al.'s (1996) study was the only one that used a standardized health questionnaire to examine parents' health status before and after a child's death. However, some studies obtained interview data from parents regarding their health. For example, Martinson et al. (1994) reported that three fathers died after heart attacks; others had heart attacks but did not die. Parents reported "not being as healthy as before," being exhausted, no longer feeling "carefree," and that mothers were "worse off than fathers." Alcohol problems were reported in 8 of 48 families (16%). It is not known whether the rates of heart attacks and alcohol abuse are excessive, because no comparison data were reported by the authors.

Coping Strategies Used by Parents Bereaved Following Their Children's Deaths Due to Cancer

Parents in Martinson et al. (1994)'s longitudinal study reported the "empty space phenomenon" left by the deceased child. Parents coped with the grief associated with emptiness by "getting over it"; "filling the emptiness" by working and keeping busy; and "keeping the connection" by integrating pain and loss, stories, and vivid memories. None of the other research reports specifically mentioned parents' coping.

CANCER DEATH BEREAVEMENT: SUMMARY

Investigators from several countries have conducted studies involving bereaved parents following a child's death associated with cancer. The majority of these studies obtained data by conducting personal interviews with parents. The data provide insights into what it is like to experience a child's extended illness and death. In some cultures, the stigma associated with having a child die from cancer apparently limits support parents obtain outside their families.

The SCL-90 was the only standardized measure used to collect data, which limits comparisons with other findings within this section. Time since the loss and before parent recruitment (up to 5 years) is a methodological concern. Potential sample bias and nonrepresentative samples need to be addressed in the future. There was no mention of concepts or theory in any of the articles reviewed for this section.

Only Birenbaum et al. (1996) collected data prior to the child's death and during bereavement, yet having a child with cancer is a prolonged, highly stressful experience for parents, with long-lasting consequences. The uncertainty and unpredictability of the children's outcomes have been shown to lead to avoidance, denial, and disengagement strategies when the child is being treated (Kazak, 2004). Caring for the ill child, watching him or her suffer, and "being on an emotional roller coaster" because of remission and relapse cycles are some of the probable causes of spillover effects on parents' bereavement that need to be taken into account in this area of research.

SIMILARITIES AND DIFFERENCES FOR SUDDEN DEATH AND EXTENDED ILLNESS PARENT BEREAVEMENT EXPERIENCES

One of the purposes of this chapter was to determine whether there are sufficient data to make comparisons of parents' experiences when bereaved by a child's sudden, violent death as opposed to being bereaved by a child's death following an extended illness. The data show that specific comparisons are not possible, but some similarities and differences can be discussed on the basis of available evidence.

Parents of very ill children and parents bereaved by a child's violent death are relatively young; on average, they are in their 30s and 40s. Undergoing these highly stressful events at these ages puts these parents at risk for serious health consequences and even their own untimely deaths (Hall & Irwin, 2001; Li et al., 2003).

Although the data defy direct comparison, parents under both bereavement circumstances reported devastating effects of the deaths of their children. Regardless of the cause of death, parents reported that their lives had changed forever. Parents in all cultures studied commented on the death of a child "being out of order," which is most difficult for them to comprehend because the death of a child violates the parents' beliefs about a just world. One Chinese mother stated that "black hair should not precede white hair." The untimely deaths of young people rob parents of the past, present, and especially the future. The parental role in both death circumstances leaves parents feeling victimized, because much of a parent's identity involves protecting and providing for his or her children and looking forward to the children's future.

It appears that not many questions were asked in regard to parents' ability to find meaning in their children's deaths following an extended illness. One interesting clue was the comment by Japanese mothers about "being tough" (Saiki-Craighill, 2001). These comments were similar to those in the

Parent Bereavement Project: "I gained strength in the face of adversity" (Murphy, 1997).

The findings from the majority of studies reported in this chapter suggest that mothers report higher rates of emotional distress than do fathers. Triggers—reminders of the child that present themselves in the bereaved parents' environment—are very painful for parents.

Important differences in a child's manner of death have yet to be examined. For example, I did not find any studies following a child's extended illness that examined the potential benefits of anticipatory grief, or studies that compared parents' responses to various types of cancer, such as leukemia versus solid tumor cancers.

RESEARCH RECOMMENDATIONS

Both areas of study addressed in this chapter can benefit from more rigorous conceptualization, study design, and measurement. Investigators of sudden, violent death bereavement continue to examine grief as a central focus of inquiry, yet there have been recommendations in the literature for at least a decade suggesting that grief is too narrow a focus for violent death bereavement—for example, that symptoms of PTSD should also be included (Amick-McMullan et al., 1991; Stevens-Guille, 1999).

More research is needed in this area regarding the marital relationship. Contrary to conventional wisdom, divorce rates were low in the Parent Bereavement Project, but in most other studies that recruited marital dyads, the marital relationship was not investigated. We need to know how marriages survive these highly stressful events, which are experienced primarily by young couples.

Future studies in the United States need to recruit samples of greater ethnic diversity. Parents of Native American, African American, Latino, and Asian youth are not being studied in the same proportions as parents of deceased Caucasians. For example, in the United States in 2002, these three ethnic groups of 15- to 24-year-olds had significantly higher rates of death by homicide compared with Caucasian young people. Deaths by homicide per 100,000 population were 5.2 for Caucasians, 83.1 for African Americans, 29.6 for Latinos, and 18.8 for Native Americans (National Center for Health Statistics, 2004).

CONCLUSION

This chapter has described parents' bereavement experiences following children's violent deaths and deaths following an extended illness resulting from cancer. These contrasting bereavement trajectories provide a context in which to determine whether one cause of a child's death influences parent outcomes in different ways from another. Available data are insufficient and not methodologically rigorous enough to make these comparisons. Research regarding violent death is increasing, whereas studies of parent bereavement following a child's death due to cancer appear to have decreased. The extreme stress brought about by anguish following violent death and death after an extended illness places parents at risk for illness and their own untimely deaths. In this chapter, I have portrayed some of the more common stressors associated with parent bereavement and examined changes over time in parents' health and well-being. More rigorous methods are recommended as investigators conduct the next generation of parent bereavement studies.

REFERENCES

American Psychiatric Association. (1987). *Diagnostic and statistical manual of mental disorders* (3rd ed., rev.). Washington, DC: Author.

Amick-McMullan, A., Kilpatrick, D. G., & Resnick, H. S. (1991). Homicide as a risk factor for PTSD among surviving family members. *Behavior Modification, 15,* 545–559.

Biondi, M., & Picardi, A. (1996). Clinical and biological aspects of bereavement and loss-induced depression: A reappraisal. *Psychotherapy and Psychosomatics, 65,* 229–245.

Birenbaum, L. K., Stewart, B., & Phillips, D. (1996). Health status of bereaved parents. *Nursing Research, 45,* 105–109.

Carver, C. S., Scheier, M. F., & Weintraub, J. K. (1989). Assessing coping strategies: A theoretically based approach. *Journal of Personality and Social Psychology, 56,* 267–283.

Centers for Disease Control and Prevention. (1997, February 7). Rates of homicide, suicide, and firearm-related death among children—26 industrialized countries. *Morbidity and Mortality Weekly Report, 46*(5), 101–105.

Cohen, S., & Rodriguez, M. (1995). Pathways linking affective disturbances and physical disorders. *Health Psychology, 14,* 374–380.

Davis, C. G., Wortman, C. B., Lehman, D. R., & Silver, R. (2000). Searching for meaning in loss: Are clinical assumptions correct? *Death Studies, 24,* 497–540.

Derogatis, L. R. (1977). *BSI—Administration, scoring, and procedures manual I.* Baltimore: Clinical Psychometric Research.

Derogatis, L. R. (1992). *BSI—Administration, scoring, and procedures manual II.* Baltimore: Clinical Psychometric Research.

Dryfoos, J. (1991). Adolescents at risk: A summation of work in the field. Programs and policies. *Journal of Adolescent Health, 12,* 630–637.

Gilbert, K. (1997). Couple coping with the death of a child. In C. Figley, B. Bride, & N. Mazza (Eds.), *Death and trauma: The traumatology of grieving* (pp. 101–122). Philadelphia: Taylor & Francis.

Green, B. L. (1990). Defining trauma: Terminology and generic stressor dimensions. *Journal of Applied Social Psychology, 20*, 1632–1642.

Hall, M., & Irwin, M. (2001). Physiological indices of functioning in bereavement. In M. Stroebe, R. Hansson, W. Stroebe, & H. Schut (Eds.), *Handbook of bereavement research: Consequences, coping, and care* (pp. 473–492). Washington, DC: American Psychological Association.

James, L., & Johnson, B. (1997). The needs of parents of pediatric oncology patients during the palliative care phase. *Journal of Pediatric Oncology Nursing, 14*, 83–95.

Janoff-Bulman, R., & Frantz, C. (1997). The impact of trauma on meaning: From meaningless world to meaningful life. In M. Power & C. Brewin (Eds.), *The transformation of meaning in psychological therapies* (pp. 91–106). New York: Wiley.

Jordan, J. R. (2001). Is suicide bereavement different? A reassessment of the literature. *Suicide and Life-Threatening Behavior, 31*, 91–101.

Kazak, A. (2004). Research priorities for family assessment and intervention in pediatric oncology. *Journal of Pediatric Oncology Nursing, 21*, 141–144.

Kessler, R. C., Sonnega, A., Bromet, E., Hughes, M., & Nelson, C. B. (1995). Posttraumatic stress disorder in the National Comorbidity Survey. *Archives of General Psychiatry, 52*, 1048–1060.

Kreicbergs, U., Valdimarsdottir, U., Onelov, E., Henter, J., & Steineck, G. (2004). Anxiety and depression in parents 4–9 years after the loss of a child owing to a malignancy: A population-based follow-up. *Psychological Medicine, 34*, 1431–1441.

Li, J., Mortensen, P., & Olsen, J. (2003). Mortality in parents after death of a child in Denmark: A nationwide follow-up study. *The Lancet, 361*, 363–367.

Martinson, I. M., & Cohen, M. (1988). Themes from a longitudinal study of family reactions to childhood cancer. *Journal of Psychosocial Oncology, 6*(3–4), 81–98.

Martinson, I. M., Guang, C., & Yi-Hua, L. (1993). Chinese families after the death of a child from cancer. *European Journal of Cancer Care, 2*, 169–173.

Martinson, I. M., McClowry, S. G., Davies, B., & Kuhlenkamp, E. J. (1994). Changes over time: A study of family bereavement following childhood cancer. *Journal of Palliative Care, 10*, 19–25.

Martinson, I. M., Lee, H., & Kim, S. (2000). Culturally based interventions for families whose child dies. *Illness, Crisis & Loss, 8*, 17–31.

Menaghan, E. (1983). Individual coping efforts and family studies: Conceptual and methodological issues. *Marriage and Family Review, 6*, 113–135.

Middleton, W., Raphael, B., Burnett, P., & Martinek, N. (1998). A longitudinal study comparing bereavement phenomena in recently bereaved spouses, adult children, and parents. *Australian and New Zealand Journal of Psychiatry, 32*, 235–241.

Murphy, S. A. (1986). Health and recovery status of natural disaster victims one and three years later. *Research in Nursing & Health, 9*, 331–340.

Murphy, S. A. (1997). *Parent bereavement stress and nursing intervention final report* (Report No. RO1 NRO1). Seattle: University of Washington.

Murphy, S. A., Johnson, L. C., Chung, I. J., & Beaton, R. D. (2003). The incidence of PTSD following the violent death of a child and predictors of change over time. *Journal of Traumatic Stress, 16,* 17–26.

Murphy, S. A., Johnson, L. C., & Lohan, J. (2000). The aftermath of the violent death of a child: An integration of the assessments of parents' mental distress and PTSD during the first 5 years of bereavement. *Journal of Loss and Trauma, 7,* 203–222.

Murphy, S. A., Johnson, L. C., & Lohan, J. (2003a). The effectiveness of coping resources and strategies used by bereaved parents 1 and 5 years after the violent deaths of their children. *Omega: The Journal of Death and Dying, 47,* 25–44.

Murphy, S. A., Johnson, L. C., & Lohan, J. (2003b). Finding meaning in a child's violent death: A five-year prospective analysis of parents' personal narratives and empirical data. *Death Studies, 27,* 381–404.

Murphy, S. A., Johnson, L. C., & Weber, N. A. (2002). Coping strategies following a child's violent death: How parents differ in their responses. *Omega: The Journal of Death and Dying, 45,* 99–118.

Murphy, S. A., Johnson, L. C., Wu, L., Fan, J. J., & Lohan, J. (2003). Bereaved parents' outcomes 4 to 60 months after their children's deaths by accident, suicide, or homicide: A comparative study demonstrating differences. *Death Studies, 27,* 39–61.

Murphy, S. A., Lohan, J., Braun, T., Johnson, L. C., Cain, K. C., Baugher, R., et al. (1999). Parents' health, health care utilization, and health behaviors following the violent deaths of their 12 to 28 year-old children: A prospective, longitudinal analysis. *Death Studies, 23,* 1–29.

National Center for Health Statistics. (2004). *Deaths: Final data for 2002. National vital statistics reports* (Vol. 53, No. 5). Washington, DC: U.S. Government Printing Office.

Parkerson, G. R., Gehlback, S. H., Wagner, E. H., James, S. A., Clapp, N. E., & Muhlbaier, L. H. (1981). The Duke–UNC Health Profile: An adult health status instrument for primary care. *Medical Care, 19,* 806–828.

Rando, T. A. (1983). An investigation of grief and adaptation in parents whose children have died from cancer. *Journal of Pediatric Psychology, 1,* 3–20.

Rando, T. A. (1996). Complications in mourning traumatic death. In K. Doka (Ed.), *Living with grief after sudden loss* (pp. 139–159). Washington, DC: Taylor & Francis.

Saiki-Craighill, S. (2001). The grieving process of Japanese mothers who have lost a child to cancer. *Journal of Pediatric Oncology Nursing, 18,* 260–275.

Sanders, C. M. (1979–1980). A comparison of adult bereavement in the death of a spouse, child, and parent. *Omega: The Journal of Death and Dying, 10,* 303–322.

Schwab, R. (1992). Effects of a child's death on the marital relationship. *Death Studies, 16,* 141–154.

Séguin, M., Lesage, A., & Kiely, M. C. (1995). Parental bereavement after suicide and accident: A comparative study. *Suicide and Life-Threatening Behavior, 25,* 489–498.

Spanier, G. B. (1976). Measuring dyadic adjustment: New scales for assessing the quality of marriage and similar dyads. *Journal of Marriage and the Family, 38,* 15–27.

Stevens-Guille, M. (1999). Intersections of grief and trauma: Family members' reactions to homicide. In C. R. Figley (Ed.), *Traumatology of grieving: Conceptual, theoretical, and treatment foundations* (pp. 53–69). Philadelphia: Brunner/Mazel.

Stroebe, W., & Schut, H. (2001). Risk factors in bereavement outcome: A methodological and empirical review. In M. S. Stroebe, R. O. Hansson, W. Stroebe, & H. Schut (Eds.), *Handbook of bereavement research: Consequences, coping, and care* (pp. 349–371). Washington, DC: American Psychological Association.

Thompson, K. E., & Range, L. M. (1990–1991). Recent bereavement from suicide and other deaths: Can people imagine it as it really is? *Omega: The Journal of Death and Dying, 22,* 249–259.

Thompson, M. P., Norris, F. H., & Ruback, R. B. (1998). Comparative distress levels of inner-city family members of homicide victims. *Journal of Traumatic Stress, 11,* 223–242.

Weisman, A. (1973). Coping with untimely death. *Psychiatry, 36,* 366–379.

19

LONG-TERM CONSEQUENCES OF PARENTAL DEATH IN CHILDHOOD: PSYCHOLOGICAL AND PHYSIOLOGICAL MANIFESTATIONS

LINDA J. LUECKEN

It has been widely theorized by researchers and clinicians that adverse childhood family experiences are linked to the development of some forms of psychopathology in adulthood. Types of adversity commonly thought to increase long-term vulnerability include abusive treatment; neglectful parenting; and family disruptions as a result of divorce, abandonment, or death of a parent. The focus of this chapter is on the long-term consequences of the early death of a parent. Although many years of research support links between childhood parental loss and the occurrence of certain forms of psychological disorder in adulthood, a number of studies have failed to find clear associations. The inconsistency in findings has led many theorists to disregard parental loss as a risk factor for later psychological disorder and others to suggest the need to go beyond main effects models to identify key pathways and moderators of outcomes (e.g., Sandler, 2001; see also chap. 25, this volume). Although less studied, recent evidence (Agid et al., 1999; Krause, 1998) also shows that early parental loss may influence physical health in later years, potentially through the development of neurobiological and physiological systems associated with stress-related illness. Like studies of psychological outcomes, some studies of

Support for this research was provided by American Heart Association Grant 0130024N.

stress-related illness have failed to find main effects of parental loss on physical health outcomes, further supporting the importance of moderating factors.

The majority of research conducted to date on moderating factors has focused on negative aspects of childhood family environments as predictors of poor mental and physical health outcomes. However, studies of adaptation failures alone cannot tell the full story of long-term adjustment following stressful early life experiences. In almost every study of early adversity a subset of children can be identified who not only avoid negative outcomes but also grow into healthy, competent adults despite having faced tremendous obstacles (Masten et al., 2004; Sandler, 2001; Werner, 1993; Werner & Smith, 1982). These children challenge researchers and practitioners to identify the factors that promote resilience in the face of the early death of a parent. The study of resilience focuses on identifying processes that account for positive outcomes in the face of adversity (Luthar, Cicchetti, & Becker, 2000; Masten & Coatsworth, 1998; Masten et al., 2004). Resilience is defined not only by the absence of pathology but also by the restoration and even advancement of health and well-being following stressful experiences. Much has been written about children's psychological resilience following traumatic experiences. Studies have found that both child- and family-level characteristics contribute to psychological resilience following parental loss. Less is known about the development of physiological resilience and long-term good physical health.

This chapter briefly reviews existing evidence concerning the short- and long-term impact of early parental loss on psychological and physiological outcomes. Many studies have defined early loss experiences as including the death of a sibling or other close relative, or separation from a parent because of death, divorce, abandonment, hospitalization, or other temporary or permanent separations. This chapter specifically focuses on losses resulting from the premature death of a parent during infancy, childhood, or adolescence. Parental death is viewed as a powerful early life experience with the potential to alter the development of biochemical, hormonal, emotional, or behavioral responses to the environment and later life stressors. Social and environmental influences present both before and after the death are considered as significant moderators of the potential impact, and I emphasize both risk and protective factors. Finally, limitations to this area of research are presented, along with directions for future research.

PSYCHOLOGICAL CONSEQUENCES OF EARLY PARENTAL LOSS

Short-Term Psychological Consequences

The long-standing research and clinical interest in the effects of early parental death on bereaved children's psychological adjustment is evidenced by the large number of studies that have been conducted over many years. In most of these studies the death is viewed as a major traumatic event that can jeopardize children's mental health. It is clear that both the child and the surviving parent typically experience the early death of a parent as an acute and profound crisis. In the short term, bereaved children are at risk of a wide range of mental health problems, including depression, anxiety, conduct problems, impaired school performance, social withdrawal, feelings of insecurity and vulnerability to their own death, and a low sense of internal control (Lutzke, Ayers, Sandler, & Barr, 1997; Tremblay & Israel, 1998; Van Eerdewegh, Bieri, Parrilla, & Clayton, 1982; Worden & Silverman, 1996).

A number of risk factors increase the child's vulnerability to poor mental health outcomes. Conjugal bereavement studies have consistently shown elevated psychological distress in the surviving parent, as evidenced by high levels of acute grief, restlessness and irritability, physical distress, and drug use (Stroebe & Stroebe, 1993). Parental depression is a significant risk factor for internalizing and externalizing disorders in children and adolescents (Langrock, Compas, Keller, Merchant, & Copeland, 2002), and considerable evidence suggests that the mental health problems experienced by bereaved parents are linked to the mental health problems of their children (Kalter et al., 2002; Kranzler, Shaffer, Wasserman, & Davies, 1990). Many studies have further focused on poor-quality or neglectful care provided by the surviving parent as a key risk factor for poor psychological outcomes. Parental stress and depression are associated with disrupted and negative parenting practices (Gelfand & Teti, 1990; Lee & Gotlib, 1991); therefore, a highly distressed bereaved parent is at risk of providing inadequate care for the bereaved child.

The death can also precipitate a series of additional stressful experiences, including financial burdens, frequent moves, lesser contact with the surviving parent, disruption of daily and social routines, and separation of family members. These negative events are associated with greater risk of child mental health problems (Sandler, Gersten, Reynolds, Kallgren, & Ramirez, 1988; Thompson, Kaslow, Price, Williams, & Kingree, 1998). Haine, Ayers, Sandler, Wolchik, and Weyer (2003) suggested that stressful events reduce a child's self-esteem, increasing the risk of internalizing problems in parentally bereaved children. Parental death can be viewed a distal major event that results in increased vulnerability to mental health problems if the environment following the loss is stressful and the child lacks the resources to effectively manage the stress. Restricted mourning behaviors and the inhibition of emotional expression may also put bereaved children at increased risk of mental health problems (Saler & Skolnick, 1992; Sandler, Wolchik, Davis, Haine, & Ayers, 2003).

Despite the evidence for risk, it is clear that many bereaved children do not experience mental health problems. Recent studies have begun to examine protective resources that promote adaptive coping and positive adjustment following parental loss. Masten et al. (2004) identified parenting quality as a "core resource" that promotes psychosocial resilience in the face of childhood adversity. Studies have consistently shown that resilient psychosocial outcomes following early parental loss are positively predicted by the primary caregiver's provision of warmth and discipline (Lin, Sandler, Ayers, Wolchik, & Luecken, 2004; Raveis, Siegel, & Karus, 1999; Sandler et al., 1992; West, Sandler, Pillow, Baca, & Gersten, 1991). *Positive parenting*, defined as caregiver warmth and consistent discipline, has been identified as an important protective factor for bereaved children (Haine, Wolchik, Sandler, Millsap, & Ayers, 2006). Haine et al. (2006) found that positive parenting served as a compensatory protective resource that exerted a beneficial effect on children's mental health independent of the effects of negative life events. Sandler et al. (1992, 2003) also have found that cohesion within the family and the consistent occurrence of positive family events contribute to resilient outcomes in bereaved children. These aspects of positive parenting are important for the adaptive development of any child, but they appear to be particularly critical for children who face the intense emotions and stressors associated with the death of a parent.

Child-level protective resources include self-efficacy beliefs, higher self-esteem, expression of feelings with understanding family members, and ability to maintain a positive sense of self in the face of adversity (Haine et al., 2003; Saler & Skolnick, 1992; Sandler et al., 2003; Worden & Silverman, 1996). Lin et al. (2004) evaluated child- and family-level protective factors in parentally bereaved children. At the family level, children's resilience was positively predicted by the surviving caregiver's warmth and ability to provide consistent discipline. At the individual level, the resilient children perceived negative events to be significantly less threatening to their well-being than did vulnerable children, and resilient children felt more able to effectively cope with life stress. Resilience may involve a chain of processes whereby adaptive coping behaviors lead to perceptions of efficacy, which improve psychological well-being (Lin et al., 2004; Sandler, Tein, Mehta, Wolchik, & Ayers, 2000).

Long-Term Psychological Consequences

A wide range of potential negative mental health outcomes in adulthood associated with early parental loss have been evaluated, with considerable inconsistency in findings. Classic psychology theories suggest that early loss of a parent is causal in the development of a number of psychological disorders over the life span (e.g., Bowlby, 1980). Vulnerability to depression and depressive disorders in adulthood have been perhaps the most commonly studied effects. Mack (2001) examined results from a large national survey and found that adults who experienced the death of a parent before age 19 had significantly higher levels of depression than those who grew up in intact families. Bifulco, Brown, and Harris (1987) reported that early loss of a mother was associated with a significantly higher incidence of depression in working-class women. Kivela, Luukinen, Koski, Viramo, and Kimmo (1998) conducted epidemiological studies of older adults (mean age = 63 years) in Finland. At the 5-year follow-up of adults who were not depressed at the study's start, parental death during childhood was an independent predictor of the development of major depression. Agid et al. (1999) found that middle-aged men and women with major depression were significantly more likely to have experienced early parental loss than were psychiatrically healthy control participants. In contrast, a number of studies have found that early parental loss is not directly or independently associated with increased risk of depression in adulthood (Kendler, Neale, Kessler, Heath, & Eaves, 1992; Kessler, Davis, & Kendler, 1997; Mireault & Bond, 1992).

A number of studies have also examined the role of early parental loss in the development of other forms of psychiatric disorders in adulthood. Agid et al. (1999) reported that patients with schizophrenia were more likely than healthy control participants to have experienced early parental death, and they proposed that genetic vulnerabilities interacted with early parental loss to predict the development of schizophrenia. Similarly, Kendler et al. (1992) evaluated the relation between parental death and the occurrence of psychiatric conditions, including major depression, generalized anxiety disorder, phobic disorders, panic disorder, and eating disorders. Premature parental death was associated only with increased risk of panic disorder or phobia.

The considerable inconsistencies in studies have led most researchers to conclude that other factors intervene in the relationship between early loss and adult psychopathology. Like conclusions drawn from studies of outcomes during childhood and adolescence, complex interactions between the loss experience and variables such as age at the time of loss, expression of grief, occurrence of stressful events following the loss, mental health of the surviving parent, and the quality of the relationship with the surviving parent, have been considered as potentially important mediators or moderators of the longer term impact of the loss. In Bifulco et al.'s (1987) study, cited previously, poor parental care proved to be a strong mediator of the relation between early parental loss and adult depression. Kendler, Gardner, and Prescott (2006) outlined a developmental model in which early parental loss serves as a pathway to major depression in men but is influenced by and influences other risk factors, including genetic risk, low parental warmth, neurotic personality, low educational attainment, substance misuse, and later stressful events. A similar model for women also found that early parental loss served as a pathway to adult depression, in this case highlighting its negative impact on educational attainment and later life interpersonal relationships (Kendler, Gardner, & Prescott, 2002).

Researchers have increasingly highlighted the importance of the family environment as a moderator of the long-term psychological consequences of parental loss. Bowlby (1980) felt that the nature of the care received by the child following the loss is a critical factor that influences the long-term impact. Similarly, Tennant (1988) suggested that studies that attempt to relate the occurrence of adult depression to childhood loss of a parent without examining the quality of the relationship with the surviving parent lack the most critical component. Such an examination is particularly critical given that the surviving parent is likely to be suffering considerable stress, increasing the potential for neglect of the child's needs. Saler and Skolnick (1992) found that adults who described their surviving parent as neglectful, lacking in affection, overcontrolling, or overprotective reported significantly more experiences of depression.

Overall, the literature is fairly consistent in finding that neglectful parenting and poor coping of the surviving parent are important risk factors in the development of depression in adulthood by children who lose a parent. Less studied have been the protective factors that promote resilience in adulthood, the exception being resilience as defined by the absence of pathology. In one study, young adults who experienced early parental loss in the presence of a strong relationship with the surviving parent had fewer depressive symptoms and higher social support than young adults from nonbereaved families who also reported strong parental relationships (Luecken, 2000a). In this study, positive parent–child relationships moderated the impact of parental loss on depression and social support outcomes. These findings suggest that successful negotiation of uncontrollable stress in childhood (promoted by a strong relationship with the caregiver) may result in enhanced adaptive abilities later in life. Masten et al. (2004) provided striking evidence that individuals who manifest resilience in emerging adulthood display adaptive capacities that promote successful negotiation of challenge over the life span.

Methodological Considerations

Two primary methodological strategies are evident in human studies of the long-term psychological consequences of early parental loss. First, many studies have examined clinically diagnosed patients or inpatients in mental health facilities. This strategy inevitably raises concerns about selection bias and the appropriate control groups to use for comparison. Second, because of the inherent difficulty of conducting prospective studies, most studies are retrospective, either by asking adults at different stages of life to relate the effects of parental loss or by correlating current adjustment with recall of early life experiences.

Interpretation of parental loss studies can be complicated by the common strategy of combining groups that recalled separation from a parent by any means (e.g., death, divorce, abandonment), making it difficult to tease apart outcomes specific to parental death. Although some studies have not found the cause of separation to differentially predict outcomes (e.g., Raphael, Cubis, Dunne, Lewin, & Kelly, 1990), others have found considerable variation in outcomes associated with parental death versus divorce (e.g., Agid et al., 1999; Kendler et al., 1992; Mack, 2001; Maier & Lachman, 2000). Although both divorce and parental death are associated with major disruption of the family environment, there is considerable variability in the types of stressors experienced by each and the impact of exposure to those stressors on mental health outcomes (Sandler et al., 2003). Finally, note that the study of resilience implies a response to an adverse event or situation. It is conceptually difficult to make comparisons regarding the impact of parenting on resilience for children from bereaved versus nonbereaved families.

PHYSIOLOGICAL OUTCOMES FOLLOWING EARLY PARENTAL LOSS

In contrast to the large number of studies that have examined long-term psychological outcomes associated with early parental loss, only recently have studies begun to consider potential consequences for the development of physiological systems and long-term physical health. Early parental loss has been linked to increased physical health problems over the life span in several epidemiological and correlational studies (Agid et al., 1999; Felitti et al., 1998; Krause, 1998; Lowman, Drossman, Cramer, & McKee, 1987). Other studies have not found a relationship between early parental loss and health problems in midlife (Maier & Lachman, 2000; Tennant, 1988), again raising the issue of intervening and moderating variables.

One pathway by which early loss may influence health over the life span is through the development of poor health behaviors, such as smoking, heavy alcohol consumption, and a sedentary lifestyle. A large body of research implicates characteristics of early family relationships in the development and maintenance of health behaviors (Repetti, Taylor, & Seeman, 2002; Taylor, Repetti, & Seeman, 1997). For example, Agid et al. (1999) reported that parental loss was associated with a stronger lifetime history of smoking behavior. Maternally separated rodents and primates show neurobiological alterations that indicate permanently altered sensitivity to drugs of abuse and consume significantly more alcohol than mother-reared animals both before and after stress exposure (Fahlke et al., 2000; Meaney, Brake, & Gratton, 2002), suggesting that disrupted care during development may form a neurobiological basis for vulnerability to substance abuse later in life.

New research on long-term physiological correlates of early parental loss raises important questions about the role of the psychosocial environment in modulating the development of bodily systems implicated in psychological and biological self-regulation over the life span. Recent evidence suggests that early loss experiences have the potential to exert long-term organizing effects on cognitive, behavioral, emotional, and physiological responses to later life stress, in a manner that may influence vulnerability to stress-related mental and physical disorders over the life span (Brotman, Gouley, Klein, Castellanos, & Pine, 2003; Luecken & Lemery, 2004; McEwen, 2003).

A biopsychosocial approach to understanding the impact of early parental loss presumes that "biological, psychological and social forces act together to determine an individual's health and vulnerability to disease" (Straub, 2002, p. 30). A growing body of evidence demonstrates the interconnectedness of physiological and psychological processes in vulnerability and resistance to both physical and psychological illness. One mechanism that may link the experience of early parental loss to physical health over the life span involves physiological stress responses (Luecken & Lemery, 2004; McEwen, 2003; Repetti et al., 2002). Stress responses prepare the body to respond to threat by mobilizing energy, increasing cardiac output, altering immune function, and inhibiting nonessential bodily functions. Stress responses involve a number of bodily systems, including the hypothalamic–pituitary–adrenocortical (HPA) axis and the sympathetico–adrenomedullary (SAM) system. The HPA axis regulates the production and release of the glucocorticoid hormone cortisol. The SAM component of the body's physiological stress response is excitatory in nature and is responsible for many of the symptoms commonly referred to as the *fight or flight response* (Bauer, Quas, & Boyce, 2002). Among other things, SAM activation results in increased blood pressure, norepinephrine, and epinephrine.

Short-term stress responses to novel situations are adaptive and facilitate behavioral strategies for responding (McEwen, 2003). However, models of the negative long-term effects of stress focus on the consequences of dysregulated stress responses, including those that are exaggerated, prolonged, or of insufficient magnitude to mount an effective response. The *allostatic load hypothesis* describes the cumulative wear and tear on the body that results from prolonged or inefficiently managed arousal of physiological stress response systems, and it provides evidence that dysregulated stress responses contribute over time to the etiology of physical and psychological illnesses, including hypertension, heart disease, depression, and infectious illnesses (McEwen, 2002, 2003). Cortisol dysregulations are also associated with increased risk of substance abuse, externalizing and internalizing disorders, and behavioral precursors to illness (Bauer et al., 2002; McEwen, 2002, 2003). The pattern of physiological responses to stress also indicates risk of later psychopathology and can provide insight into more general abilities to regulate arousal (Bauer et al., 2002), which can help identify individuals who are most vulnerable to the development of psychiatric and physical illness later in life.

The allostatic load hypothesis is primarily focused on risky patterns of physiological stress responding. Although less has been theorized regarding resilience in physiological responses, it is clear that to react quickly and flexibly, such that internal physiological systems adequately meet but do not exceed environmental demands, is highly adaptive for an organism. Equally important is for internal systems to efficiently regulate and terminate the physiological response once environmental demands lessen. The body has several mechanisms for regulation of the magnitude and duration of stress responses. Cortisol, for example, is regulated through a system of negative feedback that serves to prevent adverse effects of prolonged secretion. Cortisol also plays an important role in suppressing the initial SAM response to stress. Resilient cardiovascular responses would be evidenced by rapid initial response to challenge followed by rapid recovery to baseline after the challenge has ceased.

A number of recent reviews provide convincing evidence that early life experiences exert an important regulatory influence on the development of physiological stress response systems (Luecken & Lemery, 2004; McEwen, 2003; Nemeroff, 2004; Repetti et al., 2002). The development of the brain persists from the prenatal period well into adolescence, and it is susceptible to a wide variety of environmental influences throughout this time (Rice & Barone, 2000). In particular, early experiences with the primary caregiver can exert direct, enduring effects on the development of neurobiological stress response systems (Meaney et al., 2002). Advances in this area of research have been largely driven by animal studies, which demonstrate that stressful early life experiences can result in the development of abnormally high or low stress responses or abnormally patterned responses that lead to increased allostatic load (McEwen, 2002, 2003). Although it is clear that the long-term impact for human children may be quite different, animal models have been extremely important because they have demonstrated the powerful ability of early rearing experiences to alter the development of brain structures, brain chemistry, and neural regulation of hormonal and cardiovascular systems.

Some of the earliest indications of the profound impact of permanent separation from the caregiver were demonstrated in the 1960s and 1970s by Harry Harlow. From these seminal studies, the abnormal behavior and severe socioemotional deficits seen in animals deprived of a mother or substitute caregiver early in life became strikingly evident. Rat pups separated from their mothers show a series of behavioral and physiological changes, including decreased serum growth hormone secretion, stimulation of corticosterone (comparable to cortisol in humans) and catecholamine secretion, social withdrawal, behaviors characteristic of depression, and altered food intake (Kuhn, Pauk, & Schanberg, 1990). Less extreme deprivation studies have commonly followed paradigms that expose the animal to repeated separation from the mother (typically for 3 hours at a time) during the early postnatal period. Rat pups exposed to these types of separations exhibit hyperreactive HPA responses, coupled with elevated behavioral signs of anxiety (Plotsky et al., 2005; Plotsky, Owen, & Nemeroff, 1998). Hofer (1994) suggested that long-term physiological changes may be a direct result of deprivation from the mother's regulatory influence on the pup's developing physiology. Maternal separation may simultaneously withdraw all maternal regulators at a time when the infant's physiological and behavioral systems are dependent on them for healthy, adaptive development, with the unfortunate result being increased predisposition to disease.

For nonhuman primates, maternal separation also results in acute and long-term physiological changes, including increases in heart rate (Reite, Kaemingk, & Boccia, 1989), plasma cortisol (Gunnar, Gonzalez, Goodlin, & Levine, 1981), cerebrospinal fluid, and monoamine concentrations (Bayart, Hayashi, Faull, Barchas, & Levine, 1990). Higley, Suomi, and Linnoila (1992) reported higher baseline cortisol and cerebrospinal fluid 3-methoxy-4-hydroxyphenylglycol in monkeys separated from their mothers and reared with peers. Peer-reared animals also showed higher plasma cortisol concentrations during stress than mother-reared animals, and they showed more aggressive and less social affiliative behaviors. Sanchez et al. (2005) reported that maternally separated rhesus monkeys exhibited increased cortisol reactivity, along with a flattened diurnal cortisol rhythm. It is interesting that these monkeys also showed an increased startle response, similar to findings with patients with anxiety disorders. Across nonhuman primate species, infant responses to maternal separation are not equal in their intensity. Reite et al. (1989) suggested that differences in responses to maternal separation may be attributable to the presence and quality of alternative attachments. Boccia, Laudenslager, and Reite (1994) directly correlated the separation-related responses of infant bonnet monkeys with the size of their alternative social networks.

Also of consequence for short- and long-term physical health is the responsiveness of the immune system. Suomi (1997) provided a review of the potential for maternal separation to negatively affect immune functions. Coe and Lubach (2003) reported that in nonhuman primates, early maternal separation resulted in long-lasting immune changes that increased vulnerability to stress-related illness such as simian immunodeficiency virus (the monkey equivalent of HIV). Lewis, Gluck, Petitto, Hensley, and Ozer (2000) extended these findings by examining long-term alterations in immune status associated with separation of infant rhesus monkeys from their mothers shortly after birth. These infants were raised in partial or total isolation for the first 9 months and were evaluated approximately 20 years later. Lewis et al. reported a significant increase in overall mortality in socially isolated monkeys relative to socially reared monkeys. The isolated monkeys who survived displayed significant alterations in several aspects of immune function, leading the researchers to speculate that an increased frequency of infectious illnesses may have accounted for the premature mortality.

Despite a large and intriguing literature using animal models, surprisingly few studies have directly evaluated physiological consequences associated with early parental loss in humans. Several studies have shown the detrimental effects on cortisol regulation for severely deprived children raised in Romanian orphanages (Carlson & Earls, 1997; Gunnar, Morison, Chisholm, & Schuder, 2001). Early parental loss has also been associated with higher blood pressure in young adults (Luecken, 1998) and with elevated daily cortisol in middle-aged adults (Nicolson, 2004). Breier et al. (1988) compared resting cortisol, beta-endorphin, and adrenocorticotropic hormone levels and lifetime history of psychiatric disorder in adults who lost a parent with control participants. Participants in the loss group who had experienced a major psychiatric disorder during adulthood reported a lower quality of home life and had significantly higher levels of cortisol and beta-endorphin. Breier et al. suggested that early stress may result in long-lasting alterations in neurobiological functions, which may affect adaptability to future stress.

Like studies of psychological consequences of early parental loss, future studies will need to go beyond main effects models to consider key intervening or moderating factors that predict long-term vulnerability or resilience in physical health and the pathways by which these factors exert their influence. Ben-Shlomo and Davey-Smith (1991) suggested that early life adversity can influence cardiovascular and respiratory health later in life through a pathway of continued socioeconomic deprivation, stress exposure, and acute detrimental effects on health. Similar *cumulative adversity* or *cumulative effects* theories suggest that the experience of early loss can direct children onto a life course that increases the risk of adverse long-term health outcomes through increased exposure to contemporary stressors (e.g., Hertzman, 1999; Rutter, O'Connor, & English and Romanian Adoptees Study Team, 2004). A resilience approach seeks to identify intervening factors capable of redirecting the child onto a healthier pathway, thereby reducing exposure to later stressors and improving life span physical health.

A strong bond with the surviving parent is one moderating factor that is capable of influencing the impact of early parental death on physiological systems. In one study, early loss was associated with greater cortisol reactivity to stress only if the relationship with the surviving parent was poor (Luecken, 2000b). Luecken and Appelhans (2006) found that the combination of early parental loss and reports of abusive treatment was associated with elevated cortisol relative to participants who had experienced parental loss in the absence of abusive treatment. In contrast, young adults who experienced parental loss and reported strong family relationships had recovery of diastolic blood pressure and heart rate stress responses that were stronger than participants from intact families with strong relationships, suggesting that the combination of parental loss and positive parenting may uniquely shape self-regulatory ability, thus contributing to resilience in the face of later stress (Luecken, Rodriguez, & Appelhans, 2005).

Methodological Considerations

Numerous limitations are inherent in the conclusions that can be drawn from animal studies. Perhaps most compelling is the extent to which findings relating early separation experiences to brain and neuroendocrine development in nonhuman species can be extrapolated to form hypotheses about the consequences of early parental death for human infants. For example, what is the human infant equivalent of 180 minutes daily maternal separation for several weeks in rat pups? In early monkey studies, maternal separation was often followed by total or near-total isolation or by rearing with unrelated peer groups. Beyond separation from the mother, most of the monkeys were completely deprived of an alternative adult attachment figure, the presence of whom may have ameliorated the harsh consequences of maternal separation. These findings are arguably most comparable with those of severely deprived children raised in substandard orphanages but may be less useful in understanding more normal bereavement experiences of children. Despite these limitations, the rich animal research literature clearly demonstrates the potential for early social adversity to dramatically alter the development of the brain and stress-related physiological systems, although the corresponding predictions for human children should be considered with caution.

In most animal models of early loss, a critical period exists for the separation or stress to have any impact on developing physiology. In rat pups, maternal deprivation appears to have no effect on glucocorticoid secretion if it occurs after the first few postnatal weeks. A critical period for lasting immune changes in monkeys is approximately within the first 6 months (similar to the first 3 to 5 years in humans). Some studies have suggested that for children, losses that occur earlier in life have a greater impact, although findings are largely inconsistent, and the existence of a true critical period for humans is not clear. Although much has been speculated regarding the importance of the first 3 years of life in humans, empirical studies suggest that traumatic experiences at any age can have lasting effects on neuroendocrine and related stress response systems. Rutter et al. (2004) described follow-up studies with children adopted into British families after experiencing severe deprivation in Romanian orphanages and found "a remarkable degree of recovery after restoration of normal family rearing" (p. 89). On the basis of this and related studies, it seems there is considerable room for restoration and advancement of health following traumatic childhood events such as death of a parent.

FUTURE DIRECTIONS

As Lin et al. (2004) noted, one common limitation of their study and similar studies was the focus on a lack of mental health problems, rather than evaluation of positive outcomes, as an indication of resilience. Because *resilience* is defined as more than the absence of pathology, it will be important for future studies to evaluate positive mental and physical health outcomes, including, but not limited to, academic or social competence, life satisfaction, purpose in life, goal motivation, achievement of developmental milestones, or positive well-being. Furthermore, integration of biological perspectives into the theoretical framework of resilience, along with empirical examination of biological foundations, is imperative for research on resilience to move forward (Curtis & Cicchetti, 2003). As Curtis and Cicchetti (2003) stated, "The goal of future research on resilience should be to increasingly incorporate multiple biological measures as part of a multiple levels of analysis approach to resilience research" (p. 775). Physiological resilience can be measured by the body's ability to flexibly vary heart rate to meet environmental challenges or quickly recover cardiovascular and hormonal indices to homeostatic levels after challenge, or by the immune system's capacity to resist infection.

Another challenge for resiliency research will be to begin to define the underlying processes that contribute to adaptive capacities in children that are affected by early parental loss (Sandler et al., 2003; Wyman, Sandler, Wolchik, & Nelson, 2000). Sandler and colleagues (Sandler, 2001; Sandler et al., 2003; see also chap. 25, this volume) have presented a theoretical framework that models the influence of vulnerability and protective factors on children following parental death. In brief, their model suggests that the effects of vulnerability and protective factors are mediated through the accomplishment of age-appropriate developmental competencies and the satisfaction of basic needs and goals. In Sandler's (2001) model, the death serves as a threat to a child's maintenance of basic needs, including a sense of self-esteem, belief in one's self-efficacy to affect one's environment, and a sense of social relatedness. Protective factors promote satisfaction of needs and competencies, and vulnerability factors impede their satisfaction. Sandler's model of the mechanisms underlying resilience following parental death provides excellent guidance for future studies in this area.

This chapter has separated psychosocial outcomes from physiological outcomes, yet this is an artificial separation at best. Growing evidence clearly demonstrates the interconnected nature of emotional, behavioral, social, and physiological processes. A more complete picture of the consequences of early parental death will be facilitated by evaluation of all of these processes in concert. Some researchers have begun this process, for example, by providing evidence that the neurobiological consequences of early family adversity are influential in the development of depression and anxiety disorders in adulthood (Heim et al., 2002; Heim, Plotsky, & Nemeroff, 2004). Elsewhere, a colleague and I outlined a broad model of theoretical pathways linking family-of-origin relationships to physiological stress responses, including cognitive–affective, genetic, and psychosocial pathways (Luecken & Lemery, 2004).

Applied to parental loss, a cognitive–affective pathway suggests that the loss and parenting quality following the loss can influence the development of emotional and cognitive responses to environmental challenges that then influence the magnitude and pattern of physiological stress responses (see Luecken, Appelhans, Kraft, & Brown, 2006). A psychosocial pathway suggests that early loss and subsequent parenting quality contribute to the development of psychosocial characteristics (e.g., self-esteem, hostility, negative affect) that may alter physiological vulnerability to stress. Genetic mediation and gene–environment interactions may also be evident such that the loss experience might influence the expression of genes that may render a child more or less vulnerable to stress. Rutter et al. (2004) described similar pathways by which childhood adversity might have a persistent effect on psychosocial adversity, including a continuation of adversity over the life span, cognitive–affective processing of the experiences, and lasting biological effects brought about by the early adversity. An important direction for future research will be to more closely examine these pathways and the interrelations among them.

Cross-cultural studies have demonstrated considerable differences in parenting beliefs and practices (Bornstein et al., 1998), raising the important question of how culture interacts with the experience of parental death to predict long-term outcomes. Bifulco et al. (1987) provided a clear statement of the importance of considering cultural context given that cultures differ in important moderators, such as the availability of more developed kinship structures or support following the death. Currently, a good understanding of the role of cultural practices and context in the short- and long-term psychological and physiological consequences of early parental death is lacking, and it is hoped that future studies will address this important area.

REFERENCES

Agid, O., Shapira, B., Zislin, J., Ritsner, M., Hanin, B., Murad, H., et al. (1999). Environment and vulnerability to major psychiatric illness: A case control study of early parental loss in major depression, bipolar disorder, and schizophrenia. *Molecular Psychiatry, 4*, 163–172.

Bauer, A. M., Quas, J. A., & Boyce, W. T. (2002). Associations between physiological reactivity and children's behavior: Advantages of a multisystem approach. *Developmental and Behavioral Pediatrics, 23*, 102–113.

Bayart, F., Hayashi, K. T., Faull, K. F., Barchas, J. D., & Levine, S. (1990). Influence of maternal proximity on behavioral and physiological responses to separation in infant rhesus monkeys. *Behavioral Neuroscience, 104*, 98–107.

Ben-Shlomo, Y., & Davey-Smith, G. (1991). Deprivation in infancy or adult life: Which is more important for mortality risk? *The Lancet, 337*, 530–534.

Bifulco, A., Brown, G., & Harris, T. (1987). Childhood loss of parent, lack of adequate parental care and adult depression: A replication. *Journal of Affective Disorders, 12,* 115–128.

Boccia, M. L., Laudenslager, M. L., & Reite, M. L. (1994). Intrinsic and extrinsic factors affect infant responses to maternal separation. *Psychiatry, 57,* 43–50.

Bornstein, M. H., Haynes, O. M., Azuma, H., Galperin, C., Maital, S., Ogino, M., et al. (1998). A cross-national study of self-evaluations and attributions in parenting: Argentina, Belgium, France, Israel, Italy, Japan, and the United States. *Developmental Psychology, 34,* 662–676.

Bowlby, J. (1980). *Attachment and loss: Vol. 3. Loss: Sadness and depression.* New York: Basic Books.

Breier, A., Kelsoe, J. R., Kirwon, P. D., Bellar, S. A., Wolkowitz, O. M., & Pickar, D. (1988). Early parental loss and development of adult psychopathology. *Archives of General Psychiatry, 45,* 987–993.

Brotman, L. M., Gouley, K. K., Klein, R. G., Castellanos, X., & Pine, D. S. (2003). Children, stress, and context: Integrating basic, clinical, and experimental prevention research. *Child Development, 74,* 1053–1057.

Carlson, M., & Earls, F. (1997). Psychological and neuroendocrinological sequelae of early social deprivation in institutionalized children in Romania. In C. S. Carter, I. I. Lederhendler, & B. Kirkpatrick (Eds.), *Annals of the New York Academy of Sciences: Vol. 807. The integrative neurobiology of affiliation* (pp. 419–428). New York: New York Academy of Sciences.

Coe, C. L., & Lubach, G. R. (2003). Critical periods of special health relevance for psychoneuroimmunology. *Brain, Behavior, and Immunity, 17,* 3–12.

Curtis, W. J., & Cicchetti, D. (2003). Moving research on resilience into the 21st century: Theoretical and methodological considerations in examining the biological contributors to resilience. *Development and Psychopathology, 15,* 773–810.

Fahlke, C., Lorenz, J. G., Long, J., Champous, M., Suomi, S. J., & Higley, J. D. (2000). Rearing experiences and stress-induced plasma cortisol as early risk factors for excessive alcohol consumption in nonhuman primates. *Alcoholism: Clinical and Experimental Research, 24,* 644–650.

Felitti, V. J., Anda, R. F., Nordenberg, D., Williamson, D. F., Spitz, A. M., Edwards, V., et al. (1998). Relationship of childhood abuse and household dysfunction to many of the leading causes of death in adults. *American Journal of Preventive Medicine, 14,* 245–258.

Gelfand, D. M., & Teti, D. M. (1990). The effects of maternal depression on children. *Clinical Psychology Review, 10,* 329–353.

Gunnar, M. R., Gonzalez, C. A., Goodlin, B. L., & Levine, S. (1981). Behavioral and pituitary–adrenal responses during a prolonged separation period in infant rhesus macaques. *Psychoneuroendocrinology, 6,* 65–75.

Gunnar, M. R., Morison, S. J., Chisholm, K., & Schuder, M. (2001). Salivary cortisol levels in children adopted from Romanian orphanages. *Development and Psychopathology, 13,* 611–628.

Haine, R. A., Ayers, T., Sandler, I. N., Wolchik, S. A., & Weyer, J. L. (2003). Locus of control and self-esteem as stress-moderators or stress-mediators in parentally bereaved children. *Death Studies, 27,* 619–640.

Haine, R. A., Wolchik, S. A., Sandler, I. N., Millsap, R. E., & Ayers, T. S. (2006). Positive parenting as a protective resource for parentally bereaved children. *Death Studies, 30,* 1–28.

Heim, C., Newport, D. J., Wagner, D., Wilcox, M. M., Miller, A. H., & Nemeroff, C. B. (2002). The role of early adverse experience and adulthood stress in the prediction of neuroendocrine stress reactivity in women: A multiple regression analysis. *Depression and Anxiety, 15,* 117–125.

Heim, C., Plotsky, P. M., & Nemeroff, C. B. (2004). Importance of studying the contributions of early adverse experience to neurobiological findings in depression. *Neuropsychopharmacology, 29,* 641–648.

Hertzman, C. (1999). The biological embedding of early experience and its effects on health in adulthood. In N. E. Adler, M. Marmot, B. S. McEwen, & J. Stewart (Eds.), *Annals of the New York Academy of Sciences: Vol. 896. Socioeconomic status and health in industrial nations: Social, psychological, and biological pathways* (pp. 85–95). New York: New York Academy of Sciences.

Higley, J. D., Suomi, S. J., & Linnoila, M. (1992). A longitudinal assessment of CSF monoamine metabolite and plasma cortisol concentrations in young rhesus monkeys. *Society of Biological Psychiatry, 32,* 127–145.

Hofer, M. A. (1994). Early relationships as regulators of infant physiology and behavior. *Acta Pediatrica, 397*(Suppl.), 9–18.

Kalter, N., Lohnes, K. L., Chasin, J., Cain, A. C., Dunning, S., & Rowan, J. (2002). The adjustment of parentally bereaved children: Factors associated with short-term adjustment. *Omega: The Journal of Death and Dying, 46,* 15–34.

Kendler, K. S., Gardner, C. O., & Prescott, C. A. (2002). Toward a comprehensive developmental model for major depression in women. *American Journal of Psychiatry, 159,* 1133–1145.

Kendler, K. S., Gardner, C. O., & Prescott, C. A. (2006). Toward a comprehensive developmental model for major depression in men. *American Journal of Psychiatry, 163,* 115–124.

Kendler, K. S., Neale, M. C., Kessler, R. C., Heath, A. C., & Eaves, L. J. (1992). Childhood parental loss and adult psychopathology in women. *Archives of General Psychiatry, 49,* 109–116.

Kessler, R. C., Davis, C. G., & Kendler, K. S. (1997). Childhood adversity and adult psychiatric disorder in the U.S. National Comorbidity Survey. *Psychological Medicine, 27,* 1101–1119.

Kivela, S., Luukinen, H., Koski, K., Viramo, P., & Kimmo, P. (1998). Early loss of mother or father predicts depression in old age. *International Journal of Geriatric Psychiatry, 13,* 527–530.

Kranzler, E., Shaffer, D., Wasserman, G., & Davies, M. (1990). Early childhood bereavement. *Journal of the American Academy of Child & Adolescent Psychiatry, 29,* 513–520.

Krause, N. (1998). Early parental loss, recent life events, and changes in health among older adults. *Journal of Aging and Health, 10*, 395–421.

Kuhn, C. M., Pauk, J., & Schanberg, S. (1990). Endocrine responses to mother–infant separation in developing rats. *Developmental Psychobiology, 23*, 395–410.

Langrock, A. M., Compas, B. E., Keller, G., Merchant, M. J., & Copeland, M. E. (2002). Coping with the stress of parental depression: Parent reports of children's coping, emotional, and behavioral problems. *Journal of Clinical Child and Adolescent Psychology, 31*, 312–324.

Lee, C., & Gotlib, I. H. (1991). Adjustment of children of depressed mothers: A 10-month follow-up. *Journal of Abnormal Psychology, 100*, 473–477.

Lewis, M. H., Gluck, J. P., Petitto, J. M., Hensley, L. L., & Ozer, H. (2000). Early social deprivation in nonhuman primates: Long-term effects on survival and cell-mediated immunity. *Biological Psychiatry, 47*, 119–126.

Lin, K. K., Sandler, I. N., Ayers, T. S., Wolchik, S. A., & Luecken, L. J. (2004). Resilience in parentally bereaved children and adolescents seeking preventive services. *Journal of Clinical Child and Adolescent Psychology, 33*, 673–683.

Lowman, B. C., Drossman, D. A., Cramer, E. M., & McKee, D. C. (1987). Recollection of childhood events in adults with irritable bowel syndrome. *Journal of Clinical Gastroenterology, 9*, 324–330.

Luecken, L. J. (1998). Childhood attachment and loss experiences affect adult cardiovascular and cortisol function. *Psychosomatic Medicine, 60*, 765–772.

Luecken, L. J. (2000a). Attachment and loss experiences during childhood are associated with adult hostility, depression, and social support. *Journal of Psychosomatic Research, 49*, 85–91.

Luecken, L. J. (2000b). Parental caring and loss during childhood and adult cortisol responses to stress. *Psychology & Health, 15*, 841–851.

Luecken, L. J., & Appelhans, B. M. (2006). Early parental loss and salivary cortisol in young adulthood: The moderating role of family environment. *Development and Psychopathology, 18*, 295–308.

Luecken, L. J., Appelhans, B. M., Kraft, A., & Brown, A. (2006). Never far from home: A cognitive–affective model of the impact of early-life family relationships on physiological stress responses in adulthood. *Journal of Social and Personal Relationships, 23*, 189–203.

Luecken, L. J., & Lemery, K. (2004). Early caregiving and adult physiological stress responses. *Clinical Psychology Review, 24*, 171–191.

Luecken, L. J., Rodriguez, A., & Appelhans, B. M. (2005). Cardiovascular stress responses in young adulthood associated with family-of-origin relationships. *Psychosomatic Medicine, 67*, 514–521.

Luthar, S. S., Cicchetti, D., & Becker, B. (2000). The construct of resilience: A critical evaluation and guidelines for future work. *Child Development, 71*, 543–562.

Lutzke, J. R., Ayers, T. S., Sandler, I. N., & Barr, A. (1997). Risks and interventions for the parentally bereaved child. In S. Wolchik & I. Sandler (Eds.), *Handbook of children's coping: Linking theory and intervention* (pp. 215–244). New York: Plenum Press.

Mack, K. Y. (2001). Childhood family disruption and adult well-being: The differential effects of divorce and parental death. *Death Studies, 25,* 419–443.

Maier, E. H., & Lachman, M. E. (2000). Consequences of early parental loss and separation for health and well-being in midlife. *International Journal of Behavioral Development, 24,* 183–189.

Masten, A. S., Burt, K. B., Roisman, G. I., Obradovic, J., Long, J. D., & Tellegen, A. (2004). Resources and resilience in the transition to adulthood: Continuity and change. *Development and Psychopathology, 16,* 1071–1094.

Masten, A. S., & Coatsworth, J. D. (1998). The development of competence in favorable and unfavorable environments: Lessons from successful children. *American Psychologist, 53,* 205–220.

McEwen, B. S. (2002). Sex, stress, and the hippocampus: Allostasis, allostatic load, and the aging process. *Neurobiology of Aging, 23,* 921–939.

McEwen, B. S. (2003). Early life influences on life-long patterns of behavior and health. *Mental Retardation and Developmental Disabilities Research Reviews, 9,* 149–154.

Meaney, M. J., Brake, W., & Gratton, A. (2002). Environmental regulation of the development of mesolimbic dopamine systems: A neurobiological mechanism for vulnerability to drug abuse? *Psychoneuroendocrinology, 27,* 127–138.

Mireault, G. C., & Bond, L. A. (1992). Parental death in childhood: Perceived vulnerability and adult depression and anxiety. *American Journal of Orthopsychiatry, 62,* 517–524.

Nemeroff, C. B. (2004). Neurobiological consequences of childhood trauma. *Journal of Clinical Psychiatry, 65,* 18–28.

Nicolson, N. A. (2004). Childhood parental loss and cortisol levels in adult men. *Psychoneuroendocrinology, 29,* 1012–1018.

Plotsky, P. M., Owen, M. J., & Nemeroff, C. B. (1998). Psychoneuroendocrinology of depression: Hypothalamic–pituitary–adrenal axis. *Psychiatric Clinics of North America, 21,* 293–307.

Plotsky, P. M., Thrivikraman, K. V., Nemeroff, C. B., Caldji, C., Sharma, S., & Meaney, M. J. (2005). Long-term consequences of neonatal rearing on central corticotropin-releasing factor systems in adult male rat offspring. *Neuropsychopharmacology, 30,* 2192–2204.

Raphael, B., Cubis, J., Dunne, M., Lewin, T., & Kelly, B. (1990). The impact of parental loss on adolescents' psychosocial characteristics. *Adolescence, 25,* 689–701.

Raveis, V. H., Siegel, K., & Karus, D. (1999). Children's psychological distress following the death of a parent. *Journal of Youth and Adolescence, 28,* 165–180.

Reite, M., Kaemingk, K., & Boccia, M. L. (1989). Maternal separation in bonnet monkey infants: Altered attachment and social support. *Child Development, 60,* 473–480.

Repetti, R. L., Taylor, S. E., & Seeman, T. E. (2002). Risky families: Family social environments and the mental and physical health of offspring. *Psychological Bulletin, 128,* 330–366.

Rice, D., & Barone, S. (2000). Critical periods of vulnerability for the developing nervous system: Evidence from human and animal models. *Environmental Health Perspectives, 108*, 511–533.

Rutter, M., O'Connor, T. G., & English and Romanian Adoptees Study Team. (2004). Are there biological programming effects for psychological development? Findings from a study of Romanian adoptees. *Developmental Psychology, 40*, 81–94.

Saler, L., & Skolnick, N. (1992). Childhood parental death and depression in adulthood: Roles of surviving parent and family environment. *American Journal of Orthopsychiatry, 62*, 504–516.

Sanchez, M. M., Noble, P. M., Lyon, C. K., Plotsky, P. M., Davis, M., Nemeroff, C. B., & Winslow, J. T. (2005). Alterations in diurnal cortisol rhythm and acoustic startle response in nonhuman primates with adverse rearing. *Biological Psychiatry, 57*, 373–381.

Sandler, I. N. (2001). Quality and ecology of adversity as common mechanisms of risk and resilience. *American Journal of Community Psychology, 29*, 19–61.

Sandler, I. N., Gersten, J., Reynolds, K., Kallgren, C., & Ramirez, R. (1988). Using theory and data to plan support interventions: Design of a program for bereaved children. In B. Gottlieb (Ed.), *Marshalling social support: Formats, processes and effects* (pp. 53–83). Thousand Oaks, CA: Sage.

Sandler, I. N., Tein, J., Mehta, P., Wolchik, S., & Ayers, T. (2000). Coping efficacy and psychological problems of children of divorce. *Child Development, 71*, 1099–1118.

Sandler, I. N., West, S. G., Baca, L., Pillow, D. R., Gersten, J., Rogosch, F., et al. (1992). Linking empirically based theory and evaluation: The Family Bereavement Program. *American Journal of Community Psychology, 20*, 491–521.

Sandler, I. N., Wolchik, S. A., Davis, C. H., Haine, R. A., & Ayers, T. A. (2003). Correlational and experimental study of resilience for children of divorce and parentally-bereaved children. In S. S. Luthar (Ed.), *Resilience and vulnerability: Adaptation in the context of childhood adversities* (pp. 213–240). New York: Cambridge University Press.

Straub, R. O. (2002). *Health psychology.* New York: Worth.

Stroebe, W., & Stroebe, M. (1993). Determinants of adjustment to bereavement in younger widows and widowers. In M. Stroebe, W. Stroebe, & R. Hansson (Eds.), *Handbook of bereavement: Theory, research, and intervention* (pp. 208–226). New York: Cambridge University Press.

Suomi, S. J. (1997). Early determinants of behavior: Evidence from primate studies. *British Medical Bulletin, 53*, 170–184.

Taylor, S. E., Repetti, R. L., & Seeman, T. (1997). Health psychology: What is an unhealthy environment and how does it get under the skin? *Annual Review of Psychology, 48*, 411–447.

Tennant, C. (1988). Parent loss in childhood: Its effect in adult life. *Archives of General Psychiatry, 45*, 1045–1050.

Thompson, M. P., Kaslow, N. J., Price, A. W., Williams, K., & Kingree, J. B. (1998). Role of secondary stressors in the parental death–child distress relation. *Journal of Abnormal Child Psychology, 26*, 357–366.

Tremblay, G. C., & Israel, A. C. (1998). Children's adjustment to parental death. *Clinical Psychology: Science and Practice, 5*, 424–438.

Van Eerdewegh, M. M., Bieri, M. D., Parrilla, R. H., & Clayton, P. J. (1982). The bereaved child. *British Journal of Psychiatry, 140*, 23–29.

Werner, E. E. (1993). Risk, resilience, and recovery: Perspectives from the Kauai Longitudinal Study. *Development and Psychopathology, 5*, 503–575.

Werner, E. E., & Smith, R. S. (1982). *Vulnerable but not invincible: A study of resilient children.* New York: McGraw-Hill.

West, S. G., Sandler, I. N., Pillow, D. R., Baca, L., & Gersten, J. C. (1991). The use of structural equation modeling in generative research: Toward the design of a preventative intervention for bereaved children. *American Journal of Community Psychology, 19*, 459–480.

Worden, J. W., & Silverman, P. R. (1996). Parental death and the adjustment of school-aged children. *Omega: The Journal of Death and Dying, 33*, 91–102.

Wyman, P. A., Sandler, I. N., Wolchik, S. A., & Nelson, K. (2000). Resilience as cumulative competence promotion and stress protection: Theory and intervention. In J. R. D. Cicchetti, I. Sandler, & R. Weissberg (Eds.), *The promotion of wellness in children and adolescents* (pp. 133–184). Washington, DC: Child Welfare League of America.

20

FACTORS THAT INFLUENCE LATE-LIFE BEREAVEMENT: CONSIDERING DATA FROM THE CHANGING LIVES OF OLDER COUPLES STUDY

DEBORAH CARR

The death of a spouse is a distressing life transition that overwhelmingly strikes older adults. More than 900,000 adults are widowed each year in the United States, and nearly three quarters of them are over age 65 (Federal Interagency Forum on Aging-Related Statistics, 2004). Similar age patterns have been documented in western and central Europe (de Jong-Gierveld, de Valk, & Blommesteijn, 2002). Late-life spousal bereavement is the most common form of spousal loss, yet most theories and empirical studies of bereavement do not explicitly take into consideration the special risk factors, resources, and contextual influences that affect older widows and widowers. With the aging of the world population, scholars, practitioners, and laypersons must understand how to effectively address the challenges facing older widows and widowers.

Although widowhood has long been considered one of the most difficult stressors befalling older adults (e.g., Holmes & Rahe, 1967), most empirical studies reveal remarkable heterogeneity in older adults' adjustment to loss. Depending on the sample and assessment procedure used, most studies find that only 15% to 30% of older adults experience clinically significant depression in the year following their spouse's death (Stroebe, Hansson, & Stroebe, 1993; Zisook & Shuchter, 1991), whereas 40% to 70% experience dysphoria, or a period of 2 or more weeks marked by feelings of sadness imme-diately following the loss (e.g., Bruce, Kim, Leaf, & Jacobs, 1990; Zisook, Paulus, Shuchter, & Judd, 1997). Instead of presuming that grief and depres-sion are inevitable consequences of spousal loss, bereavement researchers must instead focus on identifying the contextual and individual-level factors that exacerbate (or buffer against) the potentially distressing consequences of late-life spousal loss.

Demographic, technological, and social conditions affect late-life mor-tality and, consequently, the nature of late-life spousal bereavement. In the United States and most developed nations today, adults are living longer than ever before, and chronically ill older adults now have access to technologies and treatments that increase the length, although not necessarily the quality, of their lives (Field & Cassel, 1997). The event of spousal death now occurs very late in life, but the process of becoming widowed may begin years prior to the actual death, starting with the onset of the spouse's illness. The months and years leading up to the death may be filled with difficult caregiving responsibilities that tax the well-being of the healthier spouse (Schulz et al., 2001; see also chap. 13, this volume). Moreover, the leading causes of deaths to older adults today—cancer and heart disease—strike men earlier and more often than women (Federal Interagency Forum on Aging-Related Statistics, 2004). As a consequence, widowhood is much more likely to befall women than men, and the extent to which spousal loss affects one's psychological, social, physical, and financial well-being varies widely by gender.

Older adults' adjustment to spousal loss also reflects the nature and qual-ity of their marital relationship prior to the loss as well as alternative sources of social support. In the United States and other individualistic societies, the nuclear family—consisting of husband, wife, and their children—is expected to be socially, economically, and residentially autonomous. As a result, when one's spouse dies the survivor must adjust emotionally to the loss of his or her partner and confidante, and he or she also must manage the practical deci-sions and responsibilities that were once shared by both spouses (Umberson, Wortman, & Kessler, 1992; Utz et al., 2004). In contrast, older adults in more collectivistic societies, including parts of Asia, Africa, and Latin America, often reside in extended family households; this integration is believed to protect against the practical and emotional losses that often cause distress for bereaved spouses (e.g., Bongaarts & Zimmer, 2002; Kim & Rhee, 2000; Morioka, 1996; Shah, Yount, Shah, & Menon, 2003).

The adjustments required by widowed spouses may be particularly diffi-cult for current cohorts of older adults in Western nations who maintained a rigid, gender-based allocation of social roles over the life course; older widows and widowers may have limited experience in managing the roles and respon-sibilities previously performed by their spouses (Spain & Bianchi, 1996). Moreover, men typically have fewer sources of friendship and social support over the life course than do women, making the loss of a wife and confidante particularly difficult for them (Antonucci, 1990).

Despite the powerful influence of macrosocial forces and maturation processes on the experiences of bereaved spouses, relatively little research has taken into consideration the distinctive risk factors, resources, and contextual factors that shape the lives of older bereaved spouses. Moreover, most empirical research on late-life bereavement explores adjustment of older adults at a single point in time after they have lost their spouses and does not take into consideration the events, experiences, and relationship dynamics that preceded the loss. Such an exploration would require prospective data that track a large sample of married older adults from the time prior to the death and that observe the surviving spouses for several observation points following the death. The Changing Lives of Older Couples (CLOC) Study, a prospective, multiwave study of widowed persons and matched control participants in the United States, offers a unique opportunity for exploring of the distinctive experiences of current cohorts of bereaved older adults.

In this chapter, I briefly review the historical, social, and psychological factors that shape the experiences of bereaved older spouses. Next, I describe the characteristics and strengths of the CLOC Study and identify reasons why the CLOC Study is ideally suited for studying late-life spousal bereavement. I summarize findings from recent studies based on the CLOC Study, with particular attention to research on how death timing and context affect bereaved older spouses, the ways that the late marital relationship affects psychological and social adjustment of the bereaved, and the practical challenges facing newly bereaved older spouses. I conclude the chapter with a discussion of the implications of recent empirical studies for theory, practice, and future research.

THE DISTINCTIVE CASE OF LATE-LIFE SPOUSAL BEREAVEMENT

Spousal bereavement may have a profoundly different meaning and set of consequences for older versus younger persons. Spousal loss may be less strongly linked to subsequent distress among older adults compared with younger adults. Older adults are more likely than younger persons to have experienced the death of a significant other prior to spousal loss, and they may be better equipped to make sense of and cope with their most recent loss (Thompson, Gallagher-Thompson, Futterman, Gilewski, & Peterson, 1991). In addition, with advanced age, spousal loss may be at least somewhat expected (Neugarten & Hagestad, 1976). Roughly 50% of women over age 65 in the United States are widowed (Fields & Casper, 2001); older women in particular may anticipate and prepare for the deaths of their husbands as they observe their peers experiencing spousal loss (Fooken, 1985; Neugarten & Hagestad, 1976). Deaths to younger adults are more likely to occur suddenly and under very distressing circumstances, such as murders or accidents (Reed, 1998; Rynearson, 1984). Given that predictable, anticipated life transitions are less stressful than unexpected ones (George, 1993), older bereaved spouses may experience a less difficult readjustment than their younger counterparts.

The purported weak relationship between widowhood and psychological distress among older adults also may reflect age-related declines in emotional reactivity. Compared with younger adults, older adults have a greater capacity to manage or "regulate" their emotional states (Lawton, Kleban, Rajagopal, & Dean, 1992); as a consequence, they report less extreme levels of both positive and negative affect and less variability in their emotional responses to stress (Mroczek & Kolarz, 1998; Stacey & Gatz, 1991). Grief reactions also are less intense and shorter lived among the elderly bereaved, compared with the younger bereaved (Nolen-Hoeksema & Ahrens, 2002; Sanders, 1993). Emotional reactivity may decline in later life because of a variety of factors: biological decreases in autonomic arousal, the greater habituation of older adults to emotional life events, adherence to cultural expectations that the elderly should not be "too emotional," and shifts in the relative salience of emotion versus cognition in late life (Carstensen & Turk-Charles, 1994). Older adults also are believed to have wisdom, which may help minimize loss-related distress; they may respond to adverse life events with equanimity and acceptance (Baltes, Smith, & Staudinger, 1992).

In later life, bereaved adults also may be better prepared to manage the practical tasks that were once managed by their spouse. The boundaries demarcating traditional "men's roles" and "women's roles" in marriage may become blurred as husbands and wives age. Although older married couples abide by a gender-typed division of household labor, just as younger couples do, this division may change as older adults face health declines and limitations to daily functioning (Szinovacz, 2000). The onset of physical health problems may render older adults less able to perform the specialized homemaking or home maintenance tasks they performed earlier in the life course. For instance, if a wife's physical limitations prevent her from preparing meals or cleaning, her husband may take over those duties. Likewise, cognitive decline in a husband may result in a wife's increased involvement in estate planning and other financial decisions that previously were managed by the husband. Older adults may gradually take on their spouses' tasks even prior to widowhood, and thus they may be better prepared on the death of a spouse.

Research on stress over the life course suggests, conversely, that spousal loss may be more strongly linked to subsequent distress for older adults because they are more likely than younger persons to experience co-occurring stressors that may overwhelm their ability to cope (Kraajj, Arensman, & Spinhoven, 2002). Older adults are more likely than younger persons to experience cognitive and physical declines; financial strains; the deaths of friends and loved ones; and the loss of other important social roles, such as employment (Norris

& Murrell, 1990). Because late-life deaths typically occur after a long illness, bereaved spouses often experience a stressful period of caregiving and may see their loved one in pain for long periods prior to the death (Schulz et al., 2001). As a result, older adults may be overwhelmed not only by their spouse's death but also by the acute and chronic stressors that accompany the death.

Studies based on age-heterogeneous samples that simply control for the bereaved person's age cannot reveal the specific consequences of spousal loss for older versus younger adults and may fail to reveal the specific pathways linking spousal loss to physical, social, and emotional well-being among younger and older adults. For these reasons, bereavement researchers require prospective data that track the experiences of older married couples through the dying process; that obtain information on the bereaved survivor at several points following spousal loss; and that include detailed information on characteristics of the survivor, the late spouse, the marital relationship, and the context of the death that may shape the experience of bereavement.

THE CHANGING LIVES OF OLDER COUPLES STUDY

Sample Characteristics

Many unresolved and unexplored questions about late-life spousal bereavement can be addressed with the CLOC Study, a large multiwave prospective study of spousal bereavement. The CLOC Study was based on a two-stage area probability sample of 1,532 married men and women from the Detroit (Michigan) Standardized Metropolitan Statistical Area.[1] To be eligible for the study, respondents had to be English-speaking members of a married couple in which the husband was age 65 or older. All sample members were not institutionalized and were capable of participating in a 2-hour face-to-face interview. Women were oversampled to increase the likelihood that sample members would become bereaved during the study period; this decision was based on the widely documented finding that men have a higher risk of mortality than do women. As a consequence, the analyses summarized in this chapter used weighted data to adjust for unequal probabilities of selection and differential response rates at the initial interview.

Baseline face-to-face interviews with the married older adults were conducted from June 1987 through April 1988. The response rate for the baseline interview was 68%, which is consistent with the response rates

---

[1]The 1,532 married persons interviewed at baseline include 423 married couples, or 846 persons for whom complete data were collected from both self and spouse. This design feature enabled researchers to undertake couple-level analyses and to explore spousal concordance in terms of their evaluation of the marriage and both their own and the spouse's health.

from other Detroit-area studies in that time period. Spousal loss was monitored subsequently using monthly death record tapes provided by the state of Michigan and by reading the daily obituaries in Detroit-area newspapers. The National Death Index and direct ascertainment of death certificates were used to confirm deaths and obtain causes of death. Of the 335 respondents known to have lost a spouse during the study period, 316 were contacted for a possible interview (19 persons, or 6%, had died during the interim). Of the 316 persons contacted, 263 (83%) participated in at least one of the three follow-up interviews, which were conducted 6 months (Wave 1), 18 months (Wave 2), and 48 months (Wave 3) after the spouse's death. Each widowed person was matched with a same-age, same-sex, nonbereaved person from the baseline sample, and this matched control participant also was interviewed at each of the three follow-ups. Adjusted and unadjusted sample sizes, organized by gender and widowhood status, across all waves of data collection, are presented in Table 20.1.[2]

Strengths of the Changing Lives of Older Couples Study

The CLOC Study has several desirable properties that make it an ideal data set for studying the context and consequences of late life spousal bereavement. First, all interviews with widowed persons (and matched control participants) were conducted 6, 18, and 48 months after the death; thus, all analyses hold constant the duration of time that had passed since the loss. Studies that fail to control the length of time since death may yield inconclusive findings; most studies concur that symptoms of psychological distress are most acute during the first 6 months after loss and then gradually return to preloss levels (e.g., Mendes de Leon, Kasl, & Jacobs, 1994). Studies that focus only on relatively long time horizons may underestimate the short-term consequences of loss, whereas studies that focus on the immediate consequences of loss may fail to reveal the consequences that emerge only in the longer term.

Second, because the data are prospective and include rich information on the widowed persons, their spouses, and their marital relationship prior to the loss, researchers have been able to study prospectively changes in psychological and social well-being after the loss. It is also possible to investigate and identify the factors that affect both one's risk of (or "selection" into) widowhood and subsequent adjustment to widowhood. The deleterious consequences of widowhood may be overstated if preloss characteristics that elevate the risk of both widowhood and poor physical and mental health, such as poverty, are not controlled.

---

[2] The variation in the number of control participants interviewed at the 6- and 18-month follow-up interviews is due solely to the availability of funding.

TABLE 20.1
Unweighted and Weighted Sample Sizes, by Widowhood Status and Gender, Changing Lives of Older Couples Study

Subgroup	Unweighted sample					Weighted sample			
	Baseline	Wave 1 (6 months)	Wave 2 (18 months)	Wave 3 (48 months)	Baseline	Wave 1 (6 months)	Wave 2 (18 months)	Wave 3 (48 months)
Total sample	1,532	333	411	208	1,532	297	370	160
Male	474	46	60	20	725	87	109	25
Female	1,058	287	351	188	807	210	261	135
Widowed		249	198	106		210	168	85
Male		35	29	10		59	51	15
Female		214	169	96		151	117	70
Matched control		84	213	102		87	202	75
Male		11	31	10		22	58	10
Female		73	182	92		65	144	65

Note. The weighted sample adjusts for unequal probabilities of selection and differential response rate at baseline.

Third, all widowed persons are assigned a same-age and same-sex matched control participant from the baseline sample; thus, the true effects of widowhood can be differentiated from those related to aging or the passage of time. Studies that focus on samples of widowed persons only, in contrast, cannot directly ascertain the effect of the widowhood transition. For instance, studies of depression rates among samples of the bereaved only cannot ascertain whether these rates are significantly different from those found among nonbereaved persons.

Fourth, the sample includes both men and women, thus allowing the exploration of gender differences in the experience of widowhood. Studies of late-life widowhood have overwhelmingly focused on women only, and gender comparisons are relatively rare.

Fifth, the CLOC Study was designed expressly to explore a wide array of outcomes, including the psychological, behavioral, cognitive, and financial consequences of loss. Because the CLOC Study includes older adults only, its content focuses on special challenges associated with aging in general, and late-life bereavement specifically. A synopsis of substantive areas included in the study is provided in Table 20.2.

Finally, the CLOC Study includes rich data on both global aspects of psychological and social adjustment, such as depressive symptoms and anxi-

TABLE 20.2
Summary of Items That Contribute to the Grief Scale and Subscales,
Changing Lives of Older Couples Study

Domain	Item
Anxiety ($\alpha = .71$)	Afraid of what is ahead.
	Felt anxious or unsettled.
	Worried about how you would manage your day to day affairs.
Despair ($\alpha = .64$)	Life seemed empty.
	Felt empty inside.
	Felt life had lost its meaning.
Shock ($\alpha = .77$)	Felt in a state of shock.
	Couldn't believe what was happening.
	Felt emotionally numb.
Anger ($\alpha = .68$)	Felt resentful or bitter about death.
	Felt death was unfair.
	Felt anger towards God.
Yearning ($\alpha = .75$)	Longing to have him or her with you.
	Painful waves of missing him or her.
	Feelings of intense pain and grief.
	Feelings of grief or loneliness.
Intrusive Thoughts ($\alpha = .66$)	Difficulty falling asleep, thoughts of him/her kept coming into your mind.
	Tried to block out memories or thoughts of him/her.
	Couldn't get thoughts about him/her out of my head.
Grief ($\alpha = .88$)	All 19 preceding items.

ety, as well as specific loss-related outcomes, such as yearning, loss-related anxiety, and practical adjustments in daily life. Specific symptoms may respond in very different ways to specific aspects of the widowhood transition, and these (potentially) competing effects may cancel out one another when only an aggregate scale is used as an outcome variable. For instance, widely used grief scales, such as the Bereavement Index (Jacobs, Kasl, & Ostfeld, 1986), Present Feelings About Loss (Singh & Raphael, 1981), and the Texas Revised Inventory of Grief (Zisook, DeVaul, & Click, 1982), comprise several symptom subscales, such as Anger or Yearning (see Table 20.3). These subscales respond differently to different aspects of loss, thus the use of an overarching grief scale may conceal patterns among specific symptoms. Moreover, the CLOC Study obtained measures of loss-related psychological outcomes at three time points (i.e., at 6, 18, and 48 months after the loss) and general psychological outcomes at four time points (i.e., baseline and at 6, 18, and 48 months after the loss). These multiple observations allow researchers to model trajectories of specific psychological symptoms over time (e.g., Bonanno et al., 2002; see also chap. 14, this volume).

The empirical studies summarized in this chapter take advantage of the unique design features of the CLOC Study and explore topics such as how, why, and for whom spousal loss affects psychological and social adjustment. The answers to these questions have important implications for policy and practice and will provide the foundation for future research on spousal bereavement in late life (for more detailed information on the CLOC Study, see Carr, Nesse, & Wortman, 2006).

RESEARCH FINDINGS FROM THE CHANGING LIVES OF OLDER COUPLES STUDY

Death Timing, Context, and Quality

For most bereaved older adults in the late 20th and early 21st centuries, spousal death occurs after a period of protracted illness and intensive caregiving. This new context of dying raises important questions about the experiences of older bereaved spouses. Are sudden, unanticipated deaths more stressful than long-anticipated deaths? Does the "quality" of a spouse's death affect the psychological adjustment of surviving spouses? Studies based on the CLOC Study reveal that answers to these questions are complex and reflect the unique resources and risk factors of older adults.

Lindemann's (1944) classic "Coconut Grove" study suggested that sudden, unexpected deaths are more distressing than anticipated deaths. Individuals who anticipate their spouse's death are believed to use the forewarning period to prepare psychologically and practically for the transition to widow-

TABLE 20.3

Summary of Ordinary Least Squares Regression Models Assessing the Effects of Selected "Death Quality" Characteristics on Psychological Adjustment to Spousal Loss, 6 Months After Loss, Changing Lives of Older Couples Study, 1987–1993

	Subscale							
	Yearning		Intrusive Thoughts		Anger		Anxiety	
	β	SE	β	SE	β	SE	β	SE
Selected "death quality" indicators								
Positive relations with spouse during final days	.467****	.175			-.325**	.171	.301*	.169
Spouse in pain prior to death	.353**	.166	.448***	.170				
Spouses were together at moment of death			-.336**	.143				
Physician or hospital contributed to the death					.698***	.274		
Dying spouse in nursing home prior to death							-.849**	.367

Note. Only death attributes that are significant predictors of psychological adjustment are presented; empty cells indicate that these attributes are not significant predictors. All models adjust for demographic characteristics (age, sex, education, income, and home ownership), confounding factors (preloss depressive symptoms, anxiety symptoms, self-rated health, and decedent's preloss health), psychological characteristics (death acceptance, religiosity, and marital quality), and objective characteristics of the death (spouse's age at death, amount of forewarning, and cause of death). From "A Good Death for Whom? Quality of Spouse's Death and Psychological Distress Among Older Widowed Persons," by D. Carr, 2003, *Journal of Health and Social Behavior, 44*, p. 225. Copyright 2003 by the American Sociological Association. Adapted with permission.

*p < .10. **p < .05. ***p < .01. ****p < .001.

hood (Blauner, 1966). However, empirical studies offer equivocal findings; some reveal that sudden deaths are more distressing than anticipated deaths (e.g., O'Bryant, 1990–1991), whereas others show that anticipated deaths are more troubling than sudden deaths (e.g., Sanders, 1982–1983). A third group of studies has found no relationship between death timing and survivors' well-being (e.g., Roach & Kitson, 1989).

These inconclusive findings are due partly to the fact that important aspects of the dying process that are correlated with anticipation of death were not controlled in past studies. As a consequence, the actual effects of anticipation of death may be either counteracted or suppressed by omitted variables. For instance, the forewarning period may be punctuated by potentially distressing experiences, such as difficult caregiving duties (Wells & Kendig, 1997), financial strains imposed by costly medical and long-term care (Field & Cassel, 1997), emotional isolation from family members and friends (Kramer, 1996–1997), and the neglect of one's own health (Sweeting & Gilhooly, 1990). The dying patient also may be subjected to physical pain, problematic medical care, and difficult decisions about future medical treatments; each of these conditions may be distressing to a spouse who is witnessing the events as they unfold.

Research based on the CLOC Study has investigated whether and how death forewarning affects older bereaved spouses' adjustment to loss while taking into consideration the special stressors and advantages associated with both sudden and anticipated deaths. Carr, House, Wortman, Nesse, and Kessler (2001) evaluated the psychological impact of three types of spousal deaths: (a) sudden deaths, (b) deaths for which the survivor had less than 6 months' forewarning, and (c) deaths for which the survivor had at least 6 months' forewarning. Other death characteristics that may be confounded with forewarning were controlled, including the spouse's age at death, whether the spouse was residing a nursing home prior to death, the intensity of spousal caregiving, whether the dying patient and spouse discussed the impending death, and whether the couple were together at the moment of death. The analyses showed that neither sudden nor anticipated deaths are uniformly distressing for older adults; instead, the psychological consequences vary across outcomes. Persons whose spouses died suddenly (compared with those who had died with some forewarning) had elevated levels of intrusive thoughts 6 months after the loss, although the effect faded by the 18-month follow up. *Intrusive thoughts*—painful, unprovoked thoughts about the deceased—are considered a symptom of posttraumatic stress disorder (e.g., Bonanno & Kaltman, 1999).

Sudden deaths affected men's and women's yearning (or longing for their deceased spouses) in different ways. Carr et al. (2001) assessed interaction terms to evaluate whether death forewarning mattered differently for men and women; they found that sudden deaths are associated with significantly lower levels of yearning among widowers yet higher levels among widows (see Figure 20.1). Widowers yearned most for their deceased wives when the wives died after a long forewarning period. This gender difference may reflect the ways that men and women relate to their spouses during marriage. For men, the forewarning period may be a time of increased closeness with their spouse and isolation from others. Men may become even more emotionally bonded to their spouse, at the expense of relationships with others. Given gender differences in mortality, men may have few same-sex peers who are also awaiting an ill wife's death. In contrast, women may rely on their female friends' direct experience with spousal illness to help them through the difficult dying process and thereafter.

Prolonged forewarning was associated with elevated anxiety levels among widows and widowers both 6 and 18 months after the death. Six months after their loss, widows and widowers who had more than 6 months' forewarning reported anxiety symptoms that were 0.5 standard deviation higher than those who had a shorter forewarning period; by

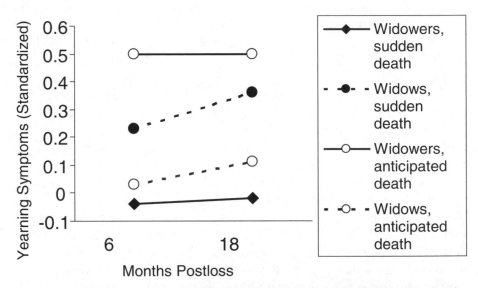

Figure 20.1. Yearning symptoms among widows and widowers, by death forewarning, 6 and 18 months postloss, Changing Lives of Older Couples Study, 1987–1993. The plotted yearning symptoms scores are based on ordinary least squares regression models, controlling for age, education, home ownership, preloss depressive symptoms, preloss anxiety symptoms, preloss self-rated health, spouse's age at death, spousal residence in nursing home prior to death, whether the widow or widower provided care to the spouse prior to death, whether the couple discussed the impending death, and whether the couple was together at the moment when the spouse died. From "Psychological Adjustment to Sudden and Anticipated Spousal Loss Among Older Widowed Persons," by D. Carr, J. S. House, C. Wortman, R. Nesse, and R. C. Kessler, 2001, *Journals of Gerontology: Social Sciences, 56B,* p. S244. Copyright 2001 by the Gerontological Society of America. Adapted with permission.

18 months, this gap had declined to 0.3 standard deviation yet remained statistically significant. These effects could not be explained away by stressors such as caregiving demands. This pattern may reflect the fact that elderly patients who are dying slowly may be suffering from long-term cognitive impairment. Unlike other anticipated deaths, which may allow time for discussions and closure, dementia and Alzheimer's disease may prevent the dying patient from communicating with loved ones during his or her final days and from finding meaning in the dying process. However, this hypothesis could not be evaluated, because the CLOC sample does not have detailed data on Alzheimer's disease or severe dementia symptoms among the decedents. Overall, this research suggests that for older adults, even sudden deaths may be anticipated and viewed as timely (Neugarten & Hagestad, 1976). As a result, sudden spousal loss among older adults may be less distressing than it is among younger and midlife widows and widowers.

Research from the CLOC Study also reveals the way that death quality shapes survivors' psychological adjustment 6 months after loss (Carr, 2003). Drawing on theoretical and philosophical writings on "dying well" and the "good death" (e.g., Byock, 1996; Field & Cassel, 1997), five aspects of death quality were considered: (a) the patient's acceptance of his or her impending death, (b) social support from loved ones, (c) degree of burden on others, (d) death timeliness, and (e) appropriate physical care. Each of these indicators characterized the dying experience of the now-deceased spouse and was based on the surviving spouse's retrospective report obtained 6 months after the death. Objective characteristics of the death, including the cause of death and duration of the illness, also were adjusted in all models.

Despite widespread belief in the clinical and religious community that a "good death" may ease psychological adjustment for widowed persons (e.g., Byock, 1996), in an earlier study (Carr, 2003) I found little empirical support for the proposed linkages between death quality and survivor adjustment. Two dimensions of death quality—(a) the dying spouse's acceptance of his or her impending death and (b) the surviving spouse's belief that the deceased had led a full life—did not predict survivor's psychological adjustment. Rather, psychological adjustment was most closely linked to physical aspects of the death (see Table 20.3). Widowed persons who reported that their spouses had considerable physical pain prior to death had significantly higher levels of yearning for their deceased spouse, significantly elevated post-loss anxiety levels, and significantly more intrusive thoughts. Those whose spouses had died because of physician or hospital negligence evidenced significantly higher levels of anger. Anger is considered a particularly difficult symptom of grief, because it is linked to social isolation and rejection of social support from friends and family. These distinctive symptom-specific patterns would have been masked if a broad outcome measure, such as overall grief, were the sole outcome measure.

One aspect of the dying process presumed to be undesirable for the patient proved protective to survivors. The spouses of persons who lived in nursing homes at the end of life showed less anxiety than survivors of those who were living at home. Placing one's husband or wife in a nursing home may psychologically prepare spouses for the permanent separation of widowhood and may spare them from the strains of providing direct care. Taken together, these findings suggest that improved medical care, affordable nursing homes, long-term or hospice care, and increased availability of pain management programs will not only benefit the dying elderly but also may enable a smoother transition to widowhood among surviving spouses.

Marital Quality

Older adults' adjustment to spousal loss is linked inextricably to the nature and quality of their late marriage. The extent to which bereaved older adults mourn the loss of their spouse, experience personal growth, or establish new romantic relationships following their loss may reflect the psychological and social benefits received (or costs incurred) in the marriage. Classic writings—guided heavily by the psychoanalytic tradition—suggest that widowed persons with the most troubled marriages suffer heightened grief and poorer adjustment following their spouse's death (Freud, 1917/1957). Survivors who had strained or conflicted marital relationships may find it hard to let go of their spouses, yet they also feel angry at the deceased for abandoning them and thus may experience elevated depression. Empirical support for this proposition is weak, however, and is undermined by a serious methodological concern: Most studies have measured marital quality retrospectively after the spouse's death, and thus widowed persons' characterizations of their marriages often are shaped by their current emotional state (Parkes & Weiss, 1983). Some bereaved spouses may retrospectively "sanctify" and offer unrealistically positive appraisals of their late spouse and marriage (Lopata, 1973), whereas depressed persons may have overly negative recollections of their marriages (Bonanno, Notarius, Gunzerath, Keltner, & Horowitz, 1998).

Research based on the CLOC project explores whether marital warmth, conflict, and dependence—assessed prior to loss—affects widowed persons' psychological and social adjustment following the loss (Carr, 2004a, 2004b; Carr et al., 2000). The analyses reveal that preloss marital warmth is positively and significantly related to postloss yearning, whereas marital conflict is negatively and significantly related to postloss yearning. These findings call into question earlier psychoanalytically based assumptions about spousal bereavement (Carr et al., 2000). Troubled marriages appear to diminish, rather than exacerbate, longing for one's lost spouse among older adults who had long-term marriages. Moreover, spouses who were highly dependent on one another for the performance of practical tasks, such as homemaking or home maintenance, report elevated anxiety symptoms following loss.

Although losing a beloved confidante and helpmate is associated with increased yearning and anxiety, respectively, these profound losses also may ultimately engender growth and resilience among the bereaved. In an earlier study (Carr, 2004b), I investigated whether practical and emotional dependence on one's late spouse affected two aspects of positive psychological functioning following loss: (a) self-esteem and (b) perceived personal growth. *Personal growth* refers to one's beliefs that he or she has become more independent, stronger, and more self-confident since the death. I assessed two-way interaction terms between gender and preloss marital dependence. The results revealed that women who reported high levels of emotional dependence on their husbands evidenced substantial increases in self-esteem after their loss, whereas men who reported high levels of instrumental dependence on their wives showed significant increases in personal growth 6 months after spousal loss. These findings suggest that bereaved persons may enjoy personal growth and self-confidence when they manage to withstand and survive an event that may have earlier seemed insurmountable. Those who were most dependent in their marriages may experience the greatest strides in skill acquisition and emotional independence following the loss, and these gains enhance their sense of self-worth.

The quality and nature of one's late marriage also are a powerful influence on one's desire to date or remarry following loss. Establishing a new romantic relationship may be a way to establish a new identity to offset the identity of widow or widower (DiGiulio, 1989). The CLOC Study assessed interest in new relationships by separately asking bereaved spouses whether they would like to remarry someday and whether they were interested in dating. I (Carr, 2004a) found that higher levels of preloss marital conflict were associated with a reduced likelihood that one was interested in dating, perhaps because individuals with troubled marriages view singlehood as preferable to being in an unrewarding relationship. I also found that widowers are much more likely than widows to both date and express interest in a new relationship, yet the sizable gender gap is conditional on aspects of the late marriage and on the availability of other sources of social support. The major reason why men form new relationships is to reestablish emotional closeness: Men who were most emotionally reliant on their wives reported the greatest desire to date and remarry. For women, this pattern was reversed: The more emotionally reliant women were on their husbands, the less interested they were in pursuing subsequent relationships. Moreover, when men and women with high levels of social support from friends were compared, the study found no gender differences in the desire to remarry, suggesting that high levels of social support enable both men and women to live happily even without the prospect of remarriage (see Figure 20.2). These findings underscore the ways

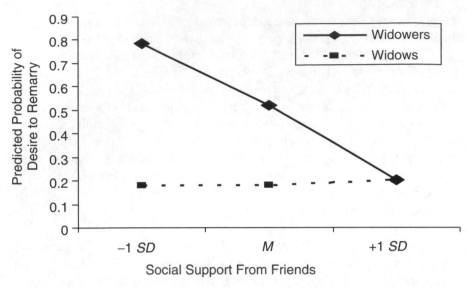

Figure 20.2. Predicted probability that bereaved spouse "would like to remarry someday," by gender and level of social support received from friends, Changing Lives of Older Couples Study, 1987–1993. Predicted probabilities are based on logistic regression models, controlling for age, education, race, home ownership, marital duration, preloss depressive symptoms, preloss anxiety symptoms, pre-loss self-rated health, spouse's preloss physical health, and preloss marital conflict. From "The Desire to Date and Remarry Among Older Widows and Widowers," by D. Carr, 2004, *Journal of Marriage and Family, 66,* p. 1061. Copyright 2004 by Wiley-Blackwell. Reprinted with permission.

that psychological and social adjustment of older bereaved spouses are closely tied to the gender roles and patterns of social interaction established years earlier.

Everyday Life Adjustments to Loss

Although the vast majority of research on late-life spousal bereavement focuses on emotional adjustment to loss, older adults also must adjust to practical challenges, such as managing household chores and finances. These practical challenges may be particularly burdensome for current cohorts of older adults, who were socialized to hold rigidly defined gender roles in the home. In older cohorts, men typically have channeled their energies into paid employment and financial management tasks, and women have specialized in child rearing, cooking, cleaning, and homemaking (Spain & Bianchi, 1996). As a consequence, bereaved older adults may be ill equipped to take on the chores and responsibilities once managed by their spouse and may need to develop new skills or increase their reliance on family members and friends for practical support.

Recognizing that older bereaved spouses must grapple with both emotional and practical issues, Stroebe and Schut (1999) developed the *dual-process model of coping*, which holds that the bereaved oscillate between two styles of coping: (a) *loss-oriented coping* and (b) *restoration-oriented coping*. Whereas loss-oriented coping focuses on "grief work" (Worden, 2002) and working through emotional aspects of loss, restoration-oriented coping focuses on managing the secondary stressors of widowhood, such as financial strains, loneliness, disruptions in one's social life, and managing chores that were once done by one's spouse. Recent studies based on CLOC data reveal tremendous heterogeneity in how older adults manage the everyday challenges of loss, with widows and widowers revealing very different strategies.

Utz et al. (2004) examined the ways that spousal loss affects the amount of time an older person spends preparing meals and doing housework in an average week. This study took advantage of the preloss data and tracked changes in housework pre- and postloss. Focusing on only a single point in time after the loss would offer an incomplete characterization of the ways that widows and widowers adjust their daily lives after spousal loss (see Figure 20.3). Widows decreased their housework by 6 hours per week postloss, and widowers increased

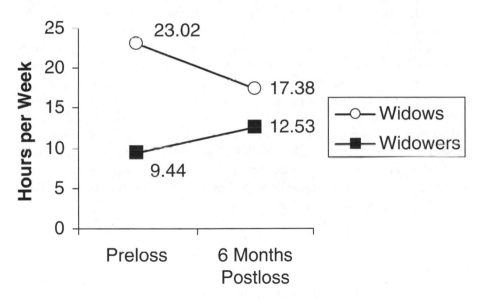

Figure 20.3. Hours spent per week preparing meals and doing housework, Changing Lives of Older Couples Study, 1987–1993. The average numbers of hours are based on ordinary least squares regression models, adjusted for age, education, income, home ownership, race, household size, functional limitations, preloss spouse health, whether one was providing spousal caregiving preloss, and dependence on children for housework. From *Spousal Bereavement in Late Life* (p. 178), by D. Carr, R. Nesse, and C. Wortman (Eds.), New York: Springer Publishing Company, LLC. Reprinted with permission of Springer Publishing Company, LLC, New York, NY 10036.

their workload by 3 hours, although women still did more housework than men at both time points. On the one hand, this pattern reflects the fact that married women typically perform more housework than their husbands, and thus the loss of a spouse adds a larger housework burden to the daily lives of men compared with women. Yet the study also revealed that recently widowed women received more help from their children than did widowers, thus reducing the amount of time that they themselves performed household chores. Because mothers maintain closer relationships with their children than do fathers at every stage in the life course, widows can easily turn to their children for practical assistance in their own time of need.

Building on this study (Utz et al., 2004), Ha, Carr, Utz, and Nesse (2006) found that widows'—but not widowers'—dependence on their adult children for financial and legal assistance also increased after the loss. On one hand, this reflects the fact that older women are believed to be inexperienced and thus in need of help in financial management matters; however, the analyses also show that women received more instrumental support from their children than men did even prior to the loss. Women's greater support from their children reflects strong reciprocity in the parent–child relationship: Although widowed women receive more practical and emotional support from their children than do their male counterparts, widowed women also are more likely than men to give emotional support to their children following loss. Recently widowed mothers maintain their role as the family's emotional and expressive caretaker, even as they work through their own grief. Taken together, these studies reveal that older widowed persons' practical adjustments to loss reflect patterns of skill development and parent–child interactions that were established years prior to the loss. These findings also underscore the importance of gender role socialization and family relations as powerful influences on older adults' adjustment to spousal loss. Studies that focus only on measures of functioning following loss will offer an incomplete or misleading portrait of the ways that gender and social relations shape the bereavement experience.

CONCLUSION AND FUTURE DIRECTIONS

In this chapter, I have presented recent research findings from the CLOC Study, which obtained detailed preloss data on older bereaved spouses and matched control participants and tracked them for 4 years after the loss; thus, it reveals the pathways linking bereavement to adjustment as well as the short- and long-term consequences of spousal loss. Taken together, studies based on the CLOC Study show that bereaved older spouses are a remarkably heterogeneous group. Some experience severe depressive and grief symptoms after their spouse dies, whereas others are psychologically resilient and can successfully manage the emotional and practical strains associated with late-life widowhood. On the whole, however, even those who experience at least some depressive symptoms bounce back within 18 months following loss. Moreover, gender is a powerful influence on the ways that men and women adjust to loss, because reactions to spousal loss often reflect lifelong processes of gender role socialization. Specifically, spousal loss does not have uniformly negative (or positive) effects on older adults' physical, emotional, and social well-being; instead, the personal consequences of spousal loss are contingent on characteristics of the bereaved, the late spouse, the context of the death, the quality of social support available, and the nature of the marital relationship. These empirical findings may help refine both theoretical approaches and practical interventions targeting spousal bereavement.

For example, many clinical interventions aimed at older bereaved persons are based loosely on psychoanalytic models of grief (e.g., Freud 1917/1957; Lindemann, 1944). A guiding assumption is that bereaved persons must confront and review their feelings about the deceased if they hope to adjust psychologically to the loss. The "work of mourning" was viewed as a critical aspect of adjustment, and failure to grieve was considered an indication of denial, lack of attachment, or emotional immaturity. Moreover, grief symptoms were believed to be most acute among persons with ambivalent relationships with the deceased (Freud 1917/1957) and those who were bereaved suddenly and without preparation (Lindemann, 1944). Although psychoanalytic perspectives on the grieving process have dominated research for much of the past century, a growing body of empirical work has started to chip away at such pervasive yet untested assumptions (e.g., Bonanno & Kaltman, 2001; Wortman & Silver, 2001). Analyses based on the CLOC Study also have contributed substantially to further theoretical refinement and our understanding of the diverse ways men and women cope with spousal loss. For example, these studies have found that persons with strained marital relations experienced fewer rather than more severe grief symptoms (Carr et al., 2000) and that sudden deaths are not necessarily associated with poorer adjustment, because anticipated deaths often are accompanied by difficult emotional and caregiving strains (Carr et al., 2001). These studies and many others coming out of the CLOC project (see Carr et al., 2006) have important implications for policy and practice and will provide the foundation for future generations of research on spousal bereavement in later life.

The CLOC project, however, describes late-life widowhood as it is currently experienced, not how it may be for future cohorts of bereaved elders. In the future, researchers will be charged with exploring additional sources of heterogeneity, including the race, ethnicity, religious, sexual orientation, and family characteristics of bereaved older spouses (see also chaps. 10, 13, 16, and 21, this volume). For example, declining fertility rates and increases in geographic mobility mean that future cohorts of older persons will have fewer children on whom they can rely for social support, and these children will be less likely than past generations to live close to their parents (Spain & Bianchi, 1996). Future cohorts of older bereaved spouses may need to develop more expansive social networks that include friends and family members who are more proximate, to counterbalance the fact that their children are fewer and less proximate than in past generations. Moreover, current cohorts of married couples are more likely than past generations to dissolve dissatisfying marriages through divorce; consequently, persons who remain married until late life may have higher levels of marital closeness and may suffer elevated grief following the loss of these close relationships.

Shifting gender roles also may reshape the bereavement experience of older spouses. Current generations of young adult women have higher levels of education, more years of work experience, and more egalitarian divisions of labor in their families than do past cohorts. Thus, they may be less dependent on their husbands for income, home repair, and financial management tasks, whereas husbands may be less dependent on their wives for homemaking chores and emotional support (Spain & Bianchi, 1996). Under this scenario, future cohorts of widowed persons may experience lower levels of anxiety than previous cohorts.

It is important to recognize the limits to generalizing findings based on the CLOC Study. Findings from the CLOC Study apply primarily to persons in Western, individualistic nations similar to the United States. Researchers should further explore prospectively how psychological reactions to loss may reflect a broader array of cultural contexts. Other cultural factors, including patterns of household structure and filial piety, and attitudes towards life and death, may condition the experience of elderly bereaved persons. As practitioners develop policies and interventions for the elderly bereaved they must take into consideration the larger cultural, social, historical, and demographic backdrop against which spousal loss occurs.

REFERENCES

Antonucci, T. C. (1990). Social supports and social relationships. In R. H. Binstock & L. K. George (Eds.), *Handbook of aging and the social sciences* (3rd ed., pp. 205–226). San Diego, CA: Academic Press.

Baltes, P., Smith, J., & Staudinger, U. (1992). Wisdom and successful aging. In T. Sonderegger (Ed.), *Nebraska Symposium on Motivation: Vol. 39. Psychology and aging* (pp. 103–21). Lincoln: University of Nebraska Press.

Blauner, R. (1966). Death and social structure. *Psychiatry, 29*, 378–394.

Bonanno, G. A., & Kaltman, S. (1999). Toward an integrative perspective on bereavement. *Psychological Bulletin, 125*, 760–776.

Bonanno, G. A., & Kaltman, S. (2001). The varieties of grief experience. *Clinical Psychology Review, 21*, 705–734.

Bonanno, G. A., Notarius, C. I., Gunzerath, L., Keltner, D., & Horowitz, M. J. (1998). Interpersonal ambivalence, perceived dyadic adjustment, and conjugal loss. *Journal of Consulting and Clinical Psychology, 66*, 1012–1022.

Bonanno, G. A., Wortman, C. B., Lehman, D. R., Tweed, R. G., Haring, M., Sonnega, J., et al. (2002). Resilience to loss and chronic grief: A prospective study from preloss to 18-months postloss. *Journal of Personality and Social Psychology, 83*, 1150–1164.

Bongaarts, J., & Zimmer, Z. (2002). Living arrangements of older adults in the developing world: An analysis of demographic and health survey households. *Journal of Gerontology: Social Sciences, 57*, 145–157.

Bruce, M. L., Kim, K., Leaf, P. J., & Jacobs, S. (1990). Depressive episodes and dysphoria resulting from conjugal bereavement in a prospective community sample. *American Journal of Psychiatry, 147*, 608–611.

Byock, I. R. (1996). The nature of suffering and the nature of opportunity at the end of life. *Clinics in Geriatric Medicine, 12*, 237–252.

Carr, D. (2003). A good death for whom? Quality of spouse's death and psychological distress among older widowed persons. *Journal of Health and Social Behavior, 44*, 215–232.

Carr, D. (2004a). The desire to date and remarry among older widows and widowers. *Journal of Marriage and the Family, 66*, 1051–1068.

Carr, D. (2004b). Gender, pre-loss marital dependence and older adults' adjustment to widowhood. *Journal of Marriage and the Family, 66*, 220–235.

Carr, D., House, J. S., Kessler, R. C., Nesse, R. M., Sonnega, J., & Wortman, C. (2000). Marital quality and psychological adjustment to widowhood among older adults: A longitudinal analysis. *Journal of Gerontology: Social Sciences, 55B*, S197–S207.

Carr, D., House, J. S., Wortman, C., Nesse, R., & Kessler, R. C. (2001). Psychological adjustment to sudden and anticipated spousal loss among older widowed persons. *Journals of Gerontology: Social Sciences, 56B*, S237–S248.

Carr, D., Nesse, R. M., & Wortman, C. B. (Eds.). (2006). *Spousal bereavement in late life*. New York: Springer Publishing Company.

Carstensen, L., & Turk-Charles, S. (1994). The salience of emotion across the adult life span. *Psychology and Aging, 9*, 259–264.

de Jong-Gierveld, J., de Valk, H., & Blommesteijn, M. (2002). Living arrangements of older persons and family support in more developed countries. *Population Bulletin of the United Nations, 42–43*, 193–217.

DiGiulio, R. (1989). *Beyond widowhood: From bereavement to emergence and hope*. New York: Free Press.

Federal Interagency Forum on Aging-Related Statistics. (2004). *Older Americans 2004: Key indicators of well-being*. Washington, DC: Author.

Field, M. J., & Cassel, C. K. (1997). *Approaching death: Improving care at the end of life*. Washington, DC: Institute of Medicine.

Fields, J., & Casper, L. M. (2001). *America's families and living arrangements: March 2000* (Current Population Reports, P20-537). Washington, DC: U.S. Census Bureau.

Fooken, I. (1985). Old and female: Psychosocial concomitants of the aging process in a group of older women. In J. Munniches, P. Mussen, E. Olbrich, & P. G. Coleman (Eds.), *Life span and change in a gerontological perspective* (pp. 7–101). Orlando, FL: Academic Press.

Freud, S. (1957). Mourning and melancholia. In J. Strachey (Ed.), *The standard edition of the complete works of Sigmund Freud* (Vol. 14, pp. 152–170). London: Hogarth Press. (Original work published 1917)

George, L. K. (1993). Sociological perspectives on life transitions. *Annual Review of Sociology, 19*, 353–373.

Ha, J., Carr, D., Utz, R., & Nesse, R. (2006). Older adults' perceptions of intergenerational support after widowhood: How do men and women differ? *Journal of Family Issues, 27*, 3–30.

Holmes, T., & Rahe, R. (1967). The Social Readjustment Scale. *Journal of Psychosomatic Research, 11*, 213–218.

Jacobs, S., Kasl, S., & Ostfeld, A. (1986). The measurement of grief: Bereaved versus non-bereaved. *The Hospice Journal, 2*, 21–36.

Kim, C., & Rhee, K. (2000). Living arrangements in old age: Views of elderly and middle-aged adults in Korea. *Hallym International Journal of Aging, 1*, 94–111.

Kraajj, V. E., Arensman, E., & Spinhoven, P. (2002). Negative life events and depression in elderly persons: A meta-analysis. *Journal of Gerontology: Medical Sciences, 57A*, M87–M94.

Kramer, D. (1996–1997). How women relate to terminally ill husbands and their subsequent adjustment to bereavement. *Omega: The Journal of Death and Dying, 34*, 93–106.

Lawton, M., Kleban, M. H., Rajagopal, D., & Dean, J. (1992). Dimensions of affective experience in three age groups. *Psychology and Aging, 7*, 171–184.

Lindemann, E. (1944). Symptomatology and management of acute grief. *American Journal of Psychiatry, 151*, 155–160.

Lopata, H. Z. (1973). *Widowhood in an American city*. Cambridge, MA: Schenkman.

Mendes de Leon, C. F., Kasl, S. V., & Jacobs, S. (1994). A prospective study of widowhood and changes in symptoms of depression in a community sample of the elderly. *Psychological Medicine, 24*, 613–624.

Morioka, K. (1996). Generational relations and their changes as they affect the status of older people in Japan. In T. Hareven (Ed.), *Aging and generational relations over the life course: A historical and cross-cultural perspective* (pp. 511–526). New York: Aldine de Gruyter.

Mroczek, D. K., & Kolarz, C. M. (1998). The effect of age on positive and negative affect: A developmental perspective on happiness. *Journal of Personality and Social Psychology, 75*, 1333–1349.

Neugarten, B., & Hagestad, G. O. (1976). Age and the life course. In G. Binstock & E. Shanas (Eds.), *Handbook of aging and the social sciences* (pp. 35–55). New York: Van Nostrand Reinhold.

Nolen-Hoeksema, S., & Ahrens, C. (2002). Age differences and similarities in the correlates of depressive symptoms. *Psychology and Aging, 17,* 116–124.

Norris, F. H., & Murrell, S. A. (1990). Social support, life events, and stress as modifiers to bereavement by older adults. *Psychology of Aging, 5,* 429–436.

O'Bryant, S. L. (1990–1991). Forewarning of husband's death: Does it make a difference? *Omega: The Journal of Death and Dying, 22,* 227–239.

Parkes, C. M., & Weiss, R. S. (1983). *Recovery from bereavement.* New York: Basic Books.

Reed, M. D. (1998). Predicting grief symptomatology among the suddenly bereaved. *Suicide and Life-Threatening Behavior, 28,* 285–301.

Roach, M. J., & Kitson, C. (1989). Impact of forewarning on adjustment to widowhood and divorce. In D. A. Lund (Ed.), *Older bereaved spouses: Research with practical applications* (pp. 185–200). New York: Hemisphere.

Rynearson, E. K. (1984). Bereavement after homicide: A descriptive study. *American Journal of Psychiatry, 141,* 1452–1454.

Sanders, C. M. (1982–1983). Effects of sudden vs. chronic illness on bereavement outcome. *Omega: The Journal of Death and Dying, 13,* 227–241.

Sanders, C. M. (1993). Risk factors in bereavement outcome. In M. S. Stroebe, W. Stroebe, & R. O. Hansson (Eds.), *Handbook of bereavement: Theory, research, and intervention* (pp. 255–267). Cambridge, England: Cambridge University Press.

Schulz, R., Beach, S., Lind, B., Martire, L., Zdaniuk, B., Hirsch, C., et al. (2001). Involvement in caregiving and adjustment to death of a spouse: Findings from the Caregiver Health Effects Study. *Journal of the American Medical Association, 285,* 3123–3129.

Shah, N., Yount, K., Shah, M., & Menon, I. (2003). Living arrangements of older women and men in Kuwait. *Journal of Cross-Cultural Gerontology, 17,* 337–355.

Singh, B., & Raphael, B. (1981). Post disaster morbidity of the bereaved: A possible role for preventive psychiatry. *Journal of Nervous and Mental Disease, 169,* 203–212.

Spain, D., & Bianchi, S. M. (1996). *Balancing act: Motherhood, marriage and employment among American women.* New York: Russell Sage Foundation.

Stacey, C. A., & Gatz, M. (1991). Cross-sectional age differences and longitudinal change on the Bradburn Affect Balance Scale. *Journal of Gerontology: Psychological Sciences, 46,* 76–78.

Stroebe, M. S., Hansson, R. O., & Stroebe, W. (1993). Contemporary themes and controversies in bereavement research. In M. S. Stroebe, W. Stroebe, & R. O. Hansson (Eds.), *Handbook of bereavement: Theory, research, and intervention* (pp. 457–476). Cambridge, England: Cambridge University Press.

Stroebe, M., & Schut, H. (1999). The dual process model of coping with bereavement: Rationale and description. *Death Studies, 23,* 197–224.

Sweeting, H. N., & Gilhooly, M. (1990). Anticipatory grief: A review. *Social Science & Medicine, 30,* 1073–1080.

Szinovacz, M. E. (2000). Changes in housework after retirement: A panel study. *Journal of Marriage and the Family, 62,* 78–92.

Thompson, L. W., Gallagher-Thompson, D., Futterman, A., Gilewski, M. J., & Peterson, J. (1991). The effects of late life spousal bereavement over a 30-month interval. *Psychology and Aging, 3,* 434–441.

Umberson, D., Wortman, C. B., & Kessler, R. C. (1992). Widowhood and depression: Explaining long-term gender differences in vulnerability. *Journal of Health and Social Behavior, 33,* 10–24.

Utz, R., Reidy, E., Carr, D., Kessler, R. C., Nesse, R. M., & Wortman, C. B. (2004). Changes in housework following widowhood: A story of gender differences and dependence on adult children. *Journal of Family Issues, 25,* 683–712.

Wells, Y. D., & Kendig, H. L. (1997). Health and well-being of spouse caregivers and the widowed. *The Gerontologist, 37,* 666–674.

Worden, J. W. (2002). *Grief counseling and grief therapy: A handbook for the mental health practitioner* (3rd ed.). New York: Springer Publishing Company.

Wortman, C. B., & Silver, R. C. (2001). The myths of coping with loss revisited. In M. S. Stroebe, R. O. Hansson, W. Stroebe, & H. Schut (Eds.), *Handbook of bereavement research: Consequences, coping, and care* (pp. 405–430). Washington, DC: American Psychological Association.

Zisook, S., DeVaul, R., & Click, M. (1982). Measuring symptoms of grief and bereavement. *American Journal of Psychiatry, 139,* 1590–1593.

Zisook, S., Paulus, M., Shuchter, S. R., & Judd, L. L. (1997). The many faces of depression following spousal bereavement. *Journal of Affective Disorders, 45,* 85–94.

Zisook, S., & Shuchter, S. R. (1991). Depression through the first year after the death of a spouse. *American Journal of Psychiatry, 148,* 1346–1352.

21

THE GRIEF OF GRANDPARENTS

BERT HAYSLIP JR. AND DIANA L. WHITE

Published empirical research specific to grandparent bereavement following the death of a child is rare. The limited attention to grieving grandparents is unfortunate because the writings of bereaved grandparents show that they are deeply affected by their loss, provide extensive support to their adult children, and may receive little attention or support from others (see Reed, 2000). Indeed, helping an adult child cope with the death of his or her own child is described as a "nearly impossible task" (Bereaved Parents of the USA, 2003, p. 2).

In this chapter, we consider persons who are grieving over the losses they have experienced in their roles as grandparents. We first discuss two frameworks that we believe to be important in understanding the experience of loss among grandparents: (a) one that emphasizes a life course perspective on intergenerational relationships and family systems and (b) disenfranchised grief. We then examine literature focusing on the death of a grandchild. Because little research has been conducted in this area, we then turn to the more extensive literature on the impact of divorce on relationships with grandchildren and the losses associated with raising a grandchild. In so doing, we identify common elements across the different types of loss experienced by grandparents and illustrate how an examination of each contributes to our understanding of grandparent bereavement. We conclude with recommendations for future directions in research with bereaved grandparents.

A LIFE COURSE PERSPECTIVE ON GRANDPARENTS AND GRIEF

The life course perspective is a dynamic approach to the study of change in families (MacMillan & Copher, 2005; O'Brien, 2005). This perspective includes the construction of social meaning surrounding life events and the social context in which transitions occur (Bengtson & Allen, 1993). The social context includes the concepts of historical time and generational time. *Generational time* refers to events or family transitions that alter interactions within families or change the ways that we view ourselves (Bengtson & Allen, 1993). Many transitions are predictable, such as adult children moving away from home and forming new partnerships and households. Changes in family structure through divorce have become an increasingly common transition as well. Transitions may also be normative or non-normative, and they reflect time or off-time events. Changing demographic patterns in the United States mean that more than half of all deaths occur after age 75 and fewer than 4% of deaths occur before age 30 (Bern-Klug & Chapin, 1999). The death of an infant or young child is clearly a non-normative and off-time event.

To understand grandparents' grief from a life course perspective, it is important to recognize the role of the adult child in mediating the degree of contact between grandparents and grandchildren (Uhlenberg & Hammill, 1998). For the most part, grandparents' interactions with adult children and grandchildren are frequent and satisfying, particularly when grandparents live nearby and the ties between parent and grandparent are strong (Mueller & Elder, 2003). Aldous (1985) suggested that it is the adult child's needs for instrumental and emotional support that activate the grandparent support system in times of family stress. When all is well with their adult children, the majority of grandparents adhere to a norm of noninterference: They enjoy grandchildren and are engaged in family activities, but they do not play an authoritative role with their grandchildren. However, when things do not go right for their adult children, grandparents come to the rescue, making their parent and grandparent roles more central to their lives (Bengtson, 1985). Grandmothers in particular are a major source of help to parents of children with disabilities (Green, 2001), and when adult children are unable to take care of their own children, it is often grandmothers who step in and fill this role (Robertson, 1995). As we discuss further later in this chapter, grandparents also provide significant aid when their grandchildren die.

Although intergenerational support from family members in times of crisis is common, it is not a universal experience. Ingersoll-Dayton, Morgan, and Antonucci (1997) stressed the importance of considering both positive and negative exchanges, finding that positive exchanges or aspects of a social network are associated with positive well-being, whereas negative aspects are associated with negative well-being. Negative aspects of a social network were particularly powerful when an individual was experiencing major stressful life events. In the present context, nearly 30% of grandparents, especially grandfathers, have been described as remote or distant from their families (Mueller et al., 2003). Some grandparents may not be helpful and indeed may cause additional pain to bereaved or divorced parents. Other examples of poor relationships between grandparent and parent generations include a son or daughter who has custody and refuses grandparents access to their grandchild, disagreements between adult children and their parents about child-rearing issues, or a history of relationship conflicts between the grandparent and adult child that culminates in parents relinquishing custody of their children. Thus, relationships between adult children and their parents are likely to influence the impact of a grandchild's death, the necessity to raise a grandchild, or (in the event of an adult child's divorce) the quality of relationships with grandchildren.

Additional life course transitions that accompany grandparenthood also influence response to the death of a grandchild or acceptance of a parenting role. Grandparents may be coping with other losses, such as the youngest child's departure from home, the loss of physical vitality, the loss of the work role through retirement or job loss (see Adams & Beehr, 2003; chap. 20, this volume; Crowley, Hayslip, & Hobdy, 2003), or the loss of a vital relationship with a spouse who has become mentally or physically incapacitated. Such life changes may overlap, leading to what Kastenbaum (1998) termed *bereavement overload*, which affects the nature and frequency of interactions with friends and other grandchildren and undermines adaptive responses to any single loss.

DISENFRANCHISED GRIEF AND GRANDPARENTHOOD

Grandparental grief can also be understood in the context of what Doka (2002; chap. 11, this volume) has termed *disenfranchised grief*. Such grief is deemed unimportant by others, and thus survivors are "not accorded a right to grieve" (Doka, 2002, p. 5). This leads to a lack of support from family, friends, or coworkers and therefore leads to diminished opportunities to reach out emotionally to others who, ironically, often not only do not (and sometimes, cannot) offer sympathy, physical, and instrumental support but also cannot understand or empathize with what the grandparent may be going through emotionally.

Doka (2002) discussed five characteristics of disenfranchised grief, each of which is relevant to this discussion. First, the relationship is not recognized.

As Ponzetti and Johnson (1991) suggested, grandparents may be "forgotten grievers" to the extent that attention is focused on the impact of the child's death on the parents as opposed to the grandparents. Second, the loss itself is not acknowledged, as when a grandchild dies shortly after birth or when the adult child has had an abortion or a miscarriage. Third, the griever is excluded, as when a grandparent who is cognitively impaired by stroke or Alzheimer's disease is denied information about the death of a grandchild, is not permitted to ask questions, or is not allowed to attend the funeral, on the assumption that he or she can no longer comprehend the nature of death. Fourth, when the circumstances of the death are construed as negative, such as when an adult child or a grandchild dies of AIDS or by suicide, or when grandparents assume caregiving responsibilities under stigmatizing social circumstances, such as in the case of the incarceration of an adult child, unemployment, divorce, parental drug use, or sexual abuse of the grandchild. The fifth characteristic of disenfranchised grief is the way individuals grieve, such as when displays of emotion are deemed appropriate and encouraged versus grief that is expressed physically, cognitively, or instrumentally (e.g., involving oneself in work) and is not recognized. Grandfathers, for example, may have particular difficulties in this respect because they are more likely to express their grief instrumentally (i.e., via their interactions with roles or tasks to be completed, as might be true for work; see Doka & Martin, 2002). The very nature of disenfranchised grief complicates bereavement adjustment by poorly defining the role of the grieving individual, leading to what has been termed *ambiguous loss* (Boss, 1999).

GRANDPARENT BEREAVEMENT

Although clinicians and researchers are increasingly focusing on ways in which death affects families (chaps. 23 and 24, this volume; Hansson, Vanzetti, Fairchild, & Berry, 1999), grandparents and other extended family members typically have not been included in studies of parental bereavement. When extended family is considered, it is often in the context of support for bereaved parents (Laakso & Paunonen-Ilmonen, 2002). Little scientific attention has been given to bereavement from a grandparent's perspective (White, 1999). We discuss here four empirical studies we found in the published literature that focused specifically on grandparent bereavement following the death of a grandchild. DeFrain and his colleagues (DeFrain, Ernst, Jakub, & Taylor; 1992; DeFrain, Jakub, & Mendoza, 1991–1992) recruited 80 grandparents to complete an open-ended questionnaire on the impact of sudden infant death syndrome (SIDS). White (2002) and White, Walker, and Richards (2007) described responses to the death of an infant as a result of SIDS, stillbirth, or a birth defect on the basis of interviews with 19 parents and 21 grandparents from 10 families. Ponzetti and Johnson (1991) gathered survey data from 45 grandparents, and Ponzetti (1992) reported further on a subset of those grandparents whose adult children had also completed a similar questionnaire; deceased grandchildren ranged in age from infancy to adolescence. Fry (1997) surveyed 152 bereaved grandparents, with in-depth interviews of a subset of 17 grandparents conducted 6 months after the survey. Her sample included grandparents whose grandchildren ranged in age from infancy into adulthood. All four studies were descriptive and used convenience samples that were predominantly White and middle class.

Grief Responses Among Grandparents

Although parents and grandparents had different role relationships with the child who died (none were identified as custodial grandparents), grandparents shared many of the same responses as the parents (White, 2002; White et al., 2007). At the same time, Ponzetti (1992) reported that parents expressed these feelings more often than grandparents. White (2002) found on the basis of scores on the Inventory of Complicated Grief (Prigerson et al., 1995) that parents as a group exhibited greater distress than grandparents. Some grandparents reported that they had not formed attachments to deceased grandchildren, usually those who were stillborn or died very early in infancy (White, 2002). None of these studies described the responses of very old or frail grandparents.

A major finding in all four studies was the trauma grandparents experienced in witnessing the pain and sorrow of their adult children and their own sense of helplessness in alleviating that pain. This was true for those without strong emotional attachments as well as for those who had been close to their grandchildren (White, 2002). This anguish was a theme that crossed many of the response categories in all studies, and it appeared to compound their own grief at the loss of their grandchild. Grandparents were mobilized to support their adult children and found their own efforts wanting because they could not "make it better."

Social Support

All four studies reported significant grandparent support. On the basis of open-ended questionnaires and interviews, Fry (1997) described grandparents who were willing to put aside their own grief to attend to the needs of their children and their surviving grandchildren. Grandparents told of supporting children by calling and visiting, being available, paying for funeral expenses, and providing other instrumental support (DeFrain et al., 1992). They identified being included by their adult children and being able to express their own feelings and emotions with their adult children as important sources of personal support. Extensive support was reported by parents and grandparents in White et al.'s (2007) study. At least one, and usually more than one, grandparent in each of the 10 families responded and provided emotional support by "being present" or by "acknowledging the significance of the loss" in ways meaningful to the parents. Grandmothers, especially maternal grandmothers, appeared to provide the highest levels of emotional support. Grandparents who had developed close attachments to their grandchildren experienced more intense grief themselves, as indicated both through interviews and the Inventory of Complicated Grief (Prigerson et al., 1995). In these families, mothers and fathers seemed more aware of grandparents' grief, and exchanges of emotional support appeared to be mutual. Ponzetti and Johnson (1991) reported that about half of the grandparents (51%) reported feeling closer to their children, and 16% reported being closer to other grandchildren after their grandchild's death.

Being "unskilled" or having "no support" were themes identified in some families (White et al., 2007). Most parents, usually mothers, identified a grandparent who was not as helpful as they wanted or had expected. In many cases, parents attributed this lack of support to clumsiness in offering support or a lack of knowledge or understanding about what was needed. This took the form of well-intentioned but unwanted advice or messages to "move on" or "get over it." Such responses are common in bereavement and often lead to conflict or friction in social relationships (Lehman & Hemphill, 1990; Nolen-Hoeksema & Larson, 1999). White et al. (2007) reported that unskilled support in the form of unwanted advice came mostly from maternal grandmothers and seemed to cause more distress to their daughters than the lack of skill demonstrated by maternal or paternal grandfathers. The mother–daughter bond is the strongest intergenerational tie (Lefkowitz & Fingerman, 2003; Rossi & Rossi, 1990; Suitor, Pillemer, Keeton, & Robison, 1995), and for this reason mothers may have had greater expectations of support from their own mothers than from their fathers or their in-laws. Therefore, they experienced greater disappointment when support was not forthcoming in the way they had expected. Fathers seemed to be somewhat more tolerant of failed efforts of support.

Although it was not surprising that most bereaved parents did not provide support to grandparents, in some families a number of grandparents did not provide support to bereaved parents. Some parents, especially fathers, had strained relationships with their parents that predated their child's death. Six of the paternal grandfathers were divorced; only 2 of these maintained relationships with adult children, and these were strained. Although these grandfathers, and 1 grandmother, did not provide support, the lack of support did not appear to cause distress because none had been expected (White et al., 2007).

Gender

Consistent with the bereavement literature, grandmothers were more likely than grandfathers to express a desire to talk about the child who died (Ponzetti & Johnson, 1991). Grandmothers also reported emotional and physical distress more often than grandfathers. The opportunity to talk about the child represented an important source of support for grandmothers (Ponzetti & Johnson, 1991). According to DeFrain et al. (1991–1992), their respondents, who were mostly grandmothers, were 3 times as likely to turn to daughters as to sons for support, a rate second only to the use of spouses as support persons. The authors offered this as evidence that fathers are neglected in their grief, suggesting that by not turning to fathers for support grandparents contribute to fathers' isolation in grief. Fry (1997) reported that grandmothers were more likely than grandfathers to seek an outlet for emotional expression; they also provided social support to others within and outside of their families as a way to foster their own healing. Religious beliefs were described more often by women as a source of comfort and recovery compared with men (Fry, 1997). Grandfathers, more than grandmothers, offered instrumental support to their children, performing tasks and offering financial assistance. Engaging in work as a means to help with their recovery was reported more by grandfathers than by grandmothers. Ponzetti and Johnson (1991) found no gender differences with respect to grandparents' feelings about adult children, anger, helplessness, and a need to make sense of the death.

Cognitive Processes

Little is known about the cognitive processes used by grandparents following their grandchild's death. DeFrain et al. (1991–1992) asked generally about grandparents' coping styles and whether they differed from those of their spouse. Although coping styles were not described, about half (52%) of the grandparents indicated that they and their spouse had different coping styles, which was less than the 93% of the SIDS parents who indicated that they had coping styles that were different from their spouses'. DeFrain et al. also found that 29% of grandparents attended a support group, and 90% reported that their religious beliefs had been important in helping them work through their grief. According to Ponzetti (1992), parents more often than grandparents indicated a need to talk to others about the death. Fry (1997) identified *recovery process* as one of six factors that emerged from her data about grandparent reactions to death of a child. The various strategies for recovery emerging from her data included reminiscing, spiritual reappraisal, focusing on others, work activities, and moving on with previously made plans.

White (2002) considered questions about the meanings parents and grandparents find following the death of a child and how meaning-making might be influenced by factors associated with the death, time since death, gender, generation, and lineage. She found support for two distinct components of meaning-making suggested by Davis, Nolen-Hoeksema, and Larson (1998): (a) making sense and (b) finding benefit. In terms of making sense of what had happened, family members talked about their efforts to understand why their babies died, drawing on both rational (i.e., medical, physiological) and spiritual or philosophical reasons. Benefits emerging from tragedy were frequently described, specifically, greater closeness in family relationships, changed perspectives or worldviews, and personal growth. The process of meaning-making was dynamic and often contradictory for parents and grand-parents alike. They were seeking to come to terms with the traumatic, non-normative family transition that had forced changes in their families, including many of the ways they enacted their roles. Meanings were socially constructed through emotional expression, storytelling, and other day-to-day interactions within and across generations. Mothers and fathers talked about similar things in their search for meaning, but gender differences were more apparent in the grandparent generation, with grandmothers reporting more active meaning-making. Although these data represent only a slice in the process, it is clear that the process was ever changing. Participants whose loss was more recent talked more about making sense of the loss than did those who were further along in their bereavement. The latter recalled their strug-gles with making sense and more frequently talked about finding benefit from the experience. Individuals struggled with conflicting meanings and were ambivalent about them, particularly early in bereavement. In general, mean-ing-making was an individual rather than a family process.

White (2002) also considered continuing bonds with the infant who died through questions about funerals, things done to remember the infant, feelings about where the infant is now, and how well parents and grandparents felt they had adjusted to or coped with the death. Funeral rituals in most families helped to define attachments that continued at the time of the inter-views. Parents and grandparents also shared memories of the child; created rituals associated with holidays, birth, and death dates; made spiritual con-nections; and held symbolic representations. This last included photographs and a wide variety of objects (e.g., animals, quilts, gardens) representing the child. Over time, many of these ways of connecting had become embedded in individual and family life. Although not all rituals and activities included grandparents, shared understandings about connections appeared to be espe-cially important. When grandparents were supportive of or shared continuing bonds, relationships between generations appeared to be strong. Because they provided common ground, shared symbols helped to smooth relationships when communication among family members was difficult. The lack of support for symbolic connections or rituals was associated with tensions between parents and extended family members. This occurred in some families in which understanding about the significance of the loss was lacking or in which grandparents were unskilled in their attempts to provide support.

GRANDPARENTS, GRIEF, AND DIVORCE

As we noted earlier, there are parallels between the grief that grandparents feel when a grandchild dies and grief associated with the permanent loss of contact with grandchildren, often because of the divorce of an adult child. If the loss is perceived as permanent, grandparents often feel powerless and vulnerable. As is the case with a grandchild's death, in the event of an adult child's divorce grandparents may lack social support, feel isolated from others, or be unable to help. Except for the death of a grandchild, it is this aspect of grief that has been the subject of the most research regarding grandparenting. Grandparents grieve over the failure of a child's marriage; worry about a grandchild's safety and well-being; fear never having contact with the grandchild ever again; and report intense feelings of depression, sadness, feeling useless, and unfulfilled (see Kruk, 1995). In the event of divorce, less physical and emotional contact with grandchildren was associated intense grief, lowered quality of life, and poorer emotional and physical health and well-being (Drew & Smith, 1999). The impact of a family feud was most negative, followed by divorce and then by geographic separation. In the context of divorce, and in contrast to the findings of Drew and Smith (1999), Edrenberg and Smith (2003) found that relationships with grandchildren were most satisfying when visits with both a daughter and a grandchild were maintained, even when contact with the latter were infrequent. Previous disagreements with the mother about child rearing may lead to limited access of maternal grandmothers and paternal grandparents to their grandchild when the mother has custody and moves away (Drew & Smith, 2002). Similarly, negative, conflictual relationships with adult children-in-law who deny access to the grandchild have profound negative physical health and emotional consequences for noncustodial grandparents, as also is the case when an adult child dies or when the adult child remarries after divorce (Kruk, 1995).

At the same time, Drew and Smith (1999) found that the impact of the loss of contact with the grandchild depended on whether the grandparent was viewed as an agent in the lives of a grandchild or whether the grandparent was viewed as a victim. For example, grandparents who acted as agents provided support and served as role models. Some of these grandparents voluntarily gave up continuing to seek contact with their grandchildren after their former daughters-in-law became angry when the grandparents allowed the grandchildren to see the fathers (the grandparents' own sons) when they visited. Although they grieved, they ultimately moved on with their own lives and discovered new interests and activities. In contrast, grandparents as victims had relationships with grandchildren described as a compensation for the lack of other sources of life satisfaction. One grandparent who was classified as a victim ultimately felt anxious and guilty over her failure to maintain contact with her son and grandchildren. She also reported that her health had suffered, and she feared that her grandchildren would never know her and benefit from the material things she could have given them. Such differences parallel the continuum of adaptive to maladaptive coping in the context of grandparents' bereavement reactions.

In discussing grandparents' grief in the event of the divorce of an adult child, it is important to recognize that consistent with the notion that coping with loss is largely an idiosyncratic emotional and social experience, contact with grandchildren may or may not diminish after divorce (e.g., see Gladstone, 1991). Thus, grief at the loss of the relationship with a grandchild after divorce is salient and profound in some cases and mild, if not absent altogether, in others. This variability in reactions to loss and separation is related to the physical proximity of the grandparent to the grandchild, the age of the grandchild (e.g., older children are more likely to demand contact with a grandparent), and the gender and lineage of the grandparent (favoring maternal grandmothers; Rossi & Rossi, 1990). For example, when one's own children have custody, grandparent–grandchild contact is less likely to be negatively affected (Jaskowski & Dellasega, 1993). Of interest is that Holladay et al. (1998) found that the likelihood of reconstructing a relationship with one's maternal grandmother among granddaughters aged 17 through 23 increased in varying degrees (as reflected in greater relational closeness) after geographical separation, death or serious illness, or family disruption. It is important to note that death; illness; or divorce, separation, or remarriage for these granddaughters were seen as opportunities to reconnect with a grandmother, just as grief may be a stimulus for personal growth (White, 2002). In contrast, relational closeness decreased in varying degrees with increased geographic separation, the granddaughter's transition to college, and with a history of negative interactions with the grandmother. In such cases, grandparents' grief may be more intense and/or more clearly defined by ambivalence.

CUSTODIAL GRANDPARENTS AS GRIEVERS

The rise in custodial grandparenting is illustrative of the historical shifts occurring in the nature of grandparenting itself (Uhlenberg & Kirby, 1998). For example, because people are living longer, grandchildren are more likely to have grandparents who are still living. Moreover, grandparents are now more highly educated; are more likely to be divorced; and because they have had fewer children, are likely to have fewer grandchildren. For these reasons, it is especially important to examine the experiences of custodial grandparenting because they provide insights into the nature of grandparent grief. Custodial grandparents provide a compelling example of disenfranchised grief as well as bereavement overload, loss of relationships, and feelings of isolation and lack of support.

Disenfranchised Grief

One of the parameters defining disenfranchised grief pertains to negative and often socially stigmatizing circumstances surrounding the death. This certainly occurs when custodial grandparenting results from incarceration; parental abuse or abandonment of the child; and, in some situations, the death or divorce of an adult child (see Hayslip & Kaminski, 2005). Grandparents may experience feelings of guilt over their perceived failures as parents in producing an adult child who has abused the grandchild, used drugs, or been incarcerated (McKelvy & Draimin, 2002). Indeed, individuals who are ashamed of their loss may feel the need to hide their grief, undermining opportunities to share their feelings about the losses they have experienced and contributing to the disenfranchised nature of their grief.

The grief of grandparents raising grandchildren who are either HIV positive or whose parents have died from HIV disease is overwhelming (Joslin, 2002; Winston, 2003), and it often has negative health consequences for grandparents (Joslin & Harrison, 2002). In the United States, HIV-infected grandchildren are stigmatized, and custodial grandparents suffer from a lack of emotional and tangible support from others (Joslin, 2002), especially where it is highly likely that the grandchild will also die. These grandparents, who are often African American, sometimes experience an overwhelming sense of loss and depression, and they even manifest behaviors and thoughts characteristic of pathological grief. Some studies (e.g., Winston, 2003) suggest that it is grandparents' own sense of a spiritual relationship with God as well as their sense of familism that enable them to cope with the profound sense of isolation, feeling different, and hopelessness that often accompanies caring for an HIV-infected child.

Feelings of not knowing what will happen to one (or one's grandchild) in the future, or feelings relating to the adult child's failures, contribute to ambiguous grief (Archibald, 2004). Grief that is ambiguous is less well defined in terms of its duration and outcome (as in the case of family members whose loved one has Alzheimer's disease). In such cases, grievers are less attuned to what they should be feeling in terms of expected emotions in light of the death and are less certain about how and when they should express their feelings as well as with whom such feelings might be shared. These uncertainties rob grieving grandparents of needed social support and undermine the likelihood that they will ask for help with their feelings, complicating the grieving process further.

The intensity of such grief has been described among Ugandan grand-mothers who, ironically, did not fear being stigmatized because AIDS occurs so frequently but who were nevertheless concerned for their children's futures if they themselves became sick and died (Poindexter & Kamya, 2003). These grandmothers took an assertive stance toward coping, maintained meaningful relationships with their grandchildren, and drew on their own inner spiritual resources. It is likely that their grief was anticipatory, given the likelihood of their own grandchildren dying from AIDS. The role such grief ultimately plays in influencing postdeath adjustment among such grandparents has yet to be explored.

Multiple Losses

Custodial grandparents typically have experienced a multitude of losses, paralleling what Kastenbaum (1998; see also chap. 4, this volume) has termed *bereavement overload*. Future plans may be permanently interrupted (parallel-ing the redefined future bereaved grandparents face without a grandchild), and the dissolution of the expected grandparent–grandchild relationship may be especially troublesome. Previous connections with a grandchild may be altered forever, much in the same way that one's relationship with a deceased grandchild is irreversibly altered and a new relationship to that child must ultimately be forged. Furthermore, custodial grandparents must also adjust to changes in their relationships with the grandchildren they are not raising, and they may experience the loss of such relationships (Shore & Hayslip, 1994).

Custodial grandparents' grief is compounded when, for example, an adult child has died. Under these circumstances, the grandchild may become a daily reminder of the loss they have suffered (de Toledo & Brown, 1995). They may grieve as well for their grandchild's loss of a parent (Reed, 2000), often to the detriment of attending to their own feelings and getting emotional support from others who recognize the seriousness of their loss.

As suggested by our earlier discussion, the losses custodial grandparents experience are often exacerbated by strained or hostile relationships with an adult child. Shore and Hayslip (1994) found that nearly two thirds of custodial grandparents expressed disappointment in their child, 28% resented their child, and more than 30% felt taken advantage of by their child. If their adult child is incarcerated, grandparents may also grieve for lost hopes and dreams for their adult child (Minkler, Fuller-Thomson, Miller, & Driver, 2000), which can be complicated by feelings of anger and resentment at having been disappointed by the child. Underscoring the emotional and physical toll that custodial grandparents experience is the greater incidence of illnesses such as depression, diabetes, hypertension, and insomnia among this population (e.g., Hayslip & Kaminski, 2005; Minkler et al., 2000).

All of these losses represent factors that are often perceived as irreversible—and indeed, quite personal—by custodial grandparents. The impact of this multitude of factors on the grief that custodial grandparents experience can be understood in terms of bereavement overload. This sense of loss overwhelms many grandparent caregivers, affecting their health, marriage, and relationships with others. As Baird (2003) stated, for a custodial grandparent "there are constant reminders of losses incurred: the retirement of a friend, watching a neighbor's grandchild come and go, lack of personal time with a spouse, lost contact with another friend" (p. 64).

Isolation

Custodial grandparents often express feelings of isolation from their age-peers (Shore & Hayslip, 1994). Indeed, this sense of being invisible and different is a powerful source of distress (Wohl, Lahner, & Jooste, 2003). Moreover, it parallels bereaved grandparents' experiences of being forgotten and ignored (Reed, 2000). The perception of oneself as different from other grandparents can be likened to the way in which many grieving persons feel different from others who have not experienced the same loss.

Such consequences may have considerable costs for custodial grandparents. Although social support cannot accelerate adaptation to the loss of others (W. Stroebe, Schut, & Stroebe, 2005), it is critical to working through one's feelings in the event of the divorce, death, or incarceration of an adult child. Thus, the dissolution of the family system and the sense of failure, sadness, or anger at an adult child's failures as a parent (or, in the case of death, anger at the deceased for dying, or guilt over unfinished business) all help to define the grief experienced by custodial grandparents. Indeed, the gravity of custodial grandparents' needs for social support and understanding are likely not to be appreciated or understood by others (Miltenberger, Hayslip, Harris, & Kaminski, 2003–2004).

Sensitivity or lack thereof to grandparents' losses is important for several reasons. First, custodial grandparents have reported that isolation from others is a major concern (Shore & Hayslip, 1994). Understanding or lack of understanding by others of the losses custodial grandparents have experienced can either lessen or exacerbate, respectively, the social distance created between the grandparents and others who have not experienced such losses. Second, custodial grandparents often have difficulty obtaining needed services for themselves and/or their grandchildren. Service providers' sensitivity to grandparents' grief can facilitate access to services. Third, custodial grandparents' recognition that their feelings of loss are not unique and that they can share them with others may increase the likelihood that they will seek both formal and informal help.

The lone published study that investigated perceptions of the losses experienced by custodial grandparents was conducted by Miltenberger et al.

(2003–2004). They sampled nearly 1,200 young adults. Such persons were randomly assigned to read about a hypothetical situation involving a caregiving grandmother (based on an actual case example) that varied in terms of grandparent ethnicity, grandchild gender, the reason for role assumption, and the presence or absence of problem behaviors and feelings in the grandchild. Miltenberger et al. found that participants were more empathic toward grandmothers who were expected to be experiencing disenfranchised grief. Indeed, participants acknowledged the innumerable losses associated with becoming a custodial grandparent because one's adult child had abandoned or abused the grandchild, abused drugs, died, or been incarcerated. Similarly, having a grandchild with behavioral and emotional problems was associated with greater sensitivity to the grandmother's loss of normalcy. However, custodial grandmothers whose children had divorced or who had lost their jobs were seen as experiencing less loss, suggesting that grief for such persons may be more disenfranchised. This may result from the prevalence of divorce and job loss, which are viewed as less stigmatizing. Grandparents' disappointments in their adult children's marriages or career success in such cases may be underestimated. These findings were generally consistent with research on responses to loss, which indicates that individuals' perceptions vary depending on how the loss has occurred and the life circumstances of the bereaved individual (M. Stroebe, Hansson, Stroebe, & Schut, 2001).

CONCLUSIONS AND RECOMMENDATIONS FOR FUTURE RESEARCH

Although little research has focused exclusively on grandparent bereavement, some descriptive findings have been consistent across studies. The limited bereavement research described in this chapter supports much of what is known generally about gender, lineage, and ambiguity in intergenerational family relationships. A focus on grandparent bereavement has expanded our understanding of family systems and how the death of one family member affects all members. Grandparents typically mobilize to support their children in need, including when a grandchild dies. Most grandparents value that role and grieve for the loss of their grandchild. At the same time, when comparisons between grandparents and parents have been made in the case of child death, it appears that grief is somewhat less intense for grandparents than it is for parents, particularly if grandparents had not formed strong attachments to the child. Given the strong intergenerational tie with their adult children, grandparents clearly grieve for their children who are in distress regardless of their own level of attachment to the grandchild. The lay and research literature have provided evidence that grandparents consistently feel helpless about their inability to make things better for their children.

Given the limited empirical literature on bereaved grandparents, much can be learned about grandparents' grief by studying their reactions to the loss of a relationship with a grandchild in the event of an adult child's divorce or when grandparents must raise an adult child's child. In each case, there are individual differences in responses to losses. These may be seen as not only highly personal but also as disenfranchised for some grandparents if circumstances are socially stigmatizing and grandparents are held responsible (e.g., had one been a better parent, the adult child would not have divorced or would have been a more competent parent). Moreover, like the loss of a grandchild through death, changed relationships with grandchildren in such circumstances may be perceived as irreversible.

Social support is critical to the well-being of grandparents who grieve because of death, who have experienced the divorce of an adult child and are cut off from a grandchild, or who have suffered the loss of a traditional grandparent–grandchild relationship because they must raise that child. At the same time, however, what is not known about grandparents' responses to grief and loss is much more extensive than is known. The studies we have described in this chapter, including all the bereavement studies, were predominantly descriptive, with small convenience samples. Larger and more representative samples with respect to gender and ethnicity are needed. Little contextual information was included in the analyses reported, in part because of small samples. As a result, little is known about other experiences that occur concurrently with bereavement, divorce, and grandparent caregiving and how they might influence grief responses.

Most studies that have focused on grandparent bereavement, divorce, and custodial grandparenting have not been theory based. Future work needs to incorporate emerging grief theories (see Neimeyer, 2006; M. Stroebe et al., 2001) that deal with the vacillating nature of bereavement adjustment, finding meaning, continuing bonds, and other cognitive processes following loss. Furthermore, because families are complex, researchers need to continue to examine family relationships across generations to better understand the relationship between family dynamics and grief processes (see Nadeau, 2001). Longitudinal designs are required to provide better understanding of the processes of adaptation within families, whether they are bereaved, engaged in caregiving, or coping with a child's divorce. Stronger understanding is also needed of what happens when grandparents put aside their own grief to support their children or grandchildren. Does this facilitate adaptation, or does it reinforce grandparents as disenfranchised grievers? What are the consequences for grandchildren?

Intervention studies that identify ways to assist grandparents in adapting to loss are sorely needed. A key factor in grandparents' adaptation to loss may be their perceptions that their adult children are coping appropriately (White, 2002). More research is needed to explore this issue and to find ways to help grandparents become more effective in supporting their adult children and surviving grandchildren. For example, with increased understanding of normal grief responses, particularly to losses during pregnancy or neonatal loss, which often go unrecognized, grandparents may be less likely to expect their children to be themselves within weeks and less likely to make hurtful comments about "moving on." In a parallel fashion, custodial grandparents and those left behind after a child's divorce might be encouraged to more openly acknowledge and talk about their grief. This in effect legitimizes grief as something worthy of one's own and others' attention; aids in the definition of the grieving role; encourages the search for help and support from others; and perhaps minimizes the negative impact of unspoken, unrecognized grief. As interventions are tested, attention needs to focus on specific approaches to help grandparents adapt to loss. It is important to note that research can identify grandparents for whom such approaches work because interventions that target grief are not equally efficacious with all persons (see Schut, Stroebe, van den Bout, & Terheggen, 2001). Such intervention studies can also increase the recognition of grandparents' grief as real and mobilize social support for them.

REFERENCES

Adams, G., & Beehr, T. (2003). *Retirement: Reasons, processes, and results*. New York: Springer Publishing Company.

Aldous, J. (1985). Parent–adult child relations as affected by the grandparent status. In V. L. Bengtson & J. F. Robertson (Eds.), *Grandparenting* (pp. 117–132). Beverly Hills, CA: Sage.

Archibald, S. (2004). An exploratory study of the experiences of ambiguous grief issues among grandparents raising grandchildren. *Dissertation Abstracts International: Humanities and Social Sciences, 64*, 1440–1441.

Baird, A. (2003). Through my eyes: Service needs of grandparents who raise their grandchildren, from the perspective of a custodial grandmother. In B. Hayslip & J. Patrick (Eds.), *Working with custodial grandparents* (pp. 59–68). New York: Springer Publishing Company.

Bengtson, V. L. (1985). Diversity and symbolism in grandparental roles. In V. L. Bengtson & J. F. Robertson (Eds.), *Grandparenting* (pp. 11–29). Beverly Hills, CA: Sage.

Bengtson, V. L., & Allen, K. R. (1993). The life course perspective applied to families over time. In P. G. Boss, W. J. Doherty, R. LaRossa, W. R. Schumm, & S. K. Steinmetz (Eds.), *Sourcebook of family theories and methods: A contextual approach* (pp. 469–498). New York: Plenum Press.

Bereaved Parents of the USA. (2003). *For bereaved grandparents*. Retrieved January 25, 2008, from http://www.bereavedparentsusa.org/images/pdfs/bpusagp.pdf

Bern-Klug, M., & Chapin, R. (1999). The changing demography of death in the United States: Implications for health care workers. In B. de Vries (Ed.), *End of life issues: Interdisciplinary and multidimensional perspectives* (pp. 265–280). New York: Springer Publishing Company.

Boss, P. (1999). *Ambiguous loss: Learning to live with unresolved grief*. Cambridge, MA: Harvard University Press.

Crowley, B., Hayslip, B., & Hobdy, J. (2003). Psychological hardiness and adjustment to life events in adulthood. *Journal of Adult Development, 10*, 237–248.

Davis, C. G., Nolen-Hoeksema, S., & Larson, J. (1998). Making sense of loss and benefiting from the experience: Two construals of meaning. *Journal of Personality and Social Psychology, 75*, 561–574.

DeFrain, J., Ernst, L., Jakub, D., & Taylor, J. (1992). *Sudden infant death: Enduring the loss*. Lexington, MA: Lexington Books.

DeFrain, J. D., Jakub, D. K., & Mendoza, B. L. (1991–1992). The psychological effects of sudden infant death on grandmothers and grandfathers. *Omega: The Journal of Death and Dying, 24*, 165–182.

de Toledo, S., & Brown, D. E. (1995). *Grandparents as parents: A survival guide for raising a second family*. New York: Guilford Press.

Doka, K. J. (2002). *Disenfranchised grief: New directions, challenges, and strategies for practice*. Champaign, IL: Research Press.

Doka, K., & Martin, T. (2002). How we grieve: Culture, class, and gender. In K. Doka (Ed.), *Disenfranchised grief: New directions, challenges, and strategies for practice* (pp. 337–348). Champaign, IL: Research Press.

Drew, L., & Smith, P. (1999). The impact of parental separation/divorce on grandparent grandchild relationships. *International Journal of Aging and Human Development, 48*, 191–216.

Drew, L., & Smith, P. (2002). Implications for grandparents when they lose contact with their grandchildren: Divorce, family feud, and geographical separation. *Journal of Mental Health and Aging, 8*, 95–119.

Edrenberg, M., & Smith, P. (2003). Grandmother–grandchild contacts before and after an adult daughter's divorce. *Journal of Divorce and Remarriage, 39*, 27–43.

Fry, P. S. (1997). Grandparents' reactions to the death of a grandchild: An exploratory factor analytic study. *Omega: The Journal of Death and Dying, 35*, 119–140.

Gladstone, J. W. (1991). An analysis of changes in grandparent–grandchild visitation following an adult child's remarriage. *Canadian Journal on Aging, 10*, 113–126.

Green, S. E. (2001). Grandma's hands: Parental perceptions of the importance of grandparents as secondary caregivers in families of children with disabilities. *International Journal of Aging and Human Development, 53*, 11–33.

Hansson, R. O., Vanzetti, N. A., Fairchild, S. K., & Berry, J. O. (1999). The impact of bereavement on families. In B. de Vries (Ed.), *End of life issues: Interdisciplinary and multidimensional perspectives* (pp. 99–117). New York: Springer Publishing Company.

Hayslip, B., Jr., & Kaminski, P. L. (2005). Grandparents raising their grandchildren: A review of literature and suggestions for practice. *The Gerontologist, 45,* 262–269.

Holladay, S., Lackovich, R., Lee, M., Coleman, M., Harding, D., & Dento, D. (1998). (Re)constructing relationships with grandparents: A turning point analysis of granddaughters' relational development with maternal grandmothers. *International Journal of Aging and Human Development, 46,* 287–303.

Ingersoll-Dayton, B., Morgan, D., & Antonucci, T. (1997). The effects of positive and negative social exchanges on aging adults. *Journal of Gerontology: Social Sciences, 52B,* S190–S199.

Jaskowski, S., & Dellasega, C. (1993). Effects of divorce on the grandparent–grandchild relationship. *Issues in Comprehensive Pediatric Nursing, 16,* 125–133.

Joslin, D. (2002). *Invisible caregivers: Older adults raising children in the wake of HIV/AIDS.* New York: Columbia University Press.

Joslin, D., & Harrison, R. (2002). Self reported physical health among older surrogate parents to children orphaned and affected by HIV disease. *AIDS Care, 14,* 619–624.

Kastenbaum, R. (1998). *Death, society, and human existence.* Boston: Allyn & Bacon.

Kruk, E. (1995). Grandparent–grandchild contact loss: Findings from a study of "grandparents' rights" members. *Canadian Journal of Aging, 14,* 737–754.

Laakso, H., & Paunonen-Ilmonen, M. (2002). Mothers' experience of social support following the death of a child. *Journal of Clinical Nursing, 11,* 176–185.

Lehman, D. R., & Hemphill, K. J. (1990). Recipients' perceptions of support attempts and attributions for support attempts that fail. *Journal of Social and Personal Relationships, 7,* 563–574.

Lefkowitz, E. S., & Fingerman, K. L. (2003). Positive and negative emotional feelings and behaviors in mother–daughter ties in late life. *Journal of Family Psychology, 17,* 607–617.

MacMillan, R., & Copher, R. (2005). Families in the life course: Interdependency of roles, role configurations, and pathways. *Journal of Marriage and Family, 67,* 858–879.

McKelvy, L., & Draimin, B. (2002). Their second chance: Grandparents caring for their grandchildren. In D. Joslin (Ed.), *Invisible caregivers: Older adults raising children in the wake of HIV/AIDS* (pp. 151–179). New York: Columbia University Press.

Miltenberger, P., Hayslip, B., Harris, B., & Kaminski, P. (2003–2004). Perceptions of the losses experienced by custodial grandmothers. *Omega: The Journal of Death and Dying, 48,* 245–262.

Minkler, M., Fuller-Thomson, E., Miller, D., & Driver, D. (2000). Grandparent caregiving and depression. In B. Hayslip & R. Goldberg-Glen (Eds.), *Grandparents raising grandchildren: Theoretical, empirical, and clinical perspectives* (pp. 207–220). New York: Springer Publishing Company.

Mueller, M. M., & Elder, G. H. (2003). Family contingencies across generations: Grandparent–grandchild relationships in holistic perspective. *Journal of Marriage and Family, 65,* 404–417.

Nadeau, J. W. (2001). Meaning making in family bereavement: A family systems approach. In M. Stroebe, R. Hansson, W. Stroebe, & H. Schut (Eds.), *Handbook of bereavement research: Consequences, coping, and care* (pp. 329–347). Washington, DC: American Psychological Association.

Neimeyer, R. A. (2006). Widowhood, grief, and the quest for meaning: A narrative perspective on resilience. In D. Carr, R. Nesse, & C. B. Wortman (Eds.), *Spousal bereavement in late life* (pp. 227–254). New York: Springer Publishing Company.

Nolen-Hoeksema, S., & Larson, J. (1999). *Coping with loss.* Mahwah, NJ: Erlbaum.

O'Brien, M. (2005). Studying individual and family development: Linking theory & research. *Journal of Marriage and Family, 67,* 880–890.

Poindexter, C. C., & Kamya, H. (2003, November). *"Mama Jaja" (Mother-Granny): The stress and strength of Ugandan grandmothers caring for AIDS orphans.* Paper presented at the Annual Meeting of the Gerontological Society of America, San Diego, CA.

Ponzetti, J. J., Jr. (1992). Bereaved families: A comparison of parents' and grandparents' reactions to the death of a child. *Omega: The Journal of Death and Dying, 25,* 63–71.

Ponzetti, J. J., Jr., & Johnson, M. (1991). The forgotten grievers: Grandparents' reactions to the death of grandchildren. *Death Studies, 15,* 157–163.

Prigerson, H. G., Maciejewski, P. K., Reynolds, C. F., III, Bierhals, A. J., Newsom, J. T., Fasiczka, A., et al. (1995). Inventory of Complicated Grief: A scale to measure maladaptive symptoms of loss. *Psychiatric Research, 59,* 65–79.

Reed, M. L. (2000). *Grandparents cry twice: Help for bereaved grandparents.* Amityville, NY: Baywood.

Robertson, J. F. (1995). Grandparenting in an era of rapid change. In R. Bleiszner & V. H. Bedford (Eds.), *Handbook of aging and the family* (pp. 243–260). Westport, CT: Greenwood Press.

Rossi, A. S., & Rossi, P. H. (1990). *Of human bonding.* New York: Aldine de Gruyter.

Schut, H., Stroebe, M., van den Bout, J., & Terheggen, M. (2001). The efficacy of bereavement interventions: Determining who benefits. In M. Stroebe, R. Hansson, W. Stroebe, & H. Schut (Eds.), *Handbook of bereavement research: Consequences, coping, and care* (pp. 705–738). Washington, DC: American Psychological Association.

Shore, R. J., & Hayslip, B. (1994). Custodial grandparenting: Implications for children's development. In A. Gottfried & A. Gottfried (Eds.), *Redefining families: Implications for children' development* (pp. 171–218). New York: Plenum Press.

Stroebe, M., Hansson, R., Stroebe, W., & Schut, H. (2001). *Handbook of bereavement research: Consequences, coping, and care.* Washington, DC: American Psychological Association.

Stroebe, W., Schut, H., & Stroebe, M. (2005). Grief work, disclosure, and counseling: Do they help the bereaved? *Clinical Psychology Review, 25,* 395–414.

Suitor, J. J., Pillemer, K., Keeton, S., & Robison, J. (1995). Aged parents and aging children: Determinants of relationship quality. In R. Bleiszner & V. H. Bedford

(Eds.), *Handbook of aging and the family* (pp. 223–242). Westport, CT: Greenwood Press.

Uhlenberg, P., & Hammill, B. (1998). Frequency of grandparent contact with grand-child sets: Six factors that make a difference. *The Gerontologist, 38,* 276–285.

Uhlenberg, P., & Kirby, J. (1998). Grandparenthood over time: Historical and demographic trends. In M. Szionovacz (Ed.), *Handbook on grandparenthood* (pp. 23–39). Westport, CT: Greenwood Press.

White, D. (1999). Grandparent participation in times of family bereavement. In B. de Vries (Ed.), *End of life issues: Interdisciplinary and multidisciplinary perspectives* (pp. 145–165). New York: Springer Publishing Company.

White, D. (2002). Intergenerational responses to the death of a child. (Doctoral dissertation, Oregon State University, 2002). *Dissertation Abstracts International, 63,* 06A.

White, D. L., Walker A. J., & Richards, L. N. (2007). *Intergenerational family support following infant death.* Manuscript submitted for publication.

Winston, C. (2003). African American grandmothers parenting grandchildren orphaned by AIDS: Grieving and coping with loss. *Illness, Crisis & Loss, 11,* 350–361.

Wohl, E., Lahner, J., & Jooste, J. (2003). Group processes among grandparents raising grandchildren. In B. Hayslip & J. Patrick (Eds.), *Working with custodial grandparents* (pp. 195–212). New York: Springer Publishing Company.

VI

DEVELOPMENT AND EFFICACY OF INTERVENTION PROGRAMS

22

BEREAVEMENT FOLLOWING DISASTERS

COLIN MURRAY PARKES

The course of bereavement can be particularly problematic when a death is sudden, unexpected, and untimely (Stroebe & Schut, 2001). Deaths caused by a disaster inevitably fit these criteria. If multiple deaths are involved, if bodies are mutilated or unrecovered, if children are among the fatalities, and if the survivors witnessed horrific events, and/or blamed themselves or others, then the process of bereavement becomes even more complex and difficult. Losses of property, homes, and livelihood, together with the social disorganization and continuing dangers that often follow disasters, add to the burden. It follows that psychological help from outside the family, often from outside the disaster-stricken community, and sometimes from outside the country, will be needed and should be given priority by caring services, both professional and voluntary.

In this chapter, I draw on experience and published research to identify the principal variables that influence the reaction of people bereaved by disasters and to examine the interventions that can be expected before, during, and after a disaster to reduce the risk of lasting problems in individuals, families, communities, and nations.

As readers of this volume will be aware, the field of bereavement is not confined to any one discipline. Psychologists, sociologists, anthropologists, psychiatrists, counselors, and leaders of various religions have all made valuable contributions to our understanding of the many problems that beset bereaved people. The simplistic methods of "bereavement counseling" of the early days are long gone. In their place are more sophisticated and broad-spectrum approaches, which include the building of trust; assessment of psychological, social, and spiritual needs; and the provision of a range of services to meet those needs. These approaches have special value in response to the many problems of disasters.

My own experience of disasters grew out of my research into the psychological consequences of bereavement and my involvement with hospice bereavement services and with the national organization Cruse Bereavement Care. Inevitably I write in this chapter about that experience and about the British scene, but this does not mean that there are not other services, in other countries, that are worthy of emulation. Anyone who has worked in a disaster area will be aware of the stream of support, goodwill, and commitment to which disasters give rise. Rivalries diminish, prejudices are put aside, and collaboration between individuals and organizations is often possible, which can bring help to large numbers of traumatized and bereaved people.

In Britain, voluntary services for bereaved people are available, without charge, in most parts of the country. The largest and most comprehensive is Cruse Bereavement Care, but there are also many independent local bereavement services, and most hospices have their own service, although some make use of their local branch of Cruse. At last count, Cruse had 5,400 volunteers, backed by 121 paid staff, to support bereaved people across England, Wales, and Northern Ireland. Cruse's bereavement volunteers (BVs), most of whom have themselves suffered losses, are carefully selected, trained, and supervised in their work. Through its central and 240 local services Cruse responded to 177,452 inquiries during 2004–2005, corresponding to approximately one third of registered deaths.[1]

Bereavement services have developed separately from the field of traumatic stress. In recent years, however, the occurrence of disasters, such as airline crashes, in which many have died but few injured people or witnesses have survived, has focused attention on bereavement and led to the inclusion of bereavement support workers in disaster teams. In Britain, this has led to a close collaboration among Cruse Bereavement Care; the Red Cross; and the police's new model family assistance teams, who provide front-line support in the face of major disasters. Staffed by family liaison officers (FLOs) with special training in the support of families at times of crisis and disaster, these elite teams set a high standard of humane support while maintaining their roles in the detection and prosecution of major crimes. Because their involvement is limited to the duration of the emergency, collaboration with other organizations that are in a position to provide longer term care is essential.

---

[1] These figures do not include Cruse Scotland, which is separately governed but closely affiliated to Cruse UK.

At the time of Britain's 1966 Aberfan disaster, in which a coal avalanche killed 144 people, most of them children, posttraumatic stress disorder (PTSD) had not been identified, psychiatrists and volunteer counselors were regarded with suspicion, and services aimed at supporting disaster victims and bereaved families were virtually nonexistent. By 2001, teams of FLOs and BVs were ready to be rapidly mobilized in response to the September 11, 2001, terrorist attacks; the December 2004 Indian Ocean tsunami; and the London bombs of July 2005. Prejudice against psychiatric services continues, but these alternatives have proved their worth and are now a regular part of the response to major incidents.

Although I have carried out little systematic research in this field, I have been involved in the planning of responses, assessment of need, and provision of help after 11 disasters over a period of 40 years. My experience ranges from small-scale disasters, such as the consequences of a helicopter crash into an oil rig, which took 12 lives, to large-scale disasters, such as the Rwandan genocide, which took more than 500,000 lives. It includes local disasters, such as the avalanche of coal slurry in Aberfan, the victims of which were all from the same small village, to international disasters, such as the bomb on Pan American Flight 103, which took the lives of 270 people from 21 different countries. Over the course of my career, major changes have taken place in the ways in which disasters are viewed, the resources available to deal with them, and the interventions that are deemed appropriate.

FACTORS INFLUENCING RESPONSE

The variables of *scale* and *spread* influence the impact of the disaster and the services necessary to cope with it. Other factors that influence the response include the duration of the event, the type of damage, and the culture and expectations of the affected population.

Differences of scale and spread are illustrated in Table 22.1. They have important implications for the organization of a response (Parkes, 1997). As a rough guide, a *small-scale disaster* is taken to mean fewer than 100 deaths, and a large-scale disaster more than 1,000 deaths. Exactly what the equivalent measures are for injuries and destruction of property has not been determined. Indeed, some floods and other disasters cause extensive damage without any loss of life. Because these lie outside the purview of this volume, they are not considered here.

After small-scale local disasters, the unit of care is the affected families, but the community will also be affected. Psychosocial support can usually be managed by local services, although it may be useful for the service providers to seek further expert advice and training.

TABLE 22.1
Differences of Scale and Spread in Recent Disasters

Size of disaster	Local	National	International
Small	Hungerford, England massacre (August 19, 1987)	Shell Oil helicopter crash, North Sea (July 17, 2002)	London bombs (July 7, 2005)
Medium	Aberfan coal avalanche (October 21, 1966)	Capsized ferry, Zeebrugge Harbour, Belgium (March 6, 1987)	Pan Am 103 explosion, Lockerbie, Scotland (December 21, 1988)
Large	Union Carbide gas leak, Bhopal, India (December 3, 1984)	Genocide, Rwanda (April–May 1994)	Terrorist attacks, United States (September 11, 2001)
			Indian Ocean tsunami (December 26, 2004)

The disaster in the small town of Hungerford, England, where in 1987 a mentally disturbed gunman killed 16 people and injured another 15 before killing himself, evoked offers of help from across the world. However, the local social services, with help from the local branch of Cruse Bereavement Care and other bodies, set up a "Family Help Unit" to provide support and advice and to accompany bereaved people at the funerals and inquest. They were backed by a psychiatrist and had no need of more extensive help. The killer was a local man, and the community as a whole suffered from becoming the center of attention by the media and from the blaming and shame that followed.

In the wake of small-scale national disasters, a local office in the disaster area and a telephone hotline are needed to provide information and short-term support as well as to liaise with local services across the country. When a helicopter crashed into an oil installation in the North Sea in 2002, the 12 people who died were from several parts of the United Kingdom. They were all, however, employees of Shell Oil, and the company rapidly mobilized its own occupational psychologist and psychiatrist to provide advice and support. I acted as a consultant to that team. In such cases, liaison with support services in other localities is needed, but such services are unlikely to become overloaded.

Liaison across national boundaries will be needed whenever an international disaster takes place, even if it is small in scale. Consulates exist to provide assistance and can be expected to respond appropriately. Leadership from the government in the country in which the disaster has taken place is the key to success, but leaders too will be caught up in the psychological consequences of the disaster and may well lack the personal support that is offered to the bereaved families.

In London, after the terrorist bombs of July 7, 2005, killed 56 people in four locations, a helpline and Family Assistance Office were set up and staffed by FLOs from the metropolitan police, selected volunteers from Cruse Bereavement Care, and the International Red Cross. They were able to provide the range of expertise that was needed by bereaved families and survivors of the bombs. In the longer term, they were able to refer persons who needed it to appropriate specialist help.

Unlike small-scale local disasters, medium-scale local disasters easily overwhelm local resources. In Aberfan, the children who died were known to the local teachers, health care team, and social workers, many of whom were themselves traumatized by the disaster. Lacking expertise in the field, they were happy to accept the help of a small team of a family caseworker, youth worker, and unattached pastoral counselor from outside the village who supplemented and supported the existing psychiatric, psychological, and social work teams. They in turn were supervised by a psychologist, a psychotherapist, and a psychiatrist.

Medium-scale national disasters necessitate a national response, although the spread of survivors across the nation may enable most of their needs to be met by local services. When the ferry boat *Herald of Free Enterprise* capsized in 1987 outside Belgium's Zeebrugge harbor, 193 people died, including both passengers and crew, most of whom lived in the United Kingdom. Members of the crew and several passengers came from the port of Dover, and it was here that a disaster office was set up with two support teams recruited from Cruse Bereavement Care and other organizations. One team, the "Home Team," manned the office and provided support to the local people, and the other team, the "Away Team," traveled throughout Britain to meet with surviving family members, assess their need for support, and introduce them to local branches of Cruse and other sources of help.

Government involvement is crucial in medium-scale international disasters. When Pan American Flight 103 was destroyed by a terrorist bomb, 4 days before Christmas 1988, over the village of Lockerbie, Scotland, there were no survivors among the 259 passengers and 16 crew. Debris and bodies were scattered over a wide area, and a large part of the plane's fuselage crashed into Lockerbie, destroying houses and killing 11 local residents. Psychological support in the locality was provided by local social services backed by Cruse. Although the dead came from 21 countries, the largest number were from the United States, and the airline helped to set up mutual support groups in the United States, including a pressure group (Victims of Pan Am Flight 103; see http://web.syr.edu/~vpaf103/about_goals.html) whose stated goals are to discover the truth behind the bombing, seek justice for their loved ones, ensure the airline industry maintains and improves safety measures, educate the public about the incident, and support one another. Pan American Airlines also set up a disaster team at Heathrow Airport to support its own air crews, who were not only grieving for the loss of colleagues but also were threatened by the possibility of further bombs and the incipient financial collapse of the airline.

Large-scale disasters are seldom confined to one locality. An exception was the Union Carbide chemical plant in Bhopal, the capital city of Madhya Pradesh, India, where 3,800 people died and 2,800 were disabled by the escape of methyl isocyanate gas in 1984. The Indian government and Union Carbide organized medical care, and an international appeal was set up to support the legal costs of the affected people, most of whom were (and still are) poverty stricken, in a series of claims for compensation that have dragged on for more than 20 years. Little bereavement support seems to have been offered.

Large-scale national disasters are also likely to benefit from help from outside the affected nation. In Rwanda, the genocide of 1994, which killed more than half a million people, was the culmination of a series of massacres. Support services from abroad were able to enter the country only after the invading Rwandese Patriotic Front troops succeeded in achieving control. The capital city, Kigali, was still under curfew and military control 1 year later, when a team from the United Nations Children's Fund was able to set up a trauma recovery program. They opened a National Trauma Centre that, over the next 5 years, provided therapeutic services to 1,146 traumatized and bereaved survivors aged 4 through 64. In addition, their trauma advisers trained 21,156 Rwandese teachers, caregivers, social workers, community and religious leaders, and local associations from across the whole of Rwanda in the provision of bereavement and trauma support to children and adults. They eventually succeeded in supporting more than 200,000 multiply traumatized and bereaved children and their surviving families (Gupta, 2000).

Large-scale international disasters inevitably require the organization of support in all of the countries involved. The destruction of the World Trade Center in New York City in the terrorist attacks of September 11, 2001, involved the loss of many people from outside as well as within the United States. To this day, the number of dead is not known for sure, and at the time, a planned response was difficult. The initial Family Assistance Center (which provided information, support, and a refuge for affected families) soon had to be moved to larger premises. The British government acted on its own initiative to organize transportation, accommodation, and support for an estimated 300 British families who were invited to visit New York to search for missing persons. An account of the support given to these people by British police and bereavement volunteers is given later in this chapter. They liaised with the work of the U.S. Federal Emergency Management Agency, whose Project Liberty made use of more than 100 mental health providers and numerous community agencies to provide free anonymous and face-to-face counseling and public education services to more than 1 million New Yorkers (see http://www.projectliberty.state.ny.us/).

The duration of a disaster can be a crucial factor in hampering support services. This is most obvious in war zones, from which the International Red Cross and other agencies may be excluded. On the other hand, human beings can learn to cope with traumatic losses. The experience of recurrent typhoons, floods, and high mortality from poverty and disease is associated with extraordinary resilience in many of the poorest parts of the world. Child bereavement adviser Ann Dent and I carried out an assessment visit to India in the wake of the Indian Ocean tsunami of December 26, 2004. By early March 2005, three months after the disaster, the symptoms of PTSD and other stress-related conditions, which had been prominent in the first few weeks, had largely disappeared, and the expectation of widespread traumatic disorder had not been fulfilled. (One regional health adviser had predicted that "almost all of the people affected by the Tsunami . . . will be suffering from some form of psycho-social trauma"; World Health Organization, 2005, ¶1.) This does not mean that there were no problems, but the problems resulted from continuing displacement, unemployment, chronic grief, and helplessness rather than from acute stress. Thus, Dent and I found evidence of subclinical or clinical depression, often associated with excessive alcohol consumption, in a substantial proportion of the fishermen who make up much of the affected population. (This finding has since been confirmed by Tharyan [2005].)

Other cultural factors that may contribute to tolerance of trauma and loss are religious beliefs that emphasize the transience of life and the promise of rewards thereafter, along with social systems that minimize individualism and emphasize identification with the family or social group. Taken in conjunction with high birth and death rates among children, which are associated with less extreme reactions to the death of a child (Scheper-Hughes, 1992), one may expect people in developing countries to be more tolerant of disaster than their counterparts in the more developed parts of the globe.

However, this should not lead us to assume that people in less developed countries are not in need of help. Cultural influences can increase as well as decrease vulnerability. For example, Yuksel and Olgun-Özpolot (2004) found remarkably high rates of persisting grief and PTSD in Turkey among parents of young men who had died or "disappeared" in the conflict between Kurds and government troops in comparison with parents whose children had died from leukemia. The attribution of martyrdom by both sides of the conflict seems to condemn these families to perpetual mourning. Consideration of a wider range of cultural variables is beyond the scope of this chapter. This important topic was covered in more detail by Parkes, Laungani, and Young (1996).

The type of damage varies widely from one disaster to another. Perhaps the most important variable is the presumed cause of the disaster. Disasters that are attributed to human agency inevitably lead to much anger, and recovery is complicated by the search for justice and/or revenge. In the immediate aftermath, outbreaks of ill-directed violence are not uncommon and may increase the risk of the initiation or perpetuation of a cycle of violence.

Most disasters give rise to a variety of traumas; these range from personal exposure to terrifying situations, witnessing horrific deaths, suffering physical injury, losing homes or property, losing one or more loved family members, and experiencing communal chaos. This means that the people who offer help need to be trained to understand and respond to this variety of needs.

CLINICAL AND ORGANIZATIONAL IMPLICATIONS

Given these great differences between disasters, is it possible to prepare in advance for them and to mobilize appropriate resources when they occur? We can no longer assume that a course in stress management, PTSD, anger management, critical incident stress debriefing, bereavement support, or community development is sufficient on its own; all may be needed. This may sound like a tall order, but most of these skills should be part of the basic training of all caring professionals and bereavement volunteers.

Mental health workers have an important contribution to make, but their training tends to focus on the diagnosis and treatment of mental illness when it arises instead of its prevention. In disaster situations, as in all major life crises, opportunities exist for preventing illness before it becomes manifest, and the services that have evolved in recent years to help people cope with bereavement and other trauma are preventive rather than psychiatric.

The focus on prevention has raised awareness of the social context in which mental health problems arise, and this is of particular importance following disasters that, as we have seen, affect not only individuals and families but also communities and nations. International disasters, such as 9/11, cause armed conflict as well as mental illness, and it is not unreasonable to hope that the right help given to afflicted communities may reduce the risk of both.

It follows that in considering the clinical implications of traumatic bereavements at times of disaster, we need to look beyond the individual to include the family, the local community, the nation, and the international scene.

Preparation for Disasters

None of us knows when or where the next disaster will occur; all we can be sure of is that it will occur. For this reason, hospitals and emergency services all have in place disaster plans, training programs, and disaster exercises. It is only in recent years, however, that proper attention has been given to the need to take into account the threats to mental health and social stability that arise after disasters or to include on the disaster teams people trained in these fields.

The management of bereavement, trauma, and stress should be part of the basic training of all members of the caring professions and all volunteers working with bereaved and/or traumatized people. Even in the absence of disasters, these skills will be needed whenever we reach out to support people who have suffered traumatic losses. In addition, special training in disaster management should ensure that there is a sufficient number of trained persons in each region to take a lead and provide the topping-up training that can enable a regular bereavement volunteer, social worker, or counselor to become part of a disaster team. This should include liaising with police and emergency and rescue services, training them in psychosocial skills, and participating in joint exercises whenever possible. In Britain, the police are now making use of psychologists and trainers from Cruse to train FLOs to support bereaved people, and Cruse has been using FLOs to help train their volunteers in crisis management.

Special problems that arise in disaster areas need special attention. For a comprehensive source of information and links to major Web sites on disaster planning and management, see the Web site maintained by Staffordshire Raynet (http://www.keele.ac.uk/depts/por/disaster.htm).

It is useful to break down the response to disasters into four phases: (a) impact, (b) recoil, (c) aftermath, and (d) long-term care. The term *impact* is here reserved for the period from the onset of the disaster to the arrival of the emergency services; *recoil* covers the period during which attempts at rescue take priority over everything else. This is followed by the *aftermath*, in which supportive services play a more active role, and *long-term care*, during which disaster services are withdrawn. These phases are not clear cut, particularly when the impact is spread out over a longer period.

Impact and Recoil

The immediate response to disasters is one of confusion and chaos. All survivors become hyperalert and, although they experience high levels of fear, most show a capacity to remain calm enough to escape from immediate dangers and/or to assist in rescue operations. Panic is most likely to occur if people are trapped and can see no escape route; this can add to the danger and may cause more deaths. An "illusion of centrality" may cause people on the periphery of the disaster to imagine that they are in the center.

Although *dissociation* (emotional numbing and the capacity to "switch off" one's feelings) may enable some people to cope in times of emergency, it can also give rise to problems, such as when people suffer episodes of amnesia, or *fugues*, in which they are found wandering in a dazed state. Removal from the scene to a supportive environment may be sufficient to enable them to regain their bearings, but psychiatric help may also be needed.

The immediate response is the responsibility of the emergency services personnel, and attempts to save lives and minimize further danger will take priority over most psychosocial needs. This said, much can be achieved by providing background support and psychological first aid as well as by using this time to assess future needs and adapt the disaster plan to this particular disaster.

Perhaps the greatest problem in the recoil phase is the chaos that is inevitable at this time and the feelings of helplessness that this evokes in would-be helpers as well as in the victims of the disaster. I remember all too well my own feelings after my first visit to Aberfan. I found myself well able to cope while in the village, but while driving away after my first day, I had to stop the car three times in order to ventilate feelings of grief, anger, and despair. I had little confidence in the value of my prior experience in this setting, little idea that my efforts would make any appreciable difference, and insufficient confidence that I could control my own feelings. It was several months before I began to feel part of a team of dedicated individuals who could see that for whatever reason, things were getting better.

Human beings evolved in a dangerous world and developed a sympathetic neuroendocrine system that would generate the adrenalin, endorphins, and other emergency responses that continue to get us through disasters. We may be surprised at the enhanced alertness, energy, and drive that we experience, and we will find ourselves working long hours without flagging.

Even so, we need to guard against overload. When we become aware that we are overstressed—for instance, if we begin to feel that we are drowning in the face of overwhelming demands—it helps to stop and wind down. I try to work out an order of priorities, deciding which tasks I must get on with now and which can be delayed, what things I can delegate and whom I can draw in to help, how long I can carry on and when I must take a break.

This process of self-monitoring can be taught to colleagues and to traumatized clients who may feel even more overwhelmed than the disaster workers do. They may snow us with information, bombarding us with one problem and not waiting for an answer before they start on the next. We need to "flag them down," pointing out that neither they nor we can cope with more than one problem at a time and inviting them to consider which issue they need to deal with now. This helps them to focus and provides them with a model of action, which they can continue to use.

Psychological First Aid

The recoil phase is not a time to provide therapy. What people need in the immediate wake of a disaster are emotional support, information, and instruction. By *emotional support* I mean the kind of reassurance that a mother can give to a frightened child; this has more to do with a touch of the hand and a smile than a facile assurance of security that may be no more than a pious hope. Information is needed to orient people and enable them to begin to adjust to the situation. Even if we are just as uncertain as they, it helps to share our uncertainty and to reassure them that nothing is being concealed. It is psychologically easier to deal with bad news than no news at all, so we should rarely overprotect people by holding back information on the grounds that it may upset them. This said, it may be necessary to deliver bad news in bite-sized chunks in order to give people time to digest and begin to process the implications of information that shatters their plans, hopes, and assumptions about the world.

Information and Instruction

On occasion, it may be necessary to give orders to take control of a situation. More often, however, it is wise to provide information first so that people can understand why a particular instruction is being given. This is no time for democratic debate, and we should recognize and fit into a military-style chain of command that can bring the situation under control as quickly as possible. The terrorist attacks of 9/11 were followed by a period of uncertainty. Despite a massive rescue operation, it was a long time before it was known who had died. Urgent attempts to prevent further attacks led to the grounding of all passenger aircraft, and the Foreign Office in Britain received numerous calls from families who were desperately seeking information about relatives who were missing in the United States. Foreign Office staff responded by offering to pay the airfares and accommodation expenses of anyone who wanted to visit the States for 4 to 5 days to check out the situation. Most of the missing persons had worked at or been visiting the World Trade Center. On November 16, 2001, I accompanied a team of FLOs to New York, on one of the first flights out of Heathrow, to prepare for the arrival next day of a team of experienced volunteers from Cruse Bereavement Care with their team leader, Arthur O'Hara. We worked closely with police officers and shared the incident room they had set up. We all stayed at the same hotel as the families who had arrived courtesy of the Foreign Office. To ensure effective liaison, we formed units of one Cruse BV and two FLOs who met each incoming family at Kennedy Airport, escorted them to the hotel, and provided the emotional support and information that they needed.

By the time the first families arrived, later on the first day, we had worked out where they might like to go and how to get them there. We protected them from the intrusions of voracious press and television teams, accompanied them on visits to the site of the World Trade Center and to the Family Assistance Center that had been set up in Manhattan. There they were able to search lists of names of patients in New York hospitals and to meet American families and families from other countries who were facing the same predicament. Most also visited the park in Union Square where candles had been lit, flowers displayed, and notices put up. These notices varied from pleas for information about missing persons, to expressions of sympathy,

exhortations for world peace, demands for justice, and nationalistic sentiments. By the time they returned to Britain, these families had formed a relationship of trust with the support workers, and this facilitated referral onward
to their local branches of Cruse Bereavement Care.

Both police and volunteers supported each other and were closely supervised and supported by their own supervisors. The value of this became apparent in the 2nd week, when the capable and trusted head of the FLO team
suffered a cardiac event and was flown back to Britain. Several FLOs subsequently expressed their appreciation of the support that they received from
the BVs at that time. There can be no doubt that this was a successful enterprise and that it was much appreciated by the families. Since then, similar
liaisons have enabled us to support families returning to Britain from the
Indian Ocean region following the tsunami of December 2004.

Aftermath

Once the rescue operations are at an end, the dead have been counted,
and the acute danger is over, psychosocial support services can play a more
prominent role. By this time, emergency personnel should have mobilized a
disaster support team or teams, depending on the scale and spread of the disaster. A chain of command should have been set up, with members clearly
apprised of their place and responsibilities within the team. An essential component is a centralized database on which is recorded relevant information
about all victims and others affected by the disaster, as well as the contact
details and qualifications of all who have offered help. The team should operate from a "disaster center," which should also act as the information point,
office, and consultation center for the affected population.

Bereavement support organizations have an important role to play at this
stage, and they should be included in all disaster teams formed in response to
events in which deaths have occurred. However, this does not mean that their
volunteers and staff should confine themselves to problems of grief and mourning. Even outside disaster areas, bereavement training and support should
include the range of traumas and life changes that often follow traumatic
losses. This makes well-trained bereavement support workers well suited to
work in disaster areas. By the same token, training in stress counseling in
industrial or other settings needs to include the field of grief and bereavement.

Disasters usually attract numerous offers of help from volunteers, most
of whom have little relevant experience or training. Indeed, some have inappropriate religious or other agendas, and there is a need for vetting to protect
victims from unqualified intrusion from these people as well as from exploitation by irresponsible representatives of the news media. On the other hand,
both well-motivated, trained volunteers and responsible media have important roles to play and need to be welcomed and cherished.

Because it takes time to organize an appropriate response to disasters, a mismatch often exists between the needs of traumatized persons and the resources available to meet their needs. Even when adequate resources are available, it is important to introduce a form of psychological assessment or triage to decide which individuals need priority attention. The illusion of centrality often means that those who are most strident in their demands for help may not be the ones most in need. The risk factors that enable us to identify individuals in need of psychological help following day-to-day bereavements are no different from the risk factors that predict psychiatric problems following disasters. They include the circumstances that make some bereavements more traumatic than others, the personal predispositions that make some individuals more vulnerable than others, and the social circumstances that give support and meaning to the lives of some but not others (Stroebe & Schut, 2001). Because bereavement workers are trained to identify these factors, this makes them well qualified to carry out triage and focus resources where they are most needed.

All too often, well-laid plans are delayed because of failure to provide the necessary resources. The Away Team in Dover took nearly 1 year to visit and assess the needs of all the families at risk after the sinking of the *Herald of Free Enterprise*. Delays in funding, recruitment, training, and deployment of staff reflect the real difficulties of creating, from scratch, a complex and expert team. Since that time (1987), public and government awareness of the need for psychosocial support after disasters has made it possible to act much more swiftly and effectively. The integration of psychiatric and psychological resources with trained BVs works very well and ensures that the majority of traumatized and bereaved people can receive the help they need without recourse to expensive and scarce psychiatric services. However, well-funded, centralized departments of psychological disaster management, such as the National Centre for Disaster Psychiatry at Uppsala University in Sweden, are needed to develop the organizational models and expertise that can prevent delays.

In the aftermath phase, psychologists and psychiatrists with experience in disaster areas are best employed in support of the front-line of bereavement volunteers and counselors, and it is essential to organize one or more training days during which they can provide the topping-up training that is needed by less experienced colleagues.

After an air crash in which more than 100 women died, a training day was organized by a local social service department, who invited doctors, social workers, and other professionals but failed to invite any volunteers or representatives of the local community. The local people subsequently set up their own support networks and ignored those provided by the local authority.

Modern information systems are an important resource in disaster areas, even in parts of the world where few people own a computer. Mobile phones enable members of the disaster team to remain in touch with the office or incident room at all times, and computers hold the database of victims and helpers and enable team leaders to access and disseminate useful documents to the affected population.

I placed on the Internet information and advice aimed at helping people bereaved by major disasters after the December 2004 tsunami; this was adapted for use after the July 2005 London bombings. Cruse BVs working in the Family Assistance Center printed it out and gave it to bereaved families. The feedback was very positive. The information covers commonly reported problems of trauma, grief, anger, guilt, and life change. The Web site is freely available (click on "Traumatic Losses" at http://www.crusebereavementcare.org.uk).

The psychological interventions needed by bereaved people in the aftermath phase are not intrinsically different from those required following other traumatic bereavements, but the specialist therapists available in normal circumstances may well be in short supply following disasters, particularly in developing countries.

High levels of anxiety and fear are often aggravated by the physiological symptoms to which they give rise (e.g., heart palpitations, breathlessness) and require traditional anxiety management programs that are part of the stock in trade of volunteer bereavement services. Medical practitioners may need to provide authoritative reassurance that the symptoms of anxiety are not an indication of an organic illness. The diagnosis of PTSD is, or should be, included in the training of every bereavement worker, if only because it is eminently treatable. The 2005 report commissioned by the National Institute for Clinical Excellence gives easily accessible guidance. The institute recommended that "all health and social care workers should be aware of the psychological impact of traumatic incidents in their immediate post-incident care of survivors and offer practical, social and emotional support to those involved" (National Collaborating Centre for Mental Health, 2005, ¶7.11.1.1). Routine screening should be carried out in all disaster areas with a suitable screening instrument such as the one developed by Chou et al. (2003).

Specialist psychological help should be considered whenever the symptoms are severe or disabling and persist for more than 1 month. (These criteria are among those necessary for the diagnosis of PTSD given in the *Diagnostic and Statistical Manual of Mental Disorders*; 4th ed.; American Psychiatric Association, 1994.) Where available, techniques such as trauma-focused cognitive behavior therapy and eye movement desensitization and reprocessing will usually reduce haunting memories and fantasies to a tolerable level.

The horrific images that characterize PTSD are so painful and terrifying that sufferers will go to great lengths to avoid anything that reminds them of the loss. They also control their thoughts by keeping busy, using distraction, and exerting rigorous self-control. Because thoughts of the lost person and the loss event can be counted on to trigger these images, people with PTSD find it difficult to talk about their loss or to grieve. This makes bereavement support difficult until the PTSD has been treated. At this point, however, the help of a BV who will hang in with the bereaved person as he or she begins, little by little, to rebuild his or her internal world, can be invaluable.

PTSD in adults and childhood can also be treated by short-term *narrative exposure therapy* (Schauer, Neuner, & Elbert, 2004). As the name implies, this provides a structured method of life review to enable traumatized persons to regain purpose and direction in lives that have been ruptured by extreme traumatic stress. It is currently undergoing a randomized control study. Schauer et al.'s (2004) manual is accessible to the general public as well as to practitioners working in the fields of mental health, disaster, conflict resolution and human rights.

Regardless of whether traumatized bereaved individuals have experienced PTSD, the risk of complicated grief (CG) is increased whenever a death is unexpected, untimely, and shattering to a person's assumptive world (Parkes, 2008, pp. 137–140). Such deaths are the rule rather than the exception in disaster areas, and they make the provision of bereavement support an essential component of disaster teams. The diagnosis and treatment of CG have been covered elsewhere in this volume (see chaps. 8 and 9). Methods of treatment that can be accessed inexpensively by large numbers of people are of particular importance. It is therefore encouraging to report the promising results of an Internet-based treatment for CG (Wagner, Knaevelsrud, & Maercker, 2006; see also chap. 26, this volume). These researchers carried out a random-allocation study of the effectiveness of exposure to three modules: (a) exposure to bereavement cues, (b) cognitive reappraisal, and (c) integration and restoration. A large treatment effect was found.

Clinical depression is another problem frequently encountered following disasters and other traumatic bereavements (Stroebe, Stroebe, & Domittner, 1988). It usually responds to cognitive behavior therapy (Sikkema, Hansen, Kochman, Tate, & Defranciesco, 2004) or to antidepressant medication (Pasternak et al., 1991; Reynolds et al., 1999; Zisook, Shuchter, Pedrelli, Sable, & Deauciuc, 2001).

Harris et al. (1999a, 1999b) have published well-conducted evaluations by random allocation of a form of befriending that can be taught to volunteers. It has been tested on two samples of women, in one to prevent postpartum depression and in the other to treat chronic depression. In both circumstances, significantly lower levels of depression were found in the intervention groups, and Harris (2006) suggested that befriending may well have special value in the wake of bereavement, particularly when trained psychologists are in short supply, as they often are after disasters in developing countries.

Anger and aggression are natural reactions to man-made disasters. They seldom cause mental illness, but they can give rise to particular difficulties if the aggression is ill directed, and they may even give rise to scapegoating, cycles of violence, and armed conflicts. People will make allowances for bereaved people if their anger is sometimes disproportionate or ill directed, but anger is not confined to the bereaved, and community leaders easily get caught up in the wave of public rage that often follows man-made disasters. These problems have been spelled out in detail by members of the International Work Group on Death, Dying and Bereavement (IWG), whose papers have examined the consequences and implications of violent death (IWG, Violence and Grief Work Group, 1997–1998) and the cycle of violence (IWG, 2005).

Anger management is a skill that should be part of the training of all individuals who are in a position to provide support after traumatic loss, be it at the individual, family, community, national, or international level. It should include an understanding of the roots of aggression in both nonhuman and human animals (Lorenz's [1966] classic *On Aggression* still has much to teach us), methods of conflict resolution, and a clear understanding of the circumstances under which necessary force should be used and the means by which its damaging effects can be minimized. Issues that increase the risk of further violence include misperceptions of the causes of violent acts, disproportionate immediate responses, the influence of legitimizing authorities, destructive codes, and polarizing inflammatory strategies. Each can feed into a loop and increase the risk of a cycle of violence. By the same token, interventions that correct the way violent behavior is perceived moderate the immediate response, support or counterbalance legitimizing authorities, replace destructive with constructive codes, support mediation, and moderate further violence (e.g., by removing weapons) can break the cycle at all levels (Parkes, 2006).

In Aberfan, several public meetings broke up in fistfights during the early months after the disaster. It was 1 year before it became possible to deal more constructively with communal rage. As one woman said to me, after attending a group meeting focused on anger management, "This is the first time I was able to stand aside from my anger and see it as an inevitable consequence of the disaster, rather than being a part of me." In that setting, attendance at the Board of Inquiry was seen as having therapeutic value. Although the board attributed blame for the disaster on several named individuals, those who listened to the evidence did not see these people as enemies to be destroyed; instead, it became evident to them that their guilt was a reflection of the human failings that we all possess.

Self-reproaches and guilt commonly coexist with anger and aggression (Parkes, 1998, p. 84). Some people seek to find someone else to blame for their own shortcomings, whereas others blame themselves unreasonably for angry acts or for feeling angry. *Survivor guilt* is common and reflects the injustice of arbitrary deaths. Self-reproaches are more likely to become serious problems if warnings of disaster were ignored or if people have become aware of their culpability. (A general practitioner told me that he had felt like a Roman Catholic confessor during the weeks that followed one man-made disaster.) Such feelings may contribute to depression at the individual level and a decline in morale at the group level. Members of a community may come to see the whole community as bad.

It is a common experience that bereaved survivors of disaster are treated as heroes. If they express their guilt, they are told, "You should not feel like that," as if they could choose how they feel. These attempts at reassurance are not helpful. Two responses that do seem to help are (a) showing nonjudgmental understanding of the "none of us is perfect" kind and (b) encouraging the person to find a worthwhile way of making restitution, perhaps by bringing something good out of the disaster—"If that's the way you feel, what are you going to do about it?" In my experience, such expressions of confidence that something can be done have therapeutic value. Likewise, at a community level, action programs may help restore faith in a community. As one survivor put it, "This disaster was caused by apathy and it is up to us to ensure that [this community] never becomes apathetic again."

Communal rituals and memorials play an important part in all bereavement but take on added meaning when it is a community that is bereaved by disaster. They help to make real the fact of loss and to help people and communities to construct a new identity. As in bereavement counseling, the aim is not to help people to forget the dead but to find a new place for them in the history of their lives and the life of their community (see also chap. 12, this volume). Community leaders play important roles by bringing home the seriousness of the situation and committing themselves to support the afflicted and involve themselves in the changes that must follow.

Ten days after 9/11, a "prayer service" was held in Saint Thomas church in New York City, to which the affected families were invited. The service was attended by Secretary General of the United Nations Kofi Annan; former U.S. President Bill Clinton; and Prime Minister of the United Kingdom Tony Blair, who read out a message of sympathy from Her Majesty the Queen. The bereaved families were accompanied throughout the day by the Cruse Bereavement Care disaster team. After the service, they had an opportunity to meet the dignitaries and receive their sympathy. Although the occasion was an ordeal for several of the families, it also brought home to everyone present the historic significance of what had happened and a feeling of being more than the center of attention—we felt loved and cared for.

Children in disaster areas are at particular risk, both as a result of the traumatic losses they have experienced and as a result of the negative influence of disasters on their parents and peers. Pynoos et al. (1987), who studied the effects on children of sniper attacks on their schools, showed that not only do children suffer posttraumatic symptoms in much the same way as adults, but also the intensity and duration of these symptoms are much greater if the child is personally bereaved. It follows that support for parents and children should be a part of all disaster services and that disaster teams should include individuals who have been selected and trained to work with children. Although space does not permit a more adequate treatment of the special problems of children in disaster areas, the U.S. National Institute of Mental Health (2001) provided useful guidance (see also chaps. 18 and 25, this volume).

All individuals who choose to work in disaster areas need to be aware of the emotional cost of the work, to monitor themselves as described earlier, and to provide and accept the mutual support that is needed at all times. *Critical incident stress debriefing*—brief, single-session interventions that focus on the traumatic incident—was originally introduced to provide support to emergency services and later widened for use with victims of disasters (Mitchell, 1983). More recently, random-allocation studies have thrown doubt on the efficacy of this type of intervention (van Emmerick, Kamphuis, Hulsbosch, & Emmelkamp, 2002; Wesseley & Deahl, 2003). However, this does not gainsay the need for regular meetings of staff at which the trust necessary to mutual support can develop, as well as the need for confidential, one-to-one support. Although line managers have primary responsibility for supporting the team, no one person can expect to be the sole supporter, and team members should be able to choose the person in whom they wish to confide. Viewed in this way, team support is a shared responsibility. Supervisors and support workers from outside the team both have useful roles to play, particularly when morale is at a low ebb or trust has been undermined.

In one disaster area, a long-standing rivalry between the education department and the health department had caused the staff of each to operate independently of the other. It was necessary for the visiting psychiatrist to initiate joint meetings between the child psychologist and the family caseworker before each realized that they were working with the same families! Prejudice soon dissolved once they began to share information and, before long, a good trusting relationship had developed.

Leaders also need support; this applies at all levels, including politicians and military leaders, who may find it difficult to acknowledge that they are not the supermen and superwomen that their juniors would like them to be. Faced with enormous responsibilities, and political pressures to take drastic action in the face of outrageous events, they need emotional support as well as reliable information and impartial advice. History suggests that they seldom get these.

Long-Term Care

As time passes, the number of bereaved people who need continuing help dwindles, and it becomes possible to withdraw any support workers who have been introduced from outside the affected community. Although it may be administratively convenient to wind up the operation on a particular day, this should be resisted, because needs do not change abruptly. Instead, the team staff should be tapered off as soon as the need declines, with the aim being to hand over control to the indigenous support systems as soon as this is reasonable. Outsiders should attempt not to colonize but to educate the local mental health and other professionals to take over.

It is unrealistic to expect that the members of the disaster team will simply return to the jobs they had before the disaster and carry on with their lives as if nothing had happened. It is not only the bereaved who are changed by disasters. Winding up a disaster team should include recognition of the fact that many members will want to review the new directions that their lives are taking and to explore the opportunities that now exist for career and personal development. Some may want to train for a caring profession; others may want to take a break from caregiving.

Just as individuals are permanently changed by disasters, so too are communities and nations. Members of disaster teams may not see it as their role to engage with the political and administrative systems that supposedly control these changes, but they often have insight into the psychology of the affected communities that these people lack. One sometimes gets the impression that, while psychologists and BVs are helping people to stand aside from their grief and make rational decisions, politicians and administrators are being blown hither and thither by the powerful emotions and pressures to which they are exposed.

As an example, during the 1st year after the Aberfan disaster, the discontent of the affected community was often expressed in attacks on "them up there." Administrators suffered so much abuse that a paralysis of decision making took place and money that had been donated to the disaster fund went unspent. The end of the 1st year, however, marked a watershed. The need for individual support to bereaved individuals diminished to the point where it became possible to withdraw the disaster team members one by one. At the same time, it became evident that the community as a whole was recovering. A comparison of the birth rate in Aberfan with the rates of neighboring villages demonstrated a sharp increase during the 2nd and 3rd years such that the number of "extra" children born in Aberfan slightly exceeded the number killed in the disaster (Parkes & Williams, 1975). These did not replace the children who died—nothing could do that—nor were they confined to parents who had lost children, most of whom were beyond reproductive age. Rather, they seemed to reflect a creative communal response to the bad thing that had happened. This did not mean that there were not individuals who continued to suffer, and a recent follow-up highlighted the extent to which we failed to provide the sophisticated care that is possible today (Morgan, Scourfield, Williams, Jasper, & Lewis, 2003).

After the first anniversary of the Aberfan disaster, two sociologists were invited to join with local disaster team and community leaders to help develop a community development plan. After a successful public meeting, a community association was initiated, and Derek Nuttall,[2] who had been the youth worker on the disaster team, was appointed as first secretary. Aberfan eventually became a forward-looking community. Five years later, it acted as host to the first of a series of conferences demonstrating the success of community development (Ballard & Jones, 1975).

CONCLUSIONS

It would be a mistake to assume that satisfactory communal development is an inevitable outcome of disasters any more than one can expect all bereaved people to make a good recovery from traumatic losses. Kai Erikson (1979) analyzed the consequences of the 1972 disaster in Buffalo Creek, West Virginia, in which a flood inundated a chain of linear villages. In many respects, this medium-scale local disaster resembled Aberfan. Erikson described the "loss of communality" that was still pervasive 2½ years later: "The people of the community no longer trust one another in the way they did before" (p. 189).

There is no space here to analyze the reasons why this happened, but the two examples, Aberfan and Buffalo Creek, do point up the possibility that things can go either way. After disasters, some individuals will grow in psychological, social, and spiritual maturity whereas others will wither; so too will some communities and some nations. It is the task of all to foster creative responses to disaster and to minimize destructive responses. Bereavement research and interventions have gone a considerable way to help individuals and families through these turning points in their lives. Is it too late to hope that the lessons learned can be successfully applied in the larger settings?

REFERENCES

American Psychiatric Association. (1994). *Diagnostic and statistical manual of mental disorders* (4th ed.). Washington, DC: Author.

Ballard, P. H., & Jones, E. (Eds.). (1975). *The year of the valleys: A self-examination by people of the South Wales valleys during the year of the valleys 1974*. Ferndale, Rhondda, Wales: Ron Jones Publications.

Chou, F. H. C., Su, T. T. P., Ou-Yang, W. C., Chien, I. C., Lu, M. K., & Chou, P. (2003). Establishment of a disaster-related psychological screening test. *Australian and New Zealand Journal of Psychiatry, 37*, 97–103.

---

[2]Nuttall remained in Aberfan for another 2 years, then left to become regional development officer and later director of Cruse Bereavement Care.

Erikson, K. T. (1979). *In the wake of the flood.* London: Allen & Unwin.

Gupta, L. (2000). Bereavement recovery following the Rwandan genocide: A community-based intervention for child survivors. *Bereavement Care, 18,* 40–42.

Harris, T. (2006). Volunteer befriending as an intervention for depression: Implications for bereavement care? *Bereavement Care, 25,* 27–30.

Harris, T., Brown, G. W., & Robinson, R. (1999a). Befriending as an intervention for chronic depression among women in an inner city: 1. Randomised control trial. *British Journal of Psychiatry, 174,* 219–224.

Harris, T., Brown, G. W., & Robinson, R. (1999b). Befriending as an intervention for chronic depression among women in an inner city: 2. Role of fresh-start experiences and baseline psycho-social factors in remission from depression. *British Medical Journal, 174,* 225–232.

International Work Group on Death, Dying and Bereavement, Violence and Grief Work Group. (1997–1998). Document on violence and grief. *Omega: The Journal of Death and Dying, 36,* 259–272.

International Work Group on Death, Dying and Bereavement. (2005). Breaking cycles of violence. *Death Studies, 29,* 585–600.

Lorenz, K. (1966). *On aggression.* London: Methuen.

Mitchell, J. T. (1983). When disaster strikes: The critical incident stress debriefing process. *Journal of Emergency Medical Services, 8,* 36–39.

Morgan, L., Scourfield, J., Williams, D., Jasper, A., & Lewis, G. (2003). The Aberfan disaster: 33-year follow-up of survivors. *British Journal of Psychiatry, 182,* 532–536.

National Collaborating Centre for Mental Health. (2005). *Post-traumatic stress disorder: The management of PTSD in adults and children in primary and secondary care* (National Clinical Practice Guideline No. 26, commissioned by the National Institute for Clinical Excellence). Retrieved January 17, 2008, from http://www.nice.org.uk/nicemedia/pdf/CG026fullguideline.pdf

National Institute of Mental Health. (2001). *Helping children and adolescents cope with violence and disasters: Fact sheet.* Washington, DC: Author.

Parkes, C. M. (1997). A typology of disasters. In D. Black, M. Newman, J. Harris-Hendriks, & G. Mezey (Eds.), *Psychological trauma: A developmental approach* (pp. 81–93). London: Gaskell.

Parkes, C. M. (1998). *Bereavement: Studies of grief in adult life.* London: Routledge.

Parkes, C. M. (2006). *Love and loss: The roots of grief and its complications.* London: Routledge.

Parkes, C. M. (2008). Breaking the cycle of violence. In R. Stevenson & G. Cox (Eds.), *Perspectives on violence* (pp. 223–238). Amityville, NY: Baywood.

Parkes, C. M., Laungani, P., & Young, B. (1996). *Death and bereavement across cultures.* London: Routledge.

Parkes, C. M., & Williams, R. M. (1975). Psychosocial effects of disaster: Birth rate in Aberfan. *British Medical Journal, 2,* 303–304.

Pasternak, R. E., Reynolds, C. F., Schlernitzauer, M., Hoch, C. C., Buysse, D. J., Houck, P. R., & Perel, J. M. (1991). Acute open trial nortriptyline therapy of bereavement-related depression in later life. *Journal of Clinical Psychiatry, 52,* 307–310.

Pynoos, R. S., Frederick, C., Nader, K., Arroyo, W., Steinberg, A., Eth, S., et al. (1987). Life threat and post-traumatic stress in school-age children. *Archives of General Psychiatry, 44,* 1057–1063.

Reynolds, C. F., Miller, M. D., Pasternak, R. E., Frank, E., Perel, J. M., Cornes, C., et al. (1999). Treatment of bereavement-related major depressive episodes in later life: A controlled study of acute and continuation treatment with nortriptyline and interpersonal psychotherapy. *American Journal of Psychiatry 156,* 202–208.

Schauer, M., Neuner, F., & Elbert, T. (2004). *Narrative exposure therapy: A short-term intervention for traumatic stress disorders after war, terrorism, or torture.* Cambridge, MA: Hogrefe & Huber.

Scheper-Hughes, N. (1992). *Death without weeping: The violence of everyday life in Brazil.* Berkeley: University of California Press.

Sikkema, K. J., Hansen, N. B., Kochman, A., Tate, D. C., & Defranciesco, W. (2004). Outcomes from a randomised controlled trial of a group intervention for HIV positive men and women coping with AIDS-related loss and bereavement. *Death Studies, 28,* 187–210.

Stroebe, W., & Schut, H. (2001). Risk factors in bereavement outcome: A methodological and empirical review. In M. S. Stroebe, R. O. Hansson, W. Stroebe, & H. Schut (Eds.), *Handbook of bereavement research: Consequences, coping, and care* (pp. 349–371). Washington, DC: American Psychological Association.

Stroebe, W., Stroebe, M., & Domittner, G. (1988). Individual and situational differences in recovery from bereavement: A risk group identified. *Journal of Social Issues, 44,* 143–158.

Tharyan, P. (2005). Traumatic bereavement and the Asian tsunami: Post-tsunami perspectives from Tamil Nadu, India. *Bereavement Care 24,* 23–26.

van Emmerick, A. A., Kamphuis, J. H., Hulsbosch, A. M., & Emmelkamp, P. M. (2002). Single session debriefing after psychological trauma: A meta-analysis. *The Lancet, 360,* 776–771.

Wagner, B., Knaevelsrud, C., & Maercker, A. (2006). Internet-based cognitive–behavioral therapy for complicated grief: A randomised controlled trial. *Death Studies, 30,* 429–453.

Wesseley, S., & Deahl, M. (2003). Psychological debriefing is a waste of time. *British Journal of Psychiatry, 183,* 12–21.

World Health Organization. (2005, January 19). *WHO warns of widespread psychological trauma among Tsunami victims* (WHO Press Release SEA/PR/1384). Retrieved January 17, 2008, from http://www.searo.who.int/EN/Section316/Section503/Section1861_8571.htm

Yuksel, S., & Olgun-Özpolot, T. (2004). Psychological problems associated with traumatic loss in Turkey. *Bereavement Care, 23,* 5–7.

Zisook, S., Shuchter, S. R., Pedrelli, P., Sable, J., & Deauciuc, S. C. (2001). Buproprion sustained release for bereavement: Results of an open trial. *Journal of Clinical Psychiatry, 62,* 227–230.

23

FAMILY FOCUSED GRIEF THERAPY: FROM PALLIATIVE CARE INTO BEREAVEMENT

DAVID W. KISSANE AND WENDY G. LICHTENTHAL

Coming to terms with the illness and eventual loss of a loved one is both a personal and communal experience. Individual experiences of mourning are in turn influenced by those of the family, the major source of social support, bringing a systemic focus to the nature of shared grief. Hospice services seek to provide bereavement support in many Western communities but meet resistance from individuals who have not met with a bereavement counselor prior to the death. A preventive and family-centered approach in which the counselor meets the family during the care of a dying patient ensures engagement and sustains continuity of care after the death. More than 15 years of research into the family's experience of grief has culminated in the model of family focused grief therapy (FFGT). In this chapter, we provide an overview of FFGT, a preventive model of family grief therapy, which begins during a terminal illness and continues beyond the death by optimizing the family's functioning and promoting their sharing of grief.

Families considered to be at some risk of a morbid bereavement outcome are selected through screening with the Family Relationships Index (FRI; Moos & Moos, 1981) and invited to meet together as a group with a facilitator. The patient dying from cancer or another progressive and serious illness initially is brought together with his or her family and caregivers at the time of referral to the palliative care service. As stated, the goal of FFGT is to optimize the family's relational functioning and mutual support, encourage the sharing of grief, and promote adaptive coping. Most typically, three to four sessions will occur before the patient dies, and the family will continue meeting with the therapist during bereavement until consolidation of gains in family functioning and adaptation are in evidence, which often requires another three to six sessions, depending on the family's needs. Having the patient present during the early phase of therapy ensures that his or her wishes are made known to the family and helps cement a strong therapeutic alliance with the therapist. The significance of the FFGT model is a paradigmatic shift from individually focused grief to shared family grief, which permits palliative care services to deliver family-centered care.

BACKGROUND

Epidemiology of Psychosocial Morbidity Within Families During Palliative Care

Distress reverberates throughout the palliative care family, whether illness is due to cancer or another serious condition such as motor neuron disease. Moderate levels of psychosocial morbidity (e.g., depression, anxiety, impaired occupational and social functioning) affect up to one half of the patients, one third of their partners, and, it is important to note, one quarter of their adult offspring (Kissane, Bloch, Burns, McKenzie, & Posterino, 1994). Although patients' distress was found to be greater at the recurrence of cancer compared with a first diagnosis (Silberfarb, Maurer, & Crouthamel, 1980), the phases of palliative and terminal care appear most demanding for the family (Cassileth et al., 1985). We identified eight studies of distress in spouses, with rates of anxiety and depression between 18% and 34% during these two phases (Buckley, 1977; Ell, Nishimoto, Mantell, & Hamovitch, 1988; Gotay, 1984; Kissane et al., 1994; Maguire, 1981; Minagawa, Uchitomi, Yamawaki, & Ishitani, 1996; Northouse, 1989; Plumb & Holland, 1977). In longitudinal studies, this distress endured for up to 18 months (Ell et al., 1988; Northouse, 1989).

Few studies have evaluated other family members, including children (Cassileth et al., 1985; Ell et al., 1988; Kissane et al., 1994) and parents (Plumb & Holland, 1977). Kissane et al. (1994) found a strikingly high level of distress in adult offspring (average age 28 years, 60% female), one quarter of whom exhibited *caseness* (when questionnaire responses exceed the threshold reaching clinical concern) on measures such as the Brief Symptom Inventory (BSI; Derogatis & Melisaratos, 1983; Derogatis & Spencer, 1982) and the Beck Depression Inventory (BDI; Beck & Beck, 1972; Beck, Steer, & Garbin, 1988).

Systematic Reviews of Family Interventions in Palliative Care

Palliative care has struggled to find an effective model to deliver family-centered care. Higginson et al. (2003) conducted a meta-analysis of 26 studies of palliative and hospice care teams and contrasted a slightly positive effect size on symptom management for patients (26 studies; weighted mean = 0.33; 95% confidence interval [CI]: 0.10, 0.56) with no benefit for the caregiver and family, including bereavement outcomes (13 studies; weighted mean = 0.17; 95% CI: −0.14, 0.48). The large U.S. National Hospice Study, for instance, failed to demonstrate any psychological effects on caregivers (Greer & Mor, 1986). A major Norwegian study randomized patients to receive comprehensive palliative care or conventional oncological care and discerned no difference in bereavement outcome despite efforts from the palliative care programs to achieve this (Ringdal, Jordhoy, Ringdal, & Kaasa, 2001).

A further systematic review of interventions to help caregivers identified 22 studies, of which 9 focused on a single carer (Harding & Higginson, 2003). Harding and Higginson (2003) lamented the methodological difficulties with many of these studies but concluded that evidence is lacking to support benefit being derived from broadly offered individual and group therapeutic interventions for carers. These researchers considered provision of information and psychological support to be key developmental agendas. In the U.S. National Hospice Study, complicated bereavement was associated with increased use of physicians, although the researchers had hoped that this could be reduced (McHorney & Mor, 1988; Mor, McHorney, & Sherwood, 1986). Intervention to promote problem-solving skills in carers was found to be effective only for a distressed subsample (Toseland, Blanchard, & McCallion, 1995). Pilot studies of carer groups showed little promise of improvement in psychosocial well-being for carers (Barg et al., 1998; Carlsson & Strang, 1996; Cawley & Gerdts, 1988; Grahn, 1996; Heinrich & Schag, 1985; Horowitz, Passik, & Malkin, 1996; Plant et al., 1987; Reele, 1994; Robinson et al., 1998). Many carers value their own independence and self-reliance. Harding and Higginson therefore argued that greater promise lies with targeted interventions that identify a significantly distressed or depressed subsample of carers and focus on these high-risk individuals. It is disappointing that palliative care interventions for caregivers, families, and the bereaved have had a negligible effect, which has resulted in the call for new approaches such as FFGT.

Family Interventions With the Bereaved

Since Paul and Grosser's (1965) pioneering work, in which they delivered family therapy to the bereaved and in so doing encouraged families to share feelings about their loss, formal studies of family interventions have yielded inconsistent findings (Kissane & Bloch, 1994). Lieberman (1978) and

Rosenthal (1980) have both reported beneficial results from family involvement. Goldstein, Alter, and Axelrod (1996) conducted an eight-session open trial of a psychoeducational family intervention in an outpatient cancer center, which helped participants adjust. In contrast, Williams and Polak (1979) intruded prematurely in having the therapist visit relatives with the coroner's assistant following motor vehicle deaths. However, pediatric family therapy (Black & Urbanowicz, 1987) produced improved child behaviors at 1 year following a parent's death, although differences waned by the 2-year follow-up. This last study did not select at-risk families and struggled with both engagement and compliance.

By the turn of the century, the promise hoped for by Paul and Grosser (1965) had unfortunately not materialized into a strong body of evidence in support of family interventions with the bereaved. This became our motivation to embark with our colleagues on a randomized controlled trial (RCT) of FFGT in 1998 (Kissane, Bloch, McKenzie, McDowall, & Nitzan, 1998; Kissane et al., 2006). Since then, another randomized intervention with adolescents and parents with HIV failed to find differences between adolescents who lost a parent when compared with nonbereaved respondents at a 2-year follow-up (Rotheram-Borus, Stein, & Lin, 2001; Rotheram-Borus, Weiss, Alber, & Lester, 2005). In the pediatric sphere, the Family Bereavement Program (Sandler et al., 2003) for parentally bereaved children and adolescents is described in chapter 25 of this volume. Let us turn now to FFGT.

THEORETICAL MODELS UNDERPINNING FAMILY FOCUSED GRIEF THERAPY

FFGT has been guided by three theories: (a) attachment theory (Bowlby, 1969), (b) cognitive processing theory in adaptation to trauma (Creamer, Burgess, & Pattison, 1992), and (c) group adaptation (Whitaker & Lieberman, 1964).

Attachment

Attachment theory is the leading conceptual model to explain grief resulting from relational losses. The most important relationships are generally found in families, whether nuclear, family of origin, or extended family (see chap. 5, this volume; Shaver & Tancredy, 2001). The principal caregiver of a dying patient is the spouse in 70% of cases, children (mostly daughters and daughters-in-law) in 20% of cases, and friends or more distant relatives in approximately 10% of cases (Ferrell, Ferrell, Rhiner, & Grant, 1991; Given & Given, 1989). Although emotional expression about the impact of the many losses associated with the illness and death is shared among family members, restorative coping responses are also activated as the family strives to reestablish some order and continuity. Our FFGT model facilitates both elements of the dual-process model (Stroebe, Hansson, Stroebe, & Schut, 2001) through inviting family members to share grief over lost attachments alongside improved family functioning, in which communication, cooperation, and mutual support are enhanced.

Cognitive Processing Theory

To accommodate new events, successful cognitive processing involves assimilating information; understanding events in accordance with one's previously established belief system; and modifying one's *assumptive world* (Parkes, 1972, 1998), a schema of ideas, values, attitudes, and beliefs that each person organizes about his or her life in the world. Illness and death, like other trauma, disrupt the assumptive world schema. At the family level, emotional disclosure and social sharing influence members' assumptive worldviews (Janoff-Bulman, 1989; Janoff-Bulman & Frantz, 1997), leading to cognitive reappraisal as confrontation or avoidance strategies unfold within the family. Family functioning through the family's basic communication processes and negotiation of differences dynamically affects members' cognitions. Families challenge negative rumination and model the way to finding positive meaning (Folkman & Moskowitz, 2000). They guide the wise or balanced regulation of grieving, recognizing when some degree of avoidance is healthy but too much is detrimental. Families pursue cognitive reframing iteratively, using the diverse views of members to test options, problem solve, and mutually support each other in finding new meaning and coping adaptively. More than any other social group, the family counters the loneliness and isolation of bereavement while forming a containing and nurturing environment that potentially optimizes the resolution of the mourning process adaptively. In this sense, the type of family functioning is a key moderator of adaptive bereavement outcome. A range of adaptive and maladaptive cognitive and social processing skills will likely mediate these outcomes for individual family members but are in turn influenced by family-as-a-whole attitudes and behaviors.

Group Adaptation

The dynamics of any group discussion move between enabling and restrictive solutions, as some members present a constructive suggestion to resolve an issue or concern while others urge caution based on a fearful perspective of what could happen (Whitaker & Lieberman, 1964). The group, in this case the family, grapples with these options. The consequent debate leads to some level of consensus, with adaptive choices generally resulting from constructive views. Sometimes, however, a dominant member may impose a deleterious point of view, or indecisive individuals are led by the majority. Difference of opinion could generate persistent conflict, with such disagreements splitting the group and reducing any perception of unity. The cohesiveness of a therapy group has long been recognized as a hallmark of its effectiveness in promoting development and maturity of its membership.

RECOGNITION OF AT-RISK FAMILIES FOR INTERVENTION WITH FAMILY FOCUSED GRIEF THERAPY

Empirical research across the past 15 years has developed a model of classifying families according to their functioning and used this to recognize families that might be considered at some risk of morbid outcome during bereavement.

Empirical Development of the Model

In 1990, we and our colleagues first studied families in whom a dying member was receiving palliative care (Kissane et al., 1994). Our second study was of bereaved families (Kissane, Bloch, Dowe, et al., 1996); our third family sample formed an intervention study (Kissane et al., 2003). We have found consistently in each of these cohorts a typology that differentiates well-functioning from dysfunctional families. We applied well-validated measures of family functioning to each sample: first to 102 families (342 participants) cross-sectionally, then to 115 families (269 participants) longitudinally, and third to a cohort of 81 families (363 participants) for the intervention. Each person completed the questionnaires independently, so that each presented his or her personal view, unbiased by the input of others. On the basis of 3 out of the 10 dimensions of the Family Environment Scale (FES; Moos & Moos, 1981)—(a) Cohesiveness, (b) Conflict, and (c) Expressiveness—five types of families were discerned. This classification has also been consistent over time (i.e., found during palliative care and at 6 weeks, 6 months, and 13 months of bereavement) and predictive of psychosocial morbidity. It is important to note that we established that there was a strong relationship between the type of family functioning and the psychosocial well-being of individual members within the family.

When the FES scores for Cohesiveness, Expressiveness, and Conflict are summed (using a reversed conflict score), the total forms the FRI. The short form of the FRI contains 4 items for each subscale, generating a possible maximum score for the FRI of 12, which indicates an optimally functioning family in the eyes of the respondent. It is a suitably brief, 12-item screening questionnaire, which can be administered as a paper-and-pencil test or via a touch-screen computer. The latter approach permits rapid computation of subscale scores.

Classification of Families: Qualitative Descriptors

We have applied descriptive names to the five classes that form our typology of family functioning. Two clusters, *supportive* and *conflict resolving*, are well functioning in their characteristics; two, *hostile* and *sullen*, are clearly dysfunctional; and we have termed the final class, which has features intermediate between its well-functioning and dysfunctional counterparts, *intermediate*. We hasten to add that we have never intended these names to be shared with families. We do not label families clinically; this would be not only pejorative but also potentially harmful. They are predictive concepts but not diagnostic categories. Nonetheless, the categories have utility in testing clinical theory. Health professionals can talk with a family about "concerns over their functioning" and, in doing this, should use the family's own descriptive language.

Supportive families have the characteristics of high cohesiveness, good expressiveness, and absent conflict. Members are intimate with each other, share their distress, and provide mutual comfort. Unbridled conflict is absent from these families as they tolerate negative emotions, disclose feelings honestly, and draw confidence from their knowledge of the family's closeness. They exhibit low levels of individual psychological morbidity, and they function competently in their social world. Supportive families win respect for their provision of care and support and do not need specialized psychological help beyond affirmation of the successful job they do. One advantage in clinical services recognizing this type of family is to empower staff to have confidence in the family's abilities, so that we avoid the unnecessary provision of limited resources.

Supportive families are impressive in that they express grief openly but without adverse consequences, ostensibly because their cohesiveness facilitates the sharing of distress while at the same time fostering mutual consolation and caring. This pattern is consonant with the clinical observation that adaptive families grieve effectively together (Kissane, 1994). Further observation of family coping style via the Family Crisis Oriented Personal Evaluation Scales (F-COPES; Olson et al., 1983)—a validated measure of family coping strategies—revealed that supportive families made regular use of mature coping strategies, such as the use of community resources, social support, and optimistic reframing of their predicament. They have the wherewithal to be assertive when they need to be.

Conflict-resolving families, the second type of well-functioning family, exhibit moderate conflict but high cohesiveness and above-average expressiveness. We surmise that their closeness and open communication are protective, providing the means to resolve differences. A degree of conflict is permissible for families to remain well functioning, but the key is surely the family's ability to tolerate this difference of opinion with respect, not destructive hostility. Members in this category carry low rates of psychosocial morbidity and the lowest levels of grief intensity.

By contrast, the *hostile* family is the most dysfunctional, characterized by high conflict, low cohesiveness, and low expressiveness. These families are fractured and chaotic, with members sometimes refusing to speak to each other for several years. They do not plan activities carefully, are not punctual, and lack structure and order. Argument destroys teamwork and inhibits any capacity for support. Offspring harbor most of the family's anger and resentment. These adult children become symptomatic with psychiatric disorders as their families find fault, blame, promote guilt, alienate and reject, or rage against one another. They have the highest rates of psychosocial morbidity. Their distress reverberates throughout the treatment system, yet key members are difficult to engage and may resist offers of help.

Palliative care services quickly recognize this hostile family type and commit considerable time and resources in response. Yet these families' coping styles are poorest, with members least able to make use of community resources, social support, cognitive reframing strategies, or religion. As such, they can be help-rejecting families. Moreover, as distress from acute grief rises, their family functioning can deteriorate across the early 3 to 4 months of bereavement. They need a defined treatment plan, a strong working alliance with the family therapist, and increased support to contain their conflict and help them to focus on the tasks at hand.

We have termed the second type of dysfunctional family *sullen* because of the muted anger and high rates of clinical depression found amid their members. These families are characterized by reduced cohesiveness, mild to moderate conflict, and poor expressiveness: an across-the-field reduction in each dimension of family functioning. They display intense levels of grief during bereavement. Members show substantial psychosocial morbidity, marginally less than hostile families, but they have the highest rates of depression (sometimes thought of psychodynamically as "anger turned in"). It is interesting that sullen families exercise the highest level of control over family life, with greater rigidity and conformity to family expectations. In their compliant way, they are less dislocated than their hostile counterparts, but expression of genuine feelings may be blocked. Disagreements remain unresolved, and anger simmers just beneath the surface. They distinctly differ from hostile families on the F-COPES in seeking assistance; appearing needy; and of all the family types making the greatest use of community resources, social support, cognitive reframing, and religion. They can therefore be engaged in therapeutic work, which is reassuring, because these families appear not only needy but also amenable to help.

The final class of family, *intermediate*, is characterized by moderate cohesiveness, but they do carry high rates of psychosocial morbidity. Members within this cluster have the lowest levels of Achievement Orientation (an FES subscale reflecting personal ambition) and Control Over Family Life (the extent to which rules are used inflexibly). These characteristics bolster the validity of this cluster as a discrete group. Individuals in intermediate families carry more symptoms of depression and anxiety, and they function less well socially than do well-functioning families. Although they do not demand attention, they have middling characteristics as "battlers," and they could be regarded as families with potential who are easily helped. They surely warrant care, can be readily engaged in therapy, and may need only a small number of sessions to help them; this work is both beneficial and appreciated.

Prevalence of Family Types

Approximately one third of families in the community function supportively, whereas another one fifth are conflict resolving in their style. Among dysfunctional families, approximately 6% are hostile and 9% sullen in nature during palliative care, but these rates double during the early months of bereavement. Approximately one third of community families display intermediate functioning during palliative care, and our longitudinal observation revealed substantial deterioration in their functioning under the stress of bereavement. We saw their movement into either of the two dysfunctional types during the early phase of bereavement. With the passage of time and waning of grief, this reversed itself by 13 months postdeath, so that one third of families again looked intermediate in their functioning (Kissane, Bloch, Dowe, et al. 1996; Kissane, Bloch, Onghena, et al., 1996).

Screening Scores Using the Family Relationships Index

Typical FRI scores generated by members of supportive families are 11 or 12: 4 for cohesiveness, 4 for reversed conflict and 3 or 4 for expressiveness. Conflict-resolving families generate scores in the range of 9 to 11, with 4 for cohesiveness, 2 or 3 for reversed conflict, and 3 or 4 for expressiveness. Among the dysfunctional families, hostile families have scores at the opposite end of the scale: 0 to 4, with a cohesiveness score of 0 to 1, an expressiveness score of 0 to 1, and a reversed conflict score of 0 to 2. Sullen families have FRI scores between 4 and 7, with typically a cohesiveness score 1 to 3, an expressiveness score 1 to 2, and a reversed conflict score of 1 to 3. Finally, intermediate families have FRI scores from 7 to 9, with cohesiveness in the range of 3 to 4, expressiveness in the range of 1 to 3, and reversed conflict in the range of 3 to 4.

Sensitivity and Specificity of the Family Relationships Index When Screening

The ability of the FRI to discriminate healthy from unhealthy families has been well established in many studies and was confirmed in our earlier

Melbourne studies through its high concurrent validity with the Family Assessment Device (FAD; Epstein, Baldwin, & Bishop, 1983). As a screening tool to detect families at risk of morbid bereavement outcome, the FRI had a sensitivity of .86 and specificity of .45 in predicting outcome correctly (Kissane et al., 2003). In using screening tools, it is customary to privilege sensitivity over specificity so that true cases are not missed. Edwards and Clarke (2005) followed 48 patients and 99 relatives across 6 months of cancer care and confirmed independently a sensitivity of 1.0 for the FRI to identify dysfunctional families using the FAD as gold standard, between 0.88 and 1.00 to detect BDI–Fastscreen "caseness" (Beck, Guth, Steer, & Ball, 1997) and between 0.77 and 1.00 for Spielberger State Anxiety caseness (Spielberger, Gorsuch, Lushene, Vagg, & Jacobs, 1983) in individual family members across three time points.

Clinical Utility of Routine Screening

Our classification of family types has been remarkably consistent across four time points through 13 months postdeath in repeated-measures multivariate analyses. Its strong association with the individual psychosocial morbidity carried by family members points to its utility as a means to better recognize those at risk. This is dependent on clinical services adopting routine screening of family functioning with a measure such as the FRI, a development we have been instituting successfully with hospice and palliative care services in New York since 2005. Recognition of at-risk families allows the introduction of a preventive intervention to reduce morbid grief.

THE FAMILY FOCUSED GRIEF THERAPY MODEL OF INTERVENTION

Goals

FFGT is a brief, time-limited, focused intervention in which the family is the recipient of care; grief and family functioning are its predominant themes. Its focus is on two major goals: to (a) improve family functioning and (b) promote adaptive grieving. The first objective is relational and is explored through attention to cohesion, communication, and conflict resolution. The second is intricately interwoven because the sharing of grief is dependent on effective communication. Family solidarity helps to counter aloneness, one of the most painful aspects of mourning. Strengths of the family are particularly affirmed as a pathway to promote change in family functioning. A "coping with cancer" and, later, "coping with bereavement" focus is sustained to avoid being drawn into long-standing problems that lie beyond the scope of this intervention. The intended benefit of FFGT is the reduction of morbid effects of grief among families at risk of poor psychosocial outcome.

Application of the model depends on the therapist achieving engagement through identification of relational concerns, which the family then owns and agrees to target as the focus of their work together. Active problem solving, conflict resolution, and the acknowledgment and sharing of grief are the mainstay of the focused treatment. Change is affirmed in the consolidation phase, with response prevention strategies considered during termination.

Course of Treatment

Therapy progresses from assessment of and mutual agreement about concerns held by the family to active treatment targeting these issues. Once progress is achieved in accomplishing the family's goals, the time between sessions is lengthened to consolidate gains before termination occurs. Longer therapy is indicated for greater dysfunction, with treatment varying between 6 and 18 months. There is not space here to provide more than a brief outline of the therapy; interested readers are referred to Kissane and Bloch's (2002) book on FFGT, which provides a comprehensive guide.

Session Outline

Session 1: Assessment

After identifying the hopes and expectations of family members, the story of illness becomes the opening theme, including the related emotional journey, understanding treatment goals, and prognosis of the cancer. As data are collected, the therapist assesses communication, cohesion, and conflict. Roles, rules, values, and beliefs are also explored. To glean information, therapists make use of open-ended questioning, which may be linear, circular, reflexive, or strategic in direction. Questioning is the primary mode of intervention. The therapist also summarizes what was understood so that a consensus is reached.

Session 2: Completion of Assessment and Negotiation of Treatment Plan

If a transgenerational picture of the family, with attention to patterns of relationship and of coping with loss, was not completed in Session 1, this continues through the construction of a genogram in Session 2. To do this, the therapist uses butcher paper or a portable whiteboard on which to draw a family tree that depicts three generations of the family, including both ancestors and descendants of the patient. Family strengths receive special focus, but loss events such as death and relational styles and alliances are the target of exploration. Again, a summary of what has been learned is used to highlight resilience, recognize what patterns of relating have been transmitted transgenerationally, and gain agreement about identified concerns so that options for treatment can be considered and family consensus negotiated. A plan and timetable of focused treatment is then agreed on.

Sessions 3 Through 8: Active Focused Therapy

The agreed foci of relationship issues are targeted with promotion of open communication, teamwork, and conflict resolution. The family's ability to accept differences of opinion and reach a negotiated compromise is promoted through formal problem-solving strategies. Themes of care provision; intimacy; the emotional challenge of suffering; discussion of death and dying; saying goodbye; the role of culture, religion, or ritual; historical or transgenerational influences; and how the family shares grief are woven into these relational reviews. Summary and affirmation of progress, with balanced attention to family strengths, are strategies common to every session. Progress with the agreed concerns is assessed and affirmed at each session.

Last Two Sessions: Consolidation and Termination

In the last two sessions, progress is again reviewed, success is affirmed, and the reemergence of old patterns is acknowledged. Response prevention strategies are discussed. Hopes and expectations for the future are considered as the family prepares for termination. Loss of therapy is grieved similarly to the death of their relative; the therapist bids the family farewell with confident reminders of its strengths, achievements, and future hopes.

Therapist Skills and Interventions

FFGT therapists should be trained in the conduct of family therapy and are commonly drawn from the disciplines of social work, psychology, and psychiatry. In FFGT, the therapist interacts warmly and authentically, manifesting both interest and concern. The ability to build a solid collaborative alliance is the first necessary skill because this models the style of relating that is a prominent objective for the family in FFGT. Second, the therapist utilizes praise and affirmation to explicitly acknowledge family strengths. This resilience model reinforces what already works well and precludes undue criticism. Third, the therapist and family must reach agreement over identified concerns, and thus a form of contract is negotiated to work collaboratively. The notion of a partnership safeguards the therapist from acting directively and builds team solutions to the family's concerns.

One of the key therapeutic skills used by an effective therapist is the ability to pose the "right" question because this invites observation, reflection, and consideration of change. Circular questioning invites members to step into each other's shoes and express opinions about each other's thoughts and feelings. As a member responds, others attend to him or her, and group discussion is stimulated. Reflexive questions propose hypotheses about relational patterns and facilitate development of insight into how family members interact. Strategic questions offer potential direction for change but leave choices about this to the family.

Another key skill is the effective use of an *integrative summary*, in which the therapist summarizes what he or she understands to have occurred; this is then agreed with or amended by the family. The therapist may invite the family to summarize—the more work they do, the more they gain. A final, vital skill is the ability to encourage expression of genuine feelings. This depends on spotting pertinent cues. The therapist then seeks to understand what lies behind the feeling, thus fostering open sharing of distress and resultant mutual comfort. In contrast with an individual model of supportive therapy, in which the therapist might empathically acknowledge and personally support a distressed individual, within FFGT the therapist's questions invite other family members to deliver the empathic support. The family learns in the session how to better comfort one another.

CHALLENGES IN DELIVERING FAMILY FOCUSED GRIEF THERAPY

Problems With Engagement

Therapists can be informed that a particular person will attend a planned session, only to discover later that the invitation was not extended. In general, the less cohesive the family, the more active the therapist needs to be in drawing its members together. Planning ahead calls for active consideration of who might attend, with benefits flowing from the therapist telephoning members and connecting with them directly.

Limits to Therapeutic Goals

Long-standing personality difficulties, chronic mental illness, and subsystem issues (e.g., marital difficulties for the offspring of the dying person) lie outside the prospects of influence by a time-limited intervention. Nevertheless, across several months, the number of issues that command attention in families is striking—pregnancy, infidelity, relationship breakdown, alcohol and drug abuse, job loss, study problems, miscarriages, and accidents are examples. Families may indeed need to talk about these events, but the therapist must monitor overall family functioning as stories unfold and deal with them in that context. Sustaining focus is crucial to the success of a brief intervention, as is the setting of realistic goals.

Therapy in the Home

Palliative care is increasingly community based. If they wish, patients are empowered to stay with their families, receive treatment in familiar settings, and die in their own homes. Disability and failing health, including cancer-induced paraplegia, significant frailty, and imminent death, make this venue an asset to members being able to attend. The patient can more readily contribute when therapist and family come, both metaphorically and literally, to the bedside. The home is not, however, necessarily the best location for every family. Those with a history of conflict are better served in a neutral location, such as the therapist's office, because there they are on equal terms and the therapist is more readily perceived as not taking sides. Approximately two thirds of therapy can occur safely in the home.

Before starting home-based therapy, rules are established to both protect and empower the process. These include stipulating the duration of the session and creating an appropriate setting by determining seating arrangements, switching off the radio or television, avoiding disruptive telephone calls and visitors, settling pets, and deferring refreshments.

Families With Young Children

When cancer afflicts a parent in his or her 30s or 40s, there is concern about death before parenting is complete. A source of additional grief is that the parent feels deprived of that pivotal role. The family may also be rendered insecure through losing a material provider. Although FFGT was established for families whose offspring were adult and often parents themselves, therapy with younger children and adolescents is common and inevitable. Genuine sharing of innermost feelings helps younger family members mature into sensitive people, but the process does not necessarily come easily. Protective barriers are often erected to shield children from harm, with the attendant risk of denying them an authentic experience of family grief. Our model promotes open sharing of thoughts and feelings to foster mutual support and commonly helps a surviving parent grow in confidence in his or her support of the children.

Ethical Issues

The intimate relations within the family correspond with the feminist contribution to ethics that stresses the sense of responsibility derived from attachment to others rather than the rights of any individual (Gilligan, 1982). Core notions of taking care of others, parenting, being responsible for an interconnected network of needs, and the protection of others capture this state of relationships. An ethic of care is at the heart of these relationship-based principles. Traits such as compassion, sympathy, fidelity, trust, discernment, sensitivity, and love take precedence over the rules and rights found in the usual medical model that privileges autonomy of the individual.

An occasional ethical quandary in family work arises from the competing needs of members. Should all members be treated equally, the needs of the dying made paramount, or might one member be occasionally privileged over others? In general, the therapist strives to be neutral and treat all equally, but pragmatic factors do prevail in circumstances of exceptional vulnerability for one family member, warranting greater attention at this time. Family decision making exists in some balance with individual choice. Open truth telling about serious illness and its prognosis is another common premise on which FFGT is built.

RESULTS OF A RANDOMIZED CONTROLLED TRIAL OF FAMILY FOCUSED GRIEF THERAPY

In the Phase 1 study of FFGT in Melbourne, Australia, 81 families gave informed consent, generating a cohort with 41 (176 individuals) intermediate, 21 (96 individuals) sullen, and 19 (81 individuals) hostile families (Kissane et al., 2006). Patients had a mean age of 57 years, 51% were male, and they suffered from cancer, with a median length of illness from diagnosis to death of 25 months and median survival time from study entry to death of 96 days. The most common tumor types were breast (25%), lung (20%), brain (12%), colorectal (9%), pancreatic (7%), esophageal (5%), prostate (4%), and other (18%). As an indication of their anticancer therapies, they had received chemotherapy in 84% of cases, radiotherapy in 74% of cases, and hormone therapy in 15% of cases (Kissane et al., 2003). Spouses were a mean age of 56 years, offspring were a mean age of 29 years, and other relatives were a mean age of 32 years. Three quarters of the families were Australian born, Christian in religious orientation, and relatively well educated; some 60% of family members were employed, and 11% were students. In 5% of families, there was one child, 51% had two children, 33% had three children, and 11% had four or more children. Randomization in a 2:1 ratio assigned 53 families to intervention and 28 to the control condition. Within the intervention arm, 45 (85%) families commenced FFGT; 2 withdrew after one session, 3 withdrew prior to termination, and 40 (75%) completed therapy. With the length of therapy adjusted to correspond with each family's clinical need, the mean number of sessions was 7.3. Intermediate families received a mean of 7.0 sessions (range: 3–13), sullen received a mean of 6.4 (range: 4–9), and hostile received a mean of 9.4 (range: 7–13). The flow of participants from screening to intervention and outcome is shown in Figure 23.1.

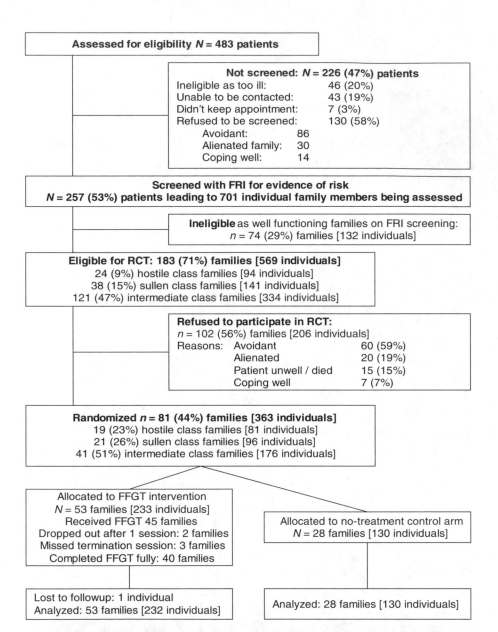

Figure 23.1. Flow diagram of enrollment, allocation, follow-up, and analysis stages of the randomized controlled trial of family focused grief therapy (FFGT). FRI = Family Relationships Index; RCT = randomized controlled trial. From "Family Focused Grief Therapy: A Randomized, Controlled Trial in Palliative Care and Bereavement," by D. W. Kissane, M. McKenzie, S. Bloch, C. Moskowitz, D. P. McKenzie, and I. O'Neill, 2006, *American Journal of Psychiatry, 163,* p.1211. Copyright 2006 by American Psychiatric Publishing, Inc. Reprinted with permission from *The American Journal of Psychiatry.*

Fidelity of Intervention

To study the treatment integrity of FFGT, a measure coding for content and process of therapy across the assessment, focused intervention, and termination phases was developed: the FFGT Treatment Integrity Measure (Chan, O'Neill, McKenzie, Love, & Kissane, 2004). Its items cover planning goals of therapy; understanding the family's style, history, ideology, and strengths; and addressing key themes. Process-based domains include providing reassurance, problem solving and assisting the family, providing direction to sessions, maintaining the agreed focus, building rapport, and terminating therapy. Eleven items code the number of questions asked on specific themes. Although items are generally therapist oriented, because FFGT is a dynamic group process some items reflect family-as-a-whole behaviors. A coding manual defines each item of the integrity measure, including explicit guidelines for rating that item, exemplars of behaviors that should or should not be considered, and important distinctions between items (Chan et al., 2004).

From the 53 families assigned to therapy in the RCT, 28 were randomly selected for this study of treatment fidelity using the FFGT Treatment Integrity Measure, leading to an appraisal of 109 family sessions. This represented a review of 62% of treated families, 38% of total therapy sessions, and 87% of the 15 participating therapists. Weighted mean percentage occurrences of therapist behaviors permitted trends in therapy application to be observed.

Interrater reliability using the FFGT Treatment Integrity Measure was satisfactory, with 88% overall agreement. Eighty-six percent of therapists adhered faithfully to core elements of the model. Therapist competence was evidenced by a strong therapeutic alliance in 94% of sessions, affirmation of family strengths in over 90% of sessions, and a focus on agreed themes in 76% of sessions. Therapists averaged 10 grief-related questions per session, 7 on communication-related issues during assessment, 7 on conflict late in therapy, and 4 on cohesiveness across the course of therapy. Discussion of loss, change, and grief was consistently comprehensive for over 78% of families in each relevant phase of therapy, highlighting its dominance as a theme. Interestingly, exploration of family communication reduced as therapy advanced and it became of less concern. On the other hand, family cohesiveness was discussed comprehensively both at the beginning and end of therapy. This contrasted with conflict, perhaps a difficult issue for therapists to address satisfactorily early on and which was explored later, when a trusting relationship had been established.

Consistent application of FFGT, with attention to its four key themes of (a) family communication, (b) cohesiveness, (c) conflict resolution, and (d) shared grief, was thus demonstrated, proving that the model is generalizable when applied by family therapists.

Outcome Findings

The concept of *intention to treat* (ITT) is the scientific standard sought in appraising the outcome of clinical trials, whereby dropouts from a study are included in the individuals being analyzed so that no bias is permitted by ignoring side effects of the intervention. The global impact of FFGT analyzed on an ITT basis was a reduction in the distress of the bereaved (BSI) when treated families were compared with control participants at 13 months postdeath (difference in change score = 0.11 [95% CI: −0.01, 0.22], $p = .02$). Significant improvement in distress and depression were demonstrated for individuals with the top 10% of BSI and BDI scores at baseline (see Table 23.1). The effect sizes for the global reduction in BDI at 6 months postdeath were a respectable 0.44 for sullen families and 0.30 for intermediate families (Kissane et al., 2006).

Analyses were also conducted of families who completed FFGT. The 179 individuals from 40 families who completed FFGT did not differ on sociodemographic, mental, or physical health variables at baseline from the 56 individuals (13 families) who did not complete the intervention (plus 2 individuals who did not attend any therapy sessions, although their families did). At the 6-month assessment, noncompleters gave ratings of the extent to which the program helped their family that were lower than rates given by completers ($p < .005$). In clinical practice, families who do not complete FFGT may be acutely or chronically dysfunctional. However, intervention effects were only marginally strengthened when analyses were focused exclusively on completers.

The effect size measuring improvements using ITT was small ($d = 0.26$; Kissane et al., 2006). This effect reached statistical significance when only individuals whose families completed the intervention were included in the analysis of the BSI at 13 months (difference in change score = 0.12; 95% CI: 0.00, 0.24; $p < .02$, $d = 0.28$). The effect size for intermediate families increased from $d = 0.30$ on ITT to $d = 0.37$ for treatment completers.

The intensity of normal grief phenomena (as measured with the Bereavement Phenomenology Questionnaire [Burnett et al., 1993; Byrne & Raphael, 1994]) reduced equivalently in both conditions of the trial. This was expected, because the phenomenology of normal grief was not the focus. Instead, the goal was the prevention of pathological grief, which is expressed clinically in terms of depressive disorders and other states associated with high distress. The striking outcome of this RCT involving 353 participants was the improvement in family members who started with high distress and depression scores at baseline.

Global family functioning (as measured with the FAD) was generally not, however, improved. Subgroup analysis of this using an ITT approach revealed a differential outcome for Intermediate and Sullen classes of families, who tended to improve, whereas the Hostile class remained unchanged,

TABLE 23.1

Comparison Using Generalized Estimating Equations of Change in Scores for the Most Distressed Family Members on Several Scales

| Scale | Time comparison | N | | Change | | | | |
		Individuals	Families	In therapy condition	In control condition	Difference	95% CI	p
BSI–GSI	Baseline to T1	22	20	0.83	0.16	0.67	0.21, 1.15	<.01**
	Baseline to T2	20	19	0.81	0.30	0.52	0.04, 1.43	<.01**
BDI	Baseline to T1	19	19	5.92	0.43	5.49	0.39, 11.79	<.01**
	Baseline to T2	18	18	5.13	3.86	1.27	0.002, 4.56	<.01**
SAS	Baseline to T1	25	20	0.48	0.33	0.15	−0.13, 0.42	.18
	Baseline to T2	24	20	0.40	0.35	0.05	−0.27, 0.36	.33
BPQ	T1 to T2	21	19	11.73	14.19	−2.46	−11.12, 6.26	.05

Note. Scores are for the 10% of family members most distressed at baseline after 6 months (T1) and 13 months (T2) of family-focused grief therapy intervention versus a control condition. CI = confidence interval; BSI–GSI = Brief Symptom Inventory General Severity Index; BDI = Beck Depression Inventory; SAS = Social Adjustment Scale; BPQ = Bereavement Phenomenology Questionnaire. From "Family Focused Grief Therapy: A Randomized, Controlled Trial in Palliative Care and Bereavement," by D. W. Kissane, S. Bloch, C. Moskowitz, D. P. McKenzie, and I. O'Neill, 2006, *American Journal of Psychiatry, 163*, p. 1213. Copyright 2006 by American Psychiatric Publishing, Inc. Adapted with permission from *The American Journal of Psychiatry.*
**p < .01.

potentially because of a dose effect. Hostile families who completed treatment did demonstrate a significant improvement in family functioning by 6 months (difference in change score = 0.22; 95% CI: 0.04, 0.39; $p < .02$), although this difference was no longer statistically significant by 13 months. Thus, a protective benefit against pathological grief was generated overall without a significant gain being formally demonstrated in the measures of family functioning. How do we explain this discrepant outcome of clinical benefit among family members, but not in their global perception of family functioning? Several explanations are possible. One lies in the nature of the measures used, with the perceptions of functioning that they capture being more trait than state characteristics: Test–retest correlations are high across 1-year time periods. Another explanation is that our impressions of family functioning may be slower to change against long-held convictions about what families are like. Furthermore, given the inevitability that death generates a perturbation in family structure and relationships, it may be too optimistic to anticipate dramatic changes in perceptions of family functioning. Nevertheless, attention to family processes of cooperation and communication may convey a protective benefit; the primary outcome of this preliminary RCT suggests that it does.

Sullen families appear to be the class most readily helped by FFGT. Our earlier work highlighted their interest in seeking help as measured by the F-COPES (Kissane, Bloch, Dowe, et al., 1996). We omitted use of the F-COPES in this first RCT but have reintroduced it in our replication study sponsored by the National Cancer Institute to explore moderators and mediators of change.

For Intermediate families, FFGT offers a modest but worthwhile prospect of benefit. Conflict tends to worsen in control families in this class, whereas those receiving FFGT improve, particularly across the first 6 months of bereavement. Distress is correspondingly reduced.

Therapeutic containment of hostile families may have been limited by an insufficient length of therapy. We plan to examine this in a replication study through formal variation in the length of treatment. Moreover, hostile families tend to be help rejecting (Kissane, Bloch, Dowe, et al., 1996). We will therefore explore such a dynamic through examination of the advantages and disadvantages that these behaviors confer on the family. At the same time, we have increased emphasis in our continuing research about the need for distance between members of hostile families, their separation being a potentially homeostatic solution to conflict. This is a necessary caveat to avoid causing harm.

It is important to note that no significant association was evident between the therapist who delivered FFGT and the outcome achieved, providing evidence that the model of therapy was indeed generalizable in being teachable to and deliverable by a variety of family therapists.

FUTURE DIRECTIONS

Considerable research is needed to develop family-centered care such as FFGT. Consideration of the following questions would have merit:

- What is the dose intensity of FFGT needed for therapeutic gain proportional to the level of dysfunction present in the family? How many sessions should be offered cost-effectively, and can this be predicted by screening?
- What are the mediators and moderators of successful outcome?
- Might FFGT be contraindicated in some very dysfunctional families for whom separation and distance are already successful solutions?
- Which therapist interventions are more successful in generating family change?
- How does the therapist discern when to promote acceptance of patterns of relating over any suggestion for change?
- What is the optimal timing of the intervention?
- How should FFGT be modified with different cultural groups?

Several replication studies are clearly needed. A large research agenda flows from this preliminary work.

CONCLUSION

Palliative care and bereavement services ultimately need to offer a range of clinical programs, for there will always be the need for individual counseling and group support alongside family therapy. Developing clear guidelines for the adoption of different therapies would be helpful. Our work has nonetheless seen tremendous benefits flow from the continuity of care that arises when an at-risk family is identified early via screening and offered preventive intervention. This is consistent with the recent bereavement literature that has argued for targeted interventions (Jordan & Neimeyer, 2003).

One key premise of our FFGT model is that bereavement care begins at entry to the palliative care or hospice program rather than being thought of as an add-on after death. Our ongoing work has been to normalize the screening of family functioning at initial assessment by the palliative care nurse as the means to initiating family-centered care as well as to further refine the model in response to specific family features and needs. We are enthusiastic about the long-term future of FFGT as a model with great clinical utility for preventing the development of prolonged grief disorder or other morbid consequences of bereavement. Rather than a sustained research focus on individual grief, we advocate for a paradigm shift to family grief. A grief that is shared can begin to be healed, and the family unit is the most natural and generally available social group to permit this sharing.

REFERENCES

Barg, F. K., Pasacreta, J. V., Nuamah, I., Robinson, K. D., Angeletti, K., Yasko, J. M., & McCorkle, R. (1998). A description of a psychoeducational intervention for family caregivers of cancer patients. *Journal of Family Nursing, 4,* 394–413.

Beck, A., & Beck, R. (1972). Screening depressed patients in family practice: A rapid technique. *Postgraduate Medicine, 52,* 81–85.

Beck, A. T., Guth, D., Steer, R. A., & Ball, R. (1997). Screening for major depression disorders in medical inpatients with the Beck Depression Inventory for primary care. *Behavioral Research and Therapy, 35,* 785–791.

Beck, A., Steer, R., & Garbin, M. (1988). Psychometric properties of the Beck Depression Inventory: Twenty-five years of evaluation. *Clinical Psychology Review, 8,* 77–100.

Black, D., & Urbanowicz, M. A. (1987). Family intervention with bereaved children. *Journal of Child Psychology and Psychiatry, 28,* 467–476.

Bowlby, J. (1969). *Attachment and loss: Vol. 1. Attachment.* New York: Basic Books.

Buckley, I. (1977). *Listen to the children: Impact on the mental health of children of a parent's catastrophic illness.* New York: Cancer Care Inc. and National Cancer Foundation.

Burnett, P., Middleton, W., Raphael, B., Dunne, M., Moylan, A., & Martinek, N. (1994). Concepts of normal bereavement. *Journal of Traumatic Stress, 7,* 123–128.

Byrne, G. J. A., & Raphael, B. (1994). A longitudinal study of bereavement phenomena in recently widowed elderly men. *Psychological Medicine, 24,* 411–421.

Carlsson, M. E., & Strang, P. M. (1996). Educational group support for patients with gynaecological cancer and their families. *Supportive Care in Cancer, 4,* 102–109.

Cassileth, B. R., Lusk, E. J., Strouse, T. B., Miller, D. S., Brown, L. L., & Cross, P. A. (1985). A psychological analysis of cancer patients and their next-of-kin. *Cancer, 55,* 72–76.

Cawley, M. M., & Gerdts, E. K. (1988). Establishing a cancer caregivers program: An interdisciplinary approach. *Cancer Nursing, 11,* 267–273.

Chan, E. K., O'Neill, I., McKenzie, M., Love, A., & Kissane, D. W. (2004). What works for therapists conducting family meetings: Treatment integrity in family-focused grief therapy during palliative care and bereavement. *Journal of Pain Symptom Management, 27,* 502–512.

Creamer, M., Burgess, P., & Pattison, P. (1992). Reaction to trauma: A cognitive processing model. *Journal of Abnormal Psychology, 101,* 452–459.

Derogatis, L. R., & Melisaratos, N. (1983). The brief symptom inventory: an introductory report. *Psychological Medicine, 13,* 595–605.

Derogatis, L. R., & Spencer, P. M. (1982). *Administration and procedures: BSI manual—I.* Baltimore: Clinical Psychometric Research.

Edwards, B., & Clarke, V. (2005). The validity of the Family Relationships Index as a screening tool for psychological risk in families of cancer patients. *Psycho-Oncology, 14*, 546–554.

Ell, K., Nishimoto, R., Mantell, J., & Hamovitch, M. (1988). Longitudinal analysis of psychological adaptation among family members of patients with cancer. *Journal of Psychosomatic Research, 32*, 429–438.

Epstein, N., Baldwin, L., & Bishop, D. (1983). The McMaster Family Assessment Device. *Journal of Marital and Family Therapy, 9*, 171–180.

Ferrell, B. R., Ferrell, B. A., Rhiner, M., & Grant, M. (1991). Family factors influencing cancer pain management. *Postgraduate Medical Journal, 67*(Suppl. 2), S64–S69.

Folkman, S., & Moskowitz, J. T. (2000). Positive affect and the other side of coping. *American Psychologist, 55*, 647–654.

Gilligan, C. (1982). *In a different voice*. Cambridge, MA: Harvard University Press.

Given, B., & Given, C. W. (1989). Cancer nursing for the elderly: A target for research. *Cancer Nursing, 12*, 71–77.

Goldstein, J., Alter, C. L., & Axelrod, R. (1996). A psychoeducational bereavement-support group for families provided in an outpatient cancer center. *Journal of Cancer Education, 11*, 233–237.

Gotay, C. C. (1984). The experience of cancer during early and advanced stages: The views of patients and their mates. *Social Science & Medicine, 18*, 605–613.

Grahn, G. (1996). Coping with the cancer experience: I. Developing an education and support programme for cancer patients and their significant others. *European Journal of Cancer Care, 5*, 176–181.

Greer, D. S., & Mor, V. (1986). An overview of national hospice study findings. *Journal of Chronic Disease, 39*, 5–7.

Harding, R., & Higginson, I. J. (2003). What is the best way to help caregivers in cancer and palliative care? A systematic literature review of interventions and their effectiveness. *Palliative Medicine, 17*, 63–74.

Heinrich, R. L., & Schag, C. C. (1985). Stress and activity management: Group treatment for cancer patients and spouses. *Journal of Consulting and Clinical Psychology, 53*, 439–446.

Higginson, I. J., Finlay, I. G., Goodwin, D. M., Hood, K., Edwards, A. G., Cook, A., et al. (2003). Is there evidence that palliative care teams alter end-of-life experiences of patients and their caregivers? *Journal of Pain Symptom Management, 25*, 150–168.

Horowitz, S., Passik, S., & Malkin, M. (1996). "In sickness and in health": A group intervention for spouses caring for patients with brain tumors. *Journal of Psychosocial Oncology, 14*, 43–56.

Janoff-Bulman, R. (1989). Assumptive worlds and the stress of traumatic events: Applications of the schema construct. *Social Cognition, 7*, 113–136.

Janoff-Bulman, R., & Frantz, C. M. (1997). The impact of trauma on meaning: From meaningless world to meaningful life. In M. J. Power & C. R. Brewin (Eds.), *The transformation of meaning in psychological therapies: Integrating theory and practice* (pp. 91–106). Chichester, England: Wiley.

Jordan, J. R., & Neimeyer, R. A. (2003). Does grief counseling work? *Death Studies, 27,* 765–786.

Kissane, D. W. (1994). Family-based grief counselling. *Australian Family Physician, 23,* 678–680.

Kissane, D. W., & Bloch, S. (1994). Family grief. *British Journal of Psychiatry, 164,* 728–740.

Kissane, D., & Bloch, S. (2002). *Family focused grief therapy: A model of family-centered care during grief and bereavement.* Buckingham, England: Open University Press.

Kissane, D. W., Bloch, S., Burns, W. I., McKenzie, D. P., & Posterino, M. (1994). Psychological morbidity in the families of patients with cancer. *Psycho-Oncology, 3,* 47–56.

Kissane, D. W., Bloch, S., Dowe, D. L., Snyder, R. D., Onghena, P., McKenzie, D. P., & Wallace, C. S. (1996). The Melbourne Family Grief Study, I: Perceptions of family functioning in bereavement. *American Journal of Psychiatry, 153,* 650–658.

Kissane, D. W., Bloch, S., Onghena, P., McKenzie, D. P., Snyder, R. D., & Dowe, D. L. (1996). The Melbourne Family Grief Study, II: Psychosocial morbidity and grief in bereaved families. *American Journal of Psychiatry, 153,* 659–666.

Kissane, D. W., Bloch, S., McKenzie, M., McDowall, A. C., & Nitzan, R. (1998). Family grief therapy: A preliminary account of a new model to promote healthy family functioning during palliative care and bereavement. *Psycho-Oncology, 7,* 14–25.

Kissane, D. W., McKenzie, M., Bloch, S., Moskowitz, C., McKenzie, D., & O'Neill, I. (2006). Family focused grief therapy: A randomized controlled trial in palliative care and bereavement. *American Journal of Psychiatry, 163,* 1208–1218.

Kissane, D. W., McKenzie, M., McKenzie, D. P., Forbes, A., O'Neill, I., & Bloch, S. (2003). Psychosocial morbidity associated with patterns of family functioning in palliative care: Baseline data from the Family Focused Grief Therapy Controlled Trial. *Palliative Medicine, 17,* 527–537.

Lieberman, S. (1978). Nineteen cases of morbid grief. *British Journal of Psychiatry, 132,* 159–163.

Maguire, P. (1981). The repercussions of mastectomy on the family. *International Journal of Family Psychiatry, 6,* 485–503.

McHorney, C. A., & Mor, V. (1988). Predictors of bereavement depression and its health services consequences. *Medical Care, 26,* 882–893.

Minagawa, H., Uchitomi, Y., Yamawaki, S., & Ishitani, K. (1996). Psychiatric morbidity in terminally ill cancer patients: A prospective study. *Cancer, 78,* 1131–1137.

Moos, R., & Moos, B. (1981). *Family Environment Scale manual.* Stanford, CA: Consulting Psychologists Press.

Mor, V., McHorney, C., & Sherwood, S. (1986). Secondary morbidity among the recently bereaved. *American Journal of Psychiatry, 143,* 158–163.

Northouse, L. (1989). A longitudinal study of the adjustment of patients and husbands to breast cancer. *Oncology Nursing Forum, 16,* 511–516.

Olson, D. H., McCubbin, H. I., Barnes, H., Larsen, A., Muxen, M. & Wilson, M. (1983). *Families: What makes them work*. Beverly Hills, CA: Sage.

Parkes, C. (1972). *Bereavement: Studies of grief in adult life*. London: Tavistock.

Parkes, C. (1998). *Bereavement studies of grief in adult life* (3rd ed.). Madison, CT: International Universities Press.

Paul, N., & Grosser, G. (1965). Operational mourning and its role in conjoint family therapy. *Community Health Journal, 1*, 339–345.

Plant, H., Richardson, J., Stubbs, L., Lynch, D., Ellwood, J., Slevin, M., et al. (1987). Evaluation of a support group for cancer patients and their families and friends. *British Journal of Hospital Medicine, 38*, 317–322.

Plumb, M. M., & Holland, J. (1977). Comparative studies of psychological function in patients with advanced cancer—I. Self-reported depressive symptoms. *Psychosomatic Medicine, 39*, 264–276.

Reele, B. L. (1994). Effect of counseling on quality of life for individuals with cancer and their families. *Cancer Nursing, 17*, 101–112.

Ringdal, G. I., Jordhoy, M. S., Ringdal, K., & Kaasa, S. (2001). The first year of grief and bereavement in close family members to individuals who have died of cancer. *Palliative Medicine, 15*, 91–105.

Robinson, K. D., Angeletti, K. A., Barg, F. K., Pasacreta, J. V., McCorkle, R., & Yasko, J. M. (1998). The development of a family caregiver cancer education program. *Journal of Cancer Education, 13*, 116–121.

Rosenthal, P. A. (1980). Short-term family therapy and pathological grief resolution with children and adolescents. *Family Process, 19*, 151–159.

Rotheram-Borus, M. J., Stein, J. A., & Lin, Y. Y. (2001). Impact of parent death and an intervention on the adjustment of adolescents whose parents have HIV/AIDS. *Journal of Consulting and Clinical Psychology, 69*, 763–773.

Rotheram-Borus, M. J., Weiss, R., Alber, S., & Lester, P. (2005). Adolescent adjustment before and after HIV-related parental death. *Journal of Consulting and Clinical Psychology, 73*, 221–228.

Sandler, I. N., Ayers, T. S., Wolchik, S. A., Tein, J.-Y., Kwok, O.-M., Haine, R. A., et al. (2003). The Family Bereavement Program: Efficacy evaluation of a theory-based prevention program for parentally bereaved children and adolescents. *Journal of Consulting and Clinical Psychology, 71*, 587–600.

Shaver, P., & Tancredy, C. (2001). Emotion, attachment, and bereavement: A conceptual commentary. In M. Stroebe, R. Hansson, W. Stroebe, & H. Schut (Eds.), *Handbook of bereavement research: Consequences, coping, and care* (pp. 63–88). Washington, DC: American Psychological Association.

Silberfarb, P. M., Maurer, L. H., & Crouthamel, C. S. (1980). Psychosocial aspects of neoplastic disease: I. Functional status of breast cancer patients during different treatment regimens. *American Journal of Psychiatry, 137*, 450–455.

Spielberger, C. D., Gorsuch, R. L., Lushene, R., Vagg, P. R., & Jacobs, G. A. (1983). *Manual for the State–Trait Anxiety Inventory*. Palo Alto, CA: Consulting Psychologists Press.

Stroebe, M., Hansson, R., Stroebe, W., & Schut, H. (2001). *Handbook of bereavement research: Consequences, coping, and care*. Washington DC: American Psychological Association.

Toseland, R. W., Blanchard, C. G., & McCallion, P. (1995). A problem solving intervention for caregivers of cancer patients. *Social Science & Medicine, 40*, 517–528.

Whitaker, D. S., & Lieberman, M. A. (1964). *Psychotherapy through the group process*. Chicago: Aldine.

Williams, W. V., & Polak, P. R. (1979). Follow-up research in primary prevention: A model of adjustment in acute grief. *Journal of Clinical Psychology, 35*, 35–45.

24

MEANING-MAKING IN BEREAVED FAMILIES: ASSESSMENT, INTERVENTION, AND FUTURE RESEARCH

JANICE WINCHESTER NADEAU

Todd, a young father, sat on the couch in my office, tears streaming down his face. He was describing the sudden death of his 4-year-old son a few weeks earlier. His wife, Lisa, sitting at the other end of the couch, stared angrily at him through tear-filled eyes. "Why didn't you listen to me when I told you Timmy was sick? I'm his mother! Mothers know things about their kids!" Timmy had been ill less than 24 hours when his life ended abruptly. There had been two trips to the emergency room, and both times Todd and Lisa had been reassured that Timmy's lethargy was not a cause for concern and so had taken him back home. As the night progressed, Timmy did not improve. Lisa told me that she had wanted to call an ambulance but that Todd became angry and insisted she not do so.

The next day, Todd insisted that they go through with their oldest son's First Communion ceremony. Lisa objected but remembers being too tired to argue. As family members congregated at the couple's home after the celebration, Lisa slipped away to check on Timmy. When she entered his room, she quickly realized he was not breathing. She screamed for help. Todd ran to her side. An ambulance was called, and chaos erupted. Rescue efforts were carried out nonetheless. Images of what was done to their son's body in attempts to revive him haunt Todd and Lisa still.

Several days later, Lisa and Todd learned that the cause of Timmy's death had been a very large, inoperable brain tumor and that nothing more could have been done for him. Still, Lisa was furious with Todd for not listening to her and trusting her instincts. Todd, in turn, felt guilty and helpless for not being able to save his son's life and for not stopping rescue efforts when he realized Timmy was already dead.

When death strikes a family, family members struggle collectively to make sense of what has happened. A family conversation begins. Members may agree with one another, disagree, ask questions, reference one another, and interrupt each other, sometimes changing the subject and sometimes finishing each other's sentences. Out of their conversations, threads of meaning start to emerge and, over time, these threads become woven into a tapestry of family meanings. The expression I use to capture the weaving together of meanings is *family meaning-making*. The term *meaning-making* was first used by Brunner (1990) nearly 2 decades ago. One meaning that Todd and Lisa made together early on was that Timmy's death had occurred because two emergency room physicians at two separate hospitals had failed to correctly diagnose their son. In other words, his death was preventable. Meanings can be as straightforward as the reason a death occurs—in this case, a misdiagnosis—or as complex as what a death means in a more existential sense.

A second meaning, born out of the couple's early tension-filled interactions, was that Timmy died because Todd had failed to do the right thing. They both believed that Todd, who had gone on the second trip to the emergency room without Lisa, should have insisted Timmy be kept in the hospital. The meaning: Timmy's death could have been prevented, if only. . . . Lisa was angry at Todd for not believing her when she had insisted that Timmy was more ill than anyone else believed. Todd felt guilty for not insisting that the rescue efforts be stopped as soon as he realized Timmy was dead and probably had been when Lisa found him. Although anger experienced by the bereaved can be projected onto anyone, this pattern of interaction was part of the couple's relationship well before Timmy's death and would prove to be integral to their grieving process. The complex mixture of grief and family dynamics is part of what makes grief a family affair.

Within the first few months, Todd and Lisa were able to make some positive sense of their son's death. Together, they construed Timmy's sudden and seemingly painless death as sparing him from the ravages of cancer treatment. They recited this meaning over and over in a litany-like manner as they retold the story of Timmy's dying. Construing Timmy's death this way, although it neutralized neither Lisa's anger at Todd nor Todd's feelings of guilt, seemed nevertheless to give them a modicum of comfort and in that way had an impact on the course and nature of their bereavement.

FAMILIES MAKING SENSE OF DEATH:
A MEANING-MAKING MODEL

The meanings that families make of their experiences are critical to understanding individual and family grief. Individual grief is profoundly shaped by the family context in which it occurs, and the grief of an individual often has profound effects on the family (Rosenblatt, 2002). Looking through a family meaning-making lens provides a greatly expanded view of the landscape of bereavement. Such an expanded view includes much of the data that are needed to deeply understand, accurately assess, and skillfully intervene with bereaved families. Furthermore, a family meaning-making model could provide the necessary scaffolding for future research on family grief and the articulation of individual and family meaning-making processes. In my opinion, meaning is at the core of family grief.

With each passing year, more researchers and scholars have addressed grief at the family systems level (Bowen, 1978; chap. 23, this volume; Gilbert, 1996, 2002; Kissane & Bloch, 2002; Murray, Toth, & Clinkinbeard, 2005; Paul & Grosser, 1965; Rosenblatt, 1983, 2000, 2002; Shapiro, 1994; Traylor, Hayslip, Kraminski, & York, 2003; Walsh & McGoldrick, 1991, 2004). They have studied a wide variety of family systems phenomena in bereaved families, but none have focused predominantly on family meanings and family meaning-making processes.

The purpose of this chapter is to present a family meaning-making model, demonstrate how grief therapists can use the model, and provide guidelines for future research to test the model. Drawing on my original research and clinical experience, the model posits that meanings are central to family grief and that meanings attached to a particular death affect bereavement outcomes. Using the family meaning-making model clinically requires that the therapist be able to think systemically, even when working with a single family member; has the skills required to work with multiple family members simultaneously; and is able to tolerate the expression of intense emotions.

PROBLEMS OF DEFINITION IN THE STUDY OF MEANING

Defining the meaning of the word *meaning* is difficult at best. Even in *Webster's New Collegiate Dictionary* (1981), it takes a long paragraph to define *meaning*. *Webster's* first definition is "the thing one intends to convey, especially by language" (p. 706). This definition is less than useful when one is studying meanings at the family level rather than the individual level. Therefore, for the purposes of this chapter and my research, on which it is based, *meanings* are defined as cognitive representations, held in the minds of family members, constructed in the context of the family, that symbolically represent various elements of reality. Meanings are products of interactions with others and are influenced by society, culture, and historical time (Nadeau, 1998).

Most of what has been written about meanings and meaning-making in bereavement has been written from an individual perspective. Researchers and scholars have focused on how individuals make sense of death, and the variables of interest have been primarily intrapersonal, intrapsychic, or cognitive. Although the focus of this chapter is on meaning-making at the family level, studies of meaning-making by individuals have implications for family-level studies. In the following paragraphs, I describe a sampling of research relevant to the development of the family meaning-making model.

Most studies of individual meaning-making processes relate meanings to bereavement outcome, but in the literature about meanings the terms *meaning* and *meaning-making* have been defined differently by various authors. Stroebe and Schut (2001a), who used the term *meaning making* in their title, stated that "how a person feels and reacts on becoming bereaved is dependent on the meaning that is assigned to the loss . . . but the problem remains that 'meaning' is a nebulous concept" (p. 56). Nearly a decade ago, Davis, Nolen-Hoeksema, and Larson (1998) argued that theoretical models of the postloss and trauma adjustment process have emphasized the critical role that finding meaning plays, but definitions of meaning have been too broad to facilitate an understanding of the psychological processes involved. They attempted to address the problem by narrowing their study to only two construals of meaning: (a) making sense of the event and (b) finding benefit in the experience (Davis et al., 1998).

More often than not, what is meant by *meaning* is searching for meaning or finding purpose in the event, as Frankl (1959) put forward in his classic book *Man's Search for Meaning*. This use limits *meaning* to only positive meaning. By contrast, when more substantive meanings are studied, such as those that families attach to a particular death, negative meanings are also found. One family in my bereavement study (Nadeau, 1998) construed their father's death as occurring because their mother failed to call an ambulance. Relationships in the family were strained, and members became more isolated from each other (Nadeau, 1998). Lisa and Todd, whose story is told at the beginning of this chapter, attached negative meanings to their son's death, initially construing Timmy's death as preventable. Lisa blamed Todd for not forcing the emergency room staff to admit Timmy and, perhaps even more damaging to the marriage, for not trusting her "mother's intuition." They entered grief therapy unable to stop attacking each other. Early therapy with this couple was more about the rift in their relationship than about their grief at the death of their son. It was not until several sessions later that they could calm themselves enough to tell the full story about Timmy's death. These examples demonstrate how negative meanings can result in more difficult or troubled bereavement (Nadeau, 1998, 2001a, 2001b, 2002, 2006).

Gamino and Sewell (2004), using the term *meaning constructs*, were among the very few who clearly identified negative meanings (constructs). They reported that focusing on negativity carried the strongest statistical relation to outcome measures and correlated with poor adjustment. By contrast, they found that the inability to make positive meanings predicts poorer outcomes in bereavement. Their study was retrospective; as a result, correlation, but not causality, could be demonstrated. For instance, individuals may have construed the death of a loved one more negatively because they were depressed. It seems, however, that the clinical reality remains the same whether negative meanings have their origin in preloss depression, originated at the time of the loss, or both. Bereaved individuals who present meanings that are negative warrant further evaluation.

Rosenblatt (2000) emphasized the prevalence of meaning-making in parental bereavement. In a narrative study of 29 couples who had experienced the death of a child, he found that "every parent narrative dealt with meaning-making related to the death" (p. 188). In a review of models of coping, Stroebe and Schut (2001b) noted that there was already a growing recognition of grief as a process of "meaning reconstruction," that bereaved people develop narratives, and that these social constructions can affect the outcome of grief.

Bonanno, Wortman, and Nesse (2004) used the term *searching for meaning*, and rather than focusing on the meanings themselves, they measured the degree to which the bereaved search for meaning. Those who did more searching had less favorable bereavement outcomes (see also chap. 14, this volume).

Neimeyer, a leading figure in postmodern, constructivist approaches to understanding bereavement, used the expression *meaning reconstruction* in his earlier work (Neimeyer, 2001) and *sense-making* in more recent publications (Neimeyer, 2005). Currier, Holland, and Neimeyer (2006), in a retrospective study, measured the degree of sense-making by 1,056 bereaved college students who had lost a friend or family member to various types of death. They found that sense-making explained the relationship between violent loss and complications in grief, suggesting that failure to find meaning in a loss was a better predictor of grief complications than were the circumstance of violent death.

There clearly is no agreed-on definition of the meaning of *meaning*. Each of the ways others have defined *meaning* seems to have been useful for their purposes. When discussing family meanings, however, the definition given earlier in this chapter seems to be the most appropriate.

FAMILY MEANING-MAKING IN BEREAVEMENT

Some researchers maintain that all meanings are created interactionally (Berger & Luckmann, 1966). Because families are primary milieus for social interaction, one could argue that they are also primary sources of meanings.

Patterson and Garwick (1994a) studied meanings in families coping with chronic illness. They conceptualized meanings as the coconstruction of family members, but they did not investigate the processes through which coconstruction occurs. They described family meanings as distinctly different from meanings held by family members and even different from consensus among family members.

Gudmundsdottir and Chesla's (2006) study revealed the most about family processes of meaning-making in bereavement. These researchers conducted an interpretive phenomenological study of grieving families in which they demonstrated how families make meaning by developing private family habits and practices to integrate their loss into everyday life. For example, one family constructed a memorial in their solarium window in memory of Agnes, their 21-month-old daughter, who had died suddenly. The family could view the clouds through the glass roof above the memorial. The clouds had special meaning to this family because their son, Norbert, had suggested that it was by riding upon the clouds that Agnes would accompany them in their move from Europe to the United States. This image enabled Anna, the mother, to leave Agnes's grave in Europe. She imagined Agnes out there on the clouds looking down on them. Through the practice of looking at the clouds and doing such things as keeping Agnes's chair at the table, this family said they were able to keep Agnes's spirit with them (Gudmundsdottir & Chesla, 2006).

In another example given by Gudmundsdottir and Chesla (2006), Christine and Bob, who had lost their firstborn daughter, Alice, kept her room just as it had been at the time of her death. Christine, for whom being a mother was self-defining, went into the room every day. Such things as the drawers still being filled with clothing and Alice's hair on the crib mattress assured Christine that she had been a mother. This practice continued until they had to prepare the room for their second child, 11 months later.

Gudmundsdottir and Chesla (2006) argued that the meaning of the death emerges from the cocreation of family narratives. They concluded that although most of the bereavement literature overwhelmingly emphasizes grief as an individual and intrapersonal phenomenon, grief is relational.

FAMILY MEANING-MAKING IN BEREAVEMENT: RESEARCH AND CLINICAL APPLICATION

Results from my family meaning-making study, subsequent research on meaning-making by others, and clinical inference from 30 years of experience working with grieving families have contributed to the evolution and application of the family meaning-making model as I present it in this chapter (Nadeau, 1998, 2001a, 2001b, 2002, 2006). Interpretations of research findings and their clinical applications presented here are speculative in nature. They invite the reader to consider what might be illuminated if families were seen through a meaning-making lens and how such a view suggests family-level assessment and interventions.

For me, interest in family meaning-making began years ago while I was working as an intensive care nurse and observing families attend their dying loved ones. In the 30 years since that time, as a hospice nurse, researcher, and marriage and family therapist, and through observing family members react and interact on receiving news of a death, I noticed that some patterns began to emerge. Family members would start almost immediately to struggle with the meaning of their experience. Over time, their conversations tended to sound like litanies, as they rehearsed the meaning phrases that emerged out of their interactions.

In a grounded theory study of meaning-making in family bereavement, members of 10 nonclinical, multigenerational families were interviewed both together and separately (Nadeau, 1998). Family systems theory provided a way to conceptualize family structure, and symbolic interaction theory provided a way to understand the relationship between mental and social processes. *Symbolic interaction theory* holds that if people define situations as real, then they are real in their consequences (Thomas, 1923). This theory would predict that if a grieving family believes that a death should not have happened, then the family's grief will have certain characteristics that are congruent with this belief. Characteristics might include feelings of anger, remorse, regret, and guilt and behaviors such as wanting to blame someone or seek revenge.

What emerged from audio recordings of 33 intensive interviews were data about sharing patterns among family members, strategies that families used in their attempt to make sense of their loss, factors that enhanced or inhibited meaning-making, and a typology of meanings constructed from sorting 250 meaning statements into 10 meaning classifications (Nadeau, 1998).

The findings included the conditions under which family members would be willing to share their experiences with each other. These included a willingness to listen, which lessened discomfort when sensitive issues were discussed (Nadeau, 1998). The clinical implications of these findings are that creating the necessary conditions could become therapy goals. Interventions that help families create a narrative about the death show promise for helping families make sense of their experience. It would seem that such interventions would be more easily implemented when the therapist has substantive data about a particular family.

Study families used six different strategies as they struggled to make sense of their loss: (a) telling their story, (b) telling about dreams, (c) characterizing the deceased, (d) comparing the death to other deaths, (e) "coincidancing," and (f) using "family speak" (Nadeau, 1998). *Coincidancing* is an expression used to capture how families attributed meaning to coincidences, and *family speak* is a descriptor used for the ordinary ways that family members conversed by agreeing, disagreeing, elaborating, questioning, referring to what others said, interrupting, and finishing each other's sentences. In a clinical context, these six strategies can be used in three ways: (a) to reveal family dynamics related to meaning-making, (b) to reveal the meanings themselves, and (c) as catalysts in the meaning-making process. Strategies reveal meanings when families use them spontaneously and when the therapist enlists them to encourage the family conversation.

For example, one of the families reported how the sun had come out just long enough for them to have a graveside service and lower their mother/grandmother into the ground (Nadeau, 1998). When asked what they made of this, they responded that it was either their deceased mother or God who caused the sun to come out. The term *coincidancing* was used to capture this strategy; that is, the family made something of co-occurring, seemingly unexplainable events. Families interacted in ways around coincidental events that were dance like. In a clinical setting, the strategy of coincidancing can be used by asking the family as a whole whether they noticed any "so-called coincidences" surrounding the death. Their answers reveal their meaning system and can stimulate the family conversation, which helps them tell their story.

Each of the study families used two other strategies: (a) characterization and (b) comparison (Nadeau, 1998). Families were asked what the person who died was like. These descriptions can be used clinically to discover important meanings. One example was a family whose member died in a much-publicized airplane crash. They said that if he had to die, he would have loved that he had a front-page spread in the newspaper.

All of the study families made meaning by comparing the death of their loved one with other deaths (Nadeau, 1998). Doing so revealed their view of the nature of the loss, which in the case of violent deaths differed greatly from the media spin. In my clinical experience, even families who have difficulty developing a coherent narrative of their loss can respond easily to a question asking them to compare the death of their family member with the deaths of others.

In one sense, all the other five strategies found in the study can be used clinically to help families tell their story (Nadeau, 1998). The strategy of telling the story as a component of narrative therapy is discussed later in this chapter. The strategy referred to as *family speak* reveals patterns of meaning among and between family members. For instance, when a family member agrees repeatedly with another member and consistently disagrees with other family members, this gives the therapist information about subsystems of meaning and about family structural characteristics, such as alliances between members. In my bereavement study, subsystems of family members were found to create their own meanings and in so doing appeared to be reinforcing subsystem boundaries. Information about family subsystems can be immensely helpful as therapy progresses and the family attempts to restructure.

Study findings also included factors that had either inhibited or stimulated family meaning-making (Nadeau, 1998). Inhibitors included family rules that prohibited talking about sensitive issues; physical and emotional distance; lack of family rituals; and *protectionism*, which meant protecting others in the family by not talking about the death. One or more of these factors of inhibition and stimulation could be used as the focus of intervention. Family-specific interventions might include helping family members learn to talk about sensitive issues in session and encouraging families to develop rituals that bring them together both emotionally and physically and reduce the need to protect one another by not talking about the loss.

Factors that acted as stimulators of meaning-making in study families included the death of a young family member, a traumatic death, or an unexpected death; family rituals; the presence of in-laws; tolerance for differences among family members; frequent interactions; and the interview itself (Nadeau, 1998). Although nothing can be done about the nature of the death (the role of ritual was discussed earlier), the other stimulators suggest interventions. Supporting tolerance for differences among family members can be both modeled and endorsed in sessions. Of particular use is inviting additional family members to the session as consultants to the therapeutic process. On the basis of both research and clinical observations, it seems that in-laws help stimulate meaning because they are not subject to the family rules that may inhibit the rest of the family. In addition, if the in-laws are unfamiliar with the family history, they can ask innocent questions with impunity.

In my family meaning-making study (Nadeau, 1998) a content analysis of the transcribed interview data netted 10 types of meanings, many of which have been reported by other researchers. Three types of meanings in the typology were more abstract in nature: (a) the philosophical, (b) the religious, and (c) those about the afterlife. These correspond roughly to the "global meanings" as reported by Patterson and Garwick (1994b) and Benore and Park (2004).

Two types of meanings from this study represented what Calhoun and Tedeschi (2001) and Tedeschi and Calhoun (2004) have described as *posttraumatic growth*. In my study, growth was expressed as "lessons learned," "truths realized," and "how our family changed" (Nadeau, 1998). Nine out of 10 families reported some positive change. Growth meanings were expressed in families in juxtaposition to negative meanings, regardless of the type of death.

Four of the 10 types of meaning included negative meanings: (a) the death was preventable, (b) the death was unfair or unjust, (c) no sense could be made of the death, and (d) what the death did not mean (Nadeau, 1998). Gamino and Sewell (2004) found that half of their 9 meaning categories were negative. Because both Gamino and Sewell's study and my family meaning-making study were retrospective, there is no way to know whether the negative meanings were made because of preloss factors, such as depression, or whether the negativity was a function of the death event itself.

When one is working clinically within the family meaning-making model, negative meanings can be seen as red flags that predict potential difficulty and a greater need for intervention. The exact nature of negative meanings can reveal nuances of family meaning and glitches in family meaning-making efforts. For example, Lisa and Todd's story, told at the start of this chapter, had at least four negative meanings attached to the death of their son: (a) Timmy had not been diagnosed correctly at two emergency rooms, (b) Todd should have insisted Timmy be held at the hospital, (c) Todd felt guilty for not stopping rescue attempts sooner, and (d) Todd should have trusted Lisa when her mother's intuition told her Timmy was more ill than anyone else thought. These meanings became the focus of therapy.

The process of making negative meanings appears to be different from saying there is no meaning to be made. Negative meanings can be clearly stated as meanings. In my family meaning-making study (Nadeau, 1998) and in my clinical practice, if family members said that there was no sense to be made, they were unable to assign a meaning, but they still carried on their search. One could hypothesize that family grief intervention could have its greatest effect around negative meanings or the failure to engage in meaning-making.

Perhaps one of the most useful findings of my study, and one that has implications for further research and the continued development of the family meaning-making model, was the collection of statements about what the deaths of loved ones did *not* mean (Nadeau, 1998). Statements about what the death did not mean were different from saying there was no meaning to be found or that the family could not find meaning. "Not" statements had content, whereas statements that they could not find meaning was more about the process of searching. It seemed that by using "not" statements, families were cutting their way through the jungle of possible interpretations, casting aside those that did not fit on their way to finding some meaning that they would not cast aside. "I know that it was not God's will," one family member proclaimed emphatically. It is interesting to note that "not" statements were made only in families who experienced sudden, unexpected deaths of younger family members.

The study concluded with my contention, yet to be tested, that a family's ability to engage in meaning-making and the nature of the meanings that families coconstruct are powerful determinants of how they will grieve and how well they will adapt to their loss (Nadeau, 1998).

USE OF THE FAMILY MEANING-MAKING MODEL FOR ASSESSMENT AND INTERVENTION

Family grief therapy differs from ordinary family therapy in at least one important way: In traditional family therapy, the therapist enters the family system in such a way as to perturb or stir up the system, making change possible; in contrast, in family grief therapy the family system is already perturbed by the loss of one of its members. The therapist's role can therefore be conceptualized as helping the perturbed family system to settle into the highest level of organization possible, including the potential for a higher level of organization than their preloss state. Because both types of family therapy start at the point of perturbation, many family therapy techniques can be adapted to family grief therapy. In fact, many of the traditional family therapy methods mirror the natural strategies families use to make sense of their loss (Nadeau, 1998, 2001a, 2001b). In the following sections, I describe therapeutic techniques that are well established within the field of psychotherapy and family therapy. What I describe here is the application of such techniques to grieving families in ways that I have found support productive family meaning-making in the face of loss.

Narrative Therapy

The most common strategy used by families to make sense of a death in the family is to tell their story. They cocreate a narrative about the time before, during, and after the death (Nadeau, 1998). Gilbert (2002), using narrative as a research method, commented that "We need to create stories to make order out of the disorder and to find meaning in the meaningless . . . we make meaning and create stories in the context of real and imagined relationships" (pp. 236, 226). There are many ways to facilitate the cocreation of a family's story. Narrative family therapy was made popular largely through the efforts of White and Epston (1990) almost 2 decades ago. It capitalizes on grieving families' inclinations to use storytelling as their main strategy (Nadeau, 1998). In narrative therapy, the story is treated as the basic unit of experience and serves to guide people in making sense of new experiences. It involves unearthing stories, understanding them, and retelling them (Sween, 1998). From a family meaning-making perspective, the focus is on how unearthing, understanding, and retelling stories occur at the family level and how these processes can be supported or engendered.

One could hypothesize that any intervention that encourages family members to tell their story has the potential to be helpful to families. Clinically speaking, the idea is to set up a therapeutic environment in which family members can "forget themselves" and tell their story, much as they would outside of formal settings and in their natural environment. Embedded in the family story are the meanings, both positive and negative, that the family has attached to a particular death. Meaning-making, according to O'Connor (2002–2003), is a bridge from negative emotion caused by negative life events to positive emotion. The ability to create positive meanings can be seen as an indicator of family resilience.

Meanings that the therapist can glean from the family story can be important to ongoing assessment and intervention. For example, troublesome meanings, such as believing that the death was the fault of someone in the family or that the death could have been prevented by someone in the family, deserve careful attention. Such powerfully negative meanings could alert helpers to the possibility of a difficult bereavement. In my own clinical experience, families in which members tend to handle stress by blaming or shaming one another will do so more intensely in the wake of a family member's death. In some cases, it can be shown that someone in the family was responsible for the death. One such situation of which I am aware was a farm accident in which a father ran over his stepson with a tractor. The parents' marriage was seriously challenged, and the couple struggled for years, wrestling with feelings of blame and guilt and searching for ways to live with the reality of what had happened.

Although family meanings are important data, the ways families tell their stories are equally important. Monitoring family dynamics as the story is told can help the therapist see family patterns that may prevent the family from being successful in their meaning-making attempts. Clinicians and researchers have shown increasing interest in family narratives as an avenue for assessing family meaning-making processes (Fiese & Wamboldt, 2003). Family grief therapy from a meaning-making perspective includes interventions that are tailor made to help correct interactive patterns that prevent successful construction of a family narrative, such as one member dominating the narrative, shy members not speaking up, or intolerance for disagreement among members.

In my clinical opinion, it is best to use the technique of *pacing* rather than leading when working with grieving families. In pacing, the therapist lets the family take the lead while he or she listens attentively, using nonverbal cues. On the other hand, it is not always wise to give the family free reign in telling their story. When a family's communication patterns are significantly dysfunctional or when the family story is overwhelmingly painful, the therapist may need to lead more and pace less. For example, the therapist may need to slow down or stop the storytelling if family members show signs of becoming overwhelmed. By the same token, if the storytelling stalls, the therapist may need to use probes to energize the narration.

Milan Family Therapy

The essential components of Milan family therapy (MFT) lend themselves well to helping bereaved families make sense of loss. MFT was developed originally in the mid-1970s by Selvini, Boscolo, Cecchin, and Prata in Milan, Italy (Boscolo, Cecchin, Hoffman, & Penn, 1987). Milan Family Therapy, with its focus on meanings and circular questioning, has been taught for 2 decades as a viable family therapy method. Although the popularity of MFT is not what it was in the late 1970s and 1980s, *circular questioning*, the central technique of MFT was further articulated by Karl Tomm (1998) and subsequently used with diverse populations, ranging from individuals with schizophrenia to troubled adolescents to Southeast Asian refugees (Bertrando et al., 2006; Kalinyak & Jones, 1999; Kelley, 1992).

MFT is useful in grief therapy for two main reasons: (a) its focus on meanings more than on behaviors and (b) its main therapeutic technique of circular questioning. Circular questioning enables therapists to collect family meanings, uncover differences among family members, and track family meanings over time. For instance, the therapist might ask a question such as, "How does your family think of your father's death?" As various family members answer, differences among members can be detected. As the family provides information, the therapist looks for openings or clues dropped by the family and, using this information, "circles" back to the family with further questions. All circular questions are about differences (Boscolo et al., 1987; Tomm, 1998).

To detect differences over time, the therapist might ask questions such as "How has the way that you think of your father's death changed since he first died?" or "How do you think it will change in the future?" It is important that the questions are directed to the family as a whole and not to any one family member. This allows the therapist to notice such things as who answers first, who chimes in, and who remains silent. When using the family meaning-making model, the clinician is interested not only in the meanings themselves but also in the processes by which the family coconstructs meanings. The therapist searches for information about the family system, changes over time, and relatedness among members (Boscolo et al., 1987). The meanings that a particular family attaches to a death at any given point in time can be treated as assessment data, and the problems a given family has in their attempts at meaning-making can become the focus of family intervention.

METAPHORS AND MEANING-MAKING

Metaphors found in the family narrative are a rich source of meanings. Metaphors are a medium through which meaning is expressed and by which new meanings are made. The bereaved often speak metaphorically about their grief, and therapists can use these metaphors to help families make sense of their loss (Nadeau, 2006).

Lakoff and Johnson (1980), in their classic book *Metaphors We Live By*, defined *metaphors* as "understanding and experiencing one kind of thing in terms of another" (p. 5). A metaphor is more than a device of poetic imagination and rhetorical flourish, and it is more than a characteristic of language alone. Metaphors structure how we perceive, how we think, and what we do. If Lakoff and Johnson are correct in their assertions, then one could hypothesize that metaphors used by families in the wake of a family death structure how the death is seen, how family members think about it, and how they will grieve.

Postmodern constructivist and narrative models of therapy rely heavily on metaphors as a means of meaning construction. Neimeyer (2005) views meaning reconstruction as the principal task of coping with loss. He asserted that new constructivist models and metaphors have the power to enhance counseling and psychotherapy with the bereaved. When working from a family meaning-making perspective, metaphors can be used in at least four ways: (a) Metaphors reveal meanings as they are initially expressed (Pardess, 2004; Rosenblatt, 2000), (b) metaphors can be extended or reworked to help a family consider alternative meanings (Neimeyer, 2005), (c) metaphors can be solicited by the therapist, (d) and metaphors can be acted out by the family to help them see themselves differently (Papp, 1983).

Family members are not always able to express meanings directly. Expression through metaphor provides a way of conveying something that is known at some level but cannot be expressed otherwise (Nadeau, 2006). In some instances, family members are unable or unwilling to give information directly (Rosenblatt, 1983). Drawing from his study of bereaved parents, Rosenblatt (2000) commented that "the key to understanding how feelings shape and are integral to parent narratives is to look at the metaphoric nature of the words parents use to talk about feelings" (p. 75). Metaphors are offered to the unconscious mind while the conscious mind remains unaware of what is going on; it thinks the conversation is about the content of the metaphor (Barker, 1985). By listening for metaphors, therapists may hear meanings that they might otherwise miss (Nadeau, 2006).

An extremely important consideration, and one that is seldom mentioned in the literature, is how to think critically about metaphors. (For a thorough discussion of the use of metaphors in grief therapy, see Nadeau, 2006.) Lakoff and Johnson (1980) emphasized the fact that although metaphors illuminate certain realities, they also obscure certain alternative realities. To use metaphors to their fullest advantage clinically, the therapist must in some ongoing way analyze metaphors as they emerge. Lakoff and Johnson suggested asking what a given metaphor illuminates, what it obscures, and what therapeutic implications it has. For example, Emily, an articulate woman in her late 50s and chief executive officer of a large company, sought help in coping with her husband's rapidly failing health and impending death. In her effort to describe their experience, she said, "We see his lymphoma as a monster that sleeps by our bed at night and, if we are lucky, it sleeps awhile in the morning before it starts clamoring to be fed. Then the rest of the day we are forced to feed it."

The use of the term *monster* illuminates how Emily and her husband, Ben, experienced the lymphoma as a terrible threat: frightening, dangerous, and insatiable. The monster lymphoma was devouring life as they had known it and literally eating up her husband's body. By using this metaphor, Emily indirectly revealed knowing that they would eventually lose the battle against the cancer. The best they could hope for was to keep it at bay for a few hours during the night. By construing the cancer as a monster, they found a way to externalize the disease and gain some respite. The fact that they could construct such a metaphor together provided data about the strength and nature of their coping skills based on their ability to coconstruct such a meaning.

When there are references to a metaphor in subsequent sessions, clients tend to elaborate, expanding their original meaning, sometimes revealing movement that they have made since the previous session (Nadeau, 2006). The monster metaphor in its original form provided a way for me to empathize with Emily about the terrifying nature of their situation and to acknowledge how skilled she and her husband were at coping—skilled enough to find a way to sleep in spite of the monster's presence. Shortly after Emily used the monster metaphor, her husband died. When Emily was asked for permission to use her monster metaphor in this chapter, she gladly assented and spontaneously expanded the metaphor by saying that at least there was one good thing about Ben's death: The monster was dead, too.

Metaphors can be useful in grief therapy because they reveal how the loss is being construed over time. Change in meanings in the positive direction can indicate progress. Metaphors that have an obvious positive effect on clients can be recalled as touchstones when the going gets rough (Nadeau, 2006).

Therapeutic use of metaphors is not without risks. Metaphors can be easily misinterpreted, not heard, or not understood by some family members. They can also be extended or reworked too soon, overwhelming the family. Therapists who use metaphors to help families make sense of their experience need to develop a trained ear, be aware of risks, and act in ways to reduce the potential harm (Nadeau, 2006).

FUTURE RESEARCH QUESTIONS AND GUIDELINES

In a broad sweep of the current literature, I found no efficacy studies of a family meaning-making approach to grief therapy. The fact that the family meaning-making approach has not been tested in any systematic way raises certain questions. For instance, one might ask whether a therapist should use an intervention that is not standardized and has not empirically been shown to be effective. Is doing so ethical, and can it be justified to third-party payers? Although it is true that the family meaning-making approach has not been tested as a model in its own right, its components have been used extensively in more standardized approaches to individual and family psychotherapy. Narrative therapy and MFT are well recognized in the psychotherapy field and have been used for a variety of individual and family problems. Narrative therapy, although generally thought of as an individual rather than a family approach, is easily adapted to families; in narrative therapy it is the story that is manipulated, not individual behaviors. Coconstructing a family story about a death is one of the main strategies grieving families use to make sense of their experience (Nadeau, 1998, 2001a, 2001b, 2006).

MFT has been in existence as a systemic family therapy model for more than 3 decades. Its primary intervention technique, circular questioning, is the component of the model that I recommend here as a viable family meaning-making method; it also is the component of the model that is most highly refined and used in couple and family therapy (Tomm, 1998).

Metaphors are part of everyday speech. In the practice of general psychotherapy, metaphors are used as a means of getting around resistance; tapping into more unconscious data; and, in some instances, serving as a cognitive behavioral technique to challenge irrational thoughts (Nadeau, 2006).

A significant amount of work needs to be done on the family meaning-making approach before it can be treated as a model in its own right. What I have described in this chapter is largely speculative and based on my own research and clinical experience (Nadeau, 1998, 2001a, 2001b, 2006). Future work needs to include the elaboration of its theoretical underpinnings, definition of terms, articulation of its assumptions, specification and standardization of family-level assessment and interventions, determination of requisite practitioner skills, and establishment of its effectiveness.

Future research on family meaning-making needs to address the relationships between and among preloss family variables, family meaning-making processes, particular meanings, and the relationship of meanings to bereavement outcomes. Family meaning-making research needs to be systemic, to treat families rather than individuals as the units of analysis, and to consider context. It will also be important to include multiple family members across generations. According to Walsh and McGoldrick (2004), "Legacies of loss find expression in continuing patterns and mutual influence among the survivors, across the generations, and over the life cycle" (p. 6).

Several technical details about family meaning-making research merit attention. The richness of family data is increased by interviewing family members both together and separately. Comparisons between the individual and family data can then be made. It appears that people say different things depending on who is present in the interview (Gudmundsdottir & Chesla, 2006; Nadeau, 1998).

Interviewing the family before interviewing individual members seems to improve the quality and quantity of data. People say things in individual interviews that they would not say with other family members present. If the family interview follows the individual interviews, then members are less at ease, perhaps fearing that the interviewer may reveal something that they would not want other family members to hear (Nadeau, 1998).

We need to know much more about why some families are successful at construing a death positively, even a violent death, whereas others are not (Gamino & Sewell, 2004). If those who make positive meanings fare better in bereavement (Currier et al., 2006), then perhaps the focus of family grief therapy should be on identifying the mechanisms that lead to negative meaning-making and finding ways of helping families develop ways of construing a death more positively.

Some of the many unanswered research questions that pertain to family meaning-making in bereavement are as follows: How do various meanings affect bereavement? How do meanings change over time? How do ethnic and cultural factors affect both the process and products of family meaning-making? How do meaning-making processes differ depending on family configuration? What is the relationship between attachment style and family meaning-making process and products? How is the meaning-making process different depending on characteristics of the death, such as when it is sudden, violent, from AIDS, from sudden infant death syndrome, or from suicide or homicide? How is meaning-making different depending on the age of the deceased, when multiple family members die at once, or when a family member is responsible for the death? How is it different depending on the role of and the family's relationship with the deceased family member? Are family meaning-making processes similar for other losses, such as divorce, disaster, chronic illness, and wartime deaths? What is the relationship between meanings or meaning-making processes and family variables over time? Finally, how is the meaning-making process affected by the family developmental stage?

All of these questions and more remain unanswered, and they are obviously beyond the scope of this chapter. The purpose of this chapter has been to present a family meaning-making approach to grief therapy, to demonstrate how grief therapists could use this approach, and to provide guidelines for future research to test its effectiveness. Although interpretations of research findings and their clinical applications presented here are speculative in nature, they show great promise. The reader is invited to consider what might be illuminated if families were seen through a meaning-making lens and how such a view can suggest family-level assessment and interventions.

The family meaning-making approach that this view affords is congruent with postmodern constructionist trends that emphasize the importance of meaning and the role meaning plays in bereavement. Furthermore, the family meaning-making approach could provide the necessary scaffolding for future research on family grief and the articulation of individual and family meaning-making processes. For this approach to become a model in its own right, more theoretical work and systematic testing are needed. Future work needs to be systemic, multigenerational, longitudinal, multimethod, multicultural, and ethnically diverse.

This model, which draws on my own original research and clinical experience, posits that meanings are central to family grief and that meanings attached to a particular death significantly affect bereavement outcomes. It is my belief that as research progresses, family meanings and meaning-making processes will emerge as essential to understanding grieving families, assessing the need for intervention, and devising interventions that are both appropriate and effective.

REFERENCES

Barker, P. (1985). *Using metaphors in psychotherapy*. New York: Brunner/Mazel.

Benore, R. B., & Park, C. L. (2004). Death-specific religious beliefs and bereavement: Belief in an afterlife and continued attachment. *International Journal for the Psychology of Religion, 14*, 1–22.

Berger, P. L., & Luckmann, T. (1966). *The social construction of reality*. Garden City, NY: Doubleday.

Bertrando, P., Cecchin, G., Clerici, M., Beltz, J., Milesi, A., & Cazzullo, C. (2006). Expressed emotion and Milan systemic intervention: A pilot study on families of people with a diagnosis of schizophrenia. *Journal of Family Therapy, 28*, 81–102.

Bonanno, G. A., Wortman, C. B., & Nesse, R. M. (2004). Prospective patterns of resilience and maladjustment during widowhood. *Psychology and Aging, 19*, 260–270.

Boscolo, L., Cecchin, G., Hoffman, L., & Penn, P. (1987). *Milan systemic family therapy*. New York: Basic Books.

Bowen, M. (1978). *Family therapy in clinical practice*. New York: Jason Aronson.

Brunner, J. (1990). *Acts of meaning*. Cambridge, MA: Harvard University Press.

Calhoun, L. G., & Tedeschi, R. G. (2001). Posttraumatic growth: The positive lessons of loss. In R. A. Neimeyer (Ed.), *Meaning reconstruction and the experience of loss* (pp. 157–172). Washington, DC: American Psychological Association.

Currier, J. M., Holland, J. M., & Neimeyer, R. A. (2006). Sense-making, grief, and the experience of violent loss: Toward a mediational model. *Death Studies, 30*, 403–428.

Davis, C. G., Nolen-Hoeksema, S., & Larson, J. (1998). Making sense of loss and benefiting from the experience: Two construals of meaning. *Journal of Personality and Social Psychology, 75*, 561–574.

Fiese, B. H., & Wamboldt, F. S. (2003). Coherent accounts of coping with a chronic illness: Convergence and divergence in family measurement using a narrative analysis. *Family Process, 42*, 439–451.

Frankl, V. E. (1959). *Man's search for meaning*. New York: Washington Square.

Gamino, L. A., & Sewell, K. W. (2004). Meaning constructs as predictors of bereavement adjustment: A report from the Scott & White Grief Study. *Death Studies, 28,* 397–421.

Gilbert, K. R. (1996). "We've had the same loss, why don't we have the same grief?" Loss and differential grief in families. *Death Studies, 20,* 269–283.

Gilbert, K. R. (2002). Taking a narrative approach to grief research: Finding meaning in stories. *Death Studies, 26,* 223–239.

Gudmundsdottir, M., & Chesla, C. A. (2006). Building a new world: Habits and practices of healing following the death of a child. *Journal of Family Nursing, 12,* 143–164.

Kalinyak, C. M., & Jones, S. L. (1999). Appropriately timed interventions with the family and the adolescent: The role of the therapist. *Issues in Mental Health Nursing, 20,* 459–472.

Kelley, P. (1992). The application of family systems theory to mental health services for Southeast Asian refugees. *Journal of Multicultural Social Work, 2,* 1–13.

Kissane, D. W., & Bloch, S. (2002). *Family focused grief therapy*. Buckingham, England: Open University Press.

Lakoff, G., & Johnson, M. (1980). *Metaphors we live by*. Chicago: University of Chicago Press.

Murray, C. I., Toth, K., & Clinkinbeard, S. S. (2005). Death, dying and grief in families. In P. C. McKenry & S. J. Price (Eds.), *Families and change: Coping with stressful events and transitions* (pp. 75–102). Thousand Oaks, CA: Sage.

Nadeau, J. W. (1998). *Families making sense of death*. Thousand Oaks, CA: Sage.

Nadeau, J. W. (2001a). Family construction of meaning. In R. A. Neimeyer (Ed.), *Meaning reconstruction and the experience of loss* (pp. 95–111). Washington, DC: American Psychological Association.

Nadeau, J. W. (2001b). Meaning making in family bereavement: A family systems approach. In M. S. Stroebe, R. O. Hansson, W. Stroebe, & H. Schut (Eds.), *Handbook of bereavement research: Consequences, coping, and care* (pp. 329–347). Washington, DC: American Psychological Association.

Nadeau, J. W. (2002). Counseling later-life families. In K. J. Doka (Ed.), *Loss in later life* (pp. 313–327). Washington, DC: Hospice Foundation of America.

Nadeau, J. W. (2006). Metaphorically speaking: The use of metaphors in grief therapy. *Illness, Crisis & Loss, 14,* 201–222.

Neimeyer, R. A. (Ed.). (2001). *Meaning reconstruction and the experience of loss*. Washington, DC: American Psychological Association.

Neimeyer, R. A. (2005). Grief, loss, and the quest for meaning: Narrative contributions to bereavement care. *Bereavement Care, 24,* 27–30.

O'Connor, M.-F. (2002–2003). Making meaning of life events: Theory, evidence, and research directions for an alternative model. *Omega: The Journal of Death and Dying, 46,* 51–75.

Papp, P. (1983). *The process of change*. New York: Guilford Press.

Pardess, E. (2004, December). *Harnessing the power of metaphors in group-work with bereaved families*. Paper presented at the Third Global Conference on Making Sense of Death and Dying, Vienna, Austria. Retrieved December 15, 2006, from http://www.inter-disciplinary.net/mso/dd/dd3/pardess%20paper.pdf

Patterson, J. M., & Garwick, A. M. (1994a). The impact of chronic illness on families: A family systems perspective. *Annals of Behavioral Medicine, 16*, 131–142.

Patterson, J. M., & Garwick, A. M. (1994b). Theoretical linkages: Family meanings and sense of coherence. In H. I. McCubbin, E. A. Thompson, A. I. Thompson, & J. E. Fromer (Eds.), *Stress, coping and health in families: Sense of coherence and resiliency* (pp. 71–89). Thousand Oaks, CA: Sage.

Paul, N., & Grosser, G. (1965). Operational mourning and its role in conjoint family therapy. *Community Mental Health Journal, 1*, 339–345.

Rosenblatt, P. C. (1983). *Bitter, bitter tears*. Minneapolis: University of Minnesota Press.

Rosenblatt, P. C. (2000). *Parent grief: Narratives of loss and relationship*. Philadelphia: Brunner/Mazel.

Rosenblatt, P. C. (2002). Grief in families. *Mortality, 7*, 125–126.

Shapiro, E. R. (1994). *Grief as a family process: A developmental approach to clinical practice*. New York: Guilford Press.

Stroebe, M., & Schut, H. (2001a). Meaning making in the dual process model. In R. Neimeyer (Ed.), *Meaning reconstruction and the experience of loss* (pp. 55–73). Washington, DC: American Psychological Association.

Stroebe, M. S., & Schut, H. (2001b). Models of coping with bereavement: A review. In M. S. Stroebe, R. O. Hansson, W. Stroebe, & H. Schut (Eds.), *Handbook of bereavement: Consequences, coping, and care* (pp. 375–403). Washington, DC: American Psychological Association.

Sween, E. (1998). One-minute question: What is narrative therapy? Some working answers. *Gecko, 2*. Retrieved January 9, 2008, from http://www.narrativespace.com/sween.html

Tedeschi, R. G., & Calhoun, L. G. (2004). Posttraumatic growth: Conceptual foundations and empirical evidence. *Psychological Inquiry, 15*, 1–18.

Thomas, W. I. (1923). *The unadjusted girl*. Boston: Little, Brown.

Tomm, K. (1998). Interventive interviewing, Part III: Intending to ask linear, circular, strategic or reflexive questions. *Family Process, 27*, 1–15.

Traylor, E. S., Hayslip, B., Kraminski, P. L., & York, C. (2003). Relationships between grief and family system characteristics: A cross lagged longitudinal analysis. *Death Studies, 27*, 575–601.

Walsh, F., & McGoldrick, M. (Eds.). (1991). *Living beyond loss: Death in the family*. New York: Norton.

Walsh, F., & McGoldrick, M. (Eds.). (2004). *Living beyond loss: Death in the family* (2nd ed.). New York: Norton.

Webster's new collegiate dictionary. (1981). Springfield, MA: Miriam.

White, M., & Epston, D. (1990). *Narrative means to therapeutic ends*. New York: Norton.

25

LINKING THEORY AND INTERVENTION TO PROMOTE RESILIENCE IN PARENTALLY BEREAVED CHILDREN

IRWIN N. SANDLER, SHARLENE A. WOLCHIK, TIM S. AYERS, JENN-YUN TEIN, STEFANY COXE, AND WAI CHOW

In this chapter, we describe the development and evaluation of the Family Bereavement Program (FBP), a theoretically derived intervention program for children who have experienced parental death. We first present a discussion of risk and protective factors for parentally bereaved children and discuss these within a general theoretical framework of resilience following adversity. We then discuss the modifiable risk and protective factors that were targeted for change in the FBP and the theoretical model underlying the program. Finally, we present evidence from the evaluation of the FBP, including assessment of mediators and moderators of program effects at posttest and short-term follow-up and findings from preliminary analyses at the 6-year follow-up. This research on a theoretically based intervention for bereaved children follows a similar program of research we have conducted with children from divorced families, and we discuss ways in which the findings with bereaved children replicate, and in some cases diverge from, findings regarding children in divorced families.

This chapter was partially funded by National Institute of Mental Health Grant 1P30 MH068685 to establish an Advanced Center for Intervention and Services Research at Arizona State University and Grant 2R01 MH49155-06 to conduct a 6-year follow-up of a preventive intervention for bereaved families.

CONTEXTUAL RESILIENCE MODEL AS A FRAMEWORK FOR IDENTIFICATION OF RISK AND PROTECTIVE FACTORS FOR PARENTALLY BEREAVED CHILDREN

Sandler, Wolchik, and Ayers (2008) described a contextual resilience model as a framework for conceptualizing the adaptation of children following major disruptions such as parental death or divorce. Although we will not repeat the details of this model here, several aspects of the model have important implications for the identification of risk and protective factors to target in intervention programs. First is the proposition that the effects of adversities, such as parental bereavement, on children's functioning can be accounted for by how well children adapt to the disruptions and restructuring of their environments after the death. Theoretically, these disruptions affect children's ability to satisfy basic needs (e.g., needs for esteem, social connectedness, and control) and their success in age-salient developmental tasks, which in turn affect their well-being (Sandler, 2001). Second, we are concerned with multiple aspects of functioning, including problem outcomes (e.g., mental health problems, problematic levels of grief) and positive outcomes (e.g., positive sense of self). Bereaved children who achieve high levels of competence and low levels of problems are considered to be resilient. The third aspect is that resilience is determined by multiple risk and protective factors that have a cumulative effect (Wyman, Sandler, Wolchik, & Nelson, 2000). Therefore, programs to promote resilience should target multiple risk and protective factors. On the basis of this conceptual framework, we and our colleagues have developed and evaluated separate programs to promote resilience for children following parental death (the FBP) and parental divorce (the New Beginnings Program [NBP]). We briefly summarize the NBP in the following paragraphs (for more detailed summaries see Sandler et al., 2003, 2008; Wolchik, Sandler, Weiss, & Winslow, 2007). In this chapter, we focus primarily on the development and evaluation of the FBP, and then we compare findings across our studies of children who have experienced these two major family disruptions.

The NBP was designed to change multiple risk and protective factors for children from divorced homes. The risk and protective factors were at the level of the family (e.g., parental warmth and discipline) and at the level of the individual child (e.g., coping). A parenting program for custodial mothers (NBP) and a child coping program were designed to change each of these factors and was subject to evaluation using a randomized experimental design. Four important findings have emerged from this study to date:

1. The NBP was successful in improving multiple risk and protective factors in the short term, most particularly parental warmth and discipline.
2. The NBP was successful in reducing externalizing problems over the first 6 months following program participation and in reduc-

ing a wide range of negative outcomes 6 years later, including diagnosed mental disorder, internalizing and externalizing problems, substance use, high-risk sexual behavior, self-esteem, and low grade-point averages.

3. The effects of the NBP on mental health outcomes were mediated by improvements in internalizing and externalizing problems (Tein, Sandler, MacKinnon, & Wolchik, 2004).

4. The effects of the NBP were stronger for the children whose families were at higher risk at the time they entered the program, which was assessed by the level of child externalizing problems and a composite index of divorce adversity (e.g., interparental conflict, negative events).

RISK AND PROTECTIVE FACTORS FOR PARENTALLY BEREAVED CHILDREN

Distinction Between Modifiable and Nonmodifiable Risk Factors

Kraemer et al. (1997) described a typology of risk and protective factors that is very useful for considering their implications for the development of theory-based interventions. In this typology, risk and protective factors that cannot be changed by an intervention such as gender, age, or cause of death are referred to as *fixed markers*. Fixed marker risk factors may be useful for identifying children or families with differential need for or ability to benefit from an intervention. For example, recent reviews of the effects of interventions for the bereaved have proposed that those who experience traumatic deaths or have higher levels of problems are more likely to benefit from intervention programs (Jordan & Neimeyer, 2003; Schut, Stroebe, van den Bout, & Terheggen, 2001), and several studies have proposed that adult men and women benefit differentially from intervention programs (Schut et al., 2001).

Risk and protective factors that can be changed by an intervention and can have effects on the outcomes targeted by the intervention are considered *causal risk factors*. From this perspective, the best evidence for a causal risk or protective factor is the demonstration in a randomized trial that a program changes a risk or protective factor and targeted outcomes and by a mediational analysis that shows that program-induced change in the risk or protective factor accounts for change in the targeted outcome.

Nonmodifiable Risk Factors for Parentally Bereaved Children: Possible Moderators of Program Impact

As noted earlier, several reviews of the effects of programs for the bereaved have found stronger program effect sizes for individuals who experienced higher levels of problems at program entry (Jordan & Neimeyer, 2003; Schut et al., 2001). Consistent with this, we have found that our intervention for children from divorced families was more effective for those who had more problems and higher levels of adversity when they entered the program (Dawson-McClure, Sandler, Wolchik, & Millsap, 2004). One potential implication of such findings is that interventions ought to be directed at the subgroup that is initially at higher risk. Consistent with this idea is the proposal that because individuals who are bereaved after more traumatic deaths, such as deaths due to suicide or violence, have higher levels of problems, they are most likely to benefit from interventions (Jordan & Neimeyer, 2003). Several studies have provided evidence that bereaved girls experience higher levels of problems than boys (Rotheram-Borus, Lee, Gwadz, & Draimin, 2001; Worden, 1996) and that programs have differential effects across gender (Schut, Stroebe, van den Bout, & de Keijser, 1997). These studies on nonmodifiable factors raise important questions concerning whether interventions for bereaved children have differential effects across initial level of problems, cause of death, and child gender.

Variable Risk and Protective Factors at the Social–Contextual and Individual Levels as Potential Modifiable Mediators of Programs to Promote Resilience

Multiple studies have found support for the relations among three potentially modifiable social–environmental factors and parentally bereaved children's functioning: (a) stressful events that follow the death, (b) positive parenting (including warmth and discipline), and (c) mental health problems of the surviving parent or caregiver (Lutzke, Ayers, Sandler, & Barr, 1997). Major stressors, such as parental death, are not singular events but rather markers for a multitude of stressful changes and disruptions in children's social and physical environments that occur before and after the death (Felner, Terre, & Rowlison, 1988). Common changes include loss of time with the surviving parent, new adults entering the family, family conflict, and health problems in the family. Researchers have consistently found positive relations between such postdeath stressful events and children's mental health problems and have found that such stressful events partially mediated the relation between parental death and children's mental health problems (Thompson, Kaslow, Price, Williams, & Kingree, 1998; West, Sandler, Pillow, Baca, & Gersten, 1991).

Parental mental health problems and the quality of parenting by the surviving parent are two interrelated social environmental factors that have implications for children's functioning. Researchers have shown that greater psychological distress in surviving parents is significantly related to higher mental health problems in bereaved children (Dowdney et al., 1999). Strong empirical support has also been found for the relation between the affective nature of the caregiver–child relationship and postdeath child mental health problems (Harris, Brown, & Bifulco, 1986). For example, Sandler, Reynolds,

Kliewer, and Ramirez (1992; see also West et al., 1991) found that higher parental warmth related to lower children's mental health problems in cross-sectional and longitudinal analyses. Saldinger, Porterfield, and Cain (2004) reported that higher levels of child-centered parenting (e.g., communication regarding feelings, responsiveness to loss-related needs, meaning-making) were related to lower internalizing problems of bereaved children. Kwok et al. (2005) found that a multireporter and multimethod measure of positive parenting that included caregiver warmth and effective discipline predicted child mental health problems 11 months later.

Multiple potentially modifiable individual factors have been found to be associated with differential levels of outcomes for bereaved children. There is evidence that higher levels of coping efficacy (Lin, Sandler, Ayers, Wolchik, & Leucken, 2004), self-esteem (e.g., Haine, Ayers, Sandler, Wolchik, & Weyer, 2003; Silverman & Worden, 1992), mastery (Bifulco, Harris, & Brown, 1992), and adaptive control beliefs (Worden, 1996) are associated with lower mental health problems in bereaved children. Lin et al. (2004) found that children who rated stressors as having negative implications for their well-being (i.e., threat appraisals for stressful events) were more likely to have mental health problems after their parents died. In addition, Lin et al. found that bereaved children with higher sense of self-efficacy in dealing with problems in their lives were less likely to have mental health problems.

Research with adults has produced conflicting evidence concerning the role of emotional expression in adaptation following bereavement (Stroebe, Schut, & Stroebe, 2005), although few studies with bereaved children have addressed this issue. Ayers, Sandler, Haine, and Wolchik (2000) studied the relations among three aspects of emotional expression and bereaved children's mental health problems: (a) inhibition of emotional expression, (b) talking with others about one's emotions, and (c) feeling that others understand one's emotions. Ayers et al. found that inhibition of emotional expression was related to higher levels of child and caregiver report of child internalizing problems and higher levels of caregiver report of externalizing problems in prospective longitudinal analyses. In addition, talking about one's feelings with members of the family and feeling understood by the primary caregiver were prospectively related to lower caregiver and child report of child mental health problems.

DESIGN AND EVALUATION OF THEORY-BASED PREVENTIVE INTERVENTIONS FOR CHILDREN WHO HAVE EXPERIENCED PARENTAL DEATH OR DIVORCE

As illustrated in Figure 25.1, the theory underlying the design of the FBP has two components. First, the program is hypothesized to improve multiple risk and protective factors. Second, changes in these risk and protective factors

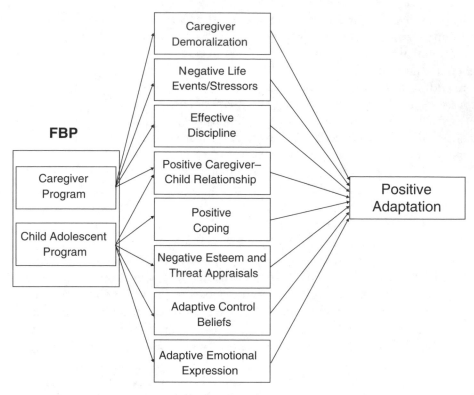

Figure 25.1. Risk and protective factors targeted for change by the Family Bereavement Program (FBP).

are hypothesized to lead to improvements in child functioning. On the basis of a cumulative risk and protection model of adversity (Wyman et al., 2000) and empirical evidence of their association with problem outcomes, we and our colleagues (Ayers et al., 2008) identified nine potentially modifiable individual and social-contextual risk and protective factors. They proposed that theoretically these risk and protective factors have a causal effect on outcomes in that change in the risk and protective factors will lead to change in the outcomes. The task of program development was to design an intervention that was feasible to implement with bereaved families and was effective in changing the identified risk and protective factors.

The Family Bereavement Program: Translation From Theory to an Intervention to Promote Resilience

Separate intervention components were designed for caregivers and children–adolescents because both these agents were seen as potentially influencing multiple targeted risk and protective factors (for a full description of

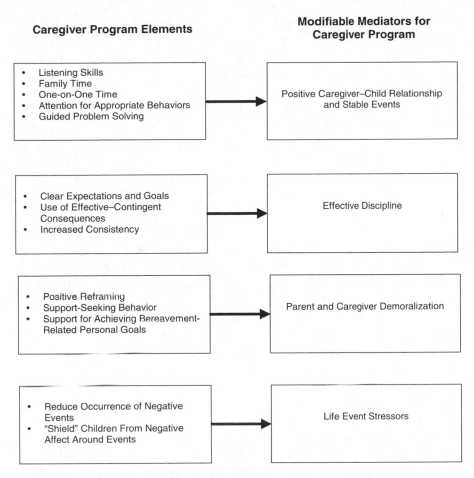

Caregiver Program Elements

Modifiable Mediators for Caregiver Program

- Listening Skills
- Family Time
- One-on-One Time
- Attention for Appropriate Behaviors
- Guided Problem Solving

Positive Caregiver–Child Relationship and Stable Events

- Clear Expectations and Goals
- Use of Effective–Contingent Consequences
- Increased Consistency

Effective Discipline

- Positive Reframing
- Support-Seeking Behavior
- Support for Achieving Bereavement-Related Personal Goals

Parent and Caregiver Demoralization

- Reduce Occurrence of Negative Events
- "Shield" Children From Negative Affect Around Events

Life Event Stressors

Figure 25.2. Modifiable mediators and illustrative program elements of the caregiver component of the Family Bereavement Program.

the intervention design, see Ayers et al., 2008). The program was designed to be delivered in 12 group sessions and 2 individual sessions, with 5 sessions including conjoint activities for the caregivers and youth. The program focused on improving skills in coping and family interactions and promoted the use of these skills to accomplish personal goals that each caregiver and child identified at the beginning of the program. Active learning strategies were used to teach the program skills, and caregivers and children practiced the program skills at home after each session. Each session included a common structure, discussion of the home practice of program skills and progress toward achieving personal goals, teaching of a new program skill, and role play practice of the new skill.

As shown in Figure 25.2, the caregiver component targeted four putative mediators: (a) caregiver–child relationship quality (positive affective quality, stability of family routines, and responsiveness of the relationship with the child), (b) effective discipline, (c) caregiver demoralization, and (d) youth exposure to stressful events that follow the death. In most cases, intervention strategies were selected on the basis of prior literature supporting their effectiveness to change the targeted mediators. To illustrate, the activities to enhance the caregiver–child relationship (e.g., family time, one-on-one time, attention for positive behaviors, and listening skills) and effective discipline (e.g., developing and communicating clear expectations, using contingent consequences, and implementing a plan to change one problem behavior) have been used to strengthen parenting in other interventions (e.g., Forehand & McMahon, 1981) as well as in a program for divorced mothers (Wolchik et al., 2007). The strategies to reduce caregiver demoralization and promote healthy grieving included methods of cognitive reframing that have been successful in treating and preventing depression (Gilham, Reivich, Jaycox, & Seligman, 1995) and in setting personal goals to deal with grief (Shear, Frank, Houck, & Reynolds, 2005). Caregivers were also taught specific strategies to help shield their children from exposure to stressful events in the family. For example, caregivers were taught to provide the children with reassurance and more hopeful cognitions (e.g., that the family is strong and will get through this difficult time) and to refrain from using their children as confidants concerning the stressors that the caregiver was experiencing (e.g., financial problems, loneliness).

The child–adolescent component targeted five putative mediators (see Figure 25.3) that theoretically could be influenced by working directly with the children themselves: (a) positive caregiver–child relationships, (b) positive coping (active coping, coping efficacy), (c) adaptive control beliefs (e.g., understanding the cause of events and making appropriate distinctions between controllable and uncontrollable events), (d) reducing appraisals that stressful events threaten their well-being or self-esteem, and (e) promoting adaptive emotional expression. Children were seen as playing a role complementary to that of caregivers in promoting positive caregiver–child relationships. For example, children were taught expression skills to share their experiences and feelings (e.g., "I-message" for feelings or "I-message" for problem solving), which complemented the listening skills taught to caregivers. Children were taught a broad range of coping skills, such as positive reframing of stressors and a four-step method of problem solving. They were taught to distinguish controllable from uncontrollable stressful events (e.g., kid's job vs. not a kid's job) and to use appropriate coping strategies for each. Children were also taught to identify depressogenic "doom and gloom" thoughts they may be using to appraise stressful events (e.g., "Everything is terrible and will never get better") and to use more "helpful and hopeful" thoughts (e.g., "Things may be bad now, but they can get better in the future"). These strategies (e.g., problem-solving skills, positive reframing, disputing negative threat appraisals) were used where prior research had demonstrated their efficacy at improving these mediators.

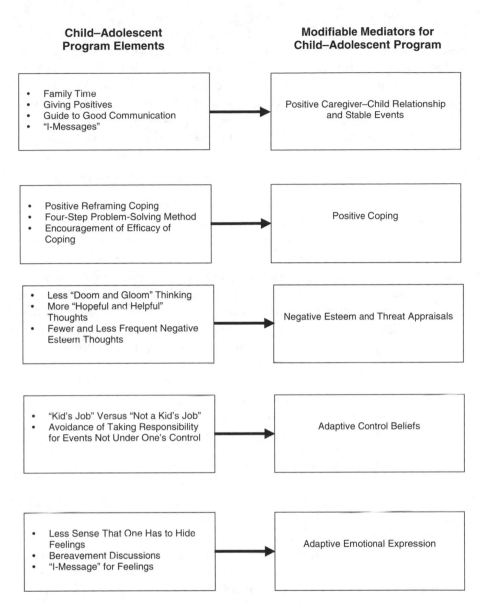

Child–Adolescent Program Elements

- Family Time
- Giving Positives
- Guide to Good Communication
- "I-Messages"

Modifiable Mediators for Child–Adolescent Program

Positive Caregiver–Child Relationship and Stable Events

- Positive Reframing Coping
- Four-Step Problem-Solving Method
- Encouragement of Efficacy of Coping

Positive Coping

- Less "Doom and Gloom" Thinking
- More "Hopeful and Helpful" Thoughts
- Fewer and Less Frequent Negative Esteem Thoughts

Negative Esteem and Threat Appraisals

- "Kid's Job" Versus "Not a Kid's Job"
- Avoidance of Taking Responsibility for Events Not Under One's Control

Adaptive Control Beliefs

- Less Sense That One Has to Hide Feelings
- Bereavement Discussions
- "I-Message" for Feelings

Adaptive Emotional Expression

Figure 25.3. Modifiable mediators and illustrative program elements of the child and adolescent component of the Family Bereavement Program.

Because the existing literature provided little guidance on the most effective approach to help children deal with grief-related emotions, we and our colleagues developed strategies consistent with our conceptualization of ways of dealing with emotions that might be helpful or harmful. On the basis of theory and research of other groups, we hypothesized that not inhibiting the expression of emotions that the child wanted to express (Pennebaker & Beall,

1986) and believing that their caregiver understood their feelings (Gottman, Katz, & Hooven, 1997) would lead to better mental health outcomes. We designed a 15-minute segment in each session that provided structured opportunities for youth to discuss a different grief-related feeling. We also encouraged the children to share their feelings with their caregivers, and we created opportunities in conjoint activities in the group meetings for them to do so and for the caregivers to show that they understood these feelings.

Evaluation of the Effects of the Family Bereavement Program

The FBP was evaluated with an experimental trial in which 156 families (involving 244 children and adolescents ages 8–14) were randomly assigned to the FBP or a self-study comparison condition. Caregivers and children–adolescents were assessed at four time points: (a) prior to being randomly assigned to either the FBP or a self-study condition, (b) immediately after the program ended, (c) 11 months after the posttest (14 months after the pretest), and (d) 6 years after the end of the intervention. The results from the first three waves have been described elsewhere (Sandler et al., 2003) and are only briefly reviewed here. At posttest, families in the program improved more than control participants on multiple risk and protective factors, including increased positive parenting (a composite of caregiver warmth and discipline); reduced stressful events; increased positive coping (a composite of active coping and coping efficacy); decreased inhibition of expression of feelings; decreased caregiver mental health problems; and positive affect in caregiver–youth interactions, as assessed by behavioral observations. At the 11-month follow-up, significant or marginally significant main effects were found indicating that the FBP reduced caregivers' mental health problems and children's inhibition of emotional expression and improved children's control beliefs. In addition, there was a significant program effect to improve positive parenting for participants who had lower scores at program entry. Significant interaction effects with gender indicated additional program effects for girls to improve positive coping and reduce threat appraisals for stressful events for those who had higher threat appraisals at program entry.

Although at posttest few significant program effects were found on children's mental health problems, at the 11-month follow-up, children who had higher levels of internalizing problems at the time they entered the program showed improvement (i.e., less internalizing) according to caregiver report. In addition, compared with girls in the self-study condition, girls who were in the FBP had lower externalizing and internalizing problems as reported by both caregivers and the girls themselves. Analyses using growth curve modeling further clarified the nature of the Gender × Program interaction effect on mental health problems (Schmiege, Khoo, Sandler, Ayers, & Wolchik, 2006). Girls in the self-study condition showed no reduction in internalizing or externalizing problems over time following parental death, whereas girls in the FBP showed reduced levels of both internalizing and externalizing problems over time. In contrast, boys in both the FBP and the self-study condition showed a decrease in internalizing and externalizing problems over time, with no significant difference between the slopes of the two program conditions.

In sum, at posttest the FBP led to improvements on a wide range of theoretical mediators for both boys and girls (e.g., positive parenting, caregiver distress, youth coping, inhibition of emotional expression, and adaptive control beliefs). Program effects on internalizing and externalizing mental health outcomes were found for girls at the 11-month follow-up and on internalizing problems for youth who had higher internalizing problems at the time they entered the program.

Mediators of the Effects of the Family Bereavement Program

Mediation analyses were conducted to test whether the effects of the FBP to reduce girls' mental health problems at the 11-month follow-up were accounted for by program-induced improvements in the risk and protective factors specified in the small theory that guided the intervention design. Mediational analyses test whether the program directly affects the theoretical mediator, which in turn directly affects the mental health outcome. The indirect effect of the mediator on the outcome is the test of mediation, that is, the test of whether the mediator accounts for a significant part of the program effect on the outcome (MacKinnon, Lockwood, Hoffman, West, & Sheets, 2002). Consistent with the program theory, each targeted mediator that was changed by the FBP at posttest was tested as a potential mediator of program effects to reduce girls' internalizing and externalizing problems at the 11-month follow-up. Because power limitations prevented the testing of all mediators simultaneously, separate models initially tested each mediator. These analyses revealed that program effects to reduce mental health problems for girls at the 11-month follow-up were mediated by program effects on three variables at posttest: (a) positive parenting, (b) negative events, and (c) active inhibition of emotional expression (Tein, Sandler, Ayers, & Wolchik, 2006). The independent effect of these three mediators was demonstrated by entering them into a single model; program effects at posttest on all three mediators mediated the program effect on girls' externalizing problems at the 11-month follow-up (see Figure 25.4).

Note that for each path the predictor variable occurred prior to the criterion variable, so that the model satisfied the condition of time precedence between the mediator and outcome (Kraemer, Wilson, Fairburn, & Agras, 2002). However, the model is a conservative one, because we do not know the time lag over which the effect of the mediator on the outcome occurs. To further probe for other significant mediators that were not detected by this model, a set of simultaneous mediation models was conducted (MacKinnon,

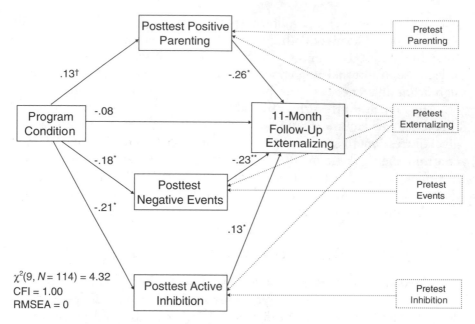

Figure 25.4. Analysis of mediators of the Family Bereavement Program to reduce externalizing problems in girls at the 11-month follow-up. CFI = comparative fit index; RMSEA = root-mean-square error of approximation.
$^\dagger p < .10.$ $^* p < .05.$ $^{**} p < .01.$

2008) that included program effects on the hypothesized mediators and mental health outcomes, both assessed at the 11-month follow-up. In these simultaneous mediation models, three additional variables mediated the program effects on girls' mental health problems: (a) positive coping, (b) threat appraisal, and (c) unknown control beliefs (Tein et al., 2006).

Moderators of the Effects of the Family Bereavement Program

As described earlier, two significant moderators of the effects of the FBP were also identified: (a) child gender and (b) baseline level of child mental health problems. The findings concerning the differential effect of the program on mental health problems across gender is consistent with evidence of gender differences in response to interventions for bereaved adults. It is important to note, however, that positive program benefits were found for both boys and girls for multiple mediator variables at posttest (e.g., positive coping, inhibition of emotional expression, positive parenting) and at the 11-month follow-up (i.e., positive parenting, control beliefs), thus supporting multiple program benefits across gender. One possible explanation for the greater program effects for girls to reduce mental health problems at the 11-month follow-up is that girls in the control group did not show a reduction in mental health problems over time, whereas boys in the control group as well as in the FBP group showed the reduction in mental health problems over time (Schmiege et al., 2006).

The findings that program effects to improve internalizing problems were stronger for individuals who had higher levels of internalizing problems at the pretest is consistent with the conclusion of several recent reviews of the bereavement intervention literature that subgroups of bereaved persons who are at elevated risk for dysfunction benefit from bereavement interventions, whereas many others do not benefit, and some may even be harmed (Jordan & Neimeyer, 2003; Schut et al., 2001). However, it is premature to apply this conclusion to the FBP for two reasons. First, because the intent of any intervention with the bereaved is to improve adaptation over time, the effects of such interventions must be evaluated over time, optimally across developmental periods. Longer term follow-up is necessary to evaluate whether the subgroup differences identified at 11 months persist over time. Second, identifying subgroups that are most at risk and thus most likely to benefit requires careful research, and commonly held beliefs about subgroups that are most at risk may not be accurate. For example, using the pretest data from the current sample, we found no evidence that cause of death (either by suicide or violence) predicted level of mental health problems of bereaved children. Furthermore, we found no evidence that the effects of the FBP were moderated by cause of death, either by suicide or violence (Brown, Sandler, Tein, Liu, & Haine, 2007).

Do the Effects of the Family Bereavement Program Change Over 6 Years?

The effects of preventive interventions theoretically may remain stable, decrease over time, or increase over time. Effects of an intervention, particularly a relatively short intervention such as the FBP, may fade over time as the short-term effects to improve risk and protective factors are counteracted by multiple life changes that occur independently of the intervention, such as new significant adults entering the family, economic changes, moving, and changes in friendships. Alternatively, immediate improvements in risk and protective factors may lead to reductions in mental health problems, which may have positive cascading effects as reductions in children's problems lead to improved interactions in the contexts of their families and communities, which lead to greater satisfaction of children's needs and further reductions in their mental health problems. Evaluation of the effects of a program for divorced families found that the magnitude of the program effects increased from 9 months after program participation to 6 years later (Wolchik et al., 2007). Similarly, as reported earlier, the effects of the FBP to reduce girls' internalizing and externalizing problems increased from posttest to 11 months later (Sandler et al., 2003).

Our research group is currently analyzing the data from the 6-year follow-up of the FBP. Although a full presentation of the results of this follow-up is beyond the scope of this chapter, we provide a preliminary picture of the nature of change in program effects over time for seven outcomes that were assessed using the same measures across all four assessment periods (pretest, posttest, 11-month follow-up, and 6-year follow-up): four measures of mental health problems (both caregiver and youth report of internalizing and externalizing problems), self-esteem, and two measures of grief as reported by the child or adolescent (general grief and intrusive grief thoughts). Analysis of covariance was used to assess program effects at each of the three postprogram assessment times on each of the seven variables, and Cohen's d was used to represent program effect size in these models (see Figure 25.5). The predictors in the model were Time 1 scores on a composite risk index (i.e., internalizing and externalizing problems), group (FBP vs. self-study condition), and the Group × Risk interaction effect. For intrusive grief thoughts, there was a significant program effect ($d = 0.325$) at the 6-year follow-up, which represented a maintenance of the main effect at 11-month follow-up, with intrusive grief thoughts being lower for children in the FBP than for those in the self-study condition. Significant small to moderate positive program main effects were found on three other variables at the 6-year follow-up; these effects were not close to significant at posttest or the 11-month follow-up (self-esteem: $d = 0.418$, $p < .01$; caregiver: $d = 0.299$, $p < .05$; youth report of externalizing: $d = 0.299$, $p < .05$). None of the Risk × Program or Gender × Program interaction effects were significant for the assessment of program effects at the 6-year follow-up. Although more in-depth analyses will be conducted to provide a more sensitive assessment of the effects of the FBP over time (e.g., by using growth curve models), these analyses provide important preliminary information concerning two issues. First, similar to the findings for the NBP, the effects of the FBP on some important outcomes grow over time. Second, the earlier findings of Program × Gender and Program × Initial Levels of Problems interaction effects are not seen at the 6-year follow-up. Given these findings, it seems premature to base conclusions about which groups do or do not gain long-term benefit from the intervention on the findings at posttest or even 1 year later. Developing robust measures through which bereaved children are helped, harmed, or unaffected by interventions is one of the most important priorities for research on interventions with bereaved children. We have previously found that an index consisting of levels of externalizing problems and social environmental adversity (e.g., stressful events, parent psychopathology) when they enter the program is a strong indicator of whether the NBP will reduce multiple child problems 6 years later (Dawson-McClure et al., 2004), and we are currently studying whether a similar index can be developed for the FBP. A second critical issue is to understand the developmental pathways by which the program affects outcomes 6 years

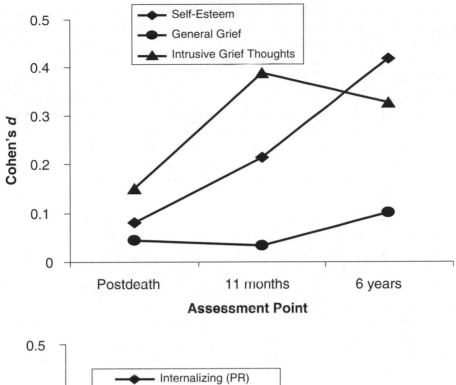

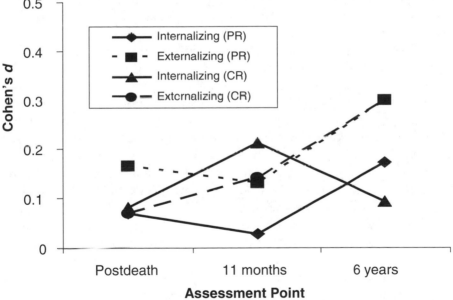

Figure 25.5. Effect sizes for the Family Bereavement Program across time. Top panel: Effect sizes on child report (CR) of self-esteem and grief-related variables across postintervention assessment points. Bottom panel: Effect sizes on parent report (PR) and CR of internalizing and externalizing problems across postintervention assessment points.

later. For example, our longitudinal research design will allow us to test whether early program effects to improve parenting influence later child behaviors (e.g., externalizing problems, control beliefs), which in turn influence children's mental health problems 6 years later. Tests of these cascading effects may enable us to better understand theory concerning how risk and protective factors influence the long-term development of problematic and positive outcomes in parentally bereaved children as well as the effects of the FBP to change these outcomes.

CONCLUDING REMARKS

Research on the FBP illustrates the value of closely integrating theoretical and intervention research in the development and evaluation of programs for bereaved families. The literatures on potentially modifiable risk and protective factors affecting adaptation after the death and fixed marker variables, such as gender, provided guidance for the design of the FBP and helped us understand the moderators of its effects. Experimental evaluation of the FBP provided information on the malleability of risk and protective factors, and mediational analysis of these effects provided rare experimental evidence to strengthen the inference of a causal relation between the risk and protective factors and mental health outcomes.

There are several consistent findings in the evaluations of the programs for parentally bereaved children and children from divorced families. First, in both trials a relatively short intervention improved mental health outcomes and self-esteem over 6 years. The persistence of program effects in these two high-risk groups 6 years later provides promising evidence of the malleability of resilience. Second, in both trials program effects were partially mediated by improvements in parenting. These findings add to a growing literature supporting the efficacy of preventive interventions that focus on strengthening parenting (e.g., DeGarmo, Patterson, & Forgatch, 2004; Spoth, Redmond, & Shin, 2001). Differences in the results from these two trials are also notable. Most prominently, although no gender differences were found in the effects of the NBP, many of the effects of the FBP on mental health outcomes at the 11-month follow-up were moderated by child gender, with girls showing greater benefits. Some prior research has reported that girls are more at risk following parental death (Reinherz, Giaconia, Hauf, Wasserman, & Silverman, 1999), and more research is needed to understand gender differences in the effects of bereavement on children. Although the initial evidence indicates that some of the effects of the FBP persist over 6 years, further probing of these effects is needed to understand the processes that mediate and moderate these long-term effects. Such findings will feed back to further our understanding of adaptation after parental death (e.g., by identifying causal risk factors) and lay the foundation for effective services to improve the adaptation of bereaved children.

REFERENCES

Ayers, T. A., Sandler, I. N., Haine, R. A., & Wolchik, S. A. (2000, June). *Emotional expression and mental health problems of parentally bereaved children*. Poster presented at the 8th annual meeting of the Society for Prevention Research, Montreal, Quebec, Canada.

Ayers, T. S., Twohey, J. L., Sandler, I. N., Wolchik, S. A., Lutzke, J. R., Padgett-Jones, S., et al. (2008). *The Family Bereavement Program: Description of a theory-based prevention program for parentally-bereaved children and adolescents*. Manuscript in preparation.

Bifulco, A., Harris, T., & Brown, G. W. (1992). Mourning or early inadequate care? Reexamining the relationship of maternal loss in childhood with adult depression and anxiety. *Development and Psychopathology, 4*, 433–449.

Brown, A. C., Sandler, I. N., Tein, J.-Y., Liu, X., & Haine, R. (2007). Implications of parental suicide and violent death for promotion of resilience of parentally-bereaved children. *Death Studies, 31*, 301–335.

Dawson-McClure, S. R., Sandler, I., Wolchik, S. A., & Millsap, R. (2004). Prediction and reduction of risk for children of divorce: A six-year longitudinal study. *Journal of Abnormal Child Psychology, 32*, 175–190.

DeGarmo, D. S., Patterson, G. R., & Forgatch, M. S. (2004). How do outcomes in a specified parent training intervention maintain or wane over time? *Prevention Science, 5*(2), 73–89.

Dowdney, L., Wilson, R., Maughan, B., Allerton, M., Schofield, P., & Skuse, D. (1999). Psychological disturbance and service provision in parentally bereaved children: Prospective case-control study. *British Medical Journal, 319*, 354–357.

Felner, R. D., Terre, L., & Rowlison, R. T. (1988). A life transition framework for understanding marital dissolution and family reorganization. In S. Wolchik & P. Karoly (Eds.), *Children of divorce: Empirical perspectives on adjustment* (pp. 35–65). New York: Gardner Press.

Forehand, R., & McMahon, R. J. (1981). *Helping the noncompliant child: A clinician's guide to parent teaching*. New York: Guilford Press.

Gilham, J. E., Reivich, K. J., Jaycox, L. H., & Seligman, M. E. P. (1995). Prevention of depressive symptoms in school children: Two-year follow-up. *Psychological Science, 6*, 343–351.

Gottman, J. M., Katz, L. F., & Hooven, C. (1997). *Meta-emotion: How families communicate emotionally*. Mahwah, NJ: Erlbaum.

Haine, R. A., Ayers, T. S., Sandler, I. N., Wolchik, S. A., & Weyer, J. L. (2003). Locus of control and self-esteem as stress-moderators or stress-mediators in parentally bereaved children. *Death Studies, 27*, 619–640.

Harris, T., Brown, G. W., & Bifulco, A. (1986). Loss of parent in childhood and adult psychiatric disorder: The role of lack of adequate parental care. *Psychological Medicine, 16*, 641–659.

Jordan, J. R., & Neimeyer, R. A. (2003). Does grief counseling work? *Death Studies, 27*, 765–786.

Kraemer, H. C., Kazdin, A. E., Offord, D. R., Kessler, R. C., Jensen, P. S., & Kupfer, D. J. (1997). Coming to terms with the terms of risk. *Archives of General Psychiatry, 54*, 337–343.

Kraemer, H. C., Wilson, T., Fairburn, C. G., & Agras, W. S. (2002). Mediators and moderators of treatment effects in randomized clinical trials. *Archives of General Psychiatry, 59*, 877–883.

Kwok, O.-M., Haine, R. A., Sandler, I. N., Ayers, T. S., Wolchik, S. A., & Tein, J.-Y. (2005). Positive parenting as mediator of the relations between parental psychological distress and mental health problems of parentally bereaved children. *Journal of Clinical Child and Adolescent Psychology, 34*, 260–271.

Lin, K., Sandler, I., Ayers, T. A., Wolchik, S. A., & Leucken, L. (2004). Resilience in parentally bereaved children and adolescents seeking preventive services. *Journal of Clinical Child and Adolescent Psychology, 33*, 673–683.

Lutzke, J. R., Ayers, T. S., Sandler, I. N., & Barr, A. (1997). Risks and interventions for the parentally bereaved child. In S. A. Wolchik & I. N. Sandler (Eds.), *Handbook of children's coping with common life stressors: Linking theory, research and interventions* (pp. 215–243). New York: Plenum Press.

MacKinnon, D. P. (2008). *Introduction to statistical mediation analyses*. Mahwah, NJ: Erlbaum.

MacKinnon, D. P., Lockwood, C. M., Hoffman, J. M., West, S. G., & Sheets, V. (2002). A comparison of methods to test mediated and other intervening variable effects. *Psychological Methods, 7*, 83–104.

Pennebaker, J. W., & Beall, S. K. (1986). Confronting a traumatic event: Toward an understanding of inhibition and disease. *Journal of Abnormal Psychology, 95*, 274–281.

Reinherz, H. Z., Giaconia, R. M., Hauf, A. M., Wasserman, M. S., & Silverman, A. B. (1999). Major depression in the transition to adulthood: Risks and impairments. *Journal of Abnormal Psychology, 108*, 500–510.

Rotheram-Borus, M. J., Lee, M. B., Gwadz, M., & Draimin, B. (2001). An intervention for parents with AIDS and their adolescent children. *American Journal of Public Health, 91*, 1294–1302.

Saldinger, A., Porterfield, K., & Cain, A. C. (2004). Meeting the needs of parentally bereaved children: A framework for child-centered parenting. *Psychiatry: Interpersonal and Biological Processes, 67*, 331–352.

Sandler, I. N. (2001). Quality and ecology of adversity as common mechanisms of risk and resilience. *American Journal of Community Psychology, 29*, 19–61.

Sandler, I. N., Ayers, T. S., Wolchik, S. A., Tein, J.-Y., Kwok, O.-M., Haine, R. A., et al. (2003). The Family Bereavement Program: Efficacy evaluation of a theory-based prevention program for parentally-bereaved children and adolescents. *Journal of Consulting and Clinical Psychology, 71*, 587–600.

Sandler, I. N., Reynolds, K. D., Kliewer, W., & Ramirez, R. (1992). Specificity of the relation between life events and psychological symptomatology. *Journal of Clinical Child Psychology, 21*, 240–248.

Sandler, I. N., Wolchik, S. A., & Ayers, T. (2008). Resilience rather than recovery: A contextual framework for adaptation following bereavement. *Death Studies, 32*, 59–73.

Schmiege, S. J., Khoo, S. T., Sandler, I. N., Ayers, T. S., & Wolchik, S. A. (2006). Symptoms of internalizing and externalizing problems: Modeling recovery curves after the death of a parent. *American Journal of Preventive Medicine, 31*, 152–160.

Schut, H. A., Stroebe, M. S., van den Bout, J., & de Keijser, J. (1997). Intervention for the bereaved: Gender differences in the efficacy of two counselling programmes. *British Journal of Clinical Psychology, 36*, 63–72.

Schut, H., Stroebe, M. S., van den Bout, J., & Terheggen, M. (2001). The efficacy of bereavement interventions: Determining who benefits. In M. S. Stroebe, R. O. Hansson, W. Stroebe, & H. Schut (Eds.), *Handbook of bereavement research: Consequences, coping, and care* (pp. 705–737). Washington, DC: American Psychological Association.

Shear, K., Frank, E., Houck, P. R., & Reynolds, C. F. (2005). Treatment of complicated grief: A randomized controlled trial. *Journal of the American Medical Association, 293*, 2601–2608.

Silverman, P. R., & Worden, J. W. (1992). Children's reactions in the early months after the death of a parent. *American Journal of Orthopsychiatry, 62*, 93–104.

Spoth, R. L., Redmond, C., & Shin, C. (2001). Randomized trial of brief family interventions for general populations: Adolescent substance use outcomes 4 years following baseline. *Journal of Consulting and Clinical Psychology, 69*, 627–642.

Stroebe, W., Schut, H., & Stroebe, M. S. (2005). Grief work, disclosure and counseling: Do they help the bereaved? *Clinical Psychology Review, 25*, 395–414.

Tein, J.-Y., Sandler, I. N., Ayers, T., & Wolchik, S. A. (2006). Mediation of the effects of the Family Bereavement Program on mental health problems of bereaved children and adolescents. *Prevention Science, 7*, 179–195.

Tein, J.-Y., Sandler, I. N., MacKinnon, D. P., & Wolchik, S. A. (2004). How did it work? Who did it work for? Mediation and mediated moderation of a preventive intervention for children of divorce. *Journal of Consulting and Clinical Psychology, 72*, 617–624.

Thompson, M. P., Kaslow, N. J., Price, A. W., Williams, K., & Kingree, J. B. (1998). Role of secondary stressors in the parental death–child distress relation. *Journal of Abnormal Child Psychology, 26*, 357–366.

West, S. G., Sandler, I. N., Pillow, D. R., Baca, L., & Gersten, J. C. (1991). The use of structural equation modeling in generative research: Toward the design of a preventive intervention for bereaved children. *American Journal of Community Psychology, 19*, 459–480.

Worden, J. W. (1996). *Children and grief: When a parent dies*. New York: Guilford Press.

Wolchik, S., Sandler, I., Weiss, L., & Winslow, E. (2007). New Beginnings: An empirically-based program to help divorced mothers promote resilience in their children. In J. M. Briesmeister & C. E. Schaefer (Eds.), *Handbook of parent training: Helping parents prevent and solve problem behaviors* (3rd ed., pp. 25–62). Hoboken, NJ: Wiley.

Wyman, P. A., Sandler, I., Wolchik, S. A., & Nelson, K. (2000). Resilience as cumulative competence promotion and stress protection: Theory and intervention. In D. Cicchetti, J. Rappaport, I. Sandler, & R. P. Weissberg (Eds.), *The promotion of wellness in children and adolescents* (pp. 133–184). Washington, DC: Child Welfare League of America.

26

BEREAVEMENT SUPPORT, INTERVENTION, AND RESEARCH ON THE INTERNET: A CRITICAL REVIEW

MARGARET S. STROEBE, KAROLIJNE VAN DER HOUWEN,
AND HENK SCHUT

Contemporary technological advances such as the World Wide Web and e-mail have drastically changed patterns of communication and the distribution of information and have influenced the shape and form of psychological research and even counseling (Kraut et al., 2004). Experts predict that Internet use will increase further, becoming even more deeply integrated into our physical and social environments (Fox, Anderson, & Rainie, 2005). In 2003, Madden reported that nearly two thirds of Americans went online to access the Internet and that information-seeking activities had increased across the board, mostly by 50% or more, since 2000. Little information is available specifically about how often the bereaved access the Internet, although a small community study conducted by Vanderwerker and Prigerson (2004) suggests that at least in the United States, they are not excluded from this trend.

The Internet offers several opportunities for bereavement-related activity. First, it offers ways of providing bereavement support (e.g., fostering interactions between bereaved people, sharing practical information) and undertaking bereavement-related activities (e.g., memorialization on the Web). Second, it extends possibilities for providing psychological intervention more formally through professionals, using a virtual medium (in the sense that there is no face-to-face encounter). Third, it creates new opportunities for conducting scientific research and/or enabling more efficient researching of traditional topics.

In this chapter, we review the impact of Internet technology within the field of bereavement and the possibilities it offers. We survey what kinds of bereavement support are available on the Web, including Web sites for remembrance of the deceased; we then discuss bereavement research and professional intervention through the Internet. Bereavement-specific research relating to use of the Internet in these areas is scarce and yet, as we illustrate in this chapter, such assessment is an essential extension of current scientific investigation. Important questions must be raised; for example, can the claims of participation benefits—say, in a bereavement support e-mail group—really be substantiated? Are there not also potentially detrimental effects? Given the future of the Internet, we need sound research to provide answers to such questions. As we hope to show in this chapter, the Internet offers huge possibilities for bereavement research: For each of the gaps in knowledge identified there is potential for extensive scientific investigation. Thus, a main aim of this chapter is to indicate limitations to contemporary knowledge and to suggest directions for future research.

INTERNET RESOURCES FOR THE BEREAVED

There has been a huge expansion in the number and types of Internet resources providing support for bereaved people. Possibilities for the various types of support can, for the most part, be located on or via general Web sites (e.g., http://www.about.com, an online source for consumer information; http://www.aarp.org, the Web site of the AARP [formerly the American Association of Retired Persons]) or bereavement-specific Web sites. Bereavement-specific Web sites may focus on bereavement in general (e.g., http://www.beyondindigo.com) or on specific losses, such as loss of a spouse (e.g., http://www.merrywidow.me.uk) or child or loss because of suicide. Many bereavement-specific Web sites have been created by persons who have suffered a loss themselves (e.g., http://www.widownet.org), some of whom are also working as mental health professionals in the area of bereavement (e.g., http://www.webhealing.com and http://www.griefnet.org). Most of these Web sites are run by volunteers. A number of bereavement-specific Web sites belong to large national or international bereavement organizations (e.g., http://www.crusebereavementcare.org.uk is the Web site of the national association for bereaved people in the United Kingdom, minus Scotland). Both general as well as bereavement-specific Web sites often include a variety of resources.

Description of Resources

Information

Most Web sites provide information about issues related to bereavement and grief, ranging from the provision of lawyers' addresses for crime victims, to listing of sources for interacting with similar others, to informing bereaved persons about the range of symptoms associated with grief. Nearly all include links that provide access to other bereavement support Web sites.

Internet Forums

Bereavement Internet forums (commonly referred to as *message boards* or *discussion boards*) are, in essence, support-oriented Web sites where discussion can take place: They contain series of messages and responses, usually by bereaved persons. An example of a typical interaction would be the following:

> **Post:** I lost my husband of [. . .] years on [. . .]. I am having a really hard time and everyone means well but they are telling me what to do. . . . I do not like living alone.
>
> **Reply:** I am so sorry and sad to hear about your loss. . . . I wish there was something I could say to help you through this, but I will say this, please post on the message board and we (I assume I can speak for all of us here) will do our best to be here for you.

Responses may either be received by private e-mail or by public posting on the forum. Registration is typically needed before messages can be posted, but messages can usually also be read by people who have not registered. Bereavement Internet forums are mostly free of charge and easily accessible, and support comes from peers, not professional facilitators, although some Web sites have skilled moderators who sometimes respond to postings and/or who delete potentially harmful messages. Forums are often divided into subforums that are dedicated to specific subjects (e.g., different types of loss). Messages are typically archived, enabling them to be studied. Bereavement Internet forums can often be accessed via general or bereavement-specific Web sites, but they can also be separate Web sites (e.g., http://www.suicidediscussionboard.com).

E-Mail Groups

E-mail grief support groups communicate through group e-mail. Group members join an e-mail list, and then e-mails of members are automatically received in one's e-mail box. One responds to the group as a whole (which is a requirement of some groups), or sometimes one can reply to individual members. It is often the case that no payment is required, although sometimes a small contribution is requested. As with bereavement Web sites, e-mails groups are usually moderated. E-mail grief support groups are a service that is frequently offered to bereaved people by some general or bereavement-specific Web sites. For example, GriefNet.org (http://www.griefnet.org) offers almost 50 e-mail support groups that are subdivided into 10 categories (e.g., the category "loss of spouse or partner" consists of four groups: "grief-widowed," "widowed-with-kids," "griefwidowed-movingon," and "young-widowed"). Sometimes, bereavement support groups that meet offline offer their members an opportunity to meet online via an e-mail grief support group. However, many e-mail groups are not associated with a particular organization or Web site. At the moment of writing, Yahoo! Groups—currently the most popular provider of electronic mailing lists—offers almost 2,000 e-mail grief support groups (with considerable variation in the number of their members and their activity level),[1] most of which have been created by individuals not associated with any Web site or organization.

Chat Rooms

A *chat room* is an online, interactive discussion forum that takes place in real time. Characteristic of chat rooms is that certain groups of bereaved people can chat with each other at specified times, sometimes with the inclusion of a professional moderator. Thus, in this case, an online typed contemporaneous conversation between (bereaved) people can take place. Whoever happens to be in a particular chat room at a certain time can see what someone has written, and anyone present (i.e., online and at the chat room Web site) can respond. To do so, one first has to register. Bereavement-specific Web sites frequently offer such a service. Also, bereavement support groups that meet offline may offer members an opportunity to meet online via chat sessions.

Online Memorial Web Sites

Online memorials are Web sites where bereaved persons—or others, for that matter—can honor their deceased loved ones (some bereaved parents, in particular, set up individual Web pages to memorialize their deceased children). Some of these Web sites charge a fee for memorial placement, but most do not. The first of these Web sites came into being in 1995, with http://www.webhealing.com and http://www.cemetery.org seemingly emerging at about the same time (Chang & Sofka, 2006; Golden, 2006). These Web sites have extended across the world; for example, they are available among Chinese communities. All of them provide the opportunity for people with computer

---

[1]This number excludes all support groups for those who are grieving the loss of their pet and memorialization groups.

access to commemorate their lost loved ones in ways that are convenient, quite personal, and often economical (Chang & Sofka, 2006), frequently by posting photographs and describing the deceased person's life and death. They often offer the opportunity for people to write a message to the person who wrote the memorial or to the deceased (although most are directed to the one who wrote the memorial).

These Web sites appeal to some bereaved people. For example, Chang and Sofka (2006), citing a government report, noted that 30,000 citizens of Peking used online services to worship their ancestors on Tomb Sweeping Day, a Chinese memorial day. They commented that those who are located far away may be able to set up a virtual space to perform traditional rituals on the Internet, for example, visiting a graveyard in cyberspace when physical distance makes visiting the actual burial or cremation place difficult (although we know of no evidence that living farther away from the place of burial or cremation is associated with more use of such Web sites). Opportunities for connectedness are varied. On one Web site (http://www.empty-cradles.com/index.html), letters can be written to heaven, and one can even select a small star to represent a deceased child (Chang & Sofka, 2006).

Do These Resources Help the Bereaved?

Information and Support Resources

What reasons do we have to assume that such resources are really worthwhile? What evidence, if any, exists? Do these resources even need to actually be helpful (as long as people want to access such them and they are not associated with huge burdens to individuals or society)? In asking this last question, we also have to consider whether they could do damage to bereaved persons, for example, by misinforming or misguiding people in distress or by leading them to harm themselves.

A primary consideration is if there are any scientific reasons to assume that the provision of bereavement-related information via the Internet can help bereaved people. Clinicians have long used the psychoeducational approach to address the need for better information for conditions such as depression, anxiety, and personality-related mental conditions such as borderline personality disorder (e.g., Colom et al., 2003). The psychoeducational approach focuses on such matters as the provision of sound information for both client and family members about a mental—or physical—condition and its treatment. If the information provided is of high quality (an assumption that also needs close examination) then, in principle, it provides knowledge and skills necessary for managing stressful health-related conditions. Although bereavement is a normal event that requires no professional intervention in most persons' lives (Schut & Stroebe, 2005;

Schut, Stroebe, van den Bout, & Terheggen, 2001), there are good reasons to argue that the psychoeducational approach also may be of relevance for this life stressor. Bereaved persons frequently need reliable information on a variety of concerns, relating not only to the loss itself but also to the management of affairs relating to changes in ongoing life during bereavement (M. Stroebe & Schut, 1999).

The Internet as a system lends itself to the widespread provision of such psychoeducational information (it is naturally also open to the placement and dissemination of any sort of information at all, from well-grounded to totally unfounded claims). However, even in the areas where considerable use has been made of such information (e.g., borderline personality disorder), researchers have deplored the lack of randomized controlled trials (Colom et al., 2003). Studies are frequently cross-sectional, precluding the possibility of making causal links. For example, Fogel, Albert, Schnabel, Ditkoff, and Neugut (2002) set out to investigate the potential benefits of using the Internet for acquiring medical information among cancer patients. They reported that 42% of the sample used the Internet in this manner. Internet use for health issues was associated with higher social support and less loneliness than when the Internet was not used or when it was used for other purposes. However, given that the study was cross-sectional, one cannot conclude that acquiring medical information on the Internet in this manner actually brings about positive effects with respect to social support or loneliness.

Turning now to the provision of support via the Internet, we must first note that differences in content and functions of Internet forums, e-mail groups, chat rooms, and so on, need to be explored in future research. At present, it is possible only to subsume them under the umbrella of "social support" for the bereaved and to consider their efficacy in general. *Social support* has typically been defined as information from others that one is loved and cared for, esteemed and valued, and part of a network of communication and mutual obligation (Cobb, 1976). Such information has traditionally come from a spouse; a lover; children; friends; or social and community contacts, such as churches or clubs.

To what extent can contacts via the Internet take over from—or supplement—traditional sources of social support? This question can be more easily addressed if one looks at the different functions social support is assumed to fulfill. Researchers have typically distinguished among emotional, instrumental, informational, and appraisal support functions (e.g., House, 1981). *Emotional support* involves providing empathy, care, love and trust. *Instrumental support* consists of behaviors that directly help the person in need (e.g., helping with work, taking care of children, or helping with transportation). *Informational support* involves providing people with information they can use in coping with their problems. *Appraisal support* is closely related to informational support. It too involves the transmission of information, but in this case it is information that is relevant to the person's self-evaluation (e.g., "How am I doing?"; "Are my feelings normal, or am I reacting abnormally?").

It seems plausible that the kind of anonymous and geographically distant contacts one makes through the Internet would be better able to fulfill informational and appraisal functions than instrumental support functions. Emotional support can clearly also be given through the Internet, albeit in a different manner (e.g., "hugs" are offered to console someone, but they do not provide bodily contact). Furthermore, relationships that started on the Internet can develop into face-to-face relationships (e.g., McKenna, Green, & Gleason, 2002), suggesting that the Internet can potentially also facilitate access to face-to-face instrumental (and emotional) support. However, given geographic distances, it seems unlikely that this happens very frequently.

As perusal of Web sites shows, claims have frequently been made that such social support resources provided by the Internet for bereaved persons are beneficial. However, scientific investigation to back up these claims falls far short of acceptable standards. Vanderwerker and Prigerson (2004) reported that technological connectedness was associated with lowering of grief and other mental health-related improvements over time. However, it is not possible to make causal statements on the basis of these associations; the study was cross-sectional, and no information was provided on the precise Internet activities of these bereaved persons. A longitudinal investigation with random assignment to Internet or non-Internet activity and the precise delineation of types of Internet activity is needed to assess the impact of the Internet on the course of grief.

The need for better methodology is further illustrated through a study of survivors of the suicides of loved ones (Hollander, 2001). On the basis of a self-report study of the efficacy of communications among these survivors, Hollander (2001) concluded that communication with similar others online was "nearly indispensable" and claimed that these interactions compensated for a lack of possibilities to have contact with other persons, for example, to interact face to face. There were no sound empirical bases for these claims. The study lacked objective measures of gains (demand characteristics and dropout biases are well-established limitations of subjective accounts), and no comparisons were made with non-Internet survivors.

Moving beyond the bereavement-specific area to research on Internet use in connection with other specific life stressors, we have found that in these areas, too, conclusions are severely compromised by poor methodology. Internet forums have been developed, for example, for women with breast cancer (Fogel et al., 2002; Lieberman & Goldstein, 2005, 2006), offering basic activities that have some parallel with bereavement Internet forums, such as reading about others' experiences and receiving support, information, and advice. Again, one example illustrates the need for caution in drawing conclusions: Lieberman and Goldstein (2005, 2006) reported improvements over 6 months in depression and well-being among women participating in cancer support Internet-based bulletin boards. They linked improvement to the expression of emotions of anger and deterioration to expressions of fear and anxiety, whereas sadness was unrelated to change scores (Lieberman & Goldstein, 2006) and yet, again, no control group of persons who did not join the bulletin board was included. Thus, no causal statements can be made about the impact of the Internet intervention. Furthermore, one cannot determine whether expressing the specific emotions caused the changes or whether these emotions were simply a manifestation of such changes.

Although there have been a number of (unsubstantiated) claims about the efficacy of online information and support, as far as we know no systematic attention has been paid to the possible negative effects that may also result from accessing such online resources. For example, Hollander (2001), in the study described earlier, gave little consideration to a possibility mentioned in passing: "There is a danger in becoming too centered on grief and forgetting the remainder of life and the living" (p. 144). Yet this is a very real risk: Research has shown that high levels of rumination about a deceased loved one are associated with poorer coping with bereavement over time (e.g., Nolen-Hoeksema, 2001). It is plausible that Internet use might increase, rather than discourage, ruminative thinking and distress.

There are two additional concerns as well. The first is the potential for exploitation or abuse of lonely, vulnerable, bereaved persons by people who try to cheat or mislead them for sexual purposes or financial gain (see Finn & Banach, 2000; Waldron, Lavitt, & Kelley, 2000). Such risks need further documentation in the bereavement field. The second concern is the possibility that the Internet socially isolates bereaved persons by decreasing face-to-face contacts. This could potentially undermine any positive impact because social isolation is strongly associated with difficulties in adjusting to bereavement (e.g., Dyregrov, Nordanger, & Dyregrov, 2003). To our knowledge, no bereavement-specific evidence is available concerning this issue, although studies in other areas have been conducted. Although caution is needed in generalizing from these studies to bereavement phenomena, the studies themselves provide useful examples of the issues to address and type of research that needs to be conducted in this specific area.

One of the first (and much-publicized) longitudinal studies of the psychological effects of high-frequency Internet use found it to be associated with decreased rates of family communication, greater loneliness, a greater number of daily life stressors, and increased depression at a later time (Kraut et al., 1998). However, a later follow-up study of the same sample revealed that these negative effects had disappeared and that instead, positive effects had appeared across the different measures of adjustment and involvement with family and friends (Kraut et al., 2002). Several other surveys conducted in the United States have also found that Internet users are either no less likely than nonusers to visit or telephone friends or that Internet users actually have a larger offline social network (e.g., Boase, Horrigan, Wellman, & Rainie, 2006; for reviews, see Bargh & McKenna, 2004; Fogel et al., 2002). As we indicated earlier, though, such studies need replication, specifically among bereaved samples.

Finally, even when (Internet) support is shown to be helpful, inadequate social support has been found to be a generic rather than bereavement-specific risk factor in that it affects the health and well-being of nonbereaved people as much as those of the bereaved (W. Stroebe, Schut, & Stroebe, 2005). Results by W. Stroebe, Stroebe, Abakoumkin, and Schut (1996) seem to indicate that the lack of a bereavement-specific effect could have to do with the fact that others cannot easily take the emotional place of the deceased person or compensate for their loss: W. Stroebe et al. (1996) showed that even with support from family and friends (their measure covered the different types of support identified earlier), bereaved persons remained highly emotionally lonely (i.e., having the sense of not having an intimate relationship, of being utterly alone). This does not mean that social support is not helpful to bereaved people, but it does suggest that one should not expect too much from it. That said, W. Stroebe et al.'s (1996) study did not analyze types of support separately (because in this study the subscales measuring different types of support correlated highly): For example, one might expect appraisal support, which is frequent on support forums, to be useful.

Psychoeducation has been acclaimed as a useful method for disseminating information about mental and physical debilities, and the scientific literature has shown beneficial effects relating to health and well-being of social support in general. However, firm conclusions about efficacy of either the provision of psychoeducation or social support within the bereavement domain, through Internet forums, e-mail groups, or chat rooms, cannot be drawn at this time: There is a complete absence of randomized controlled trials to assess the impact of programs. At an even more basic level, no criteria or procedures have been developed to differentiate high- from low-quality Internet resources.

Online Memorial Web Sites

There is widespread claim of benefits for persons who avail themselves of the possibilities for memorialization on the Internet: These resources allow emotional expression often denied in contemporary society, they allow personal tributes (from a distant place), they enable preservation of the loved one's memory and the sharing of it with others, and they provide communities for disenfranchised grievers (e.g., Golden, 2006; Moss, 2004; Roberts, 2006). These functions are similar to those of traditional memorialization (for which, as far as we know, there has also been little sound scientific investigation of benefits to the bereaved).

It is possible that the availability of online memorial Web sites compensates for the dearth of ceremonial commemoration in contemporary society, offering a new possibility to remember a deceased person. It is also possible that a memorial Web site is supplementary, adding to traditional ways of commemorating a death. It remains unclear, though, whether memorializing helps people work through grief and toward accepting that the loved one has gone, or whether it signifies a reluctance to let go and causes people to get stuck in or fixate on grieving. Yet here again, scientific investigation of the precise impact of memorializing the deceased on the Internet has lagged far behind the creation and use of these Web sites. What might one expect, on the basis of bereavement research in general, if such investigations were carried out. Two bodies of research are relevant, namely, work on (a) continuing or relinquishing bonds and (b) disenfranchised grief.

Insofar as memorialization is a way of preserving the memory of the deceased, as claimed on Web sites, it is a phenomenon addressed by the continuing-bonds literature. Moss (2004), for example, summarized contemporary views about memorialization on the Internet, acknowledging the potential function of holding onto as well as letting go of the deceased person, but she emphasized that the maintenance of the bond is central:

> These memorials repeatedly acknowledge the continuity of attachment over time, rather than its ending. Maintaining a tie with a deceased loved one can be self-affirming and comforting, and the maintenance of the bond can be more freeing than its denial. (p. 77)

The notion of *continuing bonds* denotes the presence of an ongoing inner relationship with the deceased person by the bereaved individual (see chap. 6, this volume). In contrast to earlier claims based on the analyses of Freud (1917/1957), bereavement researchers have recently argued that continuing bonds with a deceased person facilitates adjustment. Klass, Silverman, and Nickman (1996), for example, made strong claims that continuing the bond with a deceased person was of benefit: "The resolution of grief involves continuing bonds that survivors maintain with the deceased and . . . these continuing bonds can be a healthy part of the survivor's ongoing life" (p. 22). Although in general little scientific support has been provided either for this position or for the "breaking bonds" claim, researchers have recently begun to examine the specific types of continuing bonds that are associated with good versus poor adjustment to bereavement (e.g., Boelen, Stroebe, Schut, & Zijerveld, 2006; chap. 6, this volume; Schut, Stroebe, Boelen, & Zijerveld, 2006). Results have been less in favor of the benefits of continuing bonds than was previously thought to be the case. In fact, some types of retained bonds have been found to predict poorer adjustment over time. For example, in a longitudinal study of 56 bereaved individuals that controlled not only for initial levels of grief but also for conceptual overlap between the measures of grief and continuing bonds, Boelen et al. (2006) reported that continuing bonds through recovering memories was in fact a strong predictor of grief: Continuing a bond in this way was associated with poor, not better, outcome at a later time.

Continuing-bonds research has not yet provided a clear picture of the types of bonds that are adaptive or maladaptive; neither has there been sufficient empirical research to establish precisely the types of bereaved persons for whom continuing or relinquishing bonds may be more versus less advantageous. Nevertheless, some important inferences can be drawn for Internet memorialization: Investigation so far suggests that caution is needed in assuming that bereaved persons gain from memorializing their loved ones on the Internet. For many, memorialization may indeed continue the bond and preserve the memory of the deceased in a way that is meaningful and provides comfort. For others, though, it may represent an inability or disinclination to let go and move on, which is a necessary function of grieving (cf. Worden, 2002). Furthermore, it may reflect a ruminative way of grieving, which has also been shown to be predictive of poor adjustment to bereavement (Nolen-Hoeksema, 2001).

Internet memorialization has also been addressed from the perspective of *disenfranchised grief*, a term that refers to grief that results "when a person experiences a significant loss and the resultant grief is not openly acknowledged, socially validated, or publicly mourned" (see chap. 11, this volume, p. 224). Examples of disenfranchised grief range from loss of a partner in an extramarital affair to (in some societies) the death of a homosexual partner from AIDS. Provision of Internet communities and Web site memorials may compensate for societal disenfranchisement and improve the well-being of members of such stigmatized groups. In chapter 11 of this volume, Doka highlights the potential detrimental effects of having to endure a grief that is disenfranchised.

Some researchers have assumed that Internet memorialization is a useful resource for disenfranchised grievers. In fact, the theme of social sanctioning runs through many descriptive articles on memorializing loved ones on the Web (e.g., de Vries & Roberts, 2004; Moss, 2004). However, Internet memorialization is typically quite a public phenomenon, making it hard to see exceptional benefits for disenfranchised grievers. It would be easier to argue the case for the usefulness of Web sites that provide a resource for specific types of disenfranchised grief, because the Internet provides a certain degree of anonymity that may be lacking in other forms of interpersonal contact, offering opportunities to connect with similar others (Martin & Doka, 2000).

We need to learn why people memorialize loved ones (see also chaps. 4 and 12, this volume) and how their reasons for doing so relate to adaptation to bereavement. For whom does memorializing represent a gradual relinquishment of the tie and moving on through the grief process, and when does it reflect an inability to let go and an overly intense preoccupation with and clinging to the deceased loved one? Until such questions are answered, and until randomized controlled trials have been conducted to establish whether participating in memorialization activities is useful, it cannot be claimed that commemorating the deceased through the Internet is generally beneficial.

Social Support and Memorialization Through the Internet: Some General Conclusions

People who establish and report on bereavement sites repeatedly make assumptions about the usefulness of Internet resources that are offered, ranging from the benefits of using the information and support resources described earlier to the positive effects of memorializing. However, little sound empirical research in the bereavement area is available to back up these claims. The few evaluations that have been done were based on subjective evaluations and impressions of users and/or researchers and those offering the resources. Such evaluations are subject to a number of biases that raise serious doubts about the validity of conclusions about beneficial effects (e.g., dropout of those who do not find the resource useful; biased views of those offering the resource; impressionistic qualitative judgments based on small, nonrepresentative samples). In addition, studies are typically characterized by the omission of control groups and the absence of pre- and postmeasures. Rarely, if ever, has attention been paid to the possibility that there may be disadvantages, that sorrow and hurt could be increased, that the well-meant support process may (sometimes) go wrong (for some bereaved users), that using the resources offered may induce wallowing in grief.

Research from other areas also endorses the need for caution in assuming beneficial effects; again, studies are frequently weak or cannot easily be generalized to the bereavement area. Further research needs to examine a broad range of issues related to adjustment using well-controlled and longitudinal designs, for example, whether more socially isolated persons become even less integrated through reliance on Internet rather than face-to-face contacts; what types of bonds with deceased persons are associated with specific styles and intensity of memorializing; or the impact of features of Internet forum participation, such as whether a forum is professionally guided.

One can of course question whether provision of this type of support even needs to be proved efficacious as long as (a) people can access it freely (without financial cost), (b) they can choose whether to do so, and (c) if it is certain that the information provided is neither misleading nor that the support offered has adverse effects. Then again, one should be dubious about accepting such assumptions without further investigation. What emerges clearly from the preceding review is that claims should not be made about the usefulness of participating in Internet activities in the absence of any solid research basis. Also, regardless of whether effectiveness is put to empirical test, it would seem advisable to develop quality-control procedures with respect to the information and advice offered via the Internet. Some descriptive evaluations—or at least, comparisons of Web sites—can be found in the literature (e.g., for more on Web sites for bereaved children, see Aitken, 2006), but scientists could play a greater role is assessing such Web sites and publishing their findings in readily accessible sources in the future.

INTERNET-BASED RESEARCH AND INTERVENTION WITH BEREAVED PEOPLE

The Internet lends itself not only to straightforward collection of survey data but also to providing intervention (counseling and therapy) and assessing its impact. Other types of research are also conceivable—for example, research on communication between bereaved people through the content analysis of exchanges within e-mail groups or through linguistic analyses of diaries on an online journaling service (cf. Cohn, Mehl, & Pennebaker, 2004). In this section, we describe positive and negative features of conducting research on the Internet before considering additional features that more specifically relate to empirical research on the efficacy of intervention. Finally, we briefly review bereavement intervention evaluation research on the Internet, which serves as an example of the development of bereavement research on the Internet in general.

Positive Versus Negative Features of Internet Research

Conducting research through the Internet has both advantages and drawbacks. Among the advantages (see also Lange, van de Ven, Schrieken, & Emmelkamp, 2001; Schultze, 2006; Wagner, Knaevelsrud, & Maercker, 2006) is that new opportunities are opened up in recruiting and accessing respondents: The Internet provides access to samples that are beyond the reach of methods typically used in psychological research. Sampling is, to some extent, geographically independent (some countries remain relatively difficult to reach via the Internet and might therefore be underrepresented in research). Another feature that is particularly relevant to bereavement research and that is frequently mentioned as an advantage (albeit without firm foundation in research; see previous section) is that socially isolated individuals and people who for some reason are reluctant to participate in face-to-face contact may have access and be more willing to participate in research through the Internet (the same applies, perhaps to a lesser extent, to research that uses postal questionnaires). If this is the case, then respondents would be extended to people who prefer to stay on their own and more in control of their options (e.g., experiencing less social pressure to continue participation)—clearly a subgroup of persons from whom bereavement data would be useful to attain. Furthermore, participation in Internet research may encourage self-disclosure (Wagner et al., 2006); again, this needs to be tested.

Internet data can also be collected efficiently; computerized administration enables researchers to obtain sample sizes that are far larger, and recruited more easily, from many different and distant countries, than those obtained with traditional techniques. Internet research also is time saving with respect to data analysis (e.g., it dispenses with the need for data entry, although this must be weighed against the extra time needed to create a questionnaire). It is also an inexpensive way of collecting and processing data compared with traditional methods, and because data entry is automatic, the quality of the data is potentially good (e.g., there are no data entry mistakes; programs can be developed that preclude skipping of critical questions).

With respect to disadvantages, issues of sampling biases and ethical concerns are frequently raised when Internet use in bereavement research and intervention is discussed (e.g., Birnbaum, 2004; Gosling, Vazire, Srivastava, & John, 2004; Robson & Robson, 2000). On the Internet, people can more easily pretend to be who and what they are not, and possibilities for checking the reliability of the provided information are less available. With regard to sampling biases, it has often been argued that Internet samples are not sufficiently diverse. In the United States, older persons, members of ethnic minority groups (as opposed to Whites), those with modest income and education or those without jobs (among other subgroups) are all less likely to be connected to the Internet (Gosling et al., 2004; Madden, 2003). For example, in their evaluation of Internet studies Gosling et al. (2004) noted that people with lower incomes from rural areas and with less education were less likely to have access to the Internet than are high-income, urban, and educated individuals and that Internet research reaches participants who are not representative of the population at large. However, they also reported that the Internet users under investigation were relatively diverse with respect to the above socioeconomic status (SES) variables and were more representative than traditional samples. It is clear that in the bereavement research field—just as for traditionally obtained samples—the possibility of sample biasing with respect to SES factors needs careful evaluation (we return to this issue shortly), not least because this could severely limit the generalizability of results found on Internet surveys. Questions of fairness, which apply to traditional research too, must also be raised in this context: Are researchers reaching and representing the needs of the underprivileged and marginal subgroups of bereaved people in their Internet investigations?

The same concerns apply to biases other than SES ones, such as the relatively high participation rates of bereaved women rather than men or the inclusion of more younger than older bereaved persons. With regard to the latter example, the fact that Internet samples are skewed toward younger populations (Gosling et al., 2004; Madden, 2003) is a potentially severe problem for contemporary bereavement research. After all, bereavement—particularly through death of a spouse—is an experience that is more frequent in older age groups; if these age groups could not be reached through the Internet, then the applicability of using this method for studying bereaved samples must be questioned. On the other hand, the fact that younger individuals are overrepresented in Internet samples does not necessarily mean that older individuals cannot be reached. It simply reflects the fact that computer use is more frequent in the younger populations. The underrepresentation of computer users among the elderly suggests, though, that elderly samples reached through the Internet will be even more socioeconomically biased than is typical for the younger age groups. The threat to validity must be carefully weighed (and further investigated): In this case, the bias might not constitute a serious threat to the validity of Internet studies—at least for studies of the mental and physical health consequences of bereavement—because studies have not shown health differences according to SES (M. Stroebe, Schut, & Stroebe, 2007).

Review boards of Internet studies are naturally concerned about protecting the bereaved, because they are a relatively vulnerable group. Dangers inherent to Internet use for persons seeking health-related help have been documented (e.g., Finn & Banach, 2000; Waldron et al., 2000). One concern particularly inherent to Internet research (although clearly also relevant to traditional data collection) has to do with data security, confidentiality, and anonymity. Data can be secured by using adequate cryptographic protection during the transfer of data and by protecting the server against unauthorized invasions. To ensure confidentiality, researchers should behave in accordance with ethical guidelines for conducting research on the Internet. Full anonymity, although possible in theory (by making sure that no identifying markers are recorded), cannot always be ensured for administrative reasons (e.g., to prevent multiple responses from the same person; Manfreda & Vehovar, 2007). Informed consent forms need to be clear on such matters (e.g., what procedures are used to ensure data security?). Another issue concerns exclusion criteria: Are they sufficient? Saying that participants must, for example, have no serious psychopathology, or be over age 18, is no guarantee that respondents will comply with these requirements. There are also doubts as to whether vulnerable bereaved people are sufficiently protected (even if informed consent procedures are followed). These problems are clearly not all unique to Internet research, but they do need special consideration in the Internet context.

Positive Versus Negative Features of Internet Intervention

Most of the points we have just discussed apply directly or can easily be generalized to the more specific case of conducting bereavement intervention on the Internet. For example, one advantage of conducting intervention on the Internet is that the persons involved in such a program, like survey respondents, do not have to be in the same place at the same time; all that is needed for participation is a computer with a modem (this is, of course, currently easier in industrialized than in developing countries, although rapid expansion to nonindustrialized countries is occurring). Wagner et al. (2006) described further benefits of Internet therapy, although some of these could conceivably be features too of traditional treatment programs, for example, the fact that treatment protocols can be highly structured, enabling completion in a short time, and that dropout rates are reasonable. These authors also pointed out benefits inherent in the delay of feedback (this is in contrast to traditional interactions in therapy, where feedback is typically given directly), allowing respondents to reflect on and reread texts if needed. A substantial practical advantage, if the program proves effective, is the fact that Internet intervention is a low-cost method of treatment.

There are also potential dangers in using the Internet for bereavement intervention. Wagner et al. (2006) described a number of possible constraints or disadvantages, many of which reflect assumptions but that could be empirically tested. They pointed out the necessity for careful screening: A program will not suit all bereaved persons, and many with problems have to be excluded (thus limiting generalizability). This may obviously be the case for traditional therapy programs, too, although screening is likely to be conducted somewhat differently. Other concerns the authors mentioned, which are again not necessarily unique to Internet intervention but nevertheless deserve special attention, include the use of self-rated questionnaires with no independent assessment or interview of intervention participants (i.e., are they reliable?), or the potential for misunderstanding during treatment interactions (especially because there is no eye-to-eye contact or opportunity to give or receive direct feedback). Another concern may be that there is little opportunity for crisis intervention.

Finally, it is useful to consider participants' positive and negative evaluations of Internet intervention. Leibert, Archer, Munson, and York (2006) conducted a study of client perceptions of counseling. Evaluations were based on subjective accounts of online counseling versus traditional face-to-face counseling; program efficacy was not evaluated. They reported that loss of nonverbal information was considered a main disadvantage of Internet counseling (in general) but noted that anonymity was highly valued, particularly when sharing shameful information. Waldron et al. (2000) gave examples of potential harm in Internet self-help settings, including misunderstandings, excessive dependence, premature intimacy, and emotional intensity. Furthermore, there may be tendencies for Internet communities to develop normative rules that can be harmful to the participants who do not comply with them. Again, hard evidence for these claims is lacking.

Advantages and disadvantages of any particular Internet project, be it a survey, an intervention program, or an efficacy of intervention study, need to be carefully weighed. What are the particular benefits versus challenges, and what can be done to safeguard against risks for participants and researchers alike? In our view, Internet intervention programs, like their traditional counterparts, need to be subjected to rigorous efficacy evaluation procedures as part of the process of assessing advantages and disadvantages (cf. Schut et al., 2001). We turn to this issue next.

Studies of the Efficacy of Internet-Based Intervention

Internet-based intervention studies in the area of trauma and bereavement have been designed to relieve suffering and assist adaptation to bereavement (usually among individuals with relatively excessive symptomatology rates), goals that are clearly shared with traditional face-to-face counseling and therapy programs. On the Internet, intervention has typically consisted of writing tasks, with protocols giving writing instructions that often are tailored to specific needs. Feedback is usually provided (although this has not been the case in the diary intervention studies of Pennebaker and colleagues; see, e.g., Pennebaker, Zech, & Rimé, 2001). This type of intervention lends itself to implementation of cognitive behavior therapy techniques (exposure, cognitive reappraisal, and integration and restoration; Wagner et al., 2006).

To our knowledge, at this time results are available for only one Internet-based bereavement intervention study (Wagner, Knaevelsrud, & Maercker, 2005, 2006), which we describe shortly. However, studies have been conducted in the broader trauma area, notably by Lange and colleagues (Lange et al., 2001; Lange, van de Ven, & Schrieken, 2003) and Knaevelsrud and Maercker (2006). Lange and his colleagues have promoted an Internet technique they called *Interapy* (e.g., Lange et al., 2001, 2003). Interapy is an online standardized treatment for posttraumatic stress and pathological grief that includes psychoeducation, screening, measures of effects, and protocol-driven treatment for clients (exposure to bereavement cues, cognitive reappraisal, and integration and restoration). Writing assignments are an integral part of the intervention. Lange and colleagues have reported positive results from their outcome studies (see, e.g., Lange et al., 2003). Although the procedure is said to be appropriate for complicated grief, and bereaved persons have been included within their samples, separate analyses and efficacy of Interapy have not been reported specifically for this subgroup. The findings thus far combine, for instance, cases of sexual abuse, physical abuse, traffic accidents, and bereavement.

Wagner et al.'s (2005, 2006) research paves the way for further development of Internet efficacy investigation in the bereavement area. As such, it merits more detailed description although, as we discuss shortly, it lacks an important longitudinal control. These investigators extended the work of

Lange and colleagues (e.g., Lange et al., 2001, 2003) by developing an Internet-based cognitive behavioral treatment program specifically for a small sample of bereaved persons with complicated grief. This involved a writing protocol with specific and varied writing assignments, which were communicated and received via e-mail. They investigated the efficacy of this new form of bereavement intervention in a randomized controlled clinical trial (Wagner et al., 2006). Participants who responded to announcements in the printed media and bereavement Web sites were screened to assess whether they met inclusion criteria. If they did, they were assigned randomly to an immediate treatment condition or to a waiting condition, and all were given a pretreatment questionnaire. After the 5-week treatment, participants completed a posttest questionnaire and a follow-up questionnaire 3 months later (including measures of depression and anxiety and mental and physical health measures, such as the Impact of Events Scale). Participants, who were nearly all women, had suffered different types of loss (e.g., child, partner); they differed in the duration of bereavement (14 months to 29 years) and age (average age was 37 years). The 26 participants in the treatment group improved on symptoms of intrusion, avoidance, and other health measures significantly more than those in the control group ($n = 25$) at posttest. Effect sizes for treatment were reported to be large at posttest and follow-up. Improvement was maintained at 3 months, with no significant differences being discerned between posttreatment and follow-up.

The results of Wagner et al.'s (2006) Internet intervention study are promising; they suggest that the treatment was effective for bereaved people following traumatic circumstances of death and/or complicated grief. Respondents in the treatment group showed clinically significant change after the intervention (there was some decline in symptoms at posttest in the control group, consistent with usual recovery over time and possibly due to the fact that the ethical procedure required provision of bereavement information, which could have led to acquisition of knowledge and seeking of support sources). Unfortunately, there is a major limitation to this study: No follow-up data were available for the control group (who were given treatment 5 weeks after the treatment group had terminated the program), and thus no comparison with the treatment group could be made over this longer (3-month) time period. It cannot be concluded that the maintenance of improvement at 3 months in the treatment group was due to the intervention because there was no nontreatment group with which to compare the scores. Indeed, as noted earlier, the scores on dependent measures for the treatment group did not improve between posttest and follow-up (one would actually expect improvement over time without treatment). Thus, we are left not knowing whether this Internet intervention had longer term effects. A main criterion for efficacy of intervention studies is that they should evaluate long-term effects, not just immediate posttreatment effects (Schut et al., 2001). This is particularly important, because traditional grief intervention studies show considerable differences between short- and long-term effects, with less positive results in the long term.

Assessment: Impact of Bereavement Intervention on the Internet

Again, in the Internet intervention domain there is little evidence of efficacy, although we noted as a promising start Wagner et al.'s (2006) study, which merits replication and extension. There are good reasons based on previous research to believe that bereavement intervention (through the Internet) should work for some people (cf. Schut et al., 2001). There is provisional evidence from various domains (e.g., depression, anxiety disorders) that self-help Internet interventions may be a promising tool for treatment of some mental disorders (Pull, 2006). Furthermore, as we illustrate next, relevant results come from the general literature on disclosure and from the bereavement-specific literature on the efficacy of traditional techniques of intervention.

Internet bereavement programs lend themselves to so-called *written disclosure techniques*. Following the pioneering research of Pennebaker (for a review, see Pennebaker et al., 2001), the disclosure paradigm has been extensively used in recent decades as a method of intervention following stressful and/or traumatic life experiences. Instructions typically require respondents to write about their deepest thoughts and feelings about the stressful or traumatic event, each day for a number of days (often 5 to 7 days). This seemingly simple method has been shown to have positive effects on mental and physical health. Results in the case of bereavement have not been so favorable, however (M. Stroebe, Stroebe, Schut, Zech, & van den Bout, 2002). It seems likely that the technique would work better for subgroups of bereaved persons with certain maladaptive styles of coping and/or for those who suffer from complicated grief. Furthermore, techniques deriving from cognitive behavior therapy, as illustrated in Lange et al.'s (e.g., 2003) and Wagner et al.'s (2005, 2006) studies, seem more promising (e.g., including assignments that require restructuring of cognitions, as in writing a letter to the deceased).

A review of the efficacy of intervention programs conducted using traditional methods supports the preceding conclusion with respect to complicated grief (Schut et al., 2001; Schut & Stroebe, 2005). This review, which was based on the strictest methodological criteria for study selection, showed greatest efficacy of bereavement intervention for programs designed for complicated grief, grief-related depression, or posttraumatic disorders. Intervention was found to be modestly and only temporarily effective for bereaved persons who were vulnerable to the risks of bereavement (e.g., high levels of distress; traumatic circumstances of loss). It was least effective for programs directed to all bereaved persons, irrespective of whether intervention was indicated. Screening in Internet studies for high-risk individuals and those with complications in the grieving process (as in Wagner et al., 2006) probably enhances the possibility that the program will yield positive results. In addition, Schut et al. (2001) pointed out that intervention might prove more generally efficacious if the bereaved solicited help.

On the basis of the promising results of Wagner et al.'s (2005, 2006) pioneering research and results from studies of the efficacy of traditional intervention for the bereaved, one can expect well-designed Internet intervention to be effective for individuals who are at risk or who are experiencing complications in the grieving process and possibly for others who really feel the need to receive intervention. There is enormous potential for future research that has practical application (helping bereaved persons in great distress). Such research needs to conform to the stringent design and methodological criteria set out elsewhere (Schut et al., 2001).

GENERAL CONCLUSIONS

Bereaved people are free to use Internet resources that are offered to them, but they are also vulnerable. Therefore, all efforts must be made to ensure quality control and validity of claims made about the usefulness of Internet resources. There has been little research assessing the impact on individuals of any Internet-based support and intervention; the bereavement field is no exception to this. Well-controlled studies in all of the areas reviewed in this chapter are few and far between. Furthermore, there has been a tendency to sing the praises of Internet support and intervention in the bereavement area without consideration of the drawbacks and even dangers that might also be involved. It is remarkable how many claims have been made about helpful resources, including advantages of "meeting" similar bereaved others or commemorating a deceased loved one through an online Web site, without any solid evidence to back up these assumptions or to establish who will versus will not benefit (or even be adversely affected). It is disturbing that counselors and therapists are encouraged by authors describing these Web sites to include these Internet resources in their packages of care—it must be stressed yet again that the accuracy of information given or the helpfulness of many of them has not been examined.

More methodologically robust empirical research is needed, not only on provision of informal support but also on intervention programs offered by professionals. In the absence of direct evidence, we have drawn inferences in this chapter from scientific theories and related fields of empirical evidence. We have been able to indicate some positive effects of providing support, of giving information, and of intervening in the grieving process—for some people, for some troubles or ailments. On the other hand, we have had to draw attention to many limitations in empirical studies in the diverse areas.

In addition to establishing the impact of Internet resources on bereaved people, one major challenge ahead is to identify the bereaved people for whom a particular type of Internet support is effective and to guide bereaved persons selectively to using resources that are more likely to be helpful to them, including those offering professional intervention. Another challenge is to work toward ensuring that high-quality resources are available to bereaved people and that researchers find ways to help people discriminate between these and misleading or poorly informed resources.

REFERENCES

Aitken, A. (2006). Webwatch: Resources for children and young people. *Bereavement Care, 25*, 54.

Bargh, J. A., & McKenna, K. Y. A. (2004). The Internet and social life. *Annual Review of Psychology, 55*, 573–590.

Birnbaum, M. H. (2004). Data collection via the Internet. *Annual Review of Psychology, 55*, 803–832.

Boase, J., Horrigan, J., Wellman, B., & Rainie, L. (2006, January 25). *The strength of Internet ties* (Pew Internet and American Life Project). Retrieved January 25, 2008, from http://www.pewinternet.org/pdfs/PIP_Internet_ties.pdf

Boelen, P., Stroebe, M., Schut, H., & Zijerveld, A. (2006). Continuing bonds and grief: A prospective analysis. *Death Studies, 30*, 767–776.

Chang, C., & Sofka, C. (2006). Coping with loss in Chinese and North American "cyberspace" communities: E-temples and virtual cemeteries. *The Forum, 32*, 7.

Cobb, S. (1976). Social support as a moderator of life stress. *Psychosomatic Medicine, 38*, 300–314.

Cohn, M., Mehl, M., & Pennebaker, J. (2004). Linguistic markers of psychological change surrounding September 11, 2001. *Psychological Science, 15*, 687–693.

Colom, F., Vieta, E., Martinez-Aran, A., Reinares, M., Goikolea, J. M., Benabarre, A., et al. (2003). A randomized trial on the efficacy of group psychoeducation in the prophylaxis of recurrences in bipolar patients whose disease is in remission. *Archives of General Psychiatry, 60*, 402–407.

de Vries, B., & Roberts, P. (Eds.). (2004). Expressions of grief on the World Wide Web [Special issue]. *Omega: The Journal of Death and Dying, 49*(1).

Dyregrov, K., Nordanger, D., & Dyregrov, A. (2003). Predictors of psychosocial distress after suicide, SIDS and accidents. *Death Studies, 27*, 143–165.

Finn, J., & Banach, M. (2000). Victimization online: The down side of seeking human services for women on the Internet. *CyberPsychology and Behavior, 3*, 243–254.

Fogel, J., Albert, S. M., Schnabel, F., Ditkoff, B. A., & Neugut, A. (2002). Internet use and social support in women with breast cancer. *Health Psychology, 21*, 398–404.

Fox, S., Anderson, J., & Rainie, L. (2005, January 9). *The future of the Internet* (Pew Internet and American Life Project). Retrieved January 25, 2008, from http://www.pewinternet.org/pdfs/PIP_Future_of_Internet.pdf

Freud, S. (1957). Mourning and melancholia, In J. Strachey (Ed. & Trans.), *Standard edition of the complete psychological works of Sigmund Freud* (pp. 152–170). London: Hogarth Press. (Original work published 1917)

Golden, T. (2006). Healing and the Internet. *The Forum, 32,* 8.

Gosling, S., Vazire, S., Srivastava, S., & John, O. (2004). Should we trust Web-based studies? A comparative analysis of six preconceptions about Internet questionnaires. *American Psychologist, 59,* 93–104.

Hollander, E. (2001). Cyber community in the valley of the shadow of death. *Journal of Loss and Trauma, 6,* 135–146.

House, J. (1981). *Work, stress and social support.* Reading, MA: Addison-Wesley.

Klass, D., Silverman, P., & Nickman, S. L. (1996). *Continuing bonds: New understandings of grief.* Washington, DC: Taylor & Francis.

Knaevelsrud, C., & Maercker, A. (2006, December 19). Does the quality of the working alliance predict treatment outcome in online psychotherapy for traumatized patients? *Journal of Medical Internet Research, 8,* e31. Retrieved January 25, 2007, from http://www.jmir.org/2006/4/e31

Kraut, R., Kiesler, S., Boneva, B., Cummings, J., Helgeson, V., & Crawford, A. (2002). Internet paradox revisited. *Journal of Social Issues, 58,* 49–74.

Kraut, R., Olson, J., Banaji, M., Bruckman, A., Cohen, J., & Couper, M. (2004). Psychological research online: Report of Board of Scientific Affairs Advisory Group on the Conduct of Research on the Internet. *American Psychologist, 59,* 105–117.

Kraut, R., Patterson, V., Lundmark, M., Kiesler, S., Mukopadhyay, T., & Scherlis, W. (1998). Internet paradox: A social technology that reduces social involvement and psychological well-being. *American Psychologist, 53,* 1017–1031.

Lange, A., van de Ven, J., & Schrieken, B. (2003). Interapy: Treatment of post-traumatic stress via the Internet. *Cognitive Behaviour Therapy, 32,* 110–124.

Lange, A., van de Ven, J., Schrieken, B., & Emmelkamp, P. (2001). Interapy, treatment of posttraumatic stress through the Internet: A controlled trial. *Journal of Behavior Therapy and Experimental Psychiatry, 32,* 73–90.

Lieberman, M., & Goldstein, B. (2005). Self-help online: An outcome evaluation of breast cancer bulletin boards. *Journal of Health Psychology, 10,* 855–862.

Lieberman, M., & Goldstein, B. (2006). Not all negative emotions are equal: The role of emotional expression in online support groups for women with breast cancer. *Psycho-Oncology, 15,* 160–168.

Leibert, T., Archer, J., Munson, J., & York, G. (2006). An exploratory study of client perceptions of Internet counseling and the therapeutic alliance. *Journal of Mental Health Counseling, 28,* 69–83.

Madden, M. (2003). *The changing picture of who's online and what they do* (Pew Internet and American Life Project). Retrieved December 22, 2003, from http://www.pewInternet.org/reports/toc.asp?Report

Manfreda, K. L., & Vehovar, V. (2007). Internet surveys. In E. D. de Leeuw, J. J. Hox, & D. A. Dillman (Eds.), *International handbook of survey methodology* (pp. 187–204). Mahwah, NJ: Erlbaum.

Martin, T., & Doka, K. (2000). *Men don't cry, women do: Transcending gender stereotypes of grief.* Philadelphia: Brunner Mazel.

McKenna, K. Y. A., Green, A. S., & Gleason, M. J. (2002). Relationship formation on the Internet: What's the big attraction? *Journal of Social Issues, 58,* 9–31.

Moss, M. (2004). Grief on the web. *Omega: The Journal of Death and Dying, 49,* 77–81.

Nolen-Hoeksema, S. (2001). Ruminative coping and adjustment to bereavement. In M. Stroebe, R. O. Hansson, W. Stroebe, & H. Schut (Eds.), *Handbook of bereavement research: Consequences, coping, and care* (pp. 545–562). Washington, DC: American Psychological Association.

Pennebaker, J., Zech, E., & Rimé, B. (2001). Disclosing and sharing emotion: Psychological, social, and health consequences. In M. Stroebe, R. O. Hansson, W. Stroebe, & H. Schut (Eds.), *Handbook of bereavement research: Consequences, coping, and care* (pp. 517–543). Washington, DC: American Psychological Association.

Pull, C. (2006). Self-help Internet interventions for mental disorders. *Current Opinion in Psychiatry, 19,* 50–53.

Roberts, P. (2006). From my space to our space: The functions of Web memorials in bereavement. *The Forum, 32,* 1–4.

Robson, D., & Robson, M. (2000). Ethical issues in Internet counseling. *Counseling Psychology Quarterly, 13,* 249–257.

Schultze, N.-G. (2006). Success factors in Internet-based psychological counseling. *CyberPsychology & Behavior, 9,* 623–626.

Schut, H., & Stroebe, M. (2005). Interventions to enhance adaptation to bereavement. *Journal of Palliative Medicine, 8,* S140–S147.

Schut, H., Stroebe, M., Boelen, P., & Zijerveld, A. (2006). Continuing relationships with the deceased: Disentangling bonds and grief. *Death Studies, 30,* 757–766.

Schut, H., Stroebe, M., van den Bout, J., & Terheggen, M. (2001). The efficacy of bereavement interventions: Determining who benefits. In M. Stroebe, R. O. Hansson, W. Stroebe, & H. Schut (Eds.), *Handbook of bereavement research: Consequences, coping, and care* (pp. 705–737). Washington, DC: American Psychological Association.

Stroebe, M., & Schut, H. (1999). The dual process model of coping with bereavement: Rationale and description. *Death Studies, 23,* 197–224.

Stroebe, M., Schut, H., & Stroebe, W. (2007). Health consequences of bereavement: A review. *The Lancet, 370,* 1960–1973.

Stroebe, M., Stroebe, W., Schut, H., Zech, E., & van den Bout, J. (2002). Does disclosure of emotions facilitate recovery from bereavement? Evidence from two prospective studies. *Journal of Consulting and Clinical Psychology, 70,* 169–178.

Stroebe, W., Schut, H., & Stroebe, M. (2005). Grief work, disclosure and counseling: Do they help the bereaved? *Clinical Psychology Review, 25,* 395–414.

Stroebe, W., Stroebe, M., Abakoumkin, G., & Schut, H. (1996). Social and emotional loneliness: A comparison of attachment and stress theory explanations. *Journal of Personality and Social Psychology, 70,* 1241–1249.

Vanderwerker, L., & Prigerson, H. (2004). Social support and technological connectedness as protective factors in bereavement. *Journal of Loss and Trauma, 9,* 45–57.

Wagner, B., Knaevelsrud, C., & Maercker, A. (2005). Internet-based treatment for complicated grief: Concepts and case study. *Journal of Loss and Trauma, 10,* 409–432.

Wagner, B., Knaevelsrud, C., & Maercker, A. (2006). Internet-based cognitive-behavioral therapy for complicated grief: A randomized controlled train. *Death Studies, 30,* 429–453.

Waldron, V., Lavitt, M., & Kelley, D. (2000). The nature and prevention of harm in technology-mediated self-help settings: Three exemplars. *Journal of Technology in Human Services, 17,* 267–293.

Worden, W. (2002). *Grief counseling and grief therapy* (3rd ed.). New York: Springer Publishing Company.

VII

CONCLUSION

27

BEREAVEMENT RESEARCH: 21ST-CENTURY PROSPECTS

MARGARET S. STROEBE, ROBERT O. HANSSON, HENK SCHUT,
AND WOLFGANG STROEBE

Our objective for this volume has been to provide an up-to-date, state-of-the-art account of bereavement research at the start of the 21st century. We have tried as well to draw the implications of current bereavement research for contemporary societal and practice issues (although our intention has not been to provide practical guidelines either for the bereaved themselves or practitioners trying to help them). The two previous *Handbooks* in this series (Stroebe, Hansson, Stroebe, & Schut, 2001b; Stroebe, Stroebe, & Hansson, 1993) were more singularly focused on documenting the growing scientific basis for bereavement phenomena, in relationship to theory, research, and intervention. The three volumes complement one another in many ways. Many of the theoretical analyses, research reports, and guiding principles for intervention reported in the first two volumes remain relevant and provide a context for chapters in the current volume.

In this concluding chapter, we reflect on the research represented in this and the previous *Handbooks* to summarize developments and to indicate current understanding—and gaps in our knowledge—in the scientific field of bereavement. We identify core themes in relationship to scientific, societal, and practice issues. Although the chapter is divided into two main sections, covering (a) contemporary scientific and (b) societal concerns, a major thrust

577

is to draw practice implications from the scientific issues discussed as well as scientific implications from the more societally driven ones. We suggest directions for future investigation and highlight controversies in the field today, providing commentary where appropriate.

CONTEMPORARY SCIENTIFIC APPROACHES AND ISSUES

Theoretical Approaches to Grief

Contemporary bereavement research continues to be theory driven, and there is every reason to assume that this will continue to be the case through the 21st century. As both Weiss and Archer (chaps. 2 and 3, this volume) illustrate, theories are necessary to understand certain sometimes-counterintuitive phenomena and complex symptomatology. They can provide explanations of individual differences in reactions and should guide the development of care and intervention programs for alleviating distress and preventing complications. A rich body of theory, discussed in our three *Handbooks*, has made major contributions in all these respects. One important example of this is attachment theory. In chapter 5 of this volume, Mikulincer and Shaver describe how Bowlby's (e.g., 1980) insights can be tested using new methods contributed by social cognition researchers, psychophysiologists, and cognitive neuroscientists, to understand the phenomena of anxious and avoidant defenses that can be manifest during bereavement. Such an approach not only contributes to unraveling complex symptomatology but also helps to explain differences among bereaved people, and it has clear implications for intervention.

A number of important features characterize contemporary theory on bereavement. Despite earlier calls for the development of an integrative theory of bereavement (cf. also chaps. 2 and 3, this volume), we still see a multiplicity of theoretical approaches, with some cross-fertilization between theoretical positions, and theoretical analyses directed toward understanding symptomatology and coping at both the general and grief-specific levels (cf. Stroebe, Hansson, Stroebe, & Schut, 2001a). As Archer (chap. 3, this volume) notes, there is "still no comprehensive evidence-based theory to account for the way in which people move from initial high levels of distress to levels similar to those before the loss" (p. 58).

In addition, different theories address different phenomena, and on different levels of analysis. As Weiss (chap. 2, this volume) concludes,

> There now are good theories about how grief is linked to the nature of the relationship that was lost, to that relationship's meaning for the bereaved person, and to the ways in which the relationship may have served regulatory functions. Investigators have not yet integrated these

theories; neither do they fully understand the mental and emotional processes that may underlie them. However, if we have not achieved full understanding of grief in the [past] 50 years . . . we have nevertheless made a great deal of progress. (pp. 40–41)

On the other hand, researchers have increasingly come to realize the compatibility between theoretical perspectives and have addressed the potential for integration between perspectives (e.g., Rubin's [1991] two-track model and Stroebe & Schut's [1999] dual-process model with attachment theory; see chap. 5, this volume). The question is, do we really need just one integrative theory?

It is also evident that certain theories described in the *Handbooks* have continued to have a huge impact in general, whereas others have not. In particular, attachment theory, cognitive stress theory, trauma theories, and social constructionism (meaning-making) remain highly influential perspectives. To illustrate, meaning-making perspectives have been given much impetus by the work of Neimeyer (e.g., 2001), among others, and have been significant in the derivation of fundamental principles (e.g., with respect to the functioning of family systems in bereavement) and in providing guidance for therapy programming, spanning both individual and interpersonal levels of analysis (e.g., chaps. 23 and 24, this volume). In Nadeau's words,

Individual grief is profoundly shaped by the family context in which it occurs, and the grief of an individual often has profound effects on the family . . . In my opinion, meaning is at the core of family grief. (chap. 24, p. 513)

New perspectives are beginning to have an impact as well. One of these is the *life course perspective* (e.g., chaps. 20, 21, and 25, this volume; Moss, Moss, & Hansson, 2001; Oltjenbruns, 2001; Silverman & Worden, 1993), which focuses on intergenerational relationships and family systems. This perspective has been useful, for example, in understanding grandparental bereavement; it provides a dynamic approach to the study of change in families, including the construction of social meaning surrounding the life event and the social context within which it occurs (chap. 21, this volume). Furthermore, as indicated by the development of positive growth perspectives (Schaefer & Moos, 2001; chap. 15, this volume) and models of trajectories (chap. 14, this volume), bereavement research is no longer guided exclusively by a medical type of model that views grief as a pathological experience from which one must recover. Bereavement research has recently undergone a healthy expansion.

Yet there are still gaps in the range of contemporary bereavement theories. For example, with the notable exception of Archer's work (e.g., Archer, 1999, 2001; chap. 3, this volume), comparatively little attention has been paid to the evolutionary functions of grief; instead, the focus is usually on the level of psychological process. Perhaps reflecting the current demographic mix among bereavement researchers, there appears to be greater interest in issues of social constructionism, appraisal, personal and collective coping resources, and so on, than in discovering what is "wired in." However, understanding grief and grieving on the evolutionary level would seem essential, too.

We see a huge need in the field to increase the influence of theory on practice (e.g., providing guidance in settings ranging from informal support to more formal therapy). In contrast, it has become evident that clinical questions have continued to motivate researchers in conducting their work. For example, many of the chapters in this (and previous) *Handbooks* have addressed the need to clarify the meaning and functions of cognitive processes (including *grief work*) and associated implications for intervention programming (e.g., chaps. 3 and 6, this volume).

Finally, as contemporary research expands to include cultures other than Western industrialized ones, we can expect demands for theory that explains and accommodates different patterns of bereavement response. Kastenbaum's (chap. 4, this volume) examination of grief and grieving in contemporary society considers how patterns of grieving and mourning may change according to societally influenced individual experiences, circumstances, and social forces. We concur with both Kastenbaum and with Rosenblatt (chap. 10, this volume), who point out that future bereavement research in different cultures may challenge Western understanding of the emotions of grief.

Understanding the Nature of Grief

Understanding the nature of grief is one of the most fundamental tasks of scientists in our field, and given the range of issues incorporated in the general topic, it merits extensive consideration here. It is essential, for example, to understand the nature of normal and complicated forms of grief, the course of grieving across time, and the wide range of risks to mental and physical health. Later in this section, we provide examples of how contributors to this *Handbook* have addressed some of the issues (we address the more cultural and societal issues, including the diagnosis of complicated grief as a potential mental disorder, later in this chapter).

Phenomena and Manifestations of Grief

Researchers are now focusing on multiple aspects of grief. For example, we are moving toward a more differentiated understanding of the impact that different types of loss have on grief (cf. chaps. 18 and 20–22, this volume). Similarly, our focus has broadened to include a wider range of bereavement outcomes. In addition to assessing problematic outcomes (e.g., chaps. 8 and

19, this volume), researchers now often examine more positive outcomes (chap. 15, this volume). Intrapersonal approaches to understand grief and adaptation have become more balanced by interpersonal ones, particularly in relationship to coping and the provision of intervention (chaps. 23–25, this volume). We next select two topics to illustrate this more differentiated perspective.

The Course of Grief. Researchers' assumptions about the course of grief following a bereavement have changed substantially. There is now a consensus that emotional states differ considerably between bereaved people and that the temporal course of grief may reflect diverse trajectories, rather than stages or phases, both before (e.g., in the case of terminal illness) and after the death of a loved one (cf. chaps. 2, 13, 14, and 20, this volume). However, Weiss (chap. 2, this volume) points out that although bereaved individuals show great variation in the sequencing and experience of affective states, there is validity to the idea of a progression of grief states and that acknowledging this makes it easier to think about the changes in grieving that occur as time elapses. Likewise, Schulz, Boerner, and Hebert (chap. 13, this volume) conclude that despite distinct individual trajectories that provide a richer and more detailed account of bereavement (after caregiving), positive postbereavement trends were also discernable. It remains to be seen whether stage theory will regain its influence: A recent study by Maciejewski, Zhang, Block, and Prigerson (2007) on the validity of stages remains unconvincing (it was mainly retrospective, excluded persons with complicated grief or who were traumatic death survivors and used single-item measures for classification of stages).

A consensus has been reached as well regarding the heterogeneity to be found in patterns of adjustment to bereavement. In this context, researchers have endeavored to further document different types of trajectories—for example, as Murphy (chap. 18, this volume) emphasizes, among parents who are bereaved by the sudden, violent deaths of their children and the contrasting bereavement trajectories of parents whose children have died following an extended illness. It also remains important to focus "on identifying the contextual and individual-level factors that exacerbate (or buffer against) . . . potentially distressing consequences" (chap. 20, this volume, p. 418). Finally, the specification of trajectories requires greater precision, particularly given expected differences in the time course of experienced grief versus depression (cf. Boelen & Prigerson, 2007; Wijngaards-de Meij et al., 2005). Bonanno et al. (chap. 14, this volume) note that "one trajectory . . . suggested an unambiguous *chronic grief* reaction. These participants manifested low levels of *depression* prior to the loss but then showed elevated *depression* at 6 and 18 months of bereavement [italics added]" (p. 298). Future studies need to guard against equating chronic grief with depression.

Growth and Resilience. When the positive psychology movement gained momentum in the 1990s, its application to the experience of bereavement may have seemed counterintuitive. Why search for benefits, growth, and positivity when acutely bereaved people were struggling just to find their way through any single day in their lives? What was the point of studying happiness and growth when our basic motivation must ultimately be to prevent or relieve the suffering of bereaved persons, particularly those who endure extreme mental and/or physical health consequences? Also, why look at resilience?

In the meantime, researchers who examine growth and resilience have done much to demonstrate the utility of their approaches (cf. chaps. 14, 15, and 19, this volume; Folkman, 2001; Schaefer & Moos, 2001). A different picture of the grieving process emerges when we broaden our perspective to include potential for growth and resilience. For example, the research on resilience informs us about sources of strength (e.g., in coping), processes that account for positive outcomes, and individual-difference factors that contribute to repairing the damage of bereavement (e.g., chaps. 14 and 19, this volume; Folkman, 2001). However, apparent resilience may (a) camouflage symptomatology (reflecting absent grief), (b) be related to cultural norms regarding overt expression (e.g., a stoic presentation, nondisclosed grief) rather than lack of experiencing of grief, or (c) may demonstrate lack of any occasion for grieving (the deceased person was not significant in the person's life or loved). These alternatives need to be further teased apart.

Showing an awareness of such concerns, the potential value of research on growth and resilience has been shown in many areas. In the area of childhood bereavement, for example, it would be important to understand not only the long-term impact on psychopathology but also possible long-term benefits (e.g., improved self-efficacy, psychological well-being). In this connection, Luecken (chap. 19, this volume) stresses the need to examine subsets of children who grow in adversity. Luecken argues for research to "evaluate positive mental and physical health outcomes, including, but not limited to, academic or social competence, life satisfaction, purpose in life, goal motivation, achievement of developmental milestones, or positive well-being" (p. 409). Also, Luecken points out the need for integration of biological perspectives (e.g., physiological resilience) into the theoretical framework of resilience: "Physiological resilience can be measured by the body's ability to flexibly vary the heart rate to meet environmental challenges, or quickly recover cardiovascular and hormonal indices to homeostatic levels after challenge, or by the immune system's capacity to resist infection" (p. 409). Studies on the mechanisms underlying resilience are also needed (cf. chaps. 19 and 25, this volume).

Understanding of growth and resilience would also benefit from more precise, conceptual clarification. Those of us in the field need to move beyond the general categories of "posttraumatic growth" or "meaning-making" to define precisely what processes are involved. We also need to substantiate

582   STROEBE ET AL.

that growth occurs and to demonstrate its impact on adjustment (see chap. 15, this volume). Disentangling the components of growth (e.g., using Davis's [chap. 15, this volume] distinction among perceiving benefits, sustained growth, and gaining insight) in relationship to outcome variables should lead to better understanding of exactly what positive or posttraumatic growth incorporates, how it progresses, and what precisely its significance is for bereaved people. As Davis (chap. 15, this volume) notes, we will then be in a better position to help the bereaved deal with the range of changes in their lives.

Risk of Mental and Physical Health Consequences of Bereavement

It has become well established that bereavement is associated with detrimental consequences to health, but work is still needed on identifying bereaved individuals at high risk. Fortunately, theoretical models are now available to guide research and foster integration of complex and interacting variables that determine individual differences in adaptation (cf. chap. 25, this volume; Stroebe, Folkman, Hansson, & Schut, 2006). Such models, however, require further testing, and some examples are available in this *Handbook*. Sandler et al. (chap. 25, this volume) make the case for investigating multiple factors in one design: "Resilience is determined by multiple risk and protective factors that have a cumulative effect . . . Therefore, programs to promote resilience should target multiple risk and protective factors" (p. 532). Luecken (chap. 19, this volume) provides another example, examining the key pathways and moderating factors associated with long-term adaptation to early death of parent, enabling examination of how secondary losses, such as financial burdens, frequent moves, lesser contact with surviving parent, disruption of daily and social routines, and separation of family members, are associated with greater risk. Finally, Carr (chap. 20, this volume) shows how examination of multiple factors could help establish patterns of adaptation to bereavement among older adults. The picture that emerges is complex, indicating a need to take into account any age-related declines in emotional reactivity, skills and experience in dealing with adversity, and co-occurring stressors that could overwhelm an older person's abilities to cope. It becomes clear that simple age comparisons in terms of more or less impact have little meaning. It is more useful to explore multiple determinants within the unique experiences of bereavement at older and at younger ages independently than to focus on whether these groups are more versus less affected by bereavement (see also Hansson & Stroebe, 2007).

However, there is also a continuing place for in-depth analysis of single factors, such as religion. Here, appropriate complexity can be built into analyses of such variables as religious meaning-making or religious coping strategies among bereaved people. Dimensions of religious coping can be identified, religious coping measured, the impact of different faith traditions examined, and bereavement outcomes associated with religion ascertained (chap. 16, this volume).

Examinations of risk and protective factors in bereavement could also be strengthened by broadening our focus on outcome measures, beyond indexes of health and well-being, to include physiological measures (cf. Stroebe et al., 2006). For example, Luecken (chap. 19, this volume) comments on the dearth of studies that have directly evaluated physiological consequences associated with early parent loss in humans and the need to go beyond main effect models to consider key intervening or moderating factors. From an applied perspective, it also seems important to identify and distinguish between modifiable and nonmodifiable factors (chap. 25, this volume). These are useful, for example, in identifying individuals with differential needs for or ability to benefit from an intervention.

Type of Loss

Researchers have for some time considered the implications of differing forms of loss for the bereavement experience, and each of our *Handbooks* has considered a sampling of such differences. For example, considerable attention has been paid to children's loss of a parent and to parents' loss of a child. In regard to the former, in the current volume factors are identified that are likely to affect both short- and long-term consequences of the loss of a parent (chap. 19, this volume), and we have also seen how promising interventions for children can be developed (chap. 25, this volume). Further evaluation to establish intervention efficacy followed by more widespread implementation will, we hope, help to prevent both severe short- and long-term consequences.

Additional questions remain regarding the experience of losing a parent. For example, Murphy (chap. 18, this volume) reports that even within the United States, samples of greater ethnic diversity need to be included and specific needs addressed. She reports that young Native Americans, African Americans, and Latinos have higher rates of death by homicide compared with Caucasian young people. As her chapter illustrates, trajectories following this type of death are likely to be different from those that follow natural deaths. We need to understand the implications of relative excesses in such deaths for people from these different cultural groups, who may grieve in different ways (cf. chap. 10, this volume).

In our *Handbooks* we have consistently tried to increase coverage of the types of losses that had previously received relatively little attention in the literature (although further extension is still desirable, e.g., bereavement following the murder or the rare disease of a loved one). Adopting a more inclusive approach has in turn provided a number of important insights. For example, we now have a much clearer picture of the extent to which grief reactions are uniquely related not only to particular types of loss but also to characteristics of grievers and to the situation within which bereaved persons find themselves. This is especially evident in the case of the elderly bereaved, whose unique bereavement experience has received little attention, although older adults are often respondents in bereavement studies. The reports on findings from the Changing Lives of Older Couples (CLOC) Study in the current volume (chaps. 13, 14, and 20) have helped to rectify this neglect. These investigators have begun to identify how distinctive risk factors, resources, type of loss, and contextual factors combine to shape the experiences of older bereaved spouses (e.g., arduous caregiving, in combination with personal frailty, may take its toll on the surviving partner; see chap. 13, this volume). A further vivid example involving older bereaved persons is provided by Hayslip and White (chap. 21, this volume), who documented the complexity of grief following loss of a grandchild. It becomes clear that the trauma and anguish experienced by grandparents also has to do with witnessing the suffering of their adult child and their own sense of helplessness in alleviating that pain, which compounds their own grief at the loss of their grandchild.

This area of research has helped to illuminate needs for policy, support, and intervention. However, it will also be important for researchers and practitioners to remain sensitive to sociocultural, historical, health, and demographic changes that characterize older populations. As Carr (chap. 20, this volume) emphasizes, future cohorts of bereaved older persons may experience bereavement in very different ways, for example, as a result of declining family size (they will have fewer children on whom to rely for social support) and because of improving health experience and financial security. In the case of grandparental grief, lower birth rates may mean that the loss of an only grandchild—and thereby the whole new generation—occurs more frequently and seems likely to have devastating impact.

Cognitive Processes in Relationship to Bereavement Outcomes

One challenging task will be to achieve a better understanding of cognitive processes that influence good versus poor adaptation to loss. Three topics, which we discuss next, have been at the center of recent psychological research on cognitive processes.

Grief Work and Continuing Bonds. Scholars such as Archer (chap. 3, this volume) and Field (chap. 6, this volume) have rightly argued for a refinement of the notion of *grief work*, which was originally understood to mean the active process whereby attachment to the deceased is relinquished through continued confrontation of memories and thoughts associated with the loss (Freud, 1917/1957; cf. chaps. 3 and 6, this volume). One useful advance in understanding grief work, related to the concept of relinquishment in the preceding definition, has been the linking of ideas about how one works through grief with an understanding of the nature of continuing bonds and their relationship to patterns of attachment (cf. also chap. 5, this volume). Research has not consistently supported earlier conclusions (e.g., Klass, Silverman, & Nickman, 1996) that maintenance of continuing bonds is adaptive.

Other advances in this area are evident. For example, Mikulincer and Shaver (chap. 5, this volume) criticize earlier continuing-bonds formulations for being insufficiently attentive to the importance of cognitive reorganization (and the same could be said of grief work research) and have now integrated this aspect into their own analysis in terms of patterns of attachment. As contributors to the *Handbook* have also argued, the idea of continuing bonds needs to be defined and operationalized in a way that captures its multidimensionality and the complexity of its relationship to adaptation (chaps. 2 and 6, this volume). More finely grained analyses are needed of the nature of the bond, not only after bereavement but also while the person was alive (cf. chap. 20, this volume). Consideration of the cultural context has also been neglected in the past. Notions of grief work and continuing bonds must be examined in cultural and historical perspective (chaps. 10 and 12, this volume). As Rosenblatt explains in chapter 10 of this volume, some cultures welcome maintained contact with the deceased; others fear it: "There is great variety in whether and how the living and dead are thought to be in contact with each other and in what exactly *contact* means" (msp. 7). Attention to such issues would seem more likely to advance understanding than would simply prolonging discussions of whether bonds are broken or continued in normal grief process, are generally healthy or problematic, or about who maintains these opposing positions.

Meaning-Making. Many lines of research represented in the current and previous *Handbooks* can be subsumed under the general label of *meaning-making research,* including work on attributions, cognitive behavioral models, cognitive stress theory approaches, religious meaning-making, assumptive worldviews, psychosocial transitions, and growth (e.g., chaps. 15, 16, and 21, this volume). In addition, meaning-making research addresses cultural issues. For example, we now have evidence of how the meaning of death varies widely from culture to culture (chap. 10, this volume), and descriptions of the interpersonal family process that marks the discovery and negotiation of shared understandings of the death (cf. chap. 24, this volume).

Neimeyer's (2001) *meaning reconstruction perspective* has been an influential force behind much recent meaning-making research: He views meaning reconstruction as the principal task of coping with loss. This concept seems central to many types of loss. For example, Hayslip and White (chap. 21, this volume) discuss how grandparents search for meaning after the death of a grandchild, a search that is an ever-changing process and cause of mental struggle. Researchers are working toward more finely grained analyses, as illustrated in Davis's (chap. 15, this volume) approach, reported earlier. Likewise, Nadeau (chap. 24, this volume) tackles problems in defining the term *meaning-making* and comes to her own definition in the family context:

Meanings are defined as cognitive representations, held in the minds of family members, constructed in the context of the family, that symbolically represent various elements of reality. Meanings are products of interactions with others and are influenced by society, culture, and historical time. (pp. 513–514)

Of particular relevance is that empirical research is beginning to confirm previously assumed relationships between specific types of meaning-making and health. Murphy (chap. 18, this volume) reports that parents who found meaning in the deaths of their children 5 years postdeath reported better health and higher levels of marital satisfaction than those who had not found meaning 5 years after the loss, suggesting that this had to do with two meaning-related tasks that are addressed by survivors (following Janoff-Bulman & Frantz, 1997): (a) minimizing the terror of a meaning-less world and (b) maximizing value in their own lives.

In addition to the need for specification of meaning-making just noted, causal relationships between types of meaning-making and adjustment to bereavement need to be established. It is remarkable how many assumptions about the causality of meaning-making in the adjustment process are made, without proper empirical testing. This will require longitudinal research designs.

Cognitive Processing in Complicated Grief. Because the concept of complicated (prolonged) grief is being proposed for the forthcoming *Diagnostic and Statistical Manual of Mental Disorders* (e.g., 4th ed.; *DSM–IV*; American Psychiatric Association, 1994) system (see the section later in this chapter, "Complicated Grief and the *Diagnostic and Statistical Manual of Mental Disorders*"), it is of concern that research on cognitive processes associated with complicated grief is still limited. We are encouraged, however, that some of the chapters cited in the preceding section provide useful leads, as have chapters in previous *Handbooks* (e.g. Fleming & Robinson, 2001; Folkman, 2001; Nolen-Hoeksema, 2001).

However, new lines of research are needed. Recent investigations by Boelen and colleagues illustrate directions that could be followed to fill this gap (e.g., Boelen, de Keijser, van den Hout, & van den Bout, 2007; Boelen, van den Bout, & van den Hout, 2006). Adopting a cognitive–behavioral approach, Boelen and his colleagues have examined mechanisms associated with complicated grief. For example, Boelen et al. (2006) tested assumptions about the role that negative cognitions and avoidance strategies play in emotional difficulties after bereavement. Negative cognitions (about the self, life, etc.) and avoidance (e.g., of reminders of the deceased) were related to current and prospective symptomatology. The authors suggested the need for further scrutiny of these cognitive processes (e.g., to address conceptual overlap between the cognitive variables and symptomatology).

Boelen et al. (2007) also provided one of the few comparisons of different types of treatments for complicated grief (cf. also Shear, Frank, Houck, & Reynolds, 2005), examining the comparative effectiveness of cognitive–behavioral therapy with a nonspecific treatment incorporating supportive counseling. Cognitive–behavioral therapy was associated with more improvement in complicated grief and general psychopathology than supportive counseling, and the former was differentially related to exposure and cognitive restructuring treatment conditions, thus providing a first indication of how different cognitive elements in a therapy program may influence complicated grief. Future research needs to compare such treatment conditions with nontreatment control conditions, or with standard interventions with well-established and stable effects, which neither Boelen et al. nor Shear et al. (2005) did.

Research Design and Method

Many of the points made about design and methodological issues in our concluding chapter to the previous *Handbook* (Stroebe et al., 2001a) are still relevant and do not need to be repeated in detail here. In general, the field continues to be characterized by advancements in these respects, but limitations remain. For example, in the area of religious coping, Hays and Hendrix (chap. 16, this volume) note common methodological shortcomings (absence of control groups or a focus only on main effects), yet a few studies could be identified that were methodologically more sophisticated, using large samples and longitudinal models and using religious variables as predictors of health outcome over time.

In many respects, the CLOC Study serves as a model for future work in the field not only because of its rigorous design and methodological features but also because the data set has been opened for researchers in general to address their own research questions (cf. chaps. 13, 14, and 20, this volume). This prospective, multiwave study of widowed persons and matched control participants has enabled the prospective tracking of the experiences of older married couples through and after the dying process. Assessments of the bereaved survivor are available for several points in time following spousal loss. Detailed information was collected on characteristics of the survivor, the late spouse, the marital relationship, and the context of the death (cf. chap. 20, this volume). Prebereavement information has contributed greatly to understanding; for example, Bonanno et al. (chap. 14, this volume) show that some problems, such as excessive dependency, may predate conjugal loss and be associated already in marriage with excessive rates of depression, which simply persists but is not caused by bereavement.

We now turn from design to methods. Much of the data from the CLOC Study rely on well-validated written questionnaires. Questionnaire measures are still extensively used in bereavement research, and indeed, Neimeyer,

Hogan, and Laurie (chap. 7, this volume) list a number of legitimate uses for these while at the same time calling for creative application of alternative methods, including qualitative ones. They note advancements in validation and reliability of many quantitative scales of grief while urging even further psychometric rigor and extended applications to diverse cultures and communities. It is important to note that they also stressed that there is a place for generic measures of psychological distress (e.g., depressive, anxious, or posttraumatic symptoms), which may exhibit different patterns of response than measures more specific to grief.

New research techniques and procedures, as called for by Neimeyer et al. (chap. 7, this volume), are currently gaining momentum, as evidenced in functional magnetic resonance imaging studies (chap. 17, this volume) and Internet studies (chap. 26, this volume). However, cautions are raised in both chapters that report on these developments. Concerns were expressed about interpretation of functional magnetic resonance imaging data, given the pioneering nature of much of this research. In the Internet domain, cautions focused (among other things) on the validity of claims about potential benefits of participating in Internet-based formats, because far too little research has been conducted to evaluate their efficacy.

A further, highly promising development is the use of laboratory studies, as Mikulincer and Shaver illustrate (chap. 5, this volume). For example, retrieval latencies that occur when bereaved people are asked to recall memories of early childhood loss experiences can be used as measures of cognitive accessibility, or links can be made between induced negative moods associated with bereavement and cognitive processing. Techniques developed in other areas (e.g., social cognition) can usefully be applied to the bereavement research area as well. As Mikulincer and Shaver note, certain of Bowlby's (e.g., 1980) hypotheses about underlying mechanisms relating to attachment, which at the time appeared untestable, can now be examined in laboratory research.

There remain issues of sampling in bereavement research. We reviewed some sample limitations earlier, in our discussion of types of loss, but it is important to reemphasize these types of limitations again here, given their relevance to the design of studies and the generalization of results. Consider the following examples from just two areas: First, Luecken (chap. 19, this volume) notes that research on the long-term consequences of childhood loss of parent had been mainly conducted with clinically diagnosed patients and that this was retrospective. Furthermore, she cautions about generalizing from atypical samples: Too often, inferences are made about normal bereavement experiences from nonhuman species or from severely deprived children in orphanages. Second, one of the biggest challenges in the coming decades will be to adequately apply methods and techniques developed in the West to other cultural settings. As Rosenblatt (chap. 10, this volume) warns, "One cannot presume that the methods one would use in studying bereavement in cultures where psychology has flourished would be appropriate in other cultures" (p. 218). His examples are straightforward but vivid: Direct or follow-up questions may be considered rude in some cultures, and it may be difficult to recruit persons to talk about bereavement—this may be taboo. Rosenblatt's conclusions may make us less optimistic about what might ultimately be achieved in our area: Grief research "must move to a science in which not everyone can be measured on everything, in which measurement is always a matter of great skepticism, in which contradiction and difference count for a lot" (chap. 10, this volume, p. 219).

CONTEMPORARY SOCIETAL AND PRACTICAL CONCERNS

Many contributors to this *Handbook* begin their chapters with vivid examples of reactions to loss or the threat of loss, often from their own personal or clinical experience. This is not surprising because many of our contributors are practitioners as well as researchers, and as such, they are deeply steeped in narratives of grief and related phenomena. What is notable from these examples is that it is apparently easy to make the link between a scientific approach and everyday life experience in the field of bereavement, and yet there is a considerable chasm between the body of knowledge acquired by scientific means and its implementation in practice. Likewise, practice could profitably fuel research far more than it does now. Balk (2007) recently commented on this gap: "For the most part neither practitioners nor researchers take seriously the wisdom, knowledge, expertise and experience of the other while doing their work" (p. 1). On the other hand, as illustrated in the previous section, researchers are beginning to bridge this gap. For example, as Neimeyer et al. (chap. 7, this volume) show, well-normed measures have been developed, and are steadily being improved, for clinicians to use to quantify their diagnostic judgments. In the next section, we select further themes that are of particular societal relevance.

The Changing Nature of Grief in Contemporary Society

In this *Handbook*, we have been introduced to new phenomena having to do with societal changes, suggesting that what is typically understood to come under the umbrella of normal grief (and mourning) has changed in contemporary society, that new manifestations of grief may emerge, and that researchers should occasionally revisit and reconsider the spectrum of responses that grief comprises.

Examples are not hard to find: Types of disenfranchised grief have changed over recent years (chap. 11, this volume). Doka notes in chapter 11, for example, that younger people in most modern Western societies are now more accepting of the fact that loss of a partner in an unmarried cohabiting couple (whether heterosexual or homosexual) needs societal acknowledgment. There is better recognition than some decades ago of grief among the very young or those with intellectual disabilities or among bereaved persons following deaths of loved ones from AIDS or from suicide. On the other hand, some relationships may still be associated with disenfranchisement after a death; for example, former partners (e.g., divorced persons) may not be acknowledged in their grief. The concept of disenfranchisement has encouraged researchers to understand many types of loss. Now we need to assess how grief reactions vary accordingly, to assess the intensity of reactions, processes, and outcomes of disenfranchised types of loss. It is likely to continue to be an important framework, for example, as Hayslip and White (chap. 21, this volume) remark, for understanding the experience of loss among grandparents.

We are also faced with the impact of the "postmodern form of human connection" (chap. 12, this volume; see also chap. 26, this volume), such that people who "know" each other only through the news media somehow connect, for example, through sharing reactions to the death of a media figure. Walter (chap. 12, this volume) also describes the phenomenon of new public mourning. Does this reflect, as Walter asks, a phenomenon of " 'recreational grief' . . . a lightweight, undemanding image of connection, a pseudocommunity that is increasingly replacing the face-to-face connections of family, church, and neighborhood, as ephemeral as the television images that spawn it" (pp. 241–242)? More fundamentally, he asks whether private grief should really be privileged over social mourning—a contemporary view that contrasts with that of Durkheim (1915), who saw the positive functions of mourners gathering together. These clearly are new phenomena with complex functions and meanings, the theoretical, societal, and even clinical significance of which need further exploration.

Disasters at the Societal Level

Disasters can involve massive threat or loss of life, increasing the impact and complexity of the bereavement experience within a population. Such events have also challenged the assumptions of researchers (chap. 22, this volume). It is a concern, however, as Parkes notes in chapter 22, that research samples have typically been drawn from developed countries, whereas most disasters take place in the developing countries. Little systematic research has been done on the effectiveness of support, but there has been advancement in the way disasters are viewed, the resources available to deal with them, and the interventions that are deemed appropriate. Intervention needs to take into account the scale and spread of the disaster as well as the duration of the event, the type of damage, and the culture and expectations of the affected population. Problems in providing support derive also from the fact that caring professionals have limited experience across the many forms of disasters. Parkes (chap. 22, this volume) stresses that management of bereavement, trauma, and stress needs to become part of basic training of all members of caring professions and volunteers, for example, in the giving of "psychological first aid" in the early impact phase of a trauma.

Parkes (chap. 22, this volume) also expresses concern about the overemphasis on the stress and trauma approach (associated with the delineation of posttraumatic stress disorder) in guiding intervention, due in part to the influence of experience in military settings. He emphasizes the need for an integrated role of bereavement services and broad training:

> We can no longer assume that a course in stress management, [posttraumatic stress disorder], anger management, critical incident stress debriefing, bereavement support, or community development is sufficient on its own; all may be needed. This may sound like a tall order, but most of these skills should be part of the basic training of all caring professionals and bereavement volunteers. (p. 470)

The focus here can usefully be on prevention rather than treatment (of mental illness).

The Costs of Bereavement

It is surprising that at the start of the 21st century, there is practically no sound research on the costs of bereavement in the context of health care; additional research is needed to understand how systems, providers, and recipients of care are affected by these costs (Center for the Advancement of Health, 2004; Genevro & Miller, 2006).[1] Genevro and Miller (2006) referred to the "patchwork of individual studies rather than a cohesive body of evidence" (p. 1) in this area and went on to deplore the serious methodological shortcomings that limit the conclusions that can be drawn from the available studies. It seems evident, however, that the current provision of bereavement services in many contemporary societies entails considerable costs to bereaved individuals as well as the communities within which they live. In the United States, most people die in health care settings: "Death at home in the care of the family has been replaced in most instances by a technological, professional, and institutional treatment of dying" (Lunney, Foley, Smith, & Gelband, 2003, p. 3). Development of models of care at the end of life increasingly includes bereavement care, which is also reflected in policies that affect the

---

[1]We are grateful to Janice Genevro and Theresa Miller for allowing us to use their unpublished document, which notes the limited research on the costs of bereavement.

provision of care, education, and training. The economic consequences involved in provision of support and preventive treatment for the bereaved, including professional intervention for complicated grief, need to be carefully assessed, and policies must be evaluated. For example, having an intervention program available for vulnerable bereaved persons may ultimately lower costs by preventing pathology instead of having to treat it. Researchers need to show that bereavement care is effective in producing the physical and mental health outcomes that are desired: It is not enough to know how much bereavement care costs; it is also essential to know whether and under what circumstances it works (Genevro & Miller, 2006). Although governments should be committed to providing the best care for the bereaved, if researchers can provide cost-saving and cost-accounting guidelines for preventive strategies of care, this could result in improvements in caring for bereaved persons in need, and at lower costs.

Costs to informal caregivers, usually family members, are documented by Schulz et al. (chap. 13, this volume):

> Hundreds of studies carried out in the past 20 years have documented the negative health effects of caregiving, showing that caregivers are at increased risk of psychiatric and physical morbidity. . . . The challenges of caregiving become even more extreme as the care recipient nears death. (pp. 280–281)

The shift in developing as well as industrial countries in causes of death, whereby chronic diseases now account for the majority of deaths, has implications for both formal and informal (i.e., family member) health care providers. Strains on formal systems bring about increased demands on family members (chap. 13, this volume). The extent of the burden is considerable: Schulz et al. note in chapter 13 that more than 44 million adults in the United States are involved in caregiving annually and that rates are likely to be even higher in developing countries (e.g., because of the higher prevalence of some chronic diseases, such as AIDS on the African continent).

In addition to potential costs relating to the health consequences of bereavement to individuals and families, concerns exist regarding the personal and organizational costs of repeated losses and bereavements on the part of health care personnel. Yet here too it remains unclear what the emotional and economic costs are to health care providers and health care systems (extracting bereavement costs from end-of-life-care costs is frequently impossible). According to Genevro and Miller (2006), limited research indicates that health care professionals feel unprepared to provide bereavement care and that they experience grief and stress related to caring for dying patients and their families. Research also needs to determine the most effective methods for educating and supporting health care providers.

Culture and Grief

Themes relating to culture and grief arise in various contexts in this *Handbook*, and it has perhaps already become apparent that one of the great challenges for the 21st century will be to achieve a better understanding of the nature of grief in the world's different cultures. This requires becoming free of ethnocentrism. As Rosenblatt (chap. 10, this volume) states: "No knowledge about grief is culture free . . . culture creates, influences, shapes, limits, and defines grieving, sometimes profoundly" (pp. 207–208). He amply illustrates this, describing differences between cultures in how grief is expressed, in who grieves most and in what ways, and whether grieving involves remembering or forgetting. His vivid description of the people of Achuar, Ecuador, and their efforts to distance themselves from and forget the deceased provides a sharp contrast with the contemporary trend in the West to maintain relationships with a deceased person (cf. Klass et al., 1996). It becomes clear that what makes sense in one culture may make no sense in another.

Culture affects grieving in many different ways. For example, what may be considered pathological in one culture may be utterly appropriate and normal in another. Rosenblatt (chap. 10, this volume) provides important examples of this and cautions that "it is risky to take the concepts of grief pathology from one culture and apply them to people from cultures in which grief is conceptualized differently" (p. 213). The implications of cultural difference extend to the provision of intervention for complications relating to death of a loved one.

A second fascinating cultural difference concerns symptomatology. Is there really more somatization[2] of grief among Asian cultures and among immigrants to the West from Asian countries than among other cultural groups in the West? Earlier studies seemed to suggest that this was the case. Rosenblatt (1993) reported that in China and in many other societies somatization is the predominant expression of difficulties in living. However, more recent studies in the related area of depression have suggested a subtle difference in the interpretation of somatization, relating to the issue of whether somatization represents the experience or the expression of grief. In one large-scale study, the experience of depression seemed to differ little across cultures, whereas the variation in somatization was evident in presenting symptoms (Simon, VonKorff, Piccinelli, Fullerton, & Ormel, 1999): It is important to note that there was evidence that depressed persons reported somatic symptoms more frequently when seeking help from a physician with whom they had no ongoing relationship (which was more common in non-Western countries). The study authors suggested that presentation of symptoms may reflect beliefs about the appropriate

---

[2]*Somatization* denotes the presentation of personal and interpersonal distress in an idiom of physical complaints (cf. Rosenblatt, 1993).

way to seek help and have one's troubles recognized. These results raise questions about grief: Is it the case that grief is naturally experienced and responded to through the medium of the body, or is somatization a tool that enables communication of one's state of grief to others? Empirical research should probe such important distinctions in the future.

There is thus enormous potential for the expansion of bereavement research in different cultures in coming decades. It is important to understand how culture may interact, for example, with the experience of parental death, so that long-term outcomes may be predicted (e.g., in a culture in which young children may be the only remaining kin following the death of parents to AIDS). More generally, we have noted the imbalance in the relationship of research to the presence of bereavement phenomena in both Western and non-Western societies.

Complicated Grief and the *Diagnostic and Statistical Manual of Mental Disorders*

The ongoing debate about inclusion of a category of complicated grief in the *DSM* system ensures that complicated grief remains a major theme among contemporary societal issues. Before we discuss this, however, we need to address terminology. As noted in chapter 1 of this volume, most contemporary researchers and clinicians have chosen the term *complicated grief* to denote forms of grief that might be considered pathological (because of high intensity, long duration, dominant symptoms, etc.). Recently, however, Prigerson and her research team (chap. 8, this volume) have changed to using the term *prolonged grief disorder* to refer to the bereavement-specific syndrome on the grounds that this label provides greater clarity and that it better captures the nature of the disorder (points that are debatable). These authors emphasize that the term *prolonged grief* should not be taken to imply that duration is the only indicator of the pathological nature of grief—an important qualification, because it allows for inclusion of various forms of complication in the grieving process (i.e., other than what used to be called *chronic grief*, such as absent grief; see our discussion later in this section). Regardless of whether one agrees that the term *prolonged grief* is more accurate than previous labels of *complicated, traumatic,* or *pathological,* and whether other labels, such as *problematic grief,* would better cover the range of grief pathologies, this is the label currently being proposed for the forthcoming *DSM* system (as *prolonged grief disorder*).

Researchers such as Prigerson (chap. 8, this volume) and Rubin (chap. 9, this volume) argue that complicated grief is a distinguishable clinical entity whose symptom picture overlaps only slightly with other diagnostic categories, such as depression. However, is its difference from ordinary grief a matter of degree or of kind, as Weiss (chap. 2, this volume) queries? Weiss notes the overlap in symptoms of ordinary and pathological grief and that the entity complicated grief may be a way of characterizing one end of a continuum. Another consideration is that the label *complicated grief* may group the consequences of trauma together with those of loss. However desirable the recognition of complicated grief or prolonged grief may be, as Weiss concludes, its conceptualization as a distinct syndrome can be debated. Thus, research on a theoretical and conceptual level is needed to clarify precisely what complicated, or prolonged, grief is. Attachment theory has provided some leads and is compatible with proposed diagnostic categories of complicated grief (cf. chaps. 5 and 8, this volume), despite the atheoretical nature of classification systems.

The most important societal issue with respect to complicated grief involves its status as a pathological condition, as a mental disorder for inclusion in systems such as the *DSM* (e.g., American Psychiatric Association, 1994). Fundamental questions in this debate were already posed by Parkes (2005–2006) in a special issue of the scientific journal *Omega: The Journal of Death and Dying:* Is there a type of grief that can justifiably be regarded as a mental disorder? If so, how should this be classified in relationship to other disorders, and what criteria for diagnosis are best supported by research?

These questions are further addressed in the current *Handbook:* Prigerson et al. (chap. 8, this volume) answer the first of these questions in the affirmative and go on to suggest classification and criteria that are based on years of systematic research. The more skeptical position of Rubin et al. (chap. 9, this volume) is based partly on concerns deriving from their clinical work; they argue, for example, for the introduction of more relational features in a *DSM* category of complicated grief, that one should not focus on dysfunction alone but must take into account the interpersonal nature of the loss, a difficult aspect to assess. Rubin et al. argue for the representation of a broader spectrum of responses within the construct of complicated grief. They express concern about exclusion of cases of complication, arguing that a category would need to be sufficiently relevant to many forms of bereavement difficulties. Furthermore, although they recognize the need for improving services for persons in need, Rubin et al. also raise questions about the "medicalization" of responses to bereavement and the possibility that a formal diagnosis could direct attention away from indigenous supports and the natural healing of loss. Little research has examined these matters, but they deserve to be considered seriously when discussing the development of a *DSM* complicated grief category, and further efforts should be made to support or refute them empirically.

In considering the nature of complicated grief and its *DSM* status, it is also important to address the issue of subtypes (for definitions, see chap. 1, this volume). Prigerson and Jacobs (2001) noted that their concept of complicated grief for the *DSM* was close to the category of chronic grief. This left out the other original subtypes (involving absent, delayed, or inhibited grief). However, Prigerson et al. (chap. 8, this volume) now have a subtle way of including delayed and inhibited grief. Their proposed criteria for prolonged grief disorder in the *DSM* now specify that "the particular symptomatic distress must persist for at least 6 consecutive months, regardless of when those 6 months occur in relation to the loss" (chap. 8, this volume, pp. 171–172). Thus, delayed subtypes of grief are included as long as symptomatic distress persists for at least 6 months.

Questions remain, however, regarding the viability of the constructs of absent, inhibited, or delayed grief. While acknowledging that these subtypes are less frequent than chronic grief, other experts also endorse the possibility of problematic absent or delayed onset of grief (e.g., chap. 9, this volume). The experimental research of Mikulincer and Shaver (chap. 5, this volume) also speaks to this issue, showing that defensive avoidance, under conditions of high stress, may be associated with unwanted reactivation, implying that avoidance may, in a sense, backfire. Thus, they were able to demonstrate a psychodynamic phenomenon that is central to Bowlby's (e.g., 1980) theory, and the notion of absent or inhibited grief is a basic component of attachment theory (cf. chap. 5, this volume; Shaver & Tancredy, 2001). However, Bonanno et al. (chap. 14, this volume) challenge the argument that absent grief is a pathological reaction, suggesting that the absence of pronounced grief reactions may indicate resilience. Researchers who advocate a subtype of absent or inhibited grief would probably agree with Bonanno et al. that when people experience relatively mild or short-lived grief reactions, this should not be considered atypical or pathological. However, the claim that "absence of grief is not an appropriate rationale for clinical intervention" (chap. 14, this volume, p. 303) is clearly more controversial. Caution is needed when making pathological interpretations of the absence of distress, but equal caution is required in assuming no pathology among a small number of persons who are apparently resilient. The experimental approach of Mikulincer and Shaver shows great promise for further exploration of defensive, avoidant processes and their role in complicated forms of grief.

The Efficacy of Psychological Intervention

In recent years, there has been some expansion of research evaluating the efficacy of psychological intervention programs for bereavement-related distress, again one of the major, more applied challenges that researchers must address (chaps. 23 and 25, this volume; Schut & Stroebe, 2005). Studies have largely confirmed conclusions in the previous *Handbook* (Schut, Stroebe, van den Bout, & Terheggen, 2001): Programs are least effective when offered to bereaved persons in general, irrespective of indications that intervention is needed; they are more effective for those who, through screening or assessment, can be regarded as vulnerable, and they are most effective for those who have complicated grief, grief-related depression, or posttraumatic disorders.

Chapters that report intervention programs in the current *Handbook* also draw conclusions in line with these earlier ones. In particular, they support the provision of intervention to children (chap. 25, this volume) and to high-risk bereaved families (chap. 23, this volume). They also take our understanding some steps further: For example, Sandler et al.'s (chap. 25, this volume) program demonstrated efficacy among children through changing identified risk and protective factors, and it is important to note that the impact of their intervention program showed promising results at the 6-year follow-up. We have also seen how Kissane and Lichtenthal's (chap. 23, this volume) family-centered care model enables support prior to death to the patient and caregiver— a preventive and family-centered approach that sustains continuity of care. Further expansion of intervention efficacy research to caregivers is indicated by Schulz et al.'s (chap. 13, this volume) research. They have shown the need to treat prebereavement distress, which is frequently very high, and prepare individuals with caregiving responsibilities for the eventuality of death.

Although there has been a reasonable consensus in the most recent scientific literature about the validity of the patterns of effects described earlier, some disagreement exists about the possible harmfulness of bereavement intervention. Neimeyer (2000) argued that bereavement interventions could perhaps even be deleterious, at least for persons experiencing no complications in the grieving process, a claim that became much cited but has questionable empirical validation. It was contested in a recent review by Larson and Hoyt (2007). In our own reviews, we have reported no patterns of harmful effects either (Schut et al., 2001; Schut & Stroebe, 2005).

Larson and Hoyt (2007) were more positive in general about the impact of intervention for bereaved people than we have been (i.e., the patterns described at the beginning of this section from Schut et al., 2001; Schut & Stroebe, 2005). This could be due, at least in part, to the fact that Larson and Hoyt based these conclusions largely on an earlier review by Allumbaugh and Hoyt (1999) from which studies of the long-term, follow-up effects of intervention were excluded. This would give a more positive picture (because long-term effects reflect substantial relapse, short-term effects are typically stronger). In our view, an examination of follow-up effects is essential too, but here again further empirical investigation should help to establish the validity of conclusions more firmly.

Despite some developments, then, further research on the efficacy of psychological intervention programs for the bereaved remains a top priority. For example, Kissane and Lichtenthal's (chap. 23, this volume) review of studies on family intervention with bereaved families did not reveal a strong body of evidence in support of this type of intervention (although their own study contributed to this end). Studies must conform to the strictest design and methodological criteria. Publication standards need to be raised, too: Too often, what are published are pilot or partly completed investigations (reporting results only from early measurements in longitudinal designs, excluding control groups, etc.). It is not good enough to argue that one cannot assign bereaved persons in need to a control group condition (it is unethical not to investigate the efficacy of an offered program in a scientific manner). There are ways to overcome such difficulties: Sandler et al. (chap. 25, this volume), for example, showed how it is possible to use a randomized experimental design that targets multiple and protective factors for bereaved children. Nonintervention control groups are essential. Even if one compares two types of therapy, without such a control one cannot be sure whether nonintervention might not lead to even better results than either of the other interventions (e.g., the effects of the interventions might be time rather than therapy related).

Finally, apart from examining improvement or worsening of grief symptomatology following bereavement, research on intervention efficacy needs to broaden. Research could usefully include investigation of the potential indirect costs of intervention, such as withdrawal of informal support when formal support is provided (as found in a Dutch study conducted by de Keijser, 1997) and examination of processes associated with (lack of) improvement (e.g., exploring the possibility that "focusing widowers' attention to their own and others' grief—to the point where the focus may have hindered an early [and measurable] recovery from their grief" [Tudiver, Hilditch, Permaul, & McKendree, 1992, p. 160]). Ultimately (but only when a sufficient number of high-quality studies are available), meta-analysis should be used to identify differential impacts of intervention for a wider variety of subgroups.

The Efficacy of Pharmacological Intervention

There is unfortunately no body of research on the efficacy of pharmacological and medical interventions for the bereaved (for further consideration, see Alexopoulos, 2005; Raphael, Minkov, & Dobson, 2001), perhaps because medication for the bereaved was deemed a bad thing in earlier decades (and is still debatable). However, early skepticism about the value of any psychopharmacological intervention for bereaved people has given way to an effort to examine whether medication—and if so, what type(s)—may be effective in reducing psychological symptomatology relating to bereavement.

Prigerson et al. (chap. 8, this volume) identify preliminary studies suggesting differential pharmacotherapeutic indicators for bereavement-related depression versus those for the reduction of symptoms of grief per se, indicating that symptoms of grief are distinct from those of depression, differences that need to be taken into account in planning psychopharmacological intervention. Further research is needed on the impact of pharmacotherapies. Prigerson and colleagues note that there have been no randomized controlled trials of pharmacotherapies for the reduction of grief symptom severity, although there have been some promising leads for some agents. They argue the need for randomized, placebo-controlled trials before more definitive conclusions can be drawn about medications efficacy for the amelioration of prolonged grief symptomatology.

CONCLUSIONS

The first of our three *Handbooks* informed readers on a variety of fundamental issues about bereavement. The second investigated a range of new themes within the framework of consequences, coping, and care for the bereaved that could be addressed once the basics had been reasonably established. We noted in the conclusion to the second *Handbook* a need for extension rather than major change in the scope of forthcoming bereavement research. We identified a number of new research questions reflecting important continuations of the research described and issues (including controversies) raised in that volume. We noted neglected topics. We also drew attention to the fact that societal changes were likely to alter the bereavement experience and that these would affect its scientific investigation.

The current *Handbook* has continued where the last one left off. It has built on the foundations established in the first volume and addressed some of the topics that could not be included in the second. It has provided an update on controversial issues, and it has perused societal changes as a focal theme of investigation. In addition, new scientific methods have been explored, some of which could hardly be speculated on at the time the previous *Handbooks* were written. Conceptual and theoretical refinements have been documented.

Most of all, in this volume we have tried to link bereavement research to practice. As before, our efforts in this respect have been limited by space; we have had to be selective. In our view, however, bridging this gap—through studies of cultural and subgroup differences, through efficacy of intervention research, through consideration of the diagnostic status of complicated grief, and the myriad other themes where practical applications have been identified in the preceding chapters—is a major direction for future scientific investigation in our field in the 21st century.

REFERENCES

Alexopoulos, G. S. (2005). Depression in the elderly. *The Lancet, 365,* 1961–1970.

Allumbaugh, D., & Hoyt, W. (1999). Effectiveness of grief counselling: A meta-analysis. *Journal of Counseling Psychology, 46,* 370–380.

American Psychiatric Association. (1994). *Diagnostic and statistical manual of mental disorders* (4th ed.). Washington, DC: Author.

Archer, J. (1999). *The nature of grief: The evolution and psychology of reactions to loss.* London: Routledge.

Archer, J. (2001). Grief from an evolutionary perspective. In M. Stroebe, R. O. Hansson, W. Stroebe, & H. Schut (Eds.), *Handbook of bereavement research: Consequences, coping, and care* (pp. 263–283). Washington, DC: American Psychological Association.

Balk, D. (2007). Bridging the practice–research gap. *The Forum, 33,* 1–4.

Boelen, P., de Keijser, J., van den Hout, M., & van den Bout, J. (2007). Treatment of complicated grief: A comparison between cognitive–behavioral therapy and supportive counseling. *Journal of Consulting and Clinical Psychology, 75,* 277–284.

Boelen, P., & Prigerson, H. (2007). The influence of symptoms of prolonged grief disorder, depression and anxiety on quality of life among bereaved adults: A prospective study. *European Archives of Psychiatry and Clinical Neuroscience, 257,* 444–452.

Boelen, P., van den Bout, J., & van den Hout, M. (2006). Negative cognitions and avoidance in emotional problems after bereavement: A prospective study. *Behavior Research and Therapy, 44,* 1657–1672.

Bowlby, J. (1980). *Attachment and loss: Vol. 3. Sadness and depression.* New York: Basic Books.

Center for the Advancement of Health. (2004). Report on bereavement and grief research. *Death Studies, 28,* 491–575.

de Keijser, J. (1997). *Sociale steun en professionele begeleiding bij rouw* [Social support and professional counseling for the bereaved]. Amsterdam: Thesis Publishers.

Durkheim, E. (1915). *The elementary forms of the religious life.* London: Unwin.

Fleming, S., & Robinson, P. (2001). Grief and cognitive-behavioral therapy: The reconstruction of meaning. In M. Stroebe, R. O. Hansson, W. Stroebe, & H. Schut (Eds.), *Handbook of bereavement research: Consequences, coping, and care* (pp. 647–669). Washington, DC: American Psychological Association.

Folkman, S. (2001). Revised coping theory and the process of bereavement. In M. Stroebe, R. O. Hansson, W. Stroebe, & H. Schut (Eds.), *Handbook of bereavement research: Consequences, coping, and care* (pp. 563–584). Washington, DC: American Psychological Association.

Freud, S. (1957). Mourning and melancholia. In J. Strachey (Ed. & Trans.), *Standard edition of the complete works of Sigmund Freud* (pp. 152–170). London: Hogarth Press. (Original work published 1917)

Genevro, J., & Miller, T. (2006). *Health care professionals and health systems: The costs of bereavement.* Unpublished manuscript.

Hansson, R. O., & Stroebe, M. S. (2007). *Bereavement in later life: Coping, adaptation, and developmental influences.* Washington, DC: American Psychological Association.

Lunney, J., Foley, K., Smith, T., & Gelband, H. (Eds.). (2003). *Describing death in America: What we need to know.* Washington, DC: National Academies Press.

Janoff-Bulman, R., & Frantz, C. (1997). The impact of trauma on meaning: From meaningless world to meaningful life. In M. Power & C. Brewin (Eds.), *The transformation of meaning in psychological therapies* (pp. 91–106). New York: Wiley.

Klass, D., Silverman, P., & Nickman, S. (Eds.). (1996). *Continuing bonds: New under-standings of grief*. Washington, DC: Taylor & Francis.

Larson, D., & Hoyt, W. (2007). What has become of grief counselling? An evalua-tion of the empirical foundation of the new pessimism. *Professional Psychology: Research and Practice, 38*, 347–355.

Maciejewski, P., Zhang, B., Block, S., & Prigerson, H. (2007). An empirical exami-nation of the stage theory of grief. *Journal of the American Medical Association, 297*, 716–723.

Moss, M., Moss, S., & Hansson, R. (2001). Bereavement and old age. In M. Stroebe, R. O. Hansson, W. Stroebe, & H. Schut (Eds.), *Handbook of bereavement research: Consequences, coping, and care* (pp. 241–260). Washington, DC: Amer-ican Psychological Association.

Neimeyer, R. (2000). Searching for the meaning of meaning: Grief therapy and the process of reconstruction. *Death Studies, 24*, 541–558.

Neimeyer, R. (2001). *Meaning reconstruction and the experience of loss*. Washington, DC: American Psychological Association.

Nolen-Hoeksema, S. (2001). Ruminative coping and adjustment to bereavement. In M. Stroebe, R. O. Hansson, W. Stroebe, & H. Schut (Eds.), *Handbook of bereave-ment research: Consequences, coping, and care* (pp. 545–562). Washington, DC: American Psychological Association.

Oltjenbruns, K. (2001). Developmental context of childhood: Grief and regrief phe-nomena. In M. Stroebe, R. O. Hansson, W. Stroebe, & H. Schut (Eds.), *Hand-book of bereavement research: Consequences, coping, and care* (pp. 169–197). Washington, DC: American Psychological Association.

Parkes, C. M. (Ed.). (2005–2006). Complicated grief: A symposium [Special issue]. *Omega: The Journal of Death and Dying, 52*(1).

Prigerson, H., & Jacobs, S. (2001). Traumatic grief as a distinct disorder: A ration-ale, consensus criteria, and a preliminary empirical test. In M. S. Stroebe, R. O. Hansson, W. Stroebe, & H. Schut (Eds.), *Handbook of bereavement research: Con-sequences, coping, and care* (pp. 613–645). Washington, DC: American Psycho-logical Association.

Raphael, B., Minkov, C., & Dobson, M. (2001). Psychotherapeutic and pharmacologi-cal intervention for bereaved persons. In M. S. Stroebe, R. O. Hansson, W. Stroebe, & H. Schut (Eds.), *Handbook of bereavement research: Consequences, coping, and care* (pp. 587–612). Washington, DC: American Psychological Association.

Rosenblatt, P. (1993). Cross-cultural variation in the experience, expression, and understanding of grief. In D. Irish, K. Lundquist, & V. Nelsen (Eds.), *Ethnic vari-ations in dying, death, and grief* (pp. 13–19). Washington, DC: Taylor & Francis.

Rubin, S. S. (1991). Adult child loss and the two-track model of bereavement. *Omega: The Journal of Death and Dying, 24*, 183–202.

Schaefer, J., & Moos, R. (2001). Bereavement experiences and personal growth. In M. S. Stroebe, R. O. Hansson, W. Stroebe, & H. Schut (Eds.), *Handbook of bereavement research: Consequences, coping, and care* (pp. 145–167). Washington, DC: American Psychological Association.

Schut, H., & Stroebe, M. (2005). Interventions to enhance adaptation to bereavement. *Journal of Palliative Medicine, 8*, S140–S147.

Schut, H., Stroebe, M., van den Bout, J., & Terheggen, M. (2001). The efficacy of bereavement interventions: Determining who benefits. In M. Stroebe, R. O. Hansson, W. Stroebe, & H. Schut (Eds.), *Handbook of bereavement research: Consequences, coping, and care* (pp. 705–737). Washington, DC: American Psychological Association.

Shaver, P., & Tancredy, C. (2001). Emotion, attachment, and bereavement: A conceptual commentary. In M. S. Stroebe, R. O. Hansson, W. Stroebe, & H. Schut (Eds.), *Handbook of bereavement research: Consequences, coping, and care* (pp. 63–88). Washington, DC: American Psychological Association.

Shear, K., Frank, E., Houck, P., & Reynolds, C., III. (2005). Treatment of complicated grief: A randomised controlled trial. *Journal of the American Medical Association, 293*, 2601–2608.

Silverman, P., & Worden, J. W. (1993). Children's reactions to death of a parent. In M. S. Stroebe, W. Stroebe, & R. O. Hansson (Eds.), *Handbook of bereavement research: Theory, research, and intervention* (pp. 300–316). New York: Cambridge University Press.

Simon, G., VonKorff, M., Piccinelli, M., Fullerton, C., & Ormel, J. (1999). An international study of the relation between somatic symptoms and depression. *New England Journal of Medicine, 341*, 1329–1334.

Stroebe, M., Folkman, S., Hansson, R. O., & Schut, H. (2006). The prediction of bereavement outcome: Development of an integrative risk factor framework. *Social Science & Medicine, 63*, 2446–2451.

Stroebe, M., Hansson, R. O., Stroebe, W., & Schut, H. (2001a). Future directions for bereavement research. In M. Stroebe, R. O. Hansson, W. Stroebe, & H. Schut (Eds.), *Handbook of bereavement research: Consequences, coping, and care* (pp. 741–766). Washington, DC: American Psychological Association.

Stroebe, M., Hansson, R. O., Stroebe, W., & Schut, H. (Eds.). (2001b). *Handbook of bereavement research: Consequences, coping, and care.* Washington, DC: American Psychological Association Press.

Stroebe, M., & Schut, H. A. W. (1999). The dual process model of coping with bereavement: Rationale and description. *Death Studies, 23*, 1–28.

Stroebe, M., Stroebe, W., & Hansson, R. (Eds.). (1993). *Handbook of bereavement: Theory, research and intervention.* New York: Cambridge University Press.

Tudiver, F., Hilditch, J., Permaul, J. A., & McKendree, D. J. (1992). Does mutual help facilitate newly bereaved widowers? Report from a randomized controlled trial. *Evaluation & the Health Professions, 15*, 147–162.

Wijngaards-de Meij, L., Stroebe, M., Schut, H., Stroebe, W, van den Bout, J., Heijmans, P., & Dijkstra, I. (2005). Couples at risk following the death of their child: Predictors of grief versus depression. *Journal of Consulting and Clinical Psychology, 73*, 617–623.

AUTHOR INDEX

Numbers in italics refer to listings in the references.

Aron, A., 352, 354, 355, *365–369*

Aron, E. N., 355, *365*, *366*

Arroyo, W., *484*

Aslan, M., *185*

Asthana, D., *42*

Attig, T., 113, *130*, *192*, *201*

August, J., 332, *348*

Austin, D., 330, 333, 337, *344*

Averill, J. R., 4, 9, 23, *47*, *61*

Axelrod, R., 488, *507*

Ayers, T., 399, *412*, 532, 541, *549*

Ayers, T. A., 399, 400, *415*, 535, *547*, *548*

Ayers, T. S., 399, 400, *412*, *413*, *509*, 534–537, 540, *547–549*

Azhar, M. Z., 333, 338, 343, *345*

Azuma, H., *411*

Baca, L., 400, *415*, *416*, 534, *549*

Backlund, B., 232, 237, *238*

Baerends, G. P., 351, 356, *366*

Bagilishya, D., 213, 214, 218, *220*

Bailley, S. E., 145, 146, 150, *157*

Baird, A., 453, *456*

Baker, J., 142, *159*, 192, *205*

Baldewicz, T. T., *42*

Baldwin, D., *283*

Baldwin, L., 494, *507*

Baldwin, S. A., 150, *160*

Balk, D. E., 146, *159*, 334, 340, *345*, 590, *601*

Ball, R., 494, *506*

Ballard, P. H., 482, *482*

Baltes, P., 420, *436*

Balzarini, E., 269, *283*

Bambauer, K. Z., 296, *307*

Banach, M., 558, 565, *571*

Banaji, M., *572*

Banks, J. M., 218, *220*

Banner, L. L., *365*

Barchas, J. D., 406, *410*

Barg, F. K., 487, *506*, *509*

Bargh, J. A., 559, *571*

Barker, P., *528*

Barner, J. R., 71, *85*

Barnes, H., *509*

Barone, S., 405, *415*

Barr, A., 399, *413*, 534, *548*

Barrett, T. W., 145, 146, 149, *157*

Barry, L. C., 141, *158*, 167, 168, 173, *182*, 270, 278, 279, *282*

Bartels, A., 354, 355, 358, *366*

Bartholomew, K., 59, *61*, *63*, 91, 106, 108, 330, *347*

Bartholomew, M. J., 279, *283*

Bar-Tur, L., 34, *43*

Bass, D. M., 268, *282*

Batten, M., 334, 339, 340, *345*

Battin, D., 279, *283*

Bauer, A. M., 404, *410*

Baugher, R., *394*

Baumeister, R. F., 350, 364, *366*

Bayart, F., 406, *410*

Beach, S., *439*

Beach, S. R., *284*, 299, *304*

Beall, S. K., 55, *64*, 539, *548*

Bearon, L. B., 342, *346*

Beaton, R. B., *110*

Beaton, R. D., 379, *394*

Beaudoin, G., *369*

Beauregard, M., 351, *366*

Beck, A. T., 101, *108*, *158*, 486, 494, *506*

Beck, R., 486, *506*

Beck, U., 251, *259*

Becker, B., 398, *413*

Becker, E., 73, *84*

Bedard, M., 278, *282*

Beehr, T., 443, *456*

Beery, L. C., *64*, 106, *112*, 174, *184*, *186*

Bellar, S. A., *411*

Beltz, J., *528*

Benabarre, A., *571*

Ben-Ari, E., 258, *259*

Bengtson, V. L., 442, *456*, *458*

Benjamin, B., *370*

Bennett, H., 218, *221*

Benore, R. B., 519, *528*

Ben-Shlomo, Y., 407, *410*

Benson, H., 340, *346*

Ben-Ze'ev, E., 258, *259*

Berant, E., 106, *108*

Bereaved Parents of the USA, 441, *456*

Brent, S. B., 350, *370*
Breslau, N., 193, *202*
Bridge, J., 171, 174, 175, 177, *184*
Brison, K. J., 210, *220*
Brom, D., 193, *202*
Bromet, E., *393*
Brotman, L. M., 404, *411*
Brown, A., 410, *413*
Brown, A. C., 543, *547*
Brown, D. E., 452, *457*
Brown, G. W., 401, *411*, *483*, 534, *547,*
    548
Brown, L. L., 352, 365, 367, 368, *506*
Brown, S. L., 335, 340, 341, *345*
Browne, J., 71, *84*
Bruce, M. L., 174, *183*, 418, *437*
Bruckman, A., *572*
Brunner, J., 512, *528*
Bryant, B., 194, *204*
Bryant, R. A., 194, *202*
Bucciarelli, A., 302, *304*
Buchholz, H. G., *370*
Buckley, I., 486, *506*
Bunge, S. A., 88, *109*
Burgess, P., *506*
Burholt, V., 39, *44*
Burjorjee, R., 209, *220*
Burks, V. K., 58, *62*
Burlingham, D., 92, *108*
Burnett, P., 136, 138, 140, *158, 160,*
    288, 290, 306, 375, 393, 502, *506*
Burns, K., *282*
Burns, W. I., 486, *508*
Burt, K. B., *414*
Burton, L., *285*
Burton, R., 362, *366*
Butcher, J. N., 140, *158*
Butler, A. C., 299, *305*
Buysse, D. J., *184, 483*
Byock, I. R., 429, *437*
Byrne, G. J. A., 138, *158*, 502, *506*

Cain, A. C., 192, *205*, 412, 535, *548*
Cain, K. C., *110, 394*
Cait, C. A., 192, *205*
Calhoun, L. G., 311–313, 315–318,
    320–322, *322, 325*, 519, *528,*
    530

Calvi, G., 74, *84*
Campbell, W. K., 362, *366*
Campo, J., 243, *260*
Cannadine, D., 245, 255, *260*
Cardillo, V., 269, *283*
Carlson, E., *237*
Carlson, F. A., 123, *130*
Carlson, M., 407, *411*
Carlson, M. D. A., *283*
Carlsson, M. E., 487, *506*
Carpenter, B. N., 136, *159*
Carr, D., 174, *183*, 302, 305, 425–435,
    437, 438, 440
Carstensen, L., 420, *437*
Carter, C. S., 352, *366*
Cartwright, A., 279, *282*
Carver, C. S., 382, *392*
Carverhill, P. A., 154, *158*
Cascio, C., 355, 368, *371*
Caserta, M. S., 153, *158*, 174, *184*
Casey, V., *285*
Casper, L. M., 419, *438*
Cassel, C. K., 418, 427, 429, *438*
Cassidy, J., 91, 92, *108*
Cassileth, B. R., 486, *506*
Castellanos, X., 404, *411*
Catlin, E. A., 343, *347*
Cawley, M. M., 487, *506*
Cazzullo, C., *528*
Cecchin, G., 523, *528*
Center for the Advancement of Health,
    154, *158*, 592, *601*
Centers for Disease Control and Pre-
    vention, 376, *392*
Chabner, B. A., 165, *184*
Champous, M., *411*
Chan, C. L. W., 151, 156, 157, *158, 159*
Chan, E. K., 501, *506*
Chang, C., 554, 555, *571*
Chapin, R., 442, *457*
Chartier, B., 314, *325*
Chartier, B. M., 106, 107, *112*
Chasin, J., *412*
Chen, J., *347*
Chentsova-Dutton, Y., 267, 272, *282*
Cherlin, E. J., *283*
Cheshire, A., 246, *260*

Chesla, C. A., 516, 526, *529*
Chesney, M. A., 296, *305*
Chevalley, A. F., *369*
Chiang, K. H. S., 101, *111*
Chien, I. C., *482*
Childe, V. G., 252, *260*
Chisholm, K., 407, *411*
Chou, F. H. C., 469, 476, *482*
Chou, P., *482*
Chow, A., 151, 156, *158, 159*
Christakis, N. A., 272, 277, *282*
Christiano, K., 328, *348*
Christie, P., 298, *306*
Christopher-Richards, A., 296, *305*
Chung, I. J., 379, *394*
Cicchetti, D., 398, 409, *411, 413*
Cinotti, L., *371*
Clapp, N. E., *394*
Clark, C. L., 90, *108*
Clark, D. M., 298, *305*
Clark, J., 246, *260*
Clarke, V., 494, *507*
Clarridge, B. R., *285*
Clayton, P. J., 9, *23*, 174, *182*, 399, *416*
Cleary, P. A., *158*
Cleiren, M., 174, *183*
Clements, P. T., 232, *237*
Clerici, M., *528*
Click, M., 425, *440*
Clinkinbeard, S. S., 513, *529*
Coatsworth, J. D., 398, *414*
Cobb, S., 556, *571*
Coe, B., *369*
Coe, C. L., 406, *411*
Cohen, J., *572*
Cohen, L. H., 313, *324*, 330, 335, 340, *347*
Cohen, M., 386, *393*
Cohen, S., 382, *392*
Cohn, M., 563, *571*
Coleman, M., *458*
Coleman, P. G., 335, 340, *345*
Colom, F., 555, 556, *571*
Colp, R. J., 71, *84*
Compas, B. E., 399, *413*
Cook, A., *507*
Cooper, M., 246, *260*

Copeland, M. E., 399, *413*
Copher, R., 442, *458*
Corcoran, R., *371*
Cornes, C., *185, 484*
Corr, C., 232, 234, *237*
Coryell, W., 298, *307*
Costa, K. G., 330, *345*
Couper, M., *572*
Coyle, A., 332, 334, 339, 342, *346*
Coyne, J. C., 315, *322*
Crain, M. M., 218, *220*
Cramer, E. M., 403, *413*
Crandall, E. K. B., 311, *324*
Crawford, A., *572*
Crawford, C. B., 49, *62*
Creamer, M., *506*
Crofton, C., 315, *325*
Cross, P. A., *506*
Crossley, C. D., 332, *347*
Crouthamel, C. S., 486, *509*
Crowley, B., 443, *457*
Crowther, M. R., 330, *347*
Cruess, D. G., 100, *110*, 201, *203*
Cubis, J., 403, *414*
Cummings, J., *572*
Currer, C., 207, 217, *220*
Currier, J. M., 71, 84, 138, *158*, 314n3, *323*, 515, 527, *528*
Curtis, W. J., 409, *411*

Daaleman, T. P., 343, *345*
Dagan, A., 137, *159*
Dahlstrom, W. G., 140, *158*
Daie, N., 195, *202*
Danforth, L., 71, 84, 243, 251, *260*
Dang, Q., 278, *283*
Darwin, C., 29–33, *41*, 45, 47, *62*, 359, 362, 363, 365, *367*
Davey-Smith, G., 407, *410*
Davidson, J., 227, 233, *238*
Davidson, J. R. T., *185*
Davies, B., 38, *43*, 101, *111*, 386, *393*
Davies, M., 256, *261*, 399, *412*
Davis, A., 298, *306*
Davis, C. G., 56, 60, *62*, 115, *130*, 311, 313–319, *322, 323, 324*, 342, *345*, 364, *367*, 376, 384, *392*, 401, *412*, 448, *457*, 514, *528*

Eigen, H., 266, *284*
Eisenberger, N. I., 358, 361, *367*
Ekman, P., 29, 32, *41*
Elbert, T., 477, *484*
El-Dearedy, W., *371*
Elder, G. H., Jr., 442, *458*
el-Jawahri, A., 169, *186*
Ell, K., 486, *507*
Ellard, J. H., *324*
Elliot, C. L., 298, *305*
Elliott, R., 355, *367*
Ellis, B., 361, *367*
Ellison, C. G., 342, *346*
Ellwood, J., *509*
Emanuel, E. J., 267, *283*
Emanuel, L. L., *283*
Embelton, G , 330, *348*
Emmelkamp, P. M., 480, *484*, 563, *572*
Endert, E., 351, *371*
Engel, A., 246, *260*
Engel, G. L., 189, *202*, 363, *367*
Engelhardt, H. T. J., 331, *345*
English and Romanian Adoptees Study
        Team, 407, *415*
Ensing, D. S., *347*
Epstein, E. M., 55, *65*
Epstein, N., 494, *507*
Epstein, S., 310, *323*
Epston, D., 521, *530*
Erbaugh, J., *158*
Erikson, K. T., 482, *483*
Ernst, L., 444, 445, *457*
Eth, S., *484*
Evans, D. W., 356, *367*
Everett, H., 246, 250, 254–256, *260*
Excell, G., 246, 250, *260*
Eyetsemitan, F., 227, 228, 232, *238*

Fabrega, H., Jr., 212, *220*
Fabre-Nys, C., 355, *367*
Fahlke, C., 403, *411*
Fainman, D., 122, *132*
Fairburn, C. G., 541, *548*
Fairchild, S. K., 136, *159*, 444, *457*
Fairclough, D. L., *283*
Falgout, K., *347*
Fan, J. J., 380, *394*

Fan, M. Y., 302, *305*
Farberow, N. L., 279, *283*
Farr, W., 9, *23*
Faschingbauer, T. R., 136, 137, *158,
        283*
Fasiczka, A., *185, 459*
Faulkner, M., 232, *237*
Faull, K. F., 406, *410*
Federal Interagency Forum on Aging-
        Related Statistics, 417, 418, *437*
Feeny, N. C., 297, *305*
Feifel, H., *84*
Feldman, D., *239*
Feldman, S. I., 364, *367*
Felitti, V. J., 403, *411*
Felner, R. D., 534, *547*
Ferrario, S. R., 269, 273, 278, *283*
Ferrell, B. A., 488, *507*
Ferrell, B. R., *507*
Ferszt, G., 230, 237, *238*
Feudtner, C., 342, 343, *345*
Fialkow, N. J., 116, *130*
Field, M. J., 418, 427, 429, *438*
Field, N. P., 36, 37, *42*, 106, *108*, 113,
        119–121, 125, 127, 128, *130,*
        147, 150, *158*, 191, *202*, 290,
        298, 304, *306*
Fields, J., 419, *438*
Fiese, B. H., 522, *528*
Fiez, J. A., 355, *367*
Fincham, F. D., 299, *304*
Fingerman, K. L., 446, *458*
Finkenauer, C., 176, *185*
Finlay, I. G., *507*
Finn, J., 558, 565, *571*
Firth, S., 331, *345*
Fischer, E. F., 350, *368*
Fischmann, D., *185*
Fisher, H. E., 351–354, 356, 357,
        359–361, *365, 367–370*
Fisher, R. A., 49, *62*
Fissel, C., 355, *367*
Fitzgerald, R. G., *370*
Flannelly, K. J., 330, *345*
Fleissner, K., 268, *284*
Fleming, S., 280, *283*, 314, *325*, 587,
        601

Florian, V., 106, *108, 110*
Foa, E. B., 101, *109,* 293, 297, *305*
Focht-New, G., 232, *237*
Fogel, J., 556, 557, 559, *571*
Foley, K., 592, *601*
Folkman, S., 11, *24,* 268, 269, 273, 282,
        284, 294, 296, *304, 305,* 328,
        330, 333, 335–337, 340, *345,*
        347, 489, *507,* 582, 583, 587,
        601, 603
Folta, J., 230, *238*
Fonagy, P., 122, *132*
Fooken, I., 419, *438*
Forbes, A., *508*
Forde, D. R., 193, *205*
Forehand, R., 538, *547*
Forgas, J. P., 101, *109*
Forgatch, M. S., 545, *547*
Fort, C., 37, *42,* 357, *368*
Fortner, B., 192, *204*
Foster, W. J., 330, *348*
Foucault, M., 246, *260*
Fowler, J. S., *368*
Fox, S., 551, *572*
Fraley, E. C., 36, *42*
Fraley, R. C., 49, 59–61, *62,* 65, 88, 90,
        93, 96, 102, 103, 106, *109,* 113,
        130, 364, *368*
Francis, M. E., 55, *64*
Frank, E., 35, *44,* 59, *64,* 116, *132,* 172,
        173, 175, 177, 178, *184, 185,*
        190, *204, 205,* 281, 285, *484,*
        538, *549,* 588, *603*
Frankl, V. E., 320, *323,* 514, *529*
Frantz, C. M., 383, 385, *393,* 489, *507,*
        587, *601*
Frasca, A., *42, 84*
Frederick, C., *484*
Freeman, S., *24*
Frets, P. G., *159*
Freud, A., 92, *108*
Freud, S., 8, *23,* 45–47, 52, *62,* 95, 96,
        104, *109,* 114, 118, 120, *130,*
        165, 178, *183,* 189, 191, 197,
        202, 430, 435, *438,* 560, *572,*
        585, *601*
Frey, B., 343, *345*

Friedman, L. N., 52, *63*
Friedman, R., 340, *346*
Friesen, W. V., 32, *41*
Frieze, I. H., 354, *370*
Fry, P. S., 330, 333, 338, 343, *345,* 445,
        447, *457*
Fudin, C., 231, *238*
Fuller, R., 234, *238*
Fuller-Thomson, E., 452, *458*
Fullerton, C., 594, *603*
Futterman, A., 94, *109,* 419, *440*

Gagnon, J., 236, *238*
Galea, S., 302, *304*
Gallagher, D., 94, *109*
Gallagher-Thompson, D., 279, *283,*
        419, *440*
Gal-Oz, E., 37, *42,* 125, *130,* 150,
        158
Galperin, C., *411*
Gamino, L. A., 137, 142, *159,* 330, 333,
        335, 337, 340, *345, 346,* 515,
        520, 527, *529*
Gammon, V., 243, *260*
Gao, B., 36, *42,* 113, *130,* 150, *158*
Garbin, M., 486, *506*
Gardner, C. O., 401, *412*
Garner, J. P., 103, *109*
Garwick, A. M., 516, 519, *530*
Gatrad, A. R., 331, *346*
Gatz, M., 420, *439*
Gay, P., 73, *84*
Geary, P. J., 74, *84*
Gee, E., 72, *84*
Gehlback, S. H., *394*
Geis, S., 234, *238*
Gelband, H., 592, *601*
Gelfand, D. M., 399, *411*
Genevro, J., 592, 593, *601*
George, C., 98, *109,* 123, *130*
George, L. K., 342, *346,* 420, *438*
George, M., 357, *370*
Gérard, D., *371*
Gerber, I., 279, *283*
Gerdts, E. K., 487, *506*
Gergen, K., 113, *132,* 191, *205,* 244,
        262

Gergen, M., 113, *132*, 191, *205*, 244, *262*

Geron, Y., 190, *203*

Gersten, J. C., 399, 400, *415*, *416*, 534, *549*

Getz, L. L., 366

Getzel, G., 52, *63*

Giaconia, R. M., 545, *548*

Gielen, U., 5, *23*

Gilbar, O., 137, *159*

Gilbert, K. R., 376, *393*, 513, 521, *529*

Gilbert, S. M., 87, *109*

Gilewski, M. J., 279, *283*, 419, *440*

Gilham, J. E., 538, *547*

Gilhooly, M., 427, *440*

Gillath, O., 88, 103, *109*

Gillies, J., 150, 153, *159*, *160*, 310, *323*

Gilligan, C., 498, *507*

Gilliland, G., 280, *283*

Gilmartin, D., 267, *283*

Gingrich, B., 355, *368*, *371*

Gitlin, D. G., 49, *64*

Gitlin, L. N., 281, *284*

Gittings, C., 70, *84*

Given, B., *283*, 488, *507*

Given, C. W., *283*, 488, *507*

Gladstone, J. W., 450, *457*

Gleason, M. J., 557, *573*

Glover, G. H., *365*

Gluck, J. P., 406, *413*

Glymour, C., *161*

Goebel, B. I., 232, *239*

Goikolea, J. M., *571*

Golden, T., 554, 559, *572*

Goldsmith, B., 174, *183*

Goldstein, B., 557, 558, *572*

Goldstein, J., 488, *507*

Goldstein, R. Z., 356, *368*

Goldwyn, R., 120, *131*

Golsworthy, R., 332, 334, 339, 342, *346*

Gonzalez, C. A., 406, *411*

Good, B. J., 214, *220*

Good, M. D., 214, *220*

Goodkin, K., 30, 35, *42*, 72, *84*

Goodlin, B. L., 406, *411*

Goodwin, D. M., *507*

Gorsuch, R. L., 494, *509*

Gosling, S., 564, 565, *572*

Goss, R. E., 113, 126, *130*, 207, 212, 220, 245, 252, *260*

Gotay, C. C., 486, *507*

Gotlib, I. H., 399, *413*

Gottman, J. M., 540, *547*

Gouley, K. K., 404, *411*

Grafstrom, M., 269, *282*

Graham, J. R., 140, *158*

Grahn, G., 487, *507*

Grant, I., 269, 273, *283*

Grant, M., 488, *507*

Gratton, A., 403, *414*

Gray, K., 232, *238*

Grayson, C., 364, *370*

Green, A. S., 557, *573*

Green, B. L., 376, *393*

Green, F., 288, *306*

Green, K. M., 165, *184*

Green, M., 33, *43*

Green, S. E., *457*, *458*

Greenberg, J. R., 115, *131*

Greenblatt, S., 70, *84*

Greene, B. L., 298, *305*

Greenfield, D. B., 142, 146, 149, *159*

Greenwald, A. G., 310, *323*

Greer, D. S., 487, *507*

Greer, J. A., 174, *183*

Gregg, C. H., 58, *62*

Grégoire, M. C., *371*

Grevengoed, N., *347*

Grey, R., 231, *238*

Grider, S., 245, 250, 254, *260*

Griffin, D., 59, *63*

Grimes, R., 245, 246, *260*, *261*

Grosser, G., 487, 488, 509, 513, *530*

Grund, D., 107, *109*

Guang, C., 386, *393*

Guarnaccia, C. A., 278, *282*

Guba, E. G., 154, *160*

Gudmundsdottir, M., 516, 526, *529*

Gunaratnam, Y., 209, *220*

Gundel, H., 37, *42*

Gündel, H., 357, 358, *368*

Gunn, R., *371*

Gunnar, M. R., 406, 407, *411*

Gunzerath, L., 430, *437*

Gupta, L., 468, 483
Gur, R., 368
Guth, D., 494, 506
Guze, S. B., 168, 185
Gwadz, M., 534, 548

Ha, J., 434, 438
Hagestad, G. O., 279, 284, 419, 429, 439
Haine, R. A., 399, 400, 412, 415, 509, 535, 543, 547, 548
Haley, W. E., 284, 306
Halikas, J. A., 174, 182
Hall, M., 64, 71, 84, 306, 390, 393
Hallam, T., 82, 84
Hammil, S., 368
Hammill, B., 442, 460
Hamovitch, M., 486, 507
Haney, C. A., 251, 260
Haney, J., 342, 345
Hanin, B., 410
Hannon, N., 279, 283
Hansen, N. B., 477, 484
Hansson, R. O., 4, 11, 24, 30, 44, 71, 85, 93, 112, 136, 159, 417, 439, 444, 454, 459, 457, 489, 510, 577, 578, 579, 583, 601, 602, 603
Haraldsson, E., 124, 131
Harding, D., 458
Harding, R., 487, 507
Haring, M., 304, 437
Harlow, H. F., 351, 362, 368
Harlow, M. K., 351, 362, 368
Harris, B., 453, 458
Harris, T., 401, 411, 477, 483, 534, 547, 548
Harrison, R., 451, 458
Harrison, S., 350, 368
Harvey, A. G., 194, 202
Harvey, H. A., 279, 283
Hatfield, E., 352–354, 364, 368
Hathaway, W., 347
Hauf, A. M., 545, 548
Hawkins, P., 252, 260
Hayashi, K. T., 406, 410
Haynes, O. M., 411

Hayslip, B., Jr., 443, 451, 452, 453, 457–459, 513, 530
Hazan, C., 59, 63, 91, 93, 94, 109, 111
Hazelgrove, J., 70, 84
Hazen, A. L., 193, 205
Hazen, M., 237, 238
Heath, A. C., 401, 412
Hebert, R. S., 273, 278, 280, 283
Hegadoren, K. M., 193, 203
Heijmans, P., 603
Heim, C., 409, 412
Heinrich, R. L., 487, 507
Heintz, A. P., 165, 186
Helgeson, V., 572
Heller, K., 161
Helmond, F. A., 351, 371
Hembree, E. A., 297, 305
Hempel, C. G., 34, 42
Hemphill, K. J., 446, 458
Hensley, L. L., 406, 413
Henter, J., 386, 393
Herlihy, D., 74, 84
Herr, B., 232, 238
Hertz, R., 248, 249, 254, 260
Hertzman, C., 407, 412
Hesse, E., 98, 99, 102, 110, 120, 121, 123, 131
Hickling, E., 194, 201
Higgins, M. P., 330, 333, 337, 338, 342, 346
Higginson, I. J., 487, 507
Higley, J. D., 406, 411, 412
Hilditch, J., 599, 603
Hilgard, E., 121, 131
Hill, P. C., 329, 346
Hill, S., 255, 260
Hindy, C. G., 364, 368
Hinze, S., 316, 324
Hirsch, C., 284, 285, 439
Ho, S., 147, 148, 151, 156, 158, 159
Hobdy, J., 443, 457
Hoch, C. C., 184, 483
Hochschild, A. R., 225, 238
Hofer, M. A., 39, 42, 363, 368, 405, 412
Hoffman, J. M., 541, 548
Hoffman, L., 523, 528
Hoffman, R. R., III, 268, 284

Hogan, N. S., 24, 135, 138, 139, 142, 143, 146, 149, 152, 154, 157, 159, 160, 176, 183
Hokanson, J. E., 299, 305, 306
Hoklund, M., 362, 370
Holen, A., 32, 37, 41, 42, 54, 61, 125, 130, 183, 202
Holladay, S., 450, 458
Hollan, D., 211, 213, 220
Holland, J., 158, 486, 509
Holland, J. M., 71, 84, 314n3, 315, 323, 515, 528
Hollander, E., 557, 558, 572
Hollander, N. C., 214, 220
Holmes, T., 417, 438
Holst-Warhaft, G., 243, 248, 252, 256, 260
Hood, K., 507
Hooker, K., 311, 323
Hooven, C., 540, 547
Horn, R., 234, 238
Horowitz, A., 277, 282, 289, 305
Horowitz, L. M., 59, 61, 91, 106, 108
Horowitz, M. J., 32, 34, 35, 37, 41, 42, 51, 52, 54, 61, 63, 116, 125, 130, 131, 159, 178, 181, 182, 183, 185, 191, 192, 199, 200, 201, 202, 289, 291, 305, 312, 323, 430, 437
Horowitz, S., 487, 507
Horrigan, J., 559, 571
Houck, P., 190, 205, 588, 603
Houck, P. R., 35, 44, 116, 132,175, 184–186, 281, 285, 483, 538, 549
House, J., 556, 572
House, J. S., 183, 340, 345, 427, 428, 437
Houts, P. S., 279, 283
Hover, M., 342, 346
Howett, C. W., 258, 260
Hoyert, D. L., 167, 183
Hoyt, W., 598, 600, 602
Hsu, M.-T., 211, 216, 217, 218, 220
Hughes, M., 393
Hughes, P., 122, 132
Hulsbosch, A. M., 480, 484

Humphreys, K., 188, 203
Hunfeld, J. A. M., 145, 159
Hutchin, S., 282

Iltis, A. S., 331, 345
Ingersoll-Dayton, B., 458
Insel, T. R., 355, 368, 371
International Work Group on Death, Dying and Bereavement, 478, 483
International Work Group on Death, Dying and Bereavement, Violence and Grief Work Group, 478, 483
Iobst, E., 356, 367
Irish, D., 152, 159
Irwin, M. R., 71, 84, 283, 390, 393
Ishitani, K., 486, 508
Israel, A. C., 399, 416
Iwasaki, T., 126, 132
Iwashyna, T. J., 272, 277, 282

Jack, I., 257, 261
Jackson, D. A., 207, 222
Jackson, S., 285
Jacobs, G. A., 494, 509
Jacobs, S. C., 10, 23, 30, 34, 43, 106, 112, 141, 160, 169, 170, 174, 178, 179, 183–186, 196, 197, 202, 204, 300, 305, 418, 422, 425, 437, 438, 596, 602
Jacobsen, J., 284
Jacobvitz, D., 98, 110
Jakub, D. K., 444, 445, 447, 457
James, L., 376, 393
James, S. A., 394
Jang, K. L., 49, 62
Jankowiak, E. R., 350, 368
Janoff-Bulman, R., 37, 42, 47, 51, 52, 63, 309–311, 313, 315, 317, 320n5, 323, 325, 328, 346, 383, 385, 393, 489, 507, 587, 601
Janssen, H., 144, 161
Jaskowski, S., 450, 458
Jasper, A., 481, 483
Jaycox, L. H., 538, 547
Jensen, P. S., 548

John, O., 564, *572*
Johnson, B., 376, 379, *393*
Johnson, J. G., 174, *183, 185*
Johnson, L. C., 52, *63, 110,* 330, 334,
    339, 343, *347,* 380, 382, 384, *394*
Johnson, M., 444–447, *459,* 524, *529*
Johnson-Hurzler, R., *283*
Jones, E., 482, *482*
Jones, G., 247, *261*
Jones, L., 340, *348*
Jones, R., 296, *307*
Jones, S., 55, *63*
Jones, S. L., 523, *529*
Jones, W., *347*
Jooste, J., 453, *460*
Jordan, J. R., 139, 142, 143, *159, 160,*
    189, *202,* 229, 235, *239,* 303,
    305, 377, 379, 380, 385, *393,*
    505, 508, 533, 534, 543, *548*
Jordan, L., *161*
Jordhoy, M. S., 487, *509*
Joseph, S., 312, 315, 317, 318, *323*
Joslin, D., 451, *458*
Joubert, S., *369*
Judd, L. L., 418, *440*
Judd, L. W., 93, *112*
Juri, L. J., 115, *131*

Kaasa, S., 487, *509*
Kaczmarek, M., 232, 237, *238*
Kaemingk, K., 406, *414*
Kaemmer, B., 140, *158*
Kahn, D. L., 211, 216, 217, *220*
Kalinyak, C. M., 523, *529*
Kalish, R., 231, *238*
Kallgren, C., 399, *415*
Kalter, N., 399, *412*
Kaltman, S., 34, *41,* 47, 51, 57, *61,* 115,
    130, 287, 290, *304,* 427, 435,
    436, *437*
Kaltreider, N., *202*
Kamerman, J., 226, 232, 236, *238*
Kaminski, P. L., 451, 452, 453, *458*
Kamphuis, J. H., 480, *484*
Kamya, H., 452, *459*
Kaplan, N., 98, *109*
Kaprio, J., 174, *183*

Karama, S., 351, *369*
Kardiner, A., 193, *203*
Karhu, J., *371*
Karus, D., *414*
Kasl, S. V., 106, *112,* 141, *158,* 167,
    174, *182, 184–186, 204,* 278,
    282, 283, 347, 422, 425, *438*
Kaslow, N. J., 399, *416,* 534, *549*
Kass, J. D., 340, *346*
Kastenbaum, R., 69, 74–76, 78, 79, 83,
    85, 443, 452, *458*
Katz, L. F., 540, *547*
Kauffman, J., 228, 229, *238*
Kawagoe, R., *369*
Kay, W. J., 231, *238*
Kazak, A., 385, 390, *393*
Kazdin, A., 297, *305*
Kazdin, A. E., *548*
Keelan, J. P. R., 364, *369*
Keese, B. V., 192, *204*
Keeton, S., 446, *459*
Keller, G., 399, *413*
Keller, S. D., *285*
Kelley, D., 558, *574*
Kelley, P., 523, *529*
Kelly, B., 403, *414*
Kelly, J., 234, *238*
Kelsoe, J. R., *411*
Keltner, D., 32, *41,* 46, 54, 56, 60, *61,*
    115, *130,* 430, *437*
Kendig, H. L., 427, *440*
Kendler, K. S., 401, 403, *412*
Kennell, J., *347*
Keown, D., 331, *346*
Kerkhof, A. J., 174, *183*
Kessler, B. G., 320, *324*
Kessler, R. C., 33, *44, 183, 393,* 401,
    412, 418, 427, 428, *437, 440,*
    548
Khoo, S. T., 540, *549*
Kiecolt-Glaser, J. K., 289, *304*
Kiely, M. C., 376, *395*
Kiesler, S., *572*
Kilpatrick, D. G., 376, *392*
Kim, C., 418, *438*
Kim, H. K., *346*

McAdams, D. P., 319, *324*
McCallion, P., 487, *510*
McClowry, S. G., 386, *393*
McCorkle, R., 140, *160, 506, 509*
McCreery, J. M., 279, *284*
McCubbin, H. I., *509*
McCullough, M. E., 342, *346*
McDowall, A. C., 488, *508*
McEvoy, J., 232, *239*
McEwen, B. S., 404, 405, *414*
McEwen, M., 230, 235, 237, *239*
McFarland, C., 316, *324*
McGartland Rubio, D., *158*
McGlone, F., *371*
McGloshen, T. H., 279, *283*
McGoldrick, M., 513, 526, *530*
McGuire, M. T., 363, *369*
McHorney, C. A., 487, *508*
McIntosh, D. N., 55, *63*, 330, 333–335,
        338–340, *347*
McKearney, J. M., 316, *323*
McKee, D. C., 403, *413*
McKelvy, L., 451, *458*
McKendree, D. J., 599, *603*
McKenna, K. Y. A., 557, 559, *571, 573*
McKenzie, D. P., 486, 500, 503n, *508*
McKenzie, M., 488, 500, 501, 503n,
        506, 508
McKie, S., *371*
McKiernan, F., 340, *345*
McMahon, R. J., 538, *547*
McMillen, J. C., 193, *204*, 315, *324*
McMullan, J., 316, *324*
McNally, R. J., 193, *204*
Meaney, M. J., 403, 405, *414*
Mearns, J., 356, 362, 364, *370*
Meek, C., *161*
Mehl, M., 563, *571*
Mehta, P., 400, *415*
Meleis, A. I., 330, *348*
Melisaratos, N., 486, *506*
Meloy, J. R., 354, 356, 360, *370*
Melzack, R., 72, *85*
Menaghan, E., 382, *393*
Mendelsohn, A. B., *284, 306*
Mendelson, M., *158*
Mendes de Leon, C. F., 422, *438*

Mendoza, B. L., 444, 447, *457*
Mendoza, S. P., 36, *43*
Menon, I., 418, *439*
Merchant, M. J., 399, *413*
Merridale, C., 80, *85*
Merrin, W., 242, 247, *261*
Meuser, T. M., 147, 151, *160*, 280, *284*
Michael, S. T., 314n3, *324*, 330, *347*
Middleton, W., 136, 138, *158, 160*,
        288, 290, 303, *306*, 375, *393, 506*
Mikulincer, M., 88, 90–92, 97, 100–102,
        104–107, *108–111, 204*
Milbrath, C., *42, 183, 202*
Miles, M. S., 311, *324*
Milesi, A., *528*
Millay, E. S. V., 350, *370*
Miller, A. H., *412*
Miller, D., 452, *458*
Miller, D. S., *506*
Miller, L., 234, *239*
Miller, M., *161*
Miller, M. D., *185, 186, 484*
Miller, R., 232, 237, *238*
Miller, T., 592, 593, *601*
Miller, W. R., 320n5, *324*
Mills, M., 340, *345*
Millsap, R. E., 400, *412*, 534, *547*
Miltenberger, P., 453, *458*
Minagawa, H., 486, *508*
Minkler, M., 452, *458*
Minkov, C., 599, *602*
Mireault, G. C., 401, *414*
Missimer, J., *369*
Mitchell, J. T., 480, *483*
Mitchell, S. A., 115, *131*
Mitchell, S. L., 296, *307*
Mittelmark, M., *285*
Mock, J., *158*
Molina, R., *42, 84*
Moore, C. W., *185*
Moos, B., 485, 490, *508*
Moos, R., 485, 490, *508*, 579, 582, *602*
Mor, V., 487, *507, 508*
Moradi, R., 214, *220*
Morgan, D., *458*
Morgan, L., 481, *483*
Morioka, K., 418, *438*

Morison, S. J., 407, *411*

Morley, J., 243, *261*

Morrison, B., 242, 252, *261*

Morrison, R. S., 174, *183*

Mortensen, P., 19, *23*, 377, *393*

Moskowitz, C., 500, 503n, *508*

Moskowitz, J. T., 269, 282, 294, 296, 297, 300, 302, *304*, 489, *507*

Moss, M., 230, 237, *239*, 559, 560, *573*, 579, *602*

Moss, S., 230, *239*, 579, *602*

Moylan, A., 288, *306*, *506*

Mroczek, D. K., 420, *438*

Mueller, M. M., 442, 443, *458*

Muhlbaier, L. H., *394*

Mukopadhyay, T., *572*

Mullen, P., 249, *259*

Munson, J., 566, *572*

Murad, H., *410*

Murch, R. L., 313, *324*

Muriel, A. C., *185*

Murphy, A. A., 52, 60, *63*

Murphy, A. Z., 352, *369*

Murphy, S. A., 94, *110*, 330, 334, 339, 343, *347*, 377, 379–382, 384, 391, *393*, *394*

Murphy, W., *237*

Murray, A., 74, *85*

Murray, C. I., 513, *529*

Murrell, S. A., 421, *439*

Muslin, H. L., 116, *130*

Muxen, M., *509*

Nadeau, J. W., 311, *324*, 455, 459, 514, 515, 517–521, 524–527, *529*

Nader, K., *484*

Nager, E. A., 106, *110*

Najib, A., 357, 363, *370*

Najman, J. M., 330, *348*

National Alliance for Caregiving and the AARP, 267, *284*

National Cancer Institute, 168, *184*

National Center for Health Statistics, 376, 385, 391, *394*

National Collaborating Centre for Mental Health, 469, 476, *483*

National Institute of Mental Health, 480, *483*

Neale, M. C., 401, *412*

Neimeyer, R. A., *24*, 38, *43*, 71, *84*, 101, *111*, 113, *131*, 135, 143, 147, 150, 152–155, 157, *158–160*, 189, 192, 202, 204, 229, 235, 239, 303, 305, 310, 314n 3, 315, 319, *323*, *324*, 455, *459*, 505, 508, 515, *524*, 528, 529, 533, 534, 543, 548, 579, 586, 598, *602*

Nelsen, V., 152, *159*

Nelson, C. B., *393*

Nelson, K., 409, *416*, 532, *550*

Nemeroff, C. B., 362, 363, *370*, 405, 409, *412*, *414*, *415*

Nerken, I. R., 320, 321, *324*

Nesse, R. M., 48, *63*, *183*, 188, 202, 293, 302, 305, 340, 345, 425, 427, 428, 433, 434, 437, *438*, 440, 515, *528*

Neugarten, B., 279, *284*, 419, 429, *439*

Neugut, A., 556, *571*

Neuner, F., 477, *484*

Newman, J. L., 347, 355, *367*

Newport, D. J., *412*

Newsom, J. T., *184*, *185*, 268, 284, 285, *459*

Newson, J., *161*

Nichols, C., 37, *42*, 125, *130*

Nickman, S. L., 37, *43*, 96, *110*, 113, *131*, 192, *203*, 560, *572*, 586, *602*

Nicolson, N. A., 407, *414*

Nieboer, A. P., 268, *284*

Nieburg, H., 231, *238*

Nielsen, J., 332, *346*

Nishimoto, R., 486, *507*

Nitzan, R., 488, *508*

Nkosi, B. C., 215, 216, 218, *221*

Noble, P. M., *415*

Noelker, L. S., 268, *282*

Nogueira, L., *369*

Nolen-Hoeksema, S., 56, *62*, 115, *131*, 301, *306*, 311, 318, *323*, 364, *367*, *370*, 420, *439*, 446, 448, 457, *459*, 514, *528*, 558, 561, *573*, 587, *602*

Noll, D. C., 355, *367*

Noll, J. G., 46, 62
Nordanger, D., 558, 571
Nordenberg, D., 411
Norris, F. H., 376, 395, 420, 439
North, C. S., 193, 204
Northouse, L., 486, 508
Notarius, C. I., 430, 437
Nuamah, I., 506
Nugteren, A., 245, 261
Nuss, W. S., 298, 306
Nutini, H., 212, 220
Nystrom, L. E., 355, 367

Obradovic, J., 414
O'Brien, M., 442, 459
O'Bryant, S. L., 279, 283, 284, 427, 439
O'Connor, M.-F., 37, 42, 357, 358, 368, 370, 522, 529
O'Connor, T. G., 407, 415
Offord, D. R., 548
Ogino, M., 411
O'Hear, A., 251, 253, 261
O'Heeron, R. C., 53, 64
Okonogi, K., 126, 132
Olgun-Özpolot, T., 469, 484
Olsen, H., 347
Olsen, J., 19, 23, 377, 393
Olson, D. H., 491, 509
Olson, J., 572
Olson, M., 230, 235, 237, 239
Oltjenbruns, K. A., 334, 339, 340, 345, 579, 602
O'Melian, S., 84
O'Mellan, S., 42
O'Neal, B., 237
O'Neill, I., 500, 501, 503n, 506, 508
Onelov, E., 386, 393
Onghena, P., 493, 508
Opipari, L. C., 266, 284
Oram, D., 330, 347
Orbach, I., 100, 110
Ormel, J., 594, 603
Ory, M. G., 268, 284
Osterweis, M., 33, 43, 288, 299, 306
Ostfeld, A., 425, 438
Ott, C. H., 175, 177, 184
Ou-Yang, W. C., 482

Owen, M. J., 405, 414
Ozer, H., 406, 413

Paderna, L., 36, 42, 113, 130, 150, 158
Padgett-Jones, S., 547
Palmer, G. B., 218, 221
Pals, J. L., 319, 324
Panksepp, J., 350, 360–363, 370
Papa, A., 46, 62, 269, 282, 294, 304
Papp, P., 524, 529
Pardess, E., 524, 530
Pargament, K. I., 329, 332, 338, 346, 347
Paris, M., 355, 366
Park, C. L., 156, 161, 268, 269, 273, 284, 313, 324, 330, 335, 340, 347, 519, 528
Parker, L. E., 301, 306
Parkerson, G. R., 386, 394
Parkes, C. M., 4, 5, 7–10, 24, 32–35, 37, 38, 41, 43, 46, 47, 50, 51, 59, 63, 71, 80, 85, 93, 111, 117, 120, 131, 168, 170, 178, 184–186, 188, 189, 192, 197, 204, 224, 239, 288, 298, 299, 306, 309, 311, 324, 325, 349, 358, 359, 366, 370, 430, 439, 465, 469, 477, 478, 481, 483, 489, 509, 602
Parks, A. C., 321, 325
Parrilla, R. H., 399, 416
Pasacreta, J. V., 506, 509
Passchier, J., 145, 159
Passik, S., 487, 507
Pasternak, R. E., 175, 184, 185, 477, 483, 484
Patterson, G. R., 545, 547
Patterson, J. M., 516, 519, 530
Patterson, T. L., 283
Patterson, V., 572
Pattison, P., 506
Pauk, J., 405, 413
Paul, N., 487, 488, 509, 513, 530
Paulus, M. P., 93, 112, 418, 440
Paunonen-Ilmonen, M., 444, 458
Pearce, M. J., 330, 333, 336, 347
Peck, D., 232, 237, 239
Pedrelli, P., 477, 484

Penn, P., 523, 528
Pennebaker, J. W., 53, 55–58, 60, 64,
    328, 347, 539, 548, 563, 567,
    569, 571, 573
Penson, R. T., 165, 184
Peppers, L., 234, 239
Pereg, D., 101, 111
Perel, J. M., 184, 185, 483, 484
Perlman, C. A., 185
Permaul, J. A., 599, 603
Pesek, E. M., 235, 239
Peterson, J., 419, 440
Petitto, J. M., 406, 413
Pettersson, P., 245, 261
Phillips, D., 386, 392
Phillips, P. E. M., 369
Phillips, R. E., III, 332, 347
Picardi, A., 382, 392
Piccinelli, M., 594, 603
Pickar, D., 411
Pilkonis, P. A., 64, 306
Pillemer, K., 446, 459
Pillow, D. R., 400, 415, 416, 534, 549
Pine, D. S., 404, 411
Pine, V., 227, 239
Plant, H., 487, 509
Plotsky, P. M., 105, 409, 412, 414, 415
Plumb, M. M., 486, 509
Poindexter, C. C., 452, 459
Polak, P. R., 488, 510
Polan, M. L., 365
Pollack, C. E., 215, 221
Pollack, M. H., 185
Pollock, G. H., 47, 64
Pomeroy, E. C., 280, 285
Ponzetti, J. J., Jr., 444, 445, 447, 459
Porterfield, K., 192, 205, 535, 548
Post, P., 245, 246, 248, 250, 252, 254,
    256, 261
Posterino, M., 486, 508
Potvin, L., 144, 145, 160
Precht, D., 19, 23
Prescott, C. A., 401, 412
Pressman, D. L., 303, 305
Price, A. W., 399, 416, 534, 549
Prigerson, H. G., 30, 34, 38, 43, 59, 64,
    72, 85, 100, 101, 106, 110–112,

136–138, 141, 143, 158, 160,
    161, 167–181, 182–186, 188,
    189, 196–198, 201, 203, 204,
    278, 282, 283, 296, 299, 306,
    307, 347, 445, 446, 459, 551,
    557, 574, 581, 596, 601, 602
Prigerson, J., 64
Prince, R. H., 212, 218, 221
Procidano, M. E., 161
Pull, C., 569, 573
Putnam, R. D., 83, 85
Pynoos, R. S., 479, 484

Quas, J. A., 404, 410
Quesenberry, C. P., 174, 185
Quinlivan, E., 360, 369
Quittner, A. L., 266, 284

Radloff, L., 270, 284
Ragan, J. D., 55, 63
Rahe, R., 417, 438
Rainie, L., 551, 559, 571, 572
Rajagopal, D., 420, 438
Raleigh, M. M., 363, 369
Ramirez, R., 399, 415, 535, 549
Ramkalawan, T., 256, 261
Rando, T. A., 96, 111, 117–119, 128,
    132, 190, 195, 204, 227, 231,
    233, 234, 240, 291, 306, 376,
    377, 388, 394
Range, L. M., 53, 54, 64, 330, 348, 376,
    377, 395
Raphael, B., 10, 24, 93, 111, 136, 138,
    158, 160, 178, 185, 195, 197,
    204, 232, 234, 240, 288, 290,
    291, 299, 306, 375, 393, 403,
    414, 425, 439, 502, 506, 599,
    602
Rapson, R. L., 364, 368
Rashid, T., 321, 325
Raveis, V. H., 400, 414
Ravenscroft, S., 255, 261
Rawski, E. S., 252, 262
Ream, S. L., 49, 64
Reddy, S. K., 265, 284
Redmond, C., 545, 549
Reed, M. D., 334, 337, 348, 420, 439

Sable, J., 477, *484*

Sable, P., 299, *306*

Sachedina, A., 331, *348*

Safer, M. A., 298, *306*

Saiki-Craighill, S., 211, *222*, 386, 388, 390, *394*

Saldinger, A., 192, *205*, 535, *548*

Saler, L., 399, 400, 402, *415*

Salmon, J. R., 267, *284*

Salter, B. E., 49, *62*

Sanchez, M. M., 406, *415*

Sanders, C. M., 136, 137, *161*, 279, *284*, 375, 388, *394*, 420, 427, *439*

Sandler, I. N., 397–400, 403, 409, *412*, *413*, *415*, *416*, 488, 509, 532–535, 540, 541, 543, *547–550*

Santino, J., 245, 252, 254, *261*

Sapey, B., 232, 237, *240*

Sarver, R., *237*

Schachner, D. A., 100, *111*

Schaefer, C., 174, *185*

Schaefer, J., 579, 582, *602*

Schag, C. C., 487, *507*

Schanberg, S., 405, *413*

Schauer, M., 477, *484*

Scheier, M. F., 382, *392*

Scheines, R., *161*

Scheper-Hughes, N., *484*

Scherlis, W., *572*

Schieffelin, E. L., 214, *222*

Schlernitzauer, M., *184*, *483*

Schmid, B., 330, *347*

Schmidt, L. A., 138, 139, 142, *159*, 176, *183*

Schmiege, S. J., 540, 543, *549*

Schnabel, F., 556, *571*

Schneider, J., 153, *161*

Scholfield, P., *547*

Schrader, G., 298, *306*

Schreckenberger, M., 357, *370*

Schrieken, B., 563, 567, *572*

Schuder, M., 407, *411*

Schultz, W., 355, 359, 363, *370*

Schultze, N.-G., 563, *573*

Schulz, R., 266, 268–278, 281, *282–285*, 289, 296, *306*, 418, 421, *439*

Schut, H. A. W., 4, 11, *24*, 30, 34, 36, *44*, 47, 53, 54, 57, *64*, 65, 71, 85, 93, 95–97, *111*, *112*, 117, 125, 129, *130*, *132*, 150, 153, *161*, 176, *185*, *186*, 189, 191, 192, 195, *205*, 206, 208, 215, 219, *222*, 250, 262, 281, 285, 310, 321, *325*, 328, *348*, 376, 379, 395, 433, 439, 453, 454, 456, 459, 463, 475, *484*, 510, 515, *530*, 533–535, 543, 549, 555, 556, 559, 560, 565, 579, 567–570, *571*, *573*, 577, 578, 583, 597, 598, *603*

Schwab, R., 376, 385, *394*

Schwartzberg, S. S., 313, 316, *325*

Schwarz, J. C., 364, *368*

Sciorra, J., 246, *260*

Scott, S., 234, *240*

Scott, T. B., 145, 146, 149, *157*

Scourfield, J., 481, *483*

Seale, C., 210, *222*

Seamans, J. K., *369*

Sebald, W. G., 79, 81, *85*

Sedikides, C., 362, *366*

Seeman, T. E., 403, *414*, *415*

Segal, N. L., 49, *64*

Séguin, M., 376, *395*

Seligman, D., *160*

Seligman, M. E. P., 321, *325*, 538, *547*

Sellars, R. W., 258, *261*

Seltzer, M. M., 273, *285*

Sewell, K. W., 142, *159*, 330, 337, *345*, *346*, 515, 520, 527, *529*

Shackleton, C. H., 46, *64*

Shaffer, D., 399, *412*

Shah, M., 418, *439*

Shah, N., 418, *439*

Shakespeare, W., 78, *85*

Shand, A. F., 45, *64*

Shapira, B., *410*

Shapiro, E. R., 207, 209, 212, *222*, 513, *530*

Shapshak, P., *42*

Shaver, P., 36, *42*, 488, 509, 597, *603*

Shaver, P. R., 59, *62*, 63, 88, 90–93, 96, 97, 99, 100, 102–105, 107, 108–111, 113, *130*, 192, 204

Shaw, B. A., *346*

Shear, K., 35, *44*, 116, *132*, 190, *205*, 281, *284*, *285*, 538, *549*, 588, 603

Shear, M. K., 59, *64*, 175, 178, 180, *184–186*, *306*

Sheets, V., 541, *548*

Sheldon, A., *24*

Shepard, G. H., Jr., 210, 212, *222*

Sherkat, D. E., 334, 337, *348*

Sherwin, B. B., 351, *370*

Sherwood, S., 487, *508*

Shevlin, M., 256, *261*

Shield, R., *285*

Shin, C., 545, *549*

Shore, R. J., 452, 453, *459*

Shuchter, S. R., 30, 34, *44*, 52, 58, *64*, 93, 97, *112*, 173, *186*, *282*, 298, *307*, 417, 418, *440*, 477, *484*

Siddique, H., 289, *305*

Siege, B., *42*

Siegel, B., *183*, *202*

Siegel, K., 400, *414*

Siessmeier, T., *370*

Sikkema, K. J., 477, *484*

Silberfarb, P. M., 486, *509*

Silberman, R., *64*

Silver, R. C., 33, *44*, 46, 54, 55, 60, *62*, *63*, *65*, 115, *130*, *132*, 196, *206*, 289, 290, *307*, 314, 315, *323*, *325*, 330, 342, *345*, *347*, 376, *392*, 435, *440*

Silverman, A. B., 545, *548*

Silverman, G. K., 174, *185*, *347*

Silverman, P. R., 8, 24, 37, *43*, 96, *110*, 113, 115, 117, 119, *131*, *132*, 190, 192, *203*, *205*, 399, 400, *416*, 535, *549*, 572, 579, 586, *602*, *603*

Simmonds, M. A., 279, *283*

Simon, G., 594, *603*

Simon, N. M., 175, 177, *185*

Simonds, W., 251, *262*

Simpson, J. A., 364, *370*

Sinclair, H. C., 354, *370*

Singh, B., 425, *439*

Skolnick, N., 399, 400, 402, *415*

Skuse, D., *547*

Sledge, P. A., 93, *112*

Slevin, M., *509*

Sloan, D. M., 55, 65

Slutsman, J., *283*

Smith, A. M., 67, 77, 85

Smith, B. L., 167, *183*

Smith, D. A., 299, *304*

Smith, D. E., 362, *370*

Smith, E., 232, *239*

Smith, E. M., 193, *204*

Smith, J., 420, *436*

Smith, P., 449, *457*

Smith, P. C., 330, 335, 341, *348*

Smith, R. S., 398, *416*

Smith, S. H., 330, 334, 339, *348*

Smith, T., 592, *601*

Snyder, C. R., 314n3, *324*

Snyder, R. D., *508*

Sofka, C., 245, *262*, 554, 555, *571*

Sofoulis, Z., 242, 251, *262*

Solomon, A., *365*

Solomon, F., 33, *43*, 288, *306*

Solomon, J., 123, *130*, *131*

Sonnega, A., *393*

Sonnega, J., *183*, *304*, *437*

Sorenson, E. R., 32, *41*

Sormanti, M., 332, *348*

Spain, D., 418, 432, 435, *439*

Spanier, G. B., 378, *395*

Speck, P., 340, *345*

Speece, M. W., 350, *370*

Spencer, P. M., 486, *506*

Spielberger, C. D., 494, *509*

Spinhoven, P., 420, *438*

Spirtes, P., *161*

Spitz, A. M., *411*

Spoth, R. L., 545, *549*

Sprecher, S., 353, 354, *368*

Srivastava, S., 564, *572*

St. John, G., 246, *262*

Stacey, C. A., 420, *439*

Stacey, L., 218, *221*

Stader, S. R., 299, *306*

Stanis, P. I., 97, *111*

Staudinger, U., 420, *436*

Steer, R. A., 486, 494, *506*

Stefanovic, S., 298, *306*
Stegun, I. A., 180, *182*
Steiger Tebb, S., *158*
Stein, J. A., 488, *509*
Stein, M. B., 193, 194, *205*
Steinberg, A., *484*
Steineck, G., 386, *393*
Stengs, I., 252, *262*
Stevens-Guille, M., 377, 391, *395*
Stewart, B., 386, *392*
Stillwell, A. M., 350, *366*
Stinson, C. H., *42, 183, 202*
Stinson, K. M., 145, *161*
Stirling, J., *371*
Stirman, L. S., 337, *345*
Stoddard, S., 267, *283*
Stoléru, S., 351, *371*
Stone, R., 266, *285*
Strang, P. M., 487, *506*
Strang, V. R., 269, 273, *283*
Straub, R. O., 404, *415*
Strause, L., *282*
Stroebe, M. S., 4, 7, 8, 11, 12, 14, 17,
    18, 20, 22, 24, 30, 34, 36, 39, *44*,
    53, 46, 47, 52–54, 57, 60, 65, 71,
    72, 85, 93–97, 99, *111, 112*, 113,
    115, 117, 125, 128, *130, 132*,
    150, 153, *161*, 176, 177, *185*,
    186, 189, 191, 192, 195, *205*,
    206, 208, 215, 219, *222*, *244*,
    250, 251, *262*, 281, *285*, 298,
    306, 310, 321, *325*, 328, 341,
    348, 399, *415*, 417, *433, 439*,
    453–456, *459*, 477, 489, *510*,
    514, 515, *530*, 533–535, 549,
    555, 556, 559, 560, 565, 569,
    571, 573, 577–579, 583, 584,
    588, 597, 598, *601, 603*
Stroebe, W., 4, 8, *24*, 30, 34, 36, 39, *44*,
    46, 47, 52–54, 65, 71, 85, 93–95,
    112, 113, *132*, 186, 191, *205*,
    244, *262*, 298, *306*, 376, 379,
    395, 399, *415*, 417, *439*, 453,
    454, *459*, 463, 469, 475, 477,
    484, 489, *510*, 535, 549, 559,
    565, 569, *573*, 577, 578, *603*
Strong, G., 352, *365, 367, 368*

Strong, P. N., 136, *161*
Strouse, T. B., *506*
Stubbs, L., *509*
Stultz, C. H., 105, *112*
Su, T. T. P., *482*
Sudnow, D., 231, *240*
Sue, D. W., 227, 233, *240*
Sugihara, Y., *346*
Sugisawa, H., *346*
Suitor, J. J., 446, *459*
Sundin, E. C., 106, *108*
Suomi, S. J., 406, *411, 412, 415*
Swarte, N. B., 165, *186*
Sweatt, R. A., 105, *112*
Sween, E., 521, *530*
Sweeting, H. N., 427, *440*
Szinovacz, M. E., 420, *440*

Takikawa, Y., *369*
Tancredy, C. M., 49, *65*, 88, 99, *111*,
    488, *509, 597, 603*
Tate, D. C., 477, *484*
Taylor, A. C., 212, *222*
Taylor, A. N., *371*
Taylor, C. J., 105, *112*
Taylor, J., 444, 445, *457*
Taylor, L., 243, 244, *262*
Taylor, M., *302, 305*
Taylor, S. E., 310, 315, *325*, 403, *414*,
    415
Taymans, S. E., *366*
Teasdale, J. D., 298, *305*
Tedeschi, R. G., 311–313, 315–318,
    320–322, *322, 325*, 519, *528*,
    530
Tein, J.-Y., 400, *415, 509*, 543, 547,
    533, 541, 542, 548, 549
Tellegen, A., 140, *158, 414*
Tennant, C., 402, 403, *415*
Tennen, H., 321, *322*
Tennov, D., 353, *371*
Tennstedt, S., 268, *284*
Teno, J. M., 279, *285*
Terheggen, M., 189, *205*, 456, *459*, 533,
    549, 556, 573, 597, 603
Terre, L., 534, *547*
Teti, D. M., 399, *411*

SUBJECT INDEX

individual differences in grief with, 58–59

and romantic rejection, 349

Attraction, 351–352

Australia, 245

Autobiographical memories, 358

Automobile accidents. *See* Motor vehicle crashes

Automobiles, 68

Avoidance, 121, 379

Avoidant attachment style, 59, 60, 89–91

and absence of grief, 102–105

and grieving, 99

and somatic symptoms of grief, 106

A-VP-P region. *See* Accumbens–ventral pallidum–putamen region

"Away Team," 467

Balinese people, 213

Becker, Ernst, 73

Befriending, 477

"Being present," 446

Benefit(s)

caregiver, 277–278

deriving, 56

finding, 448

growth vs., 18

posttraumatic growth vs., 318–320

Bereaved

family interventions with, 487–488

and new public mourning, 255–256

Bereavement

cognitive processes in relationship to outcomes of, 585–588

costs of, 592–593

defined, 4, 72

long-term, 300–302

risk of mental/physical health consequences from, 583–584

Bereavement (Parkes), 9

Bereavement overload, 443, 452–453

Bereavement Phenomenology Questionnaire, 502

Bereavement research, 577–600

contemporary scientific approaches/ issues of, 13–15, 578–590

contemporary societal/practical concerns with, 15–16, 590–600

early developments in, 8–9

in mid-to-late 20th century, 9–10

principles of, 12–13

in 21st century, 10–11

Bereavement services, 592

Bereavement support groups, 343

Bereavement volunteers (BVs), 464, 465, 473, 474, 476

Beslan, Russia, school hostage crisis, 249

Best, George, 250, 252

Beta-endorphin, 407

Beyondindigo.com, 552

Bhopal, India, gas leak, 465, 468

Black Death. *See* Bubonic plague

Blair, Tony, 479

Blessings, 321

Blood pressure, 407

Bolan, Marc, 250

Bond(s)

caretaking, 36

continuing. *See* Continuing bonds

and mental representations, 36–37

mother–daughter, 446

pair, 36, 93, 351

security-sustaining, 40

with surviving parent, 407

symbolic, 94, 97

Bonnet monkeys, 406

Bosnian (language), 140

Bosnian Muslims, 215

Boundaries, 420

Bowlby, John, 33–34, 36–37, 46, 88–90, 96, 99, 102, 107, 119–120, 288

Boy Scouts' drowning, 242

Brain dead (term), 231

Brain dysfunction, 236

Breast cancer, 271, 557–558

Brief Symptom Inventory (BSI), 378

Bubonic plague, 74–76

Buddhism, 156, 331

Buffalo Creek, West Virginia, 482

Bulletin boards, 558

BVs. *See* Bereavement volunteers

Cairo, Egypt, 213

California, 246

and grandparent bereavement. *See* Grandparent bereavement
impact of, 19
loss of relational supports following, 39
mourners campaigning against, 255–256
parental outcomes according to cause of, 379–380, 385
and parent bereavement project. *See* Parent Bereavement Project
religious coping following, 339
sudden/violent, 376–385
China, 387, 555
Chinese Grief Reaction Assessment Form. *See* Grief Reaction Assessment Form
Christians/Christianity
and bereavement, 337
religious coping among, 331, 339
Chronic depression, 292, 297–301
Chronic disease, 265
Chronic grief, 7, 8, 34, 580
and chronic depression, 297–301
in older couples, 292
as pathological grief, 288
Chronic mourning
and anxious attachment, 100–102
and attachment style, 99
and chronic depression, 288
and prolonged grief disorder, 170
Chronic sorrow, 151
Churchill, Winston, 247
Church of England, 243
Circular questioning, 496–497, 523, 526
Clinton, Bill, 479
CLOC Study. *See* Changing Lives of Older Couples Study
Clothing, 259
Coconut Grove study, 425
Coefficient of relatedness, 49
Cognitive accessibility, 100–101
Cognitive adaptation theory, 315
Cognitive–affective pathways, 409–410
Cognitive behavior therapy, 476, 477
Cognitive dissonance, 77

Cognitive processing
in complicated grief, 587–588
and late-life bereavement, 429
and sudden infant death syndrome, 55–56
Cognitive processing theory, 489
Cognitive restructuring, 60
Cognitive stress perspective, 57
Cognitive theories, 50–51
Coincidancing, 518
Collective representations, of death, 248–249
Collectivist cultures, 58, 418
Collins, David, 87
Columbine school shootings, 249
Comatose state, 231
Combinatorics, 180
Comfort
from talking/thinking about dead spouse, 293–294
through memories, 125–126, 296
Commemorations, 245
Communality, loss of, 482
Communal rituals and memorials, 479
Community, effects of disaster on, 464
Community development plan, 482
Community leaders, 479
Companionate love, 352
Company policies, 225, 226
Comparing deaths, 518
Competence, sense of, 170
Complicated bereavement, 166
Complicated grief (CG), 72, 128, 141n1, 166. *See also* Prolonged grief disorder
after disasters, 477
cognitive processing in, 587–588
defined, 6–7
and *DSM*, 595–597
Internet-based interventions for, 568, 569
types of, 7–8
Complicated grief (CG) diagnosis, 187–201
challenges of making, 188–192
classification, 188–190
DSM–V proposal for, 197–200

Media (*continued*)
    and new public mourning, 245–249,
        254, 258
    societal changes due to, 68
    and sudden/violent deaths of chil-
        dren, 376
Medium-scale disasters, 467
Memorial Day (United States), 245,
    258
Memorial decals, 246
Memorializing evil, 257–258
Memorial murals, 246
Memorials
    for children, 383
    communal, 479
    and new public mourning, 245
    politically-controlled, 252
Memorial Web sites
    effectiveness of, 559–563
    idealization on, 106–107
    as resources, 554–555
Memory(-ies)
    active, 52
    comfort through, 125–126
Mental distress, 378, 379, 382, 385
Mental health problems
    of caregivers, 540
    of children, 542
    as consequence of bereavement, 583
    and prolonged grief disorder,
        174–175
Mental representations, 37, 122
Merridale, Catherine, 80–81
Merrin, W., 242
Merrywidow.me.uk, 552
Mesocortical system, 355
Mesolimbic pathways, 355
Message boards, 553
Metaphors, 218, 523–526
Metaphors We Live By (Lakoff &
    Johnson), 524
Mexico, 244
MFT. *See* Milan family therapy
Milan family therapy (MFT), 523, 526
Military service, 68
Millay, Edna St. Vincent, 350

Mine explosion, 316–318
Miscarriage, 144
MM-CGI. *See* Marwit–Meuser Care-
    giver Grief Inventory
Mobile phones, 475–476
Modes of dying, 74–77
Monkeys, 406, 408
Monoamine, 406
Monotropy, 89
Mood-congruent pattern of cognition,
    101
Morphine, 362
Mortality rates
    bereavement-related, 9
    of caregivers, 277
    of parents after child's death, 377
Mother–daughter bond, 446
Mothers, mortality rates of, 377
Mothers Against Drunk Driving
    (MADD), 252
Motivational system, 351, 356
Motor vehicle crashes
    delayed-onset PTSD following, 194
    parental bereavement following,
        377, 380
    roadside shrines memorializing, 246,
        256
Mourning
    and culture, 214–215
    defined, 5
    and disenfranchised grief, 226–227
    and grief, 5–6
    restricted, 399
Mourning and Melancholia (Freud), 8–9,
    45, 114
Multicultural perspective, 209
Muslim traditions, 6, 243
Myths of coping with loss, 46

Namai, 350
Narrative, 210–211, 310
Narrative therapy, 477, 521–522, 526
National Cancer Institute, 165, 504
National Centre for Disaster Psychiatry
    at Uppsala University, 475
National disasters, 467, 468

National Institute for Clinical Excellence, 476
National Institute of Mental Health, 165
National Memorial (Canberra, Australia), 245
National Trauma Centre, 468
NBP. *See* New Beginnings Program
Negative accommodation, 312
Negative beliefs, 101–102
Negative change, 317
Negative emotions, expression of, 46, 55
Negative meanings, 514–515, 520, 522, 527
Negative thinking, 105
Neglect, childhood, 174
Negligence, of physician or hospital, 429
Neonatal loss, 144
Netherlands, 228
New Beginnings Program (NBP), 532–533
New Guinea, 350
New public mourning (NPM), 16, 245–259
   clinical implications of, 254–256
   cultural explanations for, 249–252
   media explanations for, 247–249
   policy implications of, 257–258
   political explanations for, 252–253
   psychological explanations for, 253–254
   temporal components of, 245–247
   traditional vs., 259
Noninterference, 442
Norepinephrine, 360, 362, 363
Normal grief/grieving, 6, 168–169
Normative comparison approach, 297
Northern Ireland, 252
North Sea helicopter crash, 465
Nortriptyline, 175
Norwegian (language), 149
"Not" statements, 520
NPM. *See* New public mourning
Nucleus accumbens, 355

Nursing homes, 230, 430
Nuttall, Derek, 482

Object relational psychoanalytic approaches, 129
Object ties, 128–129
O'bon festival, 244
Obsessive–compulsive behaviors, 356
O'Hara, Arthur, 473
Oklahoma City bombing, 241, 249
Older adults, as excluded grievers, 232
Older couples. *See* Changing Lives of Older Couples Study
Oman, 210
Omega: The Journal of Death and Dying, 189, 197
On Aggression (Lorenz), 478
Opioid mechanisms, 355
Opioids, 362
Optimism, 364
Organismic valuing theory of growth, 312
Organized silence, 245
Oscillation, 95–96, 98
Overload, 472
Oxytocin, 352, 362

Pacing, 522
PAG. *See* Periaqueductal Gray
Pain, 72, 280, 357, 361, 429
Pair bonds, 36, 93, 351
Palliative care, 486, 487
Palme, Olaf, 250, 251
Pan American Airlines, 467–468
Pan Am Flight 103 explosion, 465, 467–468
Panic, 361–362, 471
Panic disorder, 401
Parent(s)
   depression in, 399
   mental health problems of, 399, 534
   strong bond with surviving, 407
Parental bereavement
   after extended illness of child, 385–391
   impact of, 19
   and loss of relational supports, 39
   and religious coping, 339

Parental death in childhood, 397–410
    future studies of, 408–410
    and loss of relational supports, 39
    physiological consequences of,
        403–408
    psychological consequences of,
        398–403
Parental warmth, 532
Parent Bereavement Project, 377–385
    and causes of children's death,
        379–380
    coping strategies identified in,
        381–384
    demographics of subjects in, 378
    gender differences in, 379
    meaning-making strategy in,
        383–384
    outcomes of, 378–380
    and physical health/health behaviors
        of parents, 381
Parenting programs, 532–533
Parenting quality
    and bereavement, 399–402
    and parentally bereaved children,
        534
    and unresolved loss, 123
Parkes, C. M., 9, 117, 288
Paroxysmal grief, 31–33
Partial PTSD (PPTSD), 193–194
Partner loss, 39–40
Passion of grief, 243
Past futures, 78
Pastoral care providers, 343
Past relationships, 231
Pathologic grief, 10
Peel, John, 255
Peer-reared animals, 406
Peer relationships, 428
Perceived benefits, 319n4
Periaqueductal Gray (PAG), 361, 365
Perinatal Grief Scale (PGS), 144, 145,
    149
Perinatal loss, 228
Persistent vegetative state, 75, 77
Personal growth, 431
Personal worlds, 78–79
Pets, loss of, 228, 231

PGD. See Prolonged grief disorder
PGS. See Perinatal Grief Scale
Pharmacological intervention, efficacy
    of, 599–600
Pharmacotherapy, 175
Phobias, 401
Physical health
    and bereavement, 583–584
    and early parental loss, 403–408
    and parental bereavement, 381, 389
    and prolonged grief disorder, 174
    and religious coping, 333, 336–337
Police, 227
Politics, 252–253
Ponos, 71
Positive accommodation, 312
Positive change, 317
Positive meanings, 514, 527
Positive parenting, 400, 407, 540
Positive self-view, 310
Possessions
    of deceased, 126, 381
    grief over loss of, 225–226
Posterior cingulate cortex, 354, 358
Postpartum depression, 477
Posttraumatic growth, 519–520
Posttraumatic stress disorder (PTSD)
    after disasters, 476–477, 479
    evolution of DSM criteria for,
        192–195
    following child's sudden/violent
        death, 377–380, 382, 385
    and grief theories, 52
    and late-life bereavement, 427
    and prolonged grief disorder, 173
Poverty, 73
PPTSD. See Partial PTSD
Prairie voles, 355
Prefrontal cortex, 360
Pregnancy, 73
Preloss functioning, 289–291
Premeaning phase, 383
Preoccupied attachment style, 59, 60
Preparedness, 174, 278–281
Presley, Elvis, 249–250
Primates, 406
Prisons, 230

Social isolation (*continued*)
    and online support groups, 558
    and prolonged grief, 170
Social mourning, 242
Social networks, 443
Social relationships, 376
Social support
    and disenfranchised grief, 224–229
    for grandparent bereavement, 455
    from grandparents, 445–446
    Internet-based, 556–559, 562–563
    and late-life bereavement, 431–432
    need for, 40
    and parental loss in childhood, 402
    prolonged grief and lack of, 174
    religious, 338
Societal institutions, 73
Socioeconomic status (SES), 564, 565
Socioeconomic support, of caregivers,
        278
Sociotechnological shift, 68
Soham, England, 255
Somatization, 594
Sorrow, laws of, 45–46
South Korea, 387
Soviet Union, 80–81
Spanish (language), 140–142
Specialized grief scales, 144–153
    Continuing Bonds Scale, 147, 150
    Grief Experience Questionnaire,
            146, 149–150
    Grief Reaction Assessment Form,
            148, 151–152
    Hogan Sibling Inventory of Bereave-
            ment, 146, 149
    Marwit–Meuser Caregiver Grief
            Inventory, 147, 150–151
    Perinatal Grief Scale, 144, 145, 149
Species, endangered/extinct, 82
Spirit, of deceased, 211–212
Spiritism (spiritualism), 70
"Spiritual rules," 225
Spontaneous abortion, 144
Spontaneous shrines, 245, 250,
        252–253, 257
Spouse(s)
    anticipated death of, 425, 427
    bonds of, 36

comfort derived from talking about,
        293–294
    ex-, 231, 234
    illness of, 295, 418
    social isolation with loss of, 39
    sudden death of, 279, 425, 427–428
Spread, of disaster, 464
Staffordshire Raynet, 471
Stages of grief model, 10
Stage theory(-ies) of grief, 29–30, 33–34
    Bowlby's, 33–34
    as ideal types, 34
    Malkinson and Bar-Tur's, 34
    in normal grief, 168–170
    Shuchter and Zisook's, 34
Stalin, Joseph, 80
Stalking, 354
Startle response, 406
Status, mourning and, 248–249, 254,
        259
Stigmatization
    and child's cancer, 389
    with PGD diagnosis, 176, 177
    and suicide, 377
Stillbirth
    and grandparent bereavement, 445
    grief measurement with, 144
    and syphilis, 76
    unresolved loss after, 122
Stories, about dead, 252
Storytelling, 518, 521–522
Strange Situation procedure, 122–123
Stress, 407
Stressful events
    reducing, 540
    youth exposure to, 538
Stressors, co-occurring, 420–421
Stress reduction perspective, 268
Stress response
    and early parental loss, 404–405
    and separation anxiety, 361–362
Stroebe, M., 11, 46, 95–96, 176
Stroebe, W., 95–96
Stultz, C. H., 105
Substance abuse, 403
Substance P, 360
Subsystems, of family members, 519

Trauma-focused cognitive behavior therapy, 476

Trauma perspective, 57

Traumatic events, 52

Traumatic experiences, 32

Traumatic Experiences Scale, 378

Trauma victims, 173

Treatment of Complicated Mourning (Rando), 117

TRIG. *See* Texas Revised Inventory of Grief

Triggers, 381

Tuberculosis, 75, 76

Turkish (language), 142

Twins, 49

Two Track Bereavement Questionnaire, 153

Two-track model of bereavement, 190–191

Type II errors, 189

Uganda, 452

Union Carbide gas leak, 465, 468

United Kingdom
    crisis management in, 471
    and Princess Diana's death, 247–248
    funeral songs suppressed in Victorian, 243
    lobbying groups in, 252
    mourning in, 244
    Protestant Reformation in, 70
    remembrance of war dead in, 245
    and September 11, 2001 terrorist attacks, 468, 473–474
    voluntary bereavement services in, 464

United Nations Children's Fund, 468

United States
    adolescent deaths in, 375–376
    adults involved in caregiving in, 267
    annual deaths in, 167, 265
    ethnic differences in homicide in, 391
    Internet access in, 551
    lobbying groups in, 252

    number of caregivers in, 593
    widowhood statistics in, 417, 419–420

Universals, of grief, 215–217

University of California San Francisco Coping Project, 296–297

Unresolved attachment, 98

Unresolved grief, 256

Unresolved loss
    continuing bond in, 121–123
    and maladaptive continuing bonds, 123–127

"Unresolved with respect to losses or traumas" (AAI classification), 102

Unskilled support, 446

Untimely deaths, 376

U.S. Civil War, 258

U.S. Federal Emergency Management Agency, 468

U.S. military, 165

U.S. National Hospice Study, 487

U.S. National Institute of Mental Health, 480

Vaillant, G. E., 119

Vasopressin, 352, 355

Ventral tegmental area (VTA), 354–355

Vicarious grief, 253–254

Victims of Pan Am Flight 103, 467

Victorian period, 243, 244

Vietnam Veterans, 193

Vietnam Veterans Memorial, 245, 250, 257, 258

Vigilance, 76

Violence
    and bubonic plague, 75–76
    and memory, 79–81

Violent death, of child
    coping strategies for, 381–384
    effects of, 376–377
    and grief outcomes, 378–380, 385
    PTSD following, 377–380, 382, 385
    statistics about, 375–376

Violent death, witnesses to, 256

Volunteers, 474
VTA. *See* Ventral tegmental area

War, 195–196
War dead, 70, 245, 247
War memorials, 256
Warmth
    caregiver, 400
    marital, 430
    parental, 532, 535
War zones, 469
"Wear and tear" hypothesis, 268
Webhealing.com, 552, 554
Wells, Holly, 255
Wenzlaff, R. M., 105
West, Fred and Rose, 258
Widowhood
    as stressor, 417
    in United States, 419
Widownet.org, 552
Widows and Their Families (Marris),
    40
Widow-to-Widow program, 8
Witnesses, to violent death, 256
Women, 244. *See also* Gender
    differences
Women's movement, 251
Working models, 37

Working through, 116
World Trade Center, 257, 468, 473
Worldviews
    in assumptive world theory, 309–310
    and cause of death, 313
    changes in, 315
    refinement of, 318
    and trajectory of grief, 302
World War I, 70
World War II, 79
Writing, about emotions, 53–54, 568
Written disclosure techniques, 569

Yahoo! Groups, 554
Yearning
    in grief work, 46
    as initial reaction in grief, 168–170
    and late-life bereavement, 424,
        426–430
The Year of Magical Thinking (Didion),
    87, 93
Youth (concept), 78–79
Youthful exposure, to stressful events,
    538

Zeebrugge ferry disaster, 465, 467, 475
Zisook, S., 97
Zulu people, 215, 218

ABOUT THE EDITORS

Margaret S. Stroebe, PhD, is associate professor of psychology at Utrecht University, Utrecht, the Netherlands. She received her PhD at the University of Bristol, Bristol, England. Her research interests in the bereavement area include theoretical understanding of grief and grieving, inter- and intrapersonal processes in coping with loss, and implementation and efficacy of intervention programs for bereaved people. She is coauthor (with Wolfgang Stroebe) of *Bereavement and Health* (1987) and (with Robert O. Hansson) of *Bereavement in Late Life* (2007) and editor (with the other editors of this volume) of the *Handbook of Bereavement Research: Consequences, Coping, and Care* (2001).

Robert O. Hansson, PhD, is professor emeritus at the University of Tulsa, Tulsa, Oklahoma. He earned his doctorate from the University of Washington, Seattle. His research focuses on aging families and bereavement. He has coauthored or coedited five previous books, including *Bereavement in Late Life* (with Margaret Stroebe) and two earlier editions of the *Handbook of Bereavement Research: Consequences, Coping, and Care*. He is a member of the International Work Group on Death, Dying, and Bereavement; is a fellow of the Gerontological Society of America; and has served on the editorial boards of four journals, spanning the fields of aging, relationships, and loss.

Henk Schut, PhD, is associate professor of psychology at Utrecht University. He earned his PhD in clinical psychology at Utrecht University in 1992. His research interests cover processes of coping with loss and the efficacy of bereavement care and grief therapy. He also works as a trainer for professionals (e.g., medical specialists) in dealing with bereaved people, and he supervises postdoctorate clinical psychologists in their research projects. He is one of the authors of the Dutch publication *Suicide and Grief* (1983), coauthor of *Individual Grief Counseling*, and one of the editors of the *Handbook of Bereavement Research: Consequences, Coping, and Care* (2001).

Wolfgang Stroebe, PhD, is professor of social, organizational, and health psychology at Utrecht University. He received PhDs from the University of Münster, Germany, and London University (London School of Economics), England. He has previously held academic positions in the United States, England, and Germany. His research interests span social and health psychology. He has written and edited in both these fields, including volumes on bereavement (with the editors of this volume) and the *European Review of Social Psychology* (with Miles Hewstone).